REMEDIES:
THE LAW OF DAMAGES

SECOND EDITION

Other books in the *Essentials of Canadian Law Series*

Intellectual Property Law

Income Tax Law

Immigration Law

International Trade Law

Family Law

Copyright Law

Individual Employment Law

The Law of Equitable Remedies

Administrative Law

Ethics and Canadian Criminal Law

Public International Law

Environmental Law 2/e

Securities Law

Youth Criminal Justice Law

Computer Law 2/e

The Law of Partnerships and Corporations 2/e

Media Law 2/e

Maritime Law

Criminal Law 3/e

Insurance Law

International Human Rights Law

Legal Research and Writing 2/e

The Law of Evidence 4/e

The Law of Trusts 2/e

Franchise Law

The Charter of Rights and Freedoms 3/e

Personal Property Security Law

The Law of Contracts

Pension Law

Constitutional Law 3/e

Legal Ethics and Professional Responsibility 2/e

Refugee Law

Mergers, Acquisitions, and Other Changes of Corporate Control

Bank and Customer Law in Canada

Statutory Interpretation 2/e

The Law of Torts 3/e

National Security Law: Canadian Practice in International Perspective

ESSENTIALS OF
CANADIAN LAW

REMEDIES:
THE LAW OF
DAMAGES

SECOND EDITION

JAMIE CASSELS

Professor of Law, Vice President Academic, and
Provost, University of Victoria

ELIZABETH ADJIN-TETTEY

Professor of Law, University of Victoria

Remedies: The Law of Damages, second edition
© Irwin Law Inc., 2008

Published in 2008 by

Irwin Law Inc.
14 Duncan Street
Suite 206
Toronto, ON
M5H 3G8

www.irwinlaw.com

ISBN: 978-1-55221-149-6

Library and Archives Canada Cataloguing in Publication

Cassels, Jamie
    Remedies : the law of damages / Jamie Cassels, Elizabeth Adjin-Tettey. — 2nd ed.

(Essentials of Canadian law)
Includes bibliographical references and index.
ISBN 978-1-55221-149-6

1. Remedies (Law)—Canada. 2. Damages—Canada. I. Adjin-Tettey, Elizabeth Ammah, 1965– II. Title. III. Series.

KE8532.C32 2007   347.71'077   C2007-907149-X
KF9010.C32 2007

The publisher acknowledges the financial support of the Government of Canada through the Book Publishing Industry Development Program (BPIDP) for its publishing activities.

We acknowledge the assistance of the OMDC Book Fund, an initiative of Ontario Media Development Corporation.

Printed and bound in Canada.

1 2 3 4 5   12 11 10 09 08

SUMMARY
TABLE OF CONTENTS

DETAILED
TABLE OF CONTENTS

CHAPTER 6:

COMPENSATION FOR HARM TO INTANGIBLE INTERESTS: NON-PECUNIARY AND AGGRAVATED DAMAGES   212

CHAPTER 9:

NOMINAL DAMAGES AND CONTEMPTUOUS DAMAGES

PART THREE: LIMITING PRINCIPLES

CHAPTER 10:

CERTAINTY AND CAUSATION

ACKNOWLEDGMENTS

A number of student researchers helped me with the first edition of this book during several years of research leading up to its publication. Kerry Hillier, Pam Cyr, and Phil Kennedy provided substantial assistance during this stage, and my colleague Murray Rankin furnished valuable suggestions and editorial assistance. Special thanks go to Constance Ladell, who worked with me on virtually every part of this book, and without whose help I could never have completed it on time. And, speaking of time, my greatest debt of appreciation is to Erin Shaw for helping me to find the time when I needed it and for giving me the personal support to carry through this project. I also want to recognize the huge contribution of Professor Elizabeth Adjin-Tettey to the second edition. She played the major role in bringing the work up-to-date and introduced improvements to the analysis offered in the original work.

J. Cassels

Thanks to Professor Cassels for the invitation to partner with him for the second edition of this book. It has been a truly wonderful experience for me! I also thank my partner, Paul Adjin-Tettey, and daughter, Naa Adjin-Tettey, for their support while I worked on this project.

E. Adjin-Tettey

CHAPTER 1

INTRODUCTION

A. SCOPE AND SIGNIFICANCE OF THE SUBJECT

The law of remedies provides perhaps the richest entry point into the study of the nature of judge-made law. The law of judicial remedies, which includes the law of damages, ranges over the entire field of sub-stantive private law, including the law of contract, tort, and property. An appreciation of the principles governing the choice of remedies and the methods of damages quantification provides critical insights into specific legal rules and arrangements, as well as into the nature of the common law process generally. From a pragmatic point of view, the issue of remedies is of utmost importance in civil litigation since a right has practical value only to the extent that it is vindicated by an adequate remedy. From a theoretical point of view, the law of remedies is also of primary significance because the remedies that courts choose to make available to vindicate a right reveal much about the nature, purpose, and scope of that right. To the extent that the key to understanding law lies in an examination of what legal officials do, rather than what they merely say, close scrutiny of the actual remedial outcomes of cases teaches much about law.

Despite their obvious importance, until recently, remedies have been treated more as an afterthought than as an independent area of study. Once the question of liability was established, it was assumed the appropriate remedy automatically presented itself as a reflexive outcome of the substantive law. According to this view, any discussion of remedies could be limited to a brief account of the consequences of establishing liability under a specific cause of action. As Fuller and Purdue pointed out in their famous article on damages, there is a tendency to forget that the law of damages, as much as the substantive law, can be fully understood only by uncovering the purposes served:

> In the assessment of damages the law tends to be conceived not as a purposive ordering of human affairs, but as a kind of juristic mensuration. The language of decisions sounds in terms not of command but of discovery. We *measure* the *extent* of the injury; we *determine* whether it was *caused* by the defendant's act; we *ascertain* whether the plaintiff has included the *same item* of damage twice in his complaint. One unfamiliar with the unstated premises which language of this sort conceals might almost be led to suppose that Rochester produces some ingenious instrument by which these calculations are accomplished.[1]

It is no longer possible or desirable to treat the law of damages as an afterthought. Closer study of the way in which courts formulate remedies has revealed several important insights. First, the selection of a remedy is not simply an automatic consequence of a finding of liability in a lawsuit. There is much room for judicial discretion and human choice in the determination of the appropriate remedy. The selection of remedies is every bit as much a part of the law's quest to do justice between the parties as is the application of the substantive law. As Fuller and Purdue conclude, the process of "discovering" remedies is actually the process of creating them, and the process of "measuring" losses is actually the process of choosing and affirming human interests and values.

Second, there are basic principles, purposes, and motives guiding the process of remedial selection. These can be articulated and studied in an explicit fashion and can also be used to give to the subject a unity and coherence.

Finally, because the law of remedies can be studied in terms of overarching principles, the subject need not be organized simply along the lines of the underlying causes of action. The force holding the subject together is not simply the underlying cause of action but, rather, the more general scheme of interests, policies, and purposes underlying the common law.

This work, therefore, adopts a functional and interest-based approach to the law of remedies. The subject is organized not so much ac-

---

1   L.L. Fuller & W.R. Purdue, "The Reliance Interest in Contract Damages" (1936) 46 Yale L.J. 52 [emphasis in original].

cording to whether the cause of action is in tort or contract, but instead according to the remedial purposes pursued and the interests at stake. The first part of the book deals with the principles of compensation, which is the primary function of the law of damages. Within this part, there are separate chapters focusing on the way in which courts treat different interests: economic, proprietary, physical, and intangible. Part Two then describes other non-compensatory functions of the law of damages, including restitutionary, punitive, and nominal damages. These chapters explain the other motives and policies, beyond compensation for loss, that are pursued by the law of remedies. In both Parts One and Two, the work explains when a particular remedy will be most appropriate and how that remedy is formulated and applied once chosen. Part Three deals with the limiting or balancing principles that protect the defendant from undue liability, including rules regarding proof and certainty, remoteness, and mitigation of damages.

B. THE PRINCIPLES OF REMEDIAL SELECTION

The fundamental premise underlying this work is that law, including the law of remedies, involves a purposive ordering of human affairs. In this spirit, this book attempts to point out the choices that are available to litigants and courts in respect of damages and the factors that are important in resolving those choices. The law of damages is presented as an equal partner to substantive law in doing justice between persons and equally deserving of careful analysis.

Stated at a high level of generality, this work takes as its starting point the view that the function of private law, including the law of damages, is to resolve disputes between persons in a way that is both just as between them and consistent with prevailing social values and policies. In each section an effort is made to explain why the choice of a specific remedy is deemed appropriate in the context, and how that remedy is generally formulated and applied in a way that is consistent with the judicial function suggested here.

Remedial selection and the measurement of damages are highly discretionary in nature. Civil causes of action frequently present judges with a range of acceptable remedies (e.g., the choice between specific performance and damages) and then a range of choices regarding the implementation of a particular remedy once chosen. As with substantive law, the selection of an appropriate remedy rests upon judicial choices about which interests deserve protection in the circumstances, and how that protection may be balanced against competing interests and policies.

In this work, the rules of remedial selection and damages measurement are analyzed in terms of the courts' effort to mediate between the protection of the legitimate interests of the plaintiff and the defendant. The basic principle, of which the specific rules are applications, is that the appropriate remedy is one that properly identifies and protects the plaintiff's legitimate interests without unduly oppressing the defendant or damaging other private or social interests that the law values. Oppression of the defendant may arise from an inappropriate extent of liability or an undue burden of damages that is disproportionate to the "wrong" that occurred.

An example of the balancing process referred to above is the method that courts follow in assessing damages for breach of contract. In a market economy, where the contract is an important instrument of exchange and planning, the law has chosen to devise a remedy for breach of contract that gives the plaintiff the full benefit of her bargain. In other words, where the defendant breaches a contract, the defendant is liable to pay a sum of money that puts the plaintiff in the position she would have been in had the contract been performed. This is called the expectation interest. The law has selected this interest as one that is most fair to the plaintiff and most likely to facilitate private ordering in a free market economy.[2] However, balanced against this principle are competing rules that limit the damages available to those that are reasonably foreseeable, that are not punitive, and that require the plaintiff herself to take reasonable steps to reduce the damages. In this way, the law seeks an amount of damages that compensates the plaintiff, promotes the social purpose of contract law (being the security of exchange and the promotion of private ordering), and yet does not result in an unfair degree of liability on the part of the defendant or unduly chill commercial activity in general. Throughout this work, the basic principles of damages measurement are illuminated in terms of this principle of interest balancing. It is strongly suggested that this approach provides a coherence to the entire subject, insight into the choices faced by judges, and guidance as to the principles and factors that will be important in resolving disputes.

In addition to the quest for justice between the parties, there are considerations of "legal justice" or administrative efficiency and the occasional pursuit of social interests beyond the immediate merits of the dispute between the parties. Perfect compensation for the individual plaintiff will often be sacrificed in order to achieve consistency, predictability, and administrative ease. For example, in personal injury

---

2   For elaboration on this point, see Chapter 2.

compensation, the plaintiff is entitled to lost future wages without any deduction to take into account the tax that the plaintiff might have had to pay on those wages. While this may "overcompensate" the plaintiff, it has been justified on the grounds that estimating the impact of taxation would be unduly speculative and costly.

Occasionally such administrative considerations will lead to "undercompensation." For example, while the law will sometimes grant compensation for injured feelings and pain and suffering, such claims are difficult to assess and have led courts to adopt a restrictive approach. In some cases, though the plaintiff's pain and suffering may be very real, compensation will not be forthcoming because of concerns about a flood of less well-grounded claims. At other times, such claims will be dealt with arbitrarily by awarding "conventional sums" only, to avoid the costly (and speculative) effort to individualize such awards, or for other motives, such as a desire to avoid increases in insurance rates. Where such policies are operative, this work seeks to point them out. When they appear inappropriate, it challenges them.

The interests protected by damages awards, and the approach to their measurement, will also change over time, as influenced by shifting social priorities and values and to meet new social problems and new technologies. For example, the common law of contract is the paradigm of *laissez-faire* thinking and many of its remedial rules reflect this orientation. Accordingly, until recently, courts would deny damages for emotional distress and disappointment in contract cases.[3] Contract law was confined to the protection of economic interests only, and the robust individual presupposed by the law was expected to bear a breach of contract with due emotional fortitude. This view has changed gradually with the acceptance that human relations in the marketplace may encompass more than financial interests, and the law of remedies has adapted to the new perspective. Similarly, remedial principles evolve to deal with new technologies and new social problems. Older remedial principles have adapted remarkably well, for example, to the requirement of protecting and valuing "intellectual property." And new forms of damage measurement for aesthetic and environmental harm have emerged in response to these escalating social problems. Other examples of the changing manner in which courts identify and value human interests can easily be found in the way in which courts have treated claims by women. Especially in the law regarding the assessment of personal injury damages and the valuation of property rights between spouses, the law has had to struggle mightily to keep up with

---

3   See Chapter 6.

changing social attitudes towards the characteristics of the family, the economic interests of "mothers" and "homemakers," and the nature of their losses when injured.

Because remedial principles can evolve, it is important, even on the most pragmatic level, to be aware of the historically contingent connections between specific approaches to remedies and prevailing social attitudes and values. Not just theoretical insight but also good advocacy and effective law reform proceed from the liberating discovery that law, rather than being timeless or preordained, can in fact be changed to fit better the needs of the day.

C. THE INTERESTS PROTECTED

It was suggested above that the first step in remedial choice is not *measurement* but *selection* of remedy, and that the process of selection turns on choices about the interests to be protected or the purpose to be pursued. Like other recent works on damages,[4] this book explicitly focuses on the approach of courts to different identifiable interests: economic, proprietary, physical, and intangible. In addition, it adopts a fourfold typology for organizing and explaining the different measures of damages available to protect these interests.

1) A Fourfold Typology of Damage Measures

In the article referred to earlier, Fuller and Purdue distinguished between damages designed to protect the "reliance interest," the "restitution interest," and the "expectation interest."[5] To these may be added the "retribution interest." Each of these interests corresponds to a particular goal of public policy, a particular conception of justice, and a particular measure of monetary damages. The following is a brief explanation.

Damages measured by the *expectation interest* are forward-looking and aim to give the plaintiff something he never had but expected to receive. As mentioned above, expectation damages are the primary remedy in breach of contract cases. They are an amount designed to place the plaintiff in the position he would have been in had the contract been performed.

---

4   S.M. Waddams, *The Law of Damages*, 2d ed., looseleaf (Aurora, ON: Canada Law Book, 1991–).
5   Above note 1.

Damages measured by the _reliance interest_ are backward-lookin
Available as a secondary remedy in contract cases, and a common remedy in tort cases, reliance damages aim to restore to the plaintiff any
losses suffered as a result of the defendant's breach of duty, and they are
measured by an amount that will put the plaintiff in the position she
would have been in had the wrong not been done.

Restitution damages also are backward-looking but focus not on the
plaintiff's loss but on the defendant's _gain_. Restitution damages are not
strictly compensatory, because they are aimed at preventing unjust enrichment resulting from wrongdoing. While they may incidentally compensate the plaintiff for a loss suffered, their primary purpose is to strip
the defendant of any gains earned as a result of the wrong. Thus, they are
measured not by what the plaintiff has lost but by the full amount of the
benefit obtained by the defendant as a result of the wrong.

Damages based on _retribution_ have nothing to do with compensation of the plaintiff. Rather, they are damages whose goal is to punish
the defendant or to deter certain conduct. They are available in a wide
range of cases when, owing to the particularly reprehensible nature
of the defendant's conduct, a court feels that an additional sanction
should be applied.

Each of these different types of damages protects a different interest and promotes a different form of justice. Punitive damages promote
retributive justice. They are based not only on the private interest of the
wronged plaintiff but, more important, on the public interest in deterring and punishing unacceptable behaviour. Restitutionary damages
are based upon the notion of corrective justice—that a person should not
profit from his own wrongdoing and that unjust gains must be stripped
away from him. Reliance damages are also based on a form of corrective justice—that the defendant's wrong has caused an imbalance that
must be corrected and that the plaintiff must be restored to the _status
quo ante_. Finally, _expectation_ damages are based on _distributive justice_
in that they alter the status quo. Rather than merely restoring the parties to their earlier position, expectation damages redistribute the parties' wealth according to their agreement.

2) The Measures Illustrated

The choice of remedy in any situation will turn on the court's assessment of the legitimacy of the interests asserted by the parties and the
purposes of the law in the circumstances. The following example of
the methods of damages calculation will serve to illustrate the basic
differences.

olds a garage sale after cleaning out his basement. Among the items for sale is an old wooden rocking chair, heavily coated in layers of paint. Arnold has a vague recollection of being told that the chair was one hundred years old and was called a "Royalty Rocker." He tagged the chair with a little sign saying "Royalty Rocker" and priced it at $100.

Betty sees the chair and knows that, if it is indeed a "Royalty Rocker," when properly restored it will fetch as much as $500. She asks Arnold if it really is a Royalty, and he replies that it is. Betty offers Arnold $80 for the chair, which he accepts.

Betty takes the chair home and spends one hour (and $20 worth of paint stripper) removing the paint. Underneath the paint she discovers an engraved label on the chair back indicating that the chair is nothing but a cheap replica of the Royalty, made in 1953. The most she will be able to sell it for is $50 (and the work she has done on it so far has not increased its value). Fortunately, she makes this discovery before spending the additional $100 on paint and materials and performing the three hours of labour that it would have taken to restore the chair.

Assuming that any remedy is warranted in this case (e.g., for breach of contract or negligent misrepresentation by Arnold), it is possible to articulate the different potential measures of damages. The restitutionary measure of damages is $30. This is the net benefit of the contract to Arnold, since he parted with a chair worth $50 at a price of $80 (alternatively, Betty might be entitled to the full $80 on condition that she return the chair). Awarding this amount of damages will strip Arnold of his gain, but it will not fully compensate Betty for her loss (in this case), since she spent (and wasted) an additional $20 on the chair.

The reliance damages are $50. Betty spent a total of $100 on the chair (the purchase price plus the paint stripper) and was left with an asset worth only $50. Her net loss is therefore $50, and giving her this amount will place her in the position she was in before entering into the contract (though the matter is complicated by the fact that she has also wasted her time; it is worth considering whether this might be compensated as part of her reliance claim).

The expectation measure of damages is $350. Had everything proceeded as planned, Betty would have earned a net profit of $300 (the chair would have been worth $500 after an expenditure of $200). In fact, Betty lost $50 on the transaction. In order to put her in the position she would have been in had the contract been performed, it is therefore necessary to give her $350 (once again the matter may be somewhat more complicated because Betty did not have to "spend" her time restoring the chair, so it might be argued that she has been spared an "expense").

Finally, punitive damages would involve an award that went beyond merely compensating Betty for her loss. It would be an amount awarded on top of any compensatory sum, to punish further the breach that occurred.

The choice of a particular measure of damages will turn both on the plaintiff's cause of action and on the interest that the court feels is deserving of protection in the circumstances. It is important to acknowledge that the relationship between right and remedy is not a simple one-way proposition. While certain rights (e.g., contract) generally entail particular remedies (e.g., expectation damages), the fact that a particular remedy does or does not suit the justice of the case may cause a court to reconsider the way in which it defines the right in the first instance, so as to produce a remedy that is best tailored to the situation.

To continue with the example above, the remedy for breach of contract is ordinarily expectation damages. However, a court might well feel that it would be unduly harsh to order Arnold, an "innocent" vendor, to pay $350 in damages as a result of a casual remark at a garage sale. It could conclude that his statement was not intended to be a contractual guarantee (though in more formal circumstances a guarantee might be precisely what was intended and enforced). However, a court might believe that, even though innocent, Arnold should not gain a profit on the basis of his falsehood, in which case it might order him to make restitution to Betty of the money she paid for the chair (by characterizing the claim as one based on innocent misrepresentation and permitting rescission of the contract). This would more moderately achieve some compensation of Betty and enforce the policy that a person should not gain by a falsehood. Alternatively, a court might feel that it would be unfair to leave Betty with her out-of-pocket losses as a result of her encounter with Arnold, and it might order reliance damages (based perhaps on a finding that there was a negligent misrepresentation) in order to mend her these losses. Finally, if the facts suggested that Arnold was not really so innocent but in fact committed fraud, a court might be inclined to award punitive damages.

Throughout this book, an effort is made to demonstrate when and why one of these four measures of damages will be used, as well as to explain in detail how each is formulated and applied in different contexts.

The difference between reliance and expectation damages may be further illustrated by the case of *Esso Petroleum Co. v. Mardon*.[6] The plaintiff was induced to lease a gasoline station by a careless estimate

---

6   [1976] Q.B. 801 (C.A.).

by Esso that the location's volume would be 200,000 gallons per year. In fact, the amount of business came nowhere close to this, and after several years trying to make a go of it, Mardon gave up the station and sued Esso. The court held that Mardon was not entitled to the contractual measure of damages (expectation damages based on the amount of profit that he would have earned if the representation had been true), because it was not inclined to construe the defendant's representation as a contractual guarantee that the plaintiff would sell a set amount of gasoline (it would be most unusual for a vendor of a business to give such a guarantee to the purchaser). Instead, Mardon was awarded his reliance damages, consisting of the amount of money that he had invested and lost in the venture. By awarding this sum, the plaintiff is put not in the position he would have been in had the business performed as promised, but rather in the position he would have been had he never entered into the business in the first place. The choice of the reliance measure of damages in this case can be viewed as the court's way of striking a fair balance between the interests of both parties. Mardon should be compensated for the losses he suffered as a result of the misrepresentation, but it would be unfair to the defendant to find that its estimate regarding the volume of sales could be construed as a guarantee.

An interesting illustration of the difference between expectation damages and restitution is the case of *Bollenback v. Continental Casualty Co.*[7] In this case the plaintiff had paid insurance premiums to his insurer for many years. When he made a claim for a minor injury, the claim was refused and the defendant in fact denied that he had even been insured for the past four years (owing, it would seem, to an error in the company's records). Instead of suing for his expectation damages (the amount of the claim would have been about $107), the plaintiff sued for a return of all the premiums that he had paid, an amount that was substantially in excess of the claim itself. In the circumstances the court permitted this claim on the basis that the defendant's repudiation of the contract was wrongful and that it should not be entitled to any gain as a result of its wrong. Ordinarily, the appropriate remedy for breach of contract is expectation damages. Where the amount that the plaintiff has paid for a service exceeds the value of that service, the plaintiff is not usually entitled to claim restitution of the price when the defendant breaches because that would amount to a judicial reallocation of risk. However, in this case, where the insurer did not simply breach but in fact repudiated entirely the contract, the court permitted

---

7   414 P.2d 802 (Or. Sup. Ct. 1966).

the plaintiff to claim back the full amount paid. This choice is a disincentive to the type of wrongful repudiation of which this case seems to be an example. Later in this work, similar cases are also examined in which courts award punitive damages to provide additional deterrence in such situations when it is felt that this is the only way in which to make a large corporate actor accountable.

3) General Principles

The normal measure of damages for breach of contract is the expectation measure. The purpose of contract damages is generally to put the injured party in the position as though the contract had been performed. In rare cases, the law of contract permits recovery of reliance damages as an alternative, and in other cases it may permit the recovery of the restitutionary amount. Punitive damages are seldom awarded in breach of contract cases.

The normal measure of recovery in tort law is *restitutio in integrum*: the plaintiff is entitled to be restored to the position she would have been in had the tort never been committed. This is, essentially, the reliance measure of damages. This does not mean that plaintiffs in tort cases are never entitled to future benefits. As will be seen, reliance damages may include compensation for lost future opportunities.

Punitive damages are also more at home in tort law since it is here that the law most often encounters antisocial behaviour, which courts feel merits additional deterrence.

Restitutionary remedies are not generally available for breach of contract. Instead, they are available as an alternative remedy in many tortlike actions, especially where the defendant's wrongdoing has not caused the plaintiff substantial harm but has resulted in an unjustified enrichment of the defendant. In addition, there is an important emerging body of substantive law based on the concept of unjust enrichment, which utilizes the full range of restitutionary remedies.

D. LIMITS ON THE AWARD OF DAMAGES

As explained above, the law of remedies is best understood as an effort by courts to find a just balance between the plaintiff and defendant after a wrong has been committed. While primarily concerned with making proper compensation to the plaintiff, courts are not indifferent to the interests of the defendant. The amount of compensation must be fair to *both* parties. The defendant's interests are protected, first, by ensuring that the plaintiff receives compensation only for harm to interests that are considered by courts to be worthy of protection. Even more obviously, however, the defendant's interests are further protected by a series of limiting principles that are discussed in Part Three of this book.

The onus of proof of damages is on the plaintiff. The plaintiff must show, on the balance of probabilities, that the defendant's wrong was the cause of the harm suffered, and must also prove, with a reasonable degree of certainty, the amount of the damages. The court will not burden the defendant with uncertain claims or speculative amounts of damages. Problems of proof and uncertainty are considered in Chapter 10.

In addition, even after damages have been proved with certainty, a court may still refuse to burden the defendant with those damages because they are considered too "remote." Defendants are protected against an undue extent of liability by the principle that only those damages that are reasonably foreseeable may be recovered. The principles of remoteness and foreseeability are discussed in Chapter 11.

Finally, plaintiffs may not recover damages that could have been avoided had they taken reasonable steps after the breach. This is the principle of mitigation and it places upon the plaintiff a practical burden to take measures to minimize the harm resulting from a civil wrong. The principles of mitigation are considered in Chapter 12.

Through the application of these limiting principles, courts are able to fine-tune awards of damages so that a fair balance is achieved between plaintiffs and defendants.

PART ONE

COMPENSATORY DAMAGES

CHAPTER 2

COMPENSATION FOR HARM TO ECONOMIC INTERESTS

A. INTRODUCTION

This chapter canvasses the principles of recovery for harm to economic interests. The chapter focuses primarily upon contract law, since contract is the primary means by which persons establish economic rights. However, tort law also offers protection against economic loss. For example, the action for deceit or fraud is of ancient origin. More recently, the protection of economic interests in tort has been further extended through the development of the tort of negligent misrepresentation and a cautious expansion of recovery of economic losses caused by negligence.

At one level of generality, there is no real difference in the way in which damages are calculated in contract and tort. Both are based on the principle of *restitutio in integrum*—that the plaintiff is to be made whole. This is accomplished by awarding a sum of money that will put the plaintiff in the position as though the wrong had not been done. However, in application, this principle often works differently in contract and tort. Since contracts create expectations about the future, the standard measure of recovery is expectation damages. Tort law protects interests in the present and the primary measure of damages is the reliance or restoration measure. This chapter considers the principles regarding both measures of damages.

B. BREACH OF CONTRACT: THE EXPECTATION MEASURE

1) Introduction

The ordinary measure of damages in actions for breach of contract is the expectation measure. Expectation damages are forward-ooking. They do not merely compensate persons for positive losses suffered as the result of a wrong, but give to the plaintiff the benefits expected as a result of a promise. Expectation damages aim to put the plaintiff in the position she would have been in had the contract been performed. In the case of *Wertheim v. Chicoutimi Pulp Co.*, for example, the court stated:

> [I]t is the general intention of the law that, in giving damages for breach of contract, the party complaining should, so far as it can be done by money, be placed in the same position as he would have been in if the contract had been performed.[1]

Expectation damages are designed to secure for the plaintiff the benefit of the contract. Most generally, they can be calculated by determining the *difference between the position that the plaintiff would have occupied, had the contract been performed, and the position that the plaintiff is actually in as a result of breach or non-performance of the contract.*

Sometimes, when there are no consequential or out-of-pocket losses to the plaintiff associated with the contract, the expectation measure of damages will be calculated simply by reference to the net gain that the plaintiff would have obtained as a result of the contract, subject to contingencies that would have affected the plaintiff's position even absent the defendant's breach. For example, if the contract is for the sale of goods at $100, and at the time the defendant fails to deliver the goods, they are worth $120, the expectation damages are $20 — the net benefit that would have been obtained by the plaintiff (assuming that the plaintiff has not pre-paid). Giving this amount in damages will put the plaintiff (financially) in the same position as though he had received the goods. On other occasions, the plaintiffs will have incurred additional consequential losses that must also be compensated if they are to be put in the position they would have been in had the contract been performed. For example, in the situation above, if the plaintiff had arranged and paid for transportation for the expected goods, the damages award would also have to include the wasted expenditure.

---

1   [1911] A.C. 301 at 307 (P.C.); see also *Robinson v. Harman* (1848), 1 Exch. 850 at 855, Parke B.

Alternatively, the plaintiff may have been intending to use the goods for some profit-making enterprise and as a result of the breach will have lost an opportunity to make a profit. The extent to which these additional consequential losses are recoverable is discussed in greater detail below.

2) Why Are Expectation Damages the Standard Measure in Contract Law?

Much legal scholarship has been devoted to the question of why contract law should protect the expectation interest. It has been observed that the moral force of the restitution and reliance interests is much stronger and more widely accepted than the expectation interest.[2] The restitution interest reflects the widely held sentiment that obtaining a benefit by fraud, deceit, or promise-breaking is wrong and that unjustly acquired gains should be disgorged. The reliance interest similarly rests upon a widely shared moral sentiment that injuries suffered by reason of a broken promise or misrepresentation should be made whole; that if a person relies upon another and the other fails to keep her word, any losses suffered should be compensated. But the expectation interest goes much further and grants to the plaintiff compensation not only for the loss suffered, but the gain anticipated. The plaintiff's "loss" is defined in terms of something he never had. Thus, it remains a matter of considerable interest among legal scholars why contract law pursues the protection of expectations so relentlessly.

a) Expectation Damages in a Credit Economy: Planning and Risk Allocation

There is a lively historical debate regarding the emergence of expectation damages as the standard measure of damages in contract.[3] There is some consensus that the development was related to the growing prominence of executory contracts (agreements about the future) in an increasingly market-oriented economy. There are several reasons for this. Expectation damages allow contracting parties to treat promises about the future as present values. In a complex market economy where

---

2   L.L. Fuller & W.R. Purdue, "The Reliance Interest in Contract Damages" (1936) 46 Yale L.J. 52.

3   Morton Horwitz, *The Transformation of American Law 1780–1860* (Cambridge, MA: Harvard University Press, 1977); A.W.B. Simpson, "The Horwitz Thesis and the History of Contracts" (1979) 46 U. Chicago L.R. 533; P.S. Atiyah, *The Rise and Fall of Freedom of Contract* (Oxford: Clarendon Press; New York: Oxford University Press, 1979).

actors must plan far in advance and coordinate many factors in order to produce goods and services, expectation damages provide a measure of certainty in the planning process. Mere reliance or restitution damages would not provide an adequate incentive to persons to perform their future obligations. If all that was required of contract breakers was that they restore actual losses suffered by the plaintiff, there would be little security in long-term planning.

Moreover, as Waddams points out, an important function of many executory contracts is to allocate future risks.[4] Obvious examples of such contracts include insurance contracts and commodity futures contracts. However, almost every executory contract can be seen in the same light. The parties to a contract for the sale of goods at a fixed price clearly intend to allocate the risk of a price increase to the seller and a price decrease to the buyer. To confine damages simply to out-of-pocket losses would fail to give effect to the main objective of the parties.

b)   Fuller and Purdue's Juristic Explanation

Other related explanations have been offered for the predominance of expectation damages in contract. Fuller and Purdue hypothesize that expectation damages may, in fact, simply be an administratively convenient way of protecting the full extent of reliance on contracts. The problem, they suggest, is that while it may be easy for a plaintiff to prove out-of-pocket losses suffered in reliance on a contract, it is very difficult to prove "gains prevented" as a result of such reliance. "Gains prevented" are the alternative opportunities that a person forgoes when she chooses to enter into a contract. Such opportunity costs are very much part of the price of relying on a contract, but are difficult to prove.

For example, a hotel may charge a fee when a reservation is cancelled. The hotel may appear to have incurred no positive loss in this situation and the fee appears to be compensation purely for its lost profit. However, on closer inspection, the fee may better be characterized as compensation for the loss of an opportunity to rent the room to another customer. In reliance on the first contract, the room is put aside and other transactions are prevented. Fuller and Purdue conclude that rather than requiring the hotel to prove that it actually could have rented out the room to someone else (which is difficult for the hotel to do), the law is wise simply to award the lost expectancy in such situations. Oddly, expectation damages are, on this view, the "measure of recovery most likely to reimburse the plaintiff for the (very often

---

4   S.M. Waddams, *The Law of Damages*, 2d ed., looseleaf (Aurora, ON: Canada Law Book, 1991–) at paras. 5.10–5.140.

numerous and very difficult to prove) individual acts and forbearances which make up his total reliance on the contract."[5] By protecting the full extent of reliance on contracts, the law promotes the social goal of encouraging individuals to enter into and act upon agreements. Interestingly, cancellation fees are not usually charged when the cancellation is communicated early enough to permit the hotel reasonable time to let out the room to another customer. This lends some support to the notion that what appears to be compensation for "pure" lost profit may in fact simply be compensation for lost opportunities.

c) Economic Efficiency

Economists argue that expectation damages promote efficiency by permitting contracts to take place over long periods of time, and by providing incentives to persons to make the most valuable use of resources.[6] The ability to extend an exchange or project over a period of time is of great value and allows us to accomplish things that we could not do if all exchanges had to be instantaneous. Purchasing produce from a corner grocery store may seem instantaneous, but the process whereby that produce is grown, transported, and distributed involves complex coordination over time. Allowing actors to treat future commitments as present values encourages such coordination.

More specifically, some economists argue that expectation damages ensure the most valuable use of resources by setting incentives for parties to keep contracts when it is efficient to do so and to breach them when performance would be inefficient.[7] On this view, expectation damages are preferred to alternative damage measures (either lower or higher) and to orders of specific performance.

The key concept underlying the economic view is that expectation damages permit "efficient breaches of contract." Where the cost of performing the contract to one party clearly exceeds the value of performance (or the loss on non-performance) to the other, the contract is not efficient because the total (or joint) costs of the enterprise exceed the total benefits. For example, where a supplier of goods cannot meet a customer's order (because of equipment failure, labour disruption, or the like), and the losses to the customer (or the costs of obtaining the goods elsewhere) are modest compared to the additional expense that would be incurred by the supplier, it makes economic sense to breach

---

5   Above note 2 at 60.

6   See A.T. Kronman & R.A. Posner, *The Economics of Contract Law* (Boston: Little, Brown, 1979).

7   R.A. Posner, *Economic Analysis of Law,* 6th ed. (New York: Aspen, 2003) at 118–21.

the contract. So long as the supplier is able to compensate the plaintiff for the loss, and the amount of compensation is less than the additional costs of performance, performance of the contract would waste resources and thus be inefficient. In other situations, the supplier may choose to breach simply because a more favourable offer is made for the goods. Even in these cases, so long as the additional profit from the alternative sale exceeds the loss to the first customer, the breach is "efficient" since there is a more valuable use for the resources.

By the same token, expectation damages discourage breaches of contract when the breach would be inefficient, whereas awarding anything less (such as the reliance measure of damages) would permit inefficient breaches. If the breaching party were liable only for the plaintiff's out-of-pocket losses, there would be an incentive to breach a contract any time the defendant's profit from breach exceeded the plaintiff's direct loss. But from the point of view of efficiency, the proper amounts to compare are the *total gains from breaching* the contract versus the *total gains from performing* it.

An example may clarify this point. Consider a simple contract for the sale of goods at a price of $100, where the plaintiff has paid nothing in advance and has not incurred any other expenses in relation to the contract. If, at the time of delivery, the price of the goods has risen to $120, and contract damages were limited to the reliance measure, the defendant would have an incentive to breach since the profit from breach would be $20 and the plaintiff's apparent out-of-pocket losses are zero. However, there is no guarantee that such a breach would be efficient in the sense the alternative allocation of resources is more valuable. The buyer may have needed the goods for incorporation into a product that would earn the buyer an even greater profit. Thus, the breach, which seems profitable to the defendant, is not profitable as a whole. We can only be sure that a breach is efficient if the original buyer can be fully compensated for lost gain, out of the additional gains that are offered by breach.

The efficient breach hypothesis is controversial. It reduces all considerations in contract to factors that can be measured by money (since "value" is measured by willingness to pay). It excludes the possible non-monetary harms associated with breaches of contract and assumes that a damages award is capable of fully compensating the plaintiff for all losses (i.e., that the plaintiff is truly indifferent between actual performance of the contract and damages for its breach). This is practically never the case. The theory also assumes that, where the defendant wishes to breach, the plaintiff is generally in the best position to secure alternate performance or to take steps to minimize the costs of breach. This is not always the case. Finally, and perhaps most important, there is much controversy whether "efficiency" is a social value worth pursuing so relentlessly. Since value is measured by willingness to pay, and willingness to pay is a function of *ability* to pay, it is arguable that the pursuit of efficiency gives undue weight to preferences backed simply by money.

C. EXPECTATION DAMAGES IN TYPICAL SITUATIONS

Expectation damages are the standard measure of compensation in contract law. In the following sections the application of this principle is illustrated in a variety of contexts. Problematic issues that arise in these contexts are also explained.

1) Sale of Goods

a) General Principles

While much of the law concerning the sale of goods could be covered in a chapter on property losses, it will be dealt with here since the general principles of contract damages have been highly developed in this context and provide insight into their general application.

Under both common law and statute, damages for failure by a seller to deliver goods, or a buyer to accept them, is the "loss directly and naturally resulting" from the breach of contract. Ordinarily, this will be the difference between the contract price of the goods and their market price at the time of breach. The *Sale of Goods Act* provides that both the buyer and seller are entitled to damages measured by:

(2) ... the estimated loss directly and naturally resulting, in the ordinary course of events, from the buyer's breach of contract.

(3) If there is an available market for the goods in question, the measure of damages is to be ascertained, unless there is evidence to the contrary, by the difference between the contract price and the market or current price at the time or times when the goods ought to have been accepted, or if no time was set for acceptance, then at the time of the refusal to accept.[8]

---

8   See *Sale of Goods Act*, R.S.B.C. 1996, c. 410, ss. 53: damages for non-acceptance & 54: damages for non-delivery; *Sale of Goods Act*, R.S.A. 2000, c. S-2; *Sale of Goods Act,* R.S.O. 1990, c. S.1.

Where there is an available market for the goods, the damages are usually the difference between the contract price and the market price at the time the goods ought to have been delivered or accepted. This will place the buyer or seller in the same position as if the contract had been performed. If the price of the goods has increased, the buyer will be compensated for that increase by receiving the difference in price. Similarly, in the case of seller's remedies, if the buyer breaches and the price of the goods has fallen, the seller will receive any difference in price and will therefore be just as well off by an award of damages as if the contract had been performed.

Consider the example of a seller who agrees to sell an automobile to a buyer for $5,000 and subsequently refuses to deliver the vehicle. If, at the time of the breach, the same vehicle can be purchased elsewhere for $6,000, the buyer is entitled to damages of $1,000 — the difference between the contract price and the market price. This award of damages will put the buyer in the position as though the contract had been performed. The buyer may combine the damage award with the original $5,000 and purchase the same vehicle, or will have $6,000 in cash, representing the value of the asset of which the buyer was deprived.

b)   Time of Assessment and the Relationship with Mitigation

The damages rule explained above states that the plaintiff, whether buyer or seller, is only entitled to the difference in price *at the time of the breach*. This implicitly affirms the plaintiff's obligation to *mitigate* damages (see Chapter 12 for a full discussion). The rule assumes in the case of the buyer, that he will purchase a substitute immediately, and if prices rise after that time, there will be no additional compensation. Similarly, in the case of the seller, it is assumed that she will mitigate by reselling the goods immediately. If the plaintiff buyer chooses not to purchase substitute goods at the time of breach, and the market price of those goods is rising, the plaintiff will not be permitted to recover any additional losses suffered after the breach. Similarly, if the plaintiff seller chooses not to resell the goods after the breach and their value declines, the plaintiff will not generally be able to claim the additional loss. The case law confirms that, where the seller does not immediately resell the goods, and their value declines subsequent to the breach, the seller is limited to the loss up to the time of the breach and may not claim the additional loss in value.[9]

---

9   *Roth (L.) & Co. Ltd. v. Taysen, Townsend & Co. and Grant and Grahame* (1896), 12 T.L.R. 211 (C.A.).

These timing principles are general rules, based upon the presumption that the plaintiff will take reasonable steps, at the time of the breach, to mitigate the harm caused by the breach. Only rarely will the plaintiff be permitted damages assessed at a date later than the breach. For example, where the goods are unique and the buyer has an expectation of specific performance, the buyer may be excused from the obligation to mitigate. If, for some reason, specific performance becomes unavailable, the buyer may be entitled to damages measured by the value of the goods at that later date.

The rule that damages are assessed at the date of the breach is also a rule of convenience. To crystallize damages at the time of the breach avoids the necessity of complex investigations into the precise time at which it would be reasonable to assess damages. And while somewhat arbitrary, the rule does provide certainty insofar as parties know, immediately upon breach, what their obligations are. These principles are all discussed in greater detail in Chapter 12.

The "date of breach" rule has the effect that additional losses suffered after the breach, due to further declines in the value of the goods, are not generally recoverable. The other side of this coin is that if the value of the goods *increases* after the breach, and the seller is able subsequently to sell them at a price equal to or higher than the contract price, the seller is still permitted to claim damages based upon their value at the time of the breach, despite the fact that it may appear that the seller has suffered no real loss. One example is the case of *Jamal v. Moolla Dawood Sons & Co.*[10] The defendant refused to go through with a purchase of shares from the plaintiff. At the time of the breach the market price of the shares was lower than the contract price and damages (measured by the difference in value) would have been substantial. The plaintiff, however, delayed in selling the shares until the market price recovered and in fact made a profit. The defendant claimed that the plaintiff had mitigated and avoided the loss. Despite the apparent elimination of the loss, the court awarded damages to the plaintiff based on the difference between the contract price and the market price at the time of breach. While this result may appear unduly favourable to the plaintiff, it can be defended in terms of policy. At the time of the breach the plaintiff had an option: either to sell the shares immediately or to retain them. By choosing to retain them, the plaintiff assumes the risk that their price will fall and could not claim any additional loss. By the same token, the plaintiff is permitted to retain any increase in value should the price of the shares increase. The result was fair in that the

---

10 [1916] A.C. 175 (P.C.).

plaintiff took both the risk and reward of post-breach fluctuations in the value of the shares. As Lord Wrenbury stated,

> If the seller retains the shares after the breach, the speculation as to the way the market will subsequently go is the speculation of the seller, not of the buyer; the seller cannot recover from the buyer the loss below the market price at the date of the breach if the market falls, nor is he liable to the purchaser for the profit if the market rises.[11]

Similar results have been reached in other cases involving contracts for the sale of commodities when the disappointed vendor delays in reselling. Subsequent profit earned from a favourable resale is not taken into account.[12]

c) Inflation and Interest

While damages are ordinarily assessed at the date of the breach, the plaintiff will not collect them until much later when the legal dispute is settled or the matter reaches trial. The plaintiff may, therefore, have to use her own funds, or borrowed money, in order to mitigate, and may thereby incur additional interest costs. In every province, the plaintiff is entitled to pre-judgment interest on the amount owing.[13] Even where the plaintiff incurs no direct costs, the damages award is a debt due at the time of the wrong, and where the award is not paid until much later, the plaintiff has been kept out of money that is properly hers at that time. The value of that money may have been eroded by inflation, and in any event, the plaintiff has been deprived of the opportunity to invest that money in the interim. The plaintiff is entitled to interest as compensation for this.

d) Seller's Lost Profit and the Problem of Lost Volume

The simple formula contained in the *Sale of Goods Act* does not always provide the seller with compensation for the full economic loss. In particular, the "difference in value" rule does not always compensate the plaintiff for lost profits and lost sales. Take the case of a breach by the buyer of a contract to buy an automobile for $5,000. If the vendor is able to resell the vehicle to another customer, there *appears* to be no loss. However, if the plaintiff is an automobile dealer, with a large number of automobiles to sell, the resale of the first buyer's automobile may

---

11   *Ibid.* at 179.
12   *Campbell Mostyn Ltd. v. Barnett Trading Co.*, [1954] 1 Lloyd's Rep. 65 (C.A.).
13   See M.A. Waldron, *The Law of Interest in Canada* (Scarborough, ON: Carswell Thomson Professional, 1992).

not fully cancel the vendor's loss on the first sale. The point is that the vendor might have made *both* sales, and thus earned two profits. This is called the problem of lost volume, and in such cases the expectation rule requires a different approach to the measurement of damages.

Two cases involving automobile sales illustrate the problem of lost volume. In *Thompson (W.L.) Ltd. v. Robinson (Gunmakers) Ltd.*[14] the defendant refused to accept delivery of an automobile purchased from the plaintiff. The defendant argued that there should be no damages since the plaintiff could have resold the automobile to another customer, or simply cancelled the order from the manufacturer. Because the market price had not substantially changed, there appeared to be no loss suffered, at least measured by the difference in price rule. However, the plaintiff successfully argued that it in fact lost the profits on a sale of the motor car. Had the defendant not defaulted on its contract, the plaintiff would have made *two sales instead of one*. The court held that the "difference in value rule" in the *Sale of Goods Act* is only a *prima facie* rule and if its application would lead to injustice, it should not be applied.[15] Thus, so long as the plaintiff has a sufficient supply of cars to sell to all its customers (i.e., the plaintiff's supply of goods exceeds demand), it may claim its lost profit.

The principle, and its limits, are further illustrated by contrasting *Thompson* with *Charter v. Sullivan*[16] In this case the defendant refused to accept delivery of an automobile, which the plaintiff then resold. The plaintiff admitted, however, that he could "always find purchasers for all the 'Hillman Minx' cars he was able to get." The court took this to mean that the demand for the plaintiff's automobiles exceeded supply and that the resale of the automobile did in fact replace the profit lost on the first sale. The plaintiff sold the same number of cars and earned the same amount of profit as he would have even if the defendant had fulfilled his contract. The court explained:

> The number of sales he can effect, and consequently the amount of profit he makes, will be governed, according to the state of trade, either by the number of cars he is able to obtain from the manufacturers, or by the number of purchasers he is able to find. In the former case demand exceeds supply, so that the default of one purchaser involves him in no loss, for he sells the same number of cars as he would have sold if that purchaser had not defaulted. In the latter

---

14   (1954), [1955] Ch. 177.
15   See also *Victory Motors v. Bayda*, [1973] 3 W.W.R. 747 (Sask. Dist. Ct.).
16   [1957] 2 Q.B. 117 (C.A.).

case, supply exceeds demand, so that the default of one purchaser may be said to have cost him one sale....[17]

Similar results may occur in situations where the sale is of a unique or second-hand item. The onus is on the plaintiff to prove that, but for the defendant's breach of contract, two sales could and would have been made instead of just one.[18]

The lost volume problem arises in contexts other than sales. In *Apeco of Canada Ltd. v. Windmill Place*[19] the defendant repudiated a five-year lease of space in the plaintiff's warehouse and the plaintiff claimed its lost rent. By the time of trial, the plaintiff had rented out the space to a new tenant and the defendant argued that this eliminated the loss. The Supreme Court of Canada held that the new rental did not replace the old. The crucial factor was that there was still a good deal of other vacant space in the warehouse. Had the defendant occupied the leased space under the original contract, the new tenant could also have been accommodated. The plaintiff would have had two tenants instead of one. Thus, the plaintiff was entitled to its lost rents (less a deduction from the total claim for five years' lost rent to take into account the contingency that at some point tenants would be found for the entire building). The question of lost sales is related to the problem of mitigation and the issue of "avoided loss," which are discussed in more detail in Chapter 12.

e) Buyer's Lost Profits and Other Consequential Losses

In simple sale of goods cases, consequential losses to the buyer such as lost profits can often be avoided by prompt mitigation. If the plaintiff intended to use the goods as a component of his own product, or if the goods were intended for resale, the plaintiff can go into the market and replace the goods in order to carry on with his enterprise. However, in some cases immediate mitigation may not be possible and the buyer may suffer additional losses. The goods may be specially manufactured for the buyer and not easily replaced. Or the buyer may be purchasing the goods in the course of a "string transaction" under which the specific goods must be received and re-sold to others, and no other goods will do. In these cases, the consequential loss of profit is, in principle, recoverable, subject to rules regarding mitigation and remoteness.[20]

---

17   *Ibid.* at 124–25.
18   *Lazenby Garages v. Wright*, [1976] 1 W.L.R. 459 (C.A.).
19   [1978] 2 S.C.R. 385.
20   *Kwei Tek Chao v. British Traders & Shippers Ltd.*, [1954] 2 Q.B. 459. For a discussion of the principles of remoteness and mitigation, see Chapters 11 & 12.

Lost profits are also frequently recoverable when goods are delivered late or in defective condition. In these cases the plaintiff cannot generally be expected to mitigate immediately and will therefore often lose profits or sales as a result of the breach. Subject again to rules of remoteness, lost profits are frequently awarded. For example, in *Victoria Laundry (Windsor) Ltd. v. Newman Industries Ltd.*,[21] the plaintiff was permitted to recover lost business profits due to late delivery of a boiler. In *Canlin v. Thiokol*[22] the plaintiff was awarded lost profits due to delivery of defective materials that the plaintiff used in manufacturing swimming pool covers. And in *Koufos v. C. Czarnikow Ltd.* ("*The Heron II*")[23] the plaintiff was awarded lost profits on the sale of a cargo of sugar that was delivered late. These cases, and the governing remoteness rules, are discussed in Chapter 11.

f) Contracts with Alternative Modes of Performance

Where a contract gives the defendant discretion regarding the mode of performance, the plaintiff's damages for breach of contract are limited to lost profits, based on the minimum level of performance the buyer was entitled to under the contract. In other words, damages will be assessed in the way most favourable to the breaching party.[24] For example, where a seller agrees to supply to a buyer fifty to seventy cartons of fresh vegetables every week and the seller fails to deliver as promised, the buyer's losses will be assessed based on failure to deliver fifty cartons. This may be at variance with the buyer's actual profits had the seller not repudiated the contract. Yet, because the buyer cannot insist on performance beyond the minimum level stipulated in the contract, the damages will be limited to the minimum performance on the assumption that the seller would have done the minimum required under the contract.

The only limit that may be imposed on this defendant-favourable position is that the most favourable mode of performance open to the defendant must be reasonable in the particular circumstances.[25]

2) Land Sales and Leases

Damages in respect of real estate are dealt with fully in Chapter 3 in the context of property losses. However, the principles may be briefly

---

21   [1949] 2 K.B. 528 (C.A.).
22   *Canlin v. Thiokol Fibres Canada Ltd.* (1983), 40 O.R. (2d) 687 (C.A.) [*Canlin*].
23   [1969] 1 A.C. 350 (H.L.) [*The Heron II*].
24   *Hamilton v. Open Window Bakery Ltd.*, [2004] 1 S.C.R. 303 [*Hamilton*].
25   *Paula Lee Ltd. v. Robert Zehil & Co. Ltd.*, [1983] 2 All E.R. 390 (Q.B.).

summarized here as an illustration of the expectancy principle. As in sale of goods cases, both vendor and buyer are entitled to damages measured by the difference in value between the contract price and the market price of the property (subject to a possible exception where the vendor's breach is due to a "defect in title"[26]). Thus, where the contract price for a property is $100,000 and at the date set for closing its value is $120,000, if the vendor refuses to close, the buyer's expectation damages will be $20,000 (along with the return of any deposit paid). Additionally, the buyer may have suffered other consequential losses by reason of non-delivery of the land, and these are recoverable, subject to rules of remoteness and mitigation (which are strictly applied in real estate cases).[27]

The disappointed vendor of real property is also entitled to expectation damages calculated by the difference between the contract price and the market price of the property at the time of the breach. If the value of the property at the time of the breach is less than the contract price the vendor will be able to resell the property at the reduced price and will be compensated for the loss in value.

Leases are subject to the same principles. When a tenant breaches a lease the landlord is entitled to past and future losses. This will be measured by any rent unpaid at the time of the breach, plus any remaining future unpaid rent (which will typically be measured by the difference between the rent due from the defendant and any rents that the landlord is able to obtain from a new tenant, if found).[28] Similarly, where the landlord breaches (by repudiating the lease) the tenant is entitled to be compensated for any reasonable difference in the cost of obtaining an equivalent substitute.[29]

The rules regarding the time of assessment of damages and mitigation are applied somewhat differently in real estate cases. In particular, courts are more apt to award the buyer damages assessed at a time later than the breach. For example, where the vendor breaches, and the value of the land increases following the breach, the court may award the plaintiff damages for the value of the land assessed at a date later than the breach—even up to the time of trial.[30] This compensates the plaintiff not only for any loss suffered between the time of making the con-

---

26   See discussion of the rule in *Bain v. Fothergill* in Chapter 3.
27   See Chapter 11.
28   *Highway Properties Ltd. v. Kelly, Douglas & Co.*, [1971] S.C.R. 562.
29   *R. v. Canamerican Auto Lease and Rental Ltd.* (1987), 77 N.R. 141, (*sub. nom. Canamerican Auto Lease and Rental v. Canada*) [1987] 3 F.C. 144 (C.A.).
30   See *Wroth v. Tyler*, [1974] Ch. 30; *Metropolitan Trust Co. of Canada v. Pressure Concrete Services Ltd.*, [1973] 3 O.R. 629, aff'd (1975), 9 O.R. (2d) 375 (C.A.).

tract and its breach, but also for any loss suffered after the breach. This is contrary to the usual principle regarding the crystallization of damages at the time of the breach, and displaces the buyer's usual duty to mitigate damages by purchasing substitute property. But this departure is justified by the fact that the purchaser in such instances will often be entitled to specific performance and, where the court awards damages in lieu of specific performance, those damages should put the plaintiff in the same position as though specific performance had been awarded.[31]

3) Professional Services in Relation to Land Transactions

Care must be taken in applying the expectancy measure of damages in the context of other contracts relating to real estate. In *Messineo v. Beale*[32] the issue was the proper amount of damages for a solicitor's failure to notice a defect in title in land being purchased by the plaintiff. The plaintiff purchased property that was supposed to include "Murch's Point." In fact, the vendor did not own Murch's Point and the plaintiff sued his solicitor for failing to notice the defect. The plaintiff sued for the "usual" amount of damages: the difference in value between the property that he expected to receive and the property he actually received. However, it was held that the plaintiff was entitled only to the difference between what he had paid for the land and what it was *actually worth*, not what it *would have been worth* had it met the contractual description. In fact, even without Murch's Point, the property was $8,500 more valuable than the price paid by the plaintiff. In this case, therefore, there were no damages.

The logic of this reasoning is that the solicitor's error did not *cause* the plaintiff's loss of Murch's Point. Nothing the solicitor could have done would have permitted the plaintiff to obtain the missing property. Had the error not been committed, the defect would have been noticed and the plaintiff would have avoided the transaction or would have negotiated a reduction in the purchase price. Thus, the only loss caused by the solicitor's negligence or breach of contract is the amount that the plaintiff "overpaid" for the property, and this is measured by the difference between the amount paid and the property's actual fair market value. In appropriate cases the plaintiff may also be entitled to consequential damages, including the costs of legal advice and proceedings to untangle the problems created by the error.[33]

While some have perceived the approach in *Messineo* as giving "exceptional protection"[34] to solicitors in real estate cases, the result can, in fact, be explained as an application of principles of causation. The plaintiff is *not* being denied expectation damages, but is being awarded only those damages *caused by* the wrong. This reasoning was upheld in *Toronto Industrial*.[35] The Ontario Court of Appeal affirmed that the harm flowing from a solicitor's error in a real estate transaction is measured by the amount the client overpays for the land (i.e., the difference between the purchase price and the value of the property), not by the value that the land would have had if it had been what the client had supposed. In this case the solicitor's wrong was in failing to notify his clients of an existing option on the property. His wrong did not create the option, and had he committed no wrong the option would still have existed. As Doherty J.A. concluded, the defendant's error "did not deny his clients the opportunity to purchase the property without the option.... That opportunity never existed."[36] The difference made by his wrong was that his client purchased the property for more than it was actually worth, and this is the proper measure of compensation.

Where the solicitor's error is the *cause* of the defect in title, or the solicitor is retained to cure a defect in title but fails to do so, or the solicitor simply fails properly to convey the land, the result is different. In each of these cases, the purchaser does have a right to expect a more valuable property, and the damages are measured by reference to the value that the land would have had the solicitor properly performed her contract.[37]

4) Building Contracts

When a construction contract is breached by the builder, who fails to complete, or who provides a defective performance, the owner is entitled to expectation damages. Typically these will be measured by the additional cost of completing the job (beyond the original contract price) or the cost of remedying the defect. On occasion, however, the

33   *Kienzle v. Stringer* (1980), 14 R.P.R. 29 (Ont. H.C.J.), var'd in part (1982), 35 O.R. (2d) 85 (C.A.) [*Kienzle*]; *Toronto Industrial Leaseholds Limited v. Posesorski* (1994), 21 O.R. (3d) 1 (C.A.) [*Toronto Industrial*].
34   *Kienzle, ibid.* (H.C.J.).
35   Above note 33.
36   *Ibid.* at 19.
37   *Kienzle*, above note 33 (H.C.J.).

cost of repair is unduly excessive in relation to the value of the property and the owner may be confined to a smaller sum. This issue is discussed in detail later in this chapter and in Chapter 3.[38]

5) Employment and Service Contracts

Employers and employees are entitled to expectation damages for breach of contract. The way in which expectation damages are assessed in the specific circumstances will depend upon the nature of the contract and the circumstances of the breach.

a) Claims by Employers

Where the contract is for specific services, such as a building contract or a maintenance contract, and the defendant fails to deliver, damages will be measured by the additional cost (if any) to the plaintiff of procuring those same services from someone else. Where the contract is an ordinary contract of employment with no fixed term, there will seldom be substantial damages. Where the employee quits without notice, the employer is entitled to be put in the same position it would have been in but for the breach. But because the period of notice for employees is short, and because the employer has an obligation to mitigate by finding a replacement employee expeditiously, there are seldom substantial damages. Theoretically, if the wages paid to the replacement employee are higher, the employer may have a claim for the difference, though only for the period during which the employee was contractually obliged to work for the employer. In addition, if profits are unavoidably lost before a substitute is found, the employer may have a claim for those losses.

In the case of employees or independent contractors who breach their contract, not by quitting but by failing to perform in the manner required, the employer may be entitled to an amount of money to make good the loss caused by the defective performance. Such claims are usually presented in the form of a counterclaim in an action by the employee for wrongful dismissal.[39] Damages may be assessed in the amount it costs the employer to rectify the error, the diminished value of the employer's property due to incomplete or defective work, or by the amount of a liability that the employer incurs as a result of the employee's negligence.

---

38   See Section D(2), below in this chapter, and also Chapter 3.
39   *Ferguson v. Allstate Insurance Co. of Canada* (1991), 35 C.C.E.L. 257 (Ont. Ct. Gen. Div.); *Petrone v. Marmot Concrete Services Ltd.* (1996), 37 Alta. L.R. (3d) 222 (Q.B.).

Where an employee breaches a restrictive covenant (a promise not to compete with the employer), the employer may frequently obtain an injunction to enforce the contract, and may also claim damages for lost sales or profits. Employees who accept bribes, kickbacks, or secret commissions, or who wrongly appropriate a corporate opportunity are also liable in damages for the loss suffered by the employer. Alternatively, the employer may have a restitutionary remedy to force disgorgement by the employee of the benefit. These remedies are discussed in Chapter 7.

b)   Claims by Employees for Wrongful Dismissal

Employees are also entitled to expectation damages for breach of contract by their employers. The most common type of breach is wrongful dismissal, whereby the employee is fired without cause and without sufficient notice. The employee's expectation damages are measured by lost wages during the period of lost employment. The length of that period will depend upon the terms of the contract. If the contract is for a fixed term and the employee is dismissed before the expiry of that term, he will be entitled to lost wages during the remainder. Where the contract does not fix a term the matter is left to common law. At common law an employer has the right to terminate an employee, but usually only with due notice.[40] If the employee is dismissed without notice, he or she will be entitled to damages for lost wages during the notice period. In addition to lost wages, the employee may be entitled to the monetary value of other benefits lost (pensions, insurance coverage).

If the employee finds alternate employment, he is only entitled to damages for the period of unemployment (since the loss has been mitigated). But if that new employment is at a lower salary, the employee will be entitled to the difference in salary until the end of the notice period.[41] In very limited circumstances an employee may be entitled to damages for mental suffering as a result of a wrongful dismissal. This issue is discussed in Chapter 6.

c)   Discretionary Benefits

One common issue in the context of claims by employees concerns "discretionary benefits" such as bonuses that the employee might or might not have received had she not been wrongly terminated. Are these part of the employee's expectancy? While there is no legal entitle-

---

40   See *Bardal v. Globe and Mail* (1960), 24 D.L.R. (2d) 140 (Ont. H.C.J.) [*Bardal*] for a discussion of the factors that are relevant in determining the notice period.

41   *Zylawy v. Edmonton* (1985), 60 A.R. 259 (Q.B.).

ment to such bonuses, it is arguable that as a result of the breach the employee has been deprived of the chance of receiving the benefit. In *Bardal*, the plaintiff was denied compensation for loss of a bonus on the grounds that it "was a purely voluntary gift distributed among the employees as a matter of good will."[42] In other words, if the plaintiff could not prove a legal entitlement to the sum, it is not compensable.[43] Courts now do not take such a restrictive approach. In *Ditmars v. Ross Drug Co.*[44] the wrongfully dismissed plaintiff was given compensation for lost bonuses when it was shown that he had received one every year for fourteen years and that the bonus system had become an "integral part of the employer's wage structure"[45] (by adjusting otherwise inadequate wages to prevailing levels). Thus, where the plaintiff can establish a pattern of receiving bonuses, a court is likely to consider such payments as the norm and hence automatic, thereby entitling wrongfully dismissed employees to such benefits.[46] Indeed, in principle, courts are able to go further than this. Even when there is substantial uncertainty as to whether the employee would have received a bonus, the employee should be compensated in some amount for the lost *chance* of receiving the bonus. This amount need not be the full amount of the bonus, but rather an intermediate sum reflecting the court's assessment of the probability that the bonus would have been received.[47]

D. ISSUES IN THE ASSESSMENT OF EXPECTATION DAMAGES

1) Lost Profits and Other Consequential Losses

a) General Principles

When a contract has been breached, the plaintiff may be deprived not only of the immediate benefit of the contract but may also suffer other consequential losses including wasted expenses and lost profits. Expenditures incurred in order to salvage the enterprise or minimize

---

42   Above note 40 at 146.
43   In *Carignan v. Nu Salt Corp.* (2000), 197 Sask. R. 108 (Q.B.), the court referred to the plaintiff's acknowledgment of the discretionary nature of a bonus received in the past to further support the position that no legal entitlement arose from past payment of bonuses.
44   (1970), 3 N.B.R. (2d) 139 (Q.B.).
45   *Ibid.* at 146.
46   See *Sampson v. Melanson's Waste Management Inc.* (2005), 277 N.B.R. (2d) 76 (Q.B.).
47   See Chapter 10.

the harm caused by the breach will be recoverable so long as they are reasonable.[48] For example, where defective machinery is sold to the plaintiff, the plaintiff may recover, in addition to the lost value of the machinery, reasonable sums expended to make the machinery usable.[49] Such expenses generally will be considered as reasonable attempts to mitigate (discussed in Chapter 12).

In addition, owing to the breach of contract, the plaintiff may lose future profits, or at least opportunities for profit. The failure of a real estate transaction may result in lost profits to the buyer or seller in addition to any lost value of the land (for example, where a farmer loses anticipated crops because of the failed transaction[50] or a buyer loses development profits because of the refusal of the owner of land to convey it). The repudiation of a lease may cause additional losses to the tenant beyond the mere cost of finding an alternative lease (for example, the loss of profits when the lessee is forced to shut down or relocate his business[51]). Where the contract is for the sale of goods to be resold at a profit, the plaintiff may lose the later sale if the goods are not delivered, or if they are late[52] or damaged. If the goods are for use as components in the plaintiff's own product,[53] or if the contract is for the manufacture or delivery of profit-making equipment or machinery,[54] and the defendant fails to deliver or delivers defective merchandise, the plaintiff may suffer lost profits. In each case, at least in principle, lost profits may be recovered if such recovery is necessary in order to put the plaintiff in the position as though the contract had been performed. Difficulties in estimating probable lost future profits do not preclude awarding such damages where the defendant's breach is the very cause of the uncertainty. Plaintiffs are entitled to recover projected profits subject to contingencies.[55] There are, however, important limits on recovery.

b) Limits on Recovery: Remoteness and Mitigation
Recovery of lost profits is limited by three important constraints, each of which is discussed in detail in subsequent chapters of this work. The

---

48   See *Ticketnet Corp. v. Air Canada* (1997), 154 D.L.R. (4th) 271 (Ont. C.A.), leave to appeal to S.C.C. refused (1998), 161 D.L.R. (4th) vii [*Ticketnet*].
49   *R.G. McLean Ltd. v. Canadian Vickers Ltd.*, [1971] 1 O.R. 207 (C.A.) [*Vickers*].
50   *Kienzle*, above note 33 (C.A.).
51   *Karas v. Rowlett*, [1944] S.C.R. 1.
52   *The Heron II*, above note 23: lost profit on resale of goods due to late delivery.
53   *Canlin*, above note 22.
54   *Vickers,* above note 49.
55   See *Ticketnet*, above note 48 at 298–99. This issue is discussed in more detail in Chapter 10.

first limitation on recovery of lost profits is the rule of remoteness. The risk of lost profits must be within the reasonable contemplation of the parties at the time they enter into the contract.[56] Some earlier authorities suggested that lost profits will usually fail this remoteness test because they are not foreseeable. However, more recent caselaw indicates otherwise. As Cory J.A. said in *Canlin*[57] (a claim for lost profits due to the defendant's delivery of defective material for the plaintiff's product):

> [m]ost commercial contracts pertaining to the sale and delivery of material or goods must, of necessity, be entered into with a view to making a profit in the future. To say otherwise amounts to a denial of the profit motive in the free enterprise system.[58]

Cory J.A. held that a person supplying material to another, in circumstances where it is clear that the buyer will be using that material as a component of its own goods, could easily foresee that if defective material is supplied the buyer will lose business.

Lost profits will not always be so easily foreseen, nor will the *extent* of lost profits always be foreseen. Indeed, in the leading case of *Hadley v. Baxendale*[59] it was held that it was not foreseeable to a carrier of a mill shaft that if delivery of the shaft was delayed there would be a loss of profits. And in *Victoria Laundry*,[60] the court held that, while some lost profits were foreseeable when the defendant failed to deliver a boiler to the plaintiff on time, the defendant could not have foreseen the loss to the plaintiff of the especially lucrative business that it had been expecting. The principle of remoteness of damages does, therefore, limit the circumstances in which claims for lost profits can be made, and this principle is discussed more fully in Chapter 11.

The second constraint on the recovery of lost profits is the doctrine of mitigation, which is fully discussed in Chapter 12. The principle is of particular importance in terms of limiting the period during which business losses can be claimed. Those losses are recoverable only for the period "before reasonable steps in mitigation of the loss can become effective."[61] The plaintiff is expected to mitigate damages by purchasing substitute goods or services as soon as possible, and carrying on with its business. If the lost profit accrues because the plaintiff has

---

56   *The Heron II*, above note 23: lost profit on resale of goods due to late delivery.
57   Above note 22.
58   *Ibid.* at 690.
59   (1854), 9 Exch. 341, 156 E.R. 145.
60   Above note 21.
61   In *Sunnyside Greenhouses Ltd. v. Golden West Seeds Ltd.* (1972), 27 D.L.R. (3d) 434 at 442 (Alta. C.A.).

failed to do this, it will not be recoverable.[62] To the extent that it is not practicable for the plaintiff to mitigate immediately, damages will be recoverable for the business lost. For example, in *Canlin*[63] the defendant delivered defective material to the plaintiff, who was a manufacturer of swimming pool covers. The plaintiff was permitted to recover lost profits for a period of four years. Its reputation had been so seriously harmed by the sale of defective products that it was not obliged immediately to re-enter the field and this was a reasonable period for it to recover its business.

The third constraint on recovery of lost profits is created by the onus of proof. Proving and measuring lost profits requires the plaintiff to demonstrate hypotheses about "what would have happened" had the contract not been breached. Past sales will be examined as evidence of what might have occurred and experts will be required to provide opinions regarding the plaintiff's business. Competitors' sales might be compared to determine the volume of business lost by the plaintiff. Yet all this involves a certain amount of speculation and the final measure will only be an estimate. Nevertheless, the court will not refuse to quantify damages merely because they are difficult to calculate. As Cory J.A. said in *Canlin*,

> The court, I believe, would be shirking its duty if it were to say that no damages should flow because of the difficulty of calculating and assessing such damages and that they are therefore too remote. An assessment of future loss of profits must, of necessity, be an estimate .... The task will always be difficult but not insurmountable. It poses no greater obstacle to a court than the assessment of general damages in a serious personal injury claim.[64]

This is not to say that the plaintiff will be relieved in these cases of the basic onus of proof. Courts will not speculate without evidence. Where the plaintiff claims that as a result of breach of contract they have lost sales or revenue, they must provide the court with some basis for calculating the loss (e.g., evidence of past sales) and some positive evidence that the sales or revenue would have been made (e.g., that there was some demand for their goods or services). In the absence of

---

62 *Freedhoff v. Pomalift*, [1971] 2 O.R. 773 (C.A.): lost profit not recoverable because of failure to mitigate; *Blue-Moon Logging Ltd. v. Finning Ltd.* (1995), 8 B.C.L.R. (3d) 293 (S.C.).
63 Above note 22.
64 *Ibid.* at 691.

some evidence of actual loss, and some basis for assessing its value, courts will not award lost profits.[65]

Where the plaintiff is entirely unable to prove the amount of its lost profits, it may sometimes be permitted to claim its out-of-pocket loss, wasted expenditure, or lost investment as an alternative. In these cases, the plaintiff is said to elect to claim reliance rather than expectation damages. Essentially, the plaintiff is given the benefit of a presumption that the contractual venture would at least have broken even. This principle is discussed later in this chapter as an example of the reliance interest in contract law.

In addition, sometimes the plaintiff is unable to prove lost profits because what it has lost as a result of the defendant's breach was a "chance" of earning a profit. The difficulty in these cases is that, because of the breach, there may be no way of proving whether that chance would have materialized in the plaintiff's favour. In limited circumstances the court will value the chance that has been lost. The problem of uncertainty in damages quantification and the principles regarding the valuation of lost chances are discussed more fully in Chapter 10.

c) Cumulative Claims and Avoiding Double Recovery: The Meaning of "Profit"

Claims for lost profit must be carefully prepared and analyzed so as not to overlap with other heads of damages. In principle, a plaintiff may claim all of the following: capital losses (e.g., diminished value of the property); wasted expenses; and lost profits due to a breach of contract, so long as the total amount is required to put the plaintiff in as good a position as though the contract had been performed. However, caution must be exercised in order to avoid duplicate claims. The plaintiff must not be put in a *better* position than if the contract had been performed. The problem of duplication arises when lost profits are claimed on a "gross" rather than "net" basis. In such cases, the claim for lost profits may already include capital losses and expenses.

Gross profits are the excess of total revenue from a sale or transaction over the direct costs of the sale (e.g., the cost of the goods to the vendor) without any consideration of general expenses (overhead and salaries). Net profit is the figure after all operational expenses have also been deducted from revenues. Where "gross" profits are claimed, the amount will generally include expenses that have been wasted, and it would therefore be inappropriate to claim lost profits plus wasted ex-

---

65   *Vickers*, above note 49.

penditures. Only where the claim is made on a "net profit" basis is it appropriate to add other wasted expenses.

Consider the following simple example: The buyer agrees to purchase a ton of potatoes for sale at her market stall in the city. The price for the produce is $1,000 (which has not been paid) and the buyer spends an additional $150 transporting it. She also pays $100 for the right to set up her stall in the market and hires an assistant for the day for $100. She anticipates selling the produce in units for a total price of $1,600. If the produce is tendered in a spoiled condition in breach of contract, and is entirely useless, the claim may be framed in two ways. First, the plaintiff may claim lost profit of $600. Alternatively, the buyer may claim lost "net" profit of $250 plus her wasted transportation, wages, and stall fees of $350 (to the extent that these expenditures cannot be avoided). The buyer may not, of course, claim her lost gross profits plus her wasted expenditures, because this would put her in a better position than had the contract been performed (since to earn the $600 gross profit she would have had to spend the $350 in any event).

The case of Vickers[66] provides a more complex illustration of the relevant principles. In this case the defendants sold the plaintiff a defective printing press. After fruitless attempts to repair the press the plaintiff, who had paid only $16,000 of the $76,000 purchase price, sued the defendant for expenditures wasted while trying to utilize the press on a printing project, plus an amount for lost profits. The trial judge allowed the plaintiff's claim in whole and rejected the defendant's counterclaim for the outstanding balance on the press. The Court of Appeal held that this amounted to double compensation. The plaintiff, explained Arnup J.A., is entitled to be put in the position it would have occupied had the contract been performed. While the plaintiff might have earned profits had the press worked, in order to earn those profits it would have had to pay the full purchase price for the machine. It was, therefore, inappropriate to award lost profits to the plaintiff while making no allowance for the fact that the plaintiff would have had to pay for the press: "to give the purchaser both a refund of the purchase price and expenditures made would be double compensation."[67] The court also intimated that it might have reduced the claim for lost profits further because it overlapped with the claim for wasted expenses. Since the wasted expenses claim included "overhead and supervision," these were expenditures that would have been incurred in any event in order to earn the profit claimed.

---

66 Ibid.
67 Ibid. at 214–15.

In principle, it is correct for the Court of Appeal to assert that the claim for lost profits must not be allowed to overlap with the claim for wasted expenditures. However, as commentators have pointed out,[68] the Court of Appeal's decision is also likely in error, illustrating how care must be taken when defining profit. Of course, if the plaintiff's claim is for its lost gross earnings, the cost of obtaining those earnings (e.g., the cost of purchasing equipment) must be taken into account. However, if the basis of the claim is lost "net profit" the figure claimed has been calculated *after* the costs of production have been deducted. Thus, if the claim for lost profits was made on a net basis, the Court of Appeal may have deducted the cost of the press (and possibly overhead and supervision) twice. Moreover, even if the plaintiff's claim was for gross profits, the Court of Appeal may have further erred in deducting the *entire cost* of the printing press. The plaintiff was awarded lost profits for only a two-year period and it is unfair to assume that the press would have been paid for in so short a period. As Baer points out, if the press had met contract standards, at the end of two years the plaintiff would have earned its profit and would also be left with a valuable machine. In fact, the press appears to be worthless and the court has essentially attributed "the entire capital expense to the first two years of operation."[69]

The true principle is that a plaintiff is entitled to be put in the position that she would have been in had the contract been performed. The plaintiff may claim lost profit and wasted expenses so long as the claims do not overlap. Whether they overlap will depend upon a careful examination of how the claim for lost profit is formulated. If the claim is in reality a claim for lost gross revenue, then any additional claim for lost operating or capital expenditures is redundant. However, if the claim truly is for lost profit (meaning earnings after all expenses), then to the extent that the plaintiff has incurred other costs (capital or operating) these expenditures may also be recovered since, had the contract not been breached, they would have been covered by the plaintiff's earnings.

2) Cost of Performance or Diminution in Value

a) The Issue Explained

A common issue, in the assessment of expectation damages, is whether, upon breach of contract, damages should be assessed according to the

---

68   M. Baer, "The Assessment of Damages for Breach of Contract — Loss of Profit" (1973) 51 Can. Bar Rev. 490.

69   *Ibid.* at 497.

cost of procuring substitute performance, or instead, on the basis of the diminution in the plaintiff's wealth as a result of the breach. The two measures may differ considerably. The problem typically arises in relation to contracts for the improvement or repair of property. The work may be expensive to perform, but its actual economic value is minimal. The problem is therefore discussed in more detail in the next chapter, which addresses damages in respect of property interests.

The most famous illustration of the dilemma is the U.S. case of *Peevyhouse v. Garland Coal*.[70] The defendant leased land from the plaintiff for mining operations and agreed to restore the land at the end of the lease, but failed to do so. The evidence indicated that the cost of doing the work would be $29,000, but that as a result of the failure to do the work, the plaintiff's land was worth only $300 less than it would otherwise have been. Indeed, the total value of the plaintiff's land was only $5,000. The court awarded only the diminished value of the land, reasoning that the larger amount would vastly overcompensate the plaintiff, who would be put in a much better position financially than if the contract had been performed.

The difficulty with this result, of course, is that it appears to permit the defendant deliberately to breach the contract and escape its obligations resulting in a windfall. This consideration influenced another court in the earlier and nearly identical case of *Groves v. John Wunder*[71] to award the full cost of performing the work ($60,000) though the total value of the property was only $12,000 even with the work done. The difficulty with this result is the exact converse. It appears to confer a windfall upon the plaintiff, putting him in a far better position than if the contract had been performed.

b) Factors Used to Determine the True Loss

These cases, and the relevant principles, are fully discussed in Chapter 3 in relation to the valuation of property losses. By way of summary, there is no absolute rule that expectation damages are measured by either the cost of performance or the diminished value of the property. The only rule is that the plaintiff is entitled to be put in as good a position as though the contract had been performed. This will sometimes be measured by the cost of performance, sometimes by the diminished value of the property, and sometimes by a different amount altogether. What is important is the court's assessment of the plaintiff's *true interest* in the contract and the plaintiff's *actual loss*. Where that interest is purely finan-

---

70   382 P.2d 109 (Okla. Sup. Ct. 1963).
71   286 N.W. 235 (Minn. Sup. Ct. 1939).

cial, as where the property is held only as an investment, it will be difficult for the plaintiff to argue that the loss is greater than the diminished value of the property. However, where the plaintiff has other interests (functional, aesthetic, or sentimental), the cost of actually performing the work may be justified even though it is otherwise "uneconomic."[72] Also of relevance is the question of whether the plaintiff has already done the work or genuinely intends to do so.[73] If the plaintiff intends to do the work this shows that the plaintiff does in fact value the property by the amount that will be spent. It also assures the court that the plaintiff will not simply be pocketing a windfall. Finally, the court will be influenced by considerations of economic reasonableness and unjust enrichment. Where the cost of doing the work is completely out of proportion to the benefit to be achieved, the work will be economically unreasonable and this will weigh against awarding the full cost of performance.[74] On the other hand, where the plaintiff has directly paid the defendant to do the work, the defendant will be unjustly enriched if allowed simply to walk away from the contract with the price in his pocket, saying that the work would not have increased the value of the property. These considerations are all explained in greater detail in Chapter 3.

c)   Alternative Measures

There is no reason in principle why, in assessing the plaintiff's expectancy, the courts should confine themselves to the two stark alternatives of diminished value or cost of performance. Sometimes neither of these will be an accurate measure of the plaintiff's true loss. In many cases, market values may not accurately reflect the plaintiff's loss because the plaintiff has some personal or subjective reason for wanting the work done. Yet the full cost of performance may, in the circumstances, be an over-estimate of that loss. For example, in the *Peevyhouse* case, the plaintiffs, who were farmers, likely valued the loss they suffered by a good deal more than $300. Yet it is unlikely that the cost of performance was an accurate measure of their loss, given than it was five times the total value of their property. In that case, the jury had awarded $5,000. While the Court of Appeal reduced this award, it may have been a more accurate approximation of the plaintiffs' actual subjective loss than either the cost of performance or diminution in value.

---

72   *Radford v. De Froberville*, [1978] 1 All E.R. 33 (Q.B.).
73   *Ibid.*; *Ruxley Electronics and Construction Ltd. v. Forsyth*, [1996] A.C. 344 (H.L.) [*Ruxley*].
74   *Williamson v. Joseph Baruch Construction Ltd.* (1977), 2 R.P.R. 197 (Ont. H.C.J.); *Nu-West Homes v. Thunderbird Petroleum* (1975), 59 D.L.R. (3d) 292 (Alta. C.A.).

The possibility of alternative measures, reflecting the actual loss suffered by the plaintiff has now been formally acknowledged by courts. Instead of choosing between the extreme alternatives, courts may select a midway figure where that is appropriate. For example, in *Wilson v. Sooter Studios*,[75] the defendant completely botched the plaintiffs' wedding photographs. The price that had been charged for the job was $399. Locke J.A. held that a mere refund would not adequately compensate the plaintiffs for their loss. It would not give them the lost value of the pictures. He was, however, not prepared to accept the plaintiffs' argument that the only way of protecting their expectancy would be by an award large enough to permit them to reconstitute the wedding party and re-do the photos (which would involve flying guests back to British Columbia from Eastern Canada and South America). Locke J.A. held that this would be excessive, and instead chose a mid-range figure that would approximate the *true value* of the pictures to the plaintiffs. Drawing upon the academic literature on the subject,[76] he characterized this value as the "consumer surplus":

> [T]he difference between any lower price he pays and the higher price he is prepared to pay measures the "consumer surplus" expected at the time. Therefore, willingness to pay, rather than the market price, is the appropriate measure for estimating the true value of a purchase, and the difference between the value and the market price constituted the damage.[77]

In upholding an award of $1,000, Locke J.A. stated:

> I gain some insight into the adequacy of the award when I apply the perhaps treacherous economic test outlined above, which appears to be an economist's ingenious way of measuring intrinsic value to the owner … I do not think they would have paid $7000 more than the $399 they bargained for to get the pictures. They might have paid $600 more.[78]

The concept of subjective value or consumer surplus has also been adopted by the English House of Lords in a case involving a defective

75   (1988), 33 B.C.L.R. (2d) 241 (C.A.) [*Sooter*]. Another case involving wedding pictures is *Diesen v. Samson*, [1970] 1 S.L.T. 49 (Sheriff Ct.).
76   D. Harris, A.I. Ogus, & J. Phillips, "Contract Remedies and the Consumer Surplus" (1979), 95 L.Q. Rev. 581.
77   *Sooter*, above note 75 at 245.
78   *Ibid.* at 246. See also *Dunn v. Disc Jockey Unlimited Co.* (1978), 20 O.R. (2d) 309 (Prov. Ct.), awarding damages against a disc jockey for failing to provide entertainment at a wedding measured by the amount that the plaintiff might have paid at the last minute to secure a substitute.

swimming pool.[79] Lord Mustill confirmed that the Court has greater flexibility in selecting an appropriate damages award:

> There are not two alternative measures of damage at opposite poles, but only one; namely, the loss truly suffered by the promisee. In some cases the loss cannot be fairly measured except by reference to the full cost of repairing the deficiency in performance. In others, and particularly those where the contract is designed to fulfil a purely commercial purpose, the loss will very often consist only of the monetary detriment brought about by the breach of contract. But these remedies are not exhaustive, for the law must cater for those occasions where the value of the promise to the promisee exceeds the financial enhancement of his position which full performance will secure. This excess, often referred to in the literature as the "consumer surplus" … is usually incapable of precise valuation in terms of money, because it represents a personal, subjective and non-monetary gain. Nevertheless, where it exists the law should recognize it and compensate the promisee if the misperformance takes it away.[80]

The concept of consumer surplus as a tool in damages calculations is explored fully in Chapter 6, in which intangible and non-pecuniary losses are discussed.

E. RELIANCE DAMAGES

1) Introduction

a)   General Principles and Vocabulary

The reliance measure of damages reflects the principle of corrective justice. In contract law it is based on the idea that persons should be able to rely on one another's promises. In tort law it is based on the notion that persons should be able to rely on others to take care in their word and deed. In both cases, if persons suffer harm as a result of such reliance they should be compensated for any losses.

Damages assessed with the reliance measure are designed to put the plaintiff in a "break-even" position; that is, to return the plaintiff to the position that she was in immediately prior to entering into the contract or immediately before the tort was committed. The law does this by compensating the plaintiff for any expenses or losses incurred

---

79   *Ruxley*, above note 73.
80   *Ibid.* at 360–61.

by reason of relying upon or acting upon the defendant's promise or representation. Unlike the expectation measure of damages, which is forward-looking, the reliance measure of damages is backward-looking. It seeks to restore the status quo immediately prior to the wrong and ordinarily encompasses money (and other factors of value) actually lost by the plaintiff in reliance on the defendant.

b)   The Availability of Reliance Damages

The reliance measure of damages is only a secondary remedy in contract actions. It is available when expectation damages are not suitable for some reason. However, the reliance measure of damages (though not always referred to as such) is the standard measure of recovery in tort actions in respect of economic losses. In other areas of tort law such as recovery for personal injury, damages are also measured by the reliance interest; however, they are not generally referred to as "reliance damages" since, with the exception of fraud and misrepresentation, the damages in tort actions are not typically suffered because of any conscious "reliance" on the defendant, except insofar as it might be said that persons rely upon one another to fulfill their duties. Nevertheless, damages in tort law are generally based upon the principle of "restoration," which is the equivalent of reliance damages. The object of tort damages, whether for recovery of economic, property, or physical losses, is the same—to restore the plaintiff to the position that he would have occupied had the wrong never occurred. In this chapter, the single term "reliance damages" will be used.

2)   Reliance Damages for Breach of Contract

a)   As an Alternative to Expectation Damages

Reliance damages are a secondary option in contract law. They present an attractive alternative when expectation damages are unavailable. Sometimes expectation damages (such as lost profits) are so speculative or uncertain that a court may permit the plaintiff to claim reliance damages in the alternative. Where this is the case, the rule is that a plaintiff may recover money lost in reliance on the contract, unless the defendant is able to prove that the plaintiff would have suffered that loss in any event.

The leading example of reliance recovery in contract is *Anglia Television Ltd. v. Reed*.[81] In this case, the defendant, an actor, entered into a contract with the plaintiff to star in a planned movie. The defendant

---

81   [1972] 1 Q.B. 60 (C.A.) [*Anglia Television*]. See also *CCC Films (London) Ltd. v. Impact Quadrant Films Ltd.*, [1984] 3 All E.R. 298 (Q.B.D.) [*CCC Films*].

withdrew from the project shortly after signing the contract and the plaintiff was forced to cancel the filming. There was no way of determining how much money the movie would have made and the plaintiff was therefore unable to establish a claim for lost profits. Instead, the plaintiff was awarded reliance damages — the amounts expended upon the movie and wasted as a result of the defendant's promise and breach. Lord Denning stated the principle as follows:

> It seems to me that a plaintiff in such a case as this has an election: he can either claim for loss of profits; or for his wasted expenditure. But he must elect between them. He cannot claim both. If he has not suffered any loss of profits — or if he cannot prove what his profits would have been — he can claim in the alternative the expenditure which has been thrown away, that is, wasted, by reason of the breach.[82]

It should be noted the court must have been satisfied that following the breach it was not possible for the plaintiff to find another star for the movie. Otherwise, the plaintiff might have been barred from claiming damages on the grounds that it had failed to mitigate its loss (the relevant principles are discussed in Chapter 12).

Another example of reliance damages in contract law is the case of *McRae v. Commonwealth Disposals Commission*,[83] in which the defendant sold the plaintiff salvage rights to a wrecked tanker. In preparation for the salvage expedition, the plaintiff expended funds equipping a ship and hiring a crew. These funds were, however, wasted since the supposed wreck never actually existed. Since it was impossible to say how much the venture would have earned for the plaintiff had the contract worked out as expected, the court based recovery on the amounts thrown away by the plaintiff in preparation for the expedition. The court reasoned that, despite the fact that the plaintiff could not prove that it had lost profits, it was only fair that it be permitted to claim the expenses incurred in reliance on the defendant's promise.

b)   What is Included: The Problem of Pre-Contract Expenditures

In assessing reliance damages, the general principle is that the plaintiff is entitled to losses incurred in reliance on the defendant's promise. Clearly, this includes positive expenditures made after the contract is made. But what of other losses suffered as a result of the failed venture? For example, in *Anglia Television* the court awarded the plaintiff not only the amounts expended after the contract was entered into with the

---

82   *Anglia Television, ibid.* at 63–64.
83   (1951), 84 C.L.R. 377 (H.C.A.) [*McRae*].

defendant, but also amounts that it had invested before the defendant had signed the contract. On first impression these latter losses are not strictly reliance damages since they were not incurred in "reliance" on the contract. Nevertheless, Lord Denning permitted their recovery:

> If the plaintiff claims the wasted expenditure, he is not limited to the expenditure incurred *after* the contract was concluded. He can claim also the expenditure incurred *before* the contract, provided it was such as would reasonably be in the contemplation of the parties as likely to be wasted if the contract was broken.[84]

Some commentators have criticized this aspect of the *Anglia* case.[85] They argue that the amounts spent by the plaintiff before the defendant ever agreed to do the film could hardly be called reliance losses, since they were not incurred in reliance upon the defendant's promise. While this is true, the result can be defended if several assumptions are accepted. While the amounts were not expended in reliance upon the defendant's promise, they were *lost* in reliance on that promise. The plaintiff assumed that it had found its actor, and gave up looking for another. The court seems prepared to presume that had the defendant not agreed to be in the movie, the plaintiff would have been able to find another actor, and that the movie would have earned enough at least to return the plaintiff's investment. With these presumptions in place it can truly be said that the entire investment was lost in reliance on the defendant. This interpretation provides further illustration of Fuller and Purdue's thesis that a robust definition of reliance losses, which includes "forgone opportunities," begins to converge with the concept of expectation damages.

Thus, the recovery of pre-contract expenditures under the heading of "reliance damages" may be understood as an onus-shifting principle. Essentially, the court is willing to assume that, had the contract not been breached, the plaintiff would at least have broken even and recovered its outlay. This interpretation also underlies the decision in *McRae*. There, the defendant argued that the plaintiff could not prove that its losses were caused by breach of contract because, even had a tanker existed, it might have been worthless and the plaintiff's expenses might not have been recovered. The court rejected this argument. Once the plaintiff established that the expenditures were incurred in reliance on the promise that a tanker existed, it had a *prima facie* case that the loss was caused by the breach. The burden was then shifted to

---

84   Above note 81 at 64 [emphasis in original].
85   A.I. Ogus, "Damages for Pre-Contract Expenditure" (1972) 35 Mod. L. Rev. 423.

the defendant to establish that, even had the contract not been breached (i.e., the tanker existed), the plaintiff's expenditure would nevertheless have been wasted.[86]

This interpretation suggests that an alternative way of understanding the recovery of pre-contract expenses is to view the awards made in these cases as modest expectation damages. The courts are willing to assume in the plaintiff's favour that had there been no breach of contract the plaintiff's venture would have earned sufficient revenue to at least have broken even. While the plaintiff is unable to prove that it would have earned a net profit, the court assumes that it would have earned sufficient revenue at least to cover expenses. In the face of uncertainty about the actual profits, this seems a fair way to reconcile a reasonable degree of protection for the plaintiff, without unduly burdening the defendant with unproved losses.

The interpretation of the reliance measure of damages as an onus-shifting principle suggests that the defendant may seek to rebut the presumptions. Where the defendant is able to adduce evidence that the money lost in reliance on the contract would have been lost in any event (i.e., even had the contract not been breached), the presumption that the venture would have broken even may be rebutted and the plaintiff will be unable to recover its expenditures. Another way of putting this is that, where expectation damages can be established with certainty, and they are less than the amount lost by the plaintiff in reliance on the contract, the expectation damages are a ceiling on recovery. Several cases, discussed in the following section, confirm this interpretation.

c)   The Relation between Reliance Damages and Expectation Damages

In *Anglia Television*, Lord Denning suggests that a plaintiff may always elect reliance damages. This broad statement requires some qualification. A plaintiff may claim reliance damages when expectation damages are too uncertain or impossible to prove (as in *McRae* and *Anglia Television*). However, where expectation damages can be calculated with certainty, the reliance measure may not always be available as an alternative. For example, there will be situations where the plaintiff might wish to elect to claim reliance damages when there are little or no expectation damages to claim. This would occur when the contract is not a profitable one, yet the plaintiff incurs substantial expenses in relation to it. This claim is more problematic.

---

86   *McRae*, above note 83 at 414.

For example, suppose that the plaintiff and defendant enter into a contract under which the plaintiff is to build a house for $80,000. Halfway through construction, the defendant refuses to allow the plaintiff to complete the work. At that point the plaintiff has been paid $50,000 and has spent $60,000 on the work. The cost of completing the house is $40,000. In such a case the plaintiff might wish to claim reliance damages of $10,000, since they in fact exceed expectation damages. This sum would cancel the loss incurred so far by the plaintiff on the work and put the plaintiff in the position as though the contract had not been entered. Expectation damages, on the other hand, would be nil. Had the contract run to completion, the plaintiff would have suffered a net loss of $20,000. As a result of the breach, work has been terminated at a point where the plaintiff has lost only $10,000.

Most authorities agree that reliance damages should not be awarded if they would put the plaintiff in a better position than if the contract had been performed. In the above example, permitting the plaintiff to recover reliance damages would put the plaintiff in a better position than if the contract had been performed. It would compensate the plaintiff for losses suffered not from a breach of contract (which in fact saved the plaintiff money), but from entering into an unprofitable contract in the first place.

This limitation has been confirmed in Canada in *Bowlay Logging Ltd. v. Domtar Ltd.*[87] Here, the plaintiff agreed to cut wood for the defendant for a fixed price. After the plaintiff had completed a portion of the contract, the defendant breached by failing to provide sufficient trucks to haul the wood from the wood lot. Instead of suing for its lost profits, the plaintiff sued for recovery of its costs in performing the contract to date ($233,000) less the amount that it had been paid so far ($108,000). The plaintiff relied upon *Anglia Television*, asserting that it had a right to elect between expectation damages and reliance damages. The court refused to allow the claim and confirmed that the right of election is not absolute: where the reliance claim can be shown to exceed the expectation damages to which the plaintiff would be entitled, it will fail. On the facts of the case, the court held that, even had the contract not been breached, the plaintiff would have lost money. At trial, Berger J. stated:

> The law of contract compensates a plaintiff for damages resulting from the defendant's breach; it does not compensate a plaintiff for damages resulting from his making a bad bargain. Where it can be

---

87   [1978] 4 W.W.R. 105 (B.C.S.C.), aff'd (1982), 135 D.L.R. (3d) 179 (B.C.C.A.) [*Bowlay*].

seen that the plaintiff would have incurred a loss on the contract as a whole, the expenses he has incurred are losses flowing from entering into the contract, not losses flowing from the defendant's breach ... [Otherwise] the law would run contrary to the normal expectations of the world of commerce. The burden of risk would be shifted from the plaintiff to the defendant. The defendant would become the insurer of the plaintiff's enterprise.[88]

The Court of Appeal affirmed this decision, adding that if the plaintiff could prove that its loss on the contract was *increased* by reason of the breach, the plaintiff could recover those additional losses. But it could not recover losses caused by the plaintiff's own improvident contract or inefficient work practices. Thus, in *Pacific Playground*,[89] although the plaintiff could not recover lost profits because the development was doomed even absent the defendants' breach, the plaintiff still recovered additional costs incurred in an attempt to mitigate after the breach. In this case, the plaintiff entered into a contract with Pacific Playground for the purchase of a property to be developed by the plaintiff. A subsidiary company of Pacific Playground was to deliver water for the development. The subsidiary company was unable to supply the water as expected, and the plaintiff had to incur extra expenses to secure an alternate water supply. The plaintiff ran into financial difficulties leading to foreclosure. The defendants' failure to provide an adequate water supply was found to be a significant breach, which also generated other problems for the development. However, the plaintiff faced additional problems unrelated to the defendants' breach, such as approvals for the subdivision, which also would have ultimately delayed the project and made it unprofitable. Hence, the court concluded that the plaintiff's project would have been a losing proposition even absent the defendants' breach. Expenses incurred in securing an alternate water supply were recoverable as a cost of mitigation and not in part performance of the contract. In distinguishing the result in this case from the outcome in *Bowlay*, Wilson J. noted:

> I do not consider that case to be applicable here, where I have made a finding that the expenses incurred by [the plaintiff] in search for an alternate water supply arose directly from the breach of contract by [the defendants]. They were not expenses incurred in part performance of the contract, but rather were expenses incurred as a result of

---

88 *Ibid.* at 117 (B.C.S.C.).
89 *Pacific Playground Holdings Ltd. v. Endeavour Developments Ltd.* (2002), 28 C.P.C. (5th) 85 (B.C.S.C.) [*Pacific Playground*].

the breach by [the defendants], which would not have been incurred otherwise.[90]

This confirms that where expectation damages are uncertain, and the plaintiff has lost funds in reliance on the contract, the courts are willing to shift the onus of proof to the defendant. The plaintiff is able to recover all of the funds it wasted in reliance on the contract *unless the defendant is able to demonstrate that those funds would have been lost in any event had the plaintiff completed the contract.* Where the defendant is able to demonstrate that the plaintiff would not have recovered those expenses had the contract been performed, because the contract was an unprofitable one for the plaintiff, the plaintiff may not claim those expenses. The court will not award reliance damages where this will clearly place the plaintiff in a better position than if the contract had been performed. Instead, the court will subtract from the plaintiff's reliance expenditures incurred at the time of the breach, the provable net losses that the plaintiff would have incurred by completing the contract. This principle has now been confirmed in England as well, where the Court of Appeal has adopted the reasoning in *Bowlay*.[91]

A further illustration of this principle, which provides a contrast with *Bowlay*, is the case of *Sunshine Vacation Villas Ltd. v. Hudson's Bay Co.*[92] Here the defendant breached its contract to lease space to the plaintiff for a business venture. Following *Anglia Television*, the plaintiff was permitted to claim as reliance damages its entire lost investment, though there was uncertainty about whether it would have earned any profits. The court distinguished *Bowlay* on the basis that the "crucial finding" in that case had been that plaintiff's expenditures were less than the loss that it would have incurred had the contract been completed. "The onus of establishing that state of facts rests upon the defendant. It has not been discharged in this case."[93] Thus, even where the plaintiff is unable to prove that it would have made a profit, the court will assume that it would have broken even, unless the defendant is able to show that the plaintiff would have incurred a loss.

d) Cumulative Claims: Reliance Damages as a Complement to Expectation Damages

It is sometimes said that reliance damages and expectation damages cannot be claimed together, or that "profits" and "losses" cannot both

---

90   *Ibid.* at para. 11.
91   See *CCC Films*, above note 81; *C. & P. Haulage v. Middleton*, [1983] 3 All E.R. 94 (C.A.).
92   (1984), 58 B.C.L.R. 33 (C.A.) [*Sunshine*].
93   *Ibid.* at 43.

be claimed. For example, in *Anglia Television* Lord Denning suggests that the plaintiff must "elect" between the two measures and that he cannot claim both. This issue is controversial because of an ambiguity in terminology.

As explained in an earlier part of this chapter, when expectation damages are based on "gross" profit or revenues, then it is ordinarily true that reliance damages may not also be claimed since those expenses would have been incurred in any event in order to earn the profit. To award both reliance damages and expectation damages would overcompensate the plaintiff. However, where expectation damages are based on net profit, additional reliance losses may also appropriately be claimed in some circumstances.[94]

For example, consider a situation where A agrees to sell widgets B for $1,000, which B intends to resell for $1,500. B rents warehou space for $100 to store the widgets. If A refuses to deliver, and B is u able to purchase the widgets elsewhere, B may formulate her claim two ways. First, she may claim expectation damages based on the gro revenue lost. This would be $500 assuming that the goods have n been paid for. Alternatively, the claim could be formulated as a clai for lost net profit ($400) plus wasted expenses ($100). In both cases, is placed in the position as though the contract had been performed. no event may B claim both expectation damages based on gross los plus reliance damages, since this would overcompensate B.

This account of the relation between reliance and expectation damages is, unfortunately, clearer than the caselaw suggests. Several cases have "overstated" the rule against double compensation by holding in unnecessarily broad terms that a plaintiff may never claim both lost profits and wasted expenses. One example is *Sunshine*.[95] In this case the plaintiff was seeking space in Hudson's Bay stores to operate its travel business. In breach of contract, the defendant leased space in a favourable location to the plaintiff's competitor. The plaintiff cancelled the contract and claimed its lost capital on the venture (the amount of working capital invested and not recovered) plus a sum of $100,000 for lost profit. The court denied the cumulative claim, explaining that the claims must be made in the alternative:

> One method of assessment, the return of expenses or loss of capital, approaches the matter by considering what Sunshine Vacation's position would have been had it not entered into the contract. The other, loss of profit, approaches it by considering what the position would

94   See A.I. Ogus, *The Law of Damages* (London: Butterworths, 1973).
95   Above note 92.

have been had the Bay carried out its bargain. The two approaches must be alternatives.[96]

This reasoning is correct only if the claim for lost profit is based on gross, rather than net profit. If the plaintiff is claiming the whole of its lost revenues then it is true that it should not also be entitled to its wasted expenditures, since those expenditures would have been paid from the revenues. However, if the plaintiff is claiming lost profit in the usual sense (net revenues after expenses) there is no reason why it should not be entitled to recover both. The relevant question is whether, if the contract had been performed, the plaintiff would have earned sufficient revenue both to recover its expenditures (or at least preserve the initial investment in the "value" of the business as a going concern) and earn a net return on its investment each year. If so, then it should be permitted to claim both heads of damages since this is the only way to put it in the position it would have been in had the contract been performed. The refusal in *Sunshine* to award the lost profits claim can better be defended on the ground that the claim was speculative and unproven.

To summarize, while the caselaw is somewhat confused on this point, cumulative claims for reliance expenses and lost profits should be permitted so long as they do not overlap and result in overcompensation. Whether they do overlap will depend upon whether, in the calculation of lost profits, expenses have or have not already been deducted.

F. DAMAGES FOR ECONOMIC LOSSES IN TORT

1) Bases of Liability for Economic Loss in Tort

The law of tort allows recovery of economic losses only in limited situations. Most prominently, the law permits recovery of any economic losses suffered when a person is physically injured or when his property is damaged. The principles of damages quantification in respect of personal injury are discussed in Chapter 4, and the principles of damages for harms to property are discussed in Chapter 3.

In the absence of physical injury or property damage, economic loss is recoverable in tort only in limited situations. Most clearly, economic loss can be recovered in cases of fraud and misrepresentation.[97] Certain business interests are also protected by the law of tort because

---

96   *Ibid.* at 39.
97   *Hedley Byrne & Co. Ltd. v. Heller & Partners Ltd.*, [1964] A.C. 465 (H.L.).

they are proprietary. With the expansion in this century of the concept of "intellectual property," many economic interests have received enhanced protection as property interests. Compensation in respect of these is considered in Chapter 3; and Chapter 7 describes restitutionary remedies available in respect of these same wrongs.

Beyond these categories, compensation for "pure" economic loss is rarely permitted. In particular, Canadian courts have shown a marked reluctance to permit recovery of pure economic loss suffered as a result of negligence. While there is no absolute bar against these claims, the Supreme Court has held that they will ordinarily be denied on policy grounds. It is widely accepted that the interests of citizens in their physical well-being and security of their property merit greater protection than mere financial interests. An additional reason for the restrictive approach is that the potential economic losses flowing from a single act of negligence are indeterminate and potentially enormous, and may be all out of proportion to the actual "fault" of the defendant. Liability for these losses would unduly chill commercial activity, and ordinarily it is more efficient to require persons to protect themselves from such losses by insurance, rather than through the tort system.[98]

2) Basic Principles of Damages in Tort: *Restitutio in Integrum*

In all cases where recovery of economic losses in tort is permitted, the principle is *restitutio in integrum*. The goal is to restore the plaintiff to the position that the plaintiff would have been in had the wrong not occurred. The restoration measure of damages in tort, then, is ordinarily the equivalent of the reliance measure. The plaintiff is not entitled to expectation damages since it is only by way of contract that a person is entitled to a benefit from the defendant. In *BG Checo International Ltd. v. B.C. Hydro Authority,* the Supreme Court of Canada confirmed the difference, explaining that in contract "the plaintiff is to be put in the position it would have been in had the contract been performed as agreed," whereas in tort "the plaintiff is to be put in the position it would have been in had the misrepresentation not been made."[99] The Court later explained:

---

98   *D'Amato v. Badger*, [1996] 2 S.C.R. 1071 [*D'Amato*]; *Winnipeg Condominium Corporation No. 36 v. Bird Construction Co.,* [1995] 1 S.C.R. 85 [*Winnipeg Condominium*]. See B. Feldthusen, *Economic Negligence: The Recovery of Pure Economic Loss,* 4th ed. (Toronto: Carswell, 2000).
99   [1993] 1 S.C.R. 12 at 37 [*BG Checo*].

> [T]he main reason to expect a difference between tort and contract damages is the exclusion of the bargain elements in standard tort compensation. In the terminology of L.L. Fuller and W.R. Purdue, as set out in their article, "The Reliance Interest in Contract Damages" (1936–7), 46 Yale L.J. 52 and 373, contract is normally concerned with "expectation" damages while tort is concerned with "reliance" damages."[100]

The fact that tort claims are based upon the reliance measure of damages does not mean, as we shall see, that the plaintiff is never entitled to claim lost future benefits and even lost profits. But the way in which those claims are formulated will be different from a contract claim.

3) Fraud and Misrepresentation

Damages for negligent misrepresentation[101] provide a good example of the difference between contract and tort. In cases of economic loss caused by negligent misrepresentation, damages are calculated by determining the position that the plaintiff would have been in had the misrepresentation not been made. Typically, this will involve restoring to the plaintiff any funds lost or wasted as a result of the defendant's negligence. This may include funds directly spent on the faith of the misrepresentation, plus other sums spent, or liabilities incurred as a result of the transaction. For example, where, as a result of the misrepresentation, the plaintiff has purchased goods or services from the defendant (or others), or made an investment, damages will typically be measured by the price paid by the plaintiff, less any "value received." In addition, if the plaintiff has suffered other foreseeable pecuniary losses as a result of the defendant's falsehood, those losses are recoverable as well.[102] By awarding this amount, the plaintiff can be put in the same position as though she had *never entered into the transaction*. This is different from the contractual measure, which is the difference between

---

100 *Ibid.* at 41.

101 Negligent misrepresentation has been defined by the Supreme Court of Canada in *Queen v. Cognos Inc.*, [1993] 1 S.C.R. 87 at 110:

> ... (1) there must be a duty of care based on a "special relationship" between the representor and the representee; (2) the misrepresentation in question must be untrue, inaccurate, or misleading; (3) the misrepresentor must have acted negligently in making said misrepresentation; the representee must have relied, in a reasonable manner, on said negligent misrepresentation; and (5) the reliance must have been detrimental to the representee in the sense that damages resulted.

102 *Doyle v. Olby (Ironmongers) Ltd.*, [1969] 2 Q.B. 158 [*Doyle*].

value of the goods that were received, and the value they *would have had if the misrepresentation had been true.*

The same principle applies in fraud claims. The proper remedy is an award that will place the plaintiff in the financial position she would have been in had the fraudulent statement never been made, rather than in the position the plaintiff would have been in had the statement been true.[103]

In *Beaver Lumber Co. v. McLenaghan*[104] the Saskatchewan Court of Appeal explained the difference as follows:

> Where the negligent misrepresentation induces the plaintiff to enter into a contract with the representor or a third party, is the proper measure of damages for that misrepresentation the tortious (reliance) measure or the contractual (expectation) measure? The distinction between the two measures is important and is this: the tortious measure aims at restoring the *status quo ante* and the contractual measure at putting the plaintiff in the position he would have been in had the misrepresentation been true. Thus, where a misrepresentation induces the plaintiff to enter into a contract, the tortious measure … would be the difference between the value of the property or services received under the contract and the amount paid for that property or those services, plus his consequential losses, that is, his out-of-pocket loss but not his loss of bargain or prospective profits.[105]

Goldstar Management Ltd. v. Varvis[106] provides a further illustration of the difference. The plaintiff purchased a pizza business on the faith of a misrepresentation about the volume of sales. The tort damages were assessed by the amount of money lost by the plaintiff in purchasing and operating the business ($65,000). However, the court also held that the representation could be construed as a contractual guarantee and expectation damages were assessed by the difference between what the business was actually worth, and what it would have been worth had the statement been true ($80,000).

In addition to the lost value, the plaintiff is entitled to consequential losses suffered as a result of the misrepresentation. Such losses include liabilities to third parties incurred as a result of the misrepresentation, and also additional funds wasted trying to run the business, salvage the transaction, or mitigate the damages. For example, where

---

103 *Parna v. G. & S. Properties Ltd.*, [1971] S.C.R. 306.
104 (1982), 21 Sask. R. 65 (C.A.).
105 *Ibid.* at 76.
106 (1995), 34 Alta. L.R. (3d) 74 (Q.B.).

the plaintiff purchases a business on the basis of a falsehood about its value, the plaintiff may be entitled to damages for both the diminished value of the business, and also for funds wasted attempting to run it.[107] In fraud cases it has been suggested that consequential losses are recovered so long as they are the direct result of the fraud, regardless of foreseeability, since "it does not lie in the mouth of the fraudulent person to say that they could not have been reasonably foreseen."[108] In negligent misrepresentation cases, the losses must meet the test of foreseeability.

4) Negligence Causing Pure Economic Loss

Pure economic losses caused by negligence are recoverable in tort only in limited situations. First, when a person voluntarily undertakes to perform a service, and fails to do so, that person may be liable for resulting economic loss caused by reliance on his undertaking. For example, where an insurance agent undertakes to procure insurance for a homeowner, and fails to do so, the agent may be liable to the homeowner for the loss of uninsured property.[109] Similarly, lawyers have been held liable to the intended beneficiaries of wills when, due to the lawyer's negligence, the will is invalid.[110] However, beyond these limited situations, the law is reluctant to award damages for pure economic loss caused by negligence. The Supreme Court of Canada has held, for example, that a courier is not liable to a third party for economic loss caused by late delivery of documents[111] and that a negligent driver is not liable for economic losses caused to an employer when the employee was negligently injured by the driver.[112] The courts are concerned not to open the floodgates of liability for indeterminate losses to indeterminate persons, and to "cripple [persons'] ability to do business."[113]

Despite these concerns, there are a limited number of situations where liability for pure economic loss caused by negligence will be recoverable. For example, in the case of *Rivtow Marine Ltd. v. Washington*

---

107 *Esso Petroleum v. Mardon*, [1976] Q.B. 801, [1976] 1 All E.R. 5 (C.A.) [*Esso Petroleum*].
108 *Doyle*, above note 102 at 167.
109 *Morash v. Lockhart & Ritchie Ltd.* (1978), 24 N.B.R. (2d) 180 (C.A.).
110 *Whittingham v. Crease & Co.* (1978), 88 D.L.R. (3d) 353 (B.C.S.C.); *White v. Jones*, [1995] 2 W.L.R. 187 (H.L.); *Wilhelm v. Hickson* (2000), 189 Sask. R. 71 (C.A.), leave to appeal to S.C.C. refused, [2000] S.C.C.A. No. 124.
111 *B.D.C. Ltd. v. Hoffstrand Farms Ltd.*, [1986] 1 S.C.R. 228.
112 *D'Amato*, above note 98.
113 *Canadian National Railway Co. v. Norsk Pacific Steamship Co.*, [1992] 1 S.C.R. 1021 at 1147 [*Norsk*].

Iron Works[114] the defendant was liable for the plaintiff's lost profits resulting from the defendant's failure to warn the plaintiff about a defect
in its crane (the Supreme Court reasoned that, had a timely warning
been given, the crane could have been repaired during a slower season).
The plaintiff was not awarded its expectation damages in the tort action (the cost of repairing the crane) because such damages are properly the province of the law of contract. However, it is now established
that where, as a result of the defendant's negligence, the plaintiff is
obliged to repair property in order to prevent a real and substantial
risk of harm to the occupants of the property, the reasonable costs of
restoring the structure to a non-dangerous state may be recoverable.[115]
Similarly, a plaintiff may be entitled to recover losses incurred for having to destroy or discard a product to prevent a real and substantial risk
to the health of potential consumers.[116]

In all these cases the principle of recovery is *restitutio in integrum*.
The plaintiff is entitled to be put in the position as though the negligence had not occurred. The plaintiff is entitled to recover the lost
economic benefits that it would have received, but for the defendant's
negligence (e.g., the value of the benefits under an invalid will), the expenditures incurred as a result of the negligence, and the revenues that
would have been earned had the defendant not breached its duty. For
example, in *Norsk*[117] the plaintiff was able to recover its lost revenues
resulting from damage to a bridge that it used, but did not own.

Again, while the distinction is subtle, there will still be some differences between damages in tort and damages in contract in these cases.
For example, in cases where the defendant builder's negligence neces-
sitates an expenditure to make a building safe, the plaintiff is entitled
to the reasonable cost of making the building safe, but not necessarily
to the full cost of remedying the defect or improving the building to the
standard that it would have met had the builder properly performed all
its obligations under the contract. These damages would be recoverable
only in a contract action.

5) Assessing the "but for" Situation

In tort compensation, the plaintiff is entitled to be put in the position
she would have been in but for the wrong. As is the case with expecta-

---

114 [1974] S.C.R. 1189.
115 *Winnipeg Condominium*, above note 98.
116 M. Hasegawa & Co. v. Pepsi Bottling Group (Canada), Co. (2002), 1 B.C.L.R. (4th)
     209 (C.A.).
117 Above note 113.

tion damages, the assessment of reliance damages will often require the court to make findings using hypothetical scenarios. Whereas in assessing expectation damages, a court must hypothesize what would have happened had the contract been performed, in assessing reliance damages a court must hypothesize what would have happened had the tort not been committed. For example, when the plaintiff has relied upon a negligent misrepresentation to plan a course of action (e.g., to make an investment, bid on a contract, buy a property) the court must construct an alternative scenario about what the plaintiff would have done had the misrepresentation not been made.

In most cases, where the fraud or misrepresentation induced the plaintiff to enter into a transaction, the court will simply presume that the plaintiff would not have entered into that transaction and would therefore have avoided any loss on the investment (including any consequential losses). For example, in *Rainbow Industrial Caterers v. C.N.R.*[118] the plaintiff tendered a bid to supply meals to railway crews. The bid was based on a negligent forecast by the defendant as to the volume of meals that would be required and the plaintiff lost money on the contract before terminating it. The Supreme Court of Canada granted the plaintiff its full operating loss, thus restoring it to the position that it would have occupied had it never entered into the contract.

An interesting feature of this case is that the plaintiff may have been better off as a result of claiming its reliance losses in tort rather than its expectation damages in contract. Some of the plaintiff's losses in *Rainbow* may have resulted from its own manner of carrying out the contract, or from underestimating the costs of the contract irrespective of the false information supplied by the defendant. Thus, even apart from the negligent misrepresentation, the plaintiff might have suffered a loss on the contract. Nevertheless, the Court permitted recovery of all these losses, reasoning that, whatever the cause of these losses, they would not have been incurred by the plaintiff because the plaintiff would not have entered into the contract. Thus, unlike claims in contract (as in *Bowlay*), claims for reliance damages in tort may in fact relieve the plaintiff from the consequences of having entered an unfavourable bargain. As the Supreme Court explained in a later case,

> [t]he *Rainbow* assessment of damages can obviously lead to a different quantum of damages because this method frees the parties from the burden or benefit of the rest of their bargain. The assessment of damages in a *Rainbow* situation could be lower or higher than the

---

118   [1991] 3 S.C.R. 3 [*Rainbow*].

contract damages depending on whether the contract was a good or bad bargain.[119]

The situation in England is different. The House of Lords has held that the only damages that the plaintiff may receive, even if the action is framed as one for negligent misrepresentation, are those that are caus-ally related to the breach of duty. Thus, for example, where a plaintiff purchases property on the faith of a negligent valuation, the plaintiff is entitled to recover money lost if the property is worth less than the purchase price. However, if the property also declines in value due to a slump in the market, the purchaser cannot recover the additional loss. As Lord Hoffman explained,

> A person under a duty to take reasonable care to provide information on which someone else will decide upon a course of action is, if neg-ligent, not generally regarded as responsible for all the consequences of that course of action. He is responsible only for the consequences of the information being wrong. A duty of care which imposes on the informant responsibility for losses which would have occurred even if the information had been correct is not in my view fair and reason-able as between the parties.[120]

It is submitted that the Canadian approach to this question is pref-erable. While it may appear to protect the plaintiff from risks of an investment unconnected to the defendant's wrong, the plaintiff would not have made the investment in the first place but for that wrong. Moreover, attempting to disentangle the losses caused by the defend-ant's wrong from losses that might have been suffered in any event may not be worthwhile from the point of view of judicial expediency.[121]

---

119 *BG Checo*, above note 99 at 40.
120 *South Australia Asset Management Corp. v. York Montague Ltd.*, [1996] 3 All E.R. 365 at 372 (H.L.) [*SAAMCO*].
121 In *Aneco Reinsurance Underwriting Ltd. v. Johnson & Higgens Ltd.*, [2001] UKHL 51, the House of Lords affirmed the law as stated in *SAAMCO*, *ibid.*, but noted that it will not apply in all cases. The limit of recovery is determined by the scope of the defendant's duty. In this case, where the plaintiffs had undertaken to insure a risk on the assumption of the availability of reinsurance for the risk, based on the defendant's negligently provided advice, the plaintiffs recovered not just the reinsurance cover, but the entire loss they had suffered on the transaction. Their Lordships reasoned that accurate information about the unavailability of reinsurance would have signalled to the plaintiffs the market's assessment of the risk entailed in the transaction, and they would not have pro-ceeded, and hence would have avoided the losses in question. Lord Steyn noted that it is artificial and unrealistic to distinguish between the unavailability of

There is one class of cases where the defendant may plausibly claim that damages should be reduced because some of the loss would have been incurred in any event. As seen above, in the usual case, where the plaintiff enters into a transaction on the faith of a careless statement by the defendant, the plaintiff is entitled to *all* the losses suffered on that transaction, on the assumption that "but for" the negligent advice, the plaintiff would have avoided the transaction altogether. However, in some cases the more likely scenario is that, had the information been correct, the plaintiff would still have entered into the transaction, though perhaps on different terms. In these cases, it cannot be said that all the losses suffered on the investment were caused by the defendant's wrong because even in the absence of the wrong the plaintiff might still have made the investment and might still have suffered a loss (though likely a smaller one).

This issue arose in *Rainbow*. The defendant took the position that, had a proper forecast been made, the plaintiff would still have entered into the contract (albeit with a somewhat higher bid) and would still have lost money. Thus, the damages awarded to the plaintiff put him in a better position than if no wrong had been done. The Court rejected this submission on the basis of a plaintiff-favourable presumption:

> Once the loss occasioned by the transaction is established, the plaintiff has discharged the burden of proof with respect to damages. A defendant who alleges that a plaintiff would have entered into a transaction on different terms sets up a new issue. It is an issue that requires the court to speculate as to what would have happened in a hypothetical situation. It is an area in which it is usually impossible to adduce concrete evidence. In the absence of evidence to support a finding on this issue, should the plaintiff or defendant bear the risk of non-persuasion? Must the plaintiff negate all speculative hypotheses about his position if the defendant had not committed a tort or must the tortfeasor who sets up this hypothetical situation establish it?[122]
>
> ... The appellant CN alleged that the loss was not all attributable to the misrepresentation because Rainbow would have entered into a different contract on other terms which would have resulted in at least some of the loss. What the respondent would have done had it not been for the tortious act requires a great deal of speculation, and ... I would apply the legal burden of proof against the defendant.[123]

---

reinsurance and the assessment of the risk entailed in the transaction that the plaintiffs were about to undertake. *Ibid.* at para. 41.

122 *Rainbow*, above note 118 at 15.

123 *Ibid.* at 17.

The presumption set out in *Rainbow* is rebuttable. Where the defendant is able to show that, despite the wrong, the plaintiff's course of conduct would nevertheless have resulted in a loss, the plaintiff will not be compensated for that portion of the loss that would have been incurred in any event. For example, the defendant may seek to prove that, had there been no misrepresentation, the plaintiff would have entered into another contract that would have lost money; or alternatively, that the plaintiff would have entered into the same contract, albeit on different terms. In such a case, the plaintiff will be confined to damages assessed by reference to that alternative unfavourable contract and will not be entitled to damages for profits forgone on other more favourable contracts. But the burden of persuasion on this point is on the defendant.

BG Checo[124] provides an illustration. As in *Rainbow*, the plaintiff entered into a contract on the basis of a misrepresentation about the scope of work by the defendant, and later sought to recover the losses incurred performing the contract. However, unlike *Rainbow*, there was an express finding by the Court that, had the misrepresentation not been made, the plaintiff would still have entered into the contract, though at an increased price. Thus, damages were calculated not as the entire loss suffered by the plaintiff, but rather as the difference between the loss it suffered and the loss or gain that it would have incurred had it taken the true facts into account in calculating its bid. The Court explained:

> This is not a case like *Rainbow*. Here, the evidence at trial [showed that] ... Checo would have entered the contract in any event, albeit at a higher bid. This conclusion having been reached, one would expect that the quantum of damages in tort and contract would be similar because the elements of the bargain unrelated to the misrepresentation are reintroduced. This means not giving the plaintiff compensation for any losses not related to the misrepresentation, but resulting from such factors as the plaintiff's own poor performance, or market or other forces that are a normal part of business transactions.[125]

6) Claims for Lost Profits and Forgone Opportunities: The Convergence of Reliance and Expectation Damages

Despite the conceptual difference between reliance and expectation damages, the amounts will sometimes converge. Damages in tort are

---

124 Above note 99.
125 *Ibid.* at 41.

typically based on the reliance or restoration interest. The object is to put the plaintiff in the position as though the wrong had not been committed. However, in some cases, where the reliance measure of damages includes not only direct out-of-pocket losses but also indirect losses in the nature of "forgone opportunities," reliance damages will come very close to the expectation measure of damages.

Esso Petroleum,[126] discussed earlier, provides a good illustration. The plaintiff was induced to lease a gas station by negligent misrepresentations by Esso about the amount of business that the location would attract. The court held that the plaintiff was not entitled to the contractual measure of damages (the profit that he would have earned if the representation had been true), because the defendant's representation was not a contractual guarantee that the plaintiff would sell a set amount of gasoline. The plaintiff was, therefore, confined to his claim for reliance damages (the amount of money thrown away on the venture). However, as part of his reliance damages, the plaintiff was entitled to damages representing the lost opportunities, including lost earnings, suffered by him during the years that he attempted to run the losing venture. The court held that he was a man of considerable initiative and, had he not entered upon the venture in reliance on Esso's estimate, would have earned a fair living at some other venture. The court intimated that damages on this score would take into account some return on both his capital and labour, which had been thrown away on the petrol station. Thus, while the plaintiff was not entitled to claim the lost profits on the gasoline venture, he was entitled to claim his "lost profits" in a more abstract sense. In the end, the inclusion of "lost opportunities" or "gains prevented" in the reliance measure of damages means that that measure will often be very close to the expectation measure.

Similarly, in *McRae*,[127] where the plaintiff was awarded reliance losses for expenditures wasted on a futile effort to salvage a non-existent tanker, the damages awarded included an amount that the plaintiff's vessel might have earned on a daily basis had it not been involved in the salvage expedition. The plaintiff was unable to establish what profits might have been earned had the salvage expedition been successful, but it was able to claim the notional lost profits that might have been earned on an alternate venture.

The Supreme Court of Canada has confirmed that the reliance measure of damages may include lost profits. In *V.K. Mason Construction v.*

126 Above note 107.
127 Above note 83.

Bank of Nova Scotia[128] the Court showed how reliance and expectation damages may converge. The defendant bank carelessly misrepresented to the plaintiff contractor that a developer would have sufficient financing for a construction project. On this basis the plaintiff entered into a contract with the developer to do the work but was not fully paid. The trial judge held that the bank was liable for negligent misrepresentation and awarded the plaintiff the amount owed by the developer to the plaintiff, less the portion representing the profit that the plaintiff would have earned on the project. The trial judge held that the reliance measure should include the loss incurred from performing the work, but not the profit since an award of the profit would place the plaintiff in the position as though the representation were true.

On appeal to the Supreme Court of Canada, the damages were increased to include the profit. Wilson J. agreed that there is a conceptual difference between damages in tort and contract but concluded that "in many instances the same quantum will be arrived at, albeit by somewhat different routes."[129] Wilson J. reasoned that, had the misrepresentation not been made, the plaintiff would not have entered into the contract. Thus, it is true that the plaintiff would not have earned the profit on the work. However, it is likely that, had the plaintiff not undertaken this project, it would have entered into other profitable contracts, and Wilson J. accepted that the profit lost on the first contract provided a reasonable basis for an estimate of what the plaintiff might have earned elsewhere.

Thus, reliance damages may include forgone gains. In such cases, the measure of damages in tort will in fact appear to converge with the contractual measure of damages. But the conceptual basis remains different and the two methods will not always lead to the same result. The expected profit on the first construction project is not awarded because the defendant is responsible for its loss, but simply because it serves as a convenient proxy for measuring the opportunity costs to the plaintiff. Essentially the court is adopting a plaintiff-favourable assumption that the plaintiff could have earned an equal amount of profit elsewhere. The defendant may, of course, rebut this presumption by bringing evidence to show that the expected profit on the first contract was unusually large, or that because of the state of the industry the plaintiff's opportunities elsewhere were much less valuable. Where the court accepts such evidence, the reliance and expectation measures will diverge. For example, the plaintiff in *V.K. Mason* would not be en-

---

128 [1985] 1 S.C.R. 271 [*V.K. Mason*].
129 *Ibid.* at 285.

titled to its entire lost profit where the defendant could demonstrate that this profit was unusually large in relation to what the plaintiff might have earned elsewhere.[130]

The convergence of tort and contract damages was further confirmed by the Supreme Court of Canada in *BG Checo*,[131] discussed earlier. In this case the plaintiff entered into a contract to erect a power line, based on a representation by Hydro that the right of way would be adequately cleared. The right of way was not cleared and Hydro was found liable for negligent misrepresentation and also for breach of contract. While reiterating that tort and contract damages have a different conceptual foundation, the Court held that, in cases where the negligent misrepresentation is also a breach of contract, the measure of damages will usually be the same. Considered as a breach of contract case, the goal is to put the plaintiff in the position as though Hydro had cleared the right of way. The plaintiff would have avoided the additional costs incurred in clearing the right of way and would also have avoided some overhead. Considered as a negligent misrepresentation case, had the facts been known to the plaintiff, it would have increased its bid to take into account the additional costs that it would incur on the project. Though arrived at by a different route, the amounts are roughly the same.

---

130 *Ibid.* at 286, Wilson J.
131 Above note 99.

CHAPTER 3

COMPENSATION FOR HARM TO PROPERTY INTERESTS

A. INTRODUCTION

An interest in property may be harmed in a variety of ways. The property may be stolen, damaged, or destroyed by the wrongful act of the defendant. In these cases the cause of action will be in tort (e.g., negligence, nuisance, trespass, conversion, and detinue). Alternatively, the plaintiff may be kept out of possession of property by a bailee, or by a vendor who fails to live up to a contract to sell the property; or a contractor may breach their contract to improve or preserve property. In these cases the cause of action will be in contract. This chapter outlines the basic principles of damages assessment in relation to property interests, in both contract and tort.

The first principle in respect of compensation of property interests is *restitutio in integrum*. The owner of property is entitled to be put in the position as though the wrong had not been done. The damages will be measured by the loss in value of the property to the owner.

Where the wrong is a breach of contract (e.g., a failure to deliver property that the plaintiff has purchased from the defendant, or a breach of contract to improve property), the plaintiff is entitled to expectation damages. These will be measured by the value that the property would have had to the plaintiff had the contract been performed. The same basic principle applies in tort cases. When property is damaged or destroyed, the plaintiff is entitled to full restoration; that is, to be put in the position as though the wrong had not been done. This means that, where property is *destroyed*, the owner is entitled to the actual value that the property had to her at the time of the wrong. Where the property is "fungible" and available for purchase on the market, the damages will be assessed by the cost of acquiring a substitute. Where the property is not easily replaced, courts must engage in more complex calculations to determine its value to the owner. The method is explained in the first part of this chapter.

Where the property is *damaged*, the owner is also entitled to be made whole. Typically, damages will be assessed by the reasonable cost of repairing or replacing the property. The most significant problems arise when the cost of repairing the property is out of proportion to the market value of the property. This problem is discussed in depth in a later section of this chapter.

In addition to the value of the property itself, the plaintiff is entitled to compensation for consequential losses, subject to the rules of remoteness and the duty to mitigate. For example, the purchaser of goods, or the owner, may have been intending to resell the goods or to use them in some enterprise. The breach of duty by the defendant (whether a breach of contract to deliver the goods, or a tort that damages them) may result in an additional loss of profit. Where substitute property can be immediately procured, or the property can be immediately repaired, damages will be limited to the cost of doing so since there will be no lost profits. However, in the case of many profit-earning chattels such as heavy machinery or ships, there will inevitably be a period of delay, as there will be in cases involving non-delivery of certain goods and real property. In these cases, the plaintiff is entitled to consequential losses, including lost profits, subject to the limitations imposed by the rules of remoteness and mitigation. Even where the property is not intended to be used for profit, the owner will have been deprived of its use and may have a claim for the loss of use.

B. NON-DELIVERY OF PROPERTY

Chapter 2 addressed the basic principles regarding the recovery of damages for a breach of contract. Those general principles apply to contracts to sell both real and personal property, and that chapter considered the law with respect to the sale of goods. The following section deals with contracts in respect of land.

1) Breach of Contract to Buy and Sell Real Estate

a) General Principles

Historically, the primary remedy for breach of a contract to sell land was specific performance—an order to the vendor actually to deliver the land. Land, especially residential real estate, has been considered unique and damages are presumptively inadequate. However, expectation damages are also an available remedy at the plaintiff's option; and with the diminishing availability of specific performance for the sale of land, damages are becoming a more important remedy.[1]

Expectation damages in real estate cases will be the difference between the contract price and the market price of the land.[2] For example, if the vendor refuses to deliver the property at a contract price of $100,000, and its value has increased to $110,000 at the time of the breach, the vendor will be liable for $10,000 (and the buyer will be entitled to the return of any deposit paid). Likewise, if the buyer is in breach, and the land has decreased in value, the vendor will be entitled to the loss.

If the buyer has incurred legal fees or other expenses in anticipation of closing, these are not recoverable, since they would have been incurred in any event had the contract gone through. And if the plaintiff has saved such expenses, they must be deducted from the damages for the lost value of the land since, had the contract been performed, these expenses would have been incurred in order to earn that value.[3]

b) Time of Assessment

Ordinarily, in determining compensation for breach of contract, damages are assessed at the date of the breach. This is a corollary of the rule of mitigation since it assumes that at the time of the breach the plaintiff will be able to enter into an alternate transaction. It also promotes efficiency in the assessment of damages by dictating an arbitrary but convenient point at which the valuation exercise should be done, and avoiding costly and complex litigation over the exact time at which the loss should be evaluated. These principles are discussed fully in Chapter 12.

In cases involving real estate, the rules about time of assessment are more complex, particularly in the case of the buyer's action. Since the

---

1   *Semelhago v. Paramadevan*, [1996] 2 S.C.R. 415; *Hunter's Square Developments Inc. v. 351658 Ontario Ltd.* (2002), 60 O.R. (3d) 264 (S.C.J.), aff'd (2002), 62 O.R. (3d) 302 (C.A.).

2   *Pitcher v. Shoebottom* (1970), [1971] 1 O.R. 106 (H.C.J.) [*Pitcher*].

3   *Ibid.*

buyer of real estate may be entitled to specific performance, the usual rules regarding mitigation do not apply. Obviously the law cannot be at one and the same time that the buyer is entitled to actual delivery of the property but must also mitigate by purchasing replacement property. Therefore, in the case of the buyer's action, damages are frequently assessed at the date of the trial or at the date at which any possibility of specific performance was definitively lost.[4] Where the property has increased in value from the date of the breach to the date of the trial, the buyer will therefore recover the additional lost value. This is said to be fair because, in these cases, damages should be a true equivalent of what the buyer would have received had specific performance been awarded. Even the seller of real estate may be entitled to damages measured at a date later than the breach. At the least, the seller is permitted a reasonable period of time after the breach to relist and sell the property, and any additional loss in value during that period will be recoverable.[5] The specific rules regarding time of assessment and mitigation, and their application to real estate cases, are fully discussed in Chapter 12.

c) The Rule in *Bain v. Fothergill*

There is one important exception to the usual rule regarding the recovery of expectation damages in real estate contracts. The often-cited rule in *Bain v. Fothergill* provides that the purchaser of real estate is not entitled to damages for loss of bargain where the breach is a result of a defect in title.[6] Under this rule (which was a restatement of an earlier decision in *Flureau v. Thornhill*[7]), the damages available to the purchaser in these circumstances will be restricted to the return of any deposit paid and any conveyancing costs incurred, along with applicable interest. The rule was adopted in Canada and, in addition to dispositions of fee-simple interests,[8] it has been applied to leases,[9] easements,[10] profits à prendre,[11] and options to purchase.[12]

---

4   *Wroth v. Tyler*, [1974] Ch. 30.
5   *Ansdell v. Crowther* (1984), 55 B.C.L.R. 216 (C.A.).
6   *Bain v. Fothergill* (1874), L.R. 7 H.L. 158 at 210–11.
7   (1776), 2 Wm. Bl. 1078.
8   See *Cole v. Atkins*, 209 P.2d 859 (Ariz. 1949).
9   See *Bain v. Fothergill*, above note 6; *Day v. Singleton*, [1899] 2 Ch. 320 [*Singleton*]; *J.W. Cafés, Ltd. v. Brownlow Trust Ltd.*, [1950] 1 All E.R. 894 (K.B.).
10 See *Rowe v. London School Board* (1887), 36 Ch. D. 619; *Rotman v. Pennett* (1921), 49 O.L.R. 114 (C.A.).
11 Profits à prendre is a right to take profits from the land. See *Pounsett v. Fuller* (1856), 17 C.B. 660; *Morgan v. Russell & Sons*, [1909] 1 K.B. 357.
12 See *Wright v. Dean*, [1948] Ch. 686; *Ontario Asphalt Block Co. v. Montreuil* (1915), 52 S.C.R. 541.

The rule in *Bain v. Fothergill* was developed at a time when difficulties in determining good title to land were substantial owing to the necessity of searching old records to examine the history of the property and the previous titles. Indeed, it has been suggested that the rule simply reflected the intent of the parties in these transactions that, because of the serious risk of error, damages should be limited.[13] Others have suggested that the rule was aimed at facilitating the marketability of real property by providing a limited immunity to the vendor,[14] or, in light of the complexity of real estate transactions, to limit the hardship on vendors of the usual rule of strict liability in contract law by excusing breaches that occur without the fault of the owner.[15]

i) Criticism of the Rule and Exceptions

The rule has been much criticized and is now generally regarded as an anachronism.[16] The difficulties concerning title are no longer so severe, particularly in jurisdictions with a Torrens system of land registration. If the parties truly intend to limit their potential damages, they may, as in other transactions, include a limitation or liquidated damages clause. Over the years, the rule in *Bain v. Fothergill* has been increasingly eroded by the development of exceptions.

First, the restriction on damages in *Bain v. Fothergill* was expressly confined to breach of contract *due to a defect in title*. Damages are not limited where the vendor has good title, but nonetheless repudiates the contract, or where the failure of the contract is due to a matter of conveyancing. A "matter of conveyancing" is one where the vendor has a right to obtain and convey clear title. For example, in *Re Daniel*,[17] the purchaser was awarded damages for the loss of his bargain where the conveyance failed because the vendor had insufficient funds to redeem a prior mortgage. The court held that, because the vendor had the legal right to clear the title, the rule in *Bain v. Fothergill* did not apply.

Other exceptions abound. Where the vendor is aware at the time of the contract that he does not have and cannot obtain good title, the rule does not apply (since there is deceit).[18] Where the defendant refuses to

---

13 See *Bain v. Fothergill*, above note 6 at 211, Lord Hatherley. See also S.M. Waddams, *The Law of Damages*, 2d ed., looseleaf (Aurora, ON: Canada Law Book, 1991–) at para. 1.1810.

14 *Sikes v. Wild* (1861), 1 B. & S. 587.

15 Law Reform Commission of British Columbia, *Report on the Rule in* Bain v. Fothergill (Vancouver: The Commission, 1976) at 15.

16 *Ibid.* at 18–20.

17 [1917] 2 Ch. 405.

18 For example, see *Bazin v. Bonnefoy* (1914), 16 D.L.R. 109 (Man. K.B.).

make a *bona fide* attempt to make good title, the rule does not shield him from expectation damages (unless the attempt would have been futile).[19] Another instance of the bad faith or "fault" exception occurs when the vendor himself makes it impossible to complete the transaction. This most often arises where the vendor, after agreeing to sell to the plaintiff, sells the land to a third party.[20] This exception applies even where the defendant has done so by innocent mistake.[21]

ii)   Reform of the Rule

It is said that the rule in *Bain v. Fothergill* is so anomalous, and so riddled with exceptions, that it should be abolished. In *A.V.G.*[22] the B.C. Court of Appeal invited the Supreme Court of Canada not to follow the rule in *Bain v. Fothergill*. The case was ultimately decided on the ground that the rule was inapplicable on the facts. However, Laskin C.J.C., after canvassing the many criticisms of the rule, stated in *obiter* that the mere "venerability of the rule and the fact that Legislatures have not moved long ago to abolish it, cannot be viewed as a decisive reason against a refusal by this Court to follow it. It was, after all, a judge-made rule, based on considerations that do not operate in Canada."[23] In particular, he suggested, the rule is inappropriate in jurisdictions with simpler and reliable systems of title registration.

In several jurisdictions courts have held that *A.V.G.* is binding authority for the proposition that the rule in *Bain v. Fothergill* is no longer good law. In *New Horizon Investments Ltd. v. Montroyal Estates Ltd.*,[24] the court held that the rule was inapplicable in British Columbia. In *Morrill v. Athabasca (County No. 12)*,[25] the rule was held inapplicable in Alberta. The Manitoba Court of Queen's Bench has expressed doubt as to whether the rule applies in that province,[26] and the Saskatchewan Court of Appeal relied on *A.V.G.* to come to the conclusion that "the rule in *Bain v. Fothergill* has no application to the transaction here, and

---

19   *Day v. Singleton*, above note 9.
20   See *Goffin v. Houlder* (1920), 90 L.J. Ch. 488; *Pinsonneault v. Lesperance* (1926), 58 O.L.R. 375 (C.A.); *Pitcher*, above note 2; *Stewart v. Gunn* (1974), 5 Nfld. & P.E.I.R. 291 (P.E.I.C.A.).
21   *A.V.G. Management Science Ltd. v. Barwell Developments Ltd.* (1978), [1979] 2 S.C.R. 43 [*A.V.G.*].
22   *Ibid.*
23   *Ibid.* at 57.
24   (1982), 26 R.P.R. 268 (B.C.S.C.).
25   (1980), 18 R.P.R. 196 (Alta. Q.B.).
26   *Westward Farms Ltd. v. Cadieux* (1981), 9 Man. R. (2d) 96 (Q.B.), rev'd on other grounds [1982] 5 W.W.R. 1 (Man. C.A.), leave to appeal to S.C.C. refused (1982), 18 Man. R. (2d) 269.

the general principles for assessing damages apply to a loss of bargain in an action for specific performance involving the sale of land."[27] In Ontario, the court in *Law-Woman Management Corp. v. Peel (Regional Municipality)*[28] stated:

> Although, strictly speaking, the reasons of Laskin C.J.C. on the point were *obiter*, they were a considered response to an invitation from the British Columbia Court of Appeal to overthrow the rule in *Bain*. If the rule itself is gone, it is not necessary for me to consider whether, as was the case in *A.V.G.* itself, the facts in this case take it outside of *Bain*.[29]

In effect, it would seem that the rule is no longer the law in most Canadian jurisdictions. This is certainly the case in British Columbia, where, following the proposals of the B.C. Law Reform Commission, the rule in *Bain v. Fothergill* was abolished by statute.[30] The *de facto* abolition of the rule in the rest of Canada is in accordance with a general trend within the other common law countries.[31]

d) Consequential Losses

Frequently, the loss of a real estate transaction will not only deprive the plaintiff of the value of the property but may also entail other consequential losses to the plaintiff. Where those losses are in the nature of out-of-pocket expenditures that are wasted, such expenditures are recoverable (so long as they have not already been implicitly compensated for in the award for the value of the property). More problematic are lost chances for other gains. For example, the plaintiff may have intended to develop or resell the property and will lose the anticipated profits from those transactions. In principle, such losses are also recoverable, subject to the rules of mitigation and remoteness. In practice, however, courts are wary of the potential for never-ending chains of consequential losses and tend to apply those rules fairly stringently. This is discussed fully in Chapter 11.

---

27 *Kopec v. Pyret* (1987), 36 D.L.R. (4th) 1 at 11 (Sask. C.A.). See also *Peterson v. Canadian Imperial Bank of Commerce* (1992), 105 Sask. R. 113 (C.A.).

28 (1991), 2 O.R. (3d) 567 (Gen. Div.). See also *Rondeau v. Yotis*, [1987] O.J. No. 1342 (H.C.J.); *Mitchell v. Nagoda*, [1985] O.J. No. 482 (H.C.J.); *A.V.G.*, above note 21, is authority for proposition that the rule in *Bain v. Fothergill* is not good law in Canada.

29 *Law-Woman Management Corp. v. Peel (Regional Municipality)*, ibid. at 601.

30 *Property Law Act*, R.S.B.C. 1996, c. 377, s. 37.

31 For example, the rule was abolished in England in 1989: *Law of Property (Miscellaneous Provisions) Act 1989* (U.K.), 1989, c. 34, s. 3, following the recommendations of the U.K. Law Commission in 1986.

2) Non-Delivery and Misappropriation of Chattels

a) Breach of Contract

The principles governing the buyer's remedies for breach of contract to deliver goods are discussed in Chapter 2.

b) Tort

i) General Principles: Value to the Owner

The issue of non-delivery of goods arises in tort law when the plaintiff's property is wrongfully appropriated by the defendant. The general principle in tort is that the plaintiff is entitled to be made whole and, as in the contract cases, damages are measured by the value of the goods to the owner. In addition, the plaintiff is sometimes entitled to consequential losses suffered by reason of the interference. Such losses can include lost profit and loss of use of the property.

The value of the property will be determined by its fair market value; that is, by the amount that it will cost to replace the property or, in some cases, the amount of the proceeds from sale of the property. Where the plaintiff claims the proceeds of sale, several issues recur. First, the defendant may claim that prior to the sale she had improved the value of the goods and should be entitled to retain part of the moneys. The onus is on the defendant to establish this.[32] Second, the defendant may have spent money or effort on the sale and may claim the right to deduct her "costs" from the damage award. In a series of cases involving trespass and unauthorized removal of timber, it has been held that the owner of the land from which the timber is taken is entitled to its fair market value. Where the trespass is entirely innocent, the court will deduct from the award a reasonable allowance for the cost of cutting the wood and transporting it to market. Where the trespass is intentional or reckless, the defendant will not receive any deduction for expenses (beyond the cost of transporting the goods).[33] This rule of damage assessment appears to stem from a desire to add a measure of punishment to the damages award since, from a purely commercial point of view, it provides the plaintiff with a greater financial settlement than had the plaintiff cut and sold the timber herself.

---

32   *Pathfinder Recreation Ltd. (Receiver of) v. Borg-Warner Acceptance Canada Ltd.* (1989), 77 C.B.R. (N.S.) 171 (B.C.S.C.), aff'd (1990), 52 B.C.L.R. (2d) 135 (C.A.).

33   *Shewish v. MacMillan Bloedel Ltd.* (1990), 48 B.C.L.R. (2d) 290 (C.A.) [*Shewish*]; *Craig v. North Shore Heli Logging Ltd.* (1997), 34 B.C.L.R. (3d) 330 (S.C.).

ii) Time of Assessment: Detinue and Conversion

The question of the time for assessing the value of property is complicated by the forms of action. The main tort actions for interference with goods are trespass, conversion, and detinue. The differences among the actions are the subject of much archaic caselaw and learning, which will not be repeated here.[34] *Conversion* is a substantial or total interference with the owner's rights of property.[35] Conversion typically occurs when goods are destroyed, stolen, or wrongfully sold to a third party. Mere detention of property is not necessarily conversion, and other lesser harms to goods such as unauthorized use and minor damage are simply forms of trespass. The ordinary measure of damages is the full value of the property at the time of conversion.[36] The defendant is, in effect, forced to purchase the property. In addition, the plaintiff may be awarded consequential losses (such as loss of use and lost profits) due to being deprived of his property. Where possible, the plaintiff has an obligation to mitigate by purchasing replacement property after the conversion.[37]

Detinue is also wrongful possession of the plaintiff's property—an unjustified refusal to return the plaintiff's goods on demand. Unlike conversion, which is a purely personal action for damages, detinue is a continuing wrong and one of the available remedies is an order for the return of the goods [38] or their value in lieu thereof. If the plaintiff exercises the option of having any or all of the goods returned to her, the value of the returned item(s) will be deducted from the measure of damages.[39]

The major practical difference between conversion and detinue has to do with the time of assessing the plaintiff's loss, which is important when the value of the property changes over the relevant period. A single act of conversion "crystallizes" the tort and the damages are assessed at the time of the conversion. Conversely, the wrongful detention of goods in detinue (and the damages) continues from the time the defendant refuses to deliver the goods until the goods are returned to the plaintiff

---

34 Law Reform Commission of British Columbia, *Report on Wrongful Interference with Goods* (Vancouver: The Commission, 1992).

35 See *Boma Manufacturing Ltd. v. Canadian Imperial Bank of Commerce*, [1996] 3 S.C.R. 727 at para. 3.

36 *Trusts & Guarantee Co. v. Brenner*, [1933] S.C.R. 656.

37 *Asamera Oil Corp. v. Sea Oil & General Corp.*, [1979] 1 S.C.R. 633 [*Asamera*].

38 *Rosenthal v. Alderton & Sons, Ltd.*, [1946] 1 All E.R. 583 (K.B.) [*Rosenthal*].

39 *Nagaki v. Hoppener*, [2005] B.C.J. No. 1584 at para. 23 (S.C.). The case involved an action for damages for detinue for the return of artworks the plaintiff entrusted to the defendants. The plaintiff was awarded damages and, alternatively, the court ordered that, if the missing artworks were returned to the plaintiff, their value would be deducted from the damage award.

or until the time of trial.[40] The measure of damages, therefore, is the value of the goods at the time of trial. An action in detinue is obviously advantageous to a plaintiff when the goods have increased in value in the period leading up to trial. Frequently, the same wrongful act may be both detinue and conversion. In these cases the plaintiff has a right to elect which cause of action to pursue (and thus the available remedy).[41] As Fleming suggests, "[i]f cynical, the soundest advice was accordingly to sue in detinue on a rising and in conversion on a falling market."[42]

Steiman v. Steiman[43] provides a good example of the rules regarding election and time of assessment. In this case the plaintiff brought an action in conversion of jewellery against the family of her deceased husband. From the date of the conversion until the date of the trial, the jewellery taken by the defendants had tripled in value. However, between the date of the trial and the date of the appeal, the jewellery had considerably depreciated. The trial judge assessed the value as of the trial date, but this was reversed on appeal. O'Sullivan J.A. held:

- A person whose chattels are taken wrongfully has an election. He may continue to regard the goods as his own and sue in detinue for their return or sue for damages in conversion.
- In a claim for conversion, the date of judgment may not be used as the date for assessment. If the plaintiff elects to claim damages for conversion, damages must be based on the supposition that she replaced the missing property at market prices as of the date of the conversion, or more strictly the date at which the property could reasonably have been replaced following the conversion.[44]
- The victim who sues for conversion and replaces converted goods will not lose any appreciation in value by reason of a rising market. If the victim were permitted to recover damages as of the date of trial for goods that he has in fact replaced by purchase, he would gain twice from appreciation—once on the goods converted and once on the goods purchased.
- The victim may elect to sue in detinue, in which case the value of the goods will be assessed at the date of the trial. In such a case the plaintiff is not compensated twice over because she has not replaced

40   General & Finance Facilities, Ltd. v. Cooks Cars (Romford), Ltd., [1963] 2 All E.R. 314 at 317 (C.A.) [Cooks Cars].
41   Rosenthal, above note 38 at 585.
42   J.G. Fleming, The Law of Torts, 6th ed. (Sydney: Law Book Company, 1983) at 64.
43   (1982), 18 Man. R. (2d) 203 (C.A.).
44   Alberta v. Arnold, [1971] S.C.R. 209.

the goods. In addition, the plaintiff is bound by the election and takes the risk that the value of the goods will fall, and the defendant has the option of returning the goods themselves.

Some courts have been troubled that so stark a difference in remedy should result from the different forms of action. In *Sachs v. Miklos*,[45] Lord Goddard C.J. criticized the incongruity and suggested that the measure of damages in detinue and conversion should be the same. He proposed that, in actions in conversion, any increase in value after the wrong might be added as consequential damages to the claim for their lost value at the time of the wrong (at least in situations where the owner did not become aware that the goods had been disposed until some subsequent time). In effect, the owner would be given the value of the goods at the time of the conversion, plus damages for the lost opportunity to sell the goods at their higher price at a later date. This approach would have the effect of equalizing the measure of damages in conversion and detinue, but it has been criticized.[46] At least where the goods can easily be replaced, the plaintiff in a conversion action cannot claim damages for losses suffered after a reasonable period of time in which to mitigate.

While Lord Goddard's suggestion has not been followed, another principle may serve to minimize the difference between detinue and conversion. Whatever the form of action, where the subject matter of the lawsuit is not unique, the plaintiff may have a duty to mitigate. In a rising market the owner is expected to replace the goods (thus avoiding further losses). This is suggested by the decision of the Supreme Court of Canada in *Asamera*.[47] In this case, where the defendant wrongfully refused to return the plaintiff's shares, the plaintiff's damages were calculated by the price at which replacement shares could have been purchased on the market at a reasonable time after the defendant's breach. The case does not explain precisely why the plaintiff lost the remedy of specific restitution in detinue but, as Waddams suggests, it may be because the shares are fungible and easily replaced. As explained in one case, "[t]here is always a discretion in the Court as to whether it will order restitution or give damages in lieu thereof. Restitution is never given if the articles or goods detained are ordinary goods in commerce."[48]

In the result, it may be ventured that the rules for conversion and detinue are essentially the same. In both cases, damages will be as-

---

45   [1948] 2 K.B. 23 (C.A.).
46   *Cooks Cars*, above note 40 at 317.
47   Above note 37.
48   *Mayne v. Kidd*, [1951] 2 D.L.R. 652 at 654 (Sask. C.A.), Gordon J.A.

sessed as the value of the goods at the time when the plaintiff *should have replaced them*. The plaintiff need not replace them in circumstances where he was unaware of the tort, or in situations where the goods are unique and the plaintiff has a legitimate expectation that the specific goods will actually be returned.

iii) *Consequential Losses*

Regardless of the form of action, in addition to the value of the property, the plaintiff may be able to claim damages for detention or loss of use and other consequential losses, though only when proven.[49] For example, in *Camway Trucking Ltd. v. Toronto-Dominion* Bank,[50] a creditor bank was held to have wrongfully seized trucks used by the debtor in a freight-hauling business. The bank's seizure resulted in a failure by the plaintiff to complete contracts and ultimately in the loss of its business. The court awarded damages for the lost contracts and the lost business assets, though the award was reduced by an amount reflecting the 50 percent chance that the debtor's business would have failed in any event. The plaintiff was also held to be entitled to $10,000 in exemplary damages.[51]

Consequential losses are limited by the rules of mitigation and remoteness, which are discussed fully in Chapters 11 & 12. Claims for such losses are limited, for example, to that period for which it is reasonable for a plaintiff to recover her wrongfully detained property. In *Woods v. Alberta*,[52] an owner of a logging trailer that had been wrongfully seized failed to take prompt action to recover it. The trailer was sold at auction. The damages awarded at trial were reduced on appeal and restricted to a two-week period during which the plaintiff, had he acted reasonably promptly, could have recovered the trailer.

C. DEFECTS, DAMAGE, AND DESTRUCTION OF PROPERTY

This section discusses the principles regarding "defective property." These principles are applicable in both tort cases where the plaintiff's

---

49   See, for example, *Schentag v. Gauthier* (1972), 27 D.L.R. (3d) 710 (Sask. Dist. Ct.); *Pop N' Juice Inc. v. 1203891 Ontario Ltd.*, [2004] O.J. No. 3085 (S.C.J.).

50   (1988), 9 A.C.W.S. (3d) 164 (Ont. H.C.J.).

51   See also *Sheri Dan Inc. v. Manufacturers Life Insurance Co.*, [2001] O.J. No. 1143 (S.C.J.), where the plaintiff was awarded loss of potential revenue caused by unauthorized detention of her chattels on a *per diem* basis.

52   (1989), 71 Alta. L.R. (2d) 353 (C.A.).

property has been damaged by some act of the defendant, and in contract cases where the defendant has delivered defective property or failed properly to perform a contract in respect of property (e.g., to repair or improve the property). In each case, the owner of property is entitled to the loss in the value of the property. The following sections explain how this loss is valued in different situations.

1) Contract: Sale of Defective Property and Defective Improvements

Under the common law and statute, damages available to a buyer for defects in the goods (when those defects involve a breach of warranty regarding quality) will typically be measured by the difference between the actual value of the goods at the time they were delivered and the value they would have had had they complied with the warranty.[53] This reflects the expectancy principle that the plaintiff should be placed in the same position as though the breach had not occurred. In the case of defective goods, the plaintiff will ordinarily be entitled to their diminished market value or, alternatively, to the cost of remedying any defect or repairing any damage. These measures are alternative ways of ensuring that by an award of damages the plaintiff is placed in the position as if the contract had been kept.

The same principles apply in respect of other contracts in relation to real and personal property. Where the defendant breaches a contract to do work on the plaintiff's property, the plaintiff is entitled to the diminished value of the property. This may be measured either by the difference in the market value of the property or by the cost of remedying the problem. Complications arise, however, in choosing between these two alternatives when the cost of repairs significantly exceeds the diminished market value of the goods. This problem is dealt with fully below.

2) Damage to Chattels

The general principle is the same when property is damaged (though the cause of action will most often be in tort). The owner is entitled to the property's lost value, usually measured by the reasonable cost of repair or replacement. In addition, where the repairs do not fully restore the property to its pre-accident condition, the plaintiff may also ob-

---

53   *Sale of Goods Act*, R.S.B.C. 1996, c. 410, s. 56; *Sale of Goods Act*, R.S.O. 1990, c. S.1, s. 51.

tain compensation for its remaining diminished value. And while the property is being repaired the plaintiff may also be entitled to damages for loss of its use (often measured by the cost of hiring a substitute). In *O'Grady v. Westminster Scaffolding Ltd.*,[54] involving a damaged automobile, Edmund-Davies J. stated the general principle of compensation for damage to chattels as follows:

> Where a chattel is negligently damaged, the normal measure of compensation is the difference between the value of the chattel before the damage and its value as damaged. In this case of a partial loss, this will usually be (a) the cost of repairing; (b) the difference (if any) between the value of the chattel before the accident and after it was repaired; and (c) such consequential loss as the reasonable cost of hiring another chattel while repairs are being effected.[55]

Where repairs are effected by the plaintiff, not only the direct labour and material costs are allowed but also a reasonable sum for overhead expenses arising from the repair.[56] Expenses closely associated with the cost of repair—for example, docking expenses in the case of ships,[57] towing charges,[58] increases to insurance premiums imposed because of the claim, or the insurance deductible itself[59]—can also be subsumed within the term "repair costs." Awards of interest on repair costs are also accepted by the courts as normal and appropriate.[60] Interest is calculated from the time the plaintiff pays for the repair, on the basis that the plaintiff from that point has lost the use of the money and that the original loss has not been compensated at the proper time (i.e., when it occurred).[61]

When chattels are wrongfully destroyed (or where the damage is so serious that there is a "constructive total loss"), the owner is entitled to the lost capital value of the property. In simple cases, where the property is "fungible" and available to be replaced through a purchase, the damages will be assessed by the cost of acquiring a substitute. If the destroyed property has any scrap value, the defendant is given credit for that value.

---

54   [1962] 2 Lloyd's Rep. 238 (Q.B.) [*O'Grady*].
55   *Ibid.* at 239.
56   *London Transport Executive v. Foy, Morgan & Co.*, [1955] C.L.Y. 743; *London Transport Executive v. Court*, [1954] C.L.Y. 888.
57   *The Black Prince* (1862), Lush. 568.
58   *The Inflexible H.M.S.* (1857), Sw. 200 [*Inflexible*].
59   *Ironfield v. Eastern Gas Board*, [1964] 1 W.L.R. 1125n.
60   *The Norseman*, [1957] P. 224.
61   *The Amalia* (1864), 5 New Rep. 164n at 164.

Where identical property is not available, a price may be established by reference to the market price of "comparables." Damages may include the cost of purchasing a near substitute, plus the cost of necessary adaptations to the plaintiff's use. Where there is no satisfactory market for the property in question, courts may accept other evidence of value. Experts may be permitted to provide estimates of value based upon the original cost of the property, with due allowance then made for depreciation, inflation, and other factors that would affect the value of the property.

3) Trespass to Real Property

In the case of trespass to real property, courts also compensate for any damage by awarding the diminished value of the property or the cost of repair. For example, in a series of cases in which the defendants wrongfully cut trees, courts have held that the owner is entitled to at least the diminished value of the property.[62] Where the trees had commercial value, the owner may be entitled to the market value of the timber (though, where the trespass was innocent, the defendant may deduct the cost of logging the trees).[63] Where the trees have functional or aesthetic value, the plaintiff may be entitled to the cost of replanting them, though the cost exceeds any loss in value to the land[64] or, alternatively, may be entitled to a sum of damages for loss of an amenity. Thus, a plaintiff could be entitled to damages even where the trees are "wild" and "of no practical commercial use" based on the intrinsic value of trees.[65] In addition, where the trespass is done in a high-handed or malicious fashion, the plaintiff may be entitled to punitive damages.[66]

In many cases, a technical trespass to land will not appear to cause any physical or financial harm to the plaintiff. In these cases, the plaintiff may be entitled only to nominal damages (discussed in Chapter 9). However, where the defendant has committed the trespass to save money or obtain some benefit, the owner may have a restitutionary-type remedy, even though the plaintiff would not have otherwise al-

---

62 *Scarborough (City) v. R.E.F. Homes Ltd.* (1979), 9 M.P.L.R. 255 (Ont. C.A.).

63 *Shewish*, above note 33.

64 *Dykhuizen v. Saanich (District)* (1989), 63 D.L.R. (4th) 211 (B.C.C.A.) [*Dykhuizen*].

65 *British Columbia v. Canada Forest Products*, [2004] 2 S.C.R. 74 at para. 215 [*Canada Forest Products*]. Compensation based on the intrinsic value of trees removed or destroyed by the defendant's wrongful conduct is intended to promote environmental protection, which courts have found to be a fundamental value of Canadian society. See *ibid.* at para. 217.

66 See Chapter 8.

lowed its use for profit or had the opportunity to do so during that period. For example, where the trespass is committed in the course of construction on an adjacent property, in order to save the defendant money, the plaintiff may be entitled to compensation assessed by a reasonable licence fee for the use of his property, even though no harm is done to that property.[67] Alternatively, under the rubric of punitive damages, a trespasser may be required to disgorge some or all of the profit earned by committing the trespass, though no real harm is done to the owner.[68]

4) Date for Assessing Damages

The issue of choosing a date for the assessment of damages arises whenever there has been a change in the cost of repairing the property between the time of the wrong and the time of the trial. Where the cost has increased, it will be to the plaintiff's advantage to argue for a date of assessment later than the date of the wrong. In addition, the longer the plaintiff takes to replace or repair property, the more likely it is that consequential losses, such as lost profits, will increase.

The presumptive rule in both contract and tort is that the damages are to be assessed as of the date of the wrong. Any losses arising subsequently, owing to increased repair or replacement costs, or additional consequential losses, are not recoverable. The fact that the plaintiff may have to spend her own money, or borrowed money, on repairs or replacement can be taken into account through an award of pre-judgment interest that compensates the plaintiff for the loss of use of her own capital in the period before trial (and judgment interest is available while the debt is outstanding after trial).[69] In *O'Grady*[70] the amount awarded for a car rental during the time of repair was reduced because of the plaintiff's "unreasonable delay" in commencing repairs. In *Jens v. Mannix Co.*,[71] where the plaintiff claimed the cost of repairing

---

67   *Whitwham v. Westminster Brymbo Coal & Coke Co.*, [1896] 2 Ch. 538 [*Whitwham*]. See also discussion in Chapter 7, Section E(4).

68   *Townsview Properties Ltd. v. Sun Construction & Equipment Co.* (1973), 2 O.R. (2d) 213 (H.C.J.), var'd (1974), 7 O.R. (2d) 666 (C.A.); *Austin v. Rescon Construction (1984) Ltd.* (1989), 36 B.C.L.R. (2d) 21 (C.A.) [*Austin*]. See discussion in Chapter 8, Section B(7).

69   See M.A. Waldron, *The Law of Interest in Canada* (Scarborough, ON: Carswell Thomson Professional, 1992).

70   *O'Grady,* above note 54.

71   [1978] 5 W.W.R. 486 (B.C.S.C.), rev'd (1979), 30 D.L.R. (4th) 260 (B.C.C.A.) [*Jens*].

oil damage to his home, he was confined to the cost of doing so at the time of the wrong, rather than the inflated cost at the time of trial.

There are a variety of policy reasons underlying the "time of wrong" principle. Most important, it is a corollary of the obligation to mitigate. Wrong-date valuation assumes that the plaintiff will go into the marketplace as soon as practicable after the wrong and arrange for repairs or purchase a substitute. This reduces the total costs of the breach and saves the defendant from unnecessary expense. Second, the date of the wrong-valuation rule is administratively attractive because of its simplicity. It allows courts to avoid complex inquiries into the question of when, on the facts of a particular case, it would have been reasonable to effect repairs. A fixed rule also provides a measure of certainty so the owner of damaged property will know clearly what her obligations are and the parties will be able to settle their dispute privately.

The "date of the wrong" rule is not, however, absolute. Where the plaintiff can demonstrate a reasonable excuse for her inaction, the court may accept that there was no immediate duty to mitigate and postpone the date for the assessment of damages (even to the time of trial).[72] The issue is discussed in more detail in the context of the discussion of mitigation in Chapter 12.

5) Consequential Losses

a) Necessary Expenses

Subject to the duty to mitigate and the principles of remoteness of damages, consequential losses are also recoverable when property is damaged or destroyed. The cost of hiring substitute chattels during the repair period is recoverable,[73] but plaintiffs must not exceed their reasonable requirements by the kind of substitute they obtain.[74] Where the property is an important part of the plaintiff's business, some unavoidable operating expenses, such as wages, may be wasted for a period while the property is being repaired.[75] The fact that the chattel could not have earned income because of a lack of potential customers is immaterial to an award of this type.[76] But the claim for wasted expenses

---

72   *Dodd Properties (Kent) Ltd. v. Canterbury City Council*, [1980] 1 W.L.R. 433 (C.A.).
73   *The Yorkshireman* (1827), 2 Hag. Adm. 30n; *Lagden v. O'Connor*, [2004] 1 All E.R. 277 (H.L.).
74   *Watson-Norrie Ltd. v. Shaw*, [1967] 1 Lloyd's Rep. 515 (C.A.).
75   *Inflexible*, above note 58 at 204.
76   *Edmund Handcock (1929), Ltd. v. "Ernesto" (Owners)*, [1952] 1 Lloyd's Rep. 467 (C.A.).

cannot be allowed to duplicate a claim for lost profits since to earn the profits the plaintiff would have to incur the expenses.[77]

b) Lost Profits

In addition to damages reflecting the lost value of the defective property and wasted expenses, the plaintiff may have suffered other consequential losses including lost profits. The plaintiff may have intended to use the goods for resale or as components in a product produced by the plaintiff. Or the property may have been machinery or equipment that the plaintiff intended for use in some enterprise. In each case, the delivery of defective property or the damage to the property caused by the defendant may interrupt the plaintiff's business and cause a further loss.

Lost profits due to the delivery of defective property, or wrongful damage to property, are, in principle, recoverable in both tort and contract, subject to rules about mitigation and remoteness. For example, in *Sunnyside Greenhouses Ltd. v. Golden West Seeds Ltd.*,[78] the sale of defective greenhouse panels caused a failure in the plaintiff's crop. The court held that the plaintiff was entitled to damages for the diminished value of the panels (the purchase price less any residual value) and also for lost profit for the failed crop. The court stated: "I think that the correct principle is that loss of profit (or similar loss) which is the direct and natural consequence of the breach, may be claimed for the period during which the breach is the effective cause of the loss."[79] Similarly, in tort cases where property (such as a factory or profit-earning chattels) is destroyed or damaged, profits that are lost pending repair or replacement are recoverable so long as they are a foreseeable consequence of the loss.[80]

i) Limits on the Recovery of Lost Profits

The recovery of lost profits is limited by rules of remoteness and mitigation. The risk of lost profits must be foreseeable at the time of the contract or the tort. Some earlier authorities suggested that lost profits will usually fail this remoteness test because they are not foreseeable. However, more recent authorities indicate otherwise. In *Canlin Ltd. v. Thiokol Fibres Canada Ltd.*, discussed in Chapter 2, the defendant sold the plaintiff defective material that the plaintiff used in the manufacture of swimming-pool covers. The plaintiff lost many dissatisfied cus-

---

77   See, for example, *The City of Peking* (1890), 15 App. Cas. 438 (P.C.).

78   (1972), 27 D.L.R. (3d) 434 (Alta. C.A.), aff'd (1973), 33 D.L.R. (3d) 384n (S.C.C.) [*Sunnyside*].

79   *Ibid.* at 441 (Alta. C.A.).

80   *Harbutt's "Plasticine" Ltd. v. Wayne Tank and Pump Co. Ltd.*, [1970] 1 Q.B. 447 (C.A.) [*Harbutt's "Plasticine"*].

tomers and claimed damages for lost business from the defendant. In response to the defendant's argument that such losses were too remote, Cory J.A. stated: "Most commercial contracts pertaining to the sale and delivery of material or goods must, of necessity, be entered into with a view to making a profit in the future. To say otherwise amounts to a denial of the profit motive in the free enterprise system."[81]

Lost profits will not always be so easily foreseen, nor will the *extent* of lost profits always be foreseen. The principle of remoteness of damages does, therefore, limit the circumstances in which claims for lost profits can be made, and this principle is discussed more fully in Chapter 11.

The recovery of lost profits is also limited by the principle of mitigation. Such losses are recoverable only for the period "before reasonable steps in mitigation of loss can become effective."[82] The plaintiff is expected to mitigate damages by purchasing substitute goods or services as soon as possible, and carrying on with its business. If the lost profit accrues because the plaintiff has failed to do this, it will not be recoverable.[83] To the extent that it is not practicable for the plaintiff to mitigate immediately, damages will be recoverable for the business lost. For example, in *Canlin*[84] the plaintiff was permitted to recover its lost profits for a period of four years during which it withdrew from the swimming-pool cover business. Its reputation had been so seriously harmed by the sale of defective products that it was not obliged immediately to re-enter the field and this was a reasonable period for it to recover its business. The issue of mitigation of lost profits is discussed more fully in Chapter 12.

ii)   The Relation between Lost Value and Lost Profits

When property is destroyed, and the owner seeks lost profits in addition to the lost value of the property, the quantification of damages must be approached with subtlety. One earlier approach drew a distinction between cases involving property *damage* and those involving *destruction*. In cases where the property was damaged, the owner was entitled to compensation for loss of use or lost profits during a reasonable period of repair. However, in cases of total destruction, damages for loss of use were not available. Instead, the owner was entitled to the

---

81   (1983), 40 O.R. (2d) 687 at 690 (C.A.) [*Canlin*].
82   In *Sunnyside*, above note 78 at 442.
83   *Freedhoff v. Pomalift Industries Ltd.*, [1971] 2 O.R. 773 (C.A.): lost profit not recoverable because of failure to mitigate.
84   Above note 81.

value of the property plus interest. This rule was based on a concern that lost profits were too remote and speculative, and a sense that an award of the value of the property plus interest fully compensated the owner's economic losses.

The modern approach permits lost profits to be taken into account in assessing the owner's loss in cases both of damage and of destruction, subject to rules about remoteness. However, in the case of property that is destroyed, special care must also be taken not to provide double compensation. The reason for this is that, where the owner is given the capital value of property at the time of destruction (plus interest to the time of judgment), that value may already include some compensation for lost use since the capital value of a chattel may already reflect expected profits from its use.

The leading case on this issue is the House of Lords' decision in *"Liesbosch" v. "Edison."*[85] Here, the steamship *Edison* had fouled the moorings of the dredger *Liesbosch*, dragging the latter into the open sea. The *Liesbosch* filled with water and sank. At the time of the incident, the dredger was engaged in fulfilling a contract between the plaintiff and a third party. The defendants argued that the measure of damages should be restricted to the cost of acquiring a substitute, but the plaintiffs claimed additional damages for losses incurred during the period of delay before a new dredger could start work.

Lord Wright stated: "[T]he dominant rule of law is the principle of restitutio in integrum, and subsidiary rules can only be justified if they give effect to that rule."[86] He further held that the true measure of the loss was the "value of the ship to her owner as a going concern"[87] and that damages should represent the capitalized value of the vessel as a profit-earning machine. To assess that value, it was necessary to take into account existing contractual engagements, either profitable or otherwise. But it would not be appropriate simply to add the claim for lost profits to the claim for the value of the ship for two reasons. First, those profits may already be reflected in her capital value since the value of a profit-earning property is in part a function of its expected income. Second, the award of interest on the value of the ship from the time of her destruction will to some extent offset any lost profits (since the owner would not have been earning a profit from use of the chattel plus a return on the capital at the same time). Lord Wright concluded:

---

85   *"Liesbosch," Dredger v. "Edison," S.S. (Owners)*, [1933] A.C. 449 (H.L.).
86   *Ibid.* at 463.
87   *Ibid.* at 464.

In assessing that value regard must naturally be had to her pending engagements, either profitable or the reverse. The rule, however, obviously requires some care in its application; the figure of damage is to represent the capitalized value of the vessel as a profit-earning machine, not in the abstract but in view of the actual circumstances. The value of prospective freights cannot simply be added to the market value but ought to be taken into account in order to ascertain the total value for purpose of assessing the damage, since if it is merely added to the market value of a free ship, the owner will be getting pro tanto his damages twice over. The vessel cannot be earning in the open market, while fulfilling the pending charter or charters.[88]

In the result the House of Lords instructed that the damage claim be calculated as the full capital loss to the owner, taking into account the market price of a substitute dredger and the costs of adapting, transporting, and insuring the substitute. In addition, the plaintiffs were entitled to compensation for disturbance and loss in the performance of their contract over the period between the accident and the time a replacement dredger could have been put into operation, including overhead charges and expenses of staff and equipment.

Thus, the market value of the ship and lost profits are not simply added together, but rather are both taken into account in assessing a single value: the value of the ship to her owner at the time of the loss. Where a ship is not under engagement, the owner will not be entitled to lost profits since the capitalized value of the ship will already reflect the general expectation of profits.[89] Even when the ship is under a definite engagement, the expected profits may not affect her value compared to other ships. For example, in some circumstances, where shipping is in short supply, the market value of a free vessel may be enhanced by the virtual certainty of profitable employment, and a ship under actual charter has no greater value. In such cases, it is inappropriate to award damages for loss of profits since to add the value of freights to an amount that has already anticipated them effectively compensates the owner twice over.[90] In other circumstances, the pending engagements have a value beyond what a reasonable purchaser in the market might expect, and the lost profits will in fact increase the ship's value to the owner.[91]

---

88 Ibid.
89 Voaden v. Champion (The Baltic Surveyor and the Timbuktu), [2001] 1 Lloyd's Rep. 739 at para. 76 (Q.B.D.).
90 The Llanover, [1947] P. 80.
91 Motor Cruiser Four of Hearts (Owners) v. Fortunity (Owners), [1961] 1 W.L.R. 351 [The Fortunity].

The fact that profit-earning goods are dedicated to a particular enterprise may in fact diminish their value. Chattels that may or may not be used again because of an uncertainty about the future of an enterprise may be devalued in comparison to damaged goods that form part of an unquestioned going concern. The case of *Ziehlke v. Amisk Drilling Co.*[92] illustrates the point. In an action for damage negligently caused to buildings and equipment at a non-operational mine site, the Manitoba Court of Appeal reduced the damages for the cost of replacing the property. The evidence indicated that, although the mine would likely reopen, there was a substantial chance that it would not do so, in which case the buildings and equipment would not be replaced. Further, the equipment was old and would be useful only if the mine were to become operational again. The court reduced the damages by one-third in order to reflect the chance that the mine would not reopen and the property would be valueless.

c) Loss of Use of Non-Profit-Earning Chattels

The plaintiff is entitled to consequential damages for the loss of use of property even when the property is not used to earn profits. For example, when an automobile is damaged, its owner is entitled to the costs of renting a substitute while it is being repaired. Obviously, while not being used for profit, the owner has suffered a functional loss when deprived of the use of that property.

Even when the owner does not incur an actual expense by hiring a substitute, she is still entitled to damages for loss of use. General damages for the loss of use of non-profit-earning chattels have been available at least since the 1897 decision of the House of Lords in *The Greta Holme*.[93] In this case, Lord Herschell said:

> I take it to be clear law that in general a person who has been deprived of the use of a chattel through the wrongful act of another is entitled to recover damages in respect thereof, even though he cannot prove what has been called "tangible pecuniary loss," by which I understand is meant that he is a definite sum of money out of pocket owing to the wrong he has sustained.[94]

In the later case of *The Mediana*, the same principle was defined as follows: "Where by the wrongful act of one man something belonging to another is either itself so injured as not to be capable of being used or

---

92 (1993), 92 Man. R. (2d) 83 (C.A.) [*Amisk*].
93 [1897] A.C. 596 (H.L.).
94 *Ibid.* at 604.

is taken away so that it cannot be used at all, that of itself is a ground for damages."[95]

The principle has been applied in *Birmingham Corporation v. Sowsbery.*[96] In that case, a bus operated by a not-for-profit organization was damaged by the defendant's car. During the period of repair, the bus was replaced by another bus in the plaintiff's fleet that was kept for emergencies. The corporation received general damages for the loss of use of the damaged bus. In many of these cases, the property was being used by public authorities for public works and thus no immediate "pecuniary loss" was suffered, or the owner of the property had a standby available. While it may seem that no obvious pecuniary loss has been suffered in these cases, the loss of use to the owner presumably has some economic value (otherwise the owner would not incur both the direct expenses and opportunity costs of owning and maintaining the property).

Setting the quantum of the loss in these cases is difficult because, while the use of the property was valuable to the plaintiff, it was not measured in terms of financial gain. The best measure of the value to the owner in such circumstances is the owner's opportunity cost: the amount spent or forgone by the owner to own and use the property. This could be measured by the amount that the owner could rent out the property for, or simply by the cost to the owner of the capital investment in the property (e.g., interest plus depreciation). This latter approach has been endorsed in several cases, based on the assumption that the daily "value" of the use of property is the "cost" of owning it.

There are situations where a court may reduce the award for loss of use. First, where the property is in fact owned in order to make a profit, and the defendant is able to show that the owner would not have made a profit, or would have made only a small profit, the owner is confined to the actual lost profit (or nothing if there is no profit shown).[97] This result may seem odd at first—that an owner of non-profit-earning property could recover more for lost use than the owner of profit-earning property. But the result is justifiable. Where the property is owned only to earn a profit, and has no other valuable use to the owner, then the owner loses nothing of value when the property is damaged during a period when it could not have earned profits.

Second, if the defendant is able to prove that the goods simply would not have been used for any purpose during the period of repairs, no damages will be awarded. In *Advance-Rumely Thresher Co. v.*

---

95   *The Mediana,* [1900] A.C. 113 at 116 (H.L.).
96   (1969), 113 Sol. Jo. 877.
97   *Admiralty Comrs. v. S.S. Valeria (Owners),* [1922] 2 A.C. 242 (H.L.).

Whaley,[98] the evidence showed that the plaintiff had no work for the chattel (a second-hand tractor engine) during a certain season of the year, owing to the weather. Lamont J. denied the claim for loss of use, distinguishing the shipping cases mentioned above on the basis that there was no doubt that the owners of the ships could have used them but for the collision (though not, perhaps, for profit). There were no climatic or other conditions beyond the control of the owner rendering such use impossible. In other words, there must be some "potential use" for the property. Lamont J. concluded:

> A claim for the loss of use of an engine for ploughing during the winter season in this country, where the ground is so frozen that ploughing is impossible, would carry with it on its face its own refutation, which, in my opinion, also leads to the conclusion that it was necessary to give evidence of conditions under which it would have been possible to use the engine.[99]

D. COST OF REPAIRS VERSUS DIMINUTION IN VALUE

1) The Issue Explained

Throughout the above discussion, it has been emphasized that in all cases of harm to property, the basic principle is that the owner is entitled to recover its "value." Typically, where the property is damaged, this will be the cost of repairing the property. However, such an award may not always be justified. In the case of fungible chattels, where a reasonable replacement can be purchased (and the damaged goods can be sold for scrap), it may be less expensive to purchase a replacement than to restore the damaged goods to their previous condition. In the case of real estate, the cost of actually repairing damaged land or buildings may far exceed the economic loss suffered by the owner.

The issue in each case is whether the owner is entitled to claim the full cost of repair or restoration. The question is related to the subject of mitigation: Is it reasonable of the plaintiff to expend money to repair the property after the wrong? This, in turn, depends upon whether there is, in fact, a satisfactory substitute available at a lower price, how great the difference is between the cost of repair and the cost of replace-

---

98   (1920), 52 D.L.R. 169 (Sask. C.A.).
99   *Ibid.* at 174.

ment, and whether the plaintiff has any genuine interest in pursuing the repairs in light of their expense. The following sections examine the way in which this problem arises in several different contexts.

2) Chattels

The cost of repairing damaged chattels may be recovered so long as it is "reasonable" even though that cost may exceed the apparent economic loss suffered by the owner. What is reasonable turns on how great the disparity between the figures is, and whether the owner has a "real interest" in having the repairs done. The value of the chattel to the owner may justify awarding the plaintiff the cost of repairs even if it seems uneconomical. *O'Grady*[100] provides a good example. The defendant damaged the plaintiff's M.G. automobile. The value of the car before the accident (according to the defendant) was between £185 and £200. The cost of repairs was £253. The defendants contended that the plaintiff had acted unreasonably in incurring repair costs that exceeded the value of the automobile given that similar motor vehicles were readily obtainable.

Despite the apparently uneconomical nature of the repairs, Edmund Davies J. granted the full amount and held that the plaintiff had acted reasonably in repairing the vehicle. Of particular importance in this case was the fact that the car was assiduously cared for by the plaintiff and in unique condition for a vehicle of its age. In addition, the plaintiff had demonstrated that the car did have special value to him and had in fact given it the name "Hortensia."

The cost of repairs will not always be considered reasonable. A different result was determined by the Court of Appeal in the similar case of *Darbishire v. Warran*.[101] There, the plaintiff, who had done repairs costing twice the value of his car, was held not to have "acted reasonably as between himself and the defendant ... in view of his duty to mitigate the damages."[102] Harman L.J. held that the plaintiff had breached his duty to mitigate by purchasing another vehicle, even if the particular model was not easily obtainable. This was despite evidence that the plaintiff had invested considerable personal effort in maintaining the vehicle.[103]

---

100 Above note 54. See also *Rawson v. Maher* (1982), 15 Man. R. (2d) 6 (C.A.); *Skyward Resources Ltd. v. Cessna Aircraft Co.* (2007), 44 C.C.L.T. (3d) 161 (Man. C.A.).

101 [1963] 1 W.L.R. 1067 (C.A.).

102 *Ibid.* at 1072.

103 See also *Dewees v. Morrow* (1932), 45 B.C.R. 154 (C.A.); *Scobie v. Wing* (1992), 63 B.C.L.R. (2d) 76 (C.A.).

Where the cost of repairs exceeds the diminution in market value of the property, there is no rule dictating a single choice. Instead, the cases are decided by the application of first principles. The objective of the law of damages is to restore fully the plaintiff's loss without undue hardship to the defendant. In deciding these cases, courts will be guided by the general principle of *restitutio in integrum* and will examine the evidence to determine the true nature of the owner's loss. Even when the cost of repairs appears "unreasonable," the plaintiff may be able to demonstrate that it is the best measure of the true loss. Several factors emerge from the caselaw as being clearly relevant in making this determination.

The first factor of importance is the size of the disparity between the cost of repairs and the market value of the property. Where the difference is not great (as in *O'Grady*), the court will generally defer to the plaintiff's *bona fide* choice to repair the property. However, as the disparity widens, it becomes increasingly unlikely that a reasonable person would expend the money on repairs. And while the law aims to compensate the plaintiff fully, it is not fair to permit the plaintiff to be extravagant at the defendant's expense.

The second factor is the nature of the property and the availability and equivalence of substitutes. Where the property that has been damaged is perfectly fungible, there is usually no reason for the owner to undertake repairs that are more expensive than the cost of replacing the property. Even where an identical replacement is not available, so long as there are similar goods available, it is reasonable to require the plaintiff to procure a substitute. However, where the goods are unique, or specially adapted to the plaintiff's needs, it will be more reasonable to undertake expensive repairs. In addition, even where the property is not particularly unique, the plaintiff may have a genuine subjective reason for preferring to have the repairs done. As in *O'Grady*, the plaintiff may have a sentimental attachment to the property. Many family heirlooms can easily be "replaced" in the sense that reasonable substitutes are available on the market. But their owners would prefer to have the actual article repaired because of its history or a special attachment.

The third factor is the plaintiff's intent actually to have the repairs done. In most of the cases where the plaintiff succeeds in claiming the higher cost of repairs, the plaintiff will have already had the repairs done by the time of trial. Where this is not the case, there is a danger that the plaintiff might not actually have the repairs carried out (purchasing a substitute instead and pocketing the difference). While it is not generally any concern of the court how a plaintiff spends a damage award, in these cases the plaintiff's failure actually to do the repairs may indicate an insincerity about the claim.[104] And if the plaintiff has no intention actually to do the repairs, it is difficult to argue that they are a reasonable measure of the loss. The plaintiff may be claiming the cost of repairs simply to punish the defendant or to reap a windfall. Even an undertaking to spend the money on repairs may not justify their award, since this would simply create a loss where none existed before, in order to punish the defendant.[105]

3) Real Property

Cases involving damage to real property are more complex than those involving chattels because the stakes are often much higher, and because real property has, for so long, been considered unique and thus irreplaceable on the market. In many cases, this means that the cost of repair will be allowed even when substantially in excess of market value.

In *Jens v. Mannix Co.*[106] the plaintiff's house and property were damaged by an oil spill from a broken pipeline. The defendant conceded liability for the cost of cleaning up the site but disputed the cost of rebuilding the plaintiff's house. The land was zoned for commercial use and could be sold for that purpose for more than its value with a house built upon it. In other words, the defendant argued that the market value of the land had not been diminished by the tort. Despite the "uneconomic" nature of the plaintiff's request, the court accepted that the property had special practical and sentimental value to the plaintiff. It had been his home for many years, and among other things, he ran a "car museum" from it. The property was, as such, a significant community asset. Given these facts, the court held that it was reasonable to award sufficient damages to rebuild the house.

The result in *Jens* makes good sense. The plaintiff established that the value of the property *to him* justified reconstruction of the house. His subjective valuation of the property was higher than the market's (an example of consumer surplus) and the cost of reconstruction was the true measure of his loss. The rule that emerges, however, is not that the owner is always entitled to the cost of reconstruction or repair. The rule is that the owner is entitled to the value of the loss, and this amount will vary depending upon the owner's interest in the property. Thus, in many other cases, where the cost of repair substantially

---

104 For example, see *514953 B.C. Ltd. (c.o.b. Gold Key Construction) v. Leung* (2004), 39 C.L.R. (3d) 303 (B.C.S.C.), aff'd (2007), 155 A.C.W.S. (3d) 835 (B.C.C.A.).
105 *Ruxley Electronics and Construction Ltd. v. Forsyth,* [1996] A.C. 344 (H.L.) [*Ruxley*].
106 Above note 71.

exceeds the diminished market value of the property, the court may confine the owner to the diminution in value, if any. One illustration is *C.R. Taylor (Wholesale) Ltd. v. Hepworths Ltd.*,[107] in which the plaintiff's unused billiard hall was destroyed by fire. The court refused to award the cost of rebuilding the hall given that the property was in reality a development site and the fire had only marginally affected its value. The court held that the cost of reinstatement could be claimed only where it was reasonable, having regard to the nature of the owner's interest in the property and the advantages to the plaintiff of reinstatement. Since the plaintiff's real interest in the property was solely as a commercial investment, and given that there was no intent actually to rebuild, to award the full costs of repair would confer a substantial windfall upon the plaintiff.

The Ontario Court of Appeal reached a similar result in *Montreal Trust Co. v. Hercules Sales Ltd.*[108] when it refused to award damages for destruction of a farm building in light of evidence that the plaintiff planned to subdivide and develop the property for residential use. And, in a series of cases involving the wrongful cutting of trees, courts have shown much flexibility in assessing damages. Where the trees served important functional and aesthetic purposes and the cost of replanting them is not too out of proportion, courts will award the full cost of reinstatement.[109] However, where the cost of replanting is extravagant in light of the reduction in value of the property or purpose served by the trees, courts may limit the award to a lower figure for less costly remedial work that can equally serve the plaintiff's purpose.[110] Again, the results in these cases turn on the court's assessment of the owner's true interest in the property and the genuineness of the claim to full reinstatement.

No damages have been awarded where the cost of restoration exceeds the value of the property and there is no diminution in the value of the property due to the defendant's wrongdoing. In *Dobson Estate v. Munro Homes Ltd.*,[111] involving unauthorized dumping on the plaintiff's land, the court noted that the defendants' conduct may have actually enhanced the value of the plaintiffs' property, because earth dumped on the property filled in a slump hole that would have been required to

---

107   [1977] 2 All E.R. 784 (Q.B.).

108   [1969] 1 O.R. 661 (C.A.).

109   *Peters v. Diamond*, [1964] 1 O.R. 139 (Co. Ct.); *Dykhuizen*, above note 64.

110   *Kates v. Hall* (1991), 53 B.C.L.R. (2d) 322 (C.A.) [*Kates*]; *Hutton v. Moorehouse*, [1998] B.C.J. No. 668 (S.C.); *Ovens v. Kirkman*, [2006] B.C.J. No. 540 (S.C.) [*Ovens*]; *Fondrick v. Gross* (2003), 237 Sask. R. 1 (Q.B.).

111   (2001), 212 Sask. R. 81 (Q.B.).

be filled before construction could take place on the land. The plaintiffs' claim for punitive damages was also denied because the defendants' conduct was not reprehensible enough to justify such an award.

4) Contract Cases

The same problem frequently arises in contract cases where there is a disparity between the market value of what the plaintiff has lost and the cost of substitute performance. Once again, there is no absolute rule in favour of one measure of damages over the other. The results depend very much on the facts of the case and the court's assessment of the true loss suffered by the plaintiff.

Perhaps the most famous examples of the dilemma in contract are the cases of *Peevyhouse v. Garland Coal & Mining Company*[112] and *Groves v. John Wunder Co.*[113] In both cases, the plaintiff had leased land to the defendant for mining operations. The contracts contained clauses whereby the defendants promised to do restorative work at the end of the lease, which the defendants failed to do. In both cases, the cost of actually doing the work (cost of performance) substantially exceeded the loss in value of the property due to the breach (diminution in value).

The results of the two cases illustrate how difficult the choice of values is. In *Groves*, the majority awarded the full cost of performance ($60,000), though the diminished value of the land was at most $12,000. In *Peevyhouse*, the court took the opposite approach, awarding the diminished value only.

There are three reasons offered in *Groves* in favour of the cost of performance measure. First, to permit the defendant deliberately to breach its contract and to save the costs of performing would reward bad faith and undermine the sanctity of contract. Second, to award less than the cost of doing the work would fail to give the plaintiff what was promised, and would undermine the freedom of the owner to contract for work to be done on his property (notwithstanding that the improvements might be uneconomic). Finally, the court intimated that to award the lower amount would unconscionably enrich the defendant, who had had full payment for the promised performance but sought to escape the cost of doing the work promised.

However, to each of these reasons there is a corresponding answer. First, while it is true that to award the lesser amount permits a delib-

---

112 382 P.2d 109 (Okla. Sup. Ct. 1963) [*Peevyhouse*].
113 286 N.W. 235 (Minn. Sup. Ct. 1939) [*Groves*].

erate breach of contract, it is arguable that this is, in fact, desirable in the circumstances, given that the cost of performance so substantially outweighs the cost of non-performance. Indeed, can it not be argued that it is perverse to award damages that would tend to encourage performance of such a contract at a cost of $60,000 when the total financial benefit of such performance is $12,000? Certainly from an economic point of view, the result is inefficient.[114]

Second, it is not necessarily true that awarding the lesser amount fails to respect the right of a landowner to improve his property. The judgment in *Groves* assumes throughout that the contract is a construction contract and that the work has been paid for in advance. In such a case, damages should not, of course, be limited by the value of the land. A landowner may choose to do work on her property that may even diminish the value of the property (e.g., to erect an ugly fountain) and it is no excuse for non-performance for a contractor to say that the owner has suffered no harm because the work would not have improved the land's value (indeed, stopping the work may preserve the land's value). But this was not really the case in *Groves* or *Peevyhouse*. The contract was a lease for the removal of gravel. The subsidiary agreement to leave the land level is not a construction contract, intended to improve the value of the land, but a standard term intended to ensure that the land's value is preserved after the work. The land was a commercial parcel, held by the plaintiff for investment purposes, and the owner had no apparent personal or non-financial reason for wanting the land levelled.

Third, while it is true that awarding the lesser amount would give the defendant a windfall, granting the larger amount confers an equal windfall on the plaintiff. As the dissenting judgment in *Groves* (and the majority judgment in *Peevyhouse*) points out, the general object of contract damages is to compensate the plaintiff, not to punish the defendant, and to award the full cost of performance in these cases is "unconscionable and grossly oppressive."[115] The plaintiff receives a far greater benefit from *breach* of contract than it would have received had the contract been performed. Had this contract been performed, the plaintiff would be in possession of land worth $12,000. As a result of the judgment, the plaintiff has the land (worth something less than $12,000) and $60,000 cash. From a purely financial point of view (and bearing in mind that the land was merely an investment property), the plaintiff is left in a much better position as a result of the breach.

---

114 R.A. Posner, *Economic Analysis of Law*, 6th ed. (New York: Aspen, 2003) at 121.
115 *Peevyhouse*, above note 112 at 113.

Ironically, it can be strongly argued that the decisions in both *Peevyhouse* and *Groves* are wrong! If anything, the plaintiffs in *Peevyhouse* should have been awarded the cost of fixing their land. They were farmers, had expressed special concerns about the continued usefulness of their property, and had negotiated specifically to have it restored.[116] Their loss was likely more than the mere diminution in value of the property. Conversely, in *Groves* the plaintiffs owned the property solely as a development site and had no non-pecuniary reason for wishing to restore the land. The award of the full cost of performance thus conferred upon them an amount far in excess of their actual loss. Interestingly, it has been reported that the plaintiff in *Groves* did not, in fact, use the money to level the land, but after some basic remedial work, sold the property and ended up substantially better off than had the defendant actually levelled the land.[117]

The same problem arises in many other contexts, and in none of them is there an absolute rule. Instead, courts examine the facts carefully to determine the true purpose of the contract and whether the owner has a real interest in actual performance of the contract. For example, commercial leases frequently contain a covenant to restore or repair the property at the end of the term. If the tenant fails to do so, courts will ordinarily award damages measured by the cost of actually restoring the property as required by the covenant.[118] However, where that cost is unreasonably high and will simply confer a windfall upon the owner, damages may be confined to the difference in value (if any) between the property as surrendered and as restored.[119] The problem also arises in building contracts when there is a defect in construction and the cost of curing the defect vastly exceeds the diminished value of the property due to the defect. Ordinarily the court will order the full cost of repairs,[120] but where this appears unreasonable in light of the circumstances, it will confine the owner to the diminished value.[121] In

---

116 See J.L. Maute, "*Peevyhouse v. Garland Coal & Mining Co.* Revisited: The Ballad of Willie and Lucille" (1995) 89:4 Northwestern U.L. Rev. 1341.
117 J.P. Dawson & W.B. Harvey, *Contracts and Contract Remedies* (Brooklyn: Foundation Press, 1959) at 28.
118 *Joyner v. Weeks*, [1891] 2 Q.B. 31; *Buscombe v. Stark* (1916), [1917] 1 W.W.R. 204 (B.C.C.A.); *Church of Scientology of British Columbia v. Ahmed* (1983), 44 B.C.L.R. 297 (S.C.) [*Ahmed*]; *Perentes v. Industrial Radiator Service Ltd.* (1989), 73 Sask. R. 144 (Q.B.).
119 *Miles v. Marshall* (1975), 7 O.R. (2d) 544 (H.C.J.).
120 *Radford v. De Froberville*, [1978] 1 All E.R. 33 (Q.B.) [*Radford*].
121 *Wigsell v. School for Indigent Blind* (1882), 8 Q.B.D. 357 [*Wigsell*]; *Jacobs & Young v. Kent*, 129 N.E. 889 (N.Y. Ct. App. 1921); *Williamson v. Joseph Baruch Construction Ltd.* (1977), 2 R.P.R. 197 (Ont. H.C.J.) [*Baruch*]; *Garrett v. Quality Engineering*

real estate sales the problem has arisen with respect to urea-formalde-
hyde foam insulation cases where the plaintiff claims the full cost of removing an unwanted substance when that cost exceeds the diminished
value of the house due to its presence. Again, courts have awarded the
greater amount in those situations where it truly believed the removal
was important to the owner, but they have confined the owner to damages for reduced value in other cases.[122] The problem has also arisen in
cases involving contracts to do work on mining properties. In a series
of decisions the Supreme Court of Canada has confirmed that here, too,
no fixed rule exists. Where the property can be shown to be valueless
from a mining point of view, and the work would be wasted, the court
will typically not award the full cost of doing the work.[123] But where
the work can be shown to have real value to the owner (for example,
providing useful information about the property or as a necessary part
of the overall development of the property), the cost of performing the
work may be a better measure of the owner's loss.[124] In *Insinger*,[125] Duff
J. confirmed that there was no absolute rule that the owner of property
was entitled to the full cost of performance of the work:

> If it were conclusively made out, for example, that the work to be
> done formed part and a necessary part of some plan of exploration or
> development requisite, from the miner's point of view, for develop-
> ing the property as a working mine, and necessary, from the point of
> view of businesslike managements, that it might fairly be presumed
> that in the event of the option lapsing the owner would in the ordin-
> ary course have the work completed, then the damages arising in the
> ordinary course would include the cost of doing the work.[126]

In the end, the contract cases are resolved in the same manner as
the tort cases. Courts must determine the *true nature of the plaintiff's
loss*. Of greatest importance is the nature of the plaintiff's interest in
the property. Where that interest is purely as a financial investment,
it will be difficult for the plaintiff to argue that there is any loss be-

---

    Homes Ltd. (2006), 50 C.L.R. (3d) 129 (Ont. S.C.J.); *Nu-West Homes Ltd. v. Thunder-
    bird Petroleums Ltd.* (1975), 59 D.L.R. (3d) 292 (Alta. C.A.) [*Nu-West Homes*].

122 *Mueller v. Tait* (1993), 33 R.P.R. (2d) 157 (B.C.S.C.); *Laanvere v. Johnston* (1990),
    15 R.P.R. (2d) 184 (Ont. Ct. Gen. Div.); *Vincze v. Lovegrove* (1990), 13 R.P.R. (2d)
    278 (Ont. H.C.J.).

123 *Cotter v. General Petroleums Ltd.*, [1951] S.C.R. 154 [*Cotter*].

124 *Cunningham v. Insinger*, [1924] S.C.R. 8 [*Insinger*]; *Sunshine Exploration Ltd. v.
    Dolly Varden Mines Ltd.* (N.P.L.), [1970] S.C.R. 2 [*Dolly Varden*].

125 *Ibid.*

126 *Insinger, ibid.* at 14–15.

yond the diminished market value of the property. However, where the plaintiff's interest has other dimensions (functional, aesthetic, and sentimental), the compensation will not be limited to financial loss. Courts have recognized the legitimacy of subjective value (sometimes describing it as "consumer surplus"). In Radford[127] the court awarded to the plaintiff the full cost of building a wall that the defendant had promised to build, despite the fact that the absence of the wall did not substantially affect the value of the plaintiff's property. The court emphasized the plaintiff's functional and aesthetic interest in the wall and the importance of considering whether he had a personal interest in actually completing the work. The case can be usefully contrasted with Wigsell[128] in which the court refused to award the full cost of completing a wall on the plaintiff's property. In the latter case, the purpose of the wall was to enclose a school that was never, in fact, built. There was no personal reason for wishing the wall built, and it was unlikely that it would be built. The court awarded only nominal damages to the owner for breach of the contract.

Also of critical importance is the proportionality of the cost of performance to the economic benefit to be attained. Where the cost is high, and the benefit small, courts are less likely to award the cost of performance. So, for example, in two Canadian cases, the courts refused to award large amounts of money for the demolition and replacement of cement floors that were slightly off specification, given that the substandard floors did not substantially reduce the value of the properties. In these cases, the courts found that the deviation from the contract is "inconsequential" and that the cost of repairs is unfairly out of proportion to the benefit to be obtained.[129]

Finally, the courts consider whether the owner has done the work or plans to do it. As in the tort cases, if the plaintiff has no intention of actually doing the repairs, it is difficult to argue that they are a reasonable measure of the loss. The plaintiff may be claiming the cost of repairs simply to punish the defendant or reap a windfall.[130] On the other hand, where the plaintiff seems genuinely intent on doing the work, even though its cost is very high, that intent will be good evidence of the true value of the work to the owner. In Tito v. Waddell (No. 2),[131] Megarry V.-C. said:

---

127 Above note 120.
128 Above note 121.
129 Baruch, above note 121. Nu-West Homes, above note 121.
130 Ruxley, above note 105; McGuffin v. Terry Howald Pools Inc., [2003] O.J. No. 5205 (C.A.).
131 [1977] 3 All E.R. 129 (Ch.).

The tastes and desires of the owner may be wholly out of step with the ideas of those who constitute the market; yet I cannot see why eccentricity of taste should debar him from obtaining substantial damages…. Per contra, if the plaintiff has suffered little or no monetary loss in the reduction of value of his land, and he has no intention of applying any damages towards carrying out the work contracted for, or its equivalent, I cannot see why he should recover the cost of doing work which will never be done. It would be a mere pretence to say that this cost was a loss and so should be recoverable as damages.[132]

Of some significance in this regard is whether, in the circumstances, the plaintiff has a right to request specific performance of the work and does not make this claim. The failure to claim specific performance where it is available may indicate to the court that damages measured by the diminished value of the land are an adequate remedy.[133]

The contract cases have one dimension that makes them more complicated than the tort cases. As *Groves* clearly illustrates, courts may on occasion pursue goals other than compensation. In particular, where the breach seems deliberately aimed at escaping an obligation or making a profit, in a situation where the plaintiff has actually paid to have the work done, a court may be strongly tempted to fashion an award that will strip the defendant of any unjust enrichment, even at the expense of overcompensating the plaintiff. The desire to prevent unjust enrichment has been referred to in other cases. For example, in the case of *Radford,* discussed above, the plaintiff had sold property to the defendant and the defendant had promised to build a wall between the properties. Despite the fact that the wall made little difference to the value of the property, the court awarded the full cost of building it. One factor of importance to the court was the injustice that the plaintiff had parted with his own property for a consideration that turned out to be illusory. The promise to build the wall was part of the consideration for the sale of the adjacent land. The defendant had taken the benefit of the bargain and would be unjustly enriched if allowed to keep the land without building the wall. The Supreme Court of Canada has also indicated the importance of the unjust-enrichment factor, in a case involving breach of contract to drill an oil well.[134] The ordinary rule in these cases is that the plaintiff should be entitled only to its actual economic loss. Thus, when it is proved that the well would not have produced any oil, the plaintiff is not entitled to the cost of drilling the well. However,

---

132 *Ibid.* at 316.
133 *Wigsell*, above note 121.
134 *Cotter*, above note 123 at 174, Cartwright J. See also *Dolly Varden*, above note 124.

the Court recognized that the situation might be different if the plaintiff had paid the defendant a sum of money to drill the well. Where the consideration has passed (i.e., the plaintiff has paid), the full cost of performance may be the proper measure.

In summary, there is no absolute rule favouring one measure over the other. The basic question must always be: What has the plaintiff lost by reason of the breach? The result in any case will be determined by evidence indicating the nature of the plaintiff's interest, his intent to do the work, and the size of the disparity between the two figures. Additionally, the court's desire to prevent unjust enrichment of the defendant will often tip the scale.

5) Alternate Measures

In principle there is no reason for a court to confine itself to the two stark alternatives of cost of repair or diminution in value. In some cases it may be that neither of these figures is an accurate measure of the plaintiff's loss. It may be that the diminished market value underestimates the plaintiff's loss, while the cost of repairing the property is an overestimate. This problem arose in *Kates*.[135] The plaintiff's neighbour cut down thirteen of the plaintiff's trees. While there was no apparent diminution in the value of the plaintiff's property, the plaintiff claimed $200,000 to replant mature trees. The Court of Appeal denied the full claim on the basis that the "actual benefits to the plaintiff of meticulous reinstatement"[136] did not justify the exorbitant cost. The court was influenced by, first, the enormous disparity between the cost of reinstatement and the diminished value of the land; second, the fact that the plaintiff did not use the property a great deal and that the loss of privacy could be remedied by less expensive measures; and third, a suspicion that the plaintiffs would not in fact use the award to do the work but were in fact seeking retribution. Instead, the court awarded a substantial amount for alternate remedial work, damages for "lost amenities" (privacy and aesthetics) that would not be regained, and punitive damages. This award recognizes that the subjective value of the property may lie somewhere between the cost of repair and diminution in value.[137] Only natural persons may be entitled to damages for

---

135 Above note 110.
136 *Ibid.* at 331.
137 See also *Ovens*, above note 110.

lost amenities, therefore the award is not available where the plaintiff is a corporate entity.[138]

The approach in *Kates* has also been adopted—and given a more formal theoretical basis—in England. In *Ruxley*[139] the plaintiff's swimming pool was built nine inches shallower than specified in the contract. The cost of rebuilding the pool was £21,500, yet the shallower pool was no less valuable and no less functional than a deeper pool. The House of Lords rejected the plaintiff's claim to the full cost of restoration on the basis that it was not an accurate measure of the plaintiff's actual loss and would be a "gratuitous benefit."

The House of Lords affirmed that, in determining the measure of damages, it was appropriate to take into account both the reasonableness of doing the work and the intention of the plaintiff actually to do the work. The reasonableness of the claim is ascertained by considering the proportionality between the expenditure and the benefit to be achieved. The court must consider not only the financial benefit but any non-financial interest that the plaintiff might have. In other words, it is important to look at the true interest of the plaintiff (his contractual objective), and where the contract is not merely commercial but rather involves "personal preferences," this will be a factor that may justify awarding the larger amount. However, where that objective has been substantially accomplished, as here, that will weigh against awarding the cost of reinstatement. In *Ruxley* the Court held that the cost of rebuilding the pool was wholly disproportionate to the expense, and that, since the plaintiff had no intention of rebuilding the pool, if awarded the larger amount he would end up with a pool substantially in conformity with his expectations, plus a cash windfall.

On the other hand, the Court did not hold that the plaintiff was confined to a claim based on the mere diminution in value of his property. The Court acknowledged that the "loss" suffered by the plaintiff might be somewhere in between—that the plaintiff had lost more, in terms of his own values, than could be measured by mere market prices but not so much as the full cost of replacing the swimming pool. Lord Mustill, in particular, adopted and explained the concept of consumer surplus—that improvements in property, while valuable to the owner, may not increase the monetary value of the property:

> There are not two alternative measures of damage, at opposite poles, but only one; namely, the loss truly suffered by the promisee. In some

138 *Prince Rupert (City) v. Pederson* (1994), 98 B.C.L.R. (2d) 84 at para. 27 (C.A.); *Canada Forest Products*, above note 65 at para. 218.

139 Above note 105.

cases the loss cannot be fairly measured except by reference to the full cost of repairing the deficiency in performance. In others, and particularly those where the contract is designed to fulfil a purely commercial purpose, the loss will very often consist only of the monetary detriment brought about by the breach of contract. But these remedies are not exhaustive, for the law must cater for those occasions where the value of the promise to the promisee exceeds the financial enhancement of his position which full performance will secure. This excess, often referred to in the literature as the "consumer surplus"… is usually incapable of precise valuation in terms of money, exactly because it represents a personal, subjective and non-monetary gain. Nevertheless, where it exists the law should recognise it and compensate the promisee if the misperformance takes it away.[140]

This case substantially advances the law in this area since it asserts that courts are not confined rigidly to a choice between two unreasonable extremes. Instead, courts may assess a realistic sum that more closely achieves accurate compensation for the true loss suffered by the plaintiff regardless of the amount saved and/or diminution in the value of the plaintiff's property caused by the defendant's wrongdoing. It should be emphasized that the factors influencing the court, and the result in the case, might be different in situations where the breach of contract is deliberate (e.g., to save labour and materials). In such cases, the court may be offended at the possibility that the defendant will be unjustly enriched by breach of contract and may be inclined to award the larger amount to prevent that enrichment.[141]

E. THE PROBLEM OF BETTERMENT

Where the repairs to the plaintiff's property fail to restore it to its predamaged condition, the plaintiff is entitled to damages reflecting the remaining loss in value. However, in many cases of destruction or damage to property, replacement or repair will secure for the plaintiff a better or more valuable asset than what she had lost. This is the problem of "betterment" and the issue is whether it should be taken into account in assessing damages. For example, the property that is damaged or destroyed may be old and its value depreciated already prior to the wrong.

---

140 *Ibid.* at 360–61.
141 See Chapter 7; H. Beale, "Exceptional Measures of Damages in Contract" in P. Birks, ed., *Wrongs and Remedies in the Twenty-First Century* (Oxford: Clarendon Press, 1996) at 217.

The property cannot be replaced by an exact substitute. Instead, it is replaced by a new item, or repaired with new components to a state better than at the time of the injury.

The issue of betterment poses a dilemma. On the one hand, if no deduction is made, the plaintiff will be overcompensated in the sense that at the defendant's expense she will be left with an asset that is better and more valuable than it was prior to the defendant's wrong. On the other hand, if a deduction is made, the owner of the property will have been forced to spend her own money on repairing or replacing property.

When used goods are destroyed, and an equivalent is available, the owner will be entitled only to the cost of acquiring equivalent replacement. Where an equivalent is not available, the matter is more problematic. In principle, because the plaintiff is replacing "old with new," the rebuilt property will be more valuable and the plaintiff will receive a "windfall" if no deduction is made. Following through on this logic, a deduction will sometimes be made for depreciation. For example, in *Church of Scientology of British Columbia v. Ahmed*, where it cost $166,000 to restore an old and dilapidated building and those restorations increased the value of the property by $100,000, a 66 percent deduction was made to take into account the increase in value.[142]

Despite the apparent logic of this deduction, it is hard on plaintiffs since it has the effect of forcing the plaintiff to expend his own money on repairs that would not have been required but for the defendant's wrong. This consideration has led some courts to the view that a deduction is inappropriate. A good example of this type of judicial thinking is the case of *Harbutt's "Plasticine."*[143] The plaintiff's factory was destroyed by fire as a result of the defendant's negligence and breach of contract. The plaintiff had to build the new factory to a different design to meet planning laws and, of course, replaced their old and depreciated factory with a new one. Thus, the cost of rebuilding was more than the value of their old factory. However, despite the fact that they ended up with a more valuable asset, no deduction was made for betterment. The court was not troubled by the fact that the plaintiff got "new for old" since the factory was not functionally larger or better than the old one. And, as Lord Widgery explained, to make a deduction for betterment "would be the equivalent of forcing the plaintiffs to invest their money in the modernising of their plant which might be highly inconvenient for them."[144]

---

142   *Ahmed*, above note 118; see also *Jens*, above note 71 (C.A.).
143   Above note 80.
144   *Ibid.* at 473. See also *The Clyde* (1856), S.W. 23, 166 E.R. 998; *The Gazelle* (1844), 2 Wm. Rob. 279, 166 E.R. 759; *Bacon v. Cooper (Metals Ltd.)*, [1982] 1 All E.R. 397 (C.A.).

There is no avoiding the fact that the plaintiffs obtained a windfall by this judgment. Their total wealth was greater after the trial than it was before the accident. Their building was more valuable because it was made of new materials, allowing it to last longer and to avoid certain costs of repair and upkeep that might have been incurred in respect of an old building.

Sometimes it will be obvious that a deduction for betterment should be made. Where the property is in an already damaged condition when it is damaged again by the defendant, credit will be given to the defendant for the fact that the property already required repairs. For example, in *Performance Cars Ltd. v. Abraham*,[145] the defendant damaged the front of the plaintiff's Rolls Royce automobile, requiring it to be repainted. However, the rear of the car had previously been damaged and the entire car already required repainting. In these circumstances the Court of Appeal held that the defendant was not liable for the cost, since the second accident had not imposed a new burden on the plaintiff. Similarly, when the wrong aggravates an existing problem, the defendant will be liable only for the additional repair costs created.[146]

Where the property is of the type that requires periodic replacement, credit will be given for betterment. A good example is the case of *Upper Lakes Shipping Ltd. v. St. Lawrence Cement Inc.*[147] The defendant negligently damaged the plaintiff's conveyor belt. The machinery was three years old at the time and should have lasted for fifteen years. The Ontario Court of Appeal held that, in the calculation of damages, an allowance should be made for the fact that the plaintiff would be replacing an old belt with a new one. However, it also recognized that the plaintiff was being forced to replace the conveyor belt earlier than would otherwise have been necessary. The real harm suffered by the plaintiff, therefore, was in having to replace the machinery earlier than planned. Accordingly, the plaintiff's damages were held to be the cost of accelerating the inevitable expense and could be measured by the cost of capital lost to the plaintiff (e.g., lost interest on the capital expenditure that the plaintiff was forced to make twelve years earlier than would otherwise have been necessary). Because this interest would have been earned on an annual basis over the twelve-year period, the plaintiff's

---

145 [1962] 1 Q.B. 33 (C.A.).
146 See Chapter 11.
147 (1992), 89 D.L.R. (4th) 722 (Ont. C.A.). See also *Fontaine v. Roofmart Western Ltd.* (2005), 198 Man. R. (2d) 199, var'd 2007 MBCA 44; *Rough Bay Enterprises Ltd. v. Budden* (2003), 22 B.C.L.R. (4th) 326 (S.C.).

damages were calculated as a discounted lump sum representing the present value of those future interest payments.

This decision suggests a possible compromise in cases involving even more durable property such as buildings.[148] Credit should be given to the defendant for depreciation, but the plaintiff should be compensated for having to invest its own money repairing its building. Several cases have adopted this approach. *Sunnyside Greenhouses Ltd. v. Golden West Seeds Ltd.*[149] involved the sale of defective greenhouse panels. The court held that the plaintiff was entitled to damages for the diminished value of the panels (the purchase price less any residual value) and for the wasted expense of installing them and the cost of removing them earlier than should have been necessary. The court did not award the full cost of removing the panels, since they would have had to be replaced in any event. Instead, the court awarded the interest on the early expenditure. This approach was also adopted in principle in *James Street Hardware & Furniture Co. Ltd. v. Spizziri,*[150] in which the Ontario Court of Appeal confirmed that a deduction should be made for betterment but that the plaintiff should be compensated for the loss of use of his own money.

> As Waddams suggests, the answer lies in compensating the plaintiff for the loss imposed upon him or her in being forced to spend money he or she would not otherwise have spent—at least as early as was required by the damages occasioned to him by the tort. In general terms, this loss would be the cost (if he has to borrow) or value (if he already has the money) of the money equivalent of the betterment over a particular period of time....
>
> [This approach] offers a useful guide to accommodating the interests of the defendant who wishes to avoid paying for a windfall and of a plaintiff who wishes to avoid being forced to spend money that he or she may or may not have.[151]

The onus of proof is on the defendant to demonstrate that the repairs do in fact result in betterment, and the mere fact that the cost of rebuilding a home is more than its pre-accident value does not ne-

---

148 See discussion in Waddams, above note 13 at paras. 1.2730–1.2800; *Prince George (City) v. Rahn Brothers Logging Ltd.* (2003), 9 B.C.L.R. (4th) 253 (C.A.).

149 Above note 78.

150 (1987), 62 O.R. (2d) 385 (C.A.).

151 *Ibid.* at 404–5.

cessarily indicate that the owner has been enriched.[152] The defendant must provide proof that the property is indeed more valuable. Moreover, while the interest-based approach described here is mathematically elegant, it is difficult to apply in the case of long-term assets such as a home, since there is no defined period over which a homeowner "replaces" a building.

F. RESTITUTIONARY-TYPE REMEDIES FOR INTERFERENCE WITH PROPERTY

1) Introduction

There are several remedies for interference with property that occupy the borderland between compensation and restitution. The topic of restitution is covered in detail in Chapter 7. However, this section will briefly summarize some of those remedies as they apply to interferences with property.

It will be recalled that restitutionary remedies are designed to strip the wrongdoer of ill-gotten gains. These remedies become important when the defendant's interference with the plaintiff's property appears to cause no obvious physical harm to the property, and no obvious financial loss to the plaintiff, yet the defendant has earned a profit by the interference. For example, the defendant may unlawfully use the plaintiff's property in the course of constructing a building on an adjacent lot. The trespass may cause no real financial loss to the plaintiff or harm to her property, and an action for damages would not result in substantial compensation. A restitutionary remedy focuses instead on the wrongful benefit obtained by the defendant.

2) Opportunity Cost/Savings Approaches

One common remedy in these situations derives from the old notion of "way-leave" whereby courts assess damages in an amount that the plaintiff might have charged to permit the defendant to use the property. For example, in *Whitwham*[153] the defendant trespassed on the plaintiff's property in the course of their mining operations (by dumping waste). The actual damage to the plaintiff's property was only about

---

152 *Ibid.* See also *Nan v. Black Pine Manufacturing Ltd.* (1991), 55 B.C.L.R. (2d) 241 (C.A).
153 Above note 67.

£200, but the defendant had increased its profits by £900 by committing the trespass. The Court awarded the higher sum as the quantum of damages. Lindley L.J. affirmed the principle that "if one person has without leave of another been using that other's land for his own purposes, he ought to pay for such user."[154] The "way-leave" approach has also been used in cases involving the refusal by an overholding tenant to vacate premises,[155] the unauthorized use of the plaintiff's sewer system,[156] the construction of houses on neighbouring property in violation of a restrictive covenant,[157] and construction of a home that was accessible only over the plaintiff's property.[158] In these cases the courts looked at the notional profit earned by the defendant from committing the trespass, and estimated a fair price that the plaintiff might have received from the defendant had the parties negotiated a bargain.

The opportunity-cost approach has also been used in cases involving the wrongful detention of goods. In *Strand Electric and Engineering Co. Ltd. v. Brisford Entertainments Ltd.*,[159] the defendant wrongfully retained the plaintiff's switchboards. Denning L.J. affirmed that "[i]f a wrongdoer has made use of goods for his own purposes, then he must pay a reasonable hire for them, even though the owner has in fact suffered no loss."[160] Therefore, even if the owner of goods could not have used or hired out the goods in question, he is nonetheless entitled to a reasonable hire from the defendant who has wrongfully retained them. Insofar as the damages in this case are based upon the wrongful benefit obtained by the defendant rather than the loss to the plaintiff, said Denning, it "resembles, therefore, an action for restitution rather than an action of tort."[161]

3) Full Disgorgement

On some occasions, courts will go beyond the "licence fee" approach when they consider that additional deterrence is called for. While in the case of "innocent" interferences with the plaintiff's property the parties' dispute may be properly resolved by requiring the payment of reasonable compensation, in other cases courts may not be willing to

---

154   *Ibid.* at 541–42.
155   *Swordheath Properties Ltd. v. Tabet*, [1979] 1 W.L.R. 285 (C.A.).
156   *Daniel v. O'Leary* (1976), 14 N.B.R. (2d) 564 (Q.B.).
157   *Wrotham Park Estate Co. Ltd. v. Parkside Homes Ltd.*, [1974] 1 W.L.R. 798 (Ch.).
158   *Bracewell v. Appleby*, [1975] Ch. 408.
159   [1952] 2 Q.B. 246 (C.A.).
160   *Ibid.* at 254.
161   *Ibid.* at 255.

"license" a continuing wrong. Instead, the courts "punish" the defendant or require him to disgorge the entire benefit earned as a result of the wrong. These are true restitution cases, since the sum awarded to the plaintiff has nothing to do with the plaintiff's loss. Full disgorgement of profit is often accomplished through an award of punitive damages. In *Austin*[162] the defendants trespassed by installing anchor rods below the surface of the plaintiff's property as part of the shoring for the foundation of a large building. While there was only nominal damage to the plaintiff's property, the defendant saved anywhere from $21,000 to over $30,000 by using the rods. The Court of Appeal increased the award of exemplary damages from $7,500 to $30,000 in order to eliminate the defendant's profit entirely. Punitive damages are discussed fully in Chapter 8.

4) Intellectual Property and Breach of Confidence

In cases where the defendant has misappropriated the plaintiff's intellectual property, or breached a duty of confidence, the plaintiff may obtain damages measured by its lost profits or lost sales. There are alternative measures, however, based on restitutionary notions. Where the defendant wrongfully appropriates the plaintiff's idea, in lieu of requiring the plaintiff to prove lost profits, the court may assess damages based on the value of the information wrongfully acquired. Those damages may be assessed according to the "savings" achieved by the defendant or the plaintiff's opportunity cost. This latter amount is measured by determining what the defendant would have had to pay to acquire or license that idea from the plaintiff. For example, in *Seager v. Copydex Ltd. (No. 2)*,[163] the defendant wrongfully (though innocently) used information supplied to it in confidence to design a carpet grip. The court held that, where the information is such that it could not be obtained except from the plaintiff (as opposed to a consultant), the value of the information is the price that would be paid in a sale between a willing buyer and a willing seller. In the result the court awarded a capital sum representing the stream of royalties that the plaintiff could have demanded for the sale of the idea.

An alternative measure in such cases, when the information acquired is not particularly special and could be acquired through research, is to base the award on the consulting fees or development costs

---

162 Above note 68.
163 [1969] 1 W.L.R. 809 (C.A.) [*Seager*].

that the defendant saved by reason of the breach.[164] In *Seager*, Lord Denning explained:

> The value of the confidential information depends on the nature of it. If there was nothing very special about it, that is, if it involved no particular inventive step, but was the sort of information which could be obtained by employing any competent consultant, then the value of it was the fee which a consultant would charge for it ... [but] if the information was something special, as, for instance, if it involved an inventive step or something so unusual that it could not be obtained by just going to a consultant, then the value of it is much higher. It is not merely a consultant's fee, but the price which a willing buyer—desirous of obtaining it—would pay for it. It is the value between a willing seller and a willing buyer.[165]

The approach in *Seager* will not always be appropriate. Sometimes, the actual damage to the plaintiff will be greater than a mere "licence fee." Thus, the savings method was rejected by the Supreme Court of Canada in *Cadbury Schweppes Inc. v. FBI Foods Ltd.*[166] Here, the defendant had used the plaintiff's confidential information to make a "clamato" drink. In light of a finding that the defendant would have been able to develop such a drink within a year even without the information, the trial judge awarded only $29,000, representing the amount saved by the defendant on research and development. But the Court of Appeal and Supreme Court of Canada held that, because the plaintiff was not in the business of "selling" its recipe, the mere market value of the information was not in fact an accurate measure of its loss. In fact, its loss was the loss of its monopoly position in the market during the one-year head-start period, and the compensatory damages were, therefore, based on the sales it had lost as a result of the defendant's competition.

Another alternative in intellectual property and breach of confidence cases is a full restitutionary remedy whereby a court requires the defendant to disgorge its entire profit through a remedy of accounting or a constructive trust.[167] These remedies are discussed in Chapter 7.

---

164 *Apotex Fermentation Inc. v. Novopharm Ltd.* (1998), 80 C.P.R. (3d) 449 (Man. C.A.); *ICAM Technologies Corp. v. EBCO Industries Ltd.* (1993), 85 B.C.L.R. (2d) 318 (C.A.), aff'g (1991), 6 B.C.L.R. (2d) 98 (S.C.), leave to appeal to S.C.C. abandoned, [1994] S.C.C.A. No. 23.

165 Above note 163 at 813.

166 [1999] 1 S.C.R. 142.

167 *LAC Minerals Ltd. v. International Corona Resources Ltd.*, [1989] 2 S.C.R. 574.

5) True Restitution

Finally, there are some cases in which the plaintiff may be entitled to a true restitutionary remedy in respect of misappropriation of property. When a trustee misappropriates property or a fiduciary appropriates property belonging to the plaintiff, the courts may award a full accounting or may impress that property with a constructive trust. The remedy is measured by the gain to the defendant even when this amount clearly exceeds any harm to the plaintiff. These principles are discussed fully in Chapter 7.

G. NON-PECUNIARY LOSSES IN RESPECT OF PROPERTY

While the law typically takes market prices as the basis of valuation of property, it does so only because such prices are generally good evidence of its value to the owner and an award based on market prices will generally allow the owner to obtain a substitute of equal value. However, the basic rule of compensation is not market value, but *value to the owner*, and where the owner can demonstrate that the property had greater actual value, that actual value will be compensated. The subject of intangible and non-pecuniary losses is covered fully in Chapter 6. However, this section briefly summarizes the relevant principles as they apply to property loss.

It is clear that property need not be owned for the purpose of earning a profit in order for the owner to receive compensation for loss of its use. As explained earlier in this chapter, when the property has a *functional* value to the owner, the loss of its use will be compensated.

Less obviously, the property may have sentimental, aesthetic, or *intangible* value to the owner. If properly proved, such losses are compensable under a variety of heads. Subjective value is recognized, albeit indirectly, in awards that permit the cost of "uneconomic" repairs, aggravated damages, and lost amenities. For example, in *O'Grady*,[168] discussed earlier, the owner of a car named "Hortensia" was awarded an amount to repair damage to the vehicle that exceeded the cost of actually replacing it. Additionally, where the owner attaches a subjective value to the property above its market value, this "consumer surplus" may be taken into account in assessing the owner's subjective loss. The cases on "uneconomic" repairs and consumer surplus are discussed

---

168 Above note 54.

in more detail earlier in this chapter. Also, as explained above, aesthetic and functional values can be compensated for by awards for "lost amenities," as in *Kates*,[169] where the plaintiffs were awarded substantial damages for lost amenities when their neighbour cut down their trees, despite the fact that this did not diminish the market value of their property.

Alternatively, where property has an emotional or sentimental value or use to the owner, the "intangible" loss occasioned by harm to the property may be compensated directly by an award of aggravated damages, or damages for emotional distress, subject to rules regarding remoteness. For example, in *Newell v. Canadian Pacific Airlines Ltd.*,[170] the owners of two pet dogs were awarded aggravated damages for the death of one of them and injury to another that exceeded the market value of the dogs. In several cases, disappointed purchasers of real estate have been awarded damages for emotional distress when the contract fell through (though only where the special circumstances were known to the defendant).[171] A plaintiff was awarded damages for mental distress when the defendant lost the ashes of the plaintiff's parent following cremation.[172] The topic of damages for intangible losses and emotional distress is canvassed in detail in Chapter 6.

---

169 Above note 110.
170 (1976), 14 O.R. (2d) 752 (Co. Ct.). See also *Surette v. Kingsley (c.o.b. Paws for Thoughts!)*, [2000] N.B.J. No. 532 (Small Cl. Ct.) where the plaintiff recovered damages for mental distress for uncertainty about her cat's condition following negligent treatment by the defendant.
171 *Taylor v. Gill* (1991), 13 A.R. 38 (Q.B.); *Kempling v. Hearthstone Manor Corp.* (1996), 184 A.R. 321 (C.A.). See also *Karampatos v. Torabipour*, [2004] O.J. No. 4255 (S.C.J.), where the plaintiffs were awarded damages for the emotional and physical inconvenience and hardship due to the defendant's breach of contract.
172 *Mason v. Westside Cemeteries Ltd.* (1996), 135 D.L.R. (4th) 361 (Ont. Ct. Gen. Div.).

CHAPTER 4

COMPENSATION FOR PERSONAL INJURY

A. INTRODUCTION AND TERMINOLOGY

The fundamental principle of personal injury compensation is *restitutio in integrum*: restoration of the plaintiff to her pre-accident situation, at least so far as the losses suffered can be repaired by a monetary award. Obviously, in cases of serious injury, money can never truly make up for the harm that has been suffered. But by offering a full indemnity for all economic losses, and additional compensation for non-economic losses to provide a measure of solace, the law strives to achieve this goal as nearly as possible. In *Ratych v. Bloomer*, McLachlin J. stated:

> The award is justified, not because it is appropriate to punish the de-
> fendant or enrich the plaintiff, but because it will serve the purpose
> or *function* of restoring the plaintiff as nearly as possible to his pre-
> accident state or alternatively, where this cannot be done, providing
> substitutes for what he has lost.[1]

The restoration measure of damages for personal injury may be compared with reliance damages in contract, insofar as the goal of both is to restore the plaintiff to the position as though the encounter with the defendant had not occurred.

---

1   [1990] 1 S.C.R. 940 at 963.

In three cases decided in 1978 ("the trilogy"),[2] each involving cat-astrophically injured youths, the Supreme Court of Canada set out the law regarding personal injury compensation with some precision. Damages are awarded for both *past* and *future* losses, and in both of these categories, damages are further divided into pecuniary and non-pecuniary heads. *Pecuniary damages* are intended to compensate all the plaintiff's financial losses. They cover past lost income and diminished future earning capacity, the cost of care (past and future), and expenses incurred as a result of the injury. *Non-pecuniary damages* are intended to provide a measure of consolation for intangible losses, including pain and suffering, loss of amenities, loss of enjoyment of life, and loss of expectation of life. Non-pecuniary damages may also include aggra-vated damages if the injury was caused maliciously (see Chapter 6).

Damages are also referred to as "special" and "general." *Special damages* (or "out-of-pocket" losses) are those losses and expenses (such as income loss, medical treatment) that occur before trial. These can usually be proved with some precision and supported by direct evi-dence. *General damages* are for losses that will likely arise in the future. General damages, which involve a certain amount of speculation, are generally proved through the use of expert opinion evidence.

B. GENERAL CONSIDERATIONS

This section introduces and encapsulates some general factors affecting the quantification of personal injury damages. Each of these is dealt with more extensively in a separate chapter.

1) Causation

The plaintiff has the onus of proving that the defendant's wrong was, in fact, the cause of the injury. Causation problems typically arise when the plaintiff's injury is unusual for the type of accident that occurred, or where there is evidence that the injury is one that the plaintiff was pre-disposed to or might have incurred anyway (the so-called "thin skull" situation). Causation problems are also common when the plaintiff's injury is not the result of a traumatic accident but is rather a "multi-factorial" illness or disease. Such problems arise in a particularly acute

---

2   *Andrews v. Grand & Toy Alberta Ltd.*, [1978] 2 S.C.R. 229 [*Andrews*]; *Thornton v. Prince George School District No. 57*, [1978] 2 S.C.R. 267 [*Thornton*]; *Arnold v. Teno*, [1978] 2 S.C.R. 287 [*Teno*].

fashion in the area of "toxic torts." An example would be products liability litigation over tobacco products, and the difficulty faced by smokers in proving that their cancer or respiratory illness was caused by smoking. After experimenting with a relaxed onus of proof in this area, and the awarding of "probabilistic damages," Anglo-Canadian courts have returned to the traditional requirement that the plaintiff must prove the cause of the harm on the balance of probabilities, though courts will take a robust and pragmatic approach to these questions.[3] Problems of causation are dealt with in Chapter 10.

2) Certainty

Personal injury compensation is often largely about guessing the unknowable and pondering the imponderable. The questions will frequently be as follows: What would have happened in the plaintiff's life but for the accident? And what will happen during the remainder of the plaintiff's life as a result of the accident? These questions are highly speculative. The plaintiff has the onus of proving his damages and is not entitled to recover damages that are too uncertain. However, the law has developed principles that aid the plaintiff in the face of uncertainty. Perhaps the most important is the acceptance by courts of probabilistic evidence regarding future events, and the awarding of probabilistic damages to compensate for lost chances. These principles are discussed more fully in this chapter and in Chapter 10.

3) Remoteness

The plaintiff may recover only damages that are not too remote. In personal injury law, the physical and psychosocial consequences of an injury are often far-reaching. Several cases, for example, involve personal injury plaintiffs who, as a possible result of the trauma of the accident, seek to end their lives. The physical consequences of an injury can be unexpected, and the psychological, social, and financial consequences even more so. The principles of remoteness of damages are discussed in Chapter 11.

4) Mitigation and Collateral Benefits

The plaintiff in a personal injury case has an obligation to mitigate. This means that he is obliged to take reasonable steps to achieve rehabilita-

---

3   *Snell v. Farrell*, [1990] 2 S.C.R. 311; *Athey v. Leonati*, [1996] 3 S.C.R. 458; *Resurfice Corp. v. Hanke* (2007), 45 C.C.L.T. (3d) 1 (S.C.C.).

tion and recovery, and to seek employment when he is able to do so to minimize his economic losses. The onus is on the defendant to prove that the plaintiff has not mitigated damages. The principle of mitigation does not mean that the plaintiff is obliged to accept substandard care solely to reduce the burden of damages. However, if the plaintiff fails to mitigate, his damages will be reduced. The principles of mitigation, as they apply to personal injury law, are discussed in Chapter 12.

A related issue that arises frequently in personal injury law involves the approach to collateral benefits received by the plaintiff from a third party after the injury. Such benefits include gifts, payments from disability insurance, public benefits such as welfare and employment insurance, or benefits in kind such as medical or nursing services. The question is whether these benefits should be taken into account (i.e., deducted) when assessing the plaintiff's claim. As a result of these benefits, the plaintiff's loss is reduced. However, there is much reluctance to "subsidize" the wrongdoer by treating such benefits as credits against the damages payable. The problem of collateral benefits is discussed in Chapter 13.

C. THE FORM OF THE AWARD

1) Itemizing

Formerly, personal injury damages were often awarded on a "global" basis. Canadian law now requires, however, that awards be "itemized"—namely, broken down separately into the categories of cost of care, lost earning capacity, and non-pecuniary damages—and that within each of these categories, the amounts are to be carefully analyzed. This approach makes damages quantification more rational and "scientific." It ensures more accurate compensation of the plaintiff, while not unduly burdening the defendants with unjustifiably large awards. Itemizing promotes greater uniformity among the cases and increases the calculability and predictability of awards, thereby promoting out-of-court settlements. Critics suggest that these benefits are largely illusory since the awarding of damages in a lump sum involves so many variables and imponderables that the entire exercise can be little more that "crystal ball gazing."

2) Lump Sum Awards

At common law, damages must be awarded in a single lump sum. Past losses are added up and future losses are estimated and "discounted" to a present-day capital sum. The plaintiff receives the entire amount and there are no restrictions on how it may be used and no opportunity to revise the award as the future unfolds.

a)   Advantages and Disadvantages of the Lump Sum

Lump sum awards have certain advantages. They achieve finality for the parties and promote judicial economy. The defendant (and her insurance company) needs to know her liability with certainty. At the conclusion of trial, the plaintiff receives a fixed amount and is able to plan for the future with confidence. Judicial resources are designed to resolve disputes once and for all and are insufficient to provide for any ongoing review of awards.

To determine a capital sum that compensates the plaintiff for all future losses, the court must estimate the plaintiff's pre-accident and post-accident lifespan, the earnings that the plaintiff might have made but for the accident, the earnings that the plaintiff will continue to make despite the accident, the total medical costs that will be incurred in the future as a result of the accident, and positive and negative contingencies that might have affected the plaintiff. The court must then "discount" the award to a present-day capital sum, based upon an estimate of the rate of inflation and investment return over the remaining life of the plaintiff.

Obviously such an exercise is fraught with pitfalls. Once set, the award is paid out in a single sum that may be spent in any way the plaintiff desires. There is no possibility of judicial review of the award to take into account errors in its underlying assumptions or changes in the plaintiff's circumstances or needs. If the court underestimates the rate of inflation, the available funds will run out too soon. If the plaintiff lives longer than estimated, the award will be inadequate. If the plaintiff dies earlier, the award will be a windfall to the estate. If unforeseen needs and contingencies arise, the plaintiff may be left with inadequate funds to provide the needed care. As Lord Scarman stated, "[t]here is really only one certainty: the future will prove the award to be either too high or too low."[4] And as Dickson J. stated in *Andrews*,

> it is highly irrational [for compensation] to be tied to a lump sum system and a once-and-for-all award.... It should be possible to devise some system whereby payments would be subject to periodic review and variation in the light of the continuing needs of the injured person and the cost of meeting those needs.[5]

---

4   *Lim Poh Choo v. Camden and Islington Area Health Authority*, [1980] A.C. 174 at 183 (H.L.).

5   *Andrews*, above note 2 at 236.

Notwithstanding criticisms of the lump sum system, it remains the predominant approach in personal injury claims, principally because it brings finality to legal disputes.[6]

b) Alternatives to the Lump Sum: Periodic Payments and Structured Settlements

i) Common Law

One alternative to lump sum awards is a system of periodic payments. Such payments can be in a fixed amount (e.g., purchased from an insurance company as an annuity) and can be crafted to provide adjustments in the case of certain contingencies. In *Watkins v. Olafson*[7] the Supreme Court of Canada was asked to depart from the lump sum approach and to order periodic payments. McLachlin J., on behalf of the Court, reasoned that, without legislative authority, the common law did not permit a court to order periodic payments in the place of a conventional lump sum award.[8] She was of the view that the change in the law requested was beyond the jurisdiction and competence of the Court and best left to a legislature capable of analyzing the policy issues in greater depth. Those issues include the burden on the litigants and the courts from ongoing review and adjustment of awards, the security and solvency of the defendant over time, the complications in determining when periodic payments will be ordered, and the lack of finality in the relationship between the plaintiff and the defendant.[9]

ii) Structured Settlements

Despite these objections to awards of periodic payments of damages, they have been recommended by legal commentators[10] and are increasingly used in Canada. Structured settlements, which are periodic payments negotiated by consent, have now become common. They are normally funded through the purchase of a life insurance annuity policy, which has significant tax advantages (properly structured, the income may be free of tax).[11] These policies can be designed to meet the needs of the individual plaintiff, with modifications such as variation in payments to account for infla-

---

6 See *Tsaoussis (Litigation guardian of) v. Baetz* (1998), 41 O.R. (3d) 257 (S.C.J.); *Singh v. Brar* (2002), 2 B.C.L.R. (4th) 305 (C.A.).
7 [1989] 2 S.C.R. 750 [*Olafson*].
8 *Ibid.* at 761.
9 *Ibid.*
10 Manitoba Law Reform Commission, *Report on Periodic Payment of Damages for Personal Injury and Death* (Winnipeg: The Commission, 1987).
11 J.P. Weir, *Structured Settlements* (Toronto: Carswell, 1984) at 40.

tion and occasional lump sum payments to cover extraordinary expenses such as university tuition.[12] It should be noted, however, that structured settlements and periodic payments are still offspring of the lump sum. They are ways of administering lump sums, rather than ways of departing from the lump sum award. For example, once they are in place, they do not permit for any substantial revision in light of changing circumstances or the changes in the plaintiff's medical condition or needs.

iii) Legislative Reform

Responding to the comments in *Olafson* about the need for legislative reform, several provinces have now enacted legislation to permit court-ordered structured judgments with periodic payments. In addition to the tax-related advantages, benefits of periodic payments include the pooling of mortality risks, reshaping the award to the plaintiff's ongoing situation and needs, and reducing the possibility of the award being dissipated.[13] Insurance companies can furnish the same degree of security as any other financial institution in which the plaintiff might invest. And the purchase of an annuity can provide finality for the defendant and termination of an unwanted relationship between the litigants.

Provinces that have provided legislative authority for mandatory structured judgments include Ontario,[14] British Columbia,[15] and Manitoba.[16] In British Columbia, the legislation mandates the court to award periodic payment of pecuniary damages arising from a motor-vehicle action when the amount exceeds $100,000, and the best interests of the plaintiff will be served by an award in this form.[17] In Manitoba, periodic payments may be awarded on the application of any party.[18] The court will structure the judgment to include the amount, interval, annual increase, and termination date of the payments.[19] In Ontario, the courts' ability to order periodic payments is triggered when the plaintiff requests that the award be grossed up to take account of taxes and, in medical malpractice cases, where the award for future care costs exceeds a designated amount (currently $250,000).[20]

---

12   *Ibid.* at 51.
13   *Ibid.* at 21.
14   *Courts of Justice Act*, R.S.O. 1990, c. C.43, ss. 116 & 116.1.
15   *Insurance (Vehicle) Act*, R.S.B.C. 1996, c. 231, s. 99 [*IVA*].
16   *Court of Queen's Bench Act*, S.M. 1988–89, c. 4, C.C.S.M. c. C280, amendments ss. 88.1–88.9 (en. S.M. 1993, c. 19, s. 6) [*CQBA*].
17   *IVA*, above note 15, s. 99.
18   *CQBA*, above note 16, s. 88.2.
19   *Ibid.*, s. 88.3.
20   Ontario *Rules of Civil Procedure*, R.R.O. 1990, Reg. 194, r. 53.09. See text below at notes 60 to 64. Similar legislation has been adopted in the United Kingdom—

The approach of the courts to periodic payments has been set out in *Lusignan (Litigation guardian of) v. Concordia Hospital.*[21] The defendant requested a periodic payment of damages award to a child who was mentally and physically disabled at birth owing to medical negligence. Jewers J. ruled that an award of periodic payments involved a two-stage analysis: first, verifying the desirability and feasibility of periodic payments in the particular circumstances; and second, developing a specific plan. The advantages for the plaintiff were receiving payments for life, receiving payments that were tax-free, and incurring less expense for investment needs. The advantages for the defendant were saving the cost of an award of income tax gross-up (in this case $170,000), saving a portion of an award for the expense of investment counselling, and the possibility that the premium for the annuity would be less than the lump sum assessed by the court. A periodic payment order must be in the plaintiff's best interest.[22]

3) Interest and Inflation

Because it is often many months or years from the time of an injury until the time the plaintiff receives final compensation, the subject of interest on damage awards is of considerable importance. Despite the earlier reluctance of courts to award interest, every province now provides by statute for pre-judgment interest.[23] This is interest on awards from the time of the loss until the time of trial. Additionally, where there is a delay in paying the judgment after trial, the plaintiff is entitled to judgment interest.

The precise scheme of interest varies from province to province and is beyond the scope of this book.[24] However, to summarize briefly, where the plaintiff suffers a loss at the time of the wrong (e.g., damage to the plaintiff's property), and the damage award is assessed as of that date, the plaintiff is entitled to pre-judgment interest from the date that

---

Courts Act 2003 (U.K.), 2003, c. 39, s. 100 — courts are mandated to consider making a periodic payment order in all cases involving future pecuniary losses.

21   *Lusignan (Litigation guardian of) v. Concordia Hospital,* [1997] 6 W.W.R. 185 (Man. Q.B.).

22   See *Chesher v. Monaghan* (2000), 48 O.R. (3d) 451 (C.A.), leave to appeal to S.C.C. refused, [2000] S.C.C.A. No. 399; *Lee v. Dawson* (2006), 51 B.C.L.R. (4th) 221 (C.A.), leave to appeal to S.C.C. refused, [2006] S.C.C.A. No. 192 [*Lee*]; *Yeung (Guardian ad litem of) v. Au,* 2007 BCSC 175.

23   See, for example, *Court Order Interest Act,* R.S.B.C. 1996, c. 79; *Courts of Justice Act,* above note 14.

24   See M.A. Waldron, *The Law of Interest in Canada* (Scarborough, ON: Carswell, 1992).

the cause of action arose until the date of judgment. This is fair since the plaintiff has been kept out of money properly due to her at that time. Awarding interest protects the award against the impact of inflation, and compensates the plaintiff for any need to use her own money (and thus incur interest charges or a loss of investment income) and also for the opportunity costs due to the loss of use of the money.

In many cases the loss suffered by the plaintiff is not incurred at the time of the wrong but arises at some later time. The most obvious examples are future income losses and future medical expenses. Because these are not losses incurred until after the trial, there is no need for pre-judgment interest. In fact, the converse is true. Because these expenditures will not be incurred until some time in the future, the plaintiff's award for future losses is discounted to a present value (this is discussed in more detail in a later section).

Other losses or expenses are incurred after the date of the wrong but before the date of trial. An example would be special damages for lost income or medical expenses accruing between the date of the wrong and trial. In these cases, pre-judgment interest is available but does not necessarily start running from the time of the wrong. Instead, the provincial statutes provide formulae for the treatment of such losses. Generally, pre-trial losses are grouped into categories according to three- or six-month periods during which the losses or expenses were incurred, and interest runs from the end of those periods. The precise manner of categorizing losses, and the rates of interest, vary from province to province.

Interest on damages for non-pecuniary losses are problematic because these are not losses that are easily divisible into pre- and post-judgment categories. Moreover, non-pecuniary losses are assessed in trial-date dollars (i.e., the effects of inflation are taken into account). Thus, to award the full rate of pre-judgment interest on these damages would overcompensate the plaintiff. Again, the various provinces deal with this problem in different ways, generally by permitting courts to award a lower rate of interest.

D. SPECIAL DAMAGES

The first head of damages is "specials," which are the losses and costs incurred by the plaintiff until the time of trial. Special damages are divided into pre-trial loss of working capacity and pre-trial cost of care. Pre-trial loss of working capacity includes lost earnings, lost profits, and lost homemaking capacity until the trial. Pre-trial cost of care includes expenses and services that provide medical, rehabilitation, and attendant care. Expenses incurred prior to trial must be caused by the tort, and the decision to incur them must be reasonable. Special damages are rarely controversial since they can be calculated with greater accuracy, supported by direct evidence, and require no speculation about the future.

However, claims for pre-trial economic loss can be controversial when the plaintiff's cost of care, or lost ability to engage in housework, has been ameliorated with family assistance. This raises the problem of collateral benefits, which is discussed fully in Chapter 13. Where a family member has left her employment for a period to care for the plaintiff, an award may be made for her lost wages, so long as the loss is not in excess of the cost of reasonable nursing services.[25] However, where there is no obvious "loss" either to the family member or to the plaintiff, the defendant will argue that there are no damages. Nevertheless, courts will often make an "in-trust" award for a family member who has been caring for the plaintiff prior to the time of trial. For example, in both *Thornton* and *Teno*, the plaintiffs' mothers were awarded $7,500 in trust for their caregiving, and this practice continues in many cases,[26] including situations where children care for their parents,[27] where siblings provide care for one another,[28] and where one cares for an injured partner or other extended family members.[29] The historical test is that the services must be "extraordinary" in the sense that they are beyond the ordinary work that parents, children, and spouses perform for one another and would likely be purchased by the plain-

---

25 See *Fullerton (Guardian ad litem of) v. Delair*, 2005 BCSC 204, var'd on other grounds (2006), 55 B.C.L.R. (4th) 252 (C.A.) [*Fullerton*]: income that mother gave up to care for plaintiff was less than the cost of purchasing those services. Her forgone income formed the basis of the in-trust award.

26 For examples see *Brito (Guardian ad litem of) v. Woolley*, 2001 BCSC 1178, aff'd (2003), 16 B.C.L.R. (4th) 220 (C.A.), leave to appeal to S.C.C. refused, [2003] S.C.C.A. No. 418 [*Brito*]: an in-trust award of $191,565.00 to plaintiff's parents; *Guerineau (Guardian ad litem of) v. Seger*, 2001 BCSC 291: $50,000.00 to each parent [*Guerineau*].

27 *McCloskey v. Lymn* (1996), 26 B.C.L.R. (3d) 118 (S.C.); *Suveges v. Martens*, 2000 BCSC 810 [*Suveges*]; *Miller v. Budzinski*, 2004 BCSC 1730; *Mitchell v. We Care Health Services Inc.*, 2004 BCSC 902.

28 *Jacobsen v. Nike Canada Ltd.* (1996), 19 B.C.L.R. (3d) 63 (S.C.); *Spehar (Guardian ad litem of) v. Beazley*, [2002] B.C.J. No. 1718 (S.C.), aff'd (2004), 31 B.C.L.R. (4th) 223 (C.A.), appeal to S.C.C. discontinued, [2004] S.C.C.A. No. 366 [*Spehar*].

29 *Brennan v. Singh*, [1999] B.C.J. No. 520 (S.C.) [*Brennan*]; *Grewal v. Brar*, 2004 BCSC 1157; *Wilson Estate v. Byrne*, [2004] O.J. No. 2360 (S.C.J.).

tiff if the family member had not taken them over.[30] However, some courts have taken the view that any services provided to the plaintiff by a family member, necessitated by the plaintiff's injuries, should be compensable, regardless of whether those services would ordinarily be expected of a family member.[31] In *Bystedt*, Smith J. summarized the law on "in-trust" claims as follows:

(a) the services provided must replace services necessary for the care of the plaintiff as a result of a plaintiff's injuries;

(b) if the services are rendered by a family member, they must be over and above what would be expected from the family relationship (here, the normal care of an uninjured child);

(c) the maximum value of such services is the cost of obtaining the services outside the family;

(d) where the opportunity cost to the care-giving family member is lower than the cost of obtaining the services independently, the court will award the lower amount;

(e) quantification should reflect the true and reasonable value of the services performed taking into account the time, quality and nature of those services. In this regard, the damages should reflect the wage of a substitute caregiver. There should not be a discounting or undervaluation of such services because of the nature of the relationship; and

(f) the family members providing the services need not forego other income and there need not be payment for the services rendered.[32]

In Ontario, defined family members have a direct action for any pecuniary losses resulting from injury to a family member. Under the *Fam-*

---

30 Brennan, *ibid.*; *Brito*, above note 26; *Bystedt (Guardian ad litem of) v. Hay*, [2001] B.C.J. No. 2769 (S.C.), aff'd (2004), 24 B.C.L.R. (4th) 205 (C.A.) [*Bystedt*]; *Roussin v. Bouzenad*, [2005] B.C.J. No. 2682 (S.C.) [*Roussin*]; *Dufault v. Kathed Holdings Ltd.*, [2007] B.C.J. No 252 (S.C.). *O'Ruairc (Guardian ad litem of) v. Pelletier*, 2004 BCSC 1633: no evidence that family members did anything for plaintiff to warrant in-trust award; *Madge v. Meyer* (1999), 76 Alta. L.R. (3d) 274 (Q.B.), aff'd (2001), 92 Alta. L.R. (3d) 221 (C.A.) [*Madge*]: wife awarded $75,000 for sacrificing her employment opportunities for extraordinary caregiving and companionship of husband during pre-trial period but she was not entitled to compensation for caregiving services that she performed prior to and continues to do after his injuries. *Bartosek (Litigation guardian of) v. Turret Realities Inc.*, [2001] O.J. No. 4735 (S.C.J.), aff'd (2004), 23 C.C.L.T. (3d) 161 (C.A.), leave to appeal to S.C.C. refused, [2004] S.C.C.A. No. 202 [*Bartosek*]: mother, brother, and sister compensated for making heroic efforts to care for plaintiff after accident.

31 *Bain v. Calgary Board of Education* (1993), 146 A.R. 321 (Q.B.).

32 *Bystedt*, above note 30 at para. 180 (S.C.).

ily Law Act,[33] they may claim any actual expenses incurred, and, where they provide nursing or housekeeping services, they may also claim a reasonable allowance for lost income or the value of those services. Substantial amounts have been awarded under this statute to parents, children and siblings for pre-trial care given to injured children, parents, and siblings,[34] and to spouses for care provided to their partners.[35]

E. COST OF FUTURE CARE

Personal injury victims will frequently have future care costs that will not be covered by their province's health insurance program. In serious cases the plaintiff may be placed in an institution or may require an attendant. She will have special transportation needs, drug costs, uninsured health-care services (physiotherapy, acupuncture, massage, chiropractic treatment), and rehabilitation expenses. Plaintiffs may incur substantial costs to make modifications to their living arrangements so they can remain in their homes, and they may also require ongoing homemaker and home-maintenance services. The award for cost of care is intended to provide for the plaintiff's annual needs resulting from the accident, and may also include a capital component for one-time expenses such as home renovations and vehicle modifications.

---

33   R.S.O. 1990, c. F.3, ss. 61–63.

34   *Dube (Litigation guardian of) v. Penlon Ltd.* (1994), 21 C.C.L.T. (2d) 268 (Ont. Ct. Gen. Div.): $25,000 to the plaintiff's father and $35,000 to the plaintiff's mother for four and a half years following an anaesthesia overdose rendering their three-year-old son a quadriplegic. See also *Granger (Litigation guardian of) v. Ottawa General Hospital* (1996), 7 O.T.C. 81 (Gen. Div.): $125,000 to the plaintiff's parents (claim for future damages dismissed); *Crawford (Litigation guardian of) v. Penney*, [2003] O.T.C. 16 (S.C.J.), aff'd on other grounds (2004), 26 C.C.L.T. (3d) 246 (Ont. C.A.), leave to appeal to S.C.C. refused (2005), 204 O.A.C. 398 [*Crawford*]: $375,000 to plaintiff's parents; *Carere v. Cressman* (2002), 12 C.C.L.T. (3d) 217 (Ont. S.C.J.): baby born with injuries due to negligence of midwife, mother awarded $160,000 for services and $35,000 to three sisters under the Act; *Bartosek*, above note 30: mother awarded $214,000 and two sisters awarded a total of $238,000. See also *George v. Covent Garden Market Corp.*, [2007] O.J. No. 2903 (S.C.J.); *Gordon v. Greig* (2007), 46 C.C.L.T. (3d) 212 (Ont. S.C.J.) [*Gordon*].

35   *Desbiens v. Mordini*, [2004] O.J. No. 4735 (S.C.J.); *Peddle (Litigation guardian of) v. Ontario (Minister of Transportation)*, [1997] O.J. No. 1874 (Gen. Div.), aff'd [1998] O.J. No. 5265 (C.A.) [*Peddle*].

1) The Level of Care

The primary issue regarding the costs of care is the level or standard of care to which the plaintiff is entitled. In both *Andrews*[36] *and Thornton*[37] for example, the defendant argued that the plaintiff's claim to care in his own home (following an accident that rendered him paraplegic) was too extravagant when compared to the much more moderate cost of institutional care. In both cases the Supreme Court rejected this argument. The controlling principle in assessing damages for the cost of care is that the plaintiff is entitled to compensation for all of these costs (past and future) so long as they are reasonable. What is reasonable will depend upon medical and other expert evidence (which in these cases indicated that the available institutional care would likely shorten the plaintiffs' lifespans and diminish the quality of their lives). For example, in *Dennis v. Gairdner,*[38] the plaintiff was severely injured and rendered a quadriplegic. He required a catheter to drain his bladder but his mental functions remained unaffected. Although the court found the group home where the plaintiff had been staying to be satisfactory, his desire for independent living was nevertheless held to be reasonable, among other things, because it would facilitate his physical needs and mental welfare. As well, home care was appropriate in this case because it would provide the plaintiff with a high standard of care that would ultimately give him optimum life expectancy—thirty-eight years from time of trial. The appropriate level of care should also reflect anticipated changes in the plaintiff's situation and needs, which might point to a different living arrangement in the future. Thus, in *Krangle (Guardian ad litem of) v. Brisco,*[39] although home care was appropriate for the plaintiff while he was a child, it was generally agreed that it would be in his best interest to move to a state-funded group home when he became an adult. As well, the reasonableness requirement demands that the claim must not be extravagant, in the sense that a reasonable person would consider the particular expenditure to be exorbitant.[40] The test has been stated as being expenses that a reasonably-minded person with sufficient means would be willing to incur to meet the plaintiff's needs.[41]

---

36   Above note 2.
37   *Ibid.*
38   (2002), 5 B.C.L.R. (4th) 275 (S.C.). See also *Suveges*, above note 27.
39   [2002] 1 S.C.R. 205.
40   *Ibid.* at 280.
41   *Brennan,* above note 29; *Bystedt,* above note 30 at paras. 161–63 (S.C.).

While the claim must be "reasonable" and not "extravagant," the plaintiff has no duty to "mitigate" damages in the sense of accepting less than full compensation. For example, in *Olafson*[42] the Supreme Court again overruled a lower court decision to award only the cost of institutional care to a severely injured plaintiff on the basis that, while the amount was very large from the defendant's point of view, it was not undue considering the plaintiff's legitimate needs. Similarly, while the award must be "fair to both parties," the means of the defendant are irrelevant and the plaintiff is entitled to all expenses that can be justified and supported as expenditures that would be incurred by a reasonable person in the plaintiff's circumstances. Fairness has nothing to do with the defendant's ability to pay. It is achieved by ensuring that the plaintiff's claim is reasonable and justifiable.[43]

Nor is the "social burden" of large damage awards relevant. In *Andrews* the Supreme Court rejected the argument that damages for the cost of care should be moderated in order to contain "social costs" or to reduce the social burden of accidents. In an era when such costs are widely borne through insurance, it would be unfair to an injured person to award less than full compensation simply in order to contain the cost of insurance premiums. In applying these principles in *Williams (Guardian ad litem of) v. Low*,[44] the court concluded that, given the plaintiff's age, condition, and the quality of care that she required, home care was preferable to institutional care. Interestingly, however, in *Andrews*, Dickson J. did allow that social costs might be taken into account in selecting between acceptable alternatives for care and also in assessing the amount of non-pecuniary damages (see below).

None of this is to suggest that a court will always defer to the plaintiff's plan of care. For example, where the plaintiff is severely brain damaged or totally immobile, home care may not be feasible.[45] Other evidence regarding the quality of available care, the self-reliance of the plaintiff, or the need for special facilities may also indicate institutional care as the best alternative.[46] Similarly, when presented with two acceptable alternative modes of care, the court may lean towards the less expensive.

---

42   Above note 7.
43   *Thornton*, above note 2 at 278.
44   2000 BCSC 345.
45   See, for example, *Wipfli v. Britten*, [1984] 5 W.W.R. 385 (B.C.C.A.) [*Wipfli*].
46   For example, in *Arce (Guardian ad litem of) v. Simon Fraser Health Region* (2003), 17 C.C.L.T. (3d) 97 (B.C.S.C.) [*Arce*]: home care not medically justified or reasonable for a ventilator-dependent quadriplegic. Transfer to home setting would also be risky for his health and well-being. See also *C.(H.) v. Loo* (2003), 12 Alta. L.R. (4th) 287 (Q.B.), rev'd on other grounds (2006), 384 A.R. 200 (C.A.).

2) Duration of Award: Life Expectancy

In the case of severe and permanent injuries, the costs of care must be assessed for as long as they will be required by the plaintiff. In contrast to the method adopted in regard to lost income, the figure used is the actual post-accident life expectancy. Experts utilize statistical, actuarial, and medical models to predict the plaintiff's remaining lifespan after the accident. Generally, an annual figure is settled upon and awarded for the remaining life expectancy of the plaintiff.

3) Contingencies

In settling on a final figure for the cost of care, courts will take into account the "contingencies and hazards of life" and will often make a deduction (usually in the range of 10 to 20 percent). This deduction is based on the idea that the plaintiff's circumstances may change so that the full amount of the cost of care may not be necessary. For example, the plaintiff may spend long periods in the hospital and not incur expenses during that time. Alternatively, the plaintiff may have a chance of recovery and thus face diminished expenses over time.[47] These chances are factored into the damage assessment as contingencies and valued (roughly) according to the probabilities that they will occur. In *Andrews* and *Thornton* the Court permitted a 20 percent deduction, and a figure in this range is not unusual.

As the Supreme Court said, the subject of contingencies is "fraught with difficulty."[48] To make such a large deduction is to assume that the plaintiff will not incur the full amount of the expenses assessed by the court because of a chance, for example, of early recovery. However, not all contingencies serve to reduce expenditures. There is also a chance that the plaintiff's condition will deteriorate or that new expenses will be encountered. To make a deduction of 20 percent in the case of *Andrews* was to assume that over the plaintiff's expected remaining lifespan of forty-five years, he would not face any expenses for nine of those years. There is no good reason to assume, in the absence of evidence, that the plaintiff will experience such "good luck." Some courts have recognized that contingencies may be negative as well as positive and have refused, in the absence of evidence, to make any deduction.[49] It is

---

47   *Graham v. Rourke* (1990), 75 O.R. (2d) 622 (C.A.) [*Rourke*].
48   *Andrews*, above note 2 at 249.
49   *Fenn v. Peterborough (City)* (1979), 25 O.R. (2d) 399 (C.A.), aff'd (*sub nom. Consumers' Gas Co. v. Peterborough (City)*) [1981] 2 S.C.R. 613 [*Fenn*]. See also *Bystedt*, above note 30 at para. 159 (S.C.); *Peddle*, above note 35.

strongly suggested here that no deduction should be made unless supported by the evidence. Indeed, it is increasingly the case that courts do not simply make a standard and arbitrary deduction, but rather, carefully consider the evidence about future probabilities before making any contingency adjustment.

An additional reason for moderation in contingency deductions is that they are often already embedded in the evidence. When courts accept statistical and actuarial data regarding average lifespans, average wages, and average needs of persons, many contingencies (both positive and negative) are already included in the data (since the sample cohorts are made up of persons who have experienced both bad luck and good). Thus, care must be taken not to double-count contingencies in these circumstances. For example, where the duration of the award for the cost of care is set by reference to average life expectancy tables, it would be wrong, in the absence of evidence, to reduce the award for the contingency of "early death" since that contingency is already factored into the average. Where average data are used to estimate costs, additional deductions should be made from the plaintiff's award only when there is specific evidence that the plaintiff is likely to differ from the average.[50]

4) Avoiding Overlap with the Award for Lost Income

The award for the cost of care will frequently include expenses that the plaintiff would have incurred even had he not been injured. For example, the cost of care may include transportation, food, clothing, and occasionally housing. To receive an award for such "necessaries" as part of the cost of care, and also to receive a complete indemnity for lost earnings would overcompensate the plaintiff since these are amounts that the plaintiff would have had to pay for out of income had he not been injured.

Where the court has awarded the costs of necessaries as part of the cost of care (which is the preferred approach in serious injury cases), it will generally make a corresponding deduction from the award for lost income in order to avoid overcompensation. In other words, the award for lost earnings will be made on a "net income" basis (what the plaintiff would have earned after expenses for personal necessaries). The amount of the deduction will depend upon the level of earnings that the plaintiff would have achieved, and the extent to which ordinary living expenses are covered by the award for cost of care. In serious injury cases such as the trilogy, it can be in the range of 40 to 50 percent.

---

50   *Lewis v. Todd*, [1980] 2 S.C.R. 694 [*Lewis*].

5) Collateral Benefits

One issue that commonly arises in relation to the cost of care is the extent to which family caregivers, charitable organizations, and state-funded services can be expected to provide free services to the plaintiff and thus reduce the cost of care. There are no easy rules here. On the one hand, where a person is severely injured, family members may not be "conscripted" to care for them in order to relieve the defendant of the burden of this expense. On the other hand, where an item of care will clearly be provided to the plaintiff free of charge (e.g., hospital services), there is no expense that will be incurred. To include the notional expense in the damage award is arguably a windfall to the plaintiff and unfair to the defendant.

The subject of collateral benefits is covered in depth in Chapter 13. However, the following is a brief summary. Benefits provided to the plaintiff by way of private insurance are not deducted from the claim. This does not usually result in overcompensation of the plaintiff since the insurance company will ordinarily have a right of subrogation whereby any recovery by the plaintiff will be paid over to the insurer. Similarly, where there is a right of subrogation in respect of public benefits (e.g., hospital and health care), the plaintiff may also include these amounts in the claim.[51] But, where there is no right of subrogation, and the expenses will *clearly* and *certainly* be covered by a government agency, the plaintiff may not include those items in the claim. So, for instance, future medical expenses that will be covered by a provincial health insurance plan may not be included in the plaintiff's claim since this would result in overcompensation of the plaintiff.[52]

Care provided to the plaintiff by a family member has also been problematic. The issue here is whether a deduction should be made from an award for the cost of care in situations where a spouse (or other family member) is providing "voluntary" support and care to the victim. It has long been established that care (in the form of nursing services) provided before trial may be compensated by an "in-trust" award for the caregiver (where the award is made to the plaintiff, but to be paid to the care-provider).[53] But future care is more difficult, as are

---

51 For example, *Health Services Act*, R.S.N.B. 1973, c. H-3; see also Part V of the *Hospitals Act*, R.S.A. 2000, c. H-12, Part 5.

52 *Wipfli*, above note 45; *Semenoff v. Kokan* (1990), 42 B.C.L.R. (2d) 6 (S.C.), var'd (1990), 45 B.C.L.R. (2d) 294 (S.C.), var'd (1991), 84 D.L.R. (4th) 76 (B.C.C.A.) [*Semenoff*].

53 For example, *Teno*, above note 2.

situations where the care is not specialized but rather simply day-to-day maintenance and housekeeping.

On one view, a person is entitled to claim for the cost of housekeeping only if an actual expense is likely to be incurred. If a family member will be providing those services, there is no loss. This view, which may also rest on certain assumptions about the roles of men and women in relationships, is expressed, for example, in *De Sousa v. Kuntz*.[54] In this case the B.C. Court of Appeal held that caregiving services by a spouse were part and parcel of the duties normally expected of spouses in the marital relationship and were not recoverable as a head of damages in tort. Only where "a spouse has to take on a complete function like full-time nursing, a function that is outside the usual concept of what people undertake when they take on their marriage vows, and outside the 'worse' end of the 'for better or worse' marriage scale"[55] can compensation be granted.

However, more recently the same court in *Kroeker v. Jansen*[56] recognized that "housekeeping and other spousal services have economic value for which a claim by an injured party will lie even where those services are replaced gratuitously from within the family."[57] Gibbs J.A. stated that *De Sousa* and similar cases "have been taken over by an evolution in judicial thinking."[58] While some courts continue to insist on proof of actual increased care costs,[59] the better view now is that lost housekeeping capacity is compensable even when it has been taken over by a spouse.

This issue is more fully discussed in Chapter 13.

6) Taxation

The total amount for the cost of care is awarded as a capital sum. In theory, when properly invested (on an extinguishing basis), this capital sum will provide a stream of income to cover expenses for the remainder of the plaintiff's life. However, taxation poses a problem. The capital sum itself (as a court award) is not subject to taxation, but in

---

54   (1989), 42 B.C.L.R. (2d) 186 (C.A.).
55   *Ibid.* at 196–97.
56   (1995), 4 B.C.L.R. (3d) 178 (C.A.) [*Kroeker*].
57   *Ibid.* at 183.
58   *Ibid.* at 182. See also *DiGiacomo v. Murphy*, [1995] B.C.J. No. 1886 (S.C.); *West v. Cotton* (1995), 10 B.C.L.R. (3d) 73 (C.A.); *McTavish v. MacGillivray* (2000), 74 B.C.L.R. (3d) 281 (C.A.); *Deglow v. Uffelman* (2001), 96 B.C.L.R. (3d) 130 (C.A.) [*Deglow*].
59   For example, see *Wiebe v. Neal*, 2004 BCSC 984.

the ensuing years the investment income from the capital sum will be taxable as income. While many of the expenses incurred by the plaintiff may be tax deductible as medical expenses, there will often still be serious tax consequences that may undermine the adequacy of the income from the award, ultimately depleting it too early.

Until 1989, the impact of tax was not taken into account. Courts reasoned that the adjustment would be too speculative and too difficult to calculate, and that the impact of tax was unlikely to be great because of the available deductions for medical expenses. However, in 1989, in *Olafson*,[60] the Supreme Court held that the award for the cost of care should be "grossed up" to take taxation into account. McLachlin J. stated that

> the impact of taxation on a lump sum award for cost of future care is highly significant. The sum is predicated on the assumption that the currently unused portion of the fund will be invested and earn income, for which a discount is made. That income will attract tax.... If no allowance is made for this tax, the judgement will prove insufficient to provide the care required for the predicted lifespan of the plaintiff.[61]

In this case, the Court awarded an additional $230,000 to take into account the impact of taxation.

The award to accommodate the impact of taxation, referred to as a tax gross-up, is complex. It is based on expert evidence (often conflicting), which must take into account variables such as the size of the award, the manner in which it will be invested, the rate at which it will be withdrawn, the amount of the plaintiff's income from other sources (and hence the plaintiff's marginal rate of taxation), the manner in which the income will be spent, the available deductions, and possible future changes in tax policy.[62] The unintended effect of this process can be prolonged litigation resulting in a broad range of tax gross-up awards. The Law Reform Commission of British Columbia has recommended that standardized assumptions, facilitated by legislation,[63] could reduce the time and expense of the process. Ontario has adopted such standardized assumptions regarding investments and the rate of inflation.[64]

---

60   Above note 7.

61   *Ibid.* at 764.

62   See K.D. Cooper-Stephenson, *Personal Injury Damages in Canada*, 2d ed. (Scarborough: Carswell, 1996) at 464–65.

63   Law Reform Commission of British Columbia, *Report on Standardized Assumptions for Calculating Income Tax Gross-up and Management Fees in Assessing Damages* (Vancouver: The Commission, 1994).

64   *Courts of Justice Act*, R.S.O. 1990, c. C.43; *Rules of Civil Procedure*, R.R.O. 1990, Reg. 194, r. 53.09.

F. LOST EARNING CAPACITY

The other important component of economic or pecuniary loss to the plaintiff is prospective loss of earnings or lost earning capacity. The court must assess the accident victim's earning capacity prior to the accident, measure the severity of the disability caused by the accident, estimate the extent to which the disability has impaired the victim's future income prospects, and award a capital sum representing the loss. The purpose is to put the plaintiff in the same position that he would have been in had the injury not occurred.

1) The Conceptual Basis: Earning Capacity as a Capital Asset

In the determination of what has been lost, the focus is not simply upon the plaintiff's lost future earnings. Instead, accident victims are compensated for their diminished ability or power to work productively—a capacity viewed as a capital asset. As Dickson J. stated in *Andrews*, "[i]t is not loss of earnings but, rather, loss of earning capacity for which compensation must be made.… A capital asset has been lost: what was its value?"[65]

The distinction between *lost probable earnings* and *lost earning capacity* is an important one. If compensation were for lost probable earnings only, it would be based on what the person *would have earned* had she not been injured. So, for example, a person trained as a high school teacher but working instead as a full-time (unwaged) parent of three, would have no lost earnings. If compensation is based on a person's lost earning capacity, it would be calculated on the basis of what she *could have earned* had she not been injured, regardless of whether she would in fact have made those earnings. So, for instance, a person who is trained and employable as a teacher has a certain earning capacity (say $45,000 per year), regardless of whether, at the time of the accident she is in fact working as a teacher or, indeed, whether she ever intends to work. Although the plaintiff might never have worked as a teacher, if the accident has eliminated her ability to do so, she has lost a valuable asset.

The courts are not consistent on the issue of whether they are replacing actual lost earnings, or lost earning capacity, though the choice can make an enormous difference to many plaintiffs, as illustrated in the example above. On occasion courts make awards for pure lost earn-

---

65   Above note 2 at 251.

ing capacity (even when there is no evidence that the plaintiff would in fact have earned income), but more often than not (especially where the plaintiff has a reliable work history), the award is based on a projection of the plaintiff's actual future income prospects at the time of the accident. In fact, the approach of the courts to the issue is a somewhat pragmatic compromise between these two positions.

Cooper-Stephenson suggests that, in reality, the courts have adopted a third method, which he terms "lost working capacity."[66] Courts do not confine their awards to lost probable earnings. Nor, however, do they award damages for lost earning capacity in the abstract, irrespective of how that capacity would have been exercised. The goal, he suggests, is to compensate plaintiffs for their lost capacity to *work* (whether paid or unpaid). Thus, as Smith J.A. stated in *Rowe v. Bobbell Express*, "a claim for loss of earning capacity ... is ... a claim for the loss of the value of the work that the injured plaintiff would have performed but was unable to perform because of the injury."[67] To determine this value, a court must predict how much work the plaintiff would have performed during her life, and place an economic value on that work—treating it as an economic loss even though it might not have been rewarded monetarily. Ultimately, compensation for impaired working capacity depends on real and substantial possibilities of future lost earnings or, more generally, work of economic value. The court must estimate the chance of the loss occurring. Valuation of the plaintiff's loss is based on what she would, and not could, have earned but for her injury.[68] In *M.B.*, McLachlin C.J.C. stated:

> These damages are not, then, based on a fixed value that has been assigned to an abstract capacity to earn. Rather, the value of a particular plaintiff's capacity to earn is equivalent to the value of the earnings that she or he would have received over time, had the tort not been committed.[69]

---

66 Cooper-Stephenson, above note 62 at 205.
67 (2005), 39 B.C.L.R. (4th) 185 at para. 30 (C.A.) [*Rowe*]. See also *Anderson v. Merritt (City)*, 2006 BCSC 901.
68 *Vincent v. Abu-Bakare* (2003), 259 N.B.R. (2d) 66 (C.A.) [*Vincent*]; *Sinclair v. Dines* (2005), 279 N.B.R. (2d) 227 (C.A.) [*Sinclair*]; *M.B. v. British Columbia*, [2003] 2 S.C.R. 477 at paras. 47–50 [*M.B.*]; *Rosvold v. Dunlop* (2001), 84 B.C.L.R. (3d) 158 (C.A.) [*Rosvold*]; *Reilly v. Lynn* (2003), 10 B.C.L.R. (4th) 16 (C.A.), leave to appeal to S.C.C. refused, [2003] S.C.C.A. No. 221 [*Reilly*]; *Smith v. Knudson* (2004), 33 B.C.L.R. (4th) 76 (C.A.) [*Smith*].
69 *M.B.*, *ibid.* at para. 50.

In *Vincent*, Drapeau C.J.N.B., directed trial judges to adopt a two-stage approach in the assessment of damages for impaired working capacity — courts must estimate the chance that the plaintiff will suffer loss of earnings due to the defendant's tort and, if that loss is real and substantial, then the court must determine an amount that reflects the chances of that loss occuring.[70] Finally, the court must assess the overall fairness and reasonableness of the award, and make allowance for the contingency that the assumptions that underlie the award may not unfold as expected.[71]

2) Assessing Lost Earning Capacity in Practice

It will be readily apparent that determining pre-accident earning capacity requires a large number of assumptions and hypotheses about what the plaintiff's future might have held had the accident not occurred and about what the future still holds. In order to determine a plaintiff's pre-accident capacity, a court must assess the occupation that he would have worked at, the length of time that he would have worked (starting and retiring), the wage rate for that occupation over the course of his career, and the chances that he would have changed careers or left the workforce. The Supreme Court of Canada has acknowledged that the process is akin to "crystal ball gazing." And in making these assumptions and developing these hypotheses there is much room for error.

a) Selecting the Basis for Assessing the Loss
Typically, at least in respect of serious injuries, an economist will be hired to prepare a report on the plaintiff's losses. The plaintiff's economic prospects prior to the accident, and the degree to which those prospects have been impaired as a result of the accident must be determined. The court must therefore select an income figure that the plaintiff was capable of achieving, and then determine the length of the plaintiff's working life before the accident, to arrive at a lifetime earnings figure. As a practical matter, this calculation usually begins with the plaintiff's earnings record, where one is available. The plaintiff's salary at the time of the accident will be taken as (initial) evidence of what the plaintiff's earning capacity would have been, and it is adjusted to take into account both positive and negative contingencies

---

70   *Vincent*, above note 68 at para. 61. See also *O'Donnell v. O'Blenis* (2004), 269 N.B.R. (2d) 273 (C.A.).

71   See *Rosvold*, above note 68; *Reilly*, above note 68.

that might have affected those earnings (raises, promotions, unemployment, disability, and so on). This forecasted stream of earnings is then discounted to a present-day capital sum.

Where there is no earnings record (as, for example, in the case of children and students), statistics are used. So, for instance, in the case of a young child the court may accept that he was capable of achieving the average lifetime earnings of a person of that sex, with a certain amount of education. Alternatively, courts may accept specific evidence regarding the child's family background, education, interests, motivation, and abilities in order to individualize the award. Awards to children are discussed separately below.

b) Residual Earnings

In most cases, except the most severe, the accident will not have completely eliminated the plaintiff's ability to work. Instead, the accident will simply interfere with her ability to work for a period, or may impair her ability to work full-time or to advance in her career. Where there remains a residual ability to work, the actual predicted earnings of the plaintiff are, of course, taken into account in setting the compensation figure.

In some cases, there may in fact be no appreciable diminution in the plaintiff's earnings. The plaintiff may, after the accident, continue working at the same job for the same rate of pay. Nevertheless, the plaintiff may still have a diminution in her earning *capacity* and career *options*. The injury may interfere with her ability to advance in her career, or may reduce the opportunities open to her, and she will receive some compensation for this loss.[72]

c) Accounting for Positive Contingencies and Lost Chances

Given that the court is not simply replacing lost income, the salary of the plaintiff at the time of the accident is not absolutely determinative. It is merely evidence of the value of the plaintiff's earning capacity. In many cases, the evidence will support an upwards adjustment to take into account the possibility that the plaintiff might, during the course of his working life, experience substantial wage increases, promotions, job transfers, or even a career change. For example, in *Andrews*, for the

---

72   *Pallos v. Insurance Corp. of British Columbia* (1995), 100 B.C.L.R. (2d) 260 (C.A.) [*Pallos*]; *Cochrane v. O'Brien* (2002), 225 Nfld & P.E.I.R. 285 (Nfld. C.A.); *Morel v. Bryden* (2006), 246 N.S.R. (2d) 43 (C.A.); *Fiust v. Centis*, 2005 BCSC 1067; *Letourneau v. Min* (2003), 9 B.C.L.R. (4th) 283 (C.A.); *Madge*, above note 30 at para. 12 (C.A.); *Rosvold*, above note 68; *Hamilton v. Vance*, 2007 BCSC 1001; *Sinnott v. Boggs*, 2007 BCCA 267; *Jackson v. Lai*, 2007 BCSC 1023 [*Jackson*].

purpose of estimating lost earning capacity, the figure chosen as a basis for the calculation was between his actual salary and the maximum earnings for that type of work.

In some cases, the evidence will demonstrate an unusual disparity between the plaintiff's actual wage at the time of the accident and her "real" earning capacity. The classic case is that of a young person, employed at a low-wage job at the time of the accident but on the brink of completing her education or commencing a different career. Where the evidence strongly indicates that the plaintiff would have followed a more lucrative career, the court may choose that career as the appropriate standard of measurement.

A leading illustration is the case of *Conklin v. Smith*[73] in which the plaintiff lost a leg in an accident. Prior to the accident he had intended to pursue a career as a commercial pilot and had taken steps towards this goal by leaving school to earn money to take a course. As a result of the accident, he would be able to work only in a career with wages substantially less than those of a commercial pilot. After examining evidence regarding his previous success at school, steps taken towards his goal, and overall fitness to achieve it, the Court held that the plaintiff had demonstrated a "reasonable possibility" that he might have become a pilot and assessed the loss of that chance at $5,000 per year.

An important point here is that, even where the evidence is not particularly strong or where there was only a small (though realistic) chance that the plaintiff would have changed careers, the court may nevertheless award damages for that lost chance. In contrast to proof of past losses and past events, which must be established on the *balance of probabilities*, future losses and future events are proved and valued on the basis of *reasonable possibilities* rather than *probabilities*. Future events and future losses are not treated as all-or-nothing propositions. Instead, they are treated as contingencies and valued according to the degree of probability that they might have occurred.[74] The approach is similar to that employed in contract law to value lost chances, which is discussed in Chapter 10. For the purpose of setting a figure on the value of the lost chance, the court discounts the total value of the chance by reference to the degree of probability that it would in fact have occurred. The greater the degree of probability, the greater the compensation.

---

73   [1978] 2 S.C.R. 1107. See also *Bafaro v. Jiang*, 2007 BCSC 686.

74   *Steenblok v. Funk* (1990), 46 B.C.L.R. (2d) 133 (C.A.); *Reilly*, above note 68; *Haile v. Johns* (2005), 50 B.C.L.R. (4th) 241 (C.A.).

Even small chances are compensable so long as they are reasonable possibilities and not merely speculative. In *Hearndon v. Rondeau*[75] the plaintiff suffered brain damage in an accident but was able to return to his employment as a sawmill worker. Some evidence was introduced to show that he had intended to train to become a helicopter pilot. After noting the obstacles that he would have faced, the trial judge concluded that there was no reasonable probability that he would have succeeded and declined to award damages. This decision was reversed on appeal. While the plaintiff's chance of succeeding in his goal was much smaller than the plaintiff in *Conklin*, the plaintiff had nevertheless lost a chance. Following *Chaplin v. Hicks*,[76] the plaintiff was entitled to a modest sum ($20,000) representing the value of that chance.

d) Voluntary Underemployment

A number of situations bring into focus the difference made by the conceptual basis chosen for assessing earning capacity. If courts are compensating mere lost probable earnings, then persons who do not work for a wage (homemakers and volunteers) are not entitled to compensation for lost earning capacity. However, the jurisprudence shows that the basis of the award is inability to do work of value or use the capital asset, whether paid or unpaid. The problem of homemakers is discussed in greater detail in a later section, but essentially, the value of their unpaid work is now recognized by courts as an element of lost earning capacity. It follows, then, that inability to perform volunteer work might also be compensable as a pecuniary loss rather than simply as a non-pecuniary loss. In *Rowe*,[77] Southin J.A., in her concurring judgment, raised in *obiter* the question of whether it could be said that the loss of services of a volunteer could be considered pecuniary loss for the organizations that benefitted and would likely have continued to benefit from the plaintiff's services.[78]

Another category of persons who are affected are those who are not working at "full capacity," at least when measured by their wage. Many persons choose to work fewer hours or at a lower rate of pay than their full potential. Their motives are varied. They may prefer unpaid work (volunteerism) to paid work, they may prefer leisure to long hours, or

---

75 (1984), 54 B.C.L.R. 145 (C.A.). See also *Adamson v. Charity*, 2007 BCSC 671; *Smith*, above note 68.

76 (1911), 2 K.B. 786 (C.A.).

77 *Rowe*, above note 67.

78 In *Lowe v. Guise*, [2002] 3 All E.R. 454 (C.A.), the court held, on a preliminary motion, that a plaintiff who is no longer able to gratuitously care for a disabled family member suffers a pecuniary loss for which compensation is warranted.

they may enjoy certain non-pecuniary benefits of their current employment, even though they could easily advance to a more high-paying job. In strict theory, a person's true earning capacity in these situations is not reflected in his existing earnings. A person's earning capacity is measured by what he *could* have earned but for the accident, not what he *would* have earned.

To take an oversimplified example, Sam and Janet both graduated from law school ten years ago. For five years, both worked long hours and earned $100,000 per year. However, for lifestyle reasons, Sam then chose to cut back on his working hours in order to travel and spend more time with family. Consequently, Sam's income has been substantially reduced (though he could return to the higher-income practice if he chose). If both Sam and Janet were seriously injured so they could not work, in theory, their lost earning capacity would be roughly the same. However, in practice, courts would likely base the award on their recent work history and Janet's loss would be considered greater. One example of this is *Blackstock v. Patterson*.[79] At the time she was injured, the plaintiff was a teacher who also loved to travel. The court made a substantial deduction from her claim for lost earning capacity on the basis that she would likely have taken time off work in order to travel and it would be "illogical to treat earning capacity in the abstract without giving consideration to the projected work habits of the plaintiff."[80]

There are a number of reasons for this approach. The first is pragmatic. Ordinarily, the best evidence of earning capacity is the existing earnings of the plaintiff. If it were open to plaintiffs to increase their award by arguing that at the time of the accident they were voluntarily underemployed, plaintiffs would always make this argument. Moreover, valuing earning capacity in the abstract would be a hypothetical and extremely vague exercise. Finally, some would argue that, where the plaintiff is working at less than full capacity for lifestyle reasons, then the loss suffered is not a pecuniary or economic loss but rather a non-pecuniary loss.

There is no hard and fast rule in this area. On occasion the courts will follow other courses. For example, in some cases, where the plaintiff is working under capacity because of a lifestyle preference, the court may confine the plaintiff to his actual wage loss but award an increased amount for non-economic loss. Thus, in *Varkonyi v. Canadian Pacific Railway*,[81] Kerans J. reduced the plaintiff's award on the basis that

---

79   (1982), 35 B.C.L.R. 231 (C.A.).
80   *Ibid.* at 247.
81   (1980), 26 A.R. 422 (Q.B.).

[t]his plaintiff has recently indicated willingness not to work while he pursued the more pleasurable aspects of life.... I should add that the corollary should be higher general damages. If a person chooses to enjoy life more (by not working) and then loses the ability to enjoy life, presumably the loss is greater than if he were zealously to pursue the drudgery of work.[82]

The problem with this approach is that, compared with income losses, general damages for lost enjoyment of life may offer only modest additional compensation. In addition, in the case of a catastrophically injured person, the full amount of non-pecuniary damages (which is subject to a common law upper limit) is likely to be awarded almost automatically, leaving no room for an additional amount of compensation along the lines suggested.

Some commentators have argued that the problem of compensating homemakers and other unpaid workers should be addressed by an alternative approach that takes seriously the concept of earning capacity as a capital asset and values that asset by an opportunity cost measure, based on forgone income.[83] The value of a capital asset has nothing to do with the way in which it is currently being employed. It is valued by the amount that it could command if put to its highest use in the market. In the case of people who are not in the workforce at the time of the accident, the question is not what they would have earned had they not been injured, but what they *could* have earned in the workforce, regardless of whether they would in fact have chosen to enter the workforce or to work in the home. One case describes clearly the logic of the opportunity-cost approach:

> For example, a housewife qualified as a teacher may plan a career as a home engineer, with only a reluctant notion of abandoning that position for a career in teaching. At the same time, if unfortunate circumstances demand it, or if through a change of life expectation or inclination she was compelled to do so, she might be obliged to return to the work force, and her earning capacity as a teacher represents a continuing form of insurance. Where a wrongdoer eliminates that capacity to earn a living, she is entitled to be compensated for the loss.[84]

---

82   *Ibid.* at 441. See also *Rowe*, above note 67.
83   See N. Komesar, "Towards a General Theory of Personal Injury Loss" (1974) 3:2 J. Legal Stud. 457; R.A. Posner, *Economic Analysis of Law*, 6th ed. (New York: Aspen, 2003). S.M. Waddams also endorses this approach in *The Law of Damages*, 2d ed., looseleaf (Aurora, ON: Canada Law Book, 1991–) at para. 3.800; C.J Bruce, *Assessment of Personal Injury Damages*, 2d ed. (Toronto: Butterworths, 1992) at 202–9.
84   *Benko v. Eliuk* (1991), 95 Sask. R. 161 at 165 (Q.B.) [*Benko*].

While most courts pay only lip service to the opportunity-cost approach, there are several cases in which it seems to have been applied. In the case of *Turenne v. Chung*,[85] the plaintiff had been working as a teacher in a religious order, returning her entire salary to the order each year. Because of this arrangement, the defendant argued that as a result of the accident the plaintiff had suffered no real loss. The court rejected this argument on the basis that it was irrelevant how a person chooses to spend her money. As Waddams argues, the result in such a case should not turn on whether the plaintiff returns her salary to her employer or waives it altogether.[86] The logical outcome of this approach is that a person working for a nominal wage, or no salary at all, should be compensated for her lost capacity so long as she can prove what she might have earned on the market.[87] It should be noted that the application of the opportunity-cost approach in *Turenne* was justified on the basis that the plaintiff was working, though forgoing a wage. The approach has never been used in a case where the plaintiff is simply not working.

The opportunity-cost approach is applied in several other situations. In some cases the plaintiff has been seriously injured, so that his career *options* become limited, but because he retains the same or similar job as he had prior to the accident, there is no evidence that he would suffer an actual loss of earnings. Nevertheless, in these circumstances, courts often do award damages for the loss of capacity. In *Pallos*[88] the B.C. Court of Appeal held that, even where there is no real

---

85   (1962), 40 W.W.R. 508 (Man. C.A.).

86   Waddams, above note 83 at para. 3.800.

87   The opportunity-cost approach has, on occasion, been utilized in the United States. In *Morrison v. State (of Alaska)*, 516 P.2d 402 (Alaska Sup. Ct. 1973), the Court of Appeal upheld this approach in principle. There, the trial court had based its award to a thirteen-year-old female plaintiff on the assumption that she would have worked for only five years before marrying and leaving the workforce. The Court of Appeal sent the matter back for a new trial, stating that "impairment of earning capacity is the permanent diminution of the *ability* to earn money. Appellant is correct in her contention that the trial judge should have made his award for appellant's lost earning *capacity* rather than lost earnings. It may not be assumed that because some women become housekeepers that they thereby lose their earning capacity." (at 404–5). In Australia, the courts have also considered the conceptual approach. In *Forsberg v. Maslin*, [1968] S.A.S.R. 432 (S.A.S.C.), the plaintiff had forsaken better (or more intensive) employment to race motorcycles (which was not remunerative). The court refused to limit his award for lost earning capacity to probable earnings, emphasizing the theoretical approach. This case was, however, overruled by *Mann v. Ellbourn* (1974), 8 S.A.S.R. 298 (S.A.S.C.): the plaintiff in this case was a single mother.

88   Above note 72.

possibility of diminished income, if the injury has limited the plaintiff's career options and "marketability," some compensation for the lost "capital asset" may be made (in this case $40,000).

The "capital-asset" approach was followed and elaborated upon in *Tabrizi v. Whallon Machine Inc.*[89] The plaintiff was seriously injured but following the accident had retrained and in fact improved her career prospects and income. Nevertheless, the court made a substantial award for lost earning capacity. Romilly J. stated: "The fact that the plaintiff is working at the time of trial in circumstances in which s/he earns an amount equal to or greater than his or her pre-accident earnings does not prevent the court from awarding damages to reflect that his or her capacity to earn income has been impaired."[90] He concluded that "the plaintiff must be compensated for a diminished earning capacity or employment impairment even though it is impossible to determine whether or not this diminished capacity or impairment will actually ever affect his or her income or earning ability."[91]

The logical conclusion of the capital-asset approach is that persons should be compensated for lost economic assets and opportunities, even though they would have chosen not to employ those assets or seek those opportunities. Courts are reluctant to go so far and, it is suggested, it is an overstatement to say that compensation may be had for a lost capacity that would never be exercised. There is an underlying sentiment that, if the plaintiff was not actually working, or planning to work, an award for economic loss would be a windfall. Additionally, the exercise of valuing lost capacity in the abstract is highly speculative. These concerns were summarized by Taylor J.A. (dissenting) in *Kroeker.*[92] He noted that, in actual practice, courts do not award damages for lost earning capacity in the abstract but only "for actual and anticipated pecuniary loss. Compensation is not granted for loss of future earning capacity at large, but for loss of that capacity *to the extent* that it is reasonable to expect that the particular plaintiff might, but for the accident, have employed that capacity for the purpose of generating actual income."[93] If courts were to employ the capital-asset approach, he concluded:

> Pecuniary damages would cease to reflect actual income loss, and come instead to reflect income which would have been lost had the plaintiff pursued a different, and more economically-productive, way of life.

---

89   (1996), 29 C.C.L.T. (2d) 176 (B.C.S.C.).
90   *Ibid.* at 208.
91   *Ibid.* at 211. See also *Morris v. Rose Estate* (1996), 23 B.C.L.R. (3d) 256 (C.A.).
92   Above note 56.
93   *Ibid.* at 197 [emphasis added].

This would radically change the system, and impose greatly increased cost on the public. I know of no way in which the courts, if such claims are to be allowed, could restrict or restrain awards in future.[94]

It is now understood that the basis of the award extends beyond aspects of the plaintiff's earning capacity that would have been used to generate actual income. It generally includes impairment of the ability to use that asset for all work of value, regardless of where that work occurs and whether paid or unpaid. On this basis, it is suggested that cases like *Pallos* and *Tabrizi*, discussed above, should be seen as providing compensation for the lost chance that, absent their injuries, the plaintiffs might have actually sought and achieved enhanced career prospects.[95]

3) Duration of Lost Earnings and the Problem of Lost Years

a) General Principles

Once the court has selected the basis for assessing the plaintiff's lost earnings, it must determine the duration over which the loss will be suffered. Expert testimony will be assessed to determine whether the plaintiff's injuries are temporary or permanent and, if temporary, when the plaintiff might be expected to be able to return to work (or part-time work).

In the case of permanent injuries, the court must determine how long the plaintiff would have worked had the injury not occurred. The period over which lost earnings are assessed is based on the *pre-accident* working life of the plaintiff, in contrast to the award for future care, which is based on *post-accident* lifespan. So, where the accident has shortened the plaintiff's lifespan, there is no deduction to lost earnings for "lost years." Generally, to determine the number of years of earnings, experts will rely on mortality tables that reveal the average number of working years for persons of the plaintiff's age at the time of the accident. It has occasionally been argued that, in situations where the accident has dramatically shortened the plaintiff's life, to award damages for lost earnings on a pre-accident basis will serve little purpose but to enrich the plaintiff's estate and confer a windfall on heirs. The answer given by the Supreme Court is that compensation is for loss of a capital asset destroyed by the accident, not simply to replace the

---

94 *Ibid.* at 198. See also above notes 87 and 89 and accompanying text.
95 See above section on accounting for positive contingencies and lost chances at notes 72 to 75 and Section F(2)(c), above in this chapter.

plaintiff's earnings or provide a stream of income while the plaintiff survives. Moreover, had the plaintiff died in the accident, dependants would have a claim at least to a portion of the plaintiff's lost income.

b) Partial Deduction for Lost Years

While the plaintiff is entitled to lost earnings over the entire pre-accident lifespan, where the plaintiff's life has been substantially shortened by the accident, the court will deduct from the award an amount representing the plaintiff's living expenses that will not be incurred beyond the projected date of death. The rationale for the deduction is that, if the plaintiff had lived during those years, moneys would be expended on daily "necessaries." If there is no deduction for the money that will now be "saved," the result will be a windfall to the plaintiff's estate. *Semenoff*,[96] for example, involved catastrophic injuries to a twenty-nine-year-old plaintiff, which shortened his remaining life expectancy to five years. The B.C. Court of Appeal deducted 33 percent from his lost-earnings award, representing an estimate of the personal expenses that would no longer be incurred by the plaintiff following his death. The Supreme Court of Canada confirmed this approach in *Toneguzzo-Norvell (Guardian ad litem of) v. Burnaby Hospital*.[97] A deduction for the necessaries of life (in this case 50 percent) was made from that portion of the lost-income award representing the "lost years":

> [H]ad the plaintiff been in a position to earn the monies represented by the award for lost earning capacity, she would have had to spend a portion of them for living expenses. Not to recognize this is to introduce an element of duplication and to put the plaintiff in a better position than she would have been in had she actually earned the monies in question.[98]

The Court did not analyze how it selected the figure of 50 percent. Three possible methods of calculation have been identified: the basic-necessities or poverty-line approach, the standard-of-living or available surplus approach, and the lost-savings approach.[99] The basic-necessities approach calculates the deduction on an absolute standard

---

96 Above note 52.

97 [1994] 1 S.C.R. 114 [*Toneguzzo*]. For commentary, see W.K. Branch & K.I. Price, "Case Comment Lost Years: The Compensation for Dying Young" (1994) 52 Advocate (Van.) 753. See also G. Young, "'Lost Years' as a Wrongful Death Claim" (1995) 53 Advocate (Van.) 705.

98 *Ibid.* at 127.

99 C.L. Brown, "*Duncan v. Baddeley*: Reconciling the 'Lost Years' Deduction with Fatal Accident Cases" (1997) 35 Alta. L. Rev. 1108; *Duncan Estate v. Baddeley*, [2001] 266 A.R. 323 (C.A.) [*Duncan Estate*].

of personal expense depending upon factors such as marital status and family size. The standard-of-living approach bases the deduction on the plaintiff's potential standard of living relevant to income-earning capacity, and the award for lost years is determined based on the available surplus after deductions for the reasonable amount that the plaintiff would have spent to maintain herself.[100] The lost-savings approach suggests that the only available income is what remains after a plaintiff's standard of living has been maintained, and may require deductions for all conceivable expenses.[101] The poverty-line approach has been rejected as not being a realistic reflection of what a person would spend to maintain herself.[102]

It is evident that courts are currently determining the personal living expense deduction on a case-by-case basis and it is sometimes unclear which approach they are using. Deductions have ranged as high as 85 percent on the lost-savings approach.[103] Other cases have rejected this approach, preferring instead the "conventional deduction" of one-third, often without explanation.[104] Thus far, no consistency in either the amount of the personal living expense deduction or the method of calculation has emerged in the common law. However, in *Brimacombe*, Hall J.A. cautioned that the award for lost years should be approached with great care. He stated:

---

100 See *Duncan Estate, ibid.*
101 For examples of cases in which the lost-savings approach has been applied, see *Brimacombe v. Mathews* (2001), 87 B.C.L.R. (3d) 75 (C.A.), leave to appeal to S.C.C. refused, [2001] S.C.C.A. No. 325 [*Brimacombe*]; *Fullerton, above note 25; Bohun v. Sennewald* (2007), 46 C.C.L.T. (3d) 138 (B.C.S.C.) [*Bohun*]. In *Guerineau*, above note 26, the court rejected the lost-savings approach, among other things, because it can lead to unrealistically huge deductions. See also *Duncan Estate*, above note 99, where the court rejected the lost-savings approach as resulting in unnecessarily huge deductions for lost years.
102 See *Duncan Estate, ibid.* In *Brimacombe, ibid.* at para. 248, Hall J.A. noted that the choice of appropriate method for assessing compensation for the lost years is between the lost-savings and personal-living-expenses approach.
103 *Granger (Litigation guardian of) v. Ottawa General Hospital* (1996), 7 O.T.C. 81 (Gen. Div.); *Marchand v. Public General Hospital*, [1996] O.J. No. 4420 (Gen. Div.), aff'd on other grounds (2000), 51 O.R (3d) 97 (C.A.), leave to appeal to S.C.C. refused, [2001] S.C.C.A. No. 66: 85 percent; *Bohun*, above note 104: 75 percent. In *Robb Estate v. Canadian Red Cross Society* (2001), 152 O.A.C. 60, the Ontario Court of Appeal was willing to affirm a 90 percent deduction for lost years under the lost-savings approach if it had affirmed the finding of liability in this case.
104 *Brown (Next friend of) v. University of Alberta Hospital* (1997), 145 D.L.R. (4th) 63 (Alta. Q.B.) [*Brown*]; *Brimacombe*, above note 101; *Williams (Guardian ad litem of) v. Low*, 2000 BCSC 345; *D.(M.) (Guardian ad litem of) v. British Columbia*, 2000 BCSC 700.

It seems to me that courts should be conservative in making an award under this head of damages because of the great number of variables and contingencies that enter into any assessment of earnings so far into the future, often as here, with a plaintiff who has not and in all probability will not have a proven work history.[105]

As well, in *Duncan Estate*, Fruman J.A. said that deductions for living expenses must reflect a realistic assessment of what a person at the plaintiff's income level would spend in order to live. In *Guerineau*, following *Toneguzzo*, the court noted that the standard deduction for lost years has been approximately 50 percent and deviation from this standard is justified based on evidence that the plaintiff would have spent more of his income on living expenses.[106]

4) Deductions for Negative Contingencies

In most cases, courts apply a contingency deduction to the claim for lost income. The theory is that, had the plaintiff not been injured, she would nevertheless have been exposed to contingencies that would affect her employment. Such contingencies include sickness, layoff, injury, and early retirement. Each of these might reduce income had the plaintiff not been injured. In *Thornton*, the Supreme Court approved a deduction of 10 percent and in *Andrews* it permitted a deduction of 20 percent. Additionally, certain positive contingencies may also reduce the award for lost future income. For example, where there remains a chance that the plaintiff will recover from the injuries and recommence work, that chance may be factored into the award.[107]

The contingency deduction is controversial. It should not be made automatically. As Dickson J. stated in *Thornton*, "The imposition of a contingency deduction is not mandatory.... The deduction, if any, will depend upon the facts of the case, including the age and nature of employment of the plaintiff."[108] Moreover, not all contingencies are adverse. In addition to "bad luck" a plaintiff might equally have experienced the "good luck" of unexpected wage increases, promotions, job transfers, and changes. Additionally, even when a person experiences a negative

---

105 *Brimacombe*, above note 101 at para. 248.
106 The 50 percent deduction has been applied in many cases. For examples, see *Brito*, above note 26; *Bauer (Litigation guardian of) v. Seager* (2000), 147 Man. R. (2d) 1 (Q.B.); *Osborne (Litigation guardian of) v. Bruce (County)* (1999), 39 M.V.R. (3d) 159 (Ont. Ct. Gen. Div.); *Chow (Litigation guardian of) v. Wellesley Hospital*, 1999 CarswellOnt 349 (Gen. Div.).
107 *Rourke*, above note 47.
108 Above note 2 at 283.

contingency in her employment, the impact of that contingency is often softened by private and social insurance, social assistance, termination payments, and the like. Thus, substantial contingency deductions should be made only when they are supported by the evidence. Despite these comments, many courts make contingency deductions almost automatically. Arguably, this is inappropriate, and the deductions are overly large. For example, a 20 percent contingency deduction amounts to the assumption that the plaintiff would have been unemployed one year in every five, and during that period of unemployment would have received no income, insurance, or social assistance whatsoever. Especially in cases where the trial judge has been presented with good evidence (individual and statistical) about the life prospects and needs of the plaintiff, it is better to make no further contingency deduction except to deal with specific probabilities that are relevant to the situation of the individual plaintiff and fully supported by evidence.

5) Collateral Benefits

An injured person will frequently receive some replacement for lost earnings from "collateral" sources. For example, he may have private life or disability insurance. An employer may continue his wage for a period after he is injured. His collective agreement may provide for wage continuation. He may receive social assistance benefits, unemployment insurance, and so on. The issue is whether, in assessing the wage-loss claim against the defendant, such benefits should be taken into account.

The task of the courts is to steer between two conflicting concerns. On the one hand, to deduct collateral benefits from the plaintiff's award seems to give to the defendant the benefit of charitable and other payments intended for the plaintiff. On the other hand, to ignore collateral payments in calculating damages may result in the plaintiff receiving compensation for a loss that was never really suffered—that is, double compensation. The general rule is that gifts and private charity are not deducted from the plaintiff's award. Similarly, any insurance or wage replacement for which the plaintiff has "paid" (e.g., in the form of insurance premiums) is not to be deducted when calculating the lost-income claim. The subject of collateral benefits is dealt with fully in Chapter 13.

6) Treatment of Taxation

At common law in Canada, the award for lost income is calculated without regard to tax. The defendant is not entitled to a reduction of the plaintiff's award for wage loss on the basis that those wages would have been subject to income tax. Nor is the plaintiff entitled to have the award grossed up to take into account the fact that tax will be payable on the income from the capital sum. The Supreme Court justified this approach on the basis that the award does not represent simply a replacement of lost income but rather compensation for the loss of a capital asset.[109] This approach may be contrasted with compensation of family members for their losses in fatal accident cases. In these cases, because the dependants are claiming lost income or support, the calculation is made on an after-tax basis (because the amount of family support comes only from the deceased's after-tax income).

This reasoning, while still controlling in this area, is somewhat flawed. From a pragmatic point of view, had the plaintiff not been injured, he would have earned income and inevitably have paid tax. Basing the award on gross income clearly seems to confer a windfall. Even from a conceptual point of view, while it may be true that the compensation is for a capital asset and not income, the *value* of the capital asset is substantially affected by the incidence of taxation on the income that could be generated by that asset.

Nevertheless, the most recent assault on the rule was rejected again by the Supreme Court of Canada in *Shanks v. McNee*.[110] Both the trial judge and Court of Appeal had not deducted tax from the award for lost future income, though commenting that such a deduction would be logical.[111] The Supreme Court of Canada confirmed the decision not to deduct for tax. Cory J., writing for the majority, adhered to the rule established by *Jennings*,[112] that tax on income was a matter between the state and the individual. The fact that tax was not deducted from an award was simply a reflection of the state's policy not to tax that kind of income. He concluded that it remains to the legislatures to alter the common law rule and make damages for lost income taxable, "a question of tax policy and not of tort law."[113] Subsequently, in some jurisdictions, legislation has made inroads into the common law rule. For example, in British Columbia, in automobile-accident cases, *past* income loss is calculated on an after-tax basis.[114]

---

109 *R. v. Jennings*, [1966] S.C.R. 532 [*Jennings*].
110 Known as *Cunningham v. Wheeler*, [1994] 1 S.C.R. 359.
111 *Ibid.* at 413.
112 Above note 109.
113 Above note 110 at 418.
114 *IVA*, above note 15, s. 98. In Alberta, awards for lost earnings in automobile accidents are based on net income. *Insurance Act*, R.S.A. 2000, c. I-3, s. 626.1(2).

7) Special Problems in Assessing Lost Earning Capacity

In *Andrews*, Dickson J. referred to the process of estimating lost earning capacity as akin to looking into a crystal ball. In some cases, where at the time of the accident the plaintiff is a mature individual with an established earnings record, that record can be used to determine earning capacity. However, in cases involving children, and others without a recent earnings record (e.g., homemakers), the matter is much more controversial. As Lord Denning explained in *Taylor v. Bristol Omnibus Co.*,[115]

> [a]t his very young age these [calculations] are speculative in the extreme. Who can say what a baby boy will do with his life? He may be in charge of a business and make much money. He may get into a mediocre groove and just pay his way. Or, he may be an utter failure. It is even more speculative with a baby girl. She may marry and bring up a large family, but earn nothing herself. Or, she may be a career woman, earning high wages.[116]

a)   Children

As indicated in the preceding quote, the calculation of lost earning capacity for young children is highly speculative. There is also a danger in this area, namely, that unstated or unintentional biases and assumptions will affect the award. The case of *Teno*[117] provides an illustration of the problems. In this case three levels of courts considered the problem of assessing the pecuniary loss suffered by a severely injured four-and-a-half-year-old girl. In the absence of any reliable evidence to assess this loss, the trial judge and Ontario Court of Appeal accepted the plaintiff's mother's salary as a teacher as a fair proxy and suggested a figure of $10,000 per year. The Supreme Court of Canada, however, reduced this amount to $6,000. Spence J. rightly pointed out:

> There can be no evidence whatsoever which will assist us in determining whether she ever would have become a member of the work force or whether she would have grown up in her own home and then married. There can be no evidence upon which we may assess whether she would have had a successful business future or have been a failure.[118]

---

115   [1975] 1 W.L.R. 1054 (C.A.).
116   *Ibid.* at 1059.
117   Above note 2.
118   *Ibid.* at 329.

Yet, in the absence of such evidence, Spence J. seemed prepared to assume that the plaintiff would not have achieved even the modest success of her mother. "I do not see how this Court could approve the course taken by Zuber J.A. which simply amounted to assuming ... that the infant plaintiff would follow the course of her mother who was a primary school teacher with an income of $10,000 per year."[119] The court settled on a figure of $6,000 after a contingency deduction: an amount just $1,000 above the poverty line.[120] It must be asked why, in the admitted absence of evidence one way or another, Spence J. was unwilling to assume that the plaintiff would have achieved the modest success in the workforce that her mother had. It seems probable that Spence J. was relying on certain unstated assumptions based on Diane Teno's gender—in particular, the assumption that she would marry, and that this would reduce her earning capacity.

The poverty-line approach adopted in *Teno* is not confined exclusively to female children. It has also been applied to very young male children.[121] Yet it is most prominent in the case of females, whether children or adult homemakers with little or no earnings record.[122]

The preferable—though far from perfect—approach in the case of children is to attempt to base the wage-loss prediction upon the evidence. The child may have an educational track record or career aspirations that assist the court in making assumptions about future prospects (e.g., where the court accepts a teenage child's testimony about her career aspirations).[123] Alternatively, experts will testify as to

---

119 *Ibid.*
120 *Ibid.* It is important to note that the award for lost earning capacity was not in addition to any award for the cost of care covering ordinary living expenses. As stated by Spence J.: "It should also be noted that such calculations for cost of care make no provision for the ordinary costs of living such as food, clothing and shelter but are for special care alone" (at 321).
121 In *Wipfli*, above note 45, the court rejected average male wages as the base for determining the loss suffered by an infant male and set a level of earnings between average wage for males aged twenty to twenty-four ($15,000) and poverty level ($10,000). The resulting figure of $12,500 was further reduced by 70 percent to avoid overlap with the award for care.
122 See *Fenn*, above note 49; *Webber v. Lowrie* (1978), 5 B.C.L.R. 237 (S.C.); *Penso v. Solowan* (1982), 35 B.C.L.R. 250 (C.A.).
123 *Wassell (Guardian ad litem of) v. Pile* (1994), 93 B.C.L.R. (2d) 195 (S.C.): the court accepted the testimony of the sixteen-year-old plaintiff, who aspired to obtain a degree in education and become a physical education teacher. In *MacCabe v. Board of Education of Westlock Roman Catholic Separate School District No. 110* (2001), 293 A.R. 41 (C.A.), involving a sixteen-year-old grade eleven student, the court found that, given her strong motivation, academic performance, and work ethic, she would likely have attained her desire to be a physiotherapist.

the likely educational level that the child might have attained but for the accident, either based on the plaintiff's own track record of educational achievement,[124] family history,[125] or both,[126] and will present earnings statistics for persons of that level of education as a basis for compensation. In making this prediction, experts, including developmental psychologists, may be called upon to offer their assessments. Obviously, such predictions are fraught with peril, and social assumptions are embedded in the data used.[127] For example, in one case, a court sought the aid of a developmental psychologist to determine the "life prospects" of a severely injured child, and thus determine his income loss.[128] Important traits that were held to be predictive included parental education and income, family socio-economic status, birth order, and family stability. The particular child had almost everything going against him. He was from a broken home, with low family income, and the middle child of a large number of siblings. Indeed, the Court of Appeal held that the contingency that the plaintiff might pursue advanced education because of his inability to do most types of manual labour led to the possibility that he might find an occupation that would pay him more than if the accident had not occurred. This case and others show how experts and courts often use social, economic, and racial assumptions to determine a plaintiff's life prospects, and the extent to which a tort may have impaired a plaintiff's earning potential.[129]

---

124 For example, see *Walker v. Ritchie* (2005), 31 C.C.L.T. (3d) 205 (Ont. C.A.), var'd on other grounds, [2006] 2 S.C.R. 428 [*Walker*]: The Court accepted that the plaintiff, who was seventeen years old at the time of the accident, would have completed university but for the accident, although her future career path was uncertain by the time of the accident. The Court used average earnings of university graduates in Ontario. See also *Rudd v. Hamiota Feedlot Lot Ltd.* (2006), 200 Man. R. (2d) 26 (Q.B.) [*Rudd*]; *Hartwick v. Simser*, [2004] O.J. No. 4315 (S.C.J.) [*Hartwick*].

125 *Fullerton*, above note 25; *Martin v. Listowel Memorial Hospital* (2000), 192 D.L.R. (4th) 250 (Ont. C.A.); *Rewcastle Estate v. Sieben* (2001), 296 A.R. 61 (Q.B.), rev'd in part (2003), 20 Alta. L.R. (4th) 17 (C.A.) [*Rewcastle*]; *A.C. v. Y.J.C.* (2003), 36 R.F.L. (5th) 79 (Ont. S.C.J.); *Spehar*, above note 28.

126 See *Gray v. Macklin* (2000), 4 C.C.L.T. (3d) 13 (Ont. S.C.J.); *Chow v. Hiscock* (2005), 41 C.C.L.T. (3d) 155 (B.C.S.C.).

127 In *Crawford*, above note 34 at para. 296, the Court of Appeal acknowledged that reliance on a plaintiff's family history and work ethic in determining future economic prospects could be problematic, but concluded that it is not unreasonable to assume that a child's income potential will follow that of her parents.

128 *Houle v. Calgary (City)* (1983), 44 A.R. 271 (Q.B.), var'd in part (1985), 60 A.R. 366 (C.A.), leave to appeal to S.C.C. refused (1985), 63 A.R. 79n. For a commentary see J.A. Sutherland, "Predicting a Child's Future Wage Loss" (1984) 42 Advocate 169.

129 See *Blackwater v. Plint* (2001), 93 B.C.L.R. (3d) 228 (S.C.), aff'd [2005] 3 S.C.R. 3; *H.L. v. Canada (Attorney General)*, [2005] 1 S.C.R. 401 at paras. 335–39, Basta-

While courts have cautioned against the use of stereotypes,[130] such assumptions still frequently make their way into the assessment exercise. Indeed, where the expert evidence is based upon statistics, those statistics themselves may reflect gendered, racial, and socio-economic stereotypes. This issue is addressed more fully in the next section.

b) The Use of Gendered and Racialized Statistics

Perhaps the most intractable difficulties in assessing the lost earning capacity of children have to do with the nature of the evidence relied upon (and the social realities underlying that evidence). Expert witnesses and courts use statistics as an aid to the determination of income loss, and when the statistics are "gendered" (i.e., broken down into male and female cohorts) they will result in significantly different projections for males and females. As a result of the use of gendered statistics, female plaintiffs frequently receive less compensation than their male counterparts.[131] This problem is exacerbated when negative assumptions based upon race and socio-economic status are also embedded in the statistics.

i) The Impact of Statistics

The figures presented in a British Columbia case[132] provide an illustration of this problem. The case involved an injury to a fifteen-year-old

---

rache J. (dissenting in part); *M.B. v. British Columbia*, [2003] 2 S.C.R. 477 at paras. 52–54; *M.A. v. Canada (Attorney General)* (2001), 212 Sask. R. 241 (Q.B.), var'd on other grounds (2003), 227 Sask. R. 260 (C.A.), leave to appeal to S.C.C. dismissed, [2003] S.C.C.A. No. 151; *K.L.B. v. British Columbia*, [2003] 2 S.C.R. 403 [*K.L.B.*]. For a critique of this position, see E. Adjin-Tettey, "Replicating and Perpetuating Inequalities in Personal Injury Claims through Female-Specific Contingencies" (2004) 49 McGill L.J. 309 at 333–41.

130 In *K.L.B.*, *ibid.*, at paras. 60–61, McLachlin C.J.C. cautioned trial courts not to assume that children from impoverished and difficult backgrounds are automatically predisposed to psychological difficulties that would have detrimentally affected their future prospects even absent the tort in question. Any such finding should be supported by the evidence before the court, which was present in this case. See also *A. (T.W.N.) v. Clarke* (2003), 22 B.C.L.R. (4th) 1 (C.A.).

131 See J. Cassels, "Damages for Lost Earning Capacity: Women and Children Last!" (1992) 71 Can. Bar Rev. 445, and "(In)equality and the Law of Tort: Gender, Race and the Assessment of Damages" (1995) 17 Advocates' Q. 158; E. Gibson, "The Gendered Wage Dilemma in Personal Injury Damages" in K. Cooper-Stephenson & E. Gibson, eds., *Tort Theory* (North York: Captus University Press, 1993) 185; Law Society of British Columbia, Gender Bias Committee, *Gender Equality in the Justice System* (Vancouver: Law Society of British Columbia, 1992).

132 *Mulholland (Guardian ad litem of) v. Riley*, [1993] B.C.J. No. 920 (S.C.), aff'd (1995), 12 B.C.L.R. (3d) 248 (C.A.) [*Mulholland*].

female plaintiff. The statistics presented at trial showed that the value of a female's lifetime earnings (assuming some post-secondary non-university education) would be $468,366. The comparable figure for a male in her circumstances was nearly twice as much, at $858,979. The trial judge felt constrained to use the female statistics (though he did adjust them upwards to take into account likely improvements in female wages in the future). This approach was upheld by the Court of Appeal.

Thus, when experts, lawyers, and courts forecast future earnings, gender is a major factor, and the compensation figures for women consequently incorporate and reproduce the large wage gap between men and women. When race and other social factors are mixed into the equation, the results are even more troubling. Women who are also members of visible minorities may face a double disadvantage in asserting claims for lost earning capacity if race-based statistics are used. The problem is particularly apparent when one examines the treatment of First Nations women. *Parker v. Richards* provides an example.[133] This was a fatal accident case brought on behalf of the infant daughter of a seventeen-year-old Aboriginal woman, who was killed in a motor-vehicle collision. In assessing the future income prospects of the deceased, the experts relied upon her gender (female), education (grade 6), labour-force participation (unemployed), marital status (single mother), ethnicity (Aboriginal), and socio-economic background (parents divorced). Relating these factors to the deceased, the expert asserted that the

> prospects of Cheryl Lynn would probably have been bleak, most likely below the poverty line. The composite picture of a single, lone parent female of Native ancestry, with a grade six education and never having held a job, and coming out of a broken home, would be one that would rank in Canada as one of the lowest socio-economic prospects possible in the country.[134]

Low J. adopted a welfare-payment standard for assessing financial loss and concluded that the maximum financial contribution that the deceased would have made to her daughter was $200 per month. Partially enhancing this award was an additional award for "loss of mother's services," which provided $126,238 for a live-in nanny until the infant attained fifteen years of age, $20,000 for loss of care, guidance, training, and encouragement, and $5,000 as a "nominal sum" for loss of inheritance. Courts often refer to plaintiffs' race/ethnicity and gender as

133 [1990] B.C.J. No. 1824 (S.C.).
134 *Ibid.*

negative factors in their economic prospects, but fail to recognize that, because of their economic vulnerability, the participation rates of some racialized women in the waged labour force may be higher, even if at a lower income level. For the most part, such women cannot afford to withdraw from the labour market for significant periods of time.[135]

The practice of relying upon gendered and racialized statistics, while perhaps resulting in "accurate" predictions, raises squarely the issue of whether the law of damages should seek to replicate with precision the results that would have been achieved in an unfair society. One judge, for example, remarked that "it may be as inappropriately discriminatory to discount an award solely on statistics framed on gender as it would be to discount an award on considerations of race or ethnic origin. I am doubtful of the propriety, today, of this Court basing an award of damages on a class characteristic such as gender."[136] Despite such sentiments, there is no rule of law that excludes such considerations and, indeed, such considerations are frequently embedded in the statistical and actuarial analyses that courts rely upon.

ii) De-gendering the Statistics
Courts have not been insensitive to the problems noted above. The statistics used to assess women's earning capacity are historical figures that reflect past discrimination, social roles, and economic patterns. But these roles and patterns are changing and the income gap is closing. The labour-force participation rates of males and females are expected to be roughly equal in the future. Thus, in forecasting lost earnings, it is important both to use the correct cohort and to adjust the historical figures to take into account the trend towards equalization of male and female wages. It is now standard practice, while still using female statistics, to adjust the wage-loss figure upwards to take into account the trend towards wage parity.[137] The Supreme Court of Canada has (implicitly) endorsed this approach, and other courts have followed suit.[138] Adjusting the figures in this manner is of great importance especially in cases involving young plaintiffs.

---

135 See Adjin-Tettey, above note 129 at 338–39.
136 *Terracciano (Guardian ad litem of) v. Etheridge* (1997), 33 B.C.L.R. (3d) 328 at 349 (S.C.), Saunders J. [*Terracciano*]. See also *Rudd*, above note 124.
137 *Mulholland*, above note 132. This point was raised but not acted upon in *Cherry (Guardian ad litem of) v. Borsman (sub nom. Cherry (Guardian) v. Borsman)* (1992), 70 B.C.L.R. (2d) 273 (C.A.) [*Cherry*]. It was accepted in *B.(S.M.A.) v. H.(J. N.)*, [1991] B.C.J. No. 3940 (S.C.) [*B.(S.M.A.)*].
138 In *Toneguzzo*, above note 97, the trial judge, who had been provided with comparative data on male and female wages, grossed up the award to a female

Going one step farther, it has been argued that reliance upon gendered (and racialized) statistics simply reproduces and replicates social injustice, and that the time has come to reject the practice by relying instead upon broader-based or more favourable data. This argument was tentatively accepted in the British Columbia case of *Tucker (Public Trustee) v. Asleson*.[139] This case involved a catastrophic injury to an eight-year-old girl, rendering her essentially unemployable. Counsel for the plaintiff introduced earnings figures based on the average lifetime income of male university graduates ($947,000). Counsel for the defendant objected to the plaintiff's figures, arguing that the appropriate figures were average earnings for women ($302,000). At the trial level, Finch J. appeared to accept the plaintiff's figures. He stated:

> [A]s a starting point ... the measure of the plaintiff's earning capacity should not be limited by statistics based upon her sex. Before the accident the plaintiff was a bright little girl growing up in a stable home environment. In Canada, no educational or vocational opportunities were excluded to her. She could have become a doctor, lawyer or business person. Or, in line with her childhood wish, a veterinarian.[140]

However, despite the use of the male statistics as the starting point for the calculation, the ultimate award was reduced by a staggering 63 percent for negative contingencies, thus settling on a final figure close to that suggested by the defendant.

This decision was upheld by the Court of Appeal, though without any strong endorsement of the use of male statistics.[141] Southin J., noting the speculative nature of the exercise, stated that the award would be adequate to provide comfortably for the plaintiff for the rest of her life, and that an appellate judge was in no position to gaze more accurately into the crystal ball on these matters. McEachern C.J. differed on this point and would have sent the case back for a new trial on damages. He concluded that Finch J. went too far, stating that he was "uneasy about the use of male statistics for female claimants." Indeed, he held that the use of male statistics constituted an error in law:

---

plaintiff to reflect the positive contingency of a decreasing wage gap. At the Supreme Court, the Court was asked to substitute male data as the basis of the award, but declined to do so on the basis that the argument had not been made at trial and the evidence was insufficient.

139 (1991), 86 D.L.R. (4th) 73 (B.C.S.C.), rev'd in part (1993) 102 D.L.R. (4th) 518 (B.C.C.A.) [*Tucker*].

140 Quoted from *ibid.* at 528 (C.A.).

141 *Ibid.* The appeal of the defendant Asleson was allowed (re liability) and the appeal of the Crown was dismissed. The damages award was left undisturbed.

This is not to say that female statistics should be used strictly, for they have rightly been found to reflect bias, but it is necessary, so far as may be possible, to use statistics which comport most closely with the essential facts of the case under consideration ...

While we may strive for social justice, as it is perceived from time to time, the courts must deal with the parties who are before them ... on the basis of realistic predictions about the future, and not just in accordance with understandable wishes that society, in some of its aspects, were different from what it really is.[142]

The argument made by McEachern C.J. is based on the view that, while the use of statistics may bias awards downwards, the problem is not one that can be solved by the law of remedies. The statistics accurately reflect the underlying social reality. The fact that women, and certain other groups, earn less than others may be unjust, and indeed the result of discrimination, but this systemic "injury" is not one that is caused by the defendant and should not be remedied by a more generous damage award. This view is premised on the position that it is not the function of tort law to achieve social justice in the wider sense. Traditionally, this body of law is thought to govern the relations between individuals only. It leaves little room for the recognition or remediation of the types of systemic inequality that is the focus of so much modern equality jurisprudence. Many argue that tort law is about *corrective justice*—the restoration of relationships between individuals after one of them has committed a civil wrong.[143] This model concerns itself only with the relationship between the immediate parties to the dispute and ignores the wider social context in which their encounter takes place. And the law accepts the prior status quo as the appropriate measure and goal of justice. Thus, there is little room for the application of norms of *distributive justice*—norms that might focus on wider social inequalities that are reflected in the relationship between the parties even before a wrong is committed.

Tucker has not been overruled, but some courts continue to use gender-specific statistics[144] (though generally grossing them up for im-

---

142 *Ibid.* at 531 and 533.
143 See especially the work of E.J. Weinrib. For example, "Understanding Tort Law" (1989) 23 Valparaiso U. L. Rev. 485; "Liberty, Community, and Corrective Justice" (1988) 1 Can. J. Law & Jur. 3; "Legal Formalism: On the Immanent Rationality of Law" (1988) 97 Yale L.J. 949; "Two Conceptions of Tort Law" in R.F. Devlin, ed., *Canadian Perspectives on Legal Theory* (Toronto: Emond Montgomery, 1991) at 29.
144 *D. (Guardian ad litem of) v. F.*, [1995] B.C.J. No. 2693 (S.C.): rejecting the use of male and also gender-neutral data for a female plaintiff. See also *Osborne (Litigation guardian of) v. Bruce (County)* (1999), 39 M.V.R. (3d) 159 (Ont. S.C.J.).

provements in the wage rates of women).[145] On the other hand, in several recent cases,[146] male statistics have been used for young female plaintiffs, but only on the basis of evidence that these specific individuals would likely have pursued professional careers in a typically "male" pattern[147] or that the gender wage gap is likely to have narrowed significantly or been eliminated by the time the plaintiffs would have entered the labour market, subject to a contingency deduction that pay equity may not be achieved.[148] So far, only a few cases have taken the position that, as a matter of law, gender-related factors must be filtered out of the damages calculation. For example, in *MacCabe v. Westlock Roman Catholic Separate School District No. 110*,[149] Johnstone J. stated:

> It is entirely inappropriate that any assessment I make continues to reflect historic wage inequities. I cannot agree more with Chief Justice McEachern of the British Columbia Court of Appeal in *Tucker*, *supra*, that the courts must ensure as much as possible that the appropriate weight be given to societal trends in the labour market in order that the future loss of income properly reflects future circumstances. Where we differ is that I will not sanction the "reality" of pay inequity. The societal trend is and must embrace pay equity given our fundamental right to equality which is entrenched in the constitution. The courts have judicially recognized in tort law the historical discriminatory wage practices between males and females. The courts have endeavoured to alleviate this discrimination with the use of male or female wage tables modified by either negative or positive contingencies. However, I am of the view that these approaches merely mask the problem: how can the Court embrace pay inequity between males and females? I cannot apply a flawed process which perpetuates a discriminatory practice. The application of the contingencies, although in several cases reduce the wage gap, still sanction the disparity.
>
> A growing understanding of the extent of discriminatory wage practices and the effect of this societal inequity must lead the Court to retire an antiquated or limited judicial yardstick and embrace a

---

145   The trial judgment in *Tucker*, above note 139, has been distinguished in *B.(S.M.A.)*, above note 137; *Rewcastle*, above note 125.

146   *Chu (Guardian ad litem of) v. Jacobs*, [1996] B.C.J. No. 674 (S.C.); *B.I.Z. v. Sams*, [1997] B.C.J. 793 [*B.I.Z.*]; *Terracciano*, above note 136.

147   *Spehar*, above note 28; *MacCabe v. Westlock Roman Catholic Separate School District No. 110* (1998), 226 A.R. 1 (Q.B.), rev'd in part (2001), 293 A.R. 41 (C.A.) [*MacCabe*].

148   *Gray v. Macklin*, above note 126.

149   Above note 147 at paras. 469 & 470 (Q.B.). See also *Rudd*, above note 124.

more realistic, expansive measurement legally grounded in equality. Equality is now a fundamental constitutional value in Canadian society … The Court cannot sanction future forecasting if it perpetuates the historic wage disparity between men and women. Accordingly, if there is a disparity between the male and female statistics in the employment category I have determined for the Plaintiff the male statistics shall be used, subject to the relevant contingencies. Once again if the contingencies are gender specific, then the contingencies applicable to males shall be used except in the case of life expectancy, for obvious reasons.

This was reversed on appeal.[150] The Alberta Court of Appeal held that it could not ignore the "reality" of the plaintiff's position based on statistical predictions about women's labour force participation because of their familial responsibilities. A contingency deduction was made to reflect this "reality." In support of the court's position, Whittmann J.A. stated:

> Determination of negative contingencies based upon a classification according to sex is not unreasonable in these circumstances. The situation is analogous to the use of actuarial tables based on sex, age or marital status to determine insurance premium rates for drivers of motor vehicles … application of female contingencies would not perpetuate or sanction historical and societal discrimination. Further, wage statistics perpetuate nothing. Valid data reflects historical reality.[151]

The Court of Appeal's decision is based upon the prevailing view that the purpose of tort law damage awards is "corrective" justice aimed at restoring the status quo, not distributive justice aimed at improving the status quo.

Some courts also use neutral or average income statistics that reflect the earnings of both men and women in particular categories or professions that the plaintiff would have likely attained. Even in this context, some courts continue to make female-specific contingency deductions to reflect the reality of what the plaintiffs' likely attachment to the labour force would have been.[152] However, in *Walker*, involving a sixteen-year-old plaintiff, the court refused to make gender-specific contingency deductions from the plaintiff's award for future income loss. Among other things, the court noted that gender-neutral statis-

---

150 *MacCabe, ibid.*

151 *Ibid.* at paras. 94 and 124 (C.A.). See also *Rewcastle*, above note 125 at paras. 72–74.

152 For examples, see *Audet (Guardian ad litem of) v. Bates*, [1998] B.C.J. No. 678 (S.C.); *Crawford*, above note 34; *Paxton v. Ramji*, [2006] O.J. No. 1179 (S.C.J.).

tics reflect the average earnings of men and women and already reflect negative contingencies that affect workers of both genders. A further deduction based on specific factors that affect women's labour force participation was therefore unwarranted. In fact, the purpose of using neutral earning statistics is to avoid having to choose between male and female incomes and then make the necessary adjustments to reflect what is perceived to be the plaintiff's anticipated earning prospect.

c)   Other Gender-Specific Problems: The Marriage Contingency

A related problem in the assessment of women's losses is the "marriage contingency." Even where a woman is employed at the time of the accident, and her award is based on her actual earnings rather than statistics, that award may still be reduced by certain gendered assumptions. Most significant are the "marriage contingency" and the "childbearing contingency." These are deductions made from awards because of the assumption that women will leave the workforce (for a period or permanently) in order to marry and/or raise children or look after their spouses.[153] Likewise, female plaintiffs' claims are often reduced by a contingency factor to take into account "time off for family purposes" and the development of a "family union that would allow the plaintiff to devote time from paid employment to her children."[154]

The texts and manuals relied upon by lawyers advise reductions for marriage, childbearing, and child-raising[155] and the deduction is often made by the plaintiff's own experts.[156] Even more often, the deduction is simply embedded in the average data that are used to predict female wage loss (given that this data reflects more time out of the workforce for women owing to family responsibilities). For example, in a case involving a female plaintiff who was working towards a doctoral degree at the time of the accident, the British Columbia Court of Appeal upheld an award based on gendered statistics indicating that women with such qualifications earned 10 percent less than men.[157] These figures

---

153   See, for example: *Johnston v. Bustraan* (3 March 1980), Chilliwack Reg. 57/78 (B.C.S.C.); *Bourton v. England*, [1987] B.C.J. No. 1733 (S.C.); *Downing v. Public Trustee*, [1988] B.C.J. No. 1629 (S.C.); *Botero v. Kiss*, [1991] B.C.J. No. 568 (S.C.); *Wright v. Mason*, [1991] B.C.J. No. 673 (S.C.); *Oppen v. Johnson Estate*, [1991] B.C.J. No. 3244 (S.C.) [*Oppen*]; *Waterhouse v. Fedor* (1986), 11 B.C.L.R. (2d) 56 (S.C.); *Sanderson Estate v. Betts*, [1990] B.C.J. No. 2720 (S.C.).
154   *Oppen, ibid.*
155   For example, M.L. Berenblut & H.N. Rosen, *Litigation Accounting: The Quantification of Economic Damages* (Don Mills, ON: R. De Boo, 1986).
156   *Twine v. Cyr*, [1990] B.C.J. No. 2921 (S.C.).
157   *Robinson-Phillips v. Demuth* (1994), 96 B.C.L.R. (2d) 1 (C.A.).

reflect time out of the workforce for childbearing and other reasons, despite the testimony of the plaintiff that she would have worked full-time. The court stated:

> I am not persuaded that the judge fell into error in this regard. To say after being injured in an accident what one would have done had the accident not occurred must, at best, be to give an opinion, albeit one based in this case on pre-accident intention. The judge had to take into consideration the possibility that, despite that intention, the plaintiff, had she not been in the accident, might have married and have taken time off full-time work for child-bearing or child-raising, or have taken time off for any other reason for which the average woman of her age and qualifications does so. Whatever may have been the appellant's pre-accident intention, it does not necessarily follow that she would not in fact have had the average earning experience for a woman of her age and qualifications.
>
> Having in mind that the difference between the average figures for men and women is only about ten per cent, the adoption of the latter figure does not seem unreasonable.[158]

Even in cases where courts accept a male earnings profile for a female plaintiff, a deduction may still be made for possible time away from the workforce for childrearing.[159]

At the other end of her career, a woman may also meet the assumption that she would have retired earlier than a man, even though retirement may simply be a replacement of paid work with increased unpaid work such as caregiving for aging relatives or a spouse. An example is *Boughey v. Rogers*.[160] The fifty-year-old plaintiff had been in the workforce for twelve years prior to the accident. Her compensation for lost earnings was reduced on the ground that she would have been unlikely to remain a full-time employee until retirement. The court held:

> With her husband continuing to earn a good income she may have decided at some point to cease employment outside the home and direct her energies to non-remunerative pursuits. There is also the

---

158 *Ibid.* at 4.
159 B.I.Z., above note 146.
160 [1989] B.C.J. No. 1413 (S.C). See also *Friesen v. Wood*, [1990] B.C.J. No. 1086 (S.C.). The plaintiff, a thirty-nine-year-old hospital worker, was assumed to retire at age sixty because of the physically demanding nature of that work. Paradoxically, her award for lost earnings was also reduced because of the likelihood of future earnings based on a positive assessment of her work ethic.

possibility that she may have to devote her time in the future to the care of her husband whose health is not good.[161]

Interestingly, for men, marriage is sometimes treated as a positive contingency. There is a strong correlation between marriage and a man's attachment to the workforce, and the fact (or possibility) of marriage will be taken to increase a man's award.[162] This is illustrated by a recent case in which the award to a young man with a marginal work history was significantly increased to take into account the stabilizing influence that his upcoming marriage would have had on his work habits.[163]

There is, of course, a logic to the deduction made for time out of the workforce. If the award for lost earning *capacity* is designed solely to replace lost *wages*, then the chance that a woman might leave the paid workforce for a period is relevant to the assessment of the loss. There simply is no pecuniary loss. However, if the award for lost earning capacity is designed to compensate the lost ability to *work*, then a decision to leave the paid workforce is not, in itself, relevant — unless, of course, unpaid work in the home is said to be of no value. A later section describes how courts have recently begun to place a value on "homemaking capacity" as a form of economic loss and the way in which this may partially offset the deductions described here.

Adopting an opportunity-cost approach to women's wage loss would eliminate most of the deductions discussed in this section. The voluntary choice to leave the workforce does not eliminate a person's earning capacity. The value of a person's earning capacity would be measured simply by what she could earn in the market. Nevertheless, this approach is not likely to be adopted. First, the process of estimating a person's "capacity" in the abstract is complex and speculative. Second, it is discriminatory in its own way. The Ontario Law Reform Commission has rejected it on the basis that it is unfair, because it compensates the same work at different rates.[164] In other words, two homemakers, doing identical work in the home, would receive very different awards where their previous education and work history were different. Finally, courts are concerned about the slippery slope. If women were compensated according to their opportunity costs rather than their actual

---

161 *Boughey v. Rogers, ibid.*
162 See, for example, C.J. Bruce, *Assessment of Personal Injury Damages* (Toronto: Butterworths, 1985) at 172.
163 *Lang v. Porter* (1991), 57 B.C.L.R. (2d) 253 (C.A.).
164 Ontario Law Reform Commission, *Report on Compensation for Personal Injuries and Death* (Toronto: Ministry of the Attorney General, 1987) at 46.

pecuniary losses, everyone would demand to be treated this way; for who ever works at his full capacity? This concern was well expressed by Taylor J.A. in *Kroeker:*

> The fact that the courts have spoken of earning capacity as a "capital asset" gives support to this [opportunity-cost] thesis. But the truth is that compensation is given in these cases only for actual and anticipated pecuniary loss, or for substantial possibilities of future pecuniary loss—for the loss of money which the plaintiff might reasonably have earned, but for the injury. Compensation is not granted for loss of future earning capacity at large, but for loss of that capacity *to the extent* that it is reasonable to expect that the particular plaintiff might, but for the accident, have employed that capacity for the purpose of generating actual income.
>
> ... [otherwise] compensation would justifiably be awarded not only for loss of the market value of union and other unpaid occupation-related work, church, synagogue and temple-related work, parent-teacher association, amateur sport, legion, scouts, guides, political, charitable and other public service volunteer work, gratuitous hobby activities, child-minding, chauffeuring and the like, which the plaintiff would otherwise have done and by reason of the accident can no longer do, but also for extra earnings which by more remunerative application of his or her abilities the plaintiff could have obtained but chose not to seek, and which there was no reason to expect that the plaintiff would have sought in the future. Pecuniary damages would cease to reflect actual income loss, and come instead to reflect income which would have been lost had the plaintiff pursued a different, and more economically-productive, way of life. This would radically change the system, and impose greatly increased cost on the public. I know of no way in which the courts, if such claims are to be allowed, could restrict or restrain awards in future, and the fact that a small amount is involved in this case by no means assures us that future claims, and resulting awards, would be modest. So much work of value is done without reward by all sorts of people, whether for themselves, their households, families, friends or community, and so many choose to accept for their labour lower remuneration than its real value in the market place.[165]

---

165 Above note 56 at 197–98 [emphasis in original].

G. COMPENSATION FOR LOST HOMEMAKING CAPACITY AND LOST FAMILY INCOME

1) Introduction to the Claim

To a large extent, much of the bias in awards to women results from assuming that many women leave the paid workforce to take on family responsibilities (which is true), and that this reduces their economic value or their earning capacity (which is false). While leaving the workforce certainly reduces *income*, it does not necessarily reduce the value of a person's economic *capacity* or the value of their work (as a parent or homemaker). While courts have by and large rejected the opportunity-cost approach, there is an alternative approach that does recognize the economic value of work in the home.

Even if the focus is on *actual work*, as opposed to earning capacity, leaving the workforce to work in the home (for free) does not eliminate a person's economic productivity. The work that she performs has substantial economic value and can be valued in order to arrive at a measure of her earning capacity.[166] In areas other than personal injury law, courts have recognized the unpaid contributions of homemakers. For example, in family property disputes the Supreme Court of Canada has strongly reaffirmed the economic value of household work. In *Peter v. Beblow*[167] the Court imposed a constructive trust on property to recognize the unpaid contribution of the plaintiff, who had acted as wife and mother for the previous twelve years. The Court strongly rejected the argument that such services should not be valued. McLachlin J. stated:

> The notion that household and childcare services are not worthy of recognition by the court fails to recognize the fact that these services are of great value.... The notion, moreover, is a pernicious one

---

166 Statistics Canada has estimated that the total value of unpaid household labour in Canada in 1992 amounted to somewhere between 31 percent and 46 percent of gross domestic product. The estimated annual replacement cost of the unpaid work performed by a woman is $16,580 ($9,960 for men): B. Chandler, *The Value of Household Work in Canada, 1992* (Ottawa: Statistics Canada, 1994); *General Social Survey, The 1992 General Social Survey—Cycle 7, Time Use: Microdata File Documentation and User's Guide* (Ottawa: Statistics Canada, 1993); *General Social Survey, Initial Data Release from the 1992 General Social Survey on Time Use* (Ottawa: Statistics Canada, 1993). The estimated value of unpaid work in Canada in 1998 was $297 billion. Between 1992 and 1998, the value of unpaid work increased by 183 percent: Malika Hamdad, *Valuing Households' Unpiad Work in Canada, 1992 and 1998: Trends and sources of change* (Ottawa: Statistics Canada, 2003).

167 [1993] 1 S.C.R. 980.

that systematically devalues the contributions which women tend to make to the family economy. It has contributed to the phenomenon of the feminization of poverty.[168]

It follows that awards for personal injury compensation might also reflect the economic value of housekeeping and caregiving capacity, even when unpaid. Ironically, recovery for the economic loss of housekeeping and caregiving has long been available to surviving family members in fatal accident cases.[169] Awards to the surviving spouse and children of a deceased mother solely for lost housekeeping can be in the order of $15,000 per annum.[170] Only recently has such recognition been extended to claims by women themselves when they are injured.

The leading case in the personal injury area is *Fobel v. Dean*.[171] The fifty-one-year-old female plaintiff was severely injured in an automobile accident. Prior to the accident she had worked full time in the family bakery business and was also the primary caregiver in the home. At trial no award was made specifically for lost homemaking capacity. On appeal, the award was increased on the basis that the ability to perform unpaid labour in the home should be fully compensated when lost. The court based the award on the replacement cost of such work and, using time-use studies, estimated a diminution in capacity of about fifteen hours per week, and the value of such lost capacity at $5.50 per hour.[172]

In *Benko* [173] the court explained the theoretical basis of compensation for unpaid labour in the following way:

---

168 *Ibid.* at 993.
169 *St. Lawrence & Ottawa Railway Co. v. Lett* (1885), 11 S.C.R. 422. See discussion in Chapter 5.
170 See, for example, *Kwok v. British Columbia Ferry Corp.* (1987), 20 B.C.L.R. (2d) 318 (S.C.), aff'd (1989), 37 B.C.L.R. 236 (C.A.) in which the British Columbia Supreme Court assessed the value of housework of a woman who also held down a full-time job (described as a "truly remarkable wife and mother") at $15,000 per year. See also *Grant v. Jackson* (1986), 24 D.L.R. (4th) 598 (B.C.C.A.); *Jantz v. Mulvahill*, [1989] B.C.J. No. 2346 (S.C.): value of homemaking services to the family set at $1,500 per month or $16,800 per year in addition to lost financial benefits; aff'd (1992), 11 B.C.A.C. 127 (C.A.).
171 (1991), 83 D.L.R. (4th) 385 (Sask. C.A.) [*Fobel*].
172 There was evidence that domestic services cost approximately $7.50 on a straight hourly basis, but that this amount could be reduced by 30 percent if the services were performed on a monthly basis. The judge further held that, while compensation for loss of home management services should be compensated for at a higher rate or on some other basis than the above calculation, there was no evidence before the court upon which to make such a finding. Therefore, he was confined to only being able to quantify the loss on the basis of the direct labour component. The plaintiff was awarded a total of $79,698.24 for loss of future housekeeping capacity.
173 Above note 84.

A person gains economic benefit by earnings from his occupation, and, additionally by doing for himself those things, such as building his own garage or mowing his own lawn, which produce an economic gain or saving. This multiform loss is categorized under "loss of homemaking capacity". It is an economic loss and must not duplicate the loss of the enjoyment which he would otherwise have taken from doing these things for himself, which latter loss is an amenity of life to be considered under the head "nonpecuniary damages" and is subject to the trilogy cap.[174]

Fobel has been adopted as the law in most common law provinces[175] and a number of ancillary rules have been established: (1) diminished capacity is divided into direct labour and management and calculated on the basis of a replacement-cost approach; (2) the duration of the award for diminished housekeeping capacity is based on the entire pre-accident lifespan. Retirement from the waged workforce does not mean retirement from household chores, though quantum of work may vary over time; and (3) the award is not confined to full-time homemakers but is available to anyone who can demonstrate diminished capacity, including men.[176] The principles of measuring the value of unpaid work are addressed in more detail in Chapter 5 in the context of fatal accident claims (where the principles have been better developed).

Fobel v. Dean has been rejected in one Ontario case.[177] In Ontario, where the plaintiff spends funds on a replacement homemaker, that expenditure is compensable as part of the cost of future care. Where family members provide homemaking services to an injured person, they may have an independent claim under the *Family Law Act*.[178] However, courts do not appear to be compensating persons for their "pure" loss of homemaking capacity where there is no pecuniary loss.

---

174 *Ibid.* at 165.
175 *Fobel*, above note 171, has been considered in a number of recent cases: *Knoblauch v. Biwer Estate*, [1992] 5 W.W.R. 725 (Sask. Q.B.): award made; *Mayes v. Ferguson* (1992), 102 Sask. R. 250 (Q.B.): damages for lost housekeeping capacity are available even when no loss of earnings; *Grimard v. Berry* (1992), 102 Sask. R. 137 (Q.B.) [*Grimard*]; *Silva v. Miller*, [1993] B.C.J. No. 454 (S.C.): award made; *Vykysaly v. Jablowski* (1992), 8 O.R. (3d) 181 (Gen. Div.) [*Vykysaly*]: loss of housekeeping capacity considered a non-pecuniary loss of enjoyment of life; and *Fobel*, *ibid.*, rejected in Ontario.
176 *Benko*, above note 84.
177 *Vykysaly*, above note 175.
178 R.S.O. 1990, c. F.3, s. 61.

2) Compensation for Diminished Housekeeping Capacity

The main issue of controversy is whether compensation for diminished homemaking capacity should be awarded even when the plaintiff will incur no additional expenses to obtain replacement labour. This problem is related to the issue of collateral benefits, because it usually arises when the plaintiff has suffered a loss of homemaking capacity and those functions are taken over by a family member.

One view is that the loss should be treated as a pecuniary one only where the plaintiff will actually incur housekeeping expenses in the future (i.e., that the loss is analogous to the cost of care). The other view is explained by the English Court of Appeal in *Daly v. General Steam Navigation Co. Ltd., The Dragon*,[179] which held that

> [w]here the person concerned is a housewife, who is disabled wholly or partly from doing housekeeping in her own home, she does not suffer an actual loss of earnings, and unless a substitute is employed, she may not suffer any pecuniary loss at all. Nevertheless, she is just as much disabled from doing her unpaid job as an employed person is disabled from doing his paid one, and I think that she is, in principle, entitled to be compensated separately for her loss in a similar way.[180]

This approach has been adopted by the British Columbia Court of Appeal. In *Kroeker*[181] the plaintiff was disabled from doing housework but her spouse took over those tasks and thus the plaintiff incurred no additional expenses. Nevertheless, following *Daly*, the court held that she was entitled to compensation for the pecuniary loss of diminished housekeeping capacity.

But the law in Canada is neither settled nor uniform in this area. Many judges and courts are not comfortable with the idea that the loss of housekeeping capacity is a true pecuniary loss, if money is not actually going to be needed to replace the loss. In a strongly worded dissent in *Kroeker*, Taylor J.A. disagreed that the loss should be compensated. The question, he said, is whether the plaintiff will reasonably require paid household help. To award damages for lost housekeeping capacity in these circumstances "would in my view be to alter the nature of the compensation system in a way which would, in any event, involve income redistribution rather than restitution, and thus require legislative approval."[182]

---

179 [1980] 3 All E.R. 696 (C.A.).
180 *Ibid.* at 700.
181 Above note 56.
182 *Ibid.* at 197.

Despite the fact that Taylor J.A. was speaking in dissent, the concerns he expressed are shared by others. The current state of the law is that courts appear to be following *Kroeker* in word but not always in deed. The basis of compensation is the plaintiffs' inability to perform services they were able to do prior to their injury. Entitlement to an award for future impaired housekeeping capacity as a separate head of damage therefore depends on evidence of diminished capacity and not necessarily on actual expenditure of money or the possibility of hiring replacement services to perform the services in question.[183] However, some courts continue to insist on proof that an actual pecuniary loss will be incurred before providing compensation for diminished housekeeping capacity as a separate head of damage.[184] Where there is evidence that the plaintiff might purchase household services but it is uncertain the extent of such services that may be required, some courts have awarded global sums for this head of damage.[185] Where awards are made for such losses they are generally quite modest. Where the plaintiff continues to perform the tasks but with difficulty or manages to get by without doing or intending to do those tasks, the loss may be compensated for as part of non-pecuniary damages for pain and suffering and loss of amenity.[186]

---

183 *Morel v. Bryden* (2006), 246 N.S.R. (2d) 43 (S.C.); *Carter v. Anderson* (1998), 168 N.S.R. (2d) 297 (C.A.); *Sinclair*, above note 68 at paras. 20 and 22. In *Leddicote v. Nova Scotia (Attorney General)* (2002), 203 N.S.R. (2d) 271 (C.A.) [*Leddicote*], Saunders J.A. noted that, while payment for household services in the pre-trial period may be useful evidence in support of the plaintiff's entitlment to a separate award for future impaired housekeeping capacity, this is not determinative. Courts have continued to rely on the majority decision in *Kroeker*, above note 56, to consider the plaintiff's past and future impaired housekeeping capacity as a pecuniary loss and awarded damages accordingly where services have been gratuitously performed by family members and friends. The value of work performed by those offering assistance is taken as an indication of the value of the plaintiff's loss: *McTavish v. MacGillivray* (2000), 74 B.C.L.R. (3d) 281 (C.A.) [*McTavish*]; *Deglow*, above note 58; *Bourcher v. Doiron* (2000), 230 N.B.R. (2d) 247 (C.A.); *Miller v. Folkertsma Farms Ltd.* (2001), 197 N.S.R. (2d) 282 (C.A.) [*Miller*]; *Weinmuller v. Tait*, 2006 BCSC 416; *Kartz v. Carlson*, 2006 BCSC 716.

184 *Woods v. Hubley* (1995), 146 N.S.R. (2d) 97 (C.A.); *Leddicote, ibid.*

185 *Byron v. Larson* (2004), 37 Alta. L.R. (4th) 8 (C.A.); *Banga v. Takhar* (2003), 22 B.C.L.R. (4th) 372 (S.C.); *Murphy v. 2331653 Nova Scotia Ltd. (Bulk Barn)*, 2004 NSSC 142; *Miller*, above note 183.

186 *Fobel*, above note 171; *McTavish*, above note 183 at paras. 51 and 69; *Leo (Litigation guardian of) v. Leo*, 2005 BCSC 1300; *Novakovic v. Wasylyshyn*, 2006 BCSC 338 at para. 67. *Leddicote*, above note 183; *Sinclair*, above note 68 at paras. 21 and 25. This position is potentially unfair to plaintiffs who are unable to afford to hire replacement services or who do not have family members who can step in to perform those tasks. As well, given the exercise of restraint in awarding

3) Compensation for Loss of Interdependent Relationship

If, as a result of the accident, the plaintiff is less likely to form a relationship of interdependence with another person (through marriage
or other financial interdependency), he may be able to claim compensation for this as an economic loss. The theory is that, by forming an
economic union, two people achieve higher income, generate greater
joint savings, and share household work and expenses.[187] Thus, the
lost opportunity to form such a relationship represents an economic
loss. In addition, for women who form an economic union with a man,
statistically, the male partner is likely to have greater earnings. So,
if an accident reduces the likelihood that a woman will form such a
union, compensation is sometimes made. This claim, which at one time
was referred to as "loss of marriage prospects," is now called "loss of
interdependent relationship." The amount can be substantial, typically
ranging from $50,000 to $150,000. In *Reekie v. Messervey*,[188] the British
Columbia Court of Appeal explained:

> This aspect of the damage award was called "loss of opportunity to
> marry.... But marriage itself is not the significant point. The signifi-
> cance lies in the loss of an opportunity to form a permanent inter-
> dependency relationship which may be expected to produce financial
> benefits in the form of shared family income. Such an interdepend-
> ency might have been formed with a close friend of either sex or with
> a person with whom a plaintiff might have lived as husband and wife,
> but without any marriage having taken place. Permanent financial
> interdependency, not marriage, is the gist of the claim.[189]

It is now common for courts to award damages under this head.
They may be awarded to men as well as women, and are theoretically
available to gay men and lesbians who might also be deprived of the
chance of forming an economic union. There is, however, uncertainty
in the law as to whether and when this award should be made. First,
there must be actual evidence that the tort has reduced the prospects
that the plaintiff will form a relationship of financial interdependency.
This requires judges to assess the "marriageability" of the plaintiff. The
burden of proving this is upon the plaintiff, who must lead evidence

---

non-pecuniary damages, compensation for impaired housekeeping as part of
non-pecuniary damages will be subject to the cap and, even when the cap is not
in issue, will often be modest.

187 For example, see *Walker,* above note 124.
188 (1989), 59 D.L.R. (4th) 481 (B.C.C.A.).
189 *Ibid.* at 494.

and argument that she is now less likely to form a relationship, and the approach invites arguments about other reasons why the plaintiff might be unlikely to form relationships.[190] This process is distinctly unsavoury. It has been suggested that proof of loss under this head may readily be assumed in cases involving significant or catastrophic injuries but the evidence of loss in other cases should be corroborated by testimony from family members, friends, and other acquaintances as well as expert opinion.[191] Second, the award is not available to women who, at the time of the accident, are already involved in a relationship—unless they, too, are prepared to prove that as a result of the accident that relationship is likely to dissolve; there must be a real and substantial possibility that the relationship will not last.[192] Again this could be a difficult and distasteful task (though possible as in cases where, following the accident, an existing marriage has ended).[193] Third, there must be evidence that in the circumstances such an interdependency would have enhanced the plaintiff's economic prospects. Again, the evidentiary burden is upon the plaintiff, and awards have been denied because of the impossibility of proving whether a relationship might have had positive or negative financial implications.[194]

Fourth, and most problematically, some courts refuse to make the award (or reduce it substantially) on the basis that, while the plaintiff may have reduced prospects of marrying, she will also be spared the "costs" of marriage, in particular, the costs of raising children. As one judge concluded,

> it would be improper for the present purpose to ignore the fact that were she to be married and to have children the plaintiff would be exposed to the costs of child-raising, and that from these costs she will now probably be spared. To approach the matter in the present context as counsel for the plaintiff wishes—to treat marriage, in this context, as a cost-free pecuniary gain—would in my view be to ignore basic principles of our compensation system, and to grant "overlapping" or "double" compensation.[195]

---

190 For example, *Grimard*, above note 175: no award made because the plaintiff's relationship had been deteriorating before the accident.
191 *Hartwick*, above note 124.
192 *Roussin*, above note 30.
193 *McKenzie v. Van-Kam Freightways Ltd.*, [1990] B.C.J. No. 868 (S.C.) involved a young couple who separated two years after the accident and were in the midst of divorce proceedings at the time of the trial.
194 *Gray v. Reeves* (1992), 89 D.L.R. (4th) 315 (B.C.S.C.).
195 *Newell v. Hawthornthwaite* (1988), 26 B.C.L.R. (2d) 105 at 112 (S.C.).

This reasoning, while commonly applied to reduce the award,[196] seems conceptually incorrect. The cost of having and raising children does not affect family *income*, it affects family *expenditure*. Thus, the fact that a young man may be "spared" the costs of children as the result of an injury has never been used as a basis for reducing the amount of his claim for lost income.

H. DISCOUNTING TO PRESENT VALUE

Future losses, both the cost of care and lost earning capacity, are awarded in a lump sum. Because the award compensates the plaintiff at the time of trial for a loss or expense that may not actually be incurred for many years, it must be "discounted" to present value. Otherwise the plaintiff will be overcompensated.

A dollar today is worth more than a dollar a year from now because when invested it will yield additional income. To provide an example, a court may find that a plaintiff will require $1,000 per year for a period of ten years. It would be wrong, however, simply to award $10,000 because that sum, invested in the present, is worth a good deal more than that. Thus, future losses must be "discounted" to present value.

In setting the "discount rate," two factors must be taken into account. The first is that the lump sum will be earning interest when invested. The second, however, is that at the same time, inflation will be eroding the purchasing power of money. The "real" rate of return, therefore, is the long-term rate of interest, minus the rate of inflation over that same period. In *Andrews* and *Thornton* the Supreme Court approved a 7 percent discount rate. It arrived at this figure based on evidence that long-term investment income might be in the range of 10 percent, while long-term inflation would be at 3.5 to 4 percent.

In the years after the trilogy, several commentators and law reform commissions concluded that the Supreme Court had seriously erred in setting the discount rate.[197] Most economists are of the view that the real rate of return on money is more in the neighbourhood of 3 percent. The figure of 10 percent that the Court accepted as the rate of return on investments can be seen (with the benefit of hindsight) to have been based on an expectation of inflation much higher than 3 percent. The Supreme Court later made it clear that the discount rate

---

196 *Cherry*, above note 137, var'g (1990), 75 D.L.R. (4th) 668 at 720 (B.C.S.C.). Considered in *Bates v. Nichol* (1996), 20 B.C.L.R. (3d) 248 (S.C.).
197 See D. Gibson, "Repairing the Law of Damages" (1978) 8 Man. L.J. 637.

was not fixed in stone, and in later cases it permitted the use of much lower figures.[198]

Some provinces have set a discount rate by statute, generally at a much lower figure. In Ontario, for example, the discount rate is 2.5 percent.[199] In British Columbia the rate is 2.5 percent for lost earnings and 3.5 percent for the cost of future care.[200] The difference between the rates in British Columbia is intended to take into account "productivity gains" in wage rates; that is, it incorporates an assumption that wages increase at a rate slightly higher than inflation.

The legislation of the discount rate avoids the need for protracted economic evidence and argument. In those jurisdictions without legislation, the discount rate is now usually set at a figure in the range of 3 to 4 percent, though only after the time and expense of actuarial and economic testimony.[201]

I. NON-PECUNIARY DAMAGES

Non-pecuniary damages are awarded for intangible losses, such as pain and suffering, loss of amenities, loss of enjoyment of life, and loss of expectation of life. Such damages, by their nature, are less susceptible to a "scientific" or itemized approach than are pecuniary losses. As the Supreme Court of Canada said in *Andrews,*

> [t]here is no medium of exchange for happiness. There is no market for expectation of life. The monetary evaluation of non-pecuniary losses is a philosophical and policy exercise more than a legal or logical one. The award must be fair and reasonable, fairness being gauged by earlier decisions; but the award must also of necessity be arbitrary or conventional. No money can provide true restitution.[202]

Because the elements of non-pecuniary damages are subjective, and because the categories of pain and suffering, loss of amenities, and loss

---

198 For example, in *Lewis*, above note 50, the Court adopted a discount rate of 2.25 percent.
199 *Rules of Civil Procedure*, above note 64, r. 53.09(1); see also Nova Scotia *Civil Procedure Rules* under the *Judicature Act*, R.S.N.S. 1989, c. 240, r. 31.10(2); New Brunswick *Rules of Court*, N.B. Reg. 82-73, r. 54.10(2)
200 *Law and Equity Act*, R.S.B.C. 1996, c. 253, s.56; British Columbia Reg. 352/81.
201 *Beam v. Pittman* (1994), 122 Nfld. & P.E.I.R. 181 (Nfld. T.D.), aff'd (1997) 147 Nfld. & P.E.I.R. 166 (Nfld. C.A.); *Fitch v. Willow Creek (Municipal District)*, [1993] A.J. No. 1081 (Q.B.); *Hilliard v. Grabinski*, [1998] A.J. No. 601 at para. 267 (Q.B.).
202 *Andrews*, above note 2 at 261.

of expectation of life overlap, non-pecuniary compensation is not item-ized in the same way as pecuniary losses. Instead, it is assessed globally and awarded in one lump sum.

1) The Functional Approach

In the 1978 damages trilogy, the Supreme Court adopted what it referred to as a "functional approach" to the assessment of non-pecuniary dam-ages. The Court rejected the "conceptual approach," which attempts to analogize injured faculties to lost property or assets and to place an ob-jective value on those lost assets. It also rejected the "personal approach," which attempts to measure the lost happiness subjectively experienced by the plaintiff. Instead, the Court said that a functional approach should be followed, where the primary focus is on providing a measure of "solace" for the plaintiff's misfortune. This refers to an amount that can be used for physical and other arrangements to make the plaintiff's life more tolerable and pleasurable. As the Court explained, "[m]oney is awarded because it will serve a useful function in making up for what has been lost in the only way possible, accepting that what has been lost is incapable of being replaced in any direct way."[203]

2) Non-Pecuniary Damages: The Ceiling

Despite the greater rationality promised by the functional approach, such damages will still be largely conventional and arbitrary. In the trilogy, the Supreme Court expressed grave concerns about the danger that such awards would vary too greatly among provincial jurisdictions and escalate beyond acceptable levels. Thus, based on policy considera-tions, the Court placed a ceiling of $100,000 on non-pecuniary dam-ages. It justified this ceiling by noting that, with the new attempt to provide full and generous compensation for all pecuniary losses, the award for non-pecuniary loss could be made less central to the overall compensation goal. Moreover, because there is no objective yardstick for pain and suffering, the area is open to extravagant claims. The Court viewed with some alarm stories from the United States about escalating awards that were said to be producing a "liability chill" and "insurance crisis" and concluded that the "social burden" of large awards was a genuine consideration in assessing non-pecuniary losses.

The $100,000 figure was said to be a "rough upper limit" that, except in exceptional circumstances, would establish a scale that could be used to

---

203 *Ibid.* at 262.

assess awards in less catastrophic cases.[204] In subsequent years the figure has been increased to take inflation into account, so that in 2007 the ceiling has been in the range of $310,000. While several courts have sought to justify higher awards by referring to "exceptional circumstances," these decisions have consistently been overruled.[205] Thus, notwithstanding some concerns about the continuing applicability of the conceptual basis for the cap on non-pecuniary damages, it may be said that, in ordinary personal injury cases, the "rough upper limit" is in fact a firm ceiling on awards. This is intended to limit what could otherwise be unlimited amount of damages in some cases.[206] As Hall J.A. said in *Brimacombe*, "The rough upper limit is, rather like a governor on an engine, a device that limits what otherwise could be an unlimited sum of damages."[207]

In the case of *Lindal v. Lindal*,[208] the Supreme Court overturned a British Columbia Supreme Court award in excess of the maximum. The trial judge had reasoned that the injuries of the plaintiff were more severe than those in the trilogy and were thus "exceptional circumstances." The Supreme Court reaffirmed both the functional approach and the ceiling, explaining that the relevant question was not simply how serious were the plaintiff's injuries compared to other cases, but what function money could serve in ameliorating the loss. The trial judge erred in simply comparing the severity of injuries and valuing "lost assets":

> Thus the amount of an award for non-pecuniary damage should not depend alone upon the seriousness of the injury but upon its ability to ameliorate the condition of the victim considering his or her particular situation. It therefore will not follow that in considering what part of the maximum should be awarded the gravity of the injury alone will be determinative. An appreciation of the individual's loss is the key and the "need for solace will not necessarily correlate with the seriousness of the injury."[209]

The Court also affirmed the need for a firm ceiling, reiterating the view that the claims that could be made are virtually limitless, the amounts

---

204 The rough upper limit is awarded in cases of severe or catastrophic personal injury without making distinctions between the different types of injuries. See *Spehar*, above note 28; *Aberdeen v. Langley (Township)*, 2007 BCSC 993.

205 For example, see *Lee*, above note 22: jury award of $2 million non-pecuniary damages reduced to rough upper limit.

206 See *Brimacombe*, above note 101; *Boyd v. Harris* (2004), 24 B.C.L.R. (4th) 155 (C.A.); *Fullerton*, above note 25.

207 *Brimacombe*, *ibid.* at para. 243.

208 *Lindal v. Lindal (No. 2)*, [1981] 2 S.C.R. 629 [*Lindal*].

209 *Ibid.* at 637.

are essentially arbitrary, and the social burden of damage awards must be contained.

In *ter Neuzen v. Korn*,[210] the Supreme Court again affirmed the "rough upper limit" for non-pecuniary damages and held that the infection of the plaintiff with HIV from artificial insemination was not an "exceptional case" justifying any deviation from the rule. The Court ruled that, ordinarily, jury members should not be instructed as to the upper limit in order that they not be unduly influenced by it. However, where the case is likely to produce an award at or above the upper limit, the judge is to instruct the jury as to that limit (L'Heureux-Dubé J. dissenting on this point). Where the jury awards a sum in excess of the upper limit, the trial judge is to reduce the award.

3) Application of the Functional Approach

a) General Principles

In theory, the functional approach provides a rationale and a basis for making awards. The amount of non-pecuniary damages would be calibrated by examining the seriousness of the injuries suffered by the plaintiff, and assessing the physical and other arrangements that money might usefully be spent on in order to provide a measure of solace to the plaintiff. In *Lindal*,[211] the Supreme Court reiterated that the amount of the award should be based not only on the seriousness of the injury but also on its capacity to ameliorate the condition of the plaintiff in his particular circumstances. In *ter Neuzen* the Court again confirmed that non-pecuniary damages should be awarded "to the extent that they can serve a useful purpose by providing an alternative source of satisfaction."[212] This suggests that the plaintiff should develop evidence regarding the way in which money might be used to provide solace.

However, in practice, the functional approach is applied in a more pragmatic, even mechanistic, way. Indeed, in *Andrews*[213] itself, the Supreme Court recognized that elements of both the conceptual and the personal approach would be retained in the application of the functional approach. It suggested that awards should be roughly similar for persons with similar injuries, but also that they might be different if the subjective experience of the plaintiff was different. So, for example, the loss of a finger would be a greater loss for an amateur pianist than for a person not

---

210 [1995] 3 S.C.R. 674 [*ter Neuzen*].
211 Above note 208.
212 Above note 210 at 723.
213 Above note 2.

engaged in such an activity. Greater compensation would be required to provide things and activities that would function to make up for this loss. The other variable that makes an appreciable difference is the age of the plaintiff since the younger the plaintiff, the longer the pain and suffering that will be experienced and the greater the need for solace. In addition, where the plaintiff is likely to require future painful or inconvenient surgical treatments, this is often mentioned as an aggravating factor.

Thus, despite the language of the functional approach, courts ordinarily calibrate non-pecuniary losses by examining cases in which similar injuries have been suffered, or by comparing the particular plaintiff's injuries to those suffered in the trilogy. The quantum of the award is then set on a proportionate basis. The most serious cases will attract damages at the maximum. Less serious injuries are compensated on an informal scale. Moderate soft-tissue injuries—whiplash, for example—generally fall within a range between $20,000 and $50,000,[214] with more severe cases of such injury attracting damages in the order of $50,000 to $125,000 (when there is evidence that the injury will result in a severe impairment of lifestyle owing to pain, fatigue, and psychological consequences).[215] As well, the range of non-pecuniary damages for mild traumatic brain injury with long-term effect has been $75,000 to $120,000.[216] Some provinces have also capped non-pecuniary damages for plainitffs who suffer minor injuries in motor vehicle accidents. Damages are capped at $2,500 in New Brunswick and Nova Scotia,[217] and $4,000 in Alberta.[218] Factors determining quantum include

---

214 *Cory v. Marsh* (1993), 77 B.C.L.R. (2d) 248 (C.A.); *Joyce v. Dorvault*, 2007 BCSC 786; *Kandag v. Di Vora*, 2007 BCSC 717; *Gilroy v. Schmidt*, 2006 ABQB 214; *Krause v. Gill*, 2006 BCSC 1459; *Shum v. Viveiros*, 2006 BCSC 158. In *Toor v. Toor*, 2007 BCCA 354, involving a seventy-year-old plaintiff who suffered soft-tissue injuries to her neck and back resulting in lasting effects that diminished her quality of life, the court found the award of $10,000 to be inordinately low and remitted the case back for a re-determination of the proper amount of damages.

215 For examples, see *Deglow*, above note 58; *Unger v. Singh* (2000), 72 B.C.L.R. (3d) 353 (C.A.); *Abbott v. Sharpe* (2007), 250 N.S.R. (2d) 228 (C.A.) [*Abbott*]; *Djukic v. Hahn*, 2006 BCSC 154, aff'd 2007 BCCA 203; *Parfitt v. Mayes*, 2006 BCSC 125; *Stapley v. Hejslet* (2006), 263 D.L.R. (4th) 19 (B.C.C.A.), leave to appeal to S.C.C. refused, [2006] S.C.C.A. No. 100; *Maillet v. Rosenau*, 2006 BCSC 10; *Love v. Lowden*, [2007] B.C.J. No 1506 (S.C.); *Jackson*, above note 72; *Ganderton v. Brown* (2004), 33 Alta. L.R. (4th) 271 (Q.B.).

216 See *Watt v. Meier*, 2006 BCSC 1341; *Clarke v. Hebb*, 2007 BCSC 883; *Repole v. Bakker*, 2007 BCSC 592.

217 *Injury Regulation—Insurance Act*, N.B. Reg. 2003-20, s. 4; *Automobile Insurance Tort Recovery Limitation Regulations*, N.S. Reg. 182/2003, s. 3.

218 *Minor Injury Regulation*, Alta. Reg. 123/2004, s. 6. For critques of legislative caps on non-pecuniary damages, see Barbara Billingsley, "Legislative Reform and

the ability to appreciate what has been lost; awareness of, or interest in, what was happening around the plaintiff; response to human
interaction; displays of pleasure, enjoyment, pain and sadness; attempts to communicate or initiate interaction with others; atten-
tional abilities; memory ability; and life expectancy. A determination
of the appropriate level of non-pecuniary damages will thus depend
upon the findings of fact as to the level of cognitive impairment experienced by [plaintiff].[219]

It is rare for courts to discuss the basis of the award in terms of the
functions that money might serve in the particular case, or the actual arrangements that might be made to provide solace. Indeed, such evidence
has made no difference in serious cases. For example, in *ter Neuzen*[220]
Sopinka J. acknowledged that evidence had been adduced as to the solace
that a large award for non-pecuniary loss might bring to the plaintiff,
who had contracted an HIV infection from an artificial insemination procedure. However, he preferred to compare the plaintiff's circumstances
to those of the plaintiffs in the trilogy, keeping in mind the social burden
of excessive awards, in order to justify restricting the damages for non-
pecuniary loss. The current situation is perhaps best described by Ryan
J.A. (Turnbull and Bastarache JJ.A. concurring) in *Kinsella v. Logan*:[221]
"[T]he Supreme Court of Canada has not provided much enlightenment
on the functional approach which it advocates."[222]

Thus, in the years since the trilogy, courts have by and large returned to the older "comparative" method of damages assessment. The
lasting impact of *Andrews* is that the comparison is now carried out
with a scale that has a maximum figure.

b)   The Unconscious Plaintiff

Taken to its logical extreme, the functional approach might imply that
severely brain-damaged or comatose plaintiffs should receive little or
nothing in non-pecuniary damages. In these cases, the argument would

---

Equal Access to the Justice System: An Examination of Alberta's New Minor
Injury Cap in the Context of Section 15 of the *Canadian Charter of Rights and
Freedoms*" (2005) 42 Alta. L. Rev. 711; Jeremy Taylor, "Re-thinking *Whitebread
v. Walley*: Liberal Justice and the Judicial Review of Damages Caps under Section 7 of the *Charter of Rights and Freedoms*" (2006) 29 Dalhousie L.J. 199.

219 *Bystedt*, above note 30 at para. 148. See also *Suveges*, above note 27; *Arce*, above
note 46.

220 Above note 210.

221 (1996), 179 N.B.R. (2d) 161 (C.A.).

222 *Ibid.* at para. 25.

be that money could not serve any rational function in providing solace and there is no purpose in making an award.

Some courts have applied the strict logic of the functional approach and have awarded only small sums to comatose or severely brain-damaged plaintiffs. For example, in *Semenoff*[223] the British Columbia Supreme Court awarded only $25,000 to a plaintiff who, as a result of an accident, was reduced to a "semi-vegetative state." The plaintiff was not entirely unconscious and did react to music and some stimulation. Other cases have followed this same approach.[224]

A recent case illustrating the influence of the functional approach is *Horita (Committee of) v. Graham*.[225] Following a rare jury trial of civil liability, the plaintiff's counsel submitted that the judge should refuse to accept the jury's verdict with respect to the assessment of non-pecuniary damages. The jury had assessed at zero the damages sustained by the plaintiff for non-pecuniary loss; that is, pain, suffering, and loss of enjoyment of life.[226]

The plaintiff was an eighty-six-year-old, injured while disembarking from a bus. She sustained a traumatic brain injury that permanently disabled her, requiring institutionalization. She could not consistently identify family members, although she was able to distinguish them from strangers. She felt pain and recognized "threatening behaviour" but was not fully aware of her surroundings.[227] Sigurdson J. confirmed the jury's verdict finding the plaintiff had been contributorily negligent and also that she was not entitled to non-pecuniary damages. He considered the caselaw referred to above and concluded as follows: "Under the functional approach to damages, the question of whether or not non-pecuniary damages would be useful to a severely injured plaintiff is a question of fact."[228]

Increasingly, some Canadian courts are awarding substantially higher awards, even at the rough upper limit, in cases involving severely injured plaintiffs with very limited cognitive abilities and/or appreciation of their condition and environment.[229] These awards have

---

223 Above note 52.
224 See also *Knutson v. Farr* (1984), 12 D.L.R. (4th) 658 (B.C.C.A.); *Wipfli*, above note 45; *Toneguzzo*, above note 97; *Brown*, above note 104: $35,000 to severely brain-injured child in a near-vegetative state.
225 [1997] B.C.J. No. 2880 (S.C.).
226 *Ibid.* at para. 1.
227 *Ibid.* at para. 39.
228 *Ibid.* at para. 49.
229 See *Strachan (Guardian ad litem of) v. Reynolds*, 2004 BCSC 915: severe spastic quadriplegic with minimal degree of awareness and no awareness of his condition

been justified as allowing the plaintiffs to improve their lives in small ways that, although they may seem insignificant to people not living with disabilities, mean a lot to these plaintiffs.[230]

Other common law jurisdictions have also shown reluctance to award non-economic damages to an unaware plaintiff. For example, the leading Australian case is *Skelton v. Collins*[231] in which the High Court made no award for pain and suffering to a permanently unconscious plaintiff. Windeyer J. stated:

> I am unable myself to understand how monetary compensation for the deprivation of the ability to live out life with faculties of mind and body unimpaired can be based upon an evaluation of a thing lost. It must surely be based upon solace for a condition created not upon payment for something taken away. [232]

c) Criticism and Exceptions

The ceiling on non-pecuniary damages is controversial and may someday be revisited.[233] In setting the cap in *Andrews*,[234] the Supreme Court referred to the danger of "extravagant claims" and the fact that such awards had "soared to dramatically high levels" in the United States. It concluded that the "social burden" of large damage awards should be guarded against. And in *Teno*, Spence J. reaffirmed that

> [t]he very real and serious social burden of these exorbitant awards has been illustrated graphically in the United States in cases concerning medical malpractice. We have a right to fear a situation where none but the very wealthy could own or drive automobiles because

---

and his quality of life was expected to deteriorate ($175,000); *Guerineau*, above note 26: spastic quadriplegic, cerebral palsy, epilepsy, and severe mental retardation; limited awareness ($200,000); *M.D. (Guardian ad litem of) v. British Columbia*, 2000 BCSC 700: child with severe brain injury, quadriplegic, functionally blind, and had substantially reduced mental function (upper limit); *Bystedt*, above note 30; *Strachan (Guardian ad litem of) v. Winder*, 2005 BCSC 59: child catastrophically injured at birth, resulting in severe and permanent disability (rough upper limit of $290,000); *Chow v. Hiscock* (2005), 41 C.C.L.T. (3d) 155 (B.C.S.C.): severe brain injury and in a semi-vegetative state (rough upper limit of $306,500).

230 See *Williams (Guardian ad litem of) v. Low*, 2000 BCSC 345.

231 (1966), 115 C.L.R. 94 (H.C.A.).

232 *Ibid.* at 130.

233 For example, see *Lee*, above note 22. Although the court rejected the plaintiff's argument that the rough upper limit is inconsistent with s. 15 of the *Canadian Charter of Rights and Freedoms*, it noted it is about time to re-examine the rationale for the cap.

234 Above note 2.

none but the very wealthy could afford to pay the enormous insurance premiums which would be required by insurers to meet such exorbitant awards.[235]

The Supreme Court was clearly reacting to the "insurance crisis" debate ongoing in the United States. During the relevant period, manufacturing groups and insurance companies in North America had mounted a public relations and lobbying campaign in response to a perceived "litigation explosion" causing insurance to become prohibitively expensive. The campaign was aimed at "tort reform" to restrict personal injury law.[236] For example, in a full-page advertisement in the *Wall Street Journal*, insurance companies described products liability law as an "undisguised wolf who has invaded corporate headquarters, everywhere." The advertisement continued: "The American public seems intent on going to court. 'Sue the bastards' used to be a joke. Now it's a battle cry. With the help of eager attorneys, plaintiffs are not only quick to demand justice, but 'extra' justice, because their chances of success are great."[237] Emphasizing the "frightening increase" and enormous cost of personal injury claims, the companies called for "major changes in tort laws ... to correct a disastrous trend."

The debate about whether there really is an "insurance crisis" is not settled. In some sectors, insurance has become extremely expensive (e.g., medical malpractice and some forms of environmental harm).[238] However, to put the problem in perspective, it must be noted that private liability insurance plays only a minor role in compensating injured persons compared to other systems of public and private disability insurance programs. And while some individuals do receive spectacular tort awards, the insurance problem may be due more to the *uncertainty* created by exploding technology and an unpredictable legal system than to "huge settlements."[239] Finally, the U.S. and Canadian experiences are far from comparable.

---

235 Above note 2 at 333.
236 Developments discussed in P.J. Halpern & J. Carr, *Liability Rules and Insurance Markets* (Ottawa: Consumer Research and Evaluation Branch, Consumer and Corporate Affairs Canada, 1981).
237 "The Product Liability Menace" *Wall Street Journal* (9 December 1976) B15; see also "A Life, an Industry; Who Pays?"*Globe and Mail* (17 April 1986) B21; "The Insurance Crisis" *Maclean's Magazine* (27 January 1986) 26.
238 See K.S. Abraham, "Environmental Liability and the Limits of Insurance" (1988) 88 Colum. L. Rev. 942.
239 For an analysis of the "insurance crisis" in the United States and Canada, see the Ontario Task Force on Insurance, *Final Report of the Ontario Task Force on Insurance* (Toronto: The Task Force, 1986).

The B.C. Law Reform Commission's 1984 *Report on Compensation for Non-Pecuniary Loss*[240] concluded that the insurance crisis was overstated by the media, and it questioned whether the court was the best institution to make such a determination without the benefit of public participation. The commission took issue with the court's rationale that other heads of damage already provided substantial funds for the plaintiff. Other heads of damages were designed to meet specific needs and not to justify lower non-pecuniary loss awards. The costs of litigation and legal fees, ideally, should not come from the damages allocated for future care or lost income. These expenses are often paid from a non-pecuniary loss award, which under the present regime may not be sufficient. The commission was prescient in its expectation that evolving technology could provide improved future care coupled with greater solace for the disabled plaintiff, who would need further funds beyond those awarded for future care to take full advantage of these advances.

Instead of "blaming the victims," many commentators have suggested that we re-examine our excessive reliance upon litigation and private insurance to care for the sick and injured. It is perhaps worth noting that setting a limit on personal injury damages does not in itself reduce "social costs." Rather, it simply leaves the victim to bear those costs herself. The particularly candid remarks of an Australian judge, reacting to judicial efforts to reduce damage awards, are instructive on this point:

> The judicial policy of depressing damage awards means that insurance premiums are kept within tolerable limits even with very high rates of death and injuries. It obscures the true social costs. The unintended result is a social acceptance of a high rate of road and industrial deaths and injuries, which would not be acceptable if the premiums reflected the implementation of full restitution. In practice therefore, this judicial policy has contributed to the high rate of deaths and injuries …. The sensible answer to this very serious social problem lies not in artificial transfer of the social costs to the injured persons, but in reduction of the avoidable causes.[241]

Despite these many criticisms, the cap is now probably too firmly entrenched to be changed except in a piecemeal fashion (e.g., by carving out exceptions). It has the virtue of providing some measure of predictability and consistency. Compared with the situation in the United States where jury awards can be wildly inconsistent (and sometimes unreason-

---

240 Law Reform Commission of British Columbia, *Report on Compensation for Non-Pecuniary Loss* (Vancouver: The Commission, 1984).
241 Murphy J. in *Todorovic v. Waller* (1981), 150 C.L.R. 402 at 454 (H.C.A.).

ably high), the cap does provide an important moderating effect and also contributes to greater efficiency in litigation and dispute resolution.

So far, application of the cap seems to be limited to cases involving catastrophic personal injuries.[242] The cap has been held inapplicable to cases of defamation. In *Hill v. Church of Scientology of Toronto*,[243] the Supreme Court upheld a jury award for non-pecuniary damages in excess of the cap in a libel action (general damages of $300,000, aggravated damages of $500,000, and punitive damages of $800,000). It held that the cap did not apply in defamation actions and that the jury need not be instructed on it. The Court reasoned that the function of general damages in personal injury cases is different from its function in defamation cases. In the former, there is full compensation of all pecuniary losses prior to the award of non-pecuniary damages. In libel cases, special damages for pecuniary loss are difficult to prove and the entire basis of recovery lies in the general damages award. The Court did not perceive any apparent danger in exorbitant or wildly differing levels of awards in libel cases across Canada, and it thus concluded there was no need for a judicially fashioned cap. In *Young*,[244] the Court held that the cap was inapplicable in cases of negligence causing economic loss, noting that this position does not raise social policy concerns. However, it left open the possibility of the applicability of the cap in cases not involving catastrophic personal injuries.

Courts in other cases have reconsidered the cap in light of the policy grounds upon which it is based. There is controversy among the courts in various provinces as to whether, in sexual assault cases, the cap ought to apply. In British Columbia it does not.[245] Following *Hill*, the B.C. Court of Appeal concluded that the policy bases for the cap do not apply in cases of intentional torts involving criminal behaviour. In these cases, awards made under other heads are likely to be lower and thus the primary compensation is provided under the non-pecuniary heading (under which heading are included aggravated damages). There is no indication that awards in this area are out of control or that they will result in a social burden, undue insurance rates, or a drain on public resources as they may in other categories of personal injury cases.[246] At the time of writing, in most other provinces the contrary view prevails and the cap does apply in sexual assault cases. The issue awaits final resolution by the Supreme Court of Canada.

242 *Abbott*, above note 215; *Young v. Bella*, [2006] 1 S.C.R. 108 [*Young*].
243 [1995] 2 S.C.R. 1130 [*Hill*].
244 Above note 242.
245 *Y.(S.) v. C.(F.G.)* (1996), 26 B.C.L.R. (3d) 155 (C.A.).
246 *A.(D.A.) v. B.(D.K.)* (1995), 27 C.C.L.T. (2d) 256 (Ont. Ct. Gen. Div.); *Brandner v. Brandner* (1991), 71 Man. R. (2d) 265 (Q.B.); *B.(A.) v. J.(I.)* (1991), 119 A.R. 210 (Q.B.).

J. MANAGEMENT FEES

The lump sum award is assumed to provide investment income that will provide for the plaintiff for the remainder of his life. Obviously, this assumption will bear out only if the award is carefully invested. In Teno[247] the Supreme Court affirmed that in many cases plaintiffs will require the services of skilled financial advisers to assist them in the management of their capital sum to ensure that it is properly invested and managed. It is appropriate, therefore, to provide a sum for financial services or a management fee ($35,000 in Teno).

In the later case of Mandzuk v. Vieira,[248] the Supreme Court of Canada elaborated on this concept. The award of a management fee is not automatic but is based on evidence that financial assistance is in fact necessary in the circumstances. The amount of the management fee will depend upon the severity of the plaintiff's injuries, the size of the award, the remaining lifespan of the plaintiff, and the plaintiff's abilities to fend for herself. Management fees awarded to severely injured infants with long remaining lifespans can exceed $100,000.[249] Management fees are assessed based on the initial award and not what the plaintiff actually does with the award or the amount available for investment determined at a future date.[250]

---

247 Above note 2.

248 (1988), 53 D.L.R. (4th) 606 (S.C.C.).

249 In Toneguzzo, above note 97, the Supreme Court of Canada upheld a $94,000-management fee to an injured infant. In Cherry, above note 137 (C.A.), management fees of $225,500 were awarded to a severely injured infant with an expected sixty-year life expectancy. See also Bartosek (Litigation guardian of) v. Turret Realities Inc. (2004), 23 C.C.L.T. (3d) 161 (Ont. C.A.), leave to appeal to S.C.C. refused, [2004] S.C.C.A. No. 202: the Court of Appeal reversed the trial judge's refusal to award a management fee and awarded $302,989 for a management fee; Gordon, above note 34 at paras. 72–74 and 178–79: first plaintiff was awarded $525,925 (5 percent of award for future care cost and future income loss) and second plaintff was awarded $447,164.80 (4 percent of award for future care cost and future income loss).

250 Kroppmanns v. Townsend, [2004] 1 S.C.R. 315. In this case the plaintiff received half of her damages award from personal injury, which she used to purchase a house and pay her legal fees. The appropriate discount rate, tax gross up, and management fees were not determined until five years later. The Court rejected the defendants' argument that management fees should be assessed on the actual amount available for investment after those expenses. The Court noted, among other things, that this will be inconsistent with the lump-sum approach and the plaintiffs' right to spend damage awards as they choose.

CHAPTER 5

COMPENSATION FOR DEATH

A. INTRODUCTION

At common law there was no action available either to a deceased's estate or to surviving family members for wrongful death. Courts steadfastly held that "[i]n a civil court the death of a human being cannot be complained of as an injury."[1] This state of affairs reflected two separate rules: first, that a personal action dies with the person, and second, that no one has a right of action in respect of the death of another. Both rules were much criticized. They gave rise to the anomaly that a tortfeasor was much better off killing than injuring his victim.

With increasing industrialization and mechanized transportation, these rules created even greater social hardship and were eventually altered. In 1846 the British Parliament passed *Lord Campbell's Act*, which permitted claims by close relatives for the death of a family member. Equivalent legislation in all Canadian provinces and territories now provides for compensation for family members or dependants.[2] Addi-

---

1   *Baker v. Bolton* (1808), 1 Camp. 493, 170 E.R. 1033.
2   *Family Compensation Act*, R.S.B.C. 1996, c. 126; *Fatal Accidents Act*, R.S.A. 2000, c. F-8; *Fatal Accidents Act*, R.S.S. 1978, c. F-11; *Fatal Accidents Act*, C.C.S.M. c. F50; *Fatal Accidents Act*, R.S.N.B. 1973, c. F-7; *Fatal Injuries Act*, R.S.N.S. 1989, c. 163; *Fatal Accidents Act*, R.S.P.E.I. 1988, c. F-5; *Fatal Accidents Act*, R.S.N. 1990, c. F-6; *Family Law Act*, R.S.O. 1990, c. F.3 [Ont. *FLA*]; *Fatal Accidents Act*, R.S.Y. 2002, c. 86; *Fatal Accidents Act*, R.S.N.W.T. 1988, c. F-3.

tionally, the rule against survival of actions has also been altered by legislation providing that certain rights survive the deceased and may be pursued by her estate.[3] This chapter deals primarily with compensation of dependants under fatal accident legislation. Survival actions are also briefly explained.

B. FAMILY COMPENSATION ACTIONS

1) Basis of the Claim

Under the various fatal accident and family compensation statutes, the spouse, parent, or child (and, in some cases, siblings and grandparents) of a deceased may bring an action in tort for damages. The B.C. *Family Compensation Act*[4] is typical. Section 2 provides:

> If the death of a person is caused by wrongful act, neglect or default, and the act, neglect or default is such as would, if death had not resulted, have entitled the party injured to maintain an action and recover damages for it, any person, partnership or corporation which would have been liable if death had not resulted is liable in an action for damages, despite the death of the person injured, and although the death has been caused under circumstances that amount in law to an indictable offence.

Section 3 provides:

> 3 (1) The action must be for the benefit of the spouse, parent or child of the person whose death has been caused, and must be brought by and in the name of the personal representative of the deceased.
>
> (2) The court or jury may give damages proportioned to the injury resulting from the death to the parties respectively for whose benefit the action has been brought.
>
> (3) The amount recovered, after deducting any costs not recovered from the defendant, must be divided among the parties in shares as the court or jury by their judgment or verdict directs.

---

3   *Survival of Actions Act*: R.S.A. 2000, c. S-27, s. 2; R.S.N.S. 1989, c. 453 [N.S. *SAA*], s. 2(1); R.S.P.E.I. 1988, c. S-11 [P.E.I. *SAA*], s. 4(1); R.S.N. 1990, c. S-32 [Nfld. *SAA*], s. 2; R.S.N.B. 1973, c. S-18 [N.B. *SAA*], s. 2(1); S.S. 1990–91, c. S-66.1 [Sask. *SAA*], s. 3; R.S.Y. 2002, c. 212 [Yukon *SAA*], s. 2(1); *Estate Administration Act*, R.S.B.C. 1996, c. 122 [B.C. *EAA*], s. 59; *Trustee Act*: C.C.S.M. c. T160 [Man. *TA*], s. 53(1); R.S.O. 1990, c. T.23 [Ont. *TA*], s. 38(1); R.S.N.W.T. 1988, c. T-8 [N.W.T. *TA*], s. 31.

4   R.S.B.C. 1996, c. 126, s. 2.

(4) If there is no personal representative of the deceased, or, there is a personal representative but no action has been brought within 6 months after the death of the deceased person by the personal representative, the action may be brought by and in the name or names of all or any of the persons for whose benefit the action would have been if it had been brought by the personal representative.

The Ontario *Family Law Act*[5] goes somewhat further than other provinces in that it permits third parties to recover their losses in the case of *injury* as well as death. The relevant provision reads as follows:

61. (1) If a person is injured or killed by the fault or neglect of another under circumstances where the person is entitled to recover damages, or would have been entitled if not killed, the spouse … children, grandchildren, parents, grandparents, brothers and sisters of the person are entitled to recover their pecuniary loss resulting from the injury or death from the person from whom the person injured or killed is entitled to recover or would have been entitled if not killed, and to maintain an action for the purpose in a court of competent jurisdiction.

The action for "wrongful death" is brought by the personal representative of the deceased, or failing that, directly by the surviving family members. The objective of the action is to compensate the survivors for their pecuniary losses caused by the death of a family member, and the method of assessing those damages resembles that employed in personal injury actions.[6] The compensable loss to the survivors is sometimes referred to as the value of the "dependency" and is measured by the economic contribution that the deceased would have made to the survivor had the death not occurred. The use of the word "dependency" may be misleading in the modern context. The claimant need not show that he was "dependent" upon the deceased, or that he had a legal right to financial support from the deceased. Claimants merely need to demonstrate that they fall within the ambit of the Act, and that they had a reasonable expectation of financial benefit from the deceased. The point is simply that they would have received or shared in a portion of the deceased's income. Thus, even where the deceased's lifestyle prior to his death made it unlikely that surviving family members would have benefited from his earnings, claimants may still be

---

5   R.S.O. 1990, c. F.3, ss. 61–63.
6   *Keizer v. Hanna*, [1978] 2 S.C.R. 342 [*Keizer*]; *Kennedy Estate v. Cluney (Guardian ad litem of)* (2001), 204 Nfld. & P.E.I.R. 225 (Nfld. S.C.T.D.) [*Kennedy Estate*].

entitled to some compensation based on the possibility of a change in the deceased's behaviour in the future.[7]

Recovery for wrongful death is for pecuniary or financial loss only. But this does not mean that the claims are restricted to losses of income or money. Pecuniary loss includes material non-monetary benefits that have a pecuniary value, such as homemaking services provided by a family member or the care and guidance provided by a parent to a child (both of which are discussed below). Nevertheless, lost monetary support is generally the most substantial element of the claim. As in a personal injury action, the assessment is based upon evidence regarding the deceased's probable income. The amount of the award is determined by discounting to present value the expected future stream of economic benefits from the income that the deceased would have contributed to the plaintiff, after taking into account both positive and negative contingencies that would have affected that contribution.

It is important always to keep in mind that, unlike the personal injury action, the damages are intended to compensate the *survivors* for their personal losses, not for the losses of the *deceased* (whose losses are compensated, to a limited extent, by a survival action by the estate, discussed below).[8] The focus is upon the economic contribution that the deceased would have made to the individual family members but for the tort. The consequences of this difference are that courts take a different approach to deductions, taxation, contingencies, and other issues. For example, given that the survivors are not claiming for loss of a capital asset, but only for the loss of income, the calculation of the loss is based on the deceased's net income after tax. The court will deduct from the deceased's salary any amounts that would not have gone into family income such as expenditures that the deceased would have incurred for herself.[9] Similarly, contingencies will be considered that

---

7 *Beljanski (Guardian ad litem) v. Smithwick* (2006), 56 B.C.L.R. (4th) 99 (C.A.) [*Beljanski*]. In this case the deceased, a twenty-six-year-old father of two, had a long criminal record and very limited employment history. His surviving children were held entitled to a sum for lost inheritance based on the possibility that he would have amended his ways as he grew older, as many people do, and would have been able to leave some inheritance for his children, although the bequest was unlikely to be substantial ($10,000 for each child).

8 Although the basis of the claim is the deceased's entitlement to damages for the event that led to his death had he survived, the claim under the legislation is that of the claimants themselves. The deceased would not have been entitled to maintain such a claim if he had survived. See *Ruiz v. Mount Saint Joseph Hospital*, [2001] B.C.J. No. 514 at para. 51 (C.A.) [*Ruiz*].

9 The combined damages payable to all claimants (including possible claims under survival of actions legislation) cannot exceed the total amount of the

not only affect the duration and amount of salary that the deceased would have earned (sickness, layoff, and so on), but that also affect the survivors and their relationship with the deceased. For example, the possibility that spouses might have divorced may be a contingency that affects the duration of the loss suffered by a surviving spouse. As well, factors such as illegality, that might disentitle the deceased to claim for lost earnings from criminal activities, cannot affect the dependants' claim.[10]

2) Pecuniary Losses Only

In almost all cases, the compensation that may be claimed in a wrongful death action is for financial losses only. This has been broadly interpreted to include not only pecuniary benefits that would have flowed from the deceased to the claimant but for the death, but also pecuniary advantages that claimants have lost due to the death of a family member, provided they are not too remote. This requires a case-by-case analysis to determine compensable pecuniary losses in particular cases and whether the claimant has established the necessary causal link between the loss and the death of the family member.[11] This may include potential loss of earning capacity,[12] and actual loss of income due to the death of a family member.[13]

---

deceased's net income that would have benefited the claimants. *Goudreau Estate v. Gladue Estate*, 2007 ABQB 291; *Kennedy Estate*, above note 6.

10   *Beljanski*, above note 7.

11   *Ruiz*, above note 8.

12   In *Ruiz*, *ibid.*, the deceased's daughters were awarded damages for the reduction in their earning potential due to their decision to remain in El Salvador and not to return to Canada immediately after the burial of their mother (the claimants remained in their home country to benefit from the care, guidance, and companionship of their relatives). This award was in addition to the amount they received for the loss of care, guidance, and companionship for their mother's death. The court found the award to be reasonable in light of the claimants' circumstances. They had only been in Canada for three months prior to their mother's death, had no social networks in Canada, except their stepfather, and found it difficult to live in the house they had shared with their mother.

13   Saskatchewan *Fatal Accidents Act*, above note 2, s. 4(2); *Macartney v. Warner* (2000), 46 O.R. (3d) 641 (C.A.). The plaintiffs recovered loss of income due to nervous shock caused by the death of their son. The majority of the Ontario Court of Appeal held that the wording of s. 61 of the Ont. *FLA* is sufficiently broad to include such a claim. The claim was also found to be consistent with the Saskatchewan legislation. In *Sickel Estate v. Gordy* (2004), 255 Sask. R. 246 (Q.B.), the widow's claim for past and future loss of income was dismissed be-

Aggravated and punitive damages are not available to the survivors,[14] nor may damages be awarded for grief, mental distress, or pain and suffering unless permitted under provincial legislation (discussed below). In *St. Lawrence & Ottawa Railway Co. v. Lett*,[15] the Supreme Court of Canada stated:

> [T]he injury must not be sentimental or the damages a mere solatium.... The injury must be substantial; the loss, a loss of a substantial pecuniary benefit, and the damages are not to be given to soothe the feelings of the husband or child, but are to be given for the substantial injury.[16]

An award for grief or emotional distress to surviving family members, even when there is significant disruption, illness, or hardship, will not, therefore, be made in a family compensation claim.[17] Family members have such a claim only when they are able to establish an independent cause of action for negligent infliction of mental shock; for example, where the family member actually witnesses the accident in which the deceased is killed, or witnesses the immediate aftermath.[18]

Modest non-pecuniary damages are now available in some provinces under legislation. For example, the Alberta *Fatal Accidents Act* permits limited recovery of non-pecuniary damages for "grief and loss of the guidance, care and companionship of the deceased."[19] Under the Act, a surviving spouse or parent(s) may claim $75,000 and children may claim $45,000 each. More generally, courts have sometimes expanded the definition of "pecuniary loss" to include heads of damages that do not appear, at first sight, to be monetary. In particular, for many years, courts have awarded damages to children who lose a parent for their lost "guidance, care and companionship." These awards, however, are still referred to as pecuniary damages, on the theory that guidance and care are "services" provided by the parent to the child that can be replaced, at least partially, by paid services. Such damages are now

---

cause she had failed to show that her husband's death was a proximate cause of her withdrawal from paid employment.

14   *Campbell v. Read* (1987), [1988] 3 W.W.R. 236 (B.C.C.A.); *Lord (Guardian ad litem) v. Downer* (1999), 179 D.L.R. (4th) 430 (Ont. C.A.), leave to appeal to S.C.C. refused, [1999] S.C.C.A. No. 571.

15   (1885), 11 S.C.R. 422 [*Lett*].

16   *Ibid.* at 433.

17   *Vana v. Tosta* (1967), [1968] S.C.R. 71 [*Vana*]; *Griffiths v. Canadian Pacific Railway* (1978), 6 B.C.L.R. 115 (C.A.).

18   See discussion in Chapter 6.

19   Alberta *Fatal Accidents Act*, above note 2, s. 8. See also the New Brunswick *Fatal Accidents Act*, above note 2, c. F-7, s. 3.

expressly authorized in some provincial statutes, such as the Ontario *Family Law Act*,[20] which permits an amount to compensate for the loss of "guidance, care and companionship."

3) Lost Financial Support

The primary claim in most fatal accident cases is for lost financial support. In cases where children lose a parent, this amount will be substantial. The conceptual basis for the claim is different from that in personal injury law. The dependant is not claiming for the loss of a capital asset, but rather for the loss of actual support. The question for the court, then, is what actual financial benefit the plaintiff likely would have received from the deceased. Typically, a court will accept direct evidence about the deceased's financial contributions to the plaintiff prior to the accident. But more often (because of the necessity of making the calculations over a long period into the future), courts will need to supplement such testimony with expert evidence as to the appropriate amount, based on actuarial and statistical data, applied to the family's socio-economic circumstances.

The value of lost support is determined by starting with the probable gross income of the deceased and then deducting costs and expenditures that would have been made from that income before benefiting the dependants.[21] The first substantial deduction is the personal income tax that would have been paid on the deceased's income. The second deduction is for the personal expenses related to everyday living and working that would have been incurred personally by the deceased (such as food and clothing). This deduction will be based upon the family budget and statistical data and may often be in the order of 30 percent.[22] Third, the court must determine the "hold-back" (savings) of the deceased that would not have gone to benefit the family. The issue of the "hold-back" is complicated by the fact that the deceased's personal savings might, in any event, have ultimately accrued to the surviving family members through inheritance, and might also, by reason of the law regarding family property in the province, be considered joint property.

---

20   Ont. *FLA*, above note 2.
21   *Keizer*, above note 6; *Kennedy Estate*, above note 6.
22   *MacNeil Estate v. Gillis* (*sub nom. MacNeil v. Gillis*) (1995), 138 N.S.R. (2d) 1 (C.A.) [*MacNeil*]; *McVea (Guardian ad litem of) v. T.B.* (2002), 5 B.C.L.R. (4th) 367 (S.C.) [*McVea*].

In addition to direct monetary contributions from employment, the deceased may have had other benefits from employment that were or would have been shared by the family members, such as health insurance, dental plans, and pension benefits. These benefits are economic in nature and must be factored into the calculation.

As in personal injury actions, the amounts are estimated in lump sums, capitalized over the period of the dependency. The period of the dependency is the joint life expectancy of the deceased but for the accident and of the surviving family members for the duration of their individual dependency. The stream of income over the period is then discounted to present-day value in the same manner as in a personal injury action.[23] Certain other benefits may be added back into the final sum. There will be an add-back to take into account the personal savings and other assets of the deceased that would have accrued to the survivors, discounted by the possibility of early death of survivors and further discounted to present-day value. Additionally, compensation is available if the deceased would have earned and contributed substantial retirement income to the family.

4) Treatment of Taxation

In contrast with the situation in personal injury law, taxation is taken into account in two ways in wrongful death actions. First, the loss to the survivors is calculated on the basis of the deceased's salary after tax. Unlike the personal injury claimant, family members are not claiming for loss of a capital asset. What they have lost is the prospect of financial support from funds left over from the deceased's net salary after tax. They never would have received the benefit of the deceased's gross salary. Thus, to ignore tax would be to confer a windfall upon them. As the Supreme Court has stated,

> [i]t is quite obvious that basing an award under *The Fatal Accidents Act* on gross income would fail to take into consideration the realities of life in a modern state and would, in some cases, give to the dependants a fund greatly in excess of their financial loss.[24]

To arrive at an after-tax income figure, the court will generally rely upon the deceased's pre-death salary and tax situation, and make further adjustments based on assumptions about the future rate and impact of taxation upon the plaintiff's salary during his working life.

---

23   See Chapter 4.
24   *Keizer*, above note 6 at 372. See also *Kennnedy Estate*, above note 6.

Second, an amount must be added back to the damages award to account for the impact of tax on the expected income from the lump sum once invested. While the original sum of damages itself is not taxable, that capital sum is expected to produce investment income to replicate the stream of economic benefits that the survivors would have received from the deceased. But that investment income is taxable. Thus, in order to offset the impact of taxation, a further amount must be added on. This ensures that the actual income received from the lump sum replicates as nearly as possible the pecuniary benefits that the plaintiffs would have received from the deceased but for the death.

5) Loss of Services

a) Introduction: The Conceptual Basis

It is perhaps ironic that, while persons (usually women) have only recently been permitted to claim damages for their lost ability to perform household work when they are *injured*, when a woman *dies*, the law has long recognized a claim by her surviving family members for the economic loss they suffer as a result of being deprived of the benefit of that same work.

As early as 1885, the Supreme Court of Canada had resolved the issue of whether the loss to a family of the unpaid work of a mother could be considered a pecuniary loss. *St. Lawrence and Ottawa Railway Co. v. Lett*[25] involved a claim by a husband whose wife had been killed in an accident at a railway crossing. The deceased had been a full-time homemaker, and the judges were divided on the question of whether any claim should lie for her death. Ritchie J. of the Supreme Court of Canada described both views. On the one hand, he explained, some judges do not view the loss as an economic one but characterize it as merely "sentimental."

> [T]he loss of a wife or mother, no matter how industrious, careful or attentive she might have been in looking after her husband's domestic affairs, and in promoting the material and moral condition and prospects of her children, was still sentimental, and not of a sufficiently pecuniary character to support the action.[26]

This view (that there was no real economic loss in such a case) was coupled with a concern that the loss could not easily be quantified and

---

25   *Lett*, above note 15.
26   *Ibid.* at 425.

that compensation would therefore lead to uncertainty and unfairness in damages assessment. Gwynne J. took this view:

> There is no standard, as it appears to me by which a pecuniary value could be set upon [a mother's care of her family] .... These benefits which spring from parental love and affection are neither procured nor procurable with money, and are therefore insusceptible of having a pecuniary value attached to them, and their loss, therefore, cannot be estimated in money.[27]

This perspective was rejected by the majority of judges. Ritchie J. concluded that "the loss of a mother may involve many things which may be regarded as of a pecuniary character." He continued:

> I must confess myself at a loss to understand how it can be said that the care and management of a household by an industrious, careful, frugal and intelligent woman, or the care and bringing up by a worthy loving mother of a family of children, is not a substantial benefit to the husband and children; or how it can be said that the loss of such a wife and mother is not a substantial injury but merely sentimental, is, to my mind incomprehensible ... The evidence in this case shows that the husband was receiving benefits and advantages from the services of his wife capable of pecuniary computation, and had such reasonable expectation of pecuniary benefit from the continaunce [sic] of such services by the continuance of the wife's life as would entitle him to damages.[28]

The Court awarded to the family the amount of $5,800—a substantial sum at the time.

A more contemporary example is the fatal accident claim in *Franco v. Woolfe*.[29] Here the trial judge rejected the defendant's argument that there was no, or only a very small, financial loss to the family upon the death of a homemaker. He stated:

> Marriage is not the acquisition of a cheap servant willing to perform tasks seven days a week for husband and family. While the husband may not be able to pay her, it does seem to me that her contributions demand recognition.... She is a co-equal partner in marriage and is entitled to recognition of that equality....

---

27 *Ibid.* at 445.
28 *Ibid.* at 435–36.
29 (1974), 6 O.R. (2d) 227 (H.C.J.), var'd (1976), 12 O.R. (2d) 549 (C.A.) [*Franco*].

Fortunately, economists are reconsidering whether the activities which entail the housewife's work in the household should be now evaluated in some way in terms of dollars and cents.[30]

In the 1988 case of *Kwok v. British Columbia Ferry Corp.*[31] (also a fatal accident case), the British Columbia Supreme Court assessed the value of housework done by a woman who also held down a full-time job. Cummings J. described the deceased as a "truly remarkable wife and mother" and explained her contribution to her family:

> She handled the family and business bookkeeping and accounting and assisted her husband in his garage business and his boat building venture. In addition to working at a full-time job, caring for the three children and assisting her husband, she was a busy and active home-maker performing many of the gardening chores, indoor and outdoor painting, cooking, baking, washing, ironing and laundry, as well as shopping, without any outside the household assistance. She also had the care of her elderly mother-in-law who lived with the family. Mrs. Kwok did sewing and mending for the family, preserved fish which her husband caught and fruits and vegetables which she raised in her garden or bought in season. It was her responsibility to clean and maintain both houses, the family home and the rental property, and to do the necessary redecorating of the latter when the tenants changed. She prepared lunches for the children and her husband, made their breakfasts and cleaned up before they set off for school and work each day before leaving for work herself.... She was active in the children's schools and learned sign language to assist Martin, the retarded son, to speak. She also cut her family's hair. Prior to the accident, her health was good — it had to be. All her spare time apart from work, in the evenings and on weekends, was devoted to the care of her home and family.[32]

In the result, the deceased's non-monetary contribution to her family's welfare was adjudged to be worth about $15,000 per year. Other cases

---

30   *Ibid.* at 232–33 (H.C.J.). The trial court measured the loss to the family by reference to gross national product figures and the cost of substitute labour. The Court of Appeal varied the amount on the basis that the damages should be more individualized. For a commentary, see K.D. Cooper-Stephenson & I.B. Saunders, *Personal Injury Damages in Canada: Assessment of Damages for Personal Injury and Death in Common Law Canada* (Toronto: Carswell, 1981) at 221–23.

31   (1987), 20 B.C.L.R. (2d) 318 (S.C.), aff'd (1989), 37 B.C.L.R. 236 (C.A.) [*Kwok*]. See also *McVea*, above note 22.

32   *Kwok, ibid.* at 358 (S.C.).

have adopted a similar approach.[33] It is important to note that these figures do not measure the full value of a homemaker's services but only the portion of that value that has been lost to her family.

b) Scope of the Claim

Awards for lost household services are not confined to cases involving the death of women or full-time homemakers. Claims in respect of males may also include such a component,[34] as may claims in respect of elderly persons. For example, in Riggs v. *Toronto Hospital*,[35] the husband of a woman, who was seventy-one years old at the time of her death, received substantial compensation for her death, based upon direct evidence regarding the amount of work she performed in the household and care she provided to him, as well as general statistical evidence concerning the amount of work performed by persons of her age. Ultimately, the court based the final amount of compensation upon these figures and the estimated cost to the plaintiff of paying for full-time residence in a retirement home, in recognition that without the care provided by his spouse, the plaintiff could not live independently.

c) Measurement Issues

As a result of the developments described above, it is now well established that the loss to family members of unpaid work is compensable, whether the deceased was a female or male.[36] In most jurisdictions, damages under this heading are compartmentalized into two components: loss of homemaking services; and loss of care, guidance, and companionship or affection. The latter loss is generally compensated by the

---

33 See also *Grant v. Jackson* (1986), 24 D.L.R. (4th) 598 (B.C.C.A.); *Jantz v. Mulvahill*, [1989] B.C.J. No. 2346 (S.C.), aff'd (1992), 11 B.C.A.C. 127 (C.A.) [*Jantz*]: value of homemaking services to the family set at $1,500 per month or $16,800 per year; *Rhemtulla Estate v. Pal*, [1989] B.C.J. No. 2140 (S.C.); *Murray Estate v. Advocate Contracting Ltd.* (2001), 195 N.S.R. (2d) 313 (S.C.) [*Murray Estate*].

34 For example, see *Johnson v. Milton (Town)* (2006), 25 M.P.L.R. (4th) 17 (Ont. S.C.J.) [*Johnson*]; *Millott Estate v. Reinhard* (2001), 306 A.R. 1 (Q.B.) [*Millott Estate*].

35 [1993] O.J. No. 1884 (Gen. Div.). See also *Bunting v. Li*, [2000] O.J. No. 4592 (S.C.J.) [*Bunting*], where the eighty-one-year-old plaintiff received an award for loss of services for the death of her seventy-one-year-old sister who lived with her at the time of her death; *Simpson Estate v. Cox* (2006), 32 M.V.R. (5th) 93 (N.S.S.C.), aff'd (2006), 249 N.S.R. (2d) 184 (C.A.) [*Simpson Estate*].

36 For example, in *Coe Estate v. Tennant* (1988), 31 B.C.L.R. (2d) 236 (S.C.), where both parents died, the children received an equal amount for loss of household services for each parent, as well as the conventional sum of $20,000 for the loss of each parent's love, guidance, and affection.

award of an arbitrary and modest conventional sum, and the relevant principles are discussed later in this chapter.

The determination of individual awards is obviously complex. The court must calculate the economic contribution that would have been made by the deceased to each family member had she lived. As with claims for lost financial support, this involves a large amount of speculation, since the court must estimate the expected life span of the deceased before the accident, the period over which she would have provided services to the family members, and the present value of the total economic benefit to them. The goal is to replace the services performed by the deceased, to enable the claimant(s) to maintain the standard of living they enjoyed prior to the deceased's passing, regardless of whether they have or will in fact replace those services.[37]

In determining the quantity and value of unpaid labour, courts admit the expert testimony of rehabilitation consultants, economists, actuaries, and professional caregivers, many of whom base their evidence upon statistical information. The case of *Franco*[38] considered the nature of the evidence necessary to value domestic work. The trial court had measured the loss to the family by reference to the estimated contribution to gross national product of unpaid work in the home, and the cost of substitute labour. The Court of Appeal varied the amount on the basis that the damages should be more individualized. Referring to the expert evidence regarding average contribution to GNP, the court stated:

> [T]his evidence should not have been admitted. In assessing damages for the death of a wife, the Court must determine the value of the services rendered by a particular wife to a particular husband; evidence of the value of the services rendered by the average Canadian housewife to the average Canadian husband is irrelevant to this determination.[39]

Notwithstanding its rejection of the evidence, the Court of Appeal did not overrule the award. It accepted, on the facts of the case, that the amount awarded was a defensible estimate of the deceased's actual contribution to her family, measured on a replacement cost basis. However,

---

37 See *Millott Estate*, above note 34; *Parsons Estate v. Guymer* (1998), 40 O.R. (3d) 445 (C.A.) [*Parsons Estate*].

38 Above note 29. In this case, the evidence established that average contribution to GNP was $4,000 to $4,538 per year; and that the cost of procuring a substitute would be $4,940 to $5,118 per year. On the basis of this evidence the trial judge held that the value of the services to the deceased's husband and two children was between $4,500 and $5,000 per year.

39 *Ibid.* at 551 (C.A.). See also *Parsons Estate*, above note 37.

the Court of Appeal's insistence on highly individualized evidence has significant implications for the litigation process. Some courts have been skeptical about individualized evidence as being non-objective and likely to inflate the amount of household services performed by the deceased.[40] The tendency now is to assess the extent of the deceased's household services based on statistics of the average household services performed by persons in the same category as the deceased. This may be adjusted to reflect the actual circumstances of the deceased, for instance, where supported by evidence that the deceased did and would likely have continued to do more or less housework for the claimants' benefit than the average person in the deceased's category.[41] As well, the statistical average is to be reduced by the portion of the household services that would have benefited the deceased—claimants are only entitled to recover the value of their dependency on the deceased's household services.[42]

The value of lost household services is now usually measured by determining the number of hours the deceased spent on housework and assigning a dollar value based on the "replacement cost" for those services.[43] Two different methods are possible. The first simply looks to the cost of a "replacement homemaker" for a specified number of hours. The second adopts a "catalogue of services" approach, itemizing the different functions performed by the deceased and placing a value upon each. Most often, the approach adopted consists of a mix of both approaches. The *Kwok*[44] case provides an example. The plaintiff apparently based the claim upon a catalogue of services approach, itemizing

---

40 See *Kennedy Estate*, above note 6: court refused to follow the individualized assessment in *Franco* and instead relied on Statistics Canada data on average household services provided by persons in deceased's category. See also *Hechavarria v. Reale* (2000), 51 O.R. (3d) 364 (S.C.J.) [*Hechavarria*].

41 *Murray Estate*, above note 33: deceased was an exemplary housekeeper. Award must be at the high end under this head of damages; *Kennedy Estate*, above note 6: deceased would have exceeded average by about 30 percent. See also *Hechavarria*, ibid.; *Dhillon (Guardian ad litem of) v. Mischki*, 2000 BCCA 95; *Cahoose v. Insurance Corp. of British Columbia* (1999), 63 B.C.L.R. (3d) 265 (C.A.) [*Cahoose*]. *McVea*, above note 22: given deceased's work schedule, she would have performed fewer household services than average full-time workers, resulting in a 30 percent deduction for loss of household services and remarriage contingency.

42 See *Johnson*, above note 34; *Millott Estate*, above note 34.

43 In *Parsons Estate*, above note 37, the court rejected a reimbursement approach, reasoning that claimants are entitled to an award that will replace the deceased's services. It is irrelevant whether the claimant actually uses the award to procure such services or not. A reimbursement of actual cost could undercompensate claimants.

44 Above note 31.

and valuing each component of the deceased's household functions. The judge accepted this approach as a starting point but was of the opinion that it produced an exaggerated amount ($23,342 per year); he held that, instead of breaking down the award item by item, he should make a fair estimate of a global sum ($15,000 per year). In addition, the court awarded a small sum for childcare and $20,000 for the surviving child's loss of love, guidance, and affection. A similar method was used, and a similar result reached, in *Jantz*[45] in respect of the death of the mother of three children.

In addition to direct evidence regarding the actual contribution of the deceased to the household, general evidence will be introduced regarding the value of unpaid services commonly provided by persons in the position of the deceased. Variables include, of course, the number of dependants in the family, the age of the children, and whether the deceased also worked outside the home (in which case the amount of work in the home is statistically less—though not necessarily in individual cases). The court must determine the rate at which that unpaid labour would have been performed over the deceased's lifespan. Unlike most paid labour, household production does not simply stop at age sixty or sixty-five (though the time spent will vary over a person's lifetime). Indeed, with an aging population, it may be expected that caregiving activities by the elderly may increase in the years ahead. Often, the court will make a deduction to take into account the amount of time the deceased spent on household work for her own benefit, and sometimes "credit" will be given to account for the amount of labour that surviving family members would have devoted to the deceased.[46]

The measurement of both the quantity and the value of unpaid labour is fraught with controversy. The dividing line between "labour" and "leisure" is not always clear. For example, does every moment spent with a child count as "childcare?"[47] Determining the nature of household services requires an assessment of all the functions performed by a homemaker and the adoption of "market equivalents" (cook, cleaner, manager, maintenance worker, contractor, chauffeur, nurse, planner, and so on). Even when an activity clearly counts as "work," the selection of market equivalents is, of course, fraught with value judgments. Is a homemaker a short-order cook or a dietary planner and chef? Is a parent a childcare worker or a psychologist and educator? Once these

---

45   Above note 33.

46   *Taguchi v. Stuparyk* (1994), 16 Alta. L.R. (3d) 72 (Q.B.), award reduced on appeal (1995), 169 A.R. 8 (C.A.).

47   *Bentley (Guardian ad litem of) v. Bentley*, [1994] B.C.J. No. 1118 (S.C.).

judgments have been made, a court must then assess the time devoted to each of these tasks and the portion of the total benefit that would have accrued to each individual family member. The court may make adjustments for quality differentials and must then identify appropriate wage rates.[48] The selection of monetary rates also raises difficult issues.[49] Money, of course, can never compensate for the loss of a family member. And, even accepting the limitations of money, one wonders about the accuracy of the market proxies that are typically used to measure the economic contribution of a domestic partner or parent.

6) Loss of Guidance, Care, and Companionship

a) Basis of Claim and Measurement

While survivors are entitled to compensation for pecuniary losses only, the courts have extended the definition of such losses to include claims by children (and sometimes other family members) for their loss of guidance, education, care, and companionship. Such losses may be considered pecuniary losses in the nature of unpaid but economically valuable services that were previously provided by the deceased. As the Supreme Court said in *Vana v. Tosta*, "these two children under these circumstances suffered the pecuniary loss from their mother's early death without the care, education and training (and I would also add the guidance, example and encouragement) which only a mother can give."[50] The award may be available even where the deceased did not provide moral guidance to the survivors, for example, because of his criminal behaviour, but still cared for and showed affection to them.[51]

The award for lost care, guidance, and companionship is now expressly confirmed in several provincial statutes,[52] and courts in those provinces no longer treat the award as one involving strict pecuniary

---

48   For example, see *Millott Estate*, above note 34.
49   See J. Yale, "The Valuation of Household Services in Wrongful Death Actions" (1984) 34 U.T.L.J. 283. See also J.L. Knetsch, *Legal Rules and Measurement of Economic Values: Household Production and Damage Estimates* (Toronto: Law and Economics Programme, Faculty of Law, University of Toronto, 1982).
50   *Vana*, above note 17 at 79.
51   See *Beljanski*, above note 7. Notwithstanding the deceased father's criminality, he cared for his children and spent time with them. The children were deprived of his companionship and affection with his death, and were therefore awarded a conventional sum of $5,000 each under this head.
52   *Fatal Accidents Act*, R.S.A. 2000, c. F-8, s. 8(2); R.S.S. 1978, c. F-11, s. 4.1(2); C.C.S.M. c. F50, s. 3.1; R.S.N.B. 1973, c. F-7, s. 3(4); R.S.P.E.I. 1988, c. F-5, s. 4(3); Ont. *FLA*, above note 2, s. 61(2)(e); *Fatal Injuries Act*, above note 2, s. 5(2)(d).

loss.[53] In Alberta, awards for loss of guidance, care, and companionship as well as "grief" may be awarded by statute but are strictly limited. Damages to the amount of $75,000 may be made to a spouse or cohabitant of the deceased or divided between the parents where the deceased is a minor (or if an adult was not living with a cohabitant). Damages of $45,000 may be awarded to each child of the deceased (if a minor or if an adult was not living with a cohabitant).[54]

However, this statutory head of damages has not been so broadly construed as to permit awards for mere solace. The award does not flow merely from the loss of a loved one. Rather, the claimants must prove that they in fact had a reasonable expectation of receiving care and guidance from the deceased and that they have been deprived of some tangible benefit as a result of the tort.[55]

In other provinces there is no statutory guidance, yet such awards are nevertheless regularly made. The amount will depend upon the nature of the relationship between the plaintiff and the deceased at the time of the accident, the length of time during which the plaintiff might have expected "care and guidance," and other factors, though by and large, the quantum is "conventional." In recent years, infant children have received $25,000 to $35,000 upon the death of a parent (male or female),[56]

---

53   *Mason v. Peters* (1982), 39 O.R. (2d) 27 (C.A.) [*Mason*].
54   Alberta *Fatal Accidents Act*, above note 2, s. 8(2). A 2002 amendment of the Act repealed the exclusion of adult children from obtaining compensation for grief and the loss of care, guidance, and companionship in respect of wrongful deaths occurring after the amendment came into effect (November 2002). Married adult children continue to be excluded. In *Ferraiuolo v. Olson* (2004), 357 A.R. 68 (C.A.) [*Ferraiuolo*], a decision in respect of a wrongful death that occurred before the 2002 amendment came into effect, the Alberta Court of Appeal struck down both the age and marital status restriction because they violated s. 15 of the *Canadian Charter of Rights and Freedoms* and it was not saved by s. 1. Among other things, the court noted that the exclusion ignored the needs and circumstances of adult married children in the event of a wrongful death of a parent. The New Brunswick legislation continues to restrict such damages to parent(s) of children under nineteen or who were dependent on the parent(s) for support: New Brunswick *Fatal Accidents Act*, above note 2, s. 3(4). These provisions may be contrasted with legislation in other jurisdictions where such claims are not restricted to parents of minors or unattached adults. For example, in both Saskatchewan and Manitoba, parents and children of a deceased are entitled to damages for loss of care, guidance, and companionship without reference to their age, marital, or dependency status. See *Fatal Accidents Act* Saskatchewan, above note 2, s. 4.1(2); Manitoba, above note 2, s. 3.1(2)(a).
55   *Nielsen v. Kaufmann* (1986), 54 O.R. (2d) 188 (C.A.).
56   *Plant v. Chadwick* (1986), 5 B.C.L.R. (2d) 305 (C.A): $30,000 to nine-month-old girl for loss of father; *Knutsen Estate v. Murray*, [1991] B.C.J. No. 2569 (S.C.); *Chung Estate v. King*, [1992] B.C.J. No. 1830 (S.C.); *Bentley (Guardian ad litem of) v. Bentley*,

to as high as $50,000.[57] Older children are less likely to be able to prove their dependence and loss and receive substantially less (e.g., $5,000 each to adult daughters of the deceased, though they lived with and relied heavily upon her).[58] Where there is no evidence of dependency, adult children receive nothing for the loss. For example, in *McDonnell Estate v. Royal Arch Masonic Homes Society*,[59] three middle-aged siblings claimed damages for loss of companionship when their seventy-seven-year-old mother died from a fall in the long-term care facility in which she resided. Coultas J. determined that their claim was without merit, since it essentially amounted to a claim simply for grief or sorrow, for which damages are not available.[60]

Occasionally, adults are permitted recovery under this head for loss of a parent, child, or sibling, but only when the relationship demonstrates a degree of interdependency that is out of the ordinary.[61] In *Lian v. Money*,[62] an award of $5,000 was made to the aging mother of the decedent because of the special reliance by the immigrant mother on her daughter for assistance in bridging the language and cultural gap. Modest awards have been made to adult children with a proven dependency upon their parents. In *Dewhurst v. Schmidtke*,[63] the plaintiffs were brothers aged fourteen and twenty-two who had a "special relationship" with their father, the decedent. They were awarded $25,000 and $10,000

[1994] B.C.J. No. 1118 (S.C.); *Collins (Guardian ad litem of) v. Savovich* (1996), 20 B.C.L.R. (3d) 126 (S.C.); *McVea*, above note 22 (three- and five-year-old children: $30,000 each); *Ortega v. 1005640 Ontario Inc. (c.o.b. Calypso Hut 3)*, [2002] O.J. No. 1196 (S.C.J.), aff'd (2004), 187 O.A.C. 281 (C.A.); *Foster v. Perry*, [2005] B.C.J. No. 1874 (S.C.); *Johnson v. Milton (Town)* (2006), 25 M.P.L.R. (4th) 17 (Ont. S.C.J.).

57   *Wright v. Hannon*, [2007] O.J. No. 53 (S.C.J.) [*Wright*]: children were ten and fourteen years old at time of their father's death. They were each awarded $50,000 for loss of care, guidance, and companionship.

58   *Jennings Estate v. Gibson* (1994), 48 B.C.A.C. 1 (C.A.). See also *Hoodspith v. Cook*, [1999] B.C.J. No. 1280 (S.C.): $3,500 to each child, one of whom still lived at home but no longer as dependent on the deceased as previously.

59   (1997), 41 B.C.L.R. (3d) 395 (S.C.).

60   *Ibid.* at 398. See also *Donetti v. Veillette Estate*, [2000] B.C.J. No. 1237 (S.C.).

61   In *Hechavarria*, above note 40, adult children of the deceased aged twenty-two, twenty-seven, and thirty-two who lived with their parents at the time of the death of their mother, as well as the deceased's three sisters, were awarded damages for the loss of care, guidance, and companionship given the special bond they shared with the deceased. See also *Bunting v. Li*, [2000] O.J. No. 4592 (S.C.J.) [*Bunting*]; *Cammack v. Martins Estate*, [2002] O.J. No. 4983 (S.C.): plaintiff father was awarded $30,000 for loss of care, guidance, and companionship for death of his only child, who was forty-six at time of death; *Simpson Estate*, above note 35.

62   (1994), 93 B.C.L.R. (2d) 16 (S.C.), rev'd (1996), 15 B.C.L.R. (3d) 1 (C.A.) [*Lian*].

63   [1995] B.C.J. No. 2401 (S.C.).

respectively for loss of care, guidance, and affection. Similarly, in *Bodnar v. Orban*,[64] a thirty-one-year-old daughter was awarded $30,000 for loss of care, guidance, and companionship for the death of her mother.

b) Death of a Child

Ordinarily, the loss of a child does not result in severe pecuniary loss to a parent and there are many cases involving children in which the damages have been minimal (e.g., in the range of $1,000).[65] As one judge explained, "[g]iven the realities of modern family life, the probable cost of raising and educating a son or daughter today exceeds by far the probable pecuniary value of any services they may render or financial contributions they may make in the future to parents or relatives."[66] Thus, especially when applied to children, the rules restricting recovery in fatal accident cases to economic losses mean that it truly is "cheaper to kill than to injure."

The real loss suffered when a child dies is the loss of a loved one, the deprivation of his companionship, and the accompanying grief. However, there are some circumstances in which the wrongful death of a child can result in substantial economic loss and, where the evidence supports a claim, compensation will be made. First, there are cases in which the evidence shows that the child would have provided an increasing level of care for an aging parent. In *Mason v. Peters*[67] the Ontario Court of Appeal affirmed an award of $45,000 to a mother for the death of her eleven-year-old son. The court accepted evidence indicating that the youth was mature for his years and was devoted to his mother, who was herself a paraplegic as the result of an accident. The trial judge had found that the mother was dependent upon her son and that it would be expected that he would have increasingly contributed to her welfare, both financially and non-financially over her lifetime.

The award in *Mason* was made on the basis of lost care and guidance under the *Ontario Family Law Reform Act*[68] and the court held

---

64   [2005] O.T.C. 233 (S.C.J.). See also *Hechavarria*, above note 40, where each child was awarded $30,000; *Bjornson v. McDonald*, [2005] B.C.J. No. 1873 (S.C.), a thirty-eight-year-old single mother of three, who was greatly dependent on her deceased parents, recovered $15,000 for loss of care, guidance, and companionship in addition to pecuniary losses for financial benefits that she would have received from her parents.

65   *Schroeder v. Johnson*, [1949] 4 D.L.R. 64 (Ont. H.C.); *Courtemanche v. McElwain*, [1963] 1 O.R. 472 (C.A.).

66   *Mason*, above note 53 at 33.

67   *Ibid.*

68   R.S.O. 1980, c. 152.

that it was not confined to awards for pecuniary losses. However, in principle, such an award could be made in any province since the loss of support claimed can be conceptualized as economic in character (insofar as the services have economic value).[69] There are cases in which children are clearly an asset to their families because of their contribution or intended contribution, both in kind and/or financially, and where this can be demonstrated, any losses can be recovered. These claims are often supported with evidence regarding the cultural norms of the plaintiff's community.[70] One example is a case dealing with "filial piety." In *Sum Estate v. Kan*,[71] the deceased's parents, who were of Chinese origin, were awarded $90,000 for lost future support based on a finding that their son would have observed the custom of filial piety, and that they therefore had a reasonable expectation of receiving from him a significant part of his income had he lived.[72] It is submitted that, where the expected benefit is not money but services in kind, the loss is equally compensable.[73]

7) Contingencies

a) Introduction
As in the personal injury action, contingency factors will be applied to adjust the award in fatal accident cases. Contingencies in these cases are of two general types. First, there are contingencies that would have affected the contribution of the deceased to the family had the accident not occurred. For example, in respect of a claim for lost income, the court will adjust the projection of the deceased's income to take into account the usual contingencies such as the possibilities of illness,

---

69 For example, see *Redden Estate v. Maxon* (2004), 25 C.C.L.T. (3d) 306 (B.C.S.C.).

70 For example, see *Cahoose*, above note 41. However, mere assertion that the deceased was from a cultural tradition where he was expected to have conferred some benefits on family members, without evidence of actual practice and expectation in the deceased's particular family, will not suffice to permit recovery: *Yu v. Yu* (1999), 48 M.V.R. (3d) 285 (B.C.S.C.).

71 (1995), 8 B.C.L.R. (3d) 91 (S.C.).

72 See also *Lian*, above note 62. In *To v. Toronto Board of Education* (2001), 55 O.R. (3d) 641 (C.A.), the parents of a fourteen-year-old deceased were awarded $100,000 each for loss of care, guidance, and companionship based on evidence of a strong relationship between the deceased and his parents consistent with their cultural expectations and that this would have likely continued, but for his death. See also *Osman v. 629256 Ontario Ltd.*, [2005] O.T.C. 555 (S.C.J.): the parents of a sixteen-year-old murder victim awarded $80,000 each and $20,000 to each of ten siblings for loss of guidance, care, and companionship.

73 *Graff v. Wellwood*, [1991] 5 W.W.R. 661 (Sask. C.A.).

unemployment, and early retirement. Second, there are contingencies that affect the duration and amount of the "dependency." These are contingencies that might have affected the duration of the survivor's relationship with the deceased (such as the early death of the survivor or divorce), and contingencies that might yet affect the dependency, such as remarriage.

The courts' approach to the first type of contingencies is essentially the same as in a personal injury action. Relatively modest amounts are deducted from the award to take into account the fact that the deceased's income might have been affected by illness, injury, early death, layoff, and the like. These matters are dealt with in detail in Chapter 4. The following section elaborates upon the second type of contingency deduction, which is unique to the fatal accident claim.

b) Divorce and Remarriage

In calculating an award for the lost pecuniary benefit of a relationship, courts take into account contingencies that affect such relationships and their length. These contingencies include the possible early death of the plaintiff or, more frequently in the case of spouses, the possibility that a divorce would have terminated the relationship (and thus altered the duration and economics of the relationship). The theory is that, had the accident not occurred, the marriage might have eventually broken down, and the duration (or amount) of the dependency should be adjusted to take this into account. Whether the claim is for lost income or lost household services, the possibility that the marriage might have ended may be used to reduce the economic benefits that the survivor would have received. In addition, courts may also take into account the possibility that the plaintiff might yet remarry, thus eliminating (or reducing) the loss.

An example of the application of divorce and remarriage contingencies is found in *Sharp-Barker v. Fehr*[74] in which the plaintiff brought an action following the death of her twenty-nine-year-old husband. The plaintiff claimed damages based upon a thirty-six-year joint survivorship. However, the defendant introduced statistical evidence showing that the average duration of a marriage was 11.8 years and the court accepted that the period of the dependency should be calculated with this contingency in mind. In addition, the defendant introduced evidence showing the prospects of remarriage of a twenty-six-year-old widow (52 percent) and argued that the period of the dependency should be

---

74   (1982), 39 B.C.L.R. 19 (S.C.).

further reduced because of the possibility that she would remarry and replace the loss.

The court accepted that this evidence should be given some weight. However, it also noted that marriage breakdown does not necessarily end the financial tie between spouses. After examining other evidence regarding the quality of the couple's marriage, and the plaintiff's testimony about her relations with others after the accident, the court arbitrarily concluded that "as between 11 and 39 years, a duration of 20 years for this marriage which would correspond with the adulthood of the child when that particular glue of marriage often dissolves."[75]

The court also accepted that the possibility of remarriage was a valid contingency and stated:

> I also have—may I go so far—seen in the witness stand, an attractive, young, intelligent woman who has made a living before and can do so again....
>
> [T]he lady has no obvious aversion to association with men somewhere near her own age. Again, admittedly arbitrarily, I allow a 30 per cent contingency for remarriage.[76]

The statistical evidence that is led regarding divorce and remarriage must be suitably tailored to the facts of the case, and the court may ignore it in favour of direct evidence when assessing the possibility of divorce in the actual case in front of it.[77] Moreover, any reduction in the award will be (at least partially) offset by the fact that the financial obligations of spouses to one another, and to their children, remain in existence after the end of the marriage, particularly through child support and maintenance payments. "[W]hat is being measured here is not divorce *per se* but the loss of economic contribution arising because of marriage breakdown."[78]

Where, at the time of the accident, the parties were already separated, the court will, of course, take this into account; however, even in these cases the courts may treat the effect of the separation on the loss as a contingency rather than a certainty. In *Young Estate v. Fletcher*,[79] the couple had been separated for seven months prior to the accident that killed the husband. The New Brunswick Court of Appeal found that the trial judge erred in denying the plaintiff's claim and not al-

---

75   *Ibid.* at 40.
76   *Ibid.* at 41.
77   *MacNeil*, above note 22.
78   *Schiewe Estate v. Skogan*, [1996] 8 W.W.R. 635 at 657 (Alta. Q.B.), var'd [1998] A.J. No. 1195 (C.A.).
79   (1995), 161 N.B.R. (2d) 116 (C.A.).

lowing for the possibility of reconciliation between the plaintiff and her husband. The test, said the Court of Appeal, is whether there is a reasonable possibility of reconciliation (not reasonable probability), and the court fixed the loss at 10 percent, based on its assessment of the circumstances relating to reconciliation. These included the length of the relationship; the signing of a separation agreement; the forming of extramarital relationships by both parties; the grief expressed over the separation; the desire for reconciliation expressed by both spouses; and the cultural and religious background of the parties.[80] In *Wright*, the court awarded $7,500 for loss of care, guidance, and companionship to a surviving spouse who had been separated from the deceased for four years at the time of death and their divorce would likely have been finalized, although it was uncertain when this would have occurred.[81] In Saskatchewan, parties who were separated and living apart from the deceased at the time of death are not entitled to damages for loss of care, guidance, and companionship.[82]

The other somewhat controversial contingency deduction in fatal accident cases, illustrated by the *Sharp-Barker* case described above, concerns the possibility of *remarriage* following the accident. For example, where the claim is by a surviving spouse for lost income or lost household services, there is a chance that the survivor may establish another relationship and thus regain wholly or in part the economic benefits of a relationship. In the case of children who lose a parent, there is the contingency that the surviving parent may remarry or that the children may be adopted, thus reducing their economic, though not emotional, loss.

In assessing whether the possibility of remarriage "mitigates" the plaintiff's loss, courts must assess not only the probability of remarriage but also the extent to which the financial benefits of that new relationship offset the loss. Where, at the time of trial, there has already been a remarriage, the court will take this into account.[83] However, mere remarriage does not necessarily cancel the loss, since the new partner may, for example, earn much less than the deceased.[84] In other cases, where at the time of trial there has not been a remarriage, sta-

---

80   *Ibid.* at 145–47.
81   Above note 57.
82   Saskatchewan *Fatal Accidents Act*, above note 2, s. 4.1(3).
83   *Parsons Estate*, above note 37; *Braun Estate v. Vaughan* (2000), 145 Man. R. (2d) 35 (C.A.) [*Braun Estate*].
84   *Jensen v. Guardian Insurance Co. of Canada* (1997), 37 O.T.C. 161 (Gen. Div.); *Holloway Estate v. Giles* (2001), 201 Nfld. & P.E.I.R. 181 (Nfld. S.C.), var'd on other grounds (2004), 233 Nfld. & P.E.I.R. 229 (Nfld. C.A.).

tistical evidence will be used to determine the contingency of remarriage.[85] But courts will also rely on direct and personal evidence (e.g., the testimony of the parties and others, the age of the survivors) to assess the possibility.[86] In the end, making this assessment may be "little more than a guessing game"[87] and some courts prefer to make merely a modest conventional deduction in the range of 10 to 20 percent.[88] Indeed, one province (Prince Edward Island) has legislated against taking remarriage into account at all.[89]

The possibility of remarriage also affects the claims of survivors for loss of services. In *Naeth Estate v. Warburton*,[90] the Saskatchewan Court of Appeal varied the damages awarded to the husband and minor child of the decedent, whose death had been caused by a physician's negligence during childbirth. The trial court had awarded a substantial sum for the loss of household labour. The Court of Appeal reduced the award

---

85   For example, see *MacKinnon v. Tremere*, [2000] B.C.J. No. 924 (S.C.) [*MacKinnon*]; *Murray Estate*, above note 33.

86   For example, in *Parsons Estate,* above note 37, the claimant was an elderly man (seventy-five years old by the time of the Court of Appeal decision) who also had had a stroke. Given his condition, the court concluded that there was only a slight possibility of remarriage for the third time (his second wife had also died by the time of the decision), and reduced the remarriage contingency deduction used by the trial judge from 25 percent to 5 percent. In *McVea,* above note 22, there was no remarriage contingency deduction. The evidence of a close relationship between the surviving husband and the children and the deceased's parents, as well as the husband's concern regarding how remarriage might affect his children, made remarriage unlikely. In any event, the court concluded that, even if he remarries at some point, that would not necessarily have a positive effect on the family's finances. It was actually likely to be negative.

87   *MacNeil*, above note 22 at 49. The judge said: "I endorse the view that determining an appropriate percentage for the reduction of an award for contingencies as a result of the possibilities or probabilities of divorce and remarriage is little more than a guessing game." This phrase is often used in cases involving remarriage contingency and comes from the comments of Phillimore J. in *Buckley v. John Allen & Ford (Oxford) Ltd.*, [1967] 1 All E.R. 539 at 542 (Q.B.), who said that the courts [should] be "relieved of the need to enter into this particular guessing game."

88   *Lamb v. Brandt* (1984), 56 B.C.L.R. 74 (C.A.); *Brown v. Finch* (1997), 42 B.C.L.R. (3d) 116 (C.A.) [*Finch*]; *MacKinnon*, above note 85: 20 percent contingency deduction for high likelihood of remarriage.

89   Prince Edward Island *Fatal Accidents Act*, above note 2, s. 7(1): "In assessing damages in a proceeding brought under this Act, there shall not be taken into account … the probability that a dependant may marry or the effect of such probability on any other dependant."

90   (1992), 103 Sask. R. 130 (Q.B.), rev'd in part (*sub nom. Naeth v. Warburton*) (1993), 116 Sask. R. 11 (C.A.).

on the basis that the decedent's husband, prior to trial, had begun living with a woman whom he was likely to marry. He and his child could not establish "any loss, actual or potential, of value of homemaking and domestic services" from the date of commencement of cohabitation with his new partner.[91] In 1997 the British Columbia Court of Appeal in *Brown v. Finch*[92] confirmed that the contingency of remarriage can reduce the loss of household services to the survivors.

The question of whether the "replacement" of a spouse or parent is to be taken into account is related to the issue of collateral benefits, discussed in Chapter 13. The general principle is that, where the care of children is taken over by a person who is likely to remain in the capacity of guardian, especially when that person has a legal obligation to care for the children, this will be taken into account in reducing the children's damages.[93] Where the services are provided gratuitously by someone with no obligation to do so, they will be considered "gratuitous benefits" and will not be taken into account.[94] In either case, the loss is not entirely cancelled, since there remains a contingency that the new relationship itself may not survive and the children may again find themselves without parents. A related issue is whether parental guidance can also be "replaced" through remarriage so as to eliminate or reduce the award to children for this loss. In *Comeau v. Saint John Regional Hospital*,[95] the New Brunswick Court of Appeal held that the parental guidance that the deceased father could have provided his children is unique and could not be replaced through remarriage. Parental guidance from a new parent will be in addition to, and not duplicative of, what has been lost. It is possible for a child to receive parental guidance from multiple parents; for instance, where parents remarry following separation and divorce, both step and biological parents can play that role without one necessarily replacing the other.

C. SURVIVAL ACTIONS

In addition to actions for the benefit of dependants, Canadian provinces and territories have enacted legislation providing for the "survival of

91   *Ibid.* at 12 (C.A.).
92   *Finch*, above note 88.
93   *Skelding (Guardian ad litem of) v. Skelding* (1994), 95 B.C.L.R. (2d) 201 (C.A.).
94   *Ratansi v. Abery* (1995), 5 B.C.L.R. (3d) 88 (S.C.); *Butterfield (Litigation guardian of) v. Butterfield Estate (sub nom. Butterfield v. Butterfield Estate)* (1996), 23 M.V.R. (3d) 192, 96 O.A.C. 262 (C.A.).
95   (2001), 244 N.B.R. (2d) 201 at para. 105 (C.A.).

actions" whereby the estate succeeds to the rights of the deceased.[96] By this legislation, the executor or administrator of a deceased person may bring an action for loss or damage to the person or property of the deceased. These actions are not for the benefit of dependants, but rather for the benefit of the *estate* (and hence the beneficiaries of the estate). The British Columbia *Estate Administration Act*[97] is typical. It provides that (excluding libel and slander) the estate of a person may bring or maintain "an action for all loss or damage to the person or property of the deceased in the same manner and with the same rights and remedies as the deceased would, if living, be entitled to."[98]

The scope of recovery under survival legislation varies significantly from province to province, and a comprehensive review of the legislation is beyond the scope of the present work. The relevance of survival actions goes far beyond the issue of compensation for wrongful death. Indeed, survival actions play a minor role in fatal accident litigation. Instead, such actions are typically based upon claims that existed while the deceased was alive (e.g., breach of contract), and they have nothing to do with the events that led to the deceased's death. Survival actions merely permit the estate to continue the action after the death of the plaintiff. In this sense they are not compensation for death at all, but rather compensation for other causes of action that survive death. Nevertheless, the interplay between survival actions and fatal accident claims requires brief summation.

1) Basis of Claim

Not all actions that could have been brought by the deceased while alive are capable of being brought by her estate. Survival actions are aimed primarily at compensating financial losses to the *estate*, and therefore losses of a purely personal nature are generally excluded. The theory is that the estate should be compensated for financial losses, but purely "personal" losses are cancelled by the death of the plaintiff.

In the result, most jurisdictions exclude many actions of a personal nature. For example, actions for defamation,[99] malicious prosecution,[100]

---

96 Above note 3.
97 *Ibid.*
98 *Ibid.*, s. 59(2).
99 B.C. *EAA*, above note 3, s. 59(1)(a); N.W.T. *TA*, above note 3, s. 31; Man. *TA*, above note 3, s. 53(1); Ont. *TA*, above note 3, s. 38(1); Nfld. *SAA*, above note 3, s. 11(a).
100 Man. *TA*, *ibid.*; Nfld. *SAA*, *ibid.*, s. 11(b).

and false imprisonment[101] are specifically excluded in Manitoba and Newfoundland; adultery, in Nova Scotia;[102] seduction, in Newfoundland;[103] and inducing a spouse to leave or remain apart, in Nova Scotia and Newfoundland.[104] Of more general importance, as Waddams points out, even where particular actions are not specifically excluded, most provinces restrict recovery to actual pecuniary loss (as will be discussed below), thus excluding many personal actions.[105]

2) Non-Pecuniary Losses

a) General Principles

In many provinces, survival actions are restricted to financial losses and recovery by the estate does not extend to damages in respect of physical disfigurement or pain and suffering of the deceased. Therefore, when the defendant's wrong has caused the plaintiff's death, the estate typically has no action for non-pecuniary loss suffered by the deceased. This, of course, is a substantial restriction on the use of survival actions in fatal accident claims.

The reason most commonly given for this restriction is that non-pecuniary damages would serve no useful purpose, would simply inflate the value of the estate, and would enrich its beneficiaries (who themselves did not experience the pain and suffering). Moreover, because the plaintiff has died, there is no pain and suffering experienced. Particularly in light of the Supreme Court of Canada's endorsement of the functional approach to non-pecuniary damages,[106] the inclusion of such damages in survival actions is unnecessary.

One example of the way in which these provisions operate is the case of *Lankenau v. Dutton*.[107] The plaintiff, who had been injured by the defendant's negligence, died after a trial had established liability but before the assessment of damages. Her estate continued the trial for the purpose of assessing damages. The court held that the defendant was no longer liable for damages in respect of pain and suffering, loss of amen-

---

101   Man. *TA, ibid.*; Nfld. *SAA, ibid.*, ss. 11(c) & 11(d), respectively.

102   N.S. *SAA*, above note 3, s. 2(2)(a).

103   Nfld. *SAA*, above note 3, s. 11(e).

104   N.S. *SAA*, above note 3, s. 2(2)(6); Nfld. *SAA, ibid.*, s. 11(f).

105   S.M. Waddams, *The Law of Damages*, 2d ed., looseleaf (Aurora, ON: Canada Law Book, 1991–) at para. 12.30.

106   See Chapter 4.

107   (1986), 37 C.C.L.T. 213 (B.C.S.C.), add'l reasons (1988), 27 B.C.L.R. (2d) 234 (S.C.), aff'd (1991), 55 B.C.L.R. (2d) 218 (C.A), leave to appeal to S.C.C. refused, [1991] 6 W.W.R. lxvii (note).

ities, or future income loss. Where the death is caused by the defendant's negligence, the claim for loss of expectation of life is also lost.

b) Pain and Suffering and Loss of Amenities

Thus, damages for *physical disfigurement* are specifically excluded in the Yukon, British Columbia, Alberta, Saskatchewan, New Brunswick, Prince Edward Island, and Newfoundland.[108] Similarly, damages for *pain and suffering* are excluded in Newfoundland, Yukon, British Columbia, Alberta, Saskatchewan, New Brunswick, Nova Scotia, and Prince Edward Island.[109] Damages for *loss of amenities* are also excluded, though often by implication (as covered by the more general exclusion of non-pecuniary loss). For example, in the British Columbia case of *Cromwell v. Dave Buck Ford Lease Ltd.*,[110] it was held that damages for loss of amenities experienced even during the period before the plaintiff died were foreclosed by the Act's general exclusion of damages for pain and suffering.

In the result, where the defendant's tort has caused the plaintiff's death, there is no right of recovery in the estate for non-pecuniary losses of the type that would have been recoverable had the plaintiff merely been injured. This total exclusion of non-pecuniary damages may be anomalous. Particularly where the plaintiff does not die instantly, there has been a loss suffered during a period which should be compensable. Had the plaintiff lived until trial, he would have a claim for pain and suffering even if he were to die the day after judgment. As Waddams says, "[i]t is anomalous that the plaintiff's death just before the trial should have the effect of depriving his estate of wealth represented by a valuable cause of action."[111]

---

108 Yukon *SAA*, above note 3, s. 5(1); B.C. *EAA*, above note 3, s. 59; Alta. *SAA*, above note 3, s. 5; Sask. *SAA*, above note 3, s. 6(2)(d); N.B. *SAA*, above note 3, s. 5(1); P.E.I. *SAA*, above note 3, s. 5(d); Nfld. *SAA*, above note 3, s. 11(g).

109 Nfld. *SAA*, *ibid.*, s. 4 (all non-pecuniary loss); Yukon *SAA*, *ibid.*, s. 5; B.C. *EAA*, *ibid.*, s. 59; Alta. *SAA*, *ibid.*, s. 5; Sask. *SAA*, *ibid.*, s. 6(2)(c); N.B. *SAA*, *ibid.*, s. 5(1); N.S. *SAA*, s. 4(c); P.E.I. *SAA*, *ibid.*, s. 5(c).

110 [1980] 4 W.W.R. 322 (B.C.S.C.).

111 Waddams, above note 105 at para. 12.90. In *Monahan Estate v. Nelson* (2000), 76 B.C.L.R. (3d) 109 (C.A.) [*Monahan Estate*], Newbury J.A., in dissent, expressed discomfort with excluding compensation for pain and suffering for the period between the injury and the plaintiff's death, occurring after trial but before judgment was rendered. However, she felt compelled to apply earlier authority that disentitles a deceased's estate from recovering damages for pain and suffering for the period prior to the plaintiff's death and reluctantly concluded that no such damages were recoverable by the estate of the plaintiff in that case.

Thus, in several provinces, modest damages for pain and suffering do survive the plaintiff's death. The damages awarded, however, will generally be small because they are limited to the pain and suffering experienced by the plaintiff in the period between the defendant's wrong and the plaintiff's death. Sometimes, however, these damages will be more substantial. For example, in *Booth Estate v. Sault Ste. Marie (City)*,[112] the deceased was negligently run over by a city bus and died two and a half hours later of his injuries. In an action by his estate, $12,000 in general damages were awarded on the basis that the victim had some awareness of his plight and probably suffered significant fear and pain before his death.[113] In another case, damages for pain and suffering were awarded to a deceased's estate when a negligent misdiagnosis of cancer resulted in two unnecessary surgeries.[114] Some courts have also awarded damages for pain and suffering for the period prior to the deceased's death, where death occurs after trial but before judgment, through the issuance of *nunc pro tunc* orders (which allow courts to backdate the judgment to the day prior to the victim's death) to avoid the harshness of the exclusion caused by the court's delay in issuing judgment.[115]

In some provinces, general damages are awarded only so long as the plaintiff's death was from causes other than the defendant's wrongdoing. In other words, if the defendant causes harm to the plaintiff that results in pain and suffering, and the plaintiff later dies from unrelated causes, the plaintiff's estate can maintain the original action against the defendant. For example, in *Amirault v. Westminer Canada Holdings*

---

112 [1994] O.J. No. 3105 (Gen. Div.), supp. reasons [1995] O.J. No. 2043 (Gen. Div.).

113 But see *Ordon Estate v. Grail*, [1992] O.J. No. 2847 (Gen. Div.): general damages excluded by operation of the *Trustee Act*.

114 *Mitchell Estate v. Labow*, [1995] O.J. No. 621 (Gen. Div.); general damages were also awarded in *Manitoba (Workers' Compensation Board) v. Hildebrand Estate (Public Trustee)* (1991), 29 M.V.R. (2d) 247 (Man. Q.B.). See also *Braun Estate*, above note 83: Doctor failed to inquire about a test result that could have increased the deceased's chances of survival through early diagnosis and treatment for cancer. Award of $60,000 for pain and suffering for two years prior to death; *Newman Estate v. Swales*, 2002 CarswellOnt 5581 (S.C.J.): estate awarded $60,000 for deceased's suffering for three and one-half years before her cancer diagnosis and the devastating effect of cancer on her life for twenty-two months until her death.

115 *Monahan Estate*, above note 111, Hall J.A. for the majority; *Vollrath v. Bruce* (2000), 282 A.R. 364 (Q.B.) [*Vollrath*]: deceased was awarded $50,000 but this amount was reduced by 50 percent to reflect the deceased's pre-existing conditions that would have equally caused him pain and suffering even absent the injury in question.

Ltd.,[116] the Nova Scotia Court of Appeal awarded general damages to the estate of a deceased plaintiff on the ground that the defendant's deceit and conspiracy had caused the plaintiff the loss of his "corporate life." Similarly, in *Monahan Estate*, where the plaintiff died after the trial but before judgment from factors unrelated to the defendant's wrongdoing, the majority of the British Columbia Court of Appeal limited general damages to the period prior to plaintiff's death.[117]

c)   Loss of Expectation of Life

Damages for lost expectation of life are specifically excluded by most statutes, though in some cases only when the plaintiff has died from the specific tort of the defendant. Where the plaintiff dies from some other cause, the claim for lost expectation caused by the defendant's wrong-doing may survive. In British Columbia and Ontario, damages for the death or loss of expectation of life are excluded if the death results from the tortious conduct.[118] Damages may be recoverable, however, where the defendant shortens the plaintiff's life but death is caused by an unrelated event. This claim is preserved, but its duration is measured solely by the years during which the plaintiff actually lived following the defendant's tort.

3) Punitive Damages

Generally, punitive damages are not any "loss to the estate" and they are not compensable in a survival action. For example, in Alberta, punitive damages are expressly excluded from recovery in survival actions,[119] and in British Columbia it has been held by the courts that they are excluded.[120] However, it remains unclear whether claims for punitive damages are specifically excluded from the Ontario *Trustee Act*.[121] In New Brunswick, punitive damages may be recoverable for the benefit of the estate in appropriate cases.[122]

---

116 (1994), 127 N.S.R. (2d) 241 (C.A.).
117 *Monahan Estate*, above note 111. See also *Vollrath*, above note 115.
118 B.C. *EAA*, above note 3, s. 59; Ont. *TA*, above note 3, s. 38(1).
119 Alta. *SAA*, above note 3, s. 5. See also N.S. *SAA*, s. 4(a); P.E.I. *SAA*, s. 5(a).
120 *Campbell v. Read* (1987), 22 B.C.L.R. (2d) 214 (C.A.).
121 R.S.O. 1990, c. T.23, s. 38(1). See *George v. Harris* (2001), 204 D.L.R. (4th) 218 (Ont. S.C.J.). See also *Tizard Estate v. Ontario* (2001), 41 E.T.R. (2d) 149 (S.C.J.).
122 N.B. *SAA*, above note 3, s. 5(2); New Brunswick *Fatal Accidents Act*, above note 2, s. 6(4).

4) Loss of Earning Capacity

The extent to which a claim for lost earnings survives death differs from province to province. Generally, where a person dies as the result of the defendant's wrong, the estate can claim lost earnings during the period prior to death. However, recovery of lost wages during the period after death is more complicated. In British Columbia and Saskatchewan, the legislation specifically excludes damages for lost earning capacity during the "lost years," that is, the earnings that might have been obtained had the deceased not died.[123] The reason for this rule is to avoid overcompensation of the estate or dependants. Where the plaintiff has died, it is said, the only effect of an award for lost income during the "lost years" would be a "windfall" to the estate. Since, under the fatal accident legislation, the deceased's dependants have a right to compensation for their financial losses (which is primarily a share of the deceased's income), to award the estate a sum for lost income would seriously overlap with the dependants' claims.

Several other provinces take the same approach. In *Rayner v. Knickle*,[124] the infant plaintiff was awarded damages for, *inter alia*, cost of future care, loss of future income, and general damages against the defendant doctor for negligently performing an amniocentesis that left him mentally handicapped and quadriplegic. The defendants appealed. By the time the appeal was heard, the boy had died. The Prince Edward Island Court of Appeal held that the damage awards for future care and loss of future income were not recoverable since the deceased "did not suffer any actual pecuniary loss under either of these two heads of damages."[125] In the Ontario case of *Balkos v. Cook*,[126] lost future earnings were also held to be "damages for the death" and therefore excluded under the Ontario legislation. This principle disadvantages the estates of plaintiffs who just happen to die after trial and prior to judgment, as they have to bear the brunt of the court's delay in issuing judgment. To avoid the unfairness caused by this principle, some courts will issue

---

123 B.C. *EAA*, above note 3, s. 59(3); Sask. *SAA*, above note 3, s. 6(2)(b). *Monahan Estate*, above note 111.

124 (1991), 88 Nfld. & P.E.I.R. 214 (P.E.I.C.A.) [*Rayner*]. See also *Price Estate v. Howse Estate*, 2002 NFCA 60; *MacKay Estate v. Smith* (2003), 230 Nfld & P.E.I.R. 178 (P.E.I.S.C.A.D.); *MacLean v. MacDonald* (2002), 201 N.S.R. (2d) 237 (C.A.); *Grennan Estate v. Reddoch*, 2002 YKCA 16, leave to appeal to S.C.C. refused, [2003] S.C.C.A. No. 16; Alta. *SAA*, above note 3, s. 5(2).

125 *Rayner, ibid.* at 247.

126 (1990), 75 O.R. (2d) 593 (C.A.).

nunc pro tunc judgments where the plaintiff died from a cause unrelated to the defendant's wrongdoing.[127]

The law is not uniform in respect of pecuniary losses. Waddams argues that a complete exclusion of damages for lost income goes too far. While it is true that courts should avoid double compensation, the blanket exclusion of such claims seems to apply even when there is no family compensation action. In Nunavut[128] and the Northwest Territories,[129] courts have held that damages for future earning capacity are recoverable in respect of the lost years in the same way as in personal injury claims, regardless of whether the deceased died instantly or not.[130] In *Paneak*, the court addressed the "windfall" argument, noting that it must be up to the legislature to address this issue as has been done in other jurisdictions. As well, the court noted that double recovery under the fatal accidents and survival of actions legislation can be avoided by courts' establishing rules for the assessment of damages as the Alberta Court of Appeal did in *Brooks v. Stefura*[131] following *Duncan Estate v. Baddeley*.[132]

The damages to the estate are the discounted present-day value of the deceased's future earnings, less income tax and the amount that the deceased would have spent on the necessaries of life. Double compensation of the dependants who subsequently bring a fatal accident claim can be avoided by taking their inheritance into account when calculating their loss.

---

127 *Vollrath*, above note 115.

128 *Paneak Estate v. Caron Estate* (2006), 274 D.L.R. (4th) 559 (Nu. C.A.), leave to appeal to S.C.C. refused, [2006] S.C.C.A. No. 400.

129 *Tilson Estate v. Summit Air Charters Ltd.*, [2007] 4 W.W.R. 32 (N.W.T.C.A.), leave to appeal to S.C.C. refused, [2007] S.C.C.A. No. 147.

130 *Ibid.* at paras. 5–6.

131 (2000), 266 A.R. 239 (C.A.).

132 (1997), 196 A.R. 161 (C.A.): the Alberta Court of Appeal held that loss of earning capacity was an "actual financial loss" within the meaning of the Alberta Act. In the same way that the estate can be compensated for the destruction of property, so should it be compensated for the loss of earning capacity as a capital asset. The Alta. *SAA* was subsequently amended to exclude claims for lost earnings during the lost years: Alta. *SAA*, above note 3, s. 5(2)(c). See also *Ferraiuolo v. Olson*, above note 54.

CHAPTER 6

COMPENSATION FOR HARM TO INTANGIBLE INTERESTS: NON-PECUNIARY AND AGGRAVATED DAMAGES

A. INTRODUCTION AND TERMINOLOGY

Non-pecuniary damages are an important head of compensation for civil wrongs. These damages are available in both tort and contract actions for intangible losses such as pain and suffering, mental distress, and emotional shock. There are several subheadings of non-pecuniary damages. The most common non-pecuniary damage awards are those made in personal injury actions to compensate the plaintiff for the "pain and suffering" and "lost enjoyment of life" that may accompany serious physical injury. The principles governing these awards are fully discussed in Chapter 4 in the context of personal injury damages. There are, however, many other situations in which non-pecuniary losses are compensable, in both tort and contract actions, and these form the subject matter of this chapter.

The terminology and theoretical basis of non-pecuniary damages can be confusing. One important subcategory of non-pecuniary damages is "aggravated damages." While the term is not used uniformly, aggravated damages generally refer to damages that are awarded in contract or tort actions to compensate the plaintiff for a civil wrong that is committed in a particularly callous, high-handed, or malicious fashion. In other words, the *manner* of the defendant's wrongdoing "aggravates" the damages suffered by the plaintiff. A good example is a defamation case where the defendant persists in making defamatory comments about the plaintiff even after there is reason to desist, or refuses to make an apology after it is clear that a wrong has been done. However, non-pecuniary damages are not confined to situations where the *manner* of the breach is harsh or malicious. There is another category of cases where the non-pecuniary damages flow from the *content of the duty* breached rather than the manner of its breach. An example would be the "holiday cases." Here plaintiffs are awarded damages in contract for their disappointment, anxiety, and frustration resulting from spoiled holidays, though there is nothing malicious about the breach. The damages compensate for the lost benefit suffered by the plaintiff rather than the way in which the benefit was withheld. Such damages are also, on occasion, referred to as "aggravated damages," but this is an unfortunate use of the terminology. It is better to consider these damages as a separate head of compensation for non-pecuniary loss.

Particularly when discussing aggravated damages, it is important to keep in mind that they are to be distinguished from *punitive* damages (which are discussed in Chapter 8). Non-pecuniary damages, including aggravated damages, are compensatory. Even though an award of aggravated damages may be triggered by harsh or malicious conduct, it is not designed to punish that conduct but rather to compensate the plaintiff for the additional harm caused by that conduct. In *Vorvis v. Insurance Corp. of British Columbia,* the Supreme Court of Canada explained the distinction:

> Punitive damages, as the name would indicate, are designed to punish. In this, they constitute an exception to the general common law rule that damages are designed to compensate the injured, not to punish the wrongdoer. Aggravated damages will frequently cover conduct which could also be the subject of punitive damages, but the role of aggravated damages remains compensatory.
>
> Aggravated damages are awarded to compensate for aggravated damage. As explained by Waddams, they take account of intangible injuries and by definition will generally augment damages assessed under the general rules relating to the assessment of damages. Aggravated damages are compensatory in nature and may only be awarded for that purpose. Punitive damages, on the other hand, are punitive in nature and may only be employed in circumstances where the conduct giving the cause for complaint is of such nature that it merits punishment.[1]

---

1   [1989] 1 S.C.R. 1085 at 1098–99 [*Vorvis*]. See also *Whiten v. Pilot Insurance Co.*, [2002] 1 S.C.R. 595 at paras. 116 and 156–57; *Fidler v. Sun Life Insurance Co. of Canada*, [2006] 2 S.C.R. 3 at para. 61 [*Fidler*].

The distinction between aggravated (compensatory) damages and punitive damages has been adopted throughout Canada. Obviously, however, the distinction can be blurred in practice, since the same conduct may give rise to both aggravated and punitive damages, and it is likely impossible (especially in a jury trial) to keep punitive motives entirely at bay when assessing aggravated damages.

B. NON-PECUNIARY DAMAGES IN TORT LAW

1) Compensation for Non-Pecuniary Losses as a Separate Head of Damages

In tort law, non-pecuniary losses may be compensated in a number of ways. First, physical pain and suffering, and the accompanying psychological pain, are compensated directly as a separate head of damages in personal injury cases. Whatever the cause of action (negligence or an intentional tort), where the gist of the wrong is physical injury to the plaintiff, consequential non-pecuniary losses are compensable as "pain and suffering" and "lost enjoyment of life." These losses are compensated according to the functional approach discussed in Chapter 4. In addition, where a person has been directly involved in a traumatic accident caused by the defendant's negligence, and suffers psychiatric illness as a result, she will be compensated for that illness even if her other physical injuries are minor.

Beyond torts where the essential harm is physical injury, non-pecuniary damages as a separate head of damages are rare. Until relatively recently, tort law offered no compensation for emotional and mental distress that was not accompanied by physical injury. First, courts were concerned not to open the floodgates of liability for claims to hurt feelings and emotional or mental harms resulting from various forms of interpersonal conflict short of physical violence. Second, they were concerned with the evidentiary difficulties of assessing such "intangible" injuries.

However, there are now several causes of action that directly compensate non-pecuniary harm even though it is not the consequence of physical injury. Intentional infliction of nervous shock or mental suffering is now a distinct cause of action in tort.[2] Malicious practical jokes, sexual harassment, and knowingly false accusations against a person may give rise to this action. Similarly, negligent infliction of

---

2   *Wilkinson v. Downton*, [1897] 2 Q.B. 57; See A.M. Linden & Bruce Feldthusen, *Canadian Tort Law*, 8th ed. (Markham, ON: Butterworths, 2006) at 54–57.

nervous shock or "psychiatric damage" is also sometimes compensable although within limits carefully circumscribed by courts.[3] Those limits, which are the product of continued concern not to open the floodgates to trivial claims, are more in the domain of the substantive law of torts than a book on damages. However, they include the requirement that the psychological harm manifest itself in physical symptoms or a recognizable psychiatric illness.[4] Mere fright, anxiety, or distress are not sufficient, and indeed "mere" grief and sorrow resulting from the loss of a family member are not sufficient.[5] However, where a person suffers shock because she has directly witnessed an accident involving a family member, or has come upon the immediate aftermath,[6] this is a compensable injury (though in England at least it has been held insufficient to see the accident on television).[7]

Various means have been employed over the years to restrict the availability of damages for mental distress in tort law.[8] However, the trend has been gradually to liberalize relief for non-pecuniary loss. The tests of proximity have all been widened (though cautiously). The plaintiff who suffers shock by witnessing an accident no longer needs to be a family member (however, this may assist in proving forseeability) or to be present immediately at the scene. The shock suffered must be beyond grief and sorrow and must manifest itself in some actual physical or psychiatric illness, though several courts have recently questioned this requirement. As one judge said,

> [i]t is difficult to rationalize awarding damages for physical scratches and bruises of a minor nature but refusing damages for deep emotional distress which falls short of a psychiatric condition.... I cannot see any reason to deny compensation for the emotional pain of a person who, although suffering, does not degenerate emotionally to the point of actual psychiatric illness.[9]

---

3   Linden & Feldthusen, *ibid.* at 421–40; *Devji v. Burnaby (District)* (1999), 70 B.C.L.R. (3d) 42 (C.A.), leave to appeal to S.C.C. refused, [1999] S.C.C.A. No. 608; *Mustapha v. Culligan of Canada Ltd.* (2006), 275 D.L.R. (4th) 473 (Ont. C.A.), leave to appeal to S.C.C. granted, [2007] S.C.C.A. No. 109.

4   Linden & Feldthusen, *ibid.* at 425–26; *Sant v. Jack Andrews Kirkfield Pharmacy* (2002), 161 Man. R. (2d) 121 (Q.B.).

5   *Hinz v. Berry*, [1970] 1 All E.R. 1074 (C.A.); *Satara Farms Inc. v. Parrish & Heimbecker Ltd.* (2006), 280 Sask. R. 44 (Q.B.).

6   *McLoughlin v. O'Brian*, [1982] 2 All E.R. 298 (H.L.).

7   *Alcock v. Chief Constable of South Yorkshire Police*, [1991] 4 All E.R. 907 (H.L.).

8   See the summary of the law in *Page v. Smith*, [1995] 2 All E.R. 736 (H.L.).

9   *Mason v. Westside Cemeteries Ltd.* (1996), 135 D.L.R. (4th) 361 at 379–80 (Ont. Ct. Gen. Div.) [*Mason*].

2) Compensation for Non-Pecuniary Losses by Aggravated Damages

More commonly, tort law compensates non-pecuniary harm through awards of aggravated damages. Aggravated damages are awarded for the increased harm caused when a tort is committed maliciously. They are damages for the additional emotional or psychological distress caused to the plaintiff by reason of the manner of the breach of duty. In *Hill* (a case dealing with defamation), the Supreme Court of Canada explained:

> Aggravated damages may be awarded in circumstances where the defendants' conduct has been particularly high-handed or oppressive, thereby increasing the plaintiff's humiliation and anxiety....
>
> These damages take into account the additional harm caused to the plaintiff's feelings by the defendant's outrageous and malicious conduct. Like general or special damages, they are compensatory in nature.... They represent the expression of natural indignation of right-thinking people arising from the malicious conduct of the defendant.[10]

Aggravated damages may be awarded in addition to damages for pain and suffering not only when the defendant's tort causes physical injury but also where the tort is committed in a particularly callous or malicious manner. In *Huff v. Price* the British Columbia Court of Appeal further explained:

> [A]ggravated damages are an award, or an augmentation of an award, of compensatory damages for non-pecuniary losses. They are designed to compensate the plaintiff, and they are measured by the plaintiff's suffering. Such intangible elements as pain, anguish, grief, humiliation, wounded pride, damaged self-confidence or self-esteem, loss of faith in friends or colleagues, and similar matters that are caused by the conduct of the defendant; that are of the type that the defendant should reasonably have foreseen in tort cases or had in contemplation in contract cases; that cannot be said to be fully compensated for in an award for pecuniary losses; and that are sufficiently significant in depth, or duration, or both, that they represent a significant influence on the plaintiff's life, can properly be the basis for the making of an award for non-pecuniary losses or for the augmentation of such an award. An award of that kind is frequently referred to as aggravated damages. It is, of course, not the damages that are aggravated but

---

10   *Hill v. Church of Scientology of Toronto*, [1995] 2 S.C.R. 1130 at 1205–6 [*Hill*].

the injury. The damage award is for aggravation of the injury by the defendant's high-handed conduct.[11]

a) Intentional Torts

Aggravated damages in tort are most often awarded in cases of intentional torts, where the conduct is clearly malicious and repugnant to the court's sense of propriety. Obvious examples include cases of assault and battery where the general damages may be increased because of the aggravating conduct of the defendant. As the Supreme Court of Canada explained, where the battery has occurred in "humiliating and undignified circumstances," the general damages may be increased to take into account these aggravating factors.[12] The most frequent modern use of aggravated damages in intentional tort cases occurs in cases involving sexual assault. In these cases, damages are awarded not only for physical injury but also for shock, hurt feelings, and violation of the plaintiff's autonomy.

b) Defamation

The best-established use of aggravated damages outside of assault and battery is the law of defamation under which compensation may be provided for the intangible injuries of hurt feelings and humiliation. In *Hill*[13] the Supreme Court of Canada upheld very large awards of both aggravated and punitive damages ($500,000 and $800,000 in addition to $300,000 general damages) in a case where the plaintiff, who was a Crown attorney, was defamed by the defendant. Aggravated damages in such cases depend upon a finding of malicious conduct (including recklessness) that has the effect of increasing the injury suffered by the plaintiff, "either by spreading further afield the damage to the reputation of the plaintiff, or by increasing the mental distress and humiliation of the plaintiff."[14] Applying this principle to the facts, the Court concluded that the former amount properly reflected the increased distress and humiliation to the plaintiff resulting from the defendant's actions. Furthermore, even this large award would have been insufficient to deter the defendant from its wrongful conduct and there was, therefore, space (or rational purpose) for an additional substantial award of punitive damages.

---

11 (1990), 51 B.C.L.R. (2d) 282 at 299 (C.A.).
12 *Norberg v. Wynrib*, [1992] 2 S.C.R. 226 [*Norberg*].
13 Above note 10.
14 *Ibid.* at 1206.

Aggravated damages in defamation cases require malice. "Malice" in this context includes recklessness, a concept that was further explored by the Supreme Court in *Botiuk v. Toronto Free Press Publications Ltd.*[15] The Court held that there must be something more than mere carelessness to found an action for aggravated damages, but that a reckless disregard for the reputation and dignity of a person can amount to malice. Interestingly, in this case the defendants were lawyers and the Court held that they would be presumed to be familiar with the law of libel and so should be held to a higher standard of care than a layperson: "[A]ctions which might be characterized as careless behaviour in a lay person could well become reckless behaviour in a lawyer with all the resulting legal consequences of reckless behaviour."[16]

It is noteworthy that the Supreme Court has also held that the usual cap on non-pecuniary damages[17] does not apply in defamation actions and that the jury need not be instructed on it. The amount awarded in *Hill* ($300,000 in general damages plus $500,000 in aggravated damages) vastly exceeded the amount of non-pecuniary damages permissible in a personal injury action, even where the injuries have been catastrophic. The Court reasoned that the function of general damages in personal injury cases is different from that in defamation cases. In the former, there is full compensation of all pecuniary losses prior to the award of non-pecuniary damages. In libel cases, special damages for pecuniary loss are difficult to prove, and the entire basis of recovery lies in the general damages award. The Court did not perceive any apparent danger in exorbitant or wildly differing levels of awards in libel cases across Canada, and it thus concluded that there was no need for a judicially fashioned cap.

A final example is the case of *Dixon v. British Columbia Transit*[18] in which the British Columbia Supreme Court granted aggravated and punitive damages to a plaintiff who had been wrongfully dismissed. Following *Vorvis*,[19] the court held that the employer had, in addition to breaching the employment contract, committed an "actionable wrong" justifying the extraordinary damage awards. The torts upon which the damages were based were deceit and defamation, committed by the defendants, who knowingly made the false allegation (and reported it to the media) that the plaintiff had been fired for cause.

15   [1995] 3 S.C.R. 3.
16   *Ibid.* at 35.
17   Discussed in Chapter 4, Section I(2).
18   (1995), 9 B.C.L.R. (3d) 108 (S.C.) [*Dixon*].
19   Above note 1.

c) Torts Affecting Property

Torts affecting property may also attract compensation for non-pecuniary losses, as, for example, where the interference does not diminish the value of the property but does interfere with the plaintiff's enjoyment of it. The plaintiff may claim damages for loss of use and loss of amenities.[20] Similarly, in nuisance cases, where the nuisance seriously interferes with the plaintiff's enjoyment of his property, damages may also be awarded for inconvenience and loss of amenities.[21] Where the defendant trespasses upon the plaintiff's property in a particularly high-handed or malicious manner, aggravated (and punitive) damages may be awarded.[22]

d) Aggravated Damages in Negligence Actions

Generally, aggravated damages (beyond those available for the "pain and suffering" associated with a personal injury) are awarded only when there is advertent malicious conduct by the defendant. Thus, cases involving inadvertence (negligence), while sometimes giving rise to general damages for pain and suffering, will rarely give rise to additional aggravated damages. However, where the negligence is particularly high-handed or malicious, courts have confirmed that they are able to award both aggravated and punitive damages in negligence actions.[23]

e) Form of the Award: A Separate Head of Damages?

Courts are divided on the relation between general damages for non-pecuniary loss and aggravated damages. The issue is whether aggravated damages should be a separate and distinct subheading of non-pecuniary damages or whether they should simply be included in the global sum of general damages. Sometimes, as in the case of *Norberg v. Wynrib*,[24] they are included as an unspecified amount in the global award for non-pecuniary loss. In these cases, the judge or jury takes into account the aggravated circumstances in setting on an appropriate global figure for non-pecuniary loss. Other times, as in *Hill*, aggravated damages are awarded in addition to, or as a subhead of, general damages for non-pecuniary loss. In most cases, the preferred approach is the former, given the difficulty of separating or treating distinctly the non-pecuniary harm caused by a physical injury from the non-pecuniary harm caused by the particularly malicious way in which that injury occurred.

---

20 See the discussion in Chapter 3.
21 *Bone v. Seale*, [1975] 1 W.L.R. 797 (C.A.).
22 See Chapter 8, Section B(2).
23 *Robitaille v. Vancouver Hockey Club Ltd.*, [1981] 3 W.W.R. 481 (B.C.C.A.); see discussion in Chapter 8.
24 *Norberg*, above note 12.

C. NON-PECUNIARY DAMAGES IN CONTRACT LAW

1) The Rule in *Addis v. Gramophone*

There was a time when it could be stated in nearly unqualified terms (a rare thing in law) that compensation for intangible injuries such as hurt feelings and emotional distress were not available for breach of contract. The leading case of *Addis v. Gramophone Co. Ltd.*[25] stood for the "stiff upper lip" theory of civil wrongs—that compensation in contract is for financial losses only, and that in commercial relationships (such as the employment relationship) people disappointed or distressed by breaches of contract had simply to bear the harm with whatever fortitude they could muster. As Lord Cooke stated in *Johnson v. Gore Wood & Co.*, "Contract-breaking is treated as an incident of commercial life which players in the game are expected to meet with mental fortitude."[26]

In *Addis*, the plaintiff sued for damages for wrongful dismissal from his employment. While he had been given the required six months' notice, he was prevented by the defendant from working out his contract. He sued for lost earnings and also for compensation for the harsh and humiliating manner in which he had lost his job. The jury awarded £600 in damages, a sum substantially in excess of his financial loss. The House of Lords reduced this amount, holding that, in cases of wrongful dismissal, damages are for the financial losses suffered by the plaintiff (wages for the period during which he should have received notice, loss of commissions that he would have earned). Additional damages for any pain caused by the "manner of dismissal" or for harm caused to his reputation are not available.

a)   Historical Exceptions to the *Addis* Rule

The sole exceptions to the rule in *Addis* were cases alleging breach of promise of marriage or a banker's wrongful refusal to honour a customer's cheque. In the former action, courts provided compensation not only for pecuniary loss but also for hurt feelings and wounded pride.[27] The law reflected social stereotypes, and realities, that such a breach, especially when part of a "seduction" resulting in children, could cause

---

25   [1909] A.C. 488 (H.L.) [*Addis*].
26   *Johnson v. Gore Wood & Co.*, [2001] 1 All E.R. 481, [2001] 2 W.L.R. 72 at 108 (H.L.).
27   *Lafayette v. Vignon* (1928), 23 Sask. L.R. 47 at 54 (C.A.).

serious harm to a woman's economic prospects and social standing.[28] No doubt, these damages were also motivated by punitive considerations. This action has been abolished in many common law jurisdictions.[29]

When a banker wrongfully dishonoured a customer's cheque, damages for harm to reputation were also traditionally available. Such damages can in fact be understood as compensation for pecuniary loss insofar as the imputation of insolvency against the plaintiff, and harm to the plaintiff's credit, can (at least in the case of a "trader") be presumed to injure the plaintiff's business or trade.[30]

b) Reasons for the Exclusionary Rule

Many social and commercial factors help to explain the law's traditionally restrictive approach to non-pecuniary losses as reflected in the *Addis* case. With the exceptions noted above, the exclusionary rule announced in *Addis* was firmly reiterated in numerous cases throughout the subsequent half-century.[31] Though the law has evolved since then, these considerations continue to influence the courts today and must therefore be covered to appreciate fully the ambit and application of the present law.

First, it should be noted that the Court in *Addis* did not distinguish, as courts now must, between aggravated (compensatory) and punitive damages. The claim appeared to be framed as one for exemplary damages to punish the defendant rather than to compensate the plaintiff.

---

28   In the context of seduction and illegitimate children, the court in *Berry v. Da Costa* (1866), 35 L.J.C.P. 191 commented at 192: "[T]hat part of the injury the plaintiff had sustained was the fact that in returning to her home she would do so not as a respected member of the family; that therefore the mortification she would feel in not being able to look the other members of her family in the face might be taken into consideration in estimating the amount of damages."

29   The action for breach of promise of marriage has been abolished in Ontario, British Columbia, and Manitoba. See: *Marriage Act*, R.S.O. 1990, c. M.3, s. 32(1); *Family Relations Act*, R.S.B.C. 1996, c. 128, s. 123; *Equality of Status Act*, C.C.S.M. c. 16, s. 4 (subject to the survival of an action for deceit in the case of bigamy).

30   *Rolin v. Steward* (1854), 14 C.B. 595, 139 E.R. 245; *Smith v. Commonwealth Trust Co.* (1969), 10 D.L.R. (3d) 181 (B.C.S.C.).

31   *Cook v. Swinfen*, [1967] 1 W.L.R. 457 (C.A.) refused damages for mental distress against a lawyer conducting the plaintiff's divorce case. Followed in *Kolan v. Solicitor*, [1970] 1 O.R. 41 (H.C.J.), aff'd [1970] 2 O.R. 686 (C.A.). This case involved an action against a solicitor who failed to discover that the property in the subject transaction was subject to a demolition order. Lacourcière J. followed Denning in *Cook*, holding that damages may be recoverable in contract for *nervous shock* (physical illness) when they are foreseeable, but that they may not be recovered for *injured feelings, mental distress, anger, and annoyance.* Here the plaintiff did suffer physical illness but it was not foreseeable.

As Lord Atkinson stated, "I have always understood that damages for breach of contract were in the nature of compensation, not punishment." The result can thus be explained in terms of hostility as much to exemplary damages as to aggravated damages. Viewed as a case concerning punitive damages, *Addis* can in fact be said still to be good law, but only if confined to punitive damages.

Second, the *Addis* decision reflects the commercial roots and individualist orientation of classical contract law. According to this paradigm, contracts (including employment contracts) are impersonal relationships, concerned primarily with economic exchange, and do not typically involve other elements of the parties' personalities. This conforms with the more general sociological observation that a central characteristic of the free market is its formal rationality and impersonality, meaning the absence of any room for emotional ties between persons or sentiments of altruism and fraternity.[32] Individuals are left to pursue their self-interest, free of such "irrational" obligations.

Third, the Court was obviously concerned not to introduce uncertainty into the law and commercial affairs and also not to restrict unduly the ability of employers to dismiss employees. The case is one of several (like *Hadley v. Baxendale*[33]) in which the English courts placed significant restrictions on the power of juries to set damage awards. The courts were concerned about exaggerated claims and the "floodgates" of liability. They desired to maintain predictability in damages so that individuals could be aware of the financial consequences of contract breach. The decisions in these cases all reflect the concern of courts not to surprise contracting parties unfairly, or burden them unduly, with unexpected levels of damages.

Finally, the restriction on aggravated damages reflects a concern not to upset the parties' bargain, or to "explode the contract" by reading into it obligations that the parties had not bargained for. The decision thus reflects the desire to keep separate the law of contract (assumed obligation) and the law of tort (imposed obligation). As Lord Atkinson stated, the tendency to introduce exceptions to the general principle

> ought, in my view, to be checked, rather than stimulated; inasmuch as
> to apply in their entirety the principles on which damages are meas-
> ured in tort to cases of damages for breaches of contract would lead
> to confusion and uncertainty in commercial affairs, while to apply

---

32   M. Weber, *Max Weber on Law in Economy and Society*, ed. by M. Rheinstein, translation from M. Weber, *Wirtschaft und Gesellschaft*, 2d ed. (1925) by E. Shils and M. Rheinstein (Cambridge: Harvard University Press, 1954).

33   (1854), 9 Exch. 341, 156 E.R. 145.

them only in part and in particular cases would create anomalies, lead occasionally to injustice, and make the law a still more "lawless science" than it is said to be.[34]

2) The Current Law

Today, the law of contract is more flexible in the way it approaches emotional and other intangible losses. The impersonal commercial paradigm of contract law has been relaxed somewhat as courts have come to give recognition to the "human" dimension of certain transactions. Not all contractual relations can be reduced to the simple quest for pecuniary gain, and in order to protect individuals' expectations fully, courts have partially amended the law where appropriate. In *Fidler*,[35] the Court noted that aggravated damages for mental distress arising from breach of contract have been awarded in two types of cases: "true" aggravated damages, that is, those arising from aggravating circumstances that constitute a separate cause of action, usually in tort, other than the breach of contract itself; and aggravated damages for mental distress arising out of the breach of contract itself, based on the *Hadley v. Baxendale* foreseeability test for contract damages.

a) "Intangible" Economic Losses

First, there are numerous cases in which courts have awarded what appear to be non-pecuniary damages for injuries to reputation, hurt feelings, and so on that can in fact be understood as situations involving losses that are economic in character but are simply difficult to prove or quantify. A classic example is the case of *Clayton v. Oliver*.[36] In this case the defendant had promised the plaintiff an acting engagement at the Hippodrome, with his name prominently displayed on the billboards. The House of Lords upheld a jury award not only for the plaintiff's lost income when this contract was breached but also for the intangible loss suffered by reason of damage to his reputation.

While *Clayton* is sometimes considered an early exception to the prohibition of non-pecuniary damages, in reality this "intangible" loss can easily be understood as a pecuniary loss since the promised publicity was an important part of the contract and was intended to enhance the plaintiff's career. Thus, despite the fact that the Court in *Addis* stated that damages are not available for harm to a person's reputation,

---

34   *Addis*, above note 25 at 495.
35   *Fidler*, above note 1 at paras. 51–53.
36   *Clayton (Herbert) and Jack Waller Ltd. v. Oliver*, [1930] A.C. 209 (H.L.) [*Clayton*].

they are awarded where the plaintiff is able to show that a purpose of the contract was to enhance his reputation.

Another situation where "intangible losses" have always been recoverable in contract is when the breach resulted in physical "inconvenience" or a "loss of amenities" to the plaintiff. In *Hobbs v. London and South Western Rly. Co.*,[37] the plaintiff received damages for the inconvenience of having to walk several miles in the rain owing to the defendant's breach of contract. These damages were not merely for the sentimental experience of "annoyance" or "frustration" caused by the breach, but also for the material inconvenience suffered by the plaintiff. As Mellor J. stated,

> I quite agree … that for the mere inconvenience, such as annoyance and loss of temper, or vexation, or for being disappointed in a particular thing which you have set your mind upon, without real physical inconvenience resulting, you cannot recover damages. That is purely sentimental, and not a case where the word inconvenience, as I here use it, would apply. But I must say, if it is a fact that you arrived at a place where you did not intend to go to, where you are placed, by reason of the breach of contract of the carriers, at a considerable distance from your destination, the case may be otherwise. It is admitted that if there be a carriage you may hire it and ride home and charge the expense to the defendants. The reason why you may hire a carriage and charge the expense to the company is with the view simply of mitigating the inconvenience to which you would otherwise be subject; so that where the inconvenience is real and substantial arising from being obliged to walk home, I cannot see why that should not be capable of being assessed as damages in respect of inconvenience.[38]

Like the "reputation" cases, the "inconvenience" cases can be understood narrowly as cases involving physical inconvenience and economic losses. The material inconvenience suffered by the plaintiff in *Hobbs* has a clear economic value. The plaintiff was willing to pay money to avoid having to walk!

This interpretation of the "lost amenities" cases may seem to confine these cases to their unique circumstances—that recovery is available only when the intangible benefit is economic in character. However, law and economics scholarship has increasingly shown that nearly all

---

37　(1875), L.R. 10 Q.B. 111 [*Hobbs*]. See also *Wharton v. Tom Harris Chevrolet Oldsmobile Cadillac Ltd.* (2002), 97 B.C.L.R. (3d) 307 (C.A.) [*Wharton*]; *Karampatos v. Torabipour*, [2004] O.J. No. 4255 (S.C.J.).

38　*Hobbs, ibid.* at 122–23.

"intangible" benefits can be understood in economic and even monetary terms. Intangible and psychological benefits can be monetized according to how much the plaintiff would have paid to obtain those benefits (or to avoid the loss). If we accept this, then the distinction that is intended to confine these cases is no distinction at all.

b)   Contracts with Non-Economic Subject Matter

The first significant breaches in the "stiff upper lip" theory of damages involved cases in which the contract was not an ordinary commercial exchange but instead clearly had an emotional or psychological element. These contracts cannot be assimilated to the mere commercial exchange. The very subject matter of the contract involves an intangible (psychological or emotional) benefit, and the breach clearly results in a loss of that benefit.[39] Thus, it is not appropriate to apply the restrictions developed in the commercial context. As the House of Lords explained in one case,

> [s]ince the law relating to damages for breach of contract has developed almost exclusively in a commercial context, these criteria [for measuring damages] normally proceed on the assumption that each contracting party's interest in the bargain was purely commercial and that the loss resulting from a breach of contract is measurable in purely economic terms. But this assumption may not always be appropriate.[40]

Courts now do recognize that many contracts involve substantial non-monetary benefits that, when lost, are deserving of compensation in damages. The best examples are the "holiday cases." In *Jarvis v. Swans Tours Ltd.*,[41] the plaintiff paid £63 for a two-week holiday in Switzerland. The holiday was a great disappointment, failing to live up to the representations made in the brochures, and the plaintiff was successful in asserting a breach of warranty. At trial, Mr. Jarvis was awarded only £32, being half the price of the holiday—in the judge's view, the difference between what he paid and what he got. On appeal, the amount was increased to £125 to take into account his lost enjoyment. Lord Denning considered the older cases denying damages for mental distress and stated:

---

39   See *Turczinski v. Dupont Heating & Air Conditioning Ltd.* (2004), 246 D.L.R. (4th) 95 (Ont. C.A.), leave to appeal to S.C.C. refused (2005), 252 D.L.R. (4th) vi [*Turczinski*].

40   *Ruxley Electronics and Construction Ltd. v. Forsyth*, [1996] A.C. 344 at 353 (H.L.) [*Ruxley*].

41   [1973] Q.B. 233 (C.A.) [*Jarvis*].

I think that those limitations are out of date. In a proper case damages for mental distress can be recovered in contract, just as damages for shock can be recovered in tort. One such case is a contract for a holiday, or any other contract to provide entertainment or enjoyment. If the contracting party breaks his contract, damages can be given for the disappointment, the distress, the upset and frustration caused by the breach.[42]

It has been observed by some that the plaintiff in this case was generously compensated, receiving in damages twice the original cost of the holiday.[43] But this is not necessarily true. The plaintiff not only lost the value of the holiday but was also exposed to distress, vexation, and disappointment as a result of the breach. To put him in the same position as though the contract had been performed, it would not be sufficient merely to give him back the cost of the holiday.

One way of understanding why the plaintiff was not, in fact, over-compensated is by borrowing the economist's notion of "consumer surplus." Consumer surplus is defined as the value placed on an exchange by a purchaser over and above its market price—the amount that the consumer would pay for the goods over and above their cost.[44] What the plaintiff "lost" in this case was not merely the price he paid for the holiday but its *value* to him. Merely refunding the purchase price does not put him in the position he would have been in had the contract been performed unless he is able to mitigate with no additional cost. It is significant that the plaintiff used up his yearly holiday entitlement on this vacation. In a sense, the "price" of the holiday was not only the £65 that he paid but also his time. In other words, confining his damages to the mere cost of the holiday would not even restore to him his reliance damages. While it might cancel his financial outlay, it would not make up for the fact that he had wasted his only vacation period.[45]

Jarvis has been followed in a number of other holiday cases in both England and Canada.[46] Despite earlier reservations, it has also been

---

42   *Ibid.* at 237–38.

43   D. Yates, "Damages for Non-Pecuniary Loss" (1973) 36 Mod. L. Rev. 535.

44   D. Harris, A. Ogus, & J. Phillips, "Contract Remedies and the Consumer Surplus" (1979) 95 Law Q. Rev. 581.

45   While the court did not base its calculation on this, it is significant that two weeks' wages for the plaintiff in this case was £93.27. When added to the sum awarded by the trial judge (£31.72), the total is £124.99—the amount awarded by the Court of Appeal.

46   *Jackson v. Horizon Holidays Ltd.*, [1975] 1 W.L.R. 1468 (C.A.); *Pitzel v. Saskatchewan Motor Club Travel Agency Ltd.* (1983), 149 D.L.R. (3d) 122 (Sask. Q.B.); *Fenton v. Sand & Sea Travel Ltd.* (1992), 4 Alta. L.R. (3d) 86 (Prov. Ct.) in which,

extended beyond its original context to other contracts that involve an intangible or psychological element.[47] Thus, whenever the subject matter of the contract is to provide peace of mind, enjoyment, or some other intangible benefit, damages for mental distress are available. These cases do not simply involve lost enjoyment and entertainment. In *Heywood v. Wellers*,[48] the plaintiff contracted with the defendant lawyer to obtain a restraining order against an individual who had been harassing her. When the lawyer failed properly to enforce the order, the plaintiff successfully sued for damages for mental distress. Lord Denning distinguished earlier cases refusing such damages on the ground that here the plaintiff's express purpose in employing a lawyer was to protect her from mental distress. The very subject matter of the contract involved the alleviation of mental distress and the nature of her problem should have put the lawyer on notice that a breach, especially of the type that occurred here, would result in such harm. Another contemporary example is provided by *Peters-Brown v. Regina District Health Board*.[49] In that case, the plaintiff had been treated for hepatitis at the defendant hospital. In breach of its duty of confidentiality, a list including her name was somehow posted at her workplace (a correctional centre). The list identified individuals whose body fluids should be handled with care. The court held that the hospital was liable to her both in contract (for breach of an implied term of confidentiality) and for negligence, and that she was entitled to damages for mental distress of $5,000. Again, we see here a link between the subject matter of the contract and the plaintiff's "peace of mind," with the defendant on notice of the importance of the contract to the plaintiff.

Similarly, damages for mental distress have been awarded against cemeteries and undertakers in situations where a deceased's ashes have been lost[50] or a corpse has become disinterred.[51] In these cases, the subject matter of the contract and the interests of the plaintiffs are clearly

---

contrary to earlier assurances, a disabled couple was not allowed to board their cruise ship with their scooters. They were awarded the price of their plane tickets to the departure point and $1,000 each for "distress and disappointment." *Sokolsky v. Canada 3000 Airlines Ltd.*, [2003] O.J. No. 3920 (S.C.J.); *Wolf v. Advance Fur Dressers Ltd.*, 2005 BCSC 1097.

47   See, for example, *Dunn v. Disc Jockey Unlimited Co.* (1978), 20 O.R. (2d) 309 (Prov. Ct.) [*Dunn*], awarding damages against a disc jockey for failing to provide entertainment at a wedding; *Elder v. Koppe* (1974), 15 N.S.R. (2d) 688 (S.C.T.D.), awarding damages for failure to deliver a vacation motor home.

48   [1976] Q.B. 446 (C.A.).

49   (1995), 136 Sask. R. 126 (Q.B.).

50   *Mason*, above note 9.

51   *Lamm v. Shingleton*, 55 S.E.2d 810 (N.C. 1949).

related to emotional rather than pecuniary interests. Similarly, damages for distress have been awarded against an insurer for a wrongful denial of coverage under a disability insurance policy, on the ground that one of the central purposes of such insurance is peace of mind.[52]

c) The Concept of Consumer Surplus

It is now generally accepted that many of the cases regarding non-pecuniary damages in contract are best understood as situations in which the "intangible loss" is compensated because a non-commercial benefit is the very subject matter of the contract. As mentioned above, the concept of consumer surplus provides a useful theoretical explanation for many of these cases and has been explicitly acknowledged in several judgments. For example, in *Wilson v. Sooter Studios Ltd.*,[53] the defendant completely botched the plaintiffs' wedding photographs. The price that had been charged for the job was $399. Locke J.A. held that a mere refund of the price would not adequately compensate the plaintiffs and that they were entitled to damages for their distress and disappointment as part of their expectation interest. In addressing the amount of that compensation, the plaintiffs argued that their expectations could be fully protected only by an amount of money that would enable them to obtain replacement photos. They claimed $7,000 to fly several guests back to British Columbia in order to reconstitute the wedding party for this purpose. Locke J.A. held that this would be excessive and instead opted for a mid-range figure that would approximate the true subjective value of the pictures to the plaintiffs. Drawing upon the academic literature on the subject,[54] he characterized this value as the "consumer surplus":

> [T]he difference between any lower price he pays and the higher price he is prepared to pay measures the "consumer surplus" expected at that time. Therefore, willingness to pay, rather than the market price, is the appropriate measure for estimating the true "value" of a purchase, and the differences between this value and the market price constituted the damage.[55]

---

52   *Warrington v. Great-West Life Assurance Co.* (1995), 7 B.C.L.R. (3d) 43 (S.C.) [*Warrington*]; *Fidler*, above note 1 at paras. 57–58; *Clarfield v. Crown Life Insurance Co.* (2000), 50 O.R. (3d) 696 (C.A.); *Asselstine v. Manufacturers Life Insurance Co.* (2003), 17 B.C.L.R. (4th) 107 (S.C.), aff'd (2005), 40 B.C.L.R. (4th) 226 (C.A.); *Saunders v. RBC Life Insurance Co.*, [2007] N.J. No. 186 (S.C.T.D.).
53   (1988), 33 B.C.L.R. (2d) 241 (C.A.) [*Wilson*]. Another case involving wedding pictures is *Diesen v. Samson*, [1971] S.L.T. 49 (Sheriff Ct.).
54   Harris, Ogus, & Phillips, above note 44.
55   *Wilson*, above note 53 at 245.

In upholding an award of $1,000, Locke J.A. stated,

> I gain some insight into the adequacy of the award when I apply the perhaps treacherous economic test outlined above, which appears to me to be an economist's ingenious way of measuring intrinsic value to the owner.... I do not think that they would have paid $7,000 more than the $399 they bargained for to get the pictures. They might have paid $600 more.[56]

This case can be compared with the body of law concerning divergence between market price and cost of repair, which is discussed in other places in this work.[57] In these cases, the breach of contract affects the plaintiff's property (e.g., substitute materials are used in a construction job) but there is no appreciable loss to the value of the property measured by its price on the market. Here, while there may be no diminution in the price of the property, its value to the owner is impaired. The problem, however, is to value the loss to the owner. The full cost of repairing the property will sometimes be exorbitant and will confer upon the plaintiff an undeserved windfall. In such cases, the notion of consumer surplus offers a useful mid-way measure of the "real" loss to the plaintiff.

In *Ruxley*[58] the breach of contract consisted in the defective construction of a swimming pool, which was built nine inches shallower than specified in the contract. The cost of rebuilding the pool was £21,500, yet the shallower pool was no less valuable and no less functional than a deeper pool. Thus, assessed in terms purely of market prices, the owner suffered no loss. Rather than choose between the two stark alternatives, the trial court awarded £2,500 for "loss of amenity." The Court of Appeal overruled this decision and awarded the full cost of repairing the pool, but the House of Lords restored the trial judgment.

The House of Lords held that an award of the larger amount would be punitive and would result in a windfall to the owner beyond his actual loss. "Damages are designed to compensate for an established loss and not to provide a gratuitous benefit to the aggrieved party."[59] Yet, while the defective pool was no less valuable in purely market terms, the Court accepted that it was less valuable to the owner in subjective terms. Lord

---

56 *Ibid.* at 246. See also *Dunn*, above note 47, awarding damages against a disc jockey for failing to provide entertainment at a wedding measured by the amount that the plaintiff might have paid at the last minute to secure a substitute.

57 See Chapter 2, Section D(2) and Chapter 3, Section D.

58 Above note 40.

59 *Ibid.* at 357.

Mustill, in particular, explained the concept of consumer surplus—that improvements in property, though they may have no economic value reflected in market prices, nevertheless have value to the owner.

> There are not two alternative measures of damage, at opposite poles, but only one; namely, the loss truly suffered by the promisee. In some cases the loss cannot be fairly measured except by reference to the full cost of repairing the deficiency in performance. In others, and particularly those where the contract is designed to fulfil a purely commercial purpose, the loss will very often consist only of the monetary detriment brought about by the breach of contract. But these remedies are not exhaustive, for the law must cater for those occasions where the value of the promise to the promisee exceeds the financial enhancement of his position which full performance will secure. This excess, often referred to in the literature as the "consumer surplus" ... is usually incapable of precise valuation in terms of money, exactly because it represents a personal, subjective and non-monetary gain. Nevertheless where it exists the law should recognise it and compensate the promisee if the misperformance takes it away.[60]

d) Non-Pecuniary Damages in Ordinary Contracts

The next question is whether intangible losses can be awarded in cases where the subject matter of the contract is not personal or psychological and does not involve a consumer surplus. The law has clearly come a long way since *Addis* in recognizing the psychological elements of consumer contracts. However, the fact that there now are many principled examples of situations where courts will award non-pecuniary damages does not mean that the original policy concerns behind their exclusion have been entirely rejected.

Recent English decisions have tended to be restrictive, holding that non-pecuniary damages for mental distress should be awarded only where the very object of the contract involves peace of mind or some other psychological benefit.[61] Thus, in ordinary commercial contracts, where the main object is profit, such damages should not be available (at least when not associated with actual physical injury or discomfort caused by the breach). The English decisions have referred to the policy that, in ordinary commercial contracts, defendants should be required

---

60   *Ibid.* at 360–61. For a commentary, see J. Poole, "Damages for Breach of Contract—Compensation and Personal Preferences: *Ruxley Electronics and Construction Ltd. v. Forsyth*" (1996) 59 Mod. L. Rev. 272.

61   *Bliss v. South East Thames Regional Health Authority*, [1987] I.C.R. 700 (C.A.).

to pay fair compensation for financial losses but should not be unduly surprised by additional damages.[62]

However, at least in Canada, it seems too late to close the gate quite so tightly, and the trend is to resist rigid categories. While some courts have recognized the need for limits, and while some have been swayed by the "peace of mind" test,[63] damages for emotional distress are no longer confined to cases in which the express subject matter of the contract involves a non-pecuniary benefit.

There are many cases in which non-pecuniary damages have been awarded, not because there is anything special about the subject matter of the contract itself, but simply because it was especially foreseeable that non-pecuniary damages would be the likely result of a breach. The operative test in these cases focuses less on the subject matter of the contract than on the concept of foreseeable consequences of the breach. These cases can usually be understood as an application of the "special circumstances" rule in *Hadley v. Baxendale*:[64] Damages that are otherwise too remote to be recoverable may be awarded where the defendant has notice of the special circumstances.[65] While emotional distress may not be the usual consequence of breach, the defendant has actual notice of the plaintiff's special circumstances and is therefore liable for the unusual consequences. For example, in *Newell v. Canadian Pacific Airlines Ltd.*,[66] the court awarded aggravated damages when the defendant airline, contrary to assurances, failed to carry the plaintiffs' dogs safely (one died and one was injured when carried in the cargo compartment). In considering the plaintiffs' claim, the court held that "vexation, frustration and distress" was a clearly foreseeable outcome of such a breach. The plaintiffs were awarded $500 (in addition to their

---

62   See the comments of the Court of Appeal in *Hayes v. Dodd*, [1990] 2 All E.R. 815 (C.A.), refusing to award damages for mental distress owing to solicitor's negligence in failing to disclose that leased property did not have a right of way. See also *Watts v. Morrow*, [1991] 1 W.L.R. 1421 (C.A.), in which it was held that breach of an ordinary property surveyor's contract does not permit damages for distress, except insofar as the breach causes physical discomfort; *Johnson v. Gore Wood & Co.*, above note 26.

63   See *Warrington*, above note 52. See also *McBeth v. Dalhousie College & University* (1986), 72 N.S.R. (2d) 224 (C.A.), involving a university's refusal (in breach of contract) to permit a student to write a special examination because of illness. The claim for mental distress was rejected and the case was distinguished from the "holiday type cases." The plaintiff was awarded her financial losses and general damages, which may have taken into account the difficulties the plaintiff experienced in her dealings with the defendant.

64   Above note 33.

65   *Ibid.* See discussion in Chapter 11, Section B(5).

66   (1976), 14 O.R. (2d) 752 (Co. Ct.) [*Newell*].

pecuniary loss) for their mental distress. It is significant that the plaintiffs had clearly indicated their concern for their pets and had, indeed, offered to purchase the entire first-class cabin of the airplane in order to take their dogs with them. While the subject matter of the contract was not to provide peace of mind, the special circumstances were made clear to the defendant.

Damages for mental distress have also been awarded in real estate cases, against both vendors and purchasers. In these cases, the failure of the defendant to carry out the contract significantly frustrated the plaintiffs' other plans regarding employment, personal finances, and living arrangements, resulting in upset and distress. In *Taylor v. Gill*,[67] the court rejected the distinction between commercial and non-commercial contracts and stated that damages could be awarded based upon the foreseeability of mental distress, particularly where, as in this instance, the breach substantially interfered with the plaintiff's goals and aspirations (of which the defendant was aware), and the distress manifested itself in physical symptoms. A similar result was reached in *Kempling v. Hearthstone Manor Corp.*[68] in which a disappointed purchaser of real estate was given damages for mental distress when the vendor's breach caused a "total disruption of lifestyle." In this case, Picard J. held that the availability of damages for mental distress should depend upon the general rules of remoteness set out in *Hadley v. Baxendale*.[69] Mental distress damages have also been awarded for failure to videotape a funeral service and causing a casket to slip while lowering it to the ground,[70] destroyed wedding pictures,[71] breach of a statutory warranty of fitness,[72] and negligence leading to forced guilty plea in a criminal case.[73]

In *Fidler*, the Supreme Court of Canada confirmed that the availability of mental distress damages for breach of contract in appropriate cases is consistent with, and not an exception to, the *Hadley v. Baxendale* principles of compensatory damages, while also confirming that

---

67 (1991), 13 A.R. 38 (Q.B.).
68 (1996), 41 Alta. L.R. (3d) 169 (C.A.) [*Kempling*].
69 Above note 33. See also *Tucci v. City Concepts Construction Ltd.* (2000), 2 C.L.R. (3d) 291 (Ont. S.C.J.): plaintiffs recovered mental distress damages for breach of contract for home renovations. In *Somerville v. Ashcroft Development Inc.* (2005), 35 R.P.R. (4th) 102 at para. 79 (Ont. S.C.J.), the plaintiffs recovered damages "for the stress, emotional upset and difficulties they had to endure as a result of the poor construction of [their] home."
70 *Kressin v. Memorial Gardens (BC) Ltd.*, [2004] B.C.J. No. 2363 (Prov. Ct.).
71 *Klaus v. Taylhardat*, [2007] B.C.J. No. 211 (Prov. Ct.).
72 *Wharton*, above note 37.
73 *Bordreau v. Benaiah* (2000), 46 O.R. (3d) 737 (C.A.).

distress arising from breach of an ordinary commercial contract will not normally be within the reasonable contemplation of the parties.[74] Although a breach could leave the disappointed party with feelings of frustration and anger, these cannot generally ground an award of damages unless, from the circumstances surrounding the making of the contract and any special knowledge of the defendant, those consequences are foreseeable. Foreseeability of mental distress would normally arise in relation to contracts intended to secure a particular psychological benefit for the plaintiff. This may be readily satisfied in "peace of mind" contracts. However, the expected psychological benefit need not be the very essence of the contract. It would suffice where the parties reasonably contemplated that peace of mind was part of the bargain and the mental distress resulting from the breach is sufficiently significant to justify compensation.[75]

Mental distress may be foreseeable where the defendant has actual or constructive knowledge of the plaintiff's vulnerability in the event of a breach, even if the contract was not intended to secure a psychological benefit. However, where the mental distress is largely due to a special vulnerability of the plaintiff, of which the defendant is unaware, the courts will remain reluctant to impose an unexpected liability. In *Turczinski v. Dupont Heating & Air Conditioning Ltd.*[76] the court noted that there are good reasons to limit the availability of mental distress damages in consumer contracts, including the difficulties of lay contracting parties being able to assess the mental state of strangers and how a breach of contract might affect them. As well, business people might be reluctant to deal with people with mental illness because of the possibility of being exposed to damages higher than could have been anticipated and dispropotionate to the contract price, especially where the person was unaware of the plaintiff's mental disability. In this case, the defendant's agent who dealt with the plaintiff for a home improvement contract was unaware of her mental illness, which ended up being exacerbated because of disagreements between the parties, attributable in part to the plaintiff's mental state, and resulting in delays in completing the work.[77] Mental distress damages were not foreseeable and therefore not recoverable.

Similarly, in *Wallace v. United Grain Growers*[78] (discussed more fully in the following section), the Court was called upon to consider

---

74   *Fidler*, above note 1 at paras. 43–44, 49, and 54.
75   *Ibid.* at paras. 47–48; *Wharton*, above note 37. See also *Farley v. Skinner*, [2002] A.C. 732 at para. 24 (H.L.).
76   Above note 39.
77   *Ibid.* at para. 30 (Ont. C.A.).
78   [1997] 3 S.C.R. 701 [*Wallace*].

whether aggravated damages could be awarded in a wrongful dismissal case. The Court stated that "[a]n employment contract is not one in which peace of mind is the very matter contracted for (see, for example, *Jarvis*[79] ...) and so, absent an independently actionable wrong, the foreseeability of mental distress or the fact that the parties contemplated its occurrence is of no consequence."[80] In light of later jurisprudence this statement somewhat overstates the exclusionary rule, however the basic point remains valid: that in ordinary employment contracts, where there are no special circumstances, mental distress is not ordinarily a recoverable head of damages.

It remains to be seen whether *Wallace* represents a retreat from the expansion of liability in this area. Given the developments discussed above, it is likely too late for this to happen without clearer direction. It is probable that the restrictive comments in *Wallace* will not be given general application but will be confined to contracts of employment. The special rules governing these contracts are discussed in the next section.

e)   Employment Contracts and Wrongful Dismissal

There is much jurisprudence and scholarly writing on the question whether non-pecuniary damages may be awarded in wrongful dismissal cases. *Addis*[81] itself was such a case, holding that the employee who is wrongfully terminated is entitled to compensation for pecuniary losses only, and not for harm to reputation or hurt feelings. *Addis* represents a commercial vision of the employment contract, wherein the transaction is concerned with the exchange of money for labour (as a commodity like any other). Moreover, it must be appreciated that, at common law, the foundation of the action for wrongful dismissal is simply the failure to provide due notice (or pay in lieu of notice). The damages available are confined solely to the loss suffered as a result of the employer's *failure to give proper notice*. No damages are available to the employee for loss of the job, or for the pain and distress that may be suffered as a result of the loss of the job since this is not even a breach of contract.

Addis has generally been followed by courts in Canada, including the Supreme Court of Canada, which stated: "[T]he damages cannot be increased by reason of the circumstances of dismissal whether in respect of the [employee's] wounded feelings or the prejudicial effect upon his reputation and chances of finding other employment."[82]

---

79   Above note 41.
80   Above note 78 at 734.
81   Above note 25.
82   *Peso Silver Mines Ltd. v. Cropper*, [1966] S.C.R. 673 at 684.

However, a hard and fast rule against non-pecuniary damages is difficult to justify. Courts have recognized that it is not always appropriate to reduce the employment contract to a pure commercial trade, devoid of human dimensions. Where, as part of a dismissal, an employee is unjustly accused of wrongdoing or publicly humiliated, the manner of breach might be said to aggravate the pecuniary harm suffered by making it more difficult for the employee to find new employment. Beyond this, given the importance of employment to a person's sense of security and self-esteem, such conduct can also be easily foreseen to cause non-pecuniary harm at least as serious as that suffered in the holiday cases. Thus, lawyers began to argue that employment law should recognize the same type of loss that was acknowledged in *Jarvis*. This argument has succeeded on occasion.

For example, in *Pilon v. Peugeot Canada Ltd.*,[83] the plaintiff had been employed by the defendant all his working life and had been given assurances that he had a life-time job with the company, but he was summarily dismissed without cause. The court distinguished the earlier employment cases on the basis that they dealt only with claims for loss of reputation and not whether damages for mental distress could be an element of damages in breach of contract cases. Galligan J. applied the test of reasonable forseeability of damages from *Hadley v. Baxendale*[84] and found: "In my opinion, it cannot fail to have been in the contemplation of the defendant that if it suddenly, without warning, unlawfully discharged a man whom it had led to believe was secure in his job for his working life, there would be the gravest likelihood that such a man would suffer vexation, frustration, distress and anxiety."[85] Accordingly, the plaintiff was awarded $7,500 in aggravated damages.

For several years following *Pilon*, the law remained conflicting. Some courts considered that the weight of authority and public policy was against such compensation — that it was not the function of contract damages to penalize the employer for dismissing an employee, and if the employee had an action for harm to his reputation he should sue for defamation.[86] Other courts took the position that *Jarvis* had altered the law after *Addis*, even in the area of employment contracts. Damages for mental distress were awarded in several cases involving summary

---

83   (1980), 29 O.R. (2d) 711 (H.C.J.) [*Pilon*].
84   Above note 33.
85   *Pilon*, above note 83 at 715.
86   *Abouna v. Foothills Provincial General Hospital* (1978), 8 A.R. 94 (C.A.); *Dobson v. T. Eaton Co. Ltd.* (1982), 23 Alta. L.R. (2d) 117 (Q.B.); *Ansari v. British Columbia Hydro & Power Authority* (1986), 2 B.C.L.R. (2d) 33 (S.C.).

dismissals with unjustifiable allegations of cause.[87] For example, in *Ribeiro v. Canadian Imperial Bank of Commerce*,[88] the plaintiff teller was dismissed without notice for an allegedly dishonest loan transaction, based on groundless hearsay. The court awarded $10,000 for emotional distress. Carruthers J. said:

> The defendant bank wrongfully, and I can also say wantonly and recklessly, accused the plaintiff of being otherwise and purported to terminate his employment for cause on this basis. I have concluded that this conduct on the part of the defendant bank constituted a breach of its employment agreement with the plaintiff. Having regard to the nature of the agreement, and, specifically the requirements for honesty and integrity on the part of the plaintiff, I find that it is reasonable to draw the inference that it was in the contemplation of the parties that if the plaintiff was terminated in this manner he would suffer mental distress. I have already concluded that it did, in fact, do so. Thus, the requirements for the application of the second rule in *Hadley* and *Baxendale* have been met, and the plaintiff is entitled therefore to recover damages for his "mental and emotional suffering."[89]

The court further awarded $10,000 in punitive damages since the defendant's actions called for additional condemnation. It also held that damages for loss of reputation could be recovered in a wrongful dismissal action, but that where the claim was actually one of defamation, the court should not permit it to proceed under the guise of a wrongful dismissal action.

In *Vorvis v. Insurance Corporation of British Columbia*,[90] the Supreme Court of Canada sought, with limited success, to shed light on the issue. In this case the plaintiff sued successfully for wrongful dismissal, claiming both pecuniary and non-pecuniary damages. The latter claim was based on evidence that the plaintiff had been treated harshly and unfairly by a supervisor in the period prior to his dismissal (the plain-

---

87 *Cringle v. Northern Union Insurance Co. Ltd.* (1981), 124 D.L.R. (3d) 22 (B.C.S.C.); *Brown v. Waterloo (Region) Commissioners of Police* (1982), 37 O.R. (2d) 277 (H.C.J.): case was appealed and the court disallowed the award for mental distress (1983), 43 O.R. (2d) 113 (C.A.); *Speck v. Greater Niagara General Hospital* (1983), 43 O.R. (2d) 611 (H.C.J.); *Pilato v. Hamilton Place Convention Centre Inc.* (1984), 45 O.R. (2d) 652 (H.C.J.).

88 (1989), 67 O.R. (2d) 385 (H.C.J.), var'd (1992), 13 O.R. (3d) 278 (C.A.) [*Ribeiro*]. On appeal, the award for mental distress was increased from $10,000 to $20,000, and punitive damages were increased from $10,000 to $50,000.

89 *Ibid.* at 433 (C.A.).

90 Above note 1.

tiff also claimed punitive damages in respect of this treatment). The claim for non-pecuniary damages was rejected by the Supreme Court of Canada. The Court held that the *general* rule from *Addis* has always been that an employer may terminate a contract with due notice, and that the only damages available in wrongful dismissal cases is damage from a failure to give sufficient notice. However, the Court did not entirely foreclose the possibility of aggravated damages in wrongful dismissal cases, "particularly where the acts complained of were also independently actionable."[91]

i)   The Causal Requirement
On the facts of the case, the claim in *Vorvis* for aggravated damages appears to have been dismissed by the majority of the Court because of the lack of a causal connection between the breach of contract (the termination of employment without adequate notice) and the mental distress suffered by the plaintiff. The conduct that caused the plaintiff's distress occurred mostly before the wrongful dismissal and was not itself part of the breach or otherwise actionable. As McIntyre J. stated, "[t]he conduct complained of preceded the wrongful dismissal and therefore cannot be said to have aggravated the damage incurred as a result of the dismissal."[92]

The insistence upon proof of a causal connection between the wrong (failure to give notice) and the emotional harm suffered is an important feature of *Vorvis*. A strict insistence upon a causal connection in these cases will frequently defeat a claim for mental distress. Realistically, distress is commonly felt because of the loss of one's employment or because of ill-treatment by the employer in the period leading up to the dismissal. The distress in these cases is not strictly caused by the wrongful dismissal or lack of notice, but rather by the loss of the job, which is not itself a breach of contract. Similarly, emotional distress is experienced by employees as a result of job pressures and personal treatment that may not amount to a breach of contract (as in *Vorvis*). Thus, it is only where the manner of the breach itself causes the emotional harm that it can be said to aggravate the damages.

ii)   The "Independently Actionable" Requirement
In the years following *Vorvis*, there was much debate about its proper interpretation. Many interpret the majority opinion strictly, as confining aggravated damages to cases where the acts complained of are "in-

---

91   *Ibid.* at 1103.
92   *Ibid.* at 1104.

dependently actionable" (beyond the failure to give notice). Many of these cases interpreted this as meaning that the plaintiff had to demonstrate that the breach of contract was also a tort in order to recover aggravated damages.[93] On this view, aggravated damages would be available only where the dismissal is so abusive that it coincidentally amounts to a tort, such as intentional infliction of emotional distress or the rare case where the employer assaults the employee during the dismissal,[94] wrongfully imprisons and interrogates the employee,[95] or makes false public comments about the employee that amount to deceit and defamation.[96] Somewhat more broadly, an "independently actionable wrong" might also include the breach of another term of the contract (apart from the requirement to give notice) for which mental distress damages are available under the general law of contract. For example, in *Ditchburn v. Landis & Gyr Powers Ltd.*,[97] the Ontario Court of Appeal awarded damages for mental distress against an employer for breach of its implied obligation to provide post-termination counselling to its employee. The court held that the breach of this term was an independent wrong, separate from the wrongful dismissal itself. As well, unfairly dismissing an employee and failing to find him alternate employment as required by the defendant's redundancy policy, because of the plaintiff's political affiliation, has been found to constitute an independently actionable wrong.[98]

Other courts have taken a less restrictive view of *Vorvis*, interpreting it to mean that aggravated damages are restricted but not abolished in employment contract cases, and that the "independently actionable" test is a factor to consider rather than a threshold test.[99] As one judge explained,

> I read *Vorvis* to mean not that "damages for mental distress, properly characterized as aggravated damages" will be awarded only where

---

93   *White v. F.W. Woolworth Co.* (1996), 139 Nfld. & P.E.I.R. 324 (Nfld. C.A.); *Killorn v. Healthvision Corp.* (1997), 156 N.S.R. (2d) 1 (C.A.); *Francis v. Canadian Imperial Bank of Commerce* (1994), 21 O.R. (3d) 75 (C.A.).

94   *Tannous v. Donaghue* (1995), 16 C.C.E.L. (2d) 75 (Ont. Ct. Gen. Div.), var'd on other grounds [1998] O.J. No. 2311 (C.A.); *Haggarty v. McCullough*, 2002 ABPC 3.

95   *Rahemtulla v. Vanfed Credit Union* (1984), 51 B.C.L.R. 200 (S.C.); *Bogden v. Purolator Courier Ltd.* (1996), 182 A.R. 216 (Q.B.).

96   *Dixon*, above note 18.

97   (1997), 34 O.R. (3d) 578 (C.A.).

98   *Sweetland v. Newfoundland (Minister of Development)* (2002), 221 Nfld. & P.E.I.R. 108 (S.C.) [*Sweetland*].

99   *Ribeiro*, above note 88; *Deildal v. Tod Mountain Development Ltd.* (1997), 33 B.C.L.R. (3d) 25 (C.A.).

there is an independent wrong in addition to the breach of contract
... but to leave it open to courts to develop guidelines as to the limited circumstances that will justify such awards ... [and] should be
recoverable "when the subject matter of the contract ... is to provide
peace of mind or freedom from distress."[100]

The Supreme Court of Canada has both clarified and confused the
issue further. In *Wallace*[101] the Court confirmed the strict interpretation
of *Vorvis*, holding that aggravated damages are not available in wrongful dismissal cases for breach of contract *simpliciter*. It overturned an
award by a trial judge of separate damages for mental distress, holding
that such damages are available only when the dismissal amounts to an
independently actionable wrong.[102]

In the *Wallace* case, the plaintiff's wrongful dismissal was accompanied by unfair allegations by the employer who was playing "hard-
ball." The plaintiff developed severe emotional difficulties and was
unable to secure alternate employment. The unfounded allegations of
just cause, which circulated in his profession, made it additionally difficult for him to secure new employment. Yet none of this justified an
award for mental distress, nor did it amount to a separately actionable
wrong. Iacobucci J. for the majority stated:

> Relying upon the principles enunciated in *Vorvis* ... any award of
> damages beyond compensation for breach of contract for failure to
> give reasonable notice of termination "must be founded on a separ-
> ately actionable course of conduct." Although there has been criticism
> of *Vorvis* ... this is an accurate statement of the law.... An employ-
> ment contract is not one in which peace of mind is the very matter
> contracted for ... and so, absent an independently actionable wrong,
> the foreseeability of mental distress or the fact that the parties con-
> templated its occurrence is of no consequence.[103]

However, the Court did confirm that the employer's conduct may
be taken into account in determining the length of the notice period (or
amount of pay in lieu of notice) to which the employee is entitled. Where
the termination is particularly harsh or malicious, the courts may increase the notice period (or the amount of lost salary in lieu of notice).

---

100 *Warrington*, above note 52.
101 Above note 78.
102 See also *McKinley v. BC Tel et al.* (2001), 200 D.L.R. (4th) 385 at paras. 82–83
     (S.C.C.) [*McKinley*], where the Supreme Court affirmed the separate actionable
     wrong requirement for the availability of aggravated damages.
103 *Wallace*, above note 78 at 734.

iii) *Extended Notice Periods*
Despite its apparently "hard line" in *Wallace*, the Supreme Court did leave open an indirect mechanism for compensating employees for mental distress. It restored the trial judge's award of twenty-four months' salary in lieu of notice, justifying the extraordinary amount of these damages by reference to the employer's bad faith and the emotional upset caused to the employee. The Court acknowledged that the principles enunciated in *Addis* failed to acknowledge the human dimensions of the employment contract, the importance of employment to a person's sense of self-worth, identity, and well-being, and the fact that during dismissal the employee is most vulnerable. In light of this, the Court held, the law should discourage callous and insensitive behaviour during the termination of employment. Having rejected an implied term of good faith, the Court nevertheless held that "employers ought to be held to an obligation of good faith and fair dealing in the manner of dismissal, the breach of which will be compensated for by adding to the length of the notice period."[104] Good faith, in this context, includes the requirement that the employer should be "candid, reasonable, honest and forthright"[105] and should avoid being "untruthful, misleading or unduly insensitive."[106] An employee's right to be treated fairly in the manner of dismissal is not affected by any prior agreement to terminate her employment contract pending negotiation of the terms of discharge.[107]

Generally, *Wallace* damages may be appropriate where the employer's conduct is deliberate, malicious, or shows a "blatant disregard for the employee."[108] In subsequent cases, bad faith has been held to include unfounded allegations that the employee was dishonest and abused alcohol,[109] and a dismissal delivered by a newly elected board, without any explanation, to the plaintiff's home late at night, coupled with changing the locks at the plaintiff's place of employment.[110] Maintaining unfounded allegations of unsatisfactory job performance

---

104 *Ibid.* at 742.
105 *Ibid.* at 743.
106 *Ibid.* See also *Stuart v. Navigata Communications Ltd.*, [2007] B.C.J. No. 662 (S.C.).
107 *McKinley*, above note 102 at para. 75. See also *Keays v. Honda Canada Inc.* (2006), 274 D.L.R. (4th) 107 (Ont. C.A.), appeal to S.C.C. filed, [2006] S.C.C.A. No. 470 [*Keays*].
108 *Gismondi v. Toronto (City)* (2003), 64 O.R. (3d) 688 at para. 32 (C.A.), leave to appeal to S.C.C. refused, [2003] S.C.C.A. No. 312. See also *Tanton v. Crane Canada Inc.* (2000), 278 A.R. 137 (Q.B.) [*Tanton*].
109 *Martin v. International Maple Leaf Springs Water Corp.*, [1998] B.C.J. No. 1663 (S.C.).
110 *Mrozowich v. Grandview Hospital District No. 3B* (1998), 125 Man. R. (2d) 259 (Q.B.).

almost until trial, withholding commissions, and delay in issuing a record of employment needed for employment insurance benefits have also been found to constitute bad faith in the manner of dismissal.[111] These actions were held to be unduly insensitive and demeaning. As well, summary dismissal of an employee on disability leave rather than reassigning him to a suitable position consistent with his health condition, and the employers' reduction of their severance offer during negotiation, were found to constitute unfair dealings warranting extension of the notice period.[112] In *Sweetland*,[113] the notice period was extended for the discriminatory treatment of the plaintiff based on his political affiliation, which the court found caused him humiliation, embarrassment, and damage to his sense of self-worth and self-esteem. Extension of the notice period may be appropriate even when the employee may have been dishonest in dealing with the employer in the period leading up to her dismissal, provided the dishonesty did not detrimentally affect the employment relationship.

While the law as set down in *Wallace* provides some measure of protection against emotional distress, this is achieved at the cost of contradiction and incoherence. As the dissenting judgment in *Wallace* pointed out, the *logic* of the newly fashioned award of additional notice for bad faith would appear to be that, where bad-faith dismissal makes it more difficult for the employee to secure alternate employment, the notice period will be increased to compensate for the additional pecuniary loss. The corollary would appear to be that, where the employee is unable to prove that the dismissal made securing another job more difficult, such additional compensation will not be available, notwithstanding the behaviour of the employer or the mental distress suffered by the employee. However, the Court does not follow through on this logic. Instead, Iacobucci J. states that the "humiliation, embarrassment and damage to one's sense of self-worth and self-esteem might all be

---

111 *Marshall v. Watson Wyatt & Co.* (2002), 57 O.R. (3d) 813 (C.A.); *McCulloch v. IPlatform Inc.*, [2004] O.J. No. 5237 (S.C.J.).

112 *McKinley*, above note 102 at paras. 75–77. See also *Keays*, above note 107: employer's unwillingness to accommodate the employee's disability constituted bad faith, warranting an extension of the notice period. In *Prinzo v. Baycrest Centre for Geriatric Care* (2002), 60 O.R. (3d) 474 (C.A.), the court was satisfied that harassment of an employee on disability leave, and her eventual dismissal upon resuming work that caused the employee emotional upset and affected her health, constituted an independently actionable wrong—intentional infliction of mental suffering. The court added that even absent such a finding, the plaintiff would have been entiteld to an extended notice period as per *Wallace*.

113 *Sweetland*, above note 98.

worthy of compensation"[114] in themselves, even if the bad faith of the employer did not affect the plaintiff's employment prospects. Thus, there is an apparent contradiction. The Court has stated that non-pecuniary damages may not be awarded for mental distress; however, where the breach of contract causes mental distress, the pecuniary damages can be increased to take this distress into account even if there is no increased pecuniary loss.[115]

Wallace is certainly not the last word on the matter, because it contains propositions that are difficult to reconcile and ultimately rests on a category confusion.[116] Instead of eliminating non-pecuniary damages in wrongful dismissal cases, *Wallace* has simply moved them into a different category. And they fit poorly into this category because it is one that is best suited for the analysis of pecuniary damages only. A further anomaly is that, by compensating non-pecuniary damages through an extended notice period, the distress and shock suffered by an employee will be valued according to the plaintiff's monthly salary rather than the degree of harm suffered. Injury to highly paid employees and hence their self-worth may be valued more than that of lesser-paid employees, without regard to the often vulnerable position of workers in the latter category. While this may be defensible in the case of pecuniary losses, it is not defensible when the injury complained of is not economic but affects a person's dignity and psychological well-being. Finally, by embedding the duty of good faith in the obligation to give notice, the Court unduly limits the obligation of good faith. The decision would appear to permit the employer to be as callous as it desires, so long as it gives the employee proper notice, or finds some cause (however minor) to justify the dismissal. The dissenting opinion of McLachlin J. is more logical. Damages for lack of notice should be confined to the interest they are best designed to protect (compensation for pecuniary loss during the period that the employee seeks another job). The notice period should be extended only where the employer's bad faith can be shown to have decreased the employee's re-employment prospects. Emotional distress not affecting re-employment prospects should be dealt with separately and more directly. Abusive behaviour causing mental distress should

---

114 *Wallace*, above note 78 at 745.

115 For example, in *Tanton*, above note 108, the court conceded that the callous and insensitive way in which the plaintiff's job was terminated did not affect his re-employment prospects, yet held that an extension of the notice period as per *Wallace* was appropriate in this case to compensate for the bad faith in the manner of dismissal.

116 For an effective critique of *Wallace*, see M.C. Crane, "Developments in Employment Law: The 1997–98 Term" (1999) 10 Sup. Ct. L. Rev. (2d) 341.

be separately actionable in itself, based on breach of an implied term of good faith and fair treatment during dismissal. While not completely adopting McLachlin's view, it appears that some courts will only make modest increases in the notice period where the manner of dismissal, though reprehensible, does not apparently affect the plaintiff's re-employment prospects.[117] In one case, the court suggested that entitlement to Wallace damages arises only where the manner of dismissal makes it difficult for the plaintiff to obtain alternate employment.[118]

iv) Conclusion and Summary
The independently actionable test has now been firmly entrenched in the wrongful dismissal cases, though not in non-employment cases.[119] In employment cases, after Vorvis, Wallace, and McKinley, aggravated damages will be awarded only when the dismissal also amounts to an independent wrong. However, even where there is no independent wrong, where the dismissal is in bad faith, damages for salary in lieu of notice may be increased.

Despite the restriction of non-pecuniary damages in wrongful dismissal cases, there remains one other possibility suggested by some of the caselaw. Non-pecuniary damages may be available when it can be shown that the employment relationship under consideration is different from the norm and contains an actual term (express or implied) promising the employee certain "intangible" or psychological benefits or promising to avoid distress. In this case, certain rare employment contracts might be analogous to the holiday cases or might satisfy the independently actionable test. An illustration of this possibility is the case of Pilon,[120] discussed above.

> The relationship between Pilon and Peugeot in some important respects was not a normal master-and-servant relationship. The evidence convinces me of certain things. Peugeot encouraged its employees to feel that they were part of a family in which management was a father-figure. Long-term employees in positions of responsibil-

---

117 *Clendenning v. Lowndes Lambert (B.C.) Ltd.* (2000), 82 B.C.L.R. (3d) 239 (C.A.); *Birch v. Grinnell Fire Protection a Division of Tyco International of Canada*, [1998] B.C.J. No. 1602 (S.C.); *Pauloski v. Nascor Inc.* (2002), 311 A.R. 67 (Q.B.).
118 *Cimpan v. Kolumbia Inn Daycare Society* (2006), 54 C.C.E.L. (3d) 307 (B.C.S.C.). See also *Robinson v. Fraser Wharves Ltd.* (2000), 5 C.C.E.L. (3d) 81 (B.C.S.C.), where the court justified a three-month extension of the notice period because the defendant's conduct in the manner of dismissal affected the plaintiff's re-employment prospects.
119 *Kempling*, above note 68; *Warrington*, above note 52.
120 Above note 83.

ity, such as Mr. Pilon, were paid less than the going rate in the industry for comparable jobs and in return were told that they have lifetime security. Pilon accepted that assurance and relied upon it....

He said that he thought (and I think that he was reasonable when he did so) that in a family if there was some complaint about his work he would be given some warning and opportunity to improve. In my opinion, it cannot fail to have been in the contemplation of the defendant that if it suddenly, without warning, unlawfully discharged a man whom it had led to believe was secure in his job, for his working life, there would be the gravest likelihood that such a man would suffer vexation, frustration, distress and anxiety.[121]

3) Quantum

In determining the quantum of damages for mental distress in contract, the court must make a subjective calculation of the degree of harm suffered. There is no "market" for mental distress so the awards will frequently be somewhat arbitrary and conventional. However, awards need not be entirely arbitrary. Some principles do suggest themselves. Consumer surplus value can be estimated by asking how much the consumer would have paid for the benefit or to avoid the disbenefit. By this measure, the amount awarded in *Jarvis*[122] can be defended. The plaintiff, who had only two weeks' holiday per year, had "spent" his holiday time on the vacation and that time was thus "wasted." The award made was roughly two weeks' salary. Using this test, it might be suggested that in *Newell*[123] the plaintiffs were undercompensated. They received $500 for the death of one of their dogs. They had "proved" that their value was much higher than this when they had offered to buy the entire first-class cabin of the airplane to ensure that their dogs could travel safely.

In other cases, where there is simply no "objective" way to value the loss, the award will be more conventional. Courts will examine previous cases for analogues and will seek to award a modest amount of money that will provide some solace to the plaintiff for the loss. For example, in *Mason v. Westside Cemeteries*,[124] the court held that, while damages for mental distress were appropriate, the damage actually suffered was minimal. It assessed the damages at $1,000. The plaintiff had

---

121 *Ibid.* at 715.
122 Above note 41.
123 Above note 66.
124 Above note 9.

contracted with the defendant to have his parents' ashes stored so that they could later be buried in a family plot, and when he went to check on their location some years later, he found that the defendant had lost the ashes. The loss that he incurred was held to be foreseeable and there was no doubt that he experienced real suffering, but the award was low because of the minimal suffering involved.

PART TWO

NON-COMPENSATORY DAMAGES

CHAPTER 7

AWARDS MEASURED BY BENEFIT: RESTITUTION

A. INTRODUCTION

The word "restitution" refers both to a particular type of remedy and also to a body of substantive law regarding civil liability. As a type of remedy, restitution is available in specific common law and equitable causes of action to strip unjust gains from a wrongdoer. The basis of restitution is corrective justice because it seeks to restore a disturbed equilibrium between the parties brought about by the unjust enrichment of the defendant at the plaintiff's expense.[1] As a body of substantive law, restitution has emerged as a new basis of liability or cause of action, independent of contract and tort, aimed at preventing unjust enrichment.

Both types of restitution are grounded in the principle of unjust enrichment. As a body of substantive law, the obligations encompassed in the law of restitution are organized around the moral notion that the law should prevent wrongful or unjust gains made at the expense of others. And while restitutionary *remedies* can be said to "compensate"

---

1   See *Peel (Regional Municipality) v. Canada*, [1992] 3 S.C.R. 762 at 804, McLachlin J. [*Peel*]; *Kingstreet Investments Ltd. v. New Brunswick (Department of Finance)*, 2007 SCC 1 at para. 32; James Gordley, *Foundations of Private Law: Property, Torts, Unjust Enrichment* (Oxford, New York: Oxford University Press, 2006) at 445–46; E.J. Weinrib (2000) "Restitutionary Damages As Corrective Justice" Theoretical Inquiries in Law: Vol. 1: No. 1, Article 1, online: www.bepress.com/til/default/vol1/iss1/art1.

the plaintiff for wrongdoing, they are measured by the wrongful benefit to the defendant regardless of the plaintiff's loss, if any.

Restitutionary remedies are, therefore, not strictly compensatory. While they do usually provide compensation for losses suffered by the plaintiff, they are measured not by what the plaintiff has *lost* but by what the defendant has *gained*. In the result, awards based on restitution may be more or less than the pecuniary harm suffered by the plaintiff. They are, of course, attractive to a plaintiff when it is difficult to establish a loss, but the defendant has made a wrongful profit.

The law of restitution has been developing rapidly over the past four decades. Restitutionary remedies have long been available for a number of specified common law and equitable wrongs. For example, in actions of "quasi contract" courts would imply agreements between the parties in order to justify an order for the return of money mistakenly paid by one to the other, or payment for services rendered at the defendant's request. On the equitable side, courts employed restitutionary remedies for breach of trust and rescission. Many of these historical categories of liability are illustrated later in this chapter.

More recently these disparate remedies have been aggregating under the general heading of unjust enrichment. The concept of unjust enrichment, in turn, has evolved from a mere description of these remedies to an independent body of substantive law (including principles of liability) and an autonomous basis of civil liability. In particular, the fiction that restitution turned on there being an implied contract between the parties has been abandoned. As the House of Lords stated, "The alleged contract by the blackmailer and the robber was never made and never could be. The law, in order to do justice, imputed to the wrongdoer a promise which alone as forms of action then existed could give the injured person a reasonable remedy."[2] These "fantastic resemblances of contracts invented in order to meet the requirement of the law as to forms of action"[3] are no longer necessary. Freed from the forms of action, courts now recognize that restitutionary remedies are imposed by law, not by the parties, and are grounded in unjust enrichment, not consent. Somewhat arbitrarily, this more recent trend in Canada may be traced to the 1954 case of *Deglman v. Guaranty Trust Co.*[4] in which the Supreme Court of Canada ordered a restitutionary remedy to a plaintiff who had conferred benefits on his aunt under an unenforceable contract. The Court acknowledged that the obligation to

---

2   *United Australia Ltd. v. Barclay's Bank, Ltd.*, [1941] A.C. 1 at 28 (H.L.).
3   *Ibid.* at 29.
4   *Deglman v. Guaranty Trust Co. of Canada*, [1954] S.C.R. 725 [*Deglman*].

pay was "based not on contract, but on an obligation imposed by law"[5] in order to prevent unjust enrichment.

B. THE PRINCIPLE OF UNJUST ENRICHMENT

The writers of texts have long urged that the specific remedies noted above are better understood as part of an autonomous body of law known as restitution. This body of law is organized around the principle of unjust enrichment. This is the position in the United States, and Canadian courts have moved substantially in this direction. Prominent statements of the principle of unjust enrichment include the early and famous dictum of Lord Mansfield in *Moses v. Macferlan*[6] — "the gist of this kind of action is that the defendant, upon the circumstances of the case, is obliged by the ties of natural justice and equity to refund the money." More contemporary are those found in the American Law Institute's *Restatement (Third) of the Law of Restitution and Unjust Enrichment:*[7] "A person who is unjustly enriched at the expense of another is liable in restitution to the other"; Lord Wright's speech in *Fibrosa,*[8] that "any civilized system of law is bound to provide remedies for cases of what has been called unjust enrichment or unjust benefit, that is to prevent a man from retaining the money of or some benefit derived from another which it is against conscience that he should keep."

In Canada the development of the law of unjust enrichment has been achieved primarily through the evolution of the constructive trust. In a series of cases involving the property rights of cohabiting couples (beginning with *Rathwell v. Rathwell*[9] and *Pettkus v. Becker*[10]), the Supreme Court of Canada substantially consolidated the principles of unjust enrichment.[11] In these cases the Court affirmed that, when one cohabitee contributes in money or services towards the acquisition of property by the other, the principle of unjust enrichment may

---

5   *Ibid.* at 734.
6   (1760), 2 Burr. 1005 at 1012, 97 E.R. 676 (K.B.).
7   American Law Institute, *Restatement (Third) of Restitution and Unjust Enrichment (Tentative Drafts)* (Philadelphia, PA: American Law Institute, 2000–2006) at § 1 [*Restatement (Third)*].
8   *Fibrosa Spolka Akcyjna v. Fairbairn Lawson Combe Barbour Ltd.*, [1943] A.C. 32 at 61 (H.L.).
9   [1978] 2 S.C.R. 436 [*Rathwell*].
10 [1980] 2 S.C.R. 834 [*Pettkus*].
11 See also *Sorochan v. Sorochan*, [1986] 2 S.C.R. 38 [*Sorochan*]; *Peter v. Beblow*, [1993] 1 S.C.R. 980 [*Peter*].

require a restitutionary remedy in favour of the contributor. Liability in this situation does not turn on a contract between the parties, their intent, a tort committed by one against the other, or a statute. It turns simply on the autonomous principle of unjust enrichment. The Court reiterated that the remedy was available when (a) there has been an enrichment of one party; (b) a corresponding deprivation of the other; and (c) there is no juristic reason for the deprivation. Enrichment arises from the conferral of a tangible benefit on the defendant, absent a juristic reason. The benefit may be positive (for example payment of money), or negative (for example an expense saved).[12] It is irrelevant that the defendant does not retain the benefit permanently, subject to a change of position defence. However, a change of position defence is not available to defendants who obtain the enrichment through their own wrongdoing.[13]

The three-part test is now firmly part of Canadian law, though the scope of its application is still being elaborated.[14] In *Garland*, Iacobucci J. sought to clarify the meaning of absence of juristic reason to justify restitution. This requires a two-part analysis. First, the plaintiff must show that the circumstance under which the benefit was conferred on the defendant does not fall within one of the established categories of juristic reasons. The established categories include contract, disposition of law, donative intent, and other valid common law, equitable, or statutory obligations. A *prima facie* case for restitution arises where no juristic reason from an established category exists in the circumstances.[15] Second, a *de facto* burden of proof is then placed on the defendant to show some other reason why she should retain the enrichment. Two important considerations that a defendant can evoke to rebut the *prima facie* case for restitution are the parties' reasonable expectations and public policy.[16]

---

12   *Peel*, above note 1 at 790, McLachlin J. *Restatement (Third)*, above note 7; Andrew Burrows, *Remedies for Torts and Breach of Contract*, 3d ed. (Oxford, New York: Oxford University Press, 2004) at 373.

13   *Garland v. Consumers' Gas Co.*, [2004] 1 S.C.R. 629 at paras. 63–65 [*Garland*].

14   See *ibid.* at para. 30. A similar test is emerging in England. In *B.P. Exploration Co. v. Hunt,* [1979] 1 W.L.R. 783 at 839 (Q.B.), Goff J. stated that the test was (a) receipt by the defendant of a benefit; (b) at the plaintiff's expense; (c) in such circumstances that it would be unjust to allow the defendant to retain the benefit. See also R. Goff, *The Law of Restitution*, 6th ed. by G. Jones (London: Sweet & Maxwell, 2002) at 17.

15   *Garland, ibid.* at para. 44.

16   *Ibid.* at paras. 45–46. For a critique of the two-part test for determining juristic reason, see M. McInnes, "Unjust Enrichment, Juristic Reasons and Palm Tree Justice: *Garland v. Consumers' Gas Co.*" (2004) 41 Can. Bus. L.J. 103.

C. THE AVAILABILITY OF RESTITUTIONARY REMEDIES

Restitutionary remedies have historically been available as extraordinary remedies in a limited number of situations in contract and tort, as well as in equity. The categories of restitutionary remedies have, however, grown over the years, and it would take an entire volume to list them exhaustively, and to explain the substantive principles underlying their availability.[17] The following paragraphs describe the more prominent uses of restitutionary remedies. In each case there are, of course, detailed principles of law regarding when the remedy is available and the limitations of liability. These principles are part of the substantive law of restitution and are not canvassed in detail here. Instead, the following provides a brief overview of the scope of liability for restitution.

1) Breach of Contract

Generally, restitution is not a remedy for breach of contract.[18] Plaintiffs are confined to their compensatory damages and are limited to the loss of the benefit of their bargain. If the defendant happens to make a profit by breaching that exceeds the loss suffered by the plaintiff, so be it. This is, in part, intended to promote efficient breach. In *Bank of America Canada*, the Supreme Court of Canada endorsed the idea of efficient breach: "Efficient breach should not be discouraged by the courts. This lack of disapproval emphasizes that a court will usually award money damages for breach of contract equal to the value of the bargain to the plaintiff."[19] And if the payment by the plaintiff to the defendant exceeds the expected benefit of the exchange to the plaintiff, the plaintiff is confined, on breach, to recovery of that expected benefit. The plaintiff may not, by basing his claim on unjust enrichment, place himself in a better position than if the contract had been performed, since that would alter the basis of the bargain.

---

17   See P.D. Maddaugh & J.D. McCamus, *The Law of Restitution*, looseleaf (Aurora, ON: Canada Law Book, 2004–); G.H.L. Fridman, *Restitution*, 2d ed. (Scarborough, ON: Carswell, 1992); Goff, *The Law of Restitution*, above note 14.

18   *Asamera Oil Corp. v. Sea Oil and General Corp.*, [1979] 1 S.C.R. 633; *Bank of America Canada v. Mutual Trust Co.*, [2002] 2 S.C.R. 601 at paras. 25–31 [*Bank of America Canada*].

19   *Bank of America Canada*, *ibid.* at para. 31. See Chapter 2, Section B(2)(c) for an explanation of the theory of efficient breach.

However, there are some situations where this principle would lead to injustice, and exceptions have been developed. When the plaintiff has conferred a benefit upon another pursuant to a contract, and the other repudiates or breaches the contract before fulfilling any part of their bargain, there has been a "complete failure of consideration" and the innocent party is entitled to restitution of any benefits conferred.[20] The most common situation is where the plaintiff has pre-paid for delivery of goods or services and the defendant fails to carry out the contract.[21] In these situations, recovery is based on the return to the plaintiff of what she has given the defendant, not the plaintiff's expected benefit under the contract.

As well, restitution may be an appropriate remedy to strip a defendant of profits made through the commission of a crime, which also constitutes a breach of contract. In *Attorney General v. Blake*,[22] the defendant, a former secret service agent who spied for Russia, published his memoirs using information he obtained in the course of his employment. This was in breach of his employment contract and also constituted a "crime" under the *Official Secrets Act 1989*. Although the content of the book was no longer classified information when the book was published, disclosure of the information was in violation of his employment contract. The defendant's notoriety as a former secret service agent and a spy generated considerable interest in the book and, consequently, the publisher's willingness to pay huge royalties. The House of Lords upheld the Crown's claim in restitution and awarded the outstanding royalties under the publishing agreement. However, the House of Lords noted that restitutionary remedies for breach of contract should be available only in exceptional situations.[23]

---

20 Traditionally, restitution is available only if the plaintiff has received nothing under the contract: *Hunt v. Silk* (1804), 5 East 449, 102 E.R. 1142 (K.B.). But the law is becoming more flexible in this regard. If the plaintiff has received some benefits under the contract but they are trivial, the court will likely still order restitution. See J. Beatson, *The Use and Abuse of Unjust Enrichment: Essays on the Law of Restitution* (New York: Oxford University Press, 1991) at 4.

21 *Jay Trading Corp. v. Ifax Export & Import Co.*, [1954] 2 D.L.R. 110 (N.S.T.D.).

22 [2001] 1 A.C. 268 (H.L.) [*Blake*].

23 *Ibid.* at 284–85, Lord Nicholls. See also *R. v. Attorney General of England and Wales*, [2003] UKPC 22, also involving a former agent who wrote a book in breach of his confidentiality agreement. There was no total publication ban and, in fact, some agents had also told their stories but the New Zealand Court of Appeal concluded that the Crown was entitled to an account because the Crown, rather than the defendant, is entitled to benefit from publication of the information. This was affirmed by the Privy Council.

While restitution is not available for "ordinary" breaches of contract, such a remedy may be appropriate where the defendant's conduct is cynical and calculated to make a profit, and damages will not be an adequate remedy to protect the plaintiff's interests.[24] There is also some emerging authority for the proposition that, where an equitable remedy might have been appropriate, a restitutionary remedy may be used as an alternative. Where damages would be inadequate to protect a plaintiff from a breach of contract, equity may intervene with the remedy of specific performance or an injunction. When such equitable relief is appropriate, but for some reason unavailable (e.g., because it is too late), a court might award a restitutionary measure of damages for the breach of a negative covenant. *Wrotham Park Estate Co. Ltd. v. Parkside Homes Ltd.*[25] illustrates this principle. A developer had built residential homes on a property, knowing that it was contravening a restrictive covenant prohibiting such development. The plaintiffs sought an injunction ordering the demolition of the buildings, but the injunction was refused on the grounds that this would be an unconscionable waste of needed dwellings. The plaintiff, however, suffered no actual pecuniary loss as a result of the defendant's breach. The court held that the defendants should not be unjustly enriched by the breach and assessed as damages a portion of the defendant's profit from the development, calculated by determining a sum which "might reasonably have been demanded by the plaintiffs ... as a *quid pro quo* for relaxing the covenant."[26] In *Blake*, the House of Lords affirmed the outcome in *Wrotham Park* "as... showing that in contract as well as tort damages are not always narrowly confined to recoupment of financial loss. In a suitable case damages for breach of contract may be measured by the benefit gained by the wrongdoer from the breach."[27]

Further, as Lord Nicholls noted in *Blake*, restitution may be an appropriate remedy for breach of contract in exceptional circumstances in the same way as a plaintiff's interest in performance sometimes makes it just and equitable to grant the equitable remedies of specific performance or injunction. His Lordship noted that, even when courts are awarding damages for breach of contract, they do not slavishly determine the injured party's entitlement based on her financial losses, and that in some cases damages are measured, not by the plaintiff's

---

24   See Richard Posner, *Economic Analysis of Law*, 6th ed. (New York: Aspen, 2003) at 118–19. See also *Restatement (Third)*, above note 7.
25   [1974] 1 W.L.R. 798 (Ch.) [*Wrotham Park*].
26   *Ibid.* at 815.
27   *Blake*, above note 22 at 283–84.

loss, but by reference to the defendant's benefit from wrongdoing. As well, a plaintiff is entitled to elect account of profit as an alternative to claiming damages for breach of confidence arising from a contractual relationship.[28] The House of Lords found the situation in *Blake*, unauthorized publication of information obtained in the course of the defendant's work as a secret service agent in breach of his contract, to be an appropriate case for restitution. Although the House of Lords was careful not to lay down a rigid rule of when such a relief will be appropriate, it suggested that, as a useful guide, the relief may be warranted in situations where "the plaintiff had a legitimate interest in preventing the defendant's profit-making activity and, hence, in depriving him of his profit."[29] In many such cases, the plaintiff's interest could be characterized as proprietary, for which she could have obtained injunctive relief, but the relief is not limited to property-related interests.[30]

Canadian courts have shown a willingness to award restitutionary damages for breach of contract in exceptional circumstances. In *Bank of America Canada*, the Court said one such case is where the defendant, because of her breach, profits in excess of her expected gain had the contract been performed, and the plaintiff's loss is less than the defendant's profit. Specifically, the Court noted that, where a defendant fails to pay money to the plaintiff on a specified date, the benefit to the defendant during the time payment was due and when money was actually paid, the defendant's gain would be the plaintiff's loss and a restitutionary relief may be appropriate in such circumstances.

> To prevent defendants from exploiting the time-value of money to their advantage, by delaying payment of damages so as to capitalize on the time-value of money in the interim, courts must be able to award damages which include an interest component that returns

---

28   *Ibid.* at 284–85.

29   *Ibid.* at 285. See *Esso Petroleum Co. Ltd. v. Niad Ltd.*, [2001] 1 All E.R. (D) 324 (Ch.). Maddaugh & McCamus are skeptical of the application of *Blake* in *Esso Petroleum*: Maddaugh & McCamus, above note 17 at 24-19, note 84. But see a contrary view in R. Goff, *The Law of Restitution, First Supplement to the Sixth Edition*, ed. by G. Jones (London: Sweet & Maxwell, 2004) at 77.

30   See S.M. Waddams, *The Law of Damages*, 2d ed., looseleaf (Aurora, ON: Canada Law Book, 1991)– at 9-10. The basis of restitutionary relief in *Blake* appeared to be deterrent as opposed to proprietary. Among other things, a restitutionary relief was necessary for the Crown to reinforce the importance of maintaining trust and confidence among secret service employees and to ensure the effectiveness of the service. While recognizing that damages for breach of contract may sometimes be based on the defendant's profits from the breach, Lord Hobhouse, dissenting, would prefer to limit the remedy to situations where the plaintiff has proprietary interests in the subject matter of the breach. *Blake, ibid.* at 298–99.

the value acquired by a defendant between breach and payment to the plaintiff.[31]

In this case, the respondent trust company failed to advance funds for a real estate development pursuant to contracts with the developer and the appellant. The appellant subsequently appointed a receiver and sold the project at a substantial loss. In an action against the respondent for breach of contract, the appellant recovered the value of the shortfall plus compound interest and not simple interest as argued by the respondent. In affirming this outcome, the Supreme Court of Canada held that an award of compound interest was appropriate in this case to prevent the respondent from profiting from its breach at the appellant's expense. The Court noted that loans made by the respondent since the time of the breach were based on compound interest rates. To pay the appellant money that it was entitled to receive under the contract at simple interest while the respondent earned compound interest on that money would unjustly confer on the respondent benefits that were intended for the appellant under the contract.[32]

2) Ineffective Transactions

When a contract is entirely void or voidable, the parties may seek restitution of benefits conferred under it. For example, where a contract is void because of a fundamental mistake, or where it is frustrated because of the occurrence of an event that makes performance impossible,[33] a court may order restitution of any benefits already conferred under the agreement. Additionally, when a contract is for some technical reason unenforceable (e.g., because a term is too uncertain, it is not in writing and therefore not in compliance with the statute of frauds), and one party has paid money or rendered services under the supposed contract, a court may also order restitution.[34] For example, in *Estok v. Heguy*[35] the plaintiff fertilized the defendant's fields in the mistaken belief that they had a contract of sale. The contract ultimately failed for uncertainty and the defendant was ordered to pay for the benefit received.

---

31 *Bank of America Canada*, above note 18 at para 33.
32 *Ibid.* at paras. 59–61.
33 *Fibrosa Spolka Akcyjna v. Fairbairn Lawson Combe Barbour Ltd.*, [1943] A.C. 32 at 61 (H.L.). Many provinces now have legislation permitting such restitution. See, for example, *Frustrated Contract Act*, R.S.B.C. 1996, c. 166.
34 *Deglman*, above note 4.
35 (1963), 40 D.L.R. (2d) 88 (B.C.S.C.). But see *Nicholson v. St Denis* (1975), 8 O.R. (2d) 315 (C.A.).

Similarly, where one party confers a benefit upon the other in anticipation of a contract that fails to materialize, there may also be a right to restitution[36] provided the service rendered does not exceed what would normally be performed gratuitously in the circumstances.[37] In *Palachik v. Kiss*[38] the plaintiff improved the defendant's property on the understanding that he would receive part ownership. This agreement was unenforceable because of the *Statute of Frauds*. Nevertheless, the Supreme Court of Canada ordered that the property be impressed with a constructive trust in favour of the plaintiff for the value of the improvements.

In addition, when a contract has been induced by fraud, misrepresentation, duress, or is voidable because of unconscionability, a court may permit the plaintiff to rescind the agreement. As part of rescission, the court may make an order of restitution of any benefits conferred, in order to "unwind" the contract. The order of restitution may apply to money or property transferred under the rescinded agreement. Historically, rescission and restitution could be had only when both parties could be fully restored to their original position by transferring back to each of them any property in its exact condition. Rescission was therefore not available when the benefits exchanged had been consumed or altered. Courts have gradually relaxed this requirement, especially when there is wrongdoing by one of the parties, as in the case of fraud. Where the change in property can be made up for with a monetary adjustment, rescission may still be had.[39]

3) Mistake

When a benefit is conferred by one person upon another because of a mistake (e.g., a mistake as to the identity of a creditor or where a debtor pays the same debt twice) the court may order restitution of the benefit as a matter of corrective justice.[40] Extending this principle, some courts have held that where one party discharges an obligation of another or

---

36   *William Lacey (Hounslow) Ltd. v. Davis*, [1957] 1 W.L.R. 932 (Q.B.); *Brewer v. Chrysler Canada Ltd.*, [1977] 3 W.W.R. 69 (Alta. S.C.T.D.); see G. Jones, "Claims Arising out of Anticipated Contracts Which Do Not Materialize" (1979–80) 18 U.W.O.L. Rev. 447.

37   *POS Media Online v. Queensland Investment Corporation*, [2001] FCA 809 (Aust.).

38   [1983] 1 S.C.R. 623 [*Palachik*].

39   See Maddaugh & McCamus, above note 17 at 5-46–5-47.

40   For an analysis of the theoretical and policy rationales for restitutionary remedies in mistaken conferral of benefits on others, see H. Dagan, "Mistakes" (2001) 79 Tex. L. Rev. 1795.

performs another's duty there is also a right of restitution. Examples include cases where a tenant is forced to repair a landlord's property in order to abate a nuisance. The principle is stated in *Moule v. Garrett*:[41] "Where the plaintiff has been compelled by law to pay, or being compellable by law, has paid money which the defendant was ultimately liable to pay, so that the latter obtains the benefit of the payment by the discharge of his liability; under such circumstances the defendant is held indebted to the plaintiff in the amount."[42] Where one person pays off a joint debt or liability there is a right to "contribution and indemnity" on restitutionary grounds.[43]

A leading case in this area is *Carleton (County) v. Ottawa (City)*.[44] In this case the plaintiff county had mistakenly performed the obligation of the defendant city to care for an indigent person (the city had annexed part of the county and should have assumed the obligations towards the indigent person but she was inadvertently left off the list). The Supreme Court of Canada adopted the law of restitution and ordered the defendant to reimburse the plaintiff. The city had responsibility for this individual and it would have been against conscience to allow it to escape that liability. This case expanded the scope of recovery since historically both parties had to be liable in order for one to be entitled to contribution. A person who makes a voluntary payment to discharge another's debt usually only discharges the debt if he acts with authority. A similar principle applies with respect to voluntary payments to an injured person. The payer has no direct action against the tortfeasor if the payer was not also liable.[45]

---

41   (1872) L.R. 7 Ex. 101.

42   *Ibid.* at 104.

43   According to Maddaugh & McCamus, four elements must be established:

> First, he must show that the compulsion under which the benefit was conferred was a *legal* compulsion [though this may be more liberally construed]. … Second, the plaintiff must show that his payment to the third party served to discharge a *liability* of the defendant.… Third, the plaintiff must show that both he and the defendant were subject to a *common* liability to the third party which, as between the plaintiff and the defendant, the latter was *primarily* obliged to pay.… Finally, the plaintiff must not have *officiously* made … the particular payment.…

Maddaugh & McCamus, above note 17 at 32-3–32-6.

44   [1965] S.C.R. 663.

45   *Esso Petroleum Co. Ltd. v. Hall, Russell & Co. Ltd.*, [1989] A.C. 643 (H.L.); see also Goff, *The Law of Restitution*, above note 14 at 375.

4) Unofficious Conferral of Benefits

Where goods or services are rendered at a person's request, or in circumstances where there is a clear expectation that they will be paid for, the court may order a restitutionary recovery on the basis of *quantum meruit* and *quantum valebat*. Such claims are made when there has been no price set for the services and often, no promise to pay (but a reasonable expectation of payment). These are the old quasi-contractual actions, resting upon the theory that there is an implicit contract between the parties.

Of greater complexity are claims of "necessitous intervention." If a person unofficiously confers an unequivocal benefit upon another person in a situation of necessity, the donor may be entitled to restitution. A Canadian example is *Matheson v. Smiley*.[46] Here the plaintiff doctor was called to the scene of an attempted suicide and rendered services in an unsuccessful attempt to save the life of the deceased. While there was no request by the deceased for assistance and no subsequent promise to pay, the deceased's estate was held liable to compensate the plaintiff. The court held that the response of the plaintiff was reasonable in the circumstances of the emergency and the law will imply an obligation on the estate to pay.

5) Gains from Wrongdoing

The most general category of restitutionary claims is claims in respect of profits from committing a wrong. The commission of a crime or a tort against the plaintiff, or the breach of a fiduciary obligation, may give rise to a right of restitution. In modern law, "white collar crime," including bribery, corporate espionage, breach of confidence, and theft of intellectual property, feature very prominently in the law of restitution.

a)   Waiver of Tort and Trespass
Historically, when as a result of committing certain common law torts such as trespass or misappropriation of property, a defendant acquired a sum of money or other tangible benefit, a plaintiff could "waive the tort and sue in *assumpsit*." Essentially, the law permits the plaintiff to elect to treat the defendant as an "agent" or "partner" rather than a tortfeasor, and to collect from the defendant the profits earned, rather than the damages suffered.[47] A related notion is "ratification." The victim of a

---

46   (1932), 40 Man. R. 247 (C.A.).
47   Explained in *United Australia Ltd. v. Barclay's Bank, Ltd.*, [1941] A.C. 1 (H.L.).

fraud, for example, may "ratify" the fraud and seek an accounting of the profits on the basis that the wrongdoer has become the victim's agent.[48]

Almost any tort resulting in enrichment of the defendant can be waived, including conversion (e.g., a claim for the proceeds of a wrongful sale), fraud, and trespass to goods. There is some confusion whether trespass to land can be waived. Where, as part of the trespass, the defendant removes things of value from the land (e.g., timber and minerals), the plaintiff may sue in conversion for the price received by the defendant for the timber or minerals.[49] However, where the defendant merely uses the plaintiff's land (e.g., for transportation), the remedy of waiver of tort has not been available, though it is in the United States and most authors are of the opinion that it should be.[50] Nevertheless, through the use of punitive damage awards (in which damages are measured by the total benefit to the trespasser) courts in Canada have achieved the same result. For example, in *Austin v. Rescon Const. (1984) Ltd.*[51] the defendants trespassed by installing thirty-five to thirty-nine anchor rods below the surface of the plaintiff's property as part of the shoring for the foundation of a large building. While there was only nominal damage to the plaintiff's property, the defendant saved anywhere from $21,000 to over $30,000 by using the rods. The Court of Appeal increased the award of exemplary damages from $7,500 to $30,000 in order to eliminate the defendant's profit entirely.

b) **Economic Torts, Misappropriation of Intellectual Property, and Breach of Confidence**

Economic torts, also known as business or commercial torts, include an employee or agent receiving "secret commissions" and bribes, and the misappropriation of intangible commercial values such as copyrights, patents and trademarks, and sometimes of confidential information. Many of these areas are statutorily controlled, as for example, in the case of patents, where an accounting of profits is permitted as an alternative to a damages claim.[52] Similarly, the *Copyright Act*[53] also

---

48 H. Street, *Principles of the Law of Damages* (London: Sweet & Maxwell, 1962).
49 *Shewish v. MacMillan Bloedel Ltd.* (1990), 48 B.C.L.R. (2d) 290 (C.A.).
50 Maddaugh & McCamus, above note 17 at 24-16–24-17.
51 (1989), 36 B.C.L.R. (3d) 21 (C.A.) [*Austin*]; *Townsview Properties Ltd. v. Sun Construction and Equipment Co. Ltd.* (1973), 2 O.R. (2d) 213 (H.C.J.), aff'd (1974), 7 O.R. (2d) 666 (C.A.) [*Townsview Properties*].
52 For example, the *Patent Act*, R.S.C. 1985, c. P-4. An accounting of profits may be ordered as an alternative to damages: *Teledyne Industries Ltd. v. Lido Industrial Products Ltd.* (1979), 45 C.P.R. (2d) 18 (F.C.T.D.), var'd (1981), 57 C.P.R. (2d) 29, leave to appeal to S.C.C. refused (1981), 59 C.P.R. (2d) 183n (S.C.C.).
53 R.S.C. 1985, c. C-42.

allows remedies of damages and restitution. For example, in *Pro Arts Inc. v. Campus Crafts Holdings Ltd.*[54] the claimant successfully sued for an accounting of the profits made by the defendant who had infringed the plaintiff's copyright in a highly successful poster of Farrah Fawcett-Majors. The same is true of trademarks,[55] now controlled under the *Trade-Marks Act.*[56] A Canadian trademark restitution case is *Athans v. Canadian Adventure Camps Ltd.*[57] The plaintiff, a famous water-skier, brought an action when a camp was promoted using a drawing bearing a close resemblance to the plaintiff's trademark photograph. The plaintiff recovered a percentage of the gross receipts of the camp. In *Draper v. Trist and Tristbestos Brake Linings Ltd.*,[58] a "passing off" case, Sir Wilfred Greene, M.R. stated the general principle that applies in taking an account of profits:

> [T]he damage which the plaintiff has suffered is totally immaterial. The object of the account is to give to the plaintiff the actual profits the defendants have made and of which equity strips them as soon as it establishes the profits were improperly made.[59]

Restitutionary remedies are frequently used in cases involving the misappropriation of trade secrets. In *Peter Pan Manufacturing Corporation v. Corsets Silhouette Ltd.*,[60] the defendants used techniques for manufacturing brassieres that had been learned in confidence while making some of the plaintiff's products under licence. Pennycuick J. found the plaintiff had a restitutionary right and ordered an account of all the profits made using the confidential process.

A full discussion of the scope of protection of trade secrets, and especially the newly emerging protection for confidential information, is beyond the scope of this work. But, by way of illustration, in *LAC Minerals Ltd. v. Int'l Corona Resources Ltd.*,[61] the Supreme Court of Canada affirmed the availability of restitutionary remedies in this context. LAC approached Corona for the purpose of discussing a joint venture. In the course of the discussions, Corona disclosed confidential information to LAC, which demonstrated the strong potential of significant mineral de-

54   (1980), 28 O.R. (2d) 422 (H.C.J.) [*Pro Arts*].
55   *Lever v. Goodwin* (1887), 36 Ch. D. 1 at 7 (C.A.), Cotton L.J.; *Dubiner v. Cheerio Toys and Games Ltd.* (1966), 55 D.L.R. (2d) 420 (Ex. Ct.).
56   R.S.C. 1985, c. T-13.
57   (1977), 17 O.R. (2d) 425 (H.C.J.).
58   [1939] 3 All E.R. 513 (C.A.).
59   *Ibid.* at 522.
60   [1963] 3 All E.R. 402 (Ch.) [*Peter Pan Manufacturing*].
61   [1989] 2 S.C.R. 574 [*LAC Minerals*].

posits on property adjoining property being developed by Corona. LAC purchased the adjoining property and developed a successful mine. The Supreme Court held that this was a breach of confidence and imposed a constructive trust on the defendant to ensure it did not benefit from its wrongdoing. *LAC Minerals* strikingly reveals the difference between restitutionary remedies and ordinary damage claims.

The remedy granted in *LAC Minerals* illustrates the significance of restitutionary remedies. The deal anticipated between the parties had been that, while Corona might acquire the property, the parties would probably negotiate a joint venture based on 50/50 ownership. Thus, LAC argued that the measure of compensatory damages would be 50 percent of the value of the mine. This is what Corona would have received had there been no wrong. Sopinka J. accepted this measure. The majority, however, awarded to Corona the entire property in the mine, less LAC's development costs. As La Forest J. explained,

> The essence of the imposition of fiduciary obligations is in its utility in the promotion and preservation of desired social behaviour.... The approach taken by my colleague Sopinka J. would, in my view, have the effect not of encouraging bargaining in good faith, but of encouraging the contrary. If by breaching an obligation of confidence one party is able to acquire an asset entirely for itself, at a risk of only having to compensate the other for what the other would have received if a formal relationship between them were concluded, the former would be given a strong incentive to breach the obligation and acquire the asset. In the present case, it is true that had negotiations been concluded, LAC could also have acquired an interest in the Corona land, but that is only an expectation and not a certainty. Had Corona acquired the Williams property, as they would have but for LAC's breach, it seems probable that negotiations with LAC would have resulted in a concluded agreement. However, if LAC, during the negotiations, breached a duty of confidence owed to Corona, it seems certain that Corona would have broken off negotiations and LAC would be left with nothing. In such circumstances, many business people, weighing the risks, would breach the obligation and acquire the asset. This does nothing for the preservation of the institution of good faith bargaining or relationships of trust and confidence. The imposition of a remedy which restores an asset to the party who would have acquired it but for a breach of fiduciary duties or duties of confidence acts as a deterrent to the breach of duty and strengthens the social fabric those duties are imposed to protect.[62]

---

62   *Ibid.* at 672–73.

Third parties can be liable for breach of confidence. In *A-G. v. Guardian Newspaper Ltd. (No. 2)*,[63] the House of Lords ruled that a newspaper which had aided a member of the British Secret Service to breach his lifelong obligation of confidence to the Crown, by publishing excerpts of his book *Spycatcher*,[64] was liable to account for all profits accruing to it through publishing the excerpts. Lord Keith remarked that the availability of this remedy would "lessen the temptation for recipients of confidential information to misuse it for financial gain."[65]

c) Breach of Fiduciary Duty

One of the most common uses of restitutionary remedies is to rectify breaches of fiduciary duties. The concept of a fiduciary obligation derives from equity. The best-known fiduciary is the trustee—a person who legally owns property and manages it for another's benefit. But fiduciary relationships can arise in other contexts, such as bankers and customers, employees and employers,[66] doctors and patients.[67] Indeed, the Supreme Court of Canada has been clear that the categories of fiduciaries are not closed. In *Frame v. Smith*,[68] Wilson J. explained that the three indicia of a fiduciary relationship are as follows:

(1) The fiduciary has scope for the exercise of some discretion or power.
(2) The fiduciary can unilaterally exercise that power or discretion so as to affect the beneficiary's legal or practical interests.
(3) The beneficiary is peculiarly vulnerable to or at the mercy of the fiduciary holding the discretion or power.

Where a fiduciary makes a personal profit or wrongful gain from her position, the principal may seek restitutionary remedies such as an account or constructive trust, even though the principal may have suffered no "loss." For example, where the director of a company makes a secret profit by taking advantage of a situation where the corporation is unable to act, the director may be subject to restitutionary remedies.[69] Notably, the basis of the remedy in these cases is the benefit obtained

---

63 [1988] 3 W.L.R. 776 (H.L.) [*Guardian*].
64 P. Wright, *Spycatcher: The Candid Autobiography of a Senior Intelligence Officer* (Toronto: Stoddard, 1987).
65 *Guardian*, above note 63 at 788.
66 *Pre-Cam Exploration & Development Ltd. v. McTavish*, [1966] S.C.R. 551 [*McTavish*].
67 *Norberg v. Wynrib*, [1992] 2 S.C.R. 226.
68 [1987] 2 S.C.R. 99 at 136.
69 *Regal (Hastings) Ltd. v. Gulliver*, [1942] 1 All E.R. 378 (H.L.).

by the wrongdoer, rather than the loss sustained by the plaintiff. Where a fiduciary makes a wrongful profit, a restitutionary claim will lie even though that profit might not have been available to the plaintiff. As Laskin C.J. said in *Canadian Aero Service Ltd. v. O'Malley*,

> Liability for breach of fiduciary duty does not depend upon proof by Canaero that, but for their intervention, it would have obtained the … contract; nor is it a condition of recovery of damages that Canaero establish what its profit would have been or what it has lost by failing to realize the corporate opportunity in question. It is entitled to compel the faithless fiduciaries to answer for their default according to their gain.[70]

6) Future Development

With the recognition by the Supreme Court of Canada of the general principle of unjust enrichment in the constructive trust cases, it may now be said that the categories of restitution are not closed. In a series of cases involving the property rights of cohabiting couples (beginning with *Rathwell v. Rathwell*[71] and *Pettkus v. Becker*[72]), the Supreme Court of Canada substantially consolidated the principles of unjust enrichment and confirmed that they stand as an autonomous basis of liability.[73] In *Peter v. Beblow*,[74] for example, the (female) plaintiff and (male) defendant had lived together for twelve years in a home owned by the defendant (and purchased prior to the relationship). They had merged their families (he with two children, she with four). The defendant was the primary wage earner, but the plaintiff had done nearly all the work in the home, inside and out. She also worked part-time outside the home. The Court ordered a constructive trust over the property in favour of the plaintiff. It reiterated that the remedy was available when (a) there has been an enrichment of one party; (b) a corresponding deprivation of the other; and (c) there is no juristic reason for the deprivation. The Court also affirmed that the required "benefit" or contribution need not be monetary. McLachlin J. (for the majority) held that the tests were satisfied.

> The appellant's housekeeping and child-care services constituted a benefit to the respondent (1st element), in that he received household

---

70   (1973), [1974] S.C.R. 592 at 621–22 [*Canadian Aero*].
71   Above note 9.
72   Above note 10.
73   See also *Palachik*, above note 38; *Sorochan*, above note 11.
74   Above note 11.

services without compensation, which in turn enhanced his ability to pay off his mortgage and other assets. These services also constituted a corresponding detriment to the appellant (2nd element), in that she provided services without compensation. Finally, since there was no obligation existing between the parties which would justify the unjust enrichment ... there is no juristic reason for the enrichment (3rd element).[75]

Canadian courts have consistently applied the principles articulated in these cases, although they have not always found it appropriate to impose a constructive trust in favour of the party who provided the benefit. Monetary damages have been awarded where a constructive trust is deemed inappropriate.[76]

D. REMEDIAL OPTIONS FOR UNJUST ENRICHMENT

1) Introduction

Restitutionary remedies come in many forms. Ultimately, they are all united by the theory of unjust enrichment in that their aim is to strip the defendant of wrongful gains. However, in practice the various remedies have different uses and characteristics. First, the courts may make monetary and specific orders. A monetary order simply orders the defendant to pay a sum of money to the plaintiff. A specific order relates to specific property. Courts may make both *in personam* and *in rem* orders. The latter are orders that actually affect the ownership of property and are good "against the entire world."

2) Monetary Restitution

The remedy of "restitution" generally covers the old common law *quasi-contractual* "counts." These include orders for "money had and received," *quantum meruit*, and *quantum valebat*. These are all old common law monetary remedies, available to recover money paid by mistake, under duress or as the result of fraud (money had and received), and to recover fair compensation for *goods* (*quantum valebat*) or services (*quantum meruit*). For example, in *Deglman v. Guaranty Trust Co.*[77] the Supreme

75   *Ibid.* at 989.
76   For example, see *Panara v. Di Ascenzo* (2005), 361 A.R. 382 (C.A.).
77   Above note 4.

Court of Canada awarded the plaintiff $3,000 on a *quantum meruit* basis for services rendered to his aging aunt, pursuant to an unenforceable contract (that she would leave him her house in her will).[78]

At this stage in the development of the law it is no longer necessary to distinguish among the different "counts" referred to above. It is permissible simply to use the term "restitution" to describe any *in personam* monetary order designed to require restitution of a benefit. In these cases, the restitutionary measure of damages is generally the same as the compensatory measure. The "gain" to the defendant is measured by the benefit received from (and therefore lost by) the plaintiff.

3) The Constructive Trust

Perhaps the most highly developed restitutionary remedy in Canada is the constructive trust. Historically, the constructive trust was used as a remedy against wrongdoing by trustees and fiduciaries. More recently, as explained above, the constructive trust has been used extensively in Canada as both a basis of liability and remedy in situations involving family property. However, it is certainly not confined to these situations.

The import of the constructive trust is that the defendant, who has acquired property, is declared to be a trustee for the plaintiff so that the plaintiff in effect becomes the beneficial owner. Such orders are accompanied by a decree that the defendant transfer the property to the plaintiff, or sell it and pay over the proceeds to the plaintiff. As Dickson J. explained, it "subjects the person holding title to the property ... to an equitable duty to convey it to another on the ground that he would be unjustly enriched if he were permitted to retain it."[79] The basis of constructive trust, therefore, is not the intention of the parties, whether expressed or implied. Rather, it is in accordance with good conscience. The constructive trust is not confined to situations where the defendant has taken property from the plaintiff. It may now be used in any situation where the principles of unjust enrichment indicate that the plaintiff should be entitled to property owned by the defendant.[80]

One important characteristic of the constructive trust is that it is an *in rem* remedy that gives the plaintiff ownership of specific property. As such, the plaintiff is not a mere judgment creditor. This is important when the defendant has insufficient funds to satisfy all outstanding

78   See also *Pacific National Investment Ltd. v. Victoria (City)*, [2004] 3 S.C.R. 575; *Stochinsky v. Chetner Estate* (2003), 330 A.R. 309 (C.A.).
79   *Rathwell*, above note 9 at 454.
80   *LAC Minerals*, above note 61 at 677.

debts because the effect of the constructive trust is to give the plaintiff priority over other creditors. Thus, an important consideration in making the order is whether it is appropriate that the plaintiff have priority over other creditors in bankruptcy proceedings.[81] Other factors that are important in deciding whether a constructive trust is appropriate include the "moral quality of the defendant's act" and also the difficulty of quantifying in precise terms a monetary damages award.[82]

Another form of proprietary relief is the "equitable lien." The equitable lien makes a charge on an asset in the defendant's hands, thus securing payment of a judgment against the defendant for an amount of money.[83]

4) Accounting

Accounting is a monetary remedy originally developed by the Courts of Equity to be used when neither common law damages, nor the usual equitable remedies of injunction and specific performance, would be adequate or appropriate. Its effect is to require the defendant to account to the plaintiff for an unjustly acquired profit. Accounting is an attractive remedy where the plaintiff has suffered little or no damage and the defendant has profited from her wrongdoing.

The categories of cases in which account is available are not closed. The remedy is commonly used in cases where the defendant has obtained a secret commission[84] or bribe,[85] or made a personal profit through the misuse of trust property.[86] It is frequently used when the defendant has wrongly exploited an opportunity belonging to the principal,[87] or improperly used confidential information.[88]

Accounting is a true restitutionary remedy, since it is measured by the gain to the defendant rather than the loss to the plaintiff. One illustration of the advantages of accounting is *Guardian*.[89] In this case the

---

81 *Ibid.* at 678.
82 *Ibid.*
83 *Boardman v. Phipps*, [1967] 2 A.C. 46 (H.L.); *McTavish*, above note 66; *LAC Minerals Ltd. v. Int'l Corona Resources Ltd.* (1987), 44 D.L.R. (4th) 592 (Ont. C.A.).
84 See, for example, *Turnbull v. Garden* (1869), 38 L.J. Ch. 331; *Queen of Spain v. Parr* (1869), 39 L.J. Ch. 73; *Copp v. Lynch* (1882), 26 S.J. 348.
85 See, for example, *Fawcett v. Whitehouse* (1829), 1 Russ. & M. 132, 39 E.R. 51; *Lister & Co. v. Stubbs* (1890), 45 Ch. D. 1 (C.A.); *Williams v. Barton*, [1927] 2 Ch. 9.
86 See, for example, *Solloway v. McLaughlin* (1937), [1938] A.C. 247, [1937] 4 D.L.R. 593 (P.C.); and *Zwicker v. Stanbury*, [1953] 2 S.C.R. 438.
87 See, for example, *Canadian Aero*, above note 70.
88 See, for example, *McLeod and More v. Sweezey*, [1944] S.C.R. 111.
89 Above note 63.

defendant published excerpts of the "Spycatcher" memoirs, which used secrets and confidential information from the English secret service. The defendant newspaper was ordered to disgorge all the profits that it earned from the publication. Obviously, the "damages" paid by the defendant far exceeded any monetary loss suffered by the plaintiff, and the remedy was held to be appropriate on the basis that "no one should be permitted to gain from his own wrongdoing."[90] Similarly, in *Blake*, the House of Lords applied the accounting method to strip the defendant of outstanding royalties on a book published in breach of his contract as a secret service agent, although the information was no longer classified at the time of the publication and there was no tangible loss to the Crown.

Accounting may be ordered where the defendant deliberately misappropriates the plaintiff's property in circumstances that show disregard for the plaintiff's rights and this yields substantial profits for the defendant. It is not uncommon for courts to also award punitive damages in addition to an order for accounting.[91] It follows then that courts may be less inclined to order accounting where the defendant's conduct is innocent.[92] As well, accounting may not be appropriate for breaches of ordinary commercial contracts, especially where the plaintiff's interests may be adequately protected through the use of another remedy. The exception may be where the breach results in exceptional profits for the defendant or where there is a breach of fiduciary duty.[93]

Accounting becomes complex when the profits gained have come from several sources, such as when a defendant has mixed her own and the claimant's property, or by the defendant's combining of capital and labour with the confidential information he has wrongfully employed. These difficulties are discussed below.

5) Rescission

The decree of rescission was originally an equitable remedy associated with the provision of grounds for setting aside contracts or gifts (e.g., for misrepresentation, mistake, fraud, and unconscionability). Rescission has the effect of terminating the contractual rights of the parties, and

90   *Ibid.* at 788.
91   See *Pro Arts*, above note 54; *Evocation Publishing Corp. v. Hamilton* (2002), 24 C.P.R. (4th) 52 (B.C.S.C.).
92   See *Seager v. Copydex (No. 2)*, [1969] 2 All E.R. 718 (C.A.). See also *Montreal Trust Co. v. Williston Wildcatters Corp.*, [2005] 4 W.W.R. 20 (Sask. C.A.), leave to appeal to S.C.C. refused, [2004] S.C.C.A. No. 474.
93   See *Experience Hendrix LLC v. PPX Enterprises*, [2003] EWCA Civ 323 (C.A.) [*Experience Hendrix*].

restoring the *status quo ante*. The restitutionary relief may be either proprietary (the restoration of property) or personal (repayment of money). Traditionally such relief is said to be available only when it is possible to make "perfect" restitution to both parties, and is not therefore available when benefits cannot be returned by one (e.g., because they have deteriorated or been consumed).[94] However, in practice, courts will ignore minor difficulties, or will make monetary adjustments when there has been some irreversible deterioration in the condition of property to be restored.[95] Courts will also refuse restitution if the agreement has been affirmed or if third-party rights have intervened.[96]

E. MEASURING THE ENRICHMENT: VALUATION ISSUES

Restitutionary remedies, whether framed as claims for an account or a constructive trust, are based on unjust enrichment and are measured by the benefit wrongfully obtained by the defendant. However, measuring that benefit can sometimes be a complex matter. Where the restitutionary claim is simply for the return of money had and received (e.g., a sum paid to the defendant by mistake, or the price paid for goods that are never delivered), the matter is usually quite simple. Where the claim is based on *quantum meruit* or *quantum valebat* for the reasonable value of goods and services, courts can usually ascertain a reasonable price by which the value of the benefit can be measured. However, in other cases, valuing the benefit can be more complex. The following sections outline the primary means by which courts undertake the assessment of a wrongfully acquired benefit.[97]

1) Net Profit Method

Whether the plaintiff is seeking an accounting or a constructive trust, the first, and most favourable method of measuring the extent of the benefit will be the entire net profit earned by the defendant from the

---

94   *Redican v. Nesbitt*, [1924] S.C.R. 135; *Redgrave v. Hurd* (1881), 20 Ch. D. 1 (C.A.). See *Frigidaire Corp. v. Steedman* (*sub nom. Steedman v. Frigidaire Corp.*), [1933] 1 D.L.R. 161 (P.C.), var'g [1931] O.R. 285 (C.A.) for a case where *restitutio in integrum* was not possible.

95   *Wiebe v. Butchart's Motors Ltd.*, [1949] 4 D.L.R. 838 (B.C.C.A.).

96   *Morin v. Anger* (1931), 66 O.L.R. 327 (C.A.); *Barry v. Stoney Point Canning Co.* (1917), 55 S.C.R. 51; *Kingu v. Walmar Ventures Ltd.* (1986), 10 B.C.L.R. (2d) 15 (C.A.).

97   G.B. Klippert, *Unjust Enrichment* (Toronto: Butterworths, 1983) at 221.

wrongdoing. This is the difference between the defendant's gross receipts and the expense in acquiring them.[98] The defendant is entitled to deduct its costs of doing business, but the burden rests on the defendant to establish what amounts may be deducted,[99] and where there is a chance of error, the courts will favour the claimant as a matter of principle. Although the net profit method appears to be plaintiff-favourable, it is rarely used, among other things, because of the complexities of assessing actual profit from the defendant's activities, and also because some of the profits may be due to the defendant's own efforts, time, and skill.[100] Further, sometimes what might appear to be a profitable venture could, in fact, be a losing proposition after all the deductions have been made.

In *Pro Arts*,[101] an American poster manufacturer and distributor brought an action for infringement of copyright against an Alberta company that had produced a "bootleg" version of a top-selling poster of Farrah Fawcett-Majors. In this case, there was no significant creative input by the defendant; the defendant's act was "a clear, deliberate and calculated act of piracy";[102] and the defendant, to a large extent, lived off the avails of counterfeiting. In assessing the damages, Labrosse J. explained:

> The word "profit" is not defined in the [Canadian Copyright] Act and I propose to give it its ordinary meaning: the excess of the price received over the cost of purchasing and handling or producing and marketing goods....[103]

To determine the amount of profit in this case, the total units sold (less those removed from retailers and destroyed) were multiplied by the average selling price. Proven costs, including an allowance for overheads, were deducted from this total.

At the heart of the decision to employ a net profit method is the assumption that all of the defendant's gain from an enterprise is attributable to the wrong. A useful illustration of the method is provided by *Peter Pan Manufacturing Corporation v. Corsets Silhouette Ltd.*[104] in which the plaintiff sought an accounting of the profit earned by the defend-

---

98 See the U.S. case, *Henry's Drive-In Inc. v. Anderson*, 37 Ill. App. 2d 113, 185 N.E. 2d 103 (1962).
99 *Pro Arts*, above note 54 at 437–38, Labrosse J.
100 See *Experience Hendrix*, above note 93 at para. 44, Mance L.J.
101 Above note 54 at 437–38, Labrosse J.
102 *Ibid.* at 430.
103 *Ibid.* at 437.
104 *Peter Pan Manufacturing*, above note 60.

ant from making brassieres wrongfully incorporating elements of the plaintiff's design. The profit for which the defendant was made to account was based simply on the revenue from sales, deducting what the defendant expended on manufacturing the goods. The court rejected as impracticable an alternative method urged by the defendant, where the benefit from the wrong would be measured by the *additional* profit it made from utilizing the plaintiff's intellectual property, over what it would have made by selling its own products without any wrongdoing. The court held that manufacture of the brassieres "necessarily and inevitably involved the use of confidential information"[105] and thus they could not have been manufactured without it. Where the defendant is able to prove that it could have manufactured the goods legitimately, this alternate method may be utilized (and is discussed as the savings-comparison method).

In arriving at a "net" figure, the defendant is permitted to deduct the direct costs of manufacturing, distribution, marketing, and sales. The defendant will also be allowed a proportion of administrative overhead where such costs have been increased by the manufacture of the particular product. Whether non-variable expenses such as overhead, insurance, and real estate taxes will be allowed varies depending upon the facts of the case and, in particular, whether the wrongdoing was intentional or innocent. If these expenses are in the nature of salaries to a wrongdoer, they will not be deducted.

2) Apportionment Method

Frequently, it will be inappropriate to attribute the defendant's entire net profit from an enterprise to the wrong. For example, the defendant may have misappropriated only a small component of the goods that it manufactures, utilizing its own property in the main. In these cases, the courts will award to the plaintiff that portion of the defendant's profit attributable to the wrong.

Edwards v. Lee's Administrators,[106] a U.S. waiver of tort case, is a good example of the apportionment method. The plaintiff landowner sued for an accounting of profits realized by the defendant neighbour from exhibiting "Great Onyx Cave," a cave that extended under the plaintiff's land. The plaintiff had no independent access to the cave, and the defendant had expended considerable capital and labour in attracting patrons to the cave and in improving the facilities. The court

---

105   *Ibid.* at 412.
106   *Edwards v. Sims*, 24 S.W.2d 619 (Kentucky C.A. 1929).

adopted an accounting method to determine the net profit obtained by the defendant from the trespass, taking the proportion of the cave under the plaintiff's land (30 percent) and applying it to the net proceeds received by the defendant. Moreover, only the net profits from the cave were included; those from the operation of the defendant's adjoining hotel were not counted. The plaintiffs were entitled to a proportion of cave exhibition profits, plus interest.

The defendant has the burden of separating the profits attributable to the wrong from profits attributable to other factors, such as the defendant's superior manufacturing or marketing. For the defendant, the apportionment method is often preferable to net profit, because it allows a deduction for such intangibles as goodwill, expertise, and special knowledge.

Sawatsky v. Stagecoach Publishing Co. Ltd.[107] illustrates a rather simple and mechanical application of the apportionment method. In this case, since 40 percent of the material in a book had been derived from a copyright infringement, the infringer had to pay 40 percent of his profits to the claimant. However, this kind of apportionment, while easy to calculate, does not in any meaningful way quantify the value of the misappropriated material to the success of the entire book.

3) Savings-Comparison Method

In some cases the defendant's entire net profit cannot be attributed to the wrong, because the wrong was only a small element of an otherwise lawful enterprise. In *Siddell v. Vickers*, the Court of Appeal explained that, where the defendant could have engaged in its enterprise without committing the wrong, but was able to engage in the enterprise more profitably because of the wrong, "The true test of comparison was with what the defendants would probably have used instead of the invention."[108] For example, where the wrong consists of wrongfully hiring away employees from a competitor to design a product, the defendant may often argue that the product would have been developed in any event. The only effect of the wrong is that it gave the defendant a "headstart." In these cases, the benefit to the defendant may be measured by the savings achieved by the wrong, despite the older rule that restitution was available only when the defendant had gained specific property or proceeds from the plaintiff and that a mere savings or "negative

---

107 [1981] Y.J. No. 4 (B.C.C.A. sitting as the Yukon C.A.).
108 *Siddell v. Vickers* (1892), 9 R.P.C. 152 at 153 (Eng. C.A.).

benefit" could not be the basis of restitution.[109] An illustration of the savings method is *Arbutus Park Estates Ltd. v. Fuller*.[110] Here, the defendant failed to comply with a restrictive covenant, which prohibited the construction of a garage until the plans and specifications met with the plaintiff's approval. While the plaintiff suffered no actual loss as a result of the wrong, the defendant obtained a wrongful benefit. The plaintiff was allowed to recover the amount that the defendant had *saved* by not using an architect to prepare the required plans.

The savings method has been used in cases where the defendant has wrongfully acquired confidential information making it less costly to produce a product.[111] In Chapter 3 the action for breach of confidence was discussed. There it was explained how, in an action for misusing confidential information, courts may charge the wrongdoer the research and development costs that it would have incurred to acquire the information legitimately.[112] In these cases the "benefit" to the wrongdoer is the savings on "consultancy fees." Another alternative in these cases, discussed in the next section, is to assess damages, not according to the defendant's savings, but according to the plaintiff's opportunity cost. A final possibility is a simple damages remedy compensating the plaintiff for lost profits or sales.[113]

While not framed in terms of restitution, punitive damages cases often utilize the savings method. *Townsview Properties Ltd. v. Sun Construction and Equipment Co. Ltd.*[114] is a problematic example of the savings method in this context. The plaintiff landowners sued the defendants, a construction company and a development company, who were erecting a building on adjoining property and who wrongfully excavated the plaintiff's land. This resulted in a savings for the defendants of seven to ten thousand dollars. The judge awarded "punitive damages" in the amount of five thousand dollars.

The award in *Townsview* neither strips the benefit gained nor deters such conduct, since it leaves the defendant with a net savings. It is more of a hefty licence fee for the trespass. Other cases have gone further,

109 *Phillips v. Homfray* (1883), 24 Ch. D. 439 (C.A.).
110 *Arbutus Park Estates Ltd. v. Fuller* (1976), [1977] 1 W.W.R. 729 (B.C.S.C.).
111 *Telex Corp. v. International Business Machine Corp.*, 367 F. Supp. 258 (N.D. Okla. 1973); rev'd in part 510 F.2d 894 (10th Cir. 1975).
112 *Apotex Fermentation Inc. v. Novopharm Ltd.* (1998), 129 Man. R. (2d) 161 (C.A.); *ICAM Technologies Corp. v. EBCO Industries Ltd.* (1993), 85 B.C.L.R. (2d) 318, 52 C.P.R. (3d) 61 (C.A.), aff'g (1991), 36 C.P.R. (3d) 504 (S.C.).
113 *Cadbury Schweppes Inc. v. FBI Foods Ltd.*, [1999] 1 S.C.R. 142. See discussion in Chapter 3.
114 *Townsview Properties*, above note 51.

and awarded the entire savings. In *Austin*,[115] the defendants trespassed by installing thirty-five to thirty-nine anchor rods below the surface of the plaintiff's property as part of the shoring for the foundation of a large building. While there was only nominal damage to the plaintiff's property, the defendant saved anywhere from $21,000 to over $30,000 by using the rods. The Court of Appeal increased the award of exemplary damages from $7,500 to $30,000.

4) Opportunity-Cost Method

Closely related to the savings method is the opportunity-cost method. This method of calculating damages derives from the old "way-leave" cases[116] in which the defendant has trespassed on the plaintiff's property to make a profit but caused no harm to the plaintiff's property. Damages are calculated according to what the plaintiff might have charged the defendant as a way-leave or rent. This principle was considered and extended in *Whitwam v. Westminster Brymbo Coal and Coke Co.*[117] in which the defendant trespassed on the plaintiff's property in the course of their mining operations (by dumping waste). In that case, the value of a trespass to the defendant was £900, while the diminution of the property value of the plaintiff was only £200. The court awarded the higher sum as the quantum of damages. Lindley L.J. affirmed the principle that "if one person has, without leave of another been using that other's land for his own purposes, he ought to pay for such user."[118]

This principle has also been used in cases involving the wrongful detention of goods.[119] In *Strand Electric and Engineering Co. Ltd. v. Bisford Entertainments Ltd.*,[120] Denning L.J. affirmed that, even if the owner of goods could not have used or hired out the goods in question, he is nonetheless entitled to a reasonable hire from the defendant who has wrongfully retained them. "The wrongdoer cannot be better off because he did not ask permission [if he had, reasonable remuneration would have been required]. He cannot be better off by doing wrong than

---

115 Above note 51.
116 *Martin v. Porter* (1839), 5 M. & W. 351, 151 E.R. 149; *Morgan v. Powell* (1842), 3 Q.B. 278, 114 E.R. 513; *Jegon v. Vivian* (1871), L.R. 6 Ch. 742; *Hilton v. Woods* (1867), L.R. 4 Eq. 432.
117 [1896] 2 Ch. 538.
118 *Ibid.* at 541–42.
119 *Transit Trailer Leasing Ltd. v. Robinson* (2004), 30 C.C.L.T. (3d) 227 (Ont. S.C.J.) [*Transit Trailer Leasing*].
120 [1952] 2 Q.B. 246.

he would be by doing right. He must therefore pay a reasonable hire."[121] While the action was one for "damages," Lord Denning explained, "It resembles an action for restitution rather than an action of tort. But it is unnecessary to place it into any formal category."[122] The remedy could be the same regardless of how the plaintiff's claim is characterized.[123] The "way-leave" or "licence fee" approach has also been used in cases involving the refusal by a tenant to vacate premises,[124] the unauthorized use of the plaintiff's sewer system,[125] and for trespass — removal of topsoil that was sold for revenue and the use of part of the defendant's land in the plaintiff's business.[126]

The opportunity-cost method is an instance in which the restitutionary and compensatory measures converge so long as the concept of loss is broadly conceived.[127] The "loss" to the plaintiff is the opportunity to charge a fee to the defendant. The unpaid fee is the value of the "benefit" to the defendant. In these cases the defendant's wrong may not harm or devalue the plaintiff's property, and thus there is no "loss" in terms of diminution in value. But the plaintiff is deprived of dominion and control over their property, in particular, of the right that it not be interfered with except with the owner's consent. In other words, what the plaintiff has lost is the right to bargain. *Wrotham Park*[128] illustrates this point. A developer had built homes on a property, in contravention of a restrictive covenant. The plaintiff suffered no obvious pecuniary loss as a result of the defendant's breach because its property values were not affected by the development. Relying on the basic principle in contract that the plaintiff is entitled to be put in the position as though the contract had not been broken, the defendant argued that the damages should be nominal because the plaintiff's property was not diminished in value. The court held that the defendants should not be unjustly enriched by the breach. It also re-stated the compensation rule. Had the defendant respected the contract, it would have had to bargain with the plaintiff for a relaxation of the restrictive covenant. Therefore, to place the plaintiff in the position as though the contract had not been broken, the court estimated an amount of money that

---

121 *Ibid.* at 254.
122 *Ibid.* at 255.
123 *Transit Trailer Leasing*, above note 119 at para. 85.
124 *Swordheath Properties Ltd. v. Tabet*, [1979] 1 W.L.R. 285 (C.A.).
125 *Daniel v. O'Leary* (1976), 14 N.B.R. (2d) 564 (S.C.).
126 *Wigle v. Vanderkruk*, [2005] O.T.C. 638 (S.C.J.).
127 R. Sharpe & S. Waddams, "Damages for Lost Opportunity to Bargain" (1982) 2 Oxford J. Legal Stud. 290.
128 Above note 25.

"might reasonably have been demanded by the plaintiffs … as a *quid pro quo* for relaxing the covenant."[129]

Thus, in these cases, restitution and compensation arguably converge. The cases are based on restitution in the sense that the cost avoided by the defendant is a measure of the benefit it has wrongfully obtained, and this may in fact exceed any loss proved by the plaintiff (see *Strand*). However, the method is also compensatory in that the "way-leave" fee is the amount that the plaintiff has lost as a result of the wrong. The English Court of Appeal has subsequently acknowledged that *Wrotham Park* can be explained on the basis of purely compensatory principles.[130] The House of Lords has subsequently affirmed that characterization as appropriate.[131]

5) Valuing Non-Monetary Benefits

Where the benefit to the plaintiff is in the nature of services, its value is measured on a *quantum meruit* basis. Where the services are available on the market, the court will use market value to assess the benefit. Thus, where a professional or tradesperson renders services the defendant may be made to pay a reasonable fee for the work done. Where the services are not "commercial" in nature, more difficult valuation questions arise.

The most common non-commercial cases are those involving family property. Where the law of restitution is deployed to recognize unpaid contributions to the acquisition of property there are at least two possible remedies. A court may order a cash award based on an assessment of the value of the services rendered (*quantum meruit*). Alternately, the court may order that the plaintiff has an interest in the property itself (a constructive trust). In either case, unless the court determines that an equal division is appropriate, there must be some valuation of the services. A *quantum meruit* claim is based upon the reasonable value of the services performed. Where the court chooses to impose a constructive trust, the extent of the property interest awarded is related to the amount of the claimant's contribution. McLachlin J. said in this regard:

---

129 *Ibid.* at 815. See also *Experience Hendrix*, above note 93 at para. 45.
130 *Jaggard v. Sawyer*, [1995] 1 W.L.R. 269 (C.A.).
131 *Blake*, above note 22. See also *WWF World Wide Fund for Nature v. World Wrestling Federation Entertainment Inc.*, [2006] EWHC 184 at para. 137. For a critique of the compensatory basis explanation of *Wrotham Park*, see Ralph Cullington, "A Lost Opportunity to Clarify" (2007) 123 Law Q. Rev. 48.

While agreeing that courts should avoid becoming overly technical on matters which may not be susceptible of precise monetary valuation, the principle remains that the extent of the trust must reflect the extent of the contribution.[132]

The valuation exercise is fraught with difficulties, and will likely remain a somewhat rough and ready estimate rather than a precise calculation of the exact contributions of the parties. In the *Peter v. Beblow*[133] case, the defendant argued that the plaintiff's contributions of housekeeping and childcare were not sufficiently material to ground the restitutionary remedy of a constructive trust over a portion of property that he owned. The Supreme Court of Canada affirmed that the "benefit" need not be monetary, and rejected the defendant's argument in strong terms:

> The notion that household and child care services are not worthy of recognition by the court fails to recognize the fact that these services are of great value not only to the family but to the other spouse.... The notion, moreover, is a pernicious one that systematically devalues the contributions which women tend to make to the family economy. It has contributed to the phenomenon of the feminization of poverty....[134]

Justice Cory concurred with this view. He said:

> Women no longer are expected to work exclusively in the home. It must now be recognized that when they do so, women forego outside employment to provide domestic services and child care. The granting of relief ... should adequately reflect the fact that the income earning capacity and the ability to acquire assets by one party has been enhanced by the unpaid domestic services of the other.[135]

The courts have not settled on any one method for valuing the extent of the contribution. Two general approaches compete for acceptance: the value-received approach and the value-survived approach. The former seeks to place a cash value on the services provided. The latter starts with the value of the property and goes on to determine what portion of that value is attributable to the claimant's contribution.

Where the remedy selected is the constructive trust, McLachlin J. expressed a strong preference for the value-survived approach. It avoids some of the practical problems of quantifying precisely benefits and

---

132 *Peter*, above note 11 at 998.
133 *Ibid.*
134 *Ibid.* at 993.
135 *Ibid.* at 1015.

burdens, and "arguably accords best with the expectations of most parties [since] it is more likely that a couple expects to share in the wealth generated from their partnership, rather than to receive compensation for the services performed during the relationship."[136]

In the *Peter* case itself, the trial judge had assessed the "value received" by the respondent at a modest $350 per month for twelve years ($50,400). This figure was based on the salary paid by the defendant to the last housekeeper he had hired before he and the plaintiff began living together. This amount was then reduced by 50 percent to reflect the benefit received by the claimant herself. The trial judge then awarded full ownership of the property to the plaintiff as a reasonable equivalent. The Supreme Court took a somewhat different approach, though arrived ultimately at the same conclusion.

Similar valuation problems arise when the remedy chosen is a monetary award based on *quantum meruit*. Two other cases illustrate the variety of techniques the courts have used to place a value on the services provided. The first is *Chrispen v. Topham*.[137] Here, the plaintiff and defendant lived together for a year. Shortly after moving in together, they entered into a contract whereby the (female) defendant agreed to pay the (male) plaintiff (who owned the house) $250 per month rent, and to share expenses equally. When their relationship broke down, the plaintiff sued the defendant for $3,282, which was owing under this agreement. The defendant alleged that the agreement also implicitly contained a term whereby they would share the burdens and benefits of their relationship equally, but that she had done almost all the household work. Her counterclaim was successful. The judge accepted that she had done 1,692 hours of work, and that half of the benefit of this work accrued to the plaintiff. The value of these services was determined simply by applying the minimum wage, producing a sum of $3,595. In the result, the plaintiff owed the defendant the balance of $312.

A quite different valuation method was used in *Herman v. Smith*.[138] The parties in this case lived together for six and a half years. The home was owned by the defendant and had been purchased prior to the relationship. The court held that the plaintiff's housekeeping efforts over the years had not contributed to the purchase or appreciation of the property, but did help to maintain it and provided a benefit to the defendant. The court had before it two sets of data. The first was based on hourly time allocations to domestic work and the second on annual

---

136 *Ibid.* at 999.
137 (1986), 48 Sask. R. 106 (Q.B.).
138 (1984), 34 Alta. L.R. (2d) 90 (Q.B.).

earnings for female housekeepers, servants, and related occupations on a full-time basis. The court chose the latter alternative, which produced a figure of $35,000. This figure was then reduced by 50 percent to take into account the benefits received by the plaintiff from her own work and in terms of room and board and "the other material effects of the relationship during the six or seven years that it existed."[139]

---

139 *Ibid.* at 94.

CHAPTER 8

PUNITIVE DAMAGES

A. INTRODUCTION AND TERMINOLOGY

1) Punitive Damages Distinguished from Compensatory Damages

Punitive, or exemplary, damages are distinct from compensatory, and even aggravated, damages. They are awarded against a wrongdoer, after full compensation has already been made for the harm caused. They are intended to punish the wrongdoer for particularly egregious conduct, to promote respect for the rule of law, and to provide additional deterrence.[1] Punitive damages, then, are not grounded in compensation or in corrective justice. They are grounded in retributive justice and serve the goals of punishment, deterrence, and denunciation.[2] An award should promote one or more of these objectives.[3] The Supreme Court of Canada explained, in *Vorvis v. Insurance Corp. of British Columbia*:

> Punitive damages, as the name would indicate, are designed to punish. In this, they constitute an exception to the general common law rule that damages are designed to compensate the injured, not to

---

1 See *Whiten v. Pilot Insurance Co.*, [2002] 1 S.C.R. 595 at para. 36 [*Whiten*]; *Kuddus v. Chief Constable of Leicestershire*, [2001] UKHL 29, [2001] 3 All E.R. 193 at para. 79 (H.L.), Lord Hutton [*Kuddus*].
2 *Whiten, ibid.* at paras. 43 and 68.
3 *Ibid.* at para. 71.

punish the wrongdoer. Aggravated damages will frequently cover conduct which could also be the subject of punitive damages, but the role of aggravated damages remains compensatory.[4]

As the Court noted, punitive damages will often arise out of the same malicious conduct that gave rise to aggravated damages. However, they are conceptually distinct, since aggravated damages are compensatory. One court has suggested that the distinction can be stated thus: "aggravated damage for conduct that shocks the plaintiff: exemplary (or punitive) damages for conduct which shocks the jury."[5]

2) General Principles of Availability

Punitive damages are awarded where the combined effect of compensatory, including aggravated, damages will not achieve sufficient deterrence and the defendant's actions must be further punished. They are triggered by conduct that is so high-handed, malicious, vindictive, and oppressive as to "offend the court." In *Hill v. Church of Scientology of Toronto*, the Supreme Court of Canada explained that

> [p]unitive damages may be awarded in situations where the defendant's misconduct is so malicious, oppressive and high-handed that it offends the court's sense of decency. Punitive damages bear no relation to what the plaintiff should receive by way of compensation. Their aim is not to compensate the plaintiff, but rather to punish the defendant.... They are in the nature of a fine which is meant to act as a deterrent to the defendant and to others from acting in this manner. It is important to emphasize that punitive damages should only be awarded in those circumstances where the combined award of general and aggravated damages would be insufficient to achieve the goal of punishment and deterrence.[6]

The forms of action continue to make a difference when it comes to the common law approach to punitive damages. Historically, punitive damages were never available in a simple breach of contract case unless the facts could also support a tort action. Even today, punitive damages are practically never available in simple contract actions. They are more widely available in tort claims, though still on a restricted basis. Therefore, this chapter will deal with tort and contract separately.

---

4   [1989] 1 S.C.R 1085 at 1098–99 [*Vorvis*].
5   *Muir v. Alberta* (1996), 132 D.L.R. (4th) 695 at 714 (Alta. Q.B.), citing *Salmond on the Law of Torts*.
6   [1995] 2 S.C.R. 1130 at 1208 [*Hill*].

3) Reasons for the Limited Availability of Punitive Damages

The very limited availability of punitive damages in the common law is because they deviate from the primary purpose of the common law, which is simply to compensate plaintiffs. Simple breaches of contract, and many inadvertent torts such as negligence, rarely involve serious moral turpitude. Where the defendant inadvertently harms the plaintiff, the goals of both corrective justice and deterrence are fully served by a compensatory damages award.

Even where the defendant's conduct is morally blameworthy or reprehensible, it is generally not the domain of the civil lawsuit to punish. Where wrongful activities may merit additional punishment, the matter is typically thought to be within the domain of criminal law and covered by the exhaustive provisions of the *Criminal Code*. Indeed, in Canada, common law criminal offences have long been abolished by the *Criminal Code.*[7]

It is said that punitive damages confuse the functions of civil and criminal law in that they go beyond correcting the private injustice between the individual litigants and introduce public condemnation. Punitive damages also risk unfairly penalizing the defendant without due procedural protection. The rules of evidence and burden of proof in civil litigation are not designed to protect the rights of the defendant and do not as rigorously guard against error in the judicial process. As the Supreme Court of Canada stated, punitive damages are awarded "in the absence of procedural protections for the defendant ... and upon proof on a balance of probabilities instead of the criminal standard of proof beyond a reasonable doubt."[8] In addition, punitive damages are a windfall to plaintiffs, who receive such damages after already being fully compensated for all the harm done to them. If an additional fine is thought necessary, why should the plaintiff receive it rather than the state? As Lord Reid said in *Broome v. Cassell & Co. Ltd.*:

> I think that the objections to allowing juries to go beyond compensatory damages are overwhelming. To allow pure punishment in this way contravenes almost every principle which has been evolved for the protection of offenders. There is no definition of the offence except that the conduct punished must be oppressive, high-handed, malicious, wanton or its like—terms far too vague to be admitted to any criminal code worthy of the name. There is no limit to the

---

7   *Criminal Code*, R.S.C. 1985, c. C-46, s. 9(a).
8   *Vorvis*, above note 4 at 1104.

punishment except that it must not be unreasonable.... It is no excuse to say that we need not waste sympathy on people who behave outrageously. Are we wasting sympathy on vicious criminals when we insist on proper legal safeguards for them?[9]

Despite these concerns, punitive damages are firmly entrenched in Canadian law and are more widely permitted here than in England. The Supreme Court of Canada has recognized that punishment is as much a legitimate objective of the civil law as it is of the criminal law.[10] However, the Court conceded that the principal forum for punishment remains the criminal law and that punitive damages should be awarded only in exceptional situations and with caution.[11] They are justified by the need, in some cases, to provide additional deterrence to particularly reprehensible behaviour and to express the court's sense of outrage at the defendant's conduct. This objective can only be achieved through the hybrid nature of punitive damages as straddling "the frontier between civil law ... and criminal law...."[12] As the Law Reform Commission of Ontario noted, they provide an opportunity for courts to reaffirm certain social values and, particularly when coupled with the media attention sometimes given to punitive damages cases, this serves an educative function.[13] However, because of their anomalous nature, and also the danger that juries may err in their understanding of the distinction between punitive and aggravated damages, the scope of appellate review of punitive damages awards is broader. In *Hill*, the Supreme Court of Canada affirmed that

> [t]he appellate review should be based upon the court's estimation as to whether the punitive damages serve a rational purpose. In other words, was the misconduct of the defendant so outrageous that punitive damages were rationally required to act as deterrence?[14]

4) Comparison with England and the United States

Punitive damages in Canada are more broadly available than in England, and more narrowly available than in the United States. In Eng-

9   [1972] A.C. 1027 at 1087 (H.L.) [*Broome*].
10   *Whiten*, above note 1 at para. 37.
11   *Ibid.* at para. 69; *Fidler v. Sun Life Assurance Co. of Canada*, [2006] 2 S.C.R. 3 at para. 62 [*Fidler*].
12   *Whiten*, *ibid.* at paras. 36–37.
13   Ontario Law Reform Commission, *Report on Exemplary Damages* (Toronto: The Commission, 1991) at 33.
14   *Hill*, above note 6 at 1209.

land, under the rule in *Rookes v. Barnard*,[15] apart from statute, punitive damages are limited to two situations: when there is oppressive, arbitrary, or unconstitutional action by the servants of the government; and when the defendant's conduct results in profit that is not fully offset by the award of compensatory damages. These categories were affirmed by the House of Lords in the case of *Broome*.[16] This was a case that fit within the second category, involving an intentional publication of a defamatory statement. The profits from publication would be greater than compensatory damages and, without a further award of punitive damages, the wrongdoer would still make a profit.

The decision to restrict punitive damages in England is based purely on the policy concerns explained in the previous section. The Court admitted that the narrow categories were somewhat arbitrary and even illogical, but it was unwilling to give punitive damages any wider application. The Court stated that punitive damages confer a "pure and undeserved windfall" on the plaintiff (insofar as they are awarded after full compensation); they confuse the function of civil and criminal law; the situations in which such damages may be awarded are (unlike criminal offences) only vaguely defined; and the quantum of damages (awarded by a jury) is unpredictable and not easily reviewed on appeal. This approach continues to represent the law in England,[17] though the situation there is much criticized because of the lack of any principled or coherent rationale.[18]

In contrast to England, it is notorious that awards of punitive damages in the United States are larger and more frequent than in Canada. However, the difference should not be exaggerated. Empirical studies in the United States have deflated much of the hyperbole surrounding punitive damages there.[19] Awards are not as frequent or as large as is commonly thought, and the spectacular awards sometimes reported in

---

15 [1964] A.C. 1129 (H.L.) [*Rookes*].
16 Above note 9.
17 *AB v. South-West Water Services Ltd.*, [1993] 1 All E.R. 609 (C.A.).
18 See A. Burrows, "Reforming Exemplary Damages: Expansion or Abolition?" in P. Birks, ed., *Wrongs and Remedies in the Twenty-First Century* (Oxford: Clarendon Press, 1996) at 153. The U.K. Parliament has indicated that it does not intend to enact legislation to expand the basis of exemplary damages as suggested by the Law Commission for England and Wales in its report, *Aggravated, Exemplary and Restitutionary Damages* (LC 247) (London: H.M.S.O., 1997). See *Kuddus*, above note 1 at para. 61. However, in *Kuddus*, the majority of the House of Lords favoured a broader basis for awarding exemplary damages, still within the two categories, but not limited to torts or categories for which the award had been available prior to 1964, when *Broome* was decided.
19 M.C. Rustad, "Unraveling Punitive Damages: Current Data and Further Inquiry" (1998) Wis. L. Rev. 15.

the press are frequently reduced on appeal to more moderate levels. Indeed, the U.S. Supreme Court has recently encouraged appellate courts to control jury verdicts in this respect, suggesting that excessive punitive damage awards may be unconstitutional.[20]

Nevertheless, punitive damages do feature much more prominently in U.S. law. There are at least two obvious reasons for the difference between the countries. The first is the greater prominence of the civil jury in tort cases in the United States and the more robust use of tort law to control wrongdoing. Especially in cases of corporate financial wrongdoing, juries are willing to "make an example" by awarding large sums.

The second important difference between U.S. and Canadian law is that in Canada the award for punitive damages and the evidence relating to that award must involve behaviour that is both directed towards and harmful to the specific plaintiff, and not third parties. The conduct that supports the award of punitive damages must be related to the very conduct that supports the plaintiff's cause of action.[21] This is not the case in the United States. Not only are punitive damages available in respect of more causes of action there, but it is also common, in assessing a claim for punitive damages, for the jury to hear evidence relating not only to the harm suffered by the plaintiff but also to the harm suffered by third parties from systemic wrongdoing by the defendant. The awards in these cases are to punish the defendant for wrongdoing not simply towards the plaintiff but towards all the defendant's victims. Thus, in *B.M.W. v. Gore* (see note 20), a jury awarded $4 million in punitive damages to the purchaser of a new car who was not informed of pre-delivery damage and repair to his vehicle. Clearly, the award was designed not to punish the specific wrongdoing but to deter the defendant from its general practice with respect to such repairs.

B. PUNITIVE DAMAGES IN TORT

1) General Principles

Canadian courts never adopted the English limitations on punitive damages.[22] In *H.L. Weiss Forwarding Ltd. v. Omnus*,[23] the Supreme Court

---

20 *B.M.W. of North America Inc. v. Gore*, 116 S.Ct. 1589 (1996).

21 *Guaranty Trust Co. of Canada v. Ontario (Public Trustee)* (1978), 20 O.R. (2d) 247 (H.C.J.); *Vorvis*, above note 4.

22 *Paragon Properties Ltd. v. Magna Investments Ltd.* (1972), 24 D.L.R. (3d) 156 (Alta. C.A.).

23 [1976] 1 S.C.R. 776; see also *Flame Bar-B-Q v. Hoar* (1979), 27 N.B.R. (2d) 271 (C.A.).

of Canada ignored *Rookes* in allowing punitive damages in a case involving the tort of inducing breach of contract (though the case might fit within the second category of *Rookes*). More recently, in *Vorvis*,[24] the Supreme Court of Canada explicitly held that the English restrictions on punitive damages set out in *Rookes*[25] should not apply in Canada. In place of the categorical approach in *Rookes*, the Court set out the general principles when punitive damages are available; namely, when (1) there is proof of an actionable wrong; (2) the wrong has caused the injury suffered by the plaintiff; and (3) the conduct of the defendant in committing the wrong was deserving of condemnation (because it was harsh, vindictive, reprehensible, or malicious). Yet the Court also sought to contain punitive damages within narrow limits. It insisted that such damages could be awarded only in respect of an "actionable wrong" and only in the case of "extreme" conduct.

> When then can punitive damages be awarded? … It surely cannot be merely conduct of which the Court disapproves, however strongly the judge may feel. Punishment may not be imposed in a civilized community without a justification in law. The only basis for the imposition of such punishment must be a finding of the commission of an actionable wrong which caused the injury complained of by the plaintiff.
>
> …
>
> Punitive damages may only be awarded in respect of conduct which is of such nature as to be deserving of punishment because of its harsh, vindictive, reprehensible and malicious nature. I do not suggest that I have exhausted the adjectives which could describe the conduct capable of characterizing a punitive award, but in any case where such an award is made the conduct must be extreme in its nature and such that by any reasonable standard it is deserving of full condemnation and punishment.[26]

Thus, Canadian courts have not adopted the extremely restrictive approach of their English counterparts. Yet punitive damages are still awarded only in extraordinary circumstances. Unlike England, the focus is not on the category of the wrong but on the nature of the defendant's conduct, which must be particularly deserving of punishment. Various phrases have been used to describe this standard, including "high-handed," "malicious," "vindictive," or conduct that "scandalizes the court."

---

24 *Vorvis*, above note 4. See also *Whiten*, above note 1 at para. 67.
25 Above note 15.
26 Above note 4 at 1105 and 1107–8.

2) Intentional Torts

Punitive damages are frequently awarded for intentional torts where the conduct is particularly malicious and high-handed.[27] They are awarded in cases of assault, battery,[28] defamation,[29] trespass to land,[30] fraud and deceit,[31] misappropriation of goods,[32] inducing breach of contract, malicious prosecution, and false imprisonment.[33] These cases typically involve particularly malicious or appalling conduct, such as sexual abuse, arson, violation of trust, or abuse of power, as in *Norberg v. Wynrib*,[34] in which punitive damages were awarded against a doctor who provided drugs to his addicted patient in return for sex. The Supreme Court held that this was a battery because the plaintiff's ostensible consent was vitiated by unconscionability. While the Court held that the defendant's conduct was not harsh or vindictive, it was reprehensible and required further deterrence.

Punitive damages are also sometimes available in cases involving trespass to land, especially when accompanied by a malicious destruction of the plaintiff's property. For example, in a case where the defendant cut down the plaintiff's trees in order to obtain a better ocean view, the defendant was ordered to pay $100,000 in punitive damages.[35] In this case the trespass was deliberate and aimed at enhancing the value of the defendant's own property.

Another commonly employed use of punitive damages is in defamation actions. In *Hill*[36] the Supreme Court of Canada upheld what are, by Canadian standards, large awards for both aggravated and punitive damages in an action by a lawyer who had been defamed by the defendant. The Court held that the award of $800,000 in compensatory and aggravated damages was justified by the malice underlying the tort. Furthermore, even this large award was seen by the Court as insufficient to deter the defendant from its wrongful conduct and an additional award of $800,000 in punitive damages was ordered.

---

27 See *Whiten*, above note 1 at para. 67.
28 *Delta Hotels Ltd. v. Magrum* (1975), 59 D.L.R. (3d) 126 (B.C.S.C.).
29 *Hill*, above note 6.
30 *Horseshoe Bay Retirement Society v. S.I.F. Development Corp.* (1990), 66 D.L.R. (4th) 42 (B.C.S.C.) [*Horseshoe Bay*]; *Cantera v. Eller*, [2007] O.J. No. 1899 (S.C.J.).
31 *Dixon v. British Columbia Transit* (1995), 9 B.C.L.R. (3d) 108 (S.C.) [*Dixon*].
32 *Camway Trucking Ltd. v. Toronto-Dominion Bank* (1988), 9 A.C.W.S. (3d) 164 (Ont. H.C.J.).
33 *Eagle Motors (1958) Ltd. v. Makaoff* (1970), 17 D.L.R. (3d) 222 (B.C.C.A.).
34 [1992] 2 S.C.R. 226 [*Norberg*].
35 *Horseshoe Bay*, above note 30.
36 Above note 6.

In summary, punitive damages are available in respect of most intentional torts when the conduct of the defendant merits condemnation. However, a court must be satisfied not only that the conduct calls for punishment, but also that adequate punishment and deterrence have not already been effected by the awards of compensatory and aggravated damages or by other means such as a criminal prosecution or other process. For example, in a case similar to *Norberg*, involving a sexual relationship between a doctor and his sixteen-year-old patient, punitive damages were denied on the basis that the defendant had already been punished by suspension from his professional association.[37] The issue of the proper relation between civil awards for punitive damages and criminal punishment is discussed later in this chapter.

3) Negligence

Punitive damages are rarely awarded in negligence cases since negligence is most often *inadvertent* rather than intentional or malicious. However, where the negligent conduct goes beyond carelessness and reveals a high-handed and callous disregard of the plaintiff's rights, punitive damages may be awarded. In *Robitaille v. Vancouver Hockey Club Ltd.*,[38] a hockey player's injuries were ignored by his team's manager and doctor who told him that his problems were "all in his head." These injuries were subsequently aggravated when he continued playing and he became permanently disabled. The court held that the negligence of the defendants went beyond carelessness, was "arrogant and high-handed," and thus deserving of punitive damages.

Similarly, where a medical doctor went ahead with an operation in complete disregard of current medical knowledge and performed what amounted to experimental surgery on the plaintiff, punitive damages were awarded for the negligence.[39] There, the British Columbia Court of Appeal stated that, in cases of negligence, "if the defendant has acted in good faith, then generally, exemplary damages are not awarded against him. On the other hand, where the defendant deliberately exposes the plaintiff to a risk without justification an award of exemplary damages may be appropriate."[40]

In *R.(G.B.) v. Hollett*[41] the Nova Scotia Court of Appeal awarded punitive damages against the Crown for negligence in failing to ter-

---

37   *L.T. v. McGillivray* (1993), 143 N.B.R. (2d) 241 (Q.B.).
38   (1981), 30 B.C.L.R. 286 (C.A.) [*Robitaille*].
39   *Coughlin v. Kuntz* (1989), 42 B.C.L.R. (2d) 108 (C.A.).
40   *Ibid.* at 119.
41   (1996), 154 N.S.R. (2d) 161 (C.A.) [*Hollett*].

minate a predatory and abusive employee at a reformatory in spite of his questionable conduct. The court agreed that mere negligence should not be sanctioned by an award of punitive damages, but when there is "substantially more" that shows a reckless disregard for the plaintiff or a knowing exposure to a serious risk, such damages are appropriate as a deterrent. Similarly, in *McIntyre v. Grigg*,[42] the Ontario Court of Appeal upheld an award of punitive damages against an impaired driver, but reduced the amount from $100,000 to $20,000. The court justified the award by noting that the defendant's misconduct was not merely negligent. His decision to drink excessively and then drive "demonstrated a conscious and reckless disregard for the lives and safety of others."[43] It was irrelevant that the defendant's conduct was not specifically directed at the plaintiff. Thus, despite the general rule, it is now the case that punitive damages are possible in a negligence action.

4) Products Liability Cases

Unlike the United States, punitive damages have not usually been awarded in products liability cases in Canada. There are two reasons for this. First, products liability generally involves inadvertent negligent conduct. For the reasons explained in the previous section, such conduct does not usually meet the threshold test for punitive damages. Second, in contrast to U.S. law, Canadian courts have traditionally confined the inquiry in punitive damages cases to conduct that is aimed specifically at the plaintiff, rather than conduct aimed at a class of people.[44] Thus, where the gist of the defendant's wrongdoing is disregard for the welfare of its consumers generally, this may not be as relevant in a claim by an individual plaintiff.

This requirement has been criticized by the Ontario Law Reform Commission as it renders punitive damages ineffective as a tool to "control systematic wrongdoing."[45] The rule may be fading. In *Vlchek v. Koshel*[46] the Supreme Court of British Columbia refused to strike out a claim for punitive damages though it could not be proved that the defendant intended to injure the specific plaintiff. The court held that the defendant might nevertheless be liable for punitive damages when its actions were simply directed against a class of persons, so long as

---

42   (2006), 83 O.R. (3d) 161 (C.A.) [*McIntyre*].
43   *Ibid.* at para. 57.
44   See S.M. Waddams, *Products Liability*, 4th ed. (Scarborough, ON: Carswell, 2002) at 72; *Vorvis*, above note 4.
45   Ontario Law Reform Commission, above note 13 at 14–15.
46   (1988), 30 B.C.L.R. (2d) 97 (S.C.).

those actions were "malicious or reckless to such a degree as to indicate complete indifference to the consequences that might flow therefrom, including the welfare and safety of others."[47] In *Van Oirschot v. Dow Chemical Canada Inc.*,[48] the Alberta Court of Appeal confirmed an award of $10,000 in punitive damages against the defendant who callously failed to warn the plaintiff of the risks of using a herbicide. There was an element of individual wrongdoing in this case, however, because of the high-handed conduct of the defendant after the plaintiff's crop failed and its attempt to stonewall the plaintiff's action by waiting for the evidence to decompose. In *McIntyre*, the Ontario Court of Appeal expressed support for the reasoning in *Vlchek* and *Van Oirschot*, noting that a requirement that the reprehensible conduct be specifically directed at the plaintiff could effectively bar the availability of punitive damages in product liability cases where the award may be dependent on the level of indifference to the safety of others demonstrated by a manufacturer. It would suffice where the defendant intended to do the act that caused the plaintiff's injury.[49]

5) Breach of Fiduciary Duty

Historically, punitive damages were not available for breach of equitable duties. In *Fern Brand Waxes Ltd. v. Pearl*,[50] the Ontario Court of Appeal refused to award punitive damages for breach of fiduciary duty on the ground that the action is equitable and not tortious. Many commentators, including the Law Reform Commission of Ontario, disagree with this approach. Indeed, the argument for punitive damages in cases involving fiduciary relationships seems stronger than in other cases. The special relationship between the parties, and the vulnerability usually inherent in those relationships, should expose the defendant to special liability. In several more recent cases, courts have indicated a willingness to rethink the limitation set out in *Fern Brand Waxes*. In *Norberg*[51] the Supreme Court of Canada upheld a $10,000 punitive award against the defendant doctor in respect of a wrongful sexual relationship with his patient. The doctor's actions were held by the majority to be a battery, but McLachlin J. preferred to view the wrong as a breach of fiduciary duty and held that punitive damages were, in the circumstances, avail-

---

47   *Ibid.* at 102.

48   (1995), 31 Alta. L.R. (3d) 212 (C.A.).

49   Above note 42 at paras. 67–70.

50   [1972] 3 O.R. 829 (C.A.); followed in *Worobel Estate v. Worobel* (1988), 67 O.R. (2d) 151 (H.C.J.).

51   Above note 34.

able to remedy such a breach. And in *Huff v. Price*[52] the British Columbia Court of Appeal awarded punitive damages against a fiduciary for dishonest investment practices in respect of the plaintiff's money. Finally, in the case of *M.(K.) v. M.(H.)*, a case involving incest, the Supreme Court of Canada held that, in addition to the tort action, the plaintiff could also maintain an action for breach of fiduciary duty. As well, the Court confirmed that "equitable compensation to punish the gravity of a defendant's conduct [for breach of fiduciary duty] is available on the same basis as the common law remedy of punitive damages."[53]

6) Fatal Accidents

Punitive damages are not available to dependants in fatal accident claims in Canada.[54] Nor are they available to the deceased's estate in a survival action.[55]

7) Punitive Damages to Strip Wrongful Gains

One of the purposes for which punitive damages are available even in England is to strip the defendant of ill-gotten gains when he has committed a wrong with a view to profit. For example, in *Townsview Properties Ltd. v. Sun Construction & Equipment Co.*,[56] the defendant deliberately trespassed on the plaintiff's property in order to economize on a construction project (saving between $7,000 and $11,000). The trespass did not significantly damage the plaintiff's property, and compensatory damages would have been minimal. Thus, in addition to modest compensatory damages, the court awarded $5,500 in punitive damages as the only way to deter such conduct.

Awards that fall within this category appear at first sight to be punitive and are generally treated as such by the courts. Insofar as they focus on stripping the defendant of ill-gotten gains, they are also related to the law of restitution and are discussed in greater detail in Chapter 7. On close analysis, however, in many circumstances these awards may in fact be compensatory and not punitive at all. Typically the circumstances involve breaches by the defendant of the plaintiff's

---

52   (1990), 51 B.C.L.R. (2d) 282 (C.A.) [*Huff*].

53   [1992] 3 S.C.R. 6 at 82.

54   *Campbell v. Read* (1987), 22 B.C.L.R. (2d) 214 (C.A.) [*Campbell*]; *Lord (Guardian ad litem) v. Downer* (1999), 179 D.L.R. (4th) 430 (Ont. C.A.), leave to appeal to S.C.C. refused, [1999] S.C.C.A. No. 571.

55   *Survival of Actions Act*, R.S.A. 2000, c. S-27, s. 5; *Campbell, ibid.*

56   (1973), 2 O.R. (2d) 213 (H.C.J.).

property rights. Had the defendant respected the plaintiff's rights, she would have approached the plaintiff to bargain for the right to use the plaintiff's property. The plaintiff would therefore have the right to negotiate for a share of the defendant's profits. Thus, while the plaintiff suffers no overt damage to her property, the wrong does deprive her of her right to bargain with the defendant. It has been suggested that the punitive damages awards in these cases are in fact compensation for the lost opportunity to bargain.[57]

Where the quantum of these awards does no more than strip the defendant of its wrongfully gotten gains (as in *Townsview*), the award is not really punitive at all since, arguably, it is merely giving to the plaintiff his due and taking from the defendant an amount that should have been paid in the first place (but no more). We would not call it "punishment" if the consequence to a thief was an order simply to "give it back." In more recent cases, the amount of punitive damages has been set at an amount higher than the profit made, in order to provide additional deterrence.[58]

8) Punitive Damages against Government and in *Charter* Cases

Even before the *Charter*, "oppressive, arbitrary or unconstitutional conduct by servants of the government" was one of the few recognized heads of punitive damages, even in England.[59] Punitive damages have frequently been awarded against the Crown and Crown servants in cases of assault and battery by police and other law enforcement officials;[60] wrongful search, seizure, and arrest;[61] and wrongful injuries (e.g., a fatal police shooting).[62] In addition, with the advent of the *Charter*, punitive damages are clearly available in tort-like *Charter* cases

---

57   R.J. Sharpe & S.M. Waddams, "Damages for Lost Opportunity to Bargain" (1982) 2 Oxford J. Legal Stud. 290.
58   *Austin v. Rescon Construction (1984) Ltd.* (1989), 36 B.C.L.R. (2d) 21 (C.A.) [*Austin*]. *Horseshoe Bay*, above note 30.
59   *Rookes*, above note 15.
60   *Peeters v. Canada* (1992), 54 F.T.R. (289) (T.D.), aff'd (1993), [1994] 1 F.C. 562 (C.A.), cited with approval by the High Court of Australia in *New South Wales v. Ibbett*, [2006] HCA 57 at paras. 53–54; *Ernst v. Quinonez*, 2003 CarswellOnt 3634 (S.C.J.).
61   *Rollinson v. R.* (1994), 20 C.C.L.T. (2d) 92 (F.C.T.D.); *Uni-Jet Industrial Pipe Ltd. v. Canada (Attorney General)* (2001), 156 Man. R. (2d) 14 (C.A.) [*Uni-Jet*].
62   *Patenaude v. Roy* (1988), 46 C.C.L.T. 173 (Que. S.C.), aff'd (1994), 26 C.C.L.T. (2d) 237 (Que. C.A.), increased the exemplary damages from $50,000 to $100,000.

where there is outrageous conduct.[63] In *Uni-Jet*, the court acknowledged that such awards constitute a windfall for plaintiffs but they may be necessary "from time to time … as a calculated declaration that certain conduct by public servants or agencies cannot be tolerated."[64]

Oddly, punitive damage awards against the Crown may in some cases be used as an alternative to more drastic *Charter* remedies. For example, in *R. v. F.(R.G.)*,[65] the Newfoundland Trial Division awarded punitive damages against the Crown because the length of the plaintiff's detention was too long. The proper length of the detention had been improperly calculated by the authorities and the plaintiff sought a stay of proceedings in criminal charges against him. The court refused the stay but did hold that, because the greatest care should have been used in calculating the plaintiff's detention, the mistake was deserving of punitive damages ($1,000) even though there was no malice involved.

C. QUANTUM OF AWARDS

1) General Range of Awards

Because they are "anomalous" and controversial, punitive damages are generally moderate. The Ontario Law Reform Commission conducted a study of punitive damages in 1991, concluding that awards of punitive damages had been rare and were made only at modest levels.[66] The largest award found in the study was $50,000 (though the report notes one "exceptional" case occurring shortly after the study, in which damages of over $4 million were awarded against a bank in a fraud case).[67] Awards for punitive damages are now made somewhat more frequently, but they continue to be confined largely to intentional tort cases (especially assault) and the quantum remains at or slightly above the range noted by the commission. Nevertheless, recent years have seen some courts awarding much more dramatic amounts in several cases.[68]

---

63   See K. Roach, *Constitutional Remedies in Canada* (Aurora, ON: Canada Law Book, 1994).

64   *Uni-Jet,* above note 61 at para. 84. See also *Kuddus,* above note 1 at para. 79, Lord Hutton.

65   (1991), 90 Nfld. & P.E.I.R. 113 (Nfld. T.D.).

66   Ontario Law Reform Commission, above note 13 at 22–25.

67   *Claiborne Industries Ltd. v. National Bank of Canada* (1989), 69 O.R. (2d) 65 (C.A.).

68   *Hill,* above note 6: $800,000; *Whiten,* above note 1: $1 million; *Plester v. Wawanesa Mutual Insurance Co.* (2006), 213 O.A.C. 241 (C.A.): couple awarded

2) Factors Affecting Quantum

How are punitive damage awards quantified? There is no precise "science" in the measurement of the appropriate amount of punitive damages. There are, however, certain guiding principles. The overarching questions are always the extent to which the defendant's conduct should be deterred, and the amount of the "fine" that is necessary to achieve that deterrence. The overall amount must be rationally connected to the justification for punitive damages, and the quantum must be the lowest amount necessary to achieve the purpose(s) of the award.[69]

The first factor is, of course, the nature of the defendant's conduct. The award of punitive damages must be proportionate to the wrongdoing and the degree of moral turpitude involved.[70] Actual or potential harm directed at the plaintiff is also a relevant consideration in determining the amount of damages.[71] Factors pointing to rationality may include the relative vulnerability of the plaintiff vis-à-vis the defendant, the source of that vulnerability, and any advantage gained by the defendant.[72] In setting awards, courts will often examine the facts of other cases, searching for analogous conduct and an implicit "scale" by which to measure the defendant's conduct.

The second factor is the extent to which the award of compensatory damages already given, including aggravated damages, is likely to deter such future misconduct. Compensatory damages themselves (especially when they include aggravated damages) can serve a deterrent function. Additional punishment may be unnecessary.[73] As the Ontario Court of Appeal explained (in a defamation action), if compensatory damages already satisfy the goals of deterrence and punishment, "there is then no valid reason for levying a penalty against the defendant by way of exemplary damages. To do so is simply to over-compensate the plaintiff

---

$350,000 in punitive damages against defendant insurer for unreasonable denial of claim.

69   *Whiten*, above note 1 at paras. 71, 74, and 101.
70   *Ibid.* at paras. 112–13.
71   *Ibid.* at para. 117.
72   *Ibid.* at para. 114. This explains why punitive damages may be more readily available in situations of power imbalance, but not in commercial settings involving experienced parties not in an unequal relationship. See *Whiten, ibid.* at para. 115; *Performance Industries Ltd. v. Sylvan Lake Golf & Tennis Club*, [2002] 1 S.C.R. 678 [*Sylvan Lake*]. *CivicLife.com Inc. v. Canada (Attorney General)*, [2006] O.J. No. 2474 (C.A.): plaintiff's vulnerability in relation to the defendant *per se* is not a reason for awarding punitive damages where the latter did not cause that situation.
73   See *Whiten, ibid.* at para. 123.

and provide him or her with duplicate monetary recovery."[74] Similarly, in *Sylvan Lake*, Binnie J. stated that "an award of punitive damages is rational 'if, but only if' compensatory damages do not adequately achieve the objectives of retribution, deterrence, and denunciation."[75]

In *Y.(S.) v. C.(F.G.)*,[76] the trial court awarded $250,000 in punitive and aggravated damages for a father's sexual assault, but the amount was reduced on appeal on the basis that the trial judge had not properly considered the deterrent and punitive effects of the compensatory award on its own. In the result, the best approach is to assess punitive damages only after pecuniary and non-pecuniary damages have been awarded. The British Columbia Court of Appeal explained:

> It is only after those two steps have been taken that consideration should be given to making an award of punitive damages. The reason why punitive damages should be assessed third is that the degree of punishment inflicted on the defendant by having to pay compensatory damages, including pecuniary, non-pecuniary, and aggravated damages, must first be determined before it is possible to consider whether any further penalty, by way of punishment, should be imposed on the defendant and, if so, the additional amount that is required.[77]

Other factors that a court will take into account in setting the amount of punitive damages include the "profit" earned by the defendant from committing the wrong, and the extent to which that profit exceeds the compensatory damages. In these cases, punitive damages will be assessed with reference to the profit earned, with a view to stripping the defendant's unjust enrichment and leaving no incentive or reward for the wrongdoing. In *Austin*[78] the British Columbia Court of Appeal increased a punitive damages award on this ground. The defendant had trespassed on the plaintiff's property during a construction project (by installing underground anchor rods). The trial judge had awarded $7,500 in punitive damages, though the savings to the defendant were $30,000. The Court of Appeal increased the award to the entire amount saved to teach the defendant that "tort does not pay."

The financial means of the defendant may also be relevant in determining the quantum of punitive damages where the defendant al-

---

74   *Walker v. CFTO Ltd.* (1987), 59 O.R. (2d) 104 (C.A.). See also *Sylvan Lake*, above note 72; *Whiten*, *ibid*; *Fowler v. Maritime Life Assurance* (2002), 216 Nfld. & P.E.I.R. 132 (Nfld. S.C.T.D.).

75   *Sylvan Lake*, *ibid*. at para. 87.

76   (1996), 26 B.C.L.R. (3d) 155 (C.A.).

77   *Huff*, above note 52 at 300.

78   Above note 58.

leges financial hardship, or where its wealth enabled it to sustain the misconduct in question as in *Hill*, or where a lesser amount would not adequately achieve deterrence against a wealthy defendant.[79] In *Hill*, the plaintiff was awarded $800,000 in punitive damages for defamation (in addition to general and aggravated damages of $800,000). La Forest J. commented:

> Punitive damages can and do serve a useful purpose. But for them, it would be all too easy for the large, wealthy and powerful to persist in libelling vulnerable victims. Awards of general and aggravated damages alone might simply be regarded as a licence fee for continuing a character assassination. The protection of a person's reputation arising from the publication of false and injurious statements must be effective. The most effective means of protection will be supplied by the knowledge that fines in the form of punitive damages may be awarded in cases where the defendant's conduct is truly outrageous.[80]

Corporate defendants will typically bear the brunt of larger awards.[81] In *Whiten*,[82] the Supreme Court of Canada upheld a jury award of $1 million in punitive damages against an insurance company for wrongfully withholding benefits from the plaintiffs, whose house had burned down. The Court acknowledged that this amount was high but concluded that a substantial award for punitive damages was required to punish the defendant and to reinforce the duty of good faith owed by an insurer to its insured. The Ontario Law Reform Commission agrees that the means of the defendant are relevant in assessing the amount that is necessary to achieve deterrence, but cautions that the inquiry into the defendant's wealth should be carefully controlled by the judge to eliminate undue prejudice.

Additional factors that courts take into account include the degree of moral turpitude involved in the tort and whether the defendant has apologized or expressed remorse in any way. In the defamation case of *Hill*, the fact that the defendant had not apologized and had persisted in the defamation was mentioned as a factor that increased the punitive damages.[83] By way of contrast, in *Muir v. Alberta*[84] the Crown avoided

---

79   *Whiten*, above note 1 at para. 119.
80   *Hill*, above note 6 at 1209.
81   *A.B. v. E.F.*, [2004] N.B.J. No. 261 at paras. 16–17 (Q.B.): plaintiff's claim for $3 million in punitive damages rejected because such large awards are justified only against institutional or corporate defendants.
82   *Whiten*, above note 1.
83   See also *S.(K.) v. H.(J.P.)*, 2004 BCSC 769.
84   Above note 5.

punitive damages in respect of wrongful sterilization of the plaintiff by abandoning its limitation defence and apologizing. The court held that it would be wrong to punish the defendant. However, expression of remorse and apology will not necessarily eliminate the need for punitive damages, for instance, where there were aggravating factors that warrant punishment.[85]

3) The Effect of Previous Criminal Sanctions: Double Punishment?

One of the dangers of granting punitive damages is that it encroaches upon the function of the criminal justice system. This is particularly obvious in the case of intentional torts that are also punishable by the criminal law. The issue is that for the same act (e.g., assault) the defendant may be punished criminally and also exposed to a claim for punitive damages.

It is not strictly "double jeopardy" to be both criminally and civilly liable for the same wrongful act. Indeed, section 11 of the *Criminal Code* specifically preserves the right of persons to pursue civil actions despite the fact that the wrongful act was also a criminal offence. The civil and criminal actions are compatible since the former is primarily a private action for compensation while the latter is an action involving punishment brought by the state. However, when the civil action also includes a claim for punitive damages, there is a danger that the offender is being punished twice over in respect of the same conduct.

As a general principle, courts will not award punitive damages when the defendant has already been punished criminally for exactly the same conduct. In *S.(D.) v. K.(T.)*[86] the plaintiff daughter brought an action against her father for sexual abuse. The court allowed the action and awarded compensatory damages, but it denied punitive damages because the father had been imprisoned and punitive damages would be "double punishment."[87] Similarly, in *Chow v. Hiscock*,[88] involving three teenage defendant gang members who attacked and brutally beat the plaintiff, resulting in severe brain injury that left him in a permanent semi-vegetative state, the court declined to award punitive dam-

---

85 *M.(S.) v. M.(C.L.D.)*, [2003] B.C.J. No. 964 (S.C.) [*M.(S.)*].
86 (1994), 123 Nfld. & P.E.I.R. 194 (Nfld. T.D.); see also *Loomis v. Rohan* (1974), 46 D.L.R. (3d) 423 (B.C.S.C.).
87 See also *C.(M.) v. M.(F.)* (*sub nom. C. v. M.*) (1990), 74 D.L.R. 4th 129 (Ont. Ct. Gen. Div.); *Fleury v. Fleury*, [2001] O.J. No. 1720 (C.A.).
88 (2005), 41 C.C.L.T. (3d) 155 (B.C.S.C.).

ages because the defendants had already been punished by the criminal law. The court noted that it was not for it to say that the punishment was inadequate and that it should have been harsher. Koenigsberg J. stated: "Often, the perspective of a sentencing judge is very different from those on the other side of the bench."[89]

There are many exceptions to the general rule against double punishment. If the civil case is tried first (which is rare) or if the civil offence does not exactly map onto the criminal offence, the case for a punitive award at the civil trial is stronger. For example, in *B.(A.) v. J.(I.)*,[90] the accused/defendant received a sentence for having sexually assaulted the plaintiff over the course of one year, but the civil court awarded $150,000 in punitive damages because the abuse had lasted much longer than the one year covered by the indictment. Similarly, where not all of the tortious acts against the defendant have been punished criminally, there may be room remaining for punitive damages.[91] While the defendant may be acquitted on criminal charges, there is no reason why, on the civil standard of proof, the plaintiff may not successfully prove the alleged offence and claim punitive damages.[92]

The rule against double punishment is not absolute, even when punitive damages are sought in respect of the very same conduct that has already been criminally punished. Several courts have asserted a remaining jurisdiction to award punitive damages when the criminal sanction appears inadequate.[93] In *Joanisse v. Y.(D.)*,[94] punitive damages were awarded against three defendants (young offenders) who had already been criminally punished, on the basis that there were "aggravating factors." And, an award of punitive damages was made against a defendant already sentenced to life imprisonment for murder.[95]

In the result, a more accurate statement of the law is that a criminal conviction, penalties imposed or likely to be imposed in similar proceedings against the defendant is only one of the factors to be considered in determining whether an award of punitive damages is appro-

---

89   *Ibid.* at para. 37.
90   (1991), 119 A.R. 210 (Q.B.).
91   *Flachs v. Flachs*, [2002] O.J. No. 1350 (S.C.J.).
92   *B.(P.) v. B.(W.)* (1992), 11 O.R. (3d) 161 (Gen. Div.).
93   *G.(E.D.) v. D.S. (sub nom. G. v. D.)* (1993), 77 B.C.L.R. (2d) 106 (C.A.); *McIntyre*, above note 42: court found the $500 fine for impaired driving inadequate to denounce the defendant's conduct—impaired driving. Hence, punitive damages were appropriate in this case. See also *Wilson v. Bobbie* (2006), 394 A.R. 118 (Q.B.).
94   (1995), 15 B.C.L.R. (3d) 224 (S.C.). See also *M.(S.)*, above note 85.
95   *Buxbaum (Litigation guardian of) v. Buxbaum*, [1997] O.J. No. 5166 (C.A.); see also *Cyr. v. Williams* (1995), 14 B.C.L.R. (3d) 289 (S.C.).

priate.[96] As the Court noted in *Whiten*, "The key point is that punitive damages are awarded 'if, but only if' all other penalties have been taken into account and found to be inadequate to accomplish the objectives of retribution, deterrence, and denunciation."[97] One court explained:

> Difficulties arise where the defendant, though convicted, has received a punishment considered lenient by the civil court.... For the civil Court to accept a criminal disposition as an absolute bar to exemplary damages, seems anomalous; the defendant receives a financial benefit from a criminal conviction. On the other hand, for the civil Court to add to the punishment seems a usurpation of the function of the criminal Court. If the defendant has been acquitted, on the other hand, there seems to be no bar to an award of exemplary damages.... The problems are intractable and spring from the very nature of exemplary damages. It seems that the most rational solution is for the civil Court to consider the extent of the criminal punishment and to reduce accordingly the exemplary damages that otherwise would have been appropriate.[98]

After assessing the plaintiff's aggravated general damages for battery and compensation for breach of fiduciary obligation at $60,000, the judge concluded that, in light of the criminal penalty, and the award of aggravated damages, the case was not one for punitive damages.[99] Stigmatization arising from findings of fraudulent and dishonest behaviour and publicity of the same may constitute sufficient denunciation and deterrence to make an award of punitive damages unnecessary.[100]

D. PROPER DEFENDANTS

Multiple defendants and the issue of vicarious liability pose special problems in relation to punitive damages because, even where the par-

---

96 *Whiten*, above note 1 at paras. 69 and 123; *Willington v. Marshall* (1994), 21 C.C.L.T. (2d) 198 (B.C.S.C.).
97 *Whiten*, ibid. at para. 123.
98 *B.(J.) v. B.(R.)*, [1994] O.J. No. 324 at para. 37 (Gen. Div.).
99 See also *Insurance Corp. of British Columbia v. Eurosport Auto Co.*, [2007] B.C.J. No. 972 (C.A.). The Court of Appeal reversed an order for punitive damages because, given the fines levied against the defendants in a quasi-criminal proceeding and the high likelihood of an award of special costs, no rational purpose would be served by an additional punishment through an award of punitive damages. *John Doe v. O'Dell* (2003), 230 D.L.R. (4th) 383 (Ont. S.C.J.): criminal punishment plus a large award for compensatory including aggravated damages were sufficiently deterrent. Hence an award of punitive damages was unnecessary.
100 *Sylvan Lake*, above note 72 at para. 88.

ties are jointly and severally liable for a tort, they may not be equally culpable of malicious conduct. The original rule, crafted by English courts, was that, where there are multiple defendants and some are innocent of malicious conduct, an award of punitive damages could not be made.[101] A more sensible approach has, however, been crafted in more recent cases in which the courts have asserted authority to order punitive damages against the guilty parties only.[102] The courts, by reason that it would be unjust to let a defendant who is deserving of punishment to go unpunished simply because another defendant is guiltless, have held that the English rule no longer applies in Canada.[103] The Supreme Court has affirmed in the context of a libel action that, where there are two or more parties who are liable for the same tort, their liability for aggravated and punitive damages is not typically joint and several, but rather individual, since these damages must be "assessed on the basis of the particular malice of each joint tortfeasor."[104] This rule has also been applied in tort cases involving sexual assault, where punitive damages may be awarded against the perpetrator, but not against the perpetrator's employer, even though guilty of negligence.[105]

Vicarious liability raises the same issues. Is it fair to hold an employer or principal liable for punitive damages in the case of torts committed by employees and agents? Of course, if the conduct of the employer is itself deserving of punishment, there is no problem. But where employers are innocent of any wrongdoing (but nevertheless vicariously liable for compensatory damages), it may seem unfair that they be punished. Punitive damages cannot be awarded against vicariously liable defendants in the absence of reprehensible conduct specifically referable to the employer.[106] However, such an award may be justified on the basis that it provides an incentive for employers or principals to control the behaviour of employees or agents. Moreover, corporations, of course, act only through their agents and employees, and there are

---

101 *Broome*, above note 9.
102 *Townsview Properties Ltd. v. Sun Construction & Equipment Co.* (1974), 7 O.R. (2d) 666 (C.A.); *Vogel v. Canadian Broadcasting Corp.* (1982), 35 B.C.L.R. 7 (S.C.) [*Vogel*]; *Munro v. Toronto Sun Publishing Corp.* (1982), 39 O.R. (2d) 100 (H.C.J.) [*Munro*].
103 *Vogel, ibid.*
104 *Hill*, above note 6 at 1200.
105 *K.(W.) v. Pornbacher* (1997), 32 B.C.L.R (3d) 360 (S.C.).
106 *Blackwater v. Plint* (2001), 93 B.C.L.R. (3d) 228 at paras. 416–21 (S.C.), aff'd [2005] 3 S.C.R. 3 at paras. 90–92 [*Plint*]. *A.(M.) v. Canada (Attorney General)* (2001), 212 Sask. R. 241 (Q.B.), var'd on other grounds (2003), 227 Sask. R. 260 (C.A.), application for leave to appeal to S.C.C. refused, [2003] S.C.C.A. No. 151; *S.G.H. v. Gorsline* (2001), 90 Alta. L.R. (3d) 256 (Q.B.), aff'd (2004), 29 Alta. L.R. (4th) 203 (C.A.), leave to appeal to S.C.C. refused, [2004] S.C.C.A. No. 385.

cases in which corporate defendants have been held liable for punitive damages for the acts of their employees.[107] For example, in *Robitaille*[108] the corporate defendant was liable for punitive damages in respect of callous treatment of the plaintiff by managerial-level employees. These cases appear to conform to the Ontario Law Reform Commission's suggested test that an employer should be vicariously liable for a punitive damages award against an employee only when the employer was complicit (i.e., tacitly approved) of the tort.[109] The Nova Scotia Court of Appeal in *Hollett*[110] adopted this notion and approved of the tests offered by the *Restatement of Torts*[111] that a principal or employer is liable for punitive damages when (a) the employer authorized the employee to do the acts; (b) the employer knew the employee was unfit and was reckless in employing the employee; (c) the employee or agent was employed in a managerial capacity; and (d) the employer ratified the act of the employee. The court held that the Crown was liable for the sexual assault committed by an employee in circumstances where "a managerial agent of the employer has acted recklessly in the engaging or the retaining of an employee with the resultant foreseeable danger of harm of the type which occurred here."[112]

E. PUNITIVE DAMAGES IN CONTRACT

1) Reasons for the Limited Availability of Punitive Damages

Historically, punitive damages were never available in a simple breach of contract case unless the facts could also support a tort action.[113] Even today, with very limited exceptions, this remains the rule. Numerous cases have stated categorically that "it is quite clear that punitive dam-

---

107 *Munro*, above note 102.
108 Above note 38.
109 Ontario Law Reform Commission, above note 13 at 58.
110 Above note 41.
111 *Restatement of the Law, Second, Torts* (St. Paul, MN: American Law Institute, 1979) at s. 909, "Punitive Damages against a Principal."
112 Above note 41 at 213. See also *T.W.N.A. v. Clarke* (2003), 22 B.C.L.R. (4th) 1 (C.A.): the principal of an Indian residential school was considered top management, and hence his deplorable conduct of shielding an employee who sexually abused students to protect himself and the school was attributed to his employer, Canada, to support an award of punitive damges against the government.
113 *Addis v. Gramophone Co. Ltd.*, [1909] A.C. 488 (H.L.).

ages will not be awarded in a breach of contract action in Canada"[114] and that a claim for punitive damages "may not be brought forward in an ordinary action for breach of commercial contract."[115]

The reasons for this restriction may be located in the individualism and commercial orientation of the common law of contract. Contracts are business arrangements and breach of contract is seldom considered a moral or personal wrong. As Oliver Wendell Holmes put it, "[t]he duty to keep a contract at common law means a prediction that you must pay damages if you do not keep it—and nothing else."[116] These sentiments are related to the more general positivism and individualism of the common law of contract—that it is not the function of the law to enforce morality or to teach people to be good.

The restrictive approach to punitive damages in contract has been reaffirmed by the Supreme Court of Canada. In *Vorvis*[117] the Court refused to award punitive damages in a wrongful dismissal case, holding that punitive damages are not available in contract unless the breach also amounts to an "actionable wrong" (though not limited to tortious conduct, an actionable wrong will often constitute a tort). In reaching this conclusion the Court affirmed the philosophical reasons for distinguishing between tort actions and contract actions in respect of punitive damages. Tort law involves sanctions for breach of socially imposed duties, whereas contract law (in theory) is a form of private ordering, looking only to the intent of the parties. Punitive damages in contract, based on the court's sense of wrongdoing, threatens the sanctity of the private contract. As McIntyre J. stated in *Vorvis*,

> [i]n tort cases, claims where a plaintiff asserts injury and damage caused by the defendant, the situation is different. The defendant in such a case is under a legal duty to use care not to injure his neighbour.... The compensation he is entitled to receive depends upon the nature and extent of his injuries and not upon any private arrangement made with the tortfeasor. In an action based upon a breach of contract, the only link between the parties for the purpose of defining their rights and obligations is the contract. Where the defendant has breached the contract, the remedies open to the plaintiff must arise from that contractual relationship, that "private law," which the

---

114 *Cardinal Construction Ltd. v. R.* (1981), 32 O.R. (2d) 575 at 576 (H.C.J.), aff'd (*sub nom. Cardinal Construction Ltd. v. Ontario*) (1981), 38 O.R. (2d) 161 (C.A.).

115 *Ontario (A.G.) v. Tiberius Productions Inc.* (1984), 46 O.R. (2d) 152 at 153 (H.C.J.).

116 O.W. Holmes, "The Path of the Law" (1897) 10 Harv. L. Rev. 457 at 462.

117 Above note 4; *Royal Bank of Canada v. W. Got & Associates Electric Ltd.*, [1999] 3 S.C.R. 408 at para. 26.

parties agreed to accept. The injured plaintiff then is not entitled to be made whole; he is entitled to have that which the contract provided for him or compensation for its loss. This distinction will not completely eliminate the award of punitive damages but it will make it very rare in contract cases.[118]

In *Fidler*, the Court reaffirmed this position, noting that although breaches of contract will sometimes attract condemnation, this may not necessarily ground an award of punitive damages. Punitive damages may be awarded only where the defendant's conduct significantly departs from "ordinary standards of decency ... [going] beyond the usual opprobrium that surrounds breaking a contract ... [and] it must be independently actionable."[119]

More recently, an additional reason has been given for refusing punitive damages in contract, based on the idea of economic efficiency.[120] According to this theory, so long as full compensation can be made, individuals should be left free to breach contracts at will. Sometimes a contract will simply prove too expensive to perform (i.e., the costs of performance exceed the loss from breach). In other cases, the profits from breaching a contract (to pursue a different opportunity) exceed the losses from breach. In both cases, so long as the breaching party is able to compensate fully for any losses, breaching the contract is the efficient thing to do. Requiring performance, or punishing non-performance, in these cases would be uneconomic.[121]

2) The Current Law

The leading case on punitive damages in contract is *Vorvis*[122] in which the Supreme Court of Canada denied punitive damages in an action for wrongful dismissal. McIntyre J. quoted with approval the rule from the *Restatement (2d) of the Law of Contracts* that "[p]unitive damages are not recoverable for a breach of contract unless the conduct constituting the breach is also a tort for which punitive damages are recoverable."[123]

---

118 *Vorvis, ibid.* at 1107. See also J. Swan, "Punitive Damages for Breach of Contract: A Remedy in Search of Justification" (2004) 29 Queen's L.J. 596.

119 *Fidler*, above note 11 at paras. 62–63.

120 R.A. Posner, *Economic Analysis of Law*, 6th ed. (New York: Aspen, 2003).

121 In *Bank of America Canada v. Mutual Trust Co.*, [2002] 2 S.C.R. 601, the Supreme Court of Canada endorsed the idea of efficient breach as sound in contractual dealings and not something to be condemned.

122 Above note 4.

123 *Restatement of the Law, Second, Contracts* (St. Paul, MN: American Law Institute, 1981) at s. 355.

Thus, when the facts of the dispute between the plaintiff and defendant support concurrent actions in contract and tort, punitive damages will be available. Examples include wrongful dismissal cases in which the circumstances of the dismissal are so abusive that they amount to the tort of infliction of mental distress, assault, or defamation. For example, in *Dixon*,[124] discussed above, punitive damages were awarded to a plaintiff who was wrongfully dismissed. In addition to the breach of contract (failure to give adequate notice), the employer had falsely alleged (and reported to the media) that the plaintiff had been fired for cause. The court held that this was a separate "actionable wrong" (deceit and defamation) justifying the extraordinary damage award.

In *Vorvis*, the majority judgment suggests that punitive damages will not be available in contract, unless the breach also constitutes an actionable wrong. This is not necessarily confined to cases where the defendant's conduct constitutes a tort,[125] and despite the apparently categorical refusal of courts to award punitive damages in contract *per se*, the rule is continually being tested. Many argue that the restriction is outmoded and overly formalistic. In light of the increasingly blurred line between contract and tort, it is especially difficult to see why the form of the action rather than the justice of the case should determine the remedies available. As one judge remarked,

> [a]lthough the distinction between tort and contract with respect to awards of punitive damages appears well-established, it is possible that the law may indeed have evolved to the point where punitive damages ought now to be awarded in the exceptional case of willful, wanton, malicious, or other deliberate unconscionable conduct leading to breach of a contract, particularly where such conduct is oriented to unfair profit seeking.[126]

Particularly where the subject matter of the contract is especially important to the plaintiff, the devastating consequences of breach are known to the defendant, and the breach is committed in a "high-

---

124 Above note 31.
125 In *Whiten*, above note 1 at paras. 80–81, Binnie J. noted that the requirement of actionable wrong in *Vorvis* was intended to be broader than a tort. He further noted that, although it would be rare to award punitive damages for breach of contract where the defendant's conduct does not constitute a tort, this is not impossible. In fact, insurance companies have successfully claimed punitive damages against their insureds for bad-faith dealings without grounding such claims in a separate tort. *Whiten, ibid.* at para. 83.
126 *Centennial Centre of Science & Technology v. V.S. Services Ltd.* (1982), 40 O.R. (2d) 253 at 256 (H.C.J.), DuPont J.

handed, shocking and arrogant fashion so as to demand condemnation by the court as a deterrent," some courts have indicated a willingness to reconsider the old rules.[127] For example, discriminatory conduct in violation of human rights legislation may constitute a separate actionable wrong to warrant punitive damages in wrongful dismissal cases.[128] However, it is still the case that with only a few exceptions,[129] punitive damages have not been awarded in contract actions.

3) Bad-Faith Insurance Claims

One area in which punitive damages may be available in contract is in "bad-faith" actions against insurers.[130] In these situations, wrongful refusals by insurance companies to pay valid claims, or abusive treatment of insureds, have led to punitive damage awards in U.S. cases. For example, in *Richardson v. Employers Liability Assurance Corp.*,[131] the plaintiff was injured by an uninsured motorist and submitted a claim for first-party benefits to his own insurer. The insurer adopted a policy of "payment only as a last resort" and, in spite of considerable proof

127 *Brown v. Waterloo (Region) Commissioners of Police* (1982), 37 O.R. (2d) 277 at 293 (H.C.J.), rev'd on other grounds (1983), 43 O.R. (2d) 113 (C.A.).
128 *McKinley v. BC Tel* (2001), 200 D.L.R. (4th) 385 at para. 89 (S.C.C.); *Keays v. Honda Canada Inc.* (2006), 82 O.R. (3d) 161 (C.A.), leave to appeal to S.C.C. granted, [2006] S.C.C.A. No. 470 [*Keays*]. Whereas the Court concluded that there was insufficient evidence to justify an award of punitive damages in *McKinley*, the employer's conduct in *Keays* was found to be sufficient to warrant such an award (the majority of the Ontario Court of Appeal reduced the award from $500,000 to $100,000 because the higher award was inconsistent with the evidence and did not accord with the principle of proportionality).
129 *Pilato v. Hamilton Place Convention Centre Inc.* (1984), 45 O.R. (2d) 652 (H.C.J.); *Panapers Inc. v. 1260539 Ontario Ltd.*, 2004 CarswellOnt 5466 (S.C.J.), var'd on other grounds, 2007 CarswellOnt 282 (C.A.).
130 The duty of good faith in insurance contracts is mutual as between insurers and insureds: *Ruffolo v. Sun Life Assurance Co. of Canada*, [2006] O.J. No. 3616 at para. 10 (S.C.J.). As such, punitive damages can also be awarded against an insured who engages in bad-faith conduct in dealing with the insurer, such as falsifying information on a claim or fraud. See *Andrusiw v. Aetna Life Insurance Co. of Canada* (2001), 289 A.R. 1 (Q.B.); *Industrial Alliance Insurance and Financial Services Inc. v. Skowron*, [2006] O.J. No. 2554 (S.C.J.); *Insurance Corp. of British Columbia v. Hoang* (2002), 29 M.V.R. (4th) 204 (B.C.S.C.). Approval of this practice was intimated by the Supreme Court of Canada in *Whiten*, above note 1 at para. 83.
131 25 Cal. App. 3d 232, 102 Cal. Rptr. 547 (2d Dist. 1972) [*Richardson*]. See also *Egan v. Mutual of Omaha Ins. Co.*, 620 P.2d 141 (Cal. Sup. Ct. 1979), dismissed by the Supreme Court of the United States for want of jurisdiction, 100 S.Ct. 1271 (1980).

that the negligent driver was in fact uninsured, refused to make any payment. Even when the plaintiff obtained an arbitration award for the full value of the policy, the defendant insurer still sought a "settlement." The court awarded punitive damages on the theory of the tort of bad faith, stating that the effect of the defendant's stalling tactics was to

> oppress and harass the insured needlessly and unjustifiably by refusing payment of an indisputably valid claim for the policy limits without arbitration and without judicial confirmation; it thereby created a needless uncertainty as to its ultimate payment and deferred payment from a few months after the accident to over a year thereafter.[132]

During the 1970s and 1980s several Canadian cases suggested that courts might follow the U.S. lead, noting that actions against insurers differed from the pure contract-breach cases because insurers also have a statutory obligation to pay first-party benefits.[133] In *Thompson v. Zurich Insurance Co.*,[134] the plaintiff's insurer repeatedly failed to make proper and timely payments to the plaintiff. Pennell J. suggested that punitive damages might be available in such situations:

> It seems to me (I hope with becoming deference and diffidence) that to allow the imposition of punitive damages in tort actions and to deny them without exception for breach of contract standing alone is a mechanical classification without sound and legitimate basis. I tend to the view that in certain circumstances where a breach of contract merges with and assumes the character of a wilful tort, calculated rather than inadvertent and in a wanton and reckless disregard for contractual rights of others, punitive damages may be assessed.[135]

The claim for punitive damages failed in this case for want of proof of malice. The insurer did not deny liability, but it simply failed to make timely and full payments. Pennell J. found that it did not deliberately flout its duty to make timely payments and that its position was not "so utterly unreasonable and indefensible ... [nor] so free from the possibility of *bona fide* contest and debate, as to be the equivalent of malice."[136]

Canadian law has continued to evolve in this direction. To avoid the limitations of *Vorvis*, some Canadian cases, following the U.S. ex-

---

132 *Richardson, ibid.* at 245 (Cal. Ct. App.).

133 *Jennett v. Federal Insurance Co.* (1976), 13 O.R. (2d) 617 (H.C.J.).

134 (1984), 45 O.R. (2d) 744 (H.C.J.).

135 *Ibid.* at 752–53.

136 *Ibid.* at 758.

ample, have suggested that bad-faith breach of such a contract might amount to a tort (and thus be independently actionable). Arguably, the insurance contract creates a special relationship between the parties, and the insured is in a position of vulnerability. Because of the special relationship between the parties, a "willful and calculated breach of such a contract giving rise to foreseeable harm may well be a tortious activity giving rise to liability for both compensatory and punitive damages."[137] In *Adams v. Confederation Life Insurance Co.*,[138] the defendant insurer conducted surveillance on the plaintiff when there was no evidence to support any suspicion in the plaintiff's insurance claim. The court held that this was an independently actionable wrong and thus grounds for punitive damages. Punitive damages have, however, been denied in cases where the conduct of the insurer is not independently actionable.[139]

In several subsequent cases, courts have awarded punitive damages where no tort has been committed. In *Ferguson v. National Life Assurance Co. of Canada*,[140] a court awarded punitive damages against an insurer for wrongfully and callously refusing to pay disability benefits to the plaintiff. In this case it was not the mere breach of contract (withholding benefits) that justified the award, but rather the malicious and reprehensible treatment of the plaintiff prior to the termination of benefits that constituted its breach of the duty of good faith and fair treatment. Arguably, this conduct could be said to be independently actionable insofar as the defendant made several misrepresentations and also engaged in conduct that could clearly be foreseen to cause mental distress to the plaintiff.

Most recently, in *Whiten*,[141] discussed earlier, the Supreme Court of Canada upheld a jury award of $1 million in punitive damages against an insurance company for wrongfully withholding benefits from a plaintiff whose house had burned down. The Court acknowledged that this amount was high but concluded that it was still within the rational limits necessary to punish the defendant.[142] Specifically, the Court held that the "actionable wrong" requirement for the availability of punitive damages in breach of contract cases, as stated in *Vorvis*, is not limited to conduct amounting to a tort. The Court added that, although it will

---

137 *Dale Perusse Ltd. v. Kason*, [1985] I.L.R. ¶1-1985 at 7627 (Ont. H.C.J.).
138 (1994), 152 A.R. 121 (Q.B.).
139 *Andryechen v. Transit Insurance Co.*, [1992] I.L.R. ¶1-2830 at 1820 (Ont. Ct. Gen. Div.).
140 (1996), 1 O.T.C. 81 (Gen. Div.), aff'd (1997), 102 O.A.C. 239 (C.A.).
141 Above note 1.
142 *Ibid.* at para. 128.

be rare for punitive damages to be available for breach of contract absent conduct that constitutes a tort, this is not impossible. To limit the scope of actionable wrong to tortious conduct would be unnecessarily restrictive and in any event inconsistent with the principle as set out in *Vorvis*.[143] In the context of insurance contracts, breach of an insurer's duty of good faith and fair dealings is an actionable wrong independent of the obligation to pay the insured, and can justify an award of punitive damages.[144] However, wrongful denial of a claim *per se* will not necessarily constitute a breach of the duty of good faith.[145] In *Fidler*, the insurer's denial of the plaintiff's claim for five years while it disputed her disability was found to be troubling but did not constitute bad faith on the part of the insurer. The Court found that the denial of benefits stemmed from "the difficulty Sun Life had in ascertaining whether Ms. Fidler was actually disabled … and that … its denial of benefits was the product of a real, albeit incorrect, doubt as to whether Ms. Fidler was incapable of performing *any* work, as required under the terms of the policy."[146]

It is unlikely that the bad-faith cases will remain confined to insurance contracts. It is submitted that punitive damages are appropriate in contract when (a) the contract is "personal" and of obvious importance to the plaintiff's well-being; (b) the defendant's excuse upon refusal to perform is groundless or spurious, and based on a decision or policy designed simply to enhance the defendant's profits; and (c) shows a callous disregard for the rights and welfare of the plaintiff.[147]

---

143 *Ibid.* at paras. 80–82.
144 *Ibid.* at para. 79. See also *Fidler*, above note 11 at para. 63.
145 *702535 Ontario Inc. v. Non-Marine Underwriters of Lloyds of London* (2000), 184 D.L.R. (4th) 687 (Ont. C.A.), approved in *Fidler, ibid.* at para. 63.
146 *Fidler, ibid.* at para. 74.
147 Punitive damages may be available under consumer protection legislation where a manufacturer or retailer wilfully violates the rights of consumers under the legislation even in respect of conduct falling short of what will attract punitive damages at common law. See *Prebushewski v. Dodge City Auto (1984) Ltd.*, [2005] 1 S.C.R. 649.

CHAPTER 9

NOMINAL DAMAGES AND CONTEMPTUOUS DAMAGES

A. NOMINAL DAMAGES

1) Definition and Purpose

Nominal damages serve to vindicate the plaintiff's rights even when no compensation is necessary. Nominal damages are a small sum of money, awarded when the plaintiff is able to establish a cause of action but has suffered no substantial loss, successfully mitigated the loss, or is unable to prove what that loss is. The purpose of nominal damages is to serve as a declaration of the plaintiff's rights and a minor deterrent to the defendant.

McGregor describes the purpose of nominal damages as "establishing, determining or protecting a legal right."[1] He states that they are available in two situations. The first is where the plaintiff proves that she has suffered some wrong, but no loss (or a trifling loss) has arisen from that wrong. The other, and less important, situation is when the plaintiff has shown there was a loss but the "necessary evidence as to its amount is not given."[2] An ancillary reason for awarding nominal damages is that they may be a "peg on which to hang costs."[3] This approach is no longer

---

1   H. McGregor, *McGregor on Damages*, 17th ed. (London: Sweet & Maxwell, 2003) at 362 [10-008].
2   *Ibid.* at 360 [10-004].
3   Maule J. in *Beaumont v. Greathead* (1846), 2 C.B. 494 at 499, 135 E.R. 1039.

necessary in most provinces because courts have a wide discretion as to costs and may award costs independently of any damages award.

Nominal damages are to be distinguished from both "contemptuous damages" (which are discussed later in this chapter) and also from very small awards of compensatory damages. In *Cole v. Gill*[4] the court awarded $1,000 in damages to a plaintiff who had been injured in a car accident, labelling the award "nominal damages." It explained that the small sum was chosen because the plaintiff had vastly exaggerated his injuries and lied in his testimony. This case confuses the terminology. If there had been no injuries whatsoever, the plaintiff's claim should have been dismissed (since proof of damage is an essential element of a negligence claim). The plaintiff did establish that he was injured (though minimally), and therefore the damages, while small, are compensatory and not properly called "nominal."[5]

2) Availability of Nominal Damages

Nominal damages are available whenever the plaintiff is able to establish a complete cause of action, without damage. For example, actions for breach of contract, and actions for some of the intentional torts (such as assault, battery, and trespass), do not require proof of damage as an element in the cause of action. On the other hand, actions such as negligence require proof of harm as an essential element of the cause of action, and are therefore seldom appropriate for an award of nominal damages. Nominal damages may, however, be awarded in negligence cases under McGregor's second category—where the court is satisfied that the plaintiff has suffered some harm, but there is no proof as to quantum.

In rare cases, a court has authority to refuse to award nominal damages. In *Serban v. Egolf*,[6] the defendant solicitors were sued for failing to issue a writ in time. The court found that there had been a failure of the solicitors to issue a writ but also that there had been no motor-vehicle accident in respect of which the action should have been commenced. Macdonell J. said:

> The question that concerns me in this case is whether it must follow my finding that the defendants failed to issue the writ, that the plaintiffs are entitled to judgment for nominal damages in the absence of any proven damages resulting from the breach ... I conclude, from considering the authorities, that nominal damages for a proven breach nor-

---

4   [1993] B.C.J. No. 2189 (S.C.).
5   See also *Kitney v. John Doe*, [1996] B.C.J. No. 2580 (S.C.)[*Kitney*].
6   (1983), 43 B.C.L.R. 209 (S.C.).

mally follow but that it is not invariable. The justification in the past for a judgment for nominal damages had more to do with the remedies available at the time than can be supported logically. The judgment in the case of trespass in the past was useful to defeat a prescriptive claim. Other declaratory types of judgments were useful at a time when injunctive relief was not readily available to protect a legal right....

... I consider that it would be contrary to justice and common sense to give the plaintiffs' claim the approval of the court, even to the extent of judgment for nominal damages for failing to preserve a false and meritless claim.[7]

3) Amount of Nominal Damages

The amount of nominal damages varies a great deal. Often they are set at one dollar, but can range much higher. In *Bowlay Logging*,[8] the amount awarded was $250. In this case, it will be recalled, the defendant had breached the contract, but because the plaintiff would have lost money in any event, the plaintiff suffered no "loss" as a result of the breach. The court recognized that there had been no loss; however, there was a wrong, and the right breached was seen as being important. In other recent cases, awards have been $200 (wrongful dismissal),[9] $1,500 (breach of promise of marriage),[10] $500 (minor subterranean trespass of a retaining wall),[11] $1,000 (adverse possession of land),[12] $1 (trespass to land),[13] $1,000 (wrongful detention of an airplane),[14] $1 (wrongful detention of a horse),[15] $1 (breach of contract),[16] $500 (breach of contract),[17] and $300 (trespass to goods by shoplifting).[18]

---

7   *Ibid.* at 214.
8   *Bowlay Logging Ltd. v. Domtar Ltd.* (1982), 135 D.L.R. (3d) 179 (B.C.C.A.) [*Bowlay Logging*].
9   *Beauchemin v. Universal Handling Equipment Co.* (1996), 180 A.R. 26 (Q.B.).
10 *Lakusta v. Jones* (1997), 56 Alta. L.R. (3d) 214 (Q.B.).
11 *Lim v. Titov* (1997), 208 A.R. 338 (Q.B.).
12 *Cantera v. Eller*, [2007] O.J. No. 1899 (S.C.J.).
13 *Stevens v. Pilon* (2000), 31 R.P.R. (3d) 311 (Ont. S.C.J.).
14 *No. 50 Corporate Ventures Ltd. v. Awood Air Ltd.*, [1998] B.C.J. No. 188 (S.C.).
15 *Stock v. Teske* (1997), 123 Man. R. (2d) 173 (C.A.).
16 *Health Care Developers Inc. v. Newfoundland* (1996), 141 Nfld. & P.E.I.R. 34 (Nfld. C.A.); *Place Concorde East Ltd. Partnership v. Shelter Corp. of Canada* (2006), 270 D.L.R. (4th) 181 (Ont. C.A.).
17 *Green v. Royal Bank* (1996), 28 O.R. (3d) 706 (Gen. Div.); *Blais v. Royal Bank of Canada*, [1997] O.J. No. 2288 (Gen. Div.).
18 *Hudson's Bay Co. v. White* (1997), 32 C.C.L.T. (2d) 163 (Ont. Ct. Gen. Div.), award increased [1998] O.J. No. 2383 (C.A.).

Often, fairly substantial amounts of damages have been described as "nominal." An award of $15,000 for non-pecuniary loss was described as nominal in one case where the plaintiff was felt to be exaggerating his injuries.[19] It is submitted that such an award cannot properly be described as nominal. The amount awarded, while small, is still sufficiently substantial that it cannot be justified except as compensation for a real loss. A more appropriate award of nominal damages in this context can be found in *Anderson v. Bodnarchuk*.[20] Here, the court believed that the plaintiff had suffered some pain, though it had been exaggerated. Based on the fact that the plaintiff had suffered some injury and pain, but without any evidence as to its extent, Rothery J. awarded $500 in nominal damages.

On the issue of quantum, Waddams argues that there should be a standard amount for nominal awards to increase certainty and to discourage unnecessary litigation.[21] In *Rusche v. Insurance Corp. of British Columbia*,[22] the British Columbia Supreme Court agreed with Waddams's suggestion that nominal damages should be set at the conventional sum of one dollar. This, however, was a case where the plaintiff's claim was felt to be technically correct but without merit. It involved a minor "trespass" by investigators looking into an insurance claim by the plaintiff, and the jury had awarded nominal damages of "none." In other words, the award was on the border between nominal and contemptuous damages.

It is likely that courts will continue to award somewhat larger sums, and it is submitted that this is appropriate if awards of nominal damages are not to be insulting to the plaintiff. In a later case, the British Columbia Court of Appeal awarded $500 in nominal damages for a breach of contract by an employee.[23] While there was no evidence of financial harm to the employer, the court felt that a substantial award of nominal damages was necessary to vindicate its rights. The minimal award of one dollar was, it implied, only appropriate where the court wished to express its disapprobation of the plaintiff:

> In this case, there are no grounds for expressing disapprobation of Cariboo, and the right infringed was an important one that should not be marked by an award that might be thought to express disap-

---

19   *Kitney*, above note 5.
20   [1996] S.J. No. 114 (Q.B.).
21   S.M. Waddams, *The Law of Damages*, 2d ed., looseleaf (Aurora, ON: Canada Law Book, 1991–) at para. 10.30.
22   (1992), 4 C.P.C. (3d) 12 (B.C.S.C.).
23   *Cariboo Press (1969) Ltd. v. O'Connor*, [1996] B.C.J. No. 275 (C.A.).

probation. That being so, and recognizing that the award is indeed symbolic of an important principle, I would award Cariboo damages of $500 against O'Connor.[24]

B. CONTEMPTUOUS DAMAGES

Nominal damages are not to be confused with contemptuous damages (though they often are). Contemptuous damages are awarded when the plaintiff wins the lawsuit but the court wishes to signal its disapproval of the plaintiff's conduct or action. To signal this disapproval, the award will be of the smallest amount of money possible. In these cases, the plaintiff is technically successful in the lawsuit, but the judge or jury is of the opinion that the plaintiff has suffered no real loss and the action should never have been brought. In the defamation case of *Paletta v. Lethbridge Herald Co.*, O'Byrne J. charged the jury as to contemptuous damages as follows:

> First of all there are contemptuous damages. They are awarded when the jury finds that the action should never have been brought. These arise in circumstances where the jury agrees there was libel, but is of the view that it is so petty or so minor that it did not deserve the launching of a legal action. In these cases the lowest coin of the realm is often the amount of the award.[25]

Whether a small award of damages is "nominal" or "contemptuous" becomes important when considering cost awards. While cost awards are always discretionary, where a jury awards contemptuous damages this will almost always incline a court to award costs against the "victorious" plaintiff. In *Doyle v. Sparrow*[26] the jury had awarded the plaintiff only two dollars damages in the plaintiff's defamation action. The trial judge interpreted this award as signifying nominal as opposed to contemptuous damages and awarded costs to the plaintiff in the action. The Court of Appeal confirmed the cost award, on the basis that costs

---

24 *Ibid.* at para. 28. See also *Restauronics Services Ltd. v. Forester* (2004), 23 B.C.L.R. (4th) 281 (C.A.); *Zhang v. Seymour Medical Clinic*, 2004 BCPC 355: $500 nominal damages against employer for breach of contract. Plaintiif had mitigated her losses. In *Pan Pacific Recycling Inc. v. So* (2006), 52 C.C.E.L. (3d) 261 (B.C.S.C.), the plaintiffs (two associated companies) were awarded nominal damages of $1,000 from each of the two defendants for breach of the contractual duty of loyalty to their employers.
25 (1976), 4 Alta. L.R. (2d) 97 at 105 (T.D.).
26 (1979), 27 O.R. (2d) 206 (C.A.).

are always discretionary and that there was no way of determining, after the jury's dismissal, whether it had intended to award contemptuous or nominal damages.

PART THREE

LIMITING
PRINCIPLES

CERTAINTY AND CAUSATION

A. INTRODUCTION: PROOF OF DAMAGES

The law of remedies and the substantive law are not always easily separated. Frequently, problems in substantive law resurface when the court turns to the quantification of damages, and occasionally those problems may be solved through remedial innovation. Nowhere is this more true than in the relationship between the substantive law of causation and principles of damage assessment. This chapter explains the general principles of proof regarding damages assessment, explains recovery for "lost chances," and shows how an imaginative approach to damages quantification can resolve otherwise intractable problems of proof of causation.

1) General Principles

The plaintiff may recover only damages that are caused by the defendant's wrong, and the onus of proof of this causal connection is upon the plaintiff. The test for proving causation is the "but for" test—that the loss would not have occurred but for the defendant's breach of duty. The civil standard of proof is the balance of probabilities—that it is "more probable than not" that the defendant's breach of duty caused the loss. Typically, proof of causation in this sense is a matter of substantive law. However, as will become apparent, the burden upon litigants facing such causal uncertainty has been lightened somewhat by developments in the law of remedies, especially through recovery for lost chances.

In addition to proving that the defendant caused the loss, the plaintiff must also establish the *extent* or *quantum* of the loss. This issue falls squarely within the law of remedies. In all but the simplest cases there will be some uncertainty about this. In contract cases, damages are measured by the economic benefit to the plaintiff had the contract not been breached. This requires plaintiffs to prove not only what they have directly lost as a result of the breach, but also what benefits they might have obtained, but for the defendant's wrongdoing. The extent of the plaintiff's loss may partly depend on the nature of the breach, as well as the nature of the defendant's operations or purpose of the contract. In some cases the plaintiff's entitlement will be limited to the immediate consequences of the breach,[1] whereas in other cases, the breach may have a ripple effect for future years.[2] Determining the plaintiff's entitlement involves the construction of hypothetical scenarios about what would have happened but for the breach. The same is true in tort cases. Damages are assessed by determining what the plaintiff's situation would have been, but for the tort.

In both cases the plaintiff bears the onus of proof. For example, in the case of claims for lost profit, the plaintiff must bring forward the best evidence possible to demonstrate what those profits might have been with a reasonable degree of certainty. Such evidence will be based on the plaintiff's own business records, evidence from competitors, and expert opinions. In the absence of evidence of some loss, the court may hold the burden of proof against the plaintiff and award nothing.[3] Even where the evidence shows that a loss was suffered, the court will not

---

1   See *Satara Farms Inc.* v. *Parrish & Heimbecker Ltd.* (2006), 280 Sask. R. 44 (Q.B.).

2   For example, in *Canlin Ltd.* v. *Thiokol Fibres Canada Ltd.* (1983), 40 O.R. (2d) 687 (C.A.), involving the supply of defective pool cover materials, the plaintiff's losses were not confined to losses on the sale of pool covers manufactured with the defective materials, but also covered lost profits for four years because the nature of the breach was such that it affected the plaintiff's reputation in the industry and it was not realistic for the plaintiff to have re-entered the market immediately. Similarly, in *Eggen Seed Farms Ltd.* v. *Alberta Wheat Pool* (1997), 205 A.R. 77 (Q.B.), the plaintiff, a pedigreed grain seed grower, was awarded damages for lost yield for five years following the supply of defective fertilizer. The period for future losses could be shorter depending on the nature of the plaintiff's business (*376599 Alberta Inc.* v. *Tanshaw Products Inc.* (2005), 379 A.R. 1 (Q.B): economic losses due to supply of defective entertainment product limited to six months).

3   *Cotter* v. *General Petroleums Ltd.*, [1951] S.C.R. 154. In *Pop N' Juice Inc.* v. *1203891 Ontario Ltd.*, [2004] O.J. No. 3085 (S.C.J.), claim for consequential losses for conversion was dismissed for failure to prove the losses on a balance of probabilities.

simply speculate about the amount of that loss, nor will it simply adopt the plaintiff's best-case scenario without evidentiary support.[4] Vaguely stated claims for lost profits have been denied in the absence of some compelling proof.[5]

The rule regarding onus of proof, however, must be set against another general principle: that the courts will not shirk the assessment of damages merely because the task is difficult or uncertain. Moreover, where the defendant has clearly committed a wrong that has injured the plaintiff and the plaintiff's loss is not too remote,[6] justice requires that the plaintiff should not be denied compensation for harm merely because the quantum of that harm is difficult to measure. The uncertainty may arise from the nature of the loss or from the defendant's breach that makes precise proof impossible. This occurred, for example, in *Ticketnet Corp. v. Air Canada*,[7] where the plaintiff's inability to prove its lost profit was due precisely to the defendant's breach and the subsequent injunction that prohibited Ticketnet from continuing to develop and market a software product. The plaintiff was therefore not in a position to prove its lost profits based on past performance but was held entitled to probable lost profits based on projections of what those profits would have been, subject to contingencies.[8] In *Canlin Ltd. v. Thiokol Fibres Canada Ltd.*,[9] Cory J. stated:

> The court, I believe, would be shirking its duty if it were to say that no damages should flow because of the difficulty of calculating and assessing such damages and that they are therefore too remote. An assessment of future loss of profits must, of necessity, be an estimate…. The task will always be difficult but not insurmountable. It poses no greater obstacle to a court than the assessment of general damages in a serious personal injury claim.[10]

It was noted in another case that in such situations "a court must bite the bullet and assess the damages on the basis of all available evi-

---

4   *R.G. McLean Ltd. v. Canadian Vickers Ltd.*, [1971] 1 O.R. 207 (C.A.).

5   *Sunshine Vacation Villas Ltd. v. Hudson's Bay Co.* (1984), 58 B.C.L.R. 33 (C.A.).

6   Remoteness is discussed in Chapter 11.

7   (1997), 154 D.L.R. (4th) 271 (Ont. C.A.), leave to appeal to S.C.C. refused, [1998] S.C.C.A. No. 4 [*Ticketnet*].

8   See also *Magnussen Furniture Inc. v. Mylex Ltd.* (2006), 16 B.L.R. (4th) 96 (Ont. S.C.J.) [*Magnussen*]; *Tong v. Advanced Wing Technologies Corp.*, 2001 BCSC 858.

9   (1983), 40 O.R. (2d) 687 (C.A.).

10 *Ibid.* at 691. See also *Robert McAlpine Limited v. Byrne Glass Enterprises Limited*, [2001] O.J. No. 403 (C.A.); *Plas-Tex Canada Ltd. v. Dow Chemical of Canada Ltd.* (2004), 357 A.R. 139 (C.A.), leave to appeal to S.C.C. refused, [2004] S.C.C.A. No. 542.

dence."[11] Thus, while the plaintiff should bring forward the best evidence possible to establish the extent of the loss, difficulties of proof will not bar the plaintiff's claim. Where the evidence establishes that an actual loss has been suffered, the court will not refuse to award damages merely because its extent cannot be exactly proved.[12] The court must do its best on the available evidence to quantify the loss. Moreover, the law has developed a number of rules and presumptions to aid plaintiffs in establishing the quantum of their loss. These are discussed next.

2) Plaintiff-Favourable Presumptions: Wasted Expenses in Contract and Tort

In an earlier chapter it was seen that, where profits are particularly difficult to assess in a contract action, a court may make an award to the plaintiff for the expenses incurred in performing the contract. So, for example, in *Anglia Television Ltd. v. Reed*,[13] where the plaintiff was unable to demonstrate that it had lost a profit on a movie production when the defendant actor breached his contract, the plaintiff was allowed to recover the amount it had invested in the production. In these circumstances the plaintiff has an election to claim reliance damages in place of expectation damages. This principle, it has been suggested, amounts essentially to a plaintiff-favourable assumption that, had the contract not been broken, the plaintiff would have recovered earnings on the contract at least sufficient to cover expenses—that is, that the contract was at least a break-even proposition. This principle relieves the plaintiff of the need to prove lost profits and shifts the onus of proof to the defendant to demonstrate that the plaintiff would in fact have lost money and therefore would not have covered even its expenses.[14] Only where the defendant is able to prove this on the balance of probabilities will the plaintiff's compensation be reduced below his reliance losses. This principle and the related rules are discussed fully in Chapter 2.

A similar presumption is present in tort law. In cases of fraud and negligent misstatement, for example, courts typically award to the plaintiff the entire loss suffered on a transaction or investment entered

---

11   *C & B Corrugated Containers Inc. v. Quadrant Marketing Ltd.*, [2005] O.J. No. 1665 at para. 57 (S.C.J.).
12   *Webb & Knapp (Can.) Ltd. v. Edmonton (City)*, [1970] S.C.R. 588; *B & S Publications Inc. v. Max-Contacts Inc.* (2001), 287 A.R. 201 (Q.B.).
13   [1972] 1 Q.B. 60 (C.A.).
14   *Bowlay Logging Ltd. v. Domtar Ltd.* (1982), 37 B.C.L.R. 195 (C.A.).

into by the plaintiff as a result of a misrepresentation. In such cases, damages place the plaintiff in the position she would have been in had she not entered into the losing transaction. This remedy is based upon the plaintiff-favourable presumption that the entire loss on the transaction was caused by the tort. The onus is shifted to the defendant to prove that some of the loss might have been suffered in any event.

For example, in *Rainbow Industrial Caterers v. Canadian National Railway*,[15] the plaintiff entered into a contract to supply meals to railway crews. The plaintiff's bid was based on a negligent forecast by the defendant as to the volume of meals that would be required and the plaintiff lost money on the contract before terminating it. The Supreme Court of Canada granted the plaintiff its full operating loss, thus restoring it to the position that it would have occupied had it never entered into the contract. The defendant argued that the actual loss to the plaintiff was less than this because the plaintiff would have entered into the contract in any event (though perhaps at a higher price) and would still have lost some money. The Court rejected this submission.

> Once the loss occasioned by the transaction is established, the plaintiff has discharged the burden of proof with respect to damages. A defendant who alleges that a plaintiff would have entered into a transaction on different terms sets up a new issue. It is an issue that requires the court to speculate as to what would have happened in a hypothetical situation. It is an area in which it is usually impossible to adduce concrete evidence. In the absence of evidence to support a finding on this issue, should the plaintiff or defendant bear the risk of non-persuasion? Must the plaintiff negate all speculative hypotheses about his position if the defendant had not committed a tort or must the tortfeasor who sets up this hypothetical situation establish it?[16]
>
> The appellant CN alleged that the loss was not all attributable to the misrepresentation because Rainbow would have entered into a different contract on other terms which would have resulted in at least some of the loss. What the respondent would have done had it not been for the tortious act requires a great deal of speculation, and … I would apply the legal burden of proof against the appellant.[17]

The presumption set out in *Rainbow* is rebuttable. The presumption is not applicable where the plaintiff would have entered into the trans-

---

15   [1991] 3 S.C.R. 3 [*Rainbow*].

16   *Ibid.* at 15.

17   *Ibid.* at 16. See also *Rankin v. Menzies* (2002), 47 R.P.R. (3d) 265 (Ont. S.C.J.).

action even absent the defendant's error.[18] But the burden of persuasion on this point is on the defendant to demonstrate that the plaintiff would, in fact, have entered into the same transaction and would have suffered a loss in any event.[19] These principles are discussed further in Chapter 2.

B. FUTURE UNCERTAINTY AND LOST CHANCES

1) Uncertain Future Losses

The law provides other ways in which to furnish recovery to plaintiffs when the loss is difficult to prove. In both contract and tort cases, damages are calculated by attempting to determine "what would have been" had the wrong not occurred. In many instances, the loss to the plaintiff of a past or future opportunity will be somewhat speculative. However, as explained above, so long as a real loss is proved, uncertainty as to quantum will not bar the plaintiff's claim. In claiming lost profits, where the plaintiff has direct evidence that sales were lost, the court will award the entire amount of the loss. But more often, the gist of the plaintiff's complaint will be that future sales and other opportunities for business were lost. Even though these are somewhat speculative, the court will make an award where it is likely that some such losses were suffered. In *Houweling Nurseries Ltd. v. Fisons Western Corp.*,[20] the plaintiff nursery lost numerous customers when the defendant supplied it with defective potting soil (thus killing most of the plants). The defendant argued that the lost future sales were too speculative. However, McLachlin J.A. awarded a substantial amount in respect of these uncertain losses, explaining the law in particularly clear terms:

> In my view, the law may be summarized as follows. The basic rule is that damages for lost profits, like all damages for breach of contract, must be proven on a balance of probabilities. Where it is shown with some degree of certainty that a specific contract was lost as a result of the breach, with a consequent loss of profit, that sum should be awarded. However, damages may also be awarded for loss of more

---

18   See *American Wollastonite Mining Corp. v. Scott*, [2002] B.C.J. No. 1586 (S.C.), aff'd (2003), 20 B.C.L.R. (4th) 267 (C.A.), leave to appeal to S.C.C. refused, [2004] S.C.C.A. No. 11.
19   *BG Checo International Ltd. v. British Columbia Hydro & Power Authority*, [1993] 1 S.C.R. 12.
20   (1988), 49 D.L.R. (4th) 205 (B.C.C.A.).

conjectural profits, where the evidence demonstrates the possibility that contracts have been lost because of the breach, and also establishes that it is probable that some of these possible contracts would have materialized, had the breach not occurred. In such a case, the court should make a moderate award, recognizing that some of the contracts may not have materialized had there been no breach.

The matter may be put another way. Even though the plaintiff may not be able to prove with certainty that it would have obtained specific contracts but for the breach, it may be able to establish that the defendant's breach of contract deprived it of the opportunity to obtain such business. The plaintiff is entitled to compensation for the loss of that opportunity. But it would be wrong to assess the damages for that lost opportunity as though it were a certainty.[21]

Occasionally, uncertain claims will appear so speculative that it seems impossible to assess with any degree of confidence.[22] Even in these instances, the court may make an award for the plaintiff's "lost chances." The basic principle is similar in both contract and tort.

2) Lost Chances in Contract Law

Prior to 1911, if a plaintiff was unable to prove a specific loss resulting from the breach, claims for lost opportunities (e.g., to earn a profit) were ordinarily dismissed as too conjectural or too remote. However, the case of *Chaplin v. Hicks*[23] opened the way for claims involving lost contractual benefits even in the face of substantial uncertainty. The defendant (an actor and theatrical manager) advertised a contest inviting applications from young women. Twelve winners would be selected and would be engaged for a three-year term (four at £5 per week, four at £4 per week, and four at £3 per week). The plaintiff was selected as one of fifty finalists for one of the twelve prizes (she was first in her area), but the defendant failed properly to notify her. She missed her interview and was passed over. It was held that the defendant had breached his contract by failing to use reasonable efforts to notify the plaintiff and the jury awarded £100 damages.

It was argued for the defendant that the plaintiff should receive only nominal damages since the harm suffered was too remote and speculative, that it was subject to so many contingencies that it could

---

21 *Ibid.* at 210–11. See also *Magnussen*, above note 8.
22 See *Welsh Enterprises Ltd. v. M. Milligan & Associates Ltd.*, [2005] B.C.J. No. 1668 (S.C.).
23 [1911] 2 K.B. 786 (C.A.) [*Chaplin*].

not be assessed. The Court of Appeal, however, upheld the jury verdict. The judges held that the mere fact that the prize was contingent did not mean that the chance of winning had no value or that its value could not be assessed. They all referred to the fact that the plaintiff's chance of winning was about one in four, and that the jury could take this into account in determining the value of the chance.

From one point of view, awarding damages for the value of a lost chance may seem illogical. Winning a contest is an all-or-nothing proposition. Thus, there is an argument to be made in these cases that if the plaintiff is able to prove, on the balance of probabilities, that she would have won the contest, she would receive the full value of the prize. On the other hand, if it can be shown that it is more likely than not that she would not have won, she would receive only nominal damages. While this argument may be logical, it is not fair. Instead, courts have held, as a matter of justice, that where the defendant has deprived the plaintiff of the chance of a gain of some sort, the plaintiff has been deprived of something of value (even though the chance may be a small one). The plaintiff will never know for certain whether she would have succeeded and the defendant should, in fairness, provide compensation for this loss.

Moreover, while it is true that ultimately, in the case of a contest, the plaintiff will win either nothing or the whole prize, in the face of uncertainty, the chance of winning has some value. One need simply consider a lottery ticket. The actual chance of winning may be a million to one. Thus, on the balance of probabilities, any particular ticket is likely to lose. Nevertheless, in advance of the draw, a lottery ticket has some value, and if a person wrongfully deprives another of it, he should be required to compensate the owner for the loss of its value. While most contractual rights are not bought and sold on the market like a lottery ticket (though some are, such as options and futures contracts), they do have value. As the court stated in *Chaplin*, "[i]t is true that no market can be said to exist. None of the fifty competitors could have gone into the market and sold her right ... But a jury might well take the view that such a right, if it could have been transferred, would have been of such a value that every one would recognize that a good price could be obtained for it."[24]

The same logic was adopted in the Canadian case of *Carson v. Willits*.[25] The defendant had agreed, in exchange for shares, to bore three exploratory oil wells on the plaintiff's property but abandoned the project after boring only one well. The plaintiff sued for the cost

---

24   *Ibid.* at 793.
25   (1930), 65 O.L.R. 456 (C.A.).

of boring the other two wells, whereas the defendant argued that the property was worthless and the plaintiff should receive only nominal damages. The Court of Appeal declined to adopt either approach and stated that damages should be assessed for the value of the plaintiff's lost chance. Masten J.A. stated:

> [W]hat the plaintiff has lost by the refusal of the defendant to bore two more wells was a sporting or gambling chance that valuable oil or gas would be found when the two further wells were bored. If the wells had been bored and no oil or gas had been found, the effect would be that the plaintiff has lost nothing by the refusal of the defendant to go on boring. On the other hand, if valuable oil or gas had been discovered, by the boring of these two wells, he had lost substantially. It may not be easy to compute what that chance was worth to the plaintiff, but the difficulty in estimating the quantum is no reason for refusing to award any damages.[26]

In another case on lost chances,[27] the defendant breached its contract by failing to take steps to secure zoning permission for the construction of a shopping mall on the plaintiff's property, and indeed it made that permission impossible by building another mall on nearby land. The court held that there was only a 20 percent chance that permission could have been obtained, and it awarded the plaintiff 20 percent of the profit that it would have made on the transaction. The odds of the lost chance not materializing are considered in determining the quantum of the plaintiff's loss.[28] For instance, in a case where a prime contractor, in breach of contract, failed to assign work to a subcontractor, the Court held that contingencies affecting the quantum—unanticipated job-site conditions and delays—should have been integrated into the calculation of the subcontractor's lost profit.[29] Damages for lost chances are clearly a potent solution to the problem of uncertainty.

---

26   *Ibid.* at 458.
27   *Multi-Malls Inc. v. Tex-Mall Properties Ltd.* (1980), 28 O.R. (2d) 6 (H.C.J.), aff'd (1981), 37 O.R. (2d) 133 (C.A.).
28   *Sacks v. Canada Mortgage & Housing Corp.* (2002), 98 B.C.L.R. (3d) 339 at para. 16 (S.C.) [*Sacks*]; *J.D.M. Capital Ltd. v. Asiamerica Equities Ltd.* (2001), 89 B.C.L.R. (3d) 1 (C.A.) [*J.D.M. Capital*]; *Butt v. United Steelworkers of America* (2002), 220 Nfld. & P.E.I.R. 181 (Nfld. C.A.).
29   *Naylor Group Inc. v. Ellis-Don Construction Ltd.*, [2001] 2 S.C.R. 943 at paras. 83–86.

3) The Limits of Lost Chances in Contract

In *Folland v. Reardon*,[30] the Ontario Court of Appeal summarized the
conditions for recovering loss of chance damages in contract. Doherty
J.A. stated:

> [A] plaintiff can recover damages for a lost chance if four criteria
> are met. First, the plaintiff must establish on the balance of prob-
> abilities that but for the defendant's wrongful conduct, the plaintiff
> had a chance to obtain a benefit or avoid a loss. Second, the plaintiff
> must show that the chance lost was sufficiently real and significant
> to rise above mere speculation. Third, the plaintiff must demonstrate
> that the outcome, that is, whether the plaintiff would have avoided
> the loss or made the gain depended on someone or something other
> than the plaintiff himself or herself. Fourth, the plaintiff must show
> that the lost chance had some practical value.[31]

Entitlement to compensation depends on whether the lost chance is sufficiently real and substantial.[32] Courts will not permit a plaintiff to rely
on the principle of lost chances to recover losses that are entirely speculative, or where there is simply no reliable evidence available to assess
the value of the chance.[33] In *McRae v. Commonwealth Disposals Commission*,[34] the Australian High Court refused to follow *Chaplin v. Hicks*.
In this case the defendant sold the plaintiff salvage rights to a wrecked
tanker. The plaintiff spent a large amount of money outfitting a salvage
expedition, which was entirely wasted since the supposed wreck never
actually existed. Because it was impossible to say how much the venture
would have earned the plaintiff had the contract worked out as expected, the Court based recovery on the amounts expended by the plaintiff
in preparation for the expedition. It refused to award expectation damages for lost chances, distinguishing *Chaplin* in the following way:

---

30   (2005), 74 O.R. (3d) 688 (C.A.) [*Reardon*].
31   *Ibid.* at para. 73.
32   See *Fraser Park South Estates Ltd. v. Lang Michener Lawrence & Shaw* (2001), 84
     B.C.L.R. (3d) 65 (C.A.), leave to appeal to S.C.C. refused, [2001] S.C.C.A. No.
     72. In *Toll v. Marjanovic* (2002), 46 R.P.R. (3d) 308 (Ont. S.C.J.), the vendor's
     claim for loss of opportunity to sell its property, due to a certificate of pending
     litigation that the plaintiffs had registered against the property, was dismissed
     for lack of evidence of loss of advantage of a real substantial monetary value.
33   Although there is no clear distinction between what constitutes real and sub-
     stantial chance and speculative chance, the caselaw seems to suggest that a less
     than 15 percent chance will rarely be considered significant to justify recovery.
     Reardon, above note 30 at para. 74.
34   (1951), 84 C.L.R. 377 (H.C.A.).

It does not seem possible to say that "any assessable loss has resulted from" non-delivery as such. In *Chaplin v. Hicks*, if the contract had been performed, the plaintiff would have had a real chance of winning the prize, and it seems proper enough to say that that chance was worth something. It is only in another and quite different sense that it could be said here that, if the contract had been performed, the plaintiffs would have had a chance of making a profit. The broken promise itself in *Chaplin v. Hicks* was, in effect, "to give the plaintiff a chance": here the element of chance lay in the nature of the thing contracted for itself. Here we seem to have something which cannot be assessed. If there were nothing more in this case than a promise to deliver a stranded tanker and a failure to deliver a stranded tanker, the plaintiffs would, of course, be entitled to recover the price paid by them, but beyond that, in our opinion, only nominal damages.[35]

Some courts appear to require that the plaintiff establish a "reasonable probability" that the chance would have materialized but for the breach of contract.[36] This, it is submitted, is inconsistent with the case law in this area (including *Chaplin* itself) permitting recovery when the chance is well below 50 percent.[37] The chance must be "real and substantial," but need not be "probable." Damages for lost chances should be refused only when the plaintiff provides no sound evidentiary basis for assessing the value of the chance, or when the defendant is able to establish a strong probability that the chance would not have materialized in the plaintiff's favour.

4) Lost Chances in Tort

The valuation of lost chances is common in tort law as well. For example, where a lawyer negligently misses a limitation period for filing a client's claim, or is negligent in advising a client or in the conduct of litigation, the court will assess damages based on the value of the client's lost chance.[38] Even if the chance of success is significantly less

---

35   *Ibid.* at 412.

36   *Kinkel v. Hyman*, [1939] S.C.R. 364; *Eastwalsh Homes Ltd. v. Anatal Developments Ltd.* (1993), 12 O.R. (3d) 675 (C.A.), leave to appeal to S.C.C. refused, [1993] S.C.C.A. No. 225. See also *Sacks*, above note 28; *J.D.M. Capital*, above note 28.

37   *Fasken Campbell Godfrey v. Seven-Up Canada Inc.* (2000), 47 O.R. (3d) 15 at para. 51 (C.A.).

38   *Prior v. McNab* (1976), 16 O.R. (2d) 380 (H.C.J.); *Kitchen v. Royal Air Forces Association*, [1958] 2 All E.R. 241 (C.A.); *Henderson v. Hagblom* (2003), 232 Sask. R. 81 (C.A.).

than even, the plaintiff has still lost something of value and is entitled to compensation.[39]

Even more common, and uncontroversial, is the valuation and compensation of lost chances in personal injury actions. Again, in this context, recovery of the value of lost chances is possible even when the actual probability of the chance is well under 50 percent. As explained fully in Chapter 4, the award for lost income is based upon the court's assessment of what the plaintiff *might have* earned but for the injury. Where, as a result of the injury, the plaintiff is prevented from pursuing a particular income-earning path in life, an award may be made for this loss, even though, on the balance of probabilities, the plaintiff might not have succeeded in this endeavour. For example, in *Conklin v. Smith*,[40] the plaintiff lost a leg in an accident caused by the defendant. Prior to the accident he had taken steps to commence training as a commercial pilot. The Supreme Court of Canada awarded damages for lost income based on the "reasonable possibility" that he might have succeeded in this ambition. It is important to note that in these cases the plaintiff need not establish on the balance of probabilities that it was more likely than not that he would have succeeded in his ambition. It is sufficient to demonstrate merely that there was a real chance or possibility and that as a result of the injury this chance has been destroyed. Thus, compensation will be made for lost chances even when the probability is significantly below 50 percent, provided it is not speculative. The amount of compensation will, however, reflect the degree of likelihood, and the lower the probability, the smaller the amount of compensation.[41]

The concept of chances or "contingencies" is likewise used to assess damages for the cost of care, in respect of the plaintiff's future needs and injuries in personal injury actions. When a person is injured, the full extent of her injuries and needs will rarely be known with certainty at the time of trial. In some cases evidence may indicate that the plaintiff's condition may deteriorate (thus requiring greater compensation), and in others it may improve (thus requiring less). These possible future changes are sometimes referred to as "contingencies." In assessing the quantum of damages for the cost of future care, for example, courts will take into account the future possibility that those

---

39   *Yardley v. Coombes* (1963), 107 Sol. Jo. 575.
40   [1978] 2 S.C.R. 1107.
41   *Clark v. Kereiff* (1983), 43 B.C.L.R. 157 (C.A.); *Hearndon v. Rondeau* (1984), 54 B.C.L.R. 145 (C.A.); *Freitag v. Davis*, [1984] 6 W.W.R. 188 (B.C.C.A.); *Campbell v. MacIsaac* (2004), 224 N.S.R. (2d) 315 (C.A.); *Morel v. Bryden* (2006), 246 N.S.R. (2d) 43 (C.A.).

costs may be greater because of the chance that the plaintiff's injuries will worsen, that new symptoms will become manifest, and that new procedures will become necessary.

For example, in *Schrump v. Koot*,[42] the plaintiff suffered injuries in a motor-vehicle accident that might require future back surgery. The expert evidence conflicted, though the plaintiff's doctor assessed the probability of back surgery at between 25 and 50 percent. The defendant argued that such "remote possibilities" should not be considered. The court rejected this argument, concluding that it was appropriate to take into account "chances" so long as they are real and substantial possibilities and not purely speculative: "[T]hough it may be necessary for a plaintiff to prove, on the balance of probabilities, that the tortious act or omission was the effective cause of the harm suffered, it is not necessary for him to prove, on the balance of probabilities, that future loss or damage *will* occur, but only that there is a reasonable chance of such loss or damage occurring."[43] Thus, entitlement to future losses minimally requires that there be some air of reality to the plaintiff's claim.[44]

It is important to note that the court rejected an all-or-nothing approach under which the plaintiff receives 100 percent compensation if it can be shown that the loss is "likely" to occur and nothing if it is "unlikely" to occur. Instead, uncertainty about the future is reflected in the amount of the award, "with the higher degree or the greater chance or risk of a future development attracting a higher award."[45] The damages awarded thus reflect a court's assessment of the probability that the expense will occur. In this way, uncertainty about the future is visited wholly upon neither the defendant nor the plaintiff.

5) Lost Chances to Avoid a Loss

In the same way that negative future possibilities may increase damages, positive future possibilities may be taken into account to reduce damages. For example, evidence that there is a possibility of early recovery or of successful treatment may be introduced to reduce the damage award.

The valuation of lost chances is also of importance in assessing damages when the plaintiff has failed to mitigate (or has an outstanding obligation to do so). In personal injury law, for example, if a person

---

42 (1977), 18 O.R. (2d) 337 (C.A.) [*Schrump*].
43 *Ibid.* at 339–40.
44 *Prentice (Litigation guardian of) v. Coodavia*, [2006] O.J. No. 2799 (S.C.J.).
45 *Schrump*, above note 42 at 343.

fails to follow a reasonable course of treatment or rehabilitation, damages may be reduced for his failure to mitigate, on the theory that had he mitigated his loss would have been less.[46] In these cases, however, there is seldom hard and fast evidence that a procedure would have been a success. This issue is addressed as a contingency rather than a certainty. The court must estimate the value of the chance that a particular treatment or course of action would have eliminated or reduced the plaintiff's loss. For example, in *Janiak v. Ippolito*,[47] the plaintiff's damages were reduced by 70 percent on evidence of an unreasonable refusal by the plaintiff to undergo surgery that had a 70 percent chance of effecting a complete cure.[48] Even where there is proof that, on the balance of probabilities, a particular procedure or course of treatment would succeed, the reduction of damages is still measured on the basis of the value of the chance (and the plaintiff is still entitled to some damages). The correct approach is to treat the matter as a contingency and reduce damages by the chance of a favourable outcome.[49]

C. CAUSAL UNCERTAINTY AND LOST CHANCES

1) The Problem of Causal Uncertainty

Compensation for lost chances as described above is available when the plaintiff has clearly established a cause of action by showing that the defendant's wrong caused a loss but the extent of the loss is uncertain. Courts have, on occasion, experimented with the use of probabilistic damages to solve other problems of causal uncertainty; for example, uncertainty as to whether the defendant's wrong caused any harm to the plaintiff. If a discounted damages award can be used to compensate the plaintiff for the loss of a chance, or for a possible future loss, it seems only a small extension to use a similar technique to compensate the plaintiff for losses in situations where proof of causation is impossible and an all-or-nothing approach to damages seems inappropriate.

The traditional test for the burden of proof of causation in both contract and tort is the balance of probabilities; that is, the plaintiff must establish that it is more probable than not that the defendant's wrong

---

46   See discussion of mitigation in Chapter 12.
47   [1985] 1 S.C.R. 146.
48   *Ibid.*
49   *Souto v. Anderson* (1996), 17 B.C.L.R. (3d) 238 (C.A.).

caused the plaintiff's injury. This implies that, if there is a greater than 50 percent chance that the defendant's breach caused the injury, the defendant will be liable for the full extent of the loss. If the probability is lower, the defendant escapes liability altogether. *Laferrière v. Lawson*[50] provides an illustration. In this case the defendant doctor failed to inform the plaintiff that she had cancer. The plaintiff (who had died by the time of the decision) had argued that the defendant's negligence deprived her of the chance to seek treatment and recover. The Supreme Court of Canada, however, held that she had not established that she would have recovered had such treatment been available. Thus, her claim failed the "but for" test of causation. The Ontario Court of Appeal came to a similar conclusion in *Cottrelle v. Gerrard*,[51] involving late diagnosis of a sore that ultimately became infected, leading to amputation of the plaintiff's leg. The court concluded that, given the plaintiff's medical condition, it was unlikely that an early detection would have avoided the amputation. Sharpe J.A. stated:

> ... in an action for delayed medical diagnosis and treatment, a plaintiff must prove on a balance of probabilities that the delay caused or contributed to the unfavourable outcome. In other words, if, on a balance of probabilities, the plaintiff fails to prove that the unfavourable outcome would have been avoided with prompt diagnosis and treatment, then the plaintiff's claim must fail. It is not sufficient to prove that adequate diagnosis and treatment would have afforded a chance of avoiding the unfavourable outcome unless that chance surpasses the threshold of "more likely than not."[52]

Another example is a case in which a hospital emergency department failed to detect arsenic in a patient who was sent away and died. In subsequent litigation it was held that there was no proof that treatment would have saved him. In other words, he would have died anyway.[53]

---

50 [1991] 1 S.C.R. 541 [*Laferrière*]. See also *St.-Jean v. Mercier*, [2002] 1 S.C.R. 491. In this case, the Court found that the nature of the damage the plaintiff sustained upon impact in a car accident was such that she did not have a significant chance of recovery. Thus, the doctor's negligent treatment could not be said to have caused her injuries on a balance of probabilities.

51 (2003), 67 O.R. (3d) 737 (C.A.), leave to appeal to S.C.C. dismissed, [2003] S.C.C.A. No. 549.

52 *Ibid.* at para. 25.

53 *Barnett v. Chelsea and Kensington Hospital Management Committee*, [1969] 1 Q.B. 428. However, a claim will not be considered loss of a chance for a favourable outcome where there is a known and proven cure/treatment for the condition that was not properly diagnosed. In *Gemoto v. Calgary Regional Hospital* (2006), 67 Alta. L. R. (4th) 226 (Q.B.), Martin J. held that failure to properly monitor,

The usual approach to causation will therefore frequently defeat claims where there is great causal uncertainty. Particularly because the onus of proof is upon the plaintiff, the law may be biased against compensation in complex personal injury cases. There is consequently a lively debate in the law about extending the principle of recovery for lost chances or probabilistic damages to these situations.

The cases on "lost chances" discussed in the previous sections generally involve situations where the defendant's negligence clearly caused the plaintiff some loss or injury but there is uncertainty about the extent of that injury or the amount of the loss suffered. The class of cases now under consideration are more difficult. These involve situations where there is uncertainty whether the defendant's negligence was causally linked to any injury at all. In these cases, the most that can sometimes be said is that the defendant's negligence was a "contributing factor" to the injury, or that it deprived the plaintiff of a "chance" of recovery in cases of medical negligence.

These cases arise in a variety of contexts. Particularly when the negligence and injury are non-traumatic (as in the case of disease caused by exposure to a toxic substance), proof of the causal connection can be very speculative. Unlike traumatic injury, illness and disease can be difficult to trace to their sources. The understanding of the link between particular factors and diseases is often based upon statistical and probabilistic evidence rather than mechanical chains. For example, it may be statistically true that 40 percent of all cancers in smokers is caused by cigarettes. However, applying the traditional rule of causation in any particular case will lead to the conclusion that in any one individual the cancer was not caused by smoking (since there is only a 40 percent chance that smoking caused the cancer). By insisting on individualized proof in these cases, the law will be systematically biased against compensation.

2) Experiments with Reversed Onus Rules

Some courts have experimented with onus-shifting rules to ease the burden of proof of causation in these cases. For a period, Canadian

---

assess, and care for the plaintiff, and thereby not recognizing that he had developed appendicitis, was distinguishable from the loss of chance cases that involve misdiagnosis or late diagnosis that robs the plaintiff of the opportunity to seek treatment that could have been successful. In this case, because there is a known treatment for the plaintiff's condition—surgery—negligent conduct that resulted in the plaintiff's not getting that known treatment was compensable injury and not loss of a chance. See para. 501.

courts, following the English case of *McGhee v. National Coal Board*,[54] appeared to be relaxing the burden of proof of causation in personal injury cases. *McGhee* involved an employee who developed dermatitis from coal dust. He was unable to establish that the provision of washing facilities by his employer (the negligence alleged) would have prevented the dermatitis. Yet the House of Lords held that he had shown that the failure had materially increased the risk of injury and that this was sufficient to shift the burden of proof to the defendant. Lord Wilberforce stated:

> But the question remains whether a pursuer must necessarily fail if, after he has shown a breach of duty, involving an increase of risk of disease, he cannot positively prove that this increase of risk caused or materially contributed to the disease while his employers cannot positively prove the contrary ... it is a sound principle that where a person has, by breach of duty of care, created a risk, and injury occurs within the area of that risk, the loss should be borne by him unless he shows that it had some other cause.[55]

McGhee had been interpreted by Canadian courts as reversing the onus of proof in certain situations where medical or scientific knowledge about causation was inadequate. Courts held that, where a certain conduct materially contributes to the risk of injury, the defendant engages in that conduct in breach of a duty, and the relevant injury results, then the defendant will be taken to have caused the injury.[56] However, the English House of Lords has retreated from its position in *McGhee* in *Wilsher v. Essex Area Health Authority*,[57] holding that the onus of proof may not be reversed. The Supreme Court of Canada has likewise retreated from a reversed burden of proof and has rejected *McGhee* in the case of *Snell v. Farrell*.[58] In that case, Sopinka J. stated:

> I have examined the alternatives arising out of the *McGhee* case. They were that the plaintiff simply prove that the defendant created a risk that the injury which occurred would occur. Or, what amounts to the same thing, that the defendant has the burden of disproving causation. If I were convinced that defendants who have a substantial connection to the injury were escaping liability because plaintiffs cannot prove

---

54   [1972] 3 All E.R. 1008 (H.L.) [*McGhee*].
55   *Ibid.* at 1012.
56   See, for example, *Nowsco Well Service Ltd. v. Canadian Propane Gas & Oil Ltd.* (1981), 122 D.L.R. (3d) 228 (Sask. C.A.).
57   [1988] A.C. 1074 (H.L.).
58   [1990] 2 S.C.R. 311.

causation under currently applied principles, I would not hesitate to adopt one of these alternatives. In my opinion, however, properly applied, the principles relating to causation are adequate to the task.[59]

One of the stated reasons for rejecting *McGhee* was "[t]he experience in the United States tells us that liberalization of rules for recovery in malpractice suits contributed to the medical malpractice crisis of the 1970s."[60] While perhaps unduly cautious, the reaffirmation of traditional rules of causation does not mean the plaintiff must provide irrefutable scientific evidence of causation. The Supreme Court has confirmed that judges and juries are entitled to draw common-sense inferences from the evidence. In medical malpractice cases, especially where the facts lie particularly within the knowledge of the defendant, some positive evidence of causation will be sufficient to create an inference of causation in the absence of proof to the contrary.[61] Judges and juries are entitled to take a "robust and pragmatic" view of causation in situations of uncertainty.[62] However, the burden of proof remains firmly upon the plaintiff, and the mere fact that an injury occurs within the area of risk created by the defendant's negligent conduct is not sufficient to infer causation.[63]

Though not reviving the reversal of onus suggested in *McGhee*, English and Canadian courts have lightened the evidentiary burden for plaintiffs in certain cases of causal uncertainties. In *Fairchild*,[64] the House of Lords held that conduct that materially increases a plaintiff's risk of suffering an injury may be sufficient to establish causation in limited circumstances. Causation will be established where each of multiple defendants, in breach of their duty of care to the plaintiff, exposed her to a risk of injury at different times that materializes, and it is impossible for the plaintiff to prove that each defendant's negligence caused her injury on a balance of probabilities, due to inadequate scientific or medical knowledge. The principle has been extended to include situations where the plaintiff's contributory negligence also exposes her to the same risk of injury.[65] The Supreme Court of Canada has held that a material contribution test should be used where there are independent multiple factors,

---

59   *Ibid.* at 326–27.
60   *Ibid.* at 327.
61   *Ibid.* at 330.
62   *Lankenau v. Dutton* (1991), 55 B.C.L.R. (2d) 218 (C.A.).
63   *Stewart v. Pettie*, [1995] 1 S.C.R. 131.
64   *Fairchild v. Glenhaven Funeral Services*, [2002] 3 All E.R. 305 (H.L.). See J. Cassels & C. Jones, "Rethinking Ends and Means in Mass Tort: Probabilistic Causation and Risk-Based Mass Tort Claims After *Fairchild v. Glenhaven Funeral Services*" (2003) 82 Can. Bar Rev. 597.
65   *Barker v. Corus UK Plc*, [2006] UKHL 20.

none of which is a sufficient cause of the plaintiff's injuries; the plaintiff's injury is within the scope of risk created by the defendant's negligence; and it is impossible for the plaintiff to prove causation on a balance of probabilities due to factors beyond the plaintiff's control.[66]

3) Causal Uncertainty and Probabilistic Damages

In light of the difficulties of proving causation, especially given the rejection of onus-reversing rules, some have suggested that difficulties of proof might be solved through the extension of probabilistic damages to these cases. Under this theory, causal uncertainty is dealt with not at the liability stage but at the remedies stage. Where there is causal uncertainty, the defendant is held liable, but the quantum of damages is determined in accordance with the likelihood that the defendant's negligence harmed the plaintiff, even where that probability is under 50 percent. In other words, in the absence of conclusive proof of actual causation, a court will rely on epidemiological evidence and statistics. For example, on the evidence there may be a 40 percent chance that a particular disease is caused by exposure to a product. The plaintiff would therefore receive 40 percent damages. This approach is particularly useful in class actions where all the claims are aggregated. If the class consists of 100 cancer victims who smoked, there may be statistical evidence that 40 percent of those cancers were caused by smoking. Damages would be assessed at 40 percent.

For a time there was some indication that the courts might adopt this approach. One example of probabilistic or proportional damages is the case of *Seyfert v. Burnaby Hospital Society*.[67] The plaintiff, who was being treated for an injury, was misdiagnosed and developed complications from the injury. It was unclear, however, that the medical negligence caused the complications because they may have developed in any event. Nevertheless, relying on *McGhee*, McEachern C.J. held that the negligence had materially contributed to the risk of the complications and awarded 25 percent of the damages, representing the lost chance of avoiding the complications and the longer period of convalescence. However, this approach to alleviating the burden of proof of causation has not been followed in England[68] and in other parts of Canada.[69]

---

66 *Resurfice Corp. v. Hanke*, [2007] SCC 7.

67 (1986), 27 D.L.R. (4th) 96 (B.C.S.C.).

68 In England, see *Hotson v. East Berkshire Area Health Authority*, [1987] 2 All E.R. 909 (H.L.); *Gregg v. Scott*, [2005] 4 All E.R. 812 (H.L.).

69 See *Cabral v. Gupta* (1992), 83 Man. R. (2d) 2 (C.A.).

In *Laferrière*,[70] the Supreme Court of Canada foreclosed an award for loss of a chance under Quebec civil law (and expressed doubt about the availability of such an award at common law). Here, the defendant doctor failed, following a biopsy in 1971, to inform the plaintiff that she had cancer. In 1978 the plaintiff died of generalized cancer. There was no doubt that the defendant was negligent, but substantial doubt existed whether any additional treatment would have increased the plaintiff's chance of survival. Notwithstanding this doubt, the Quebec Court of Appeal awarded the plaintiff substantial damages based on the theory that she had been deprived of the opportunity or chance to seek additional treatment and improve her health. The Supreme Court of Canada reversed this element of the decision. The Court reaffirmed the traditional principles of causation whereby the plaintiff must establish causation on the balance of probabilities. Gonthier J. concluded: "I do not feel that it is appropriate to focus on the degree of probability of success and to compensate accordingly."[71] He explained:

> [I]t is only in exceptional loss of chance cases that a judge is presented with a situation where the damage can only be understood in probabilistic or statistical terms and where it is impossible to evaluate sensibly whether or how the chance would have been realized in that particular case. The purest example of such a lost chance is that of the lottery ticket which is not placed in the draw due to the negligence of the seller of the ticket. The judge has no factual context in which to evaluate the likely result other than the realm of pure statistical chance. Effectively, the pool of factual evidence regarding the various eventualities in the particular case is dry in such cases, and the plaintiff has nothing other than statistics to elaborate the claim in damages.
>
> ...
>
> ... I am not prepared to conclude that particular medical conditions should be treated for purposes of causation as the equivalent of diffuse elements of pure chance, analogous to the non-specific factors of fate or fortune which influence the outcome of a lottery.[72]

Even more recently, in the case of *Athey v. Leonati*,[73] the Supreme Court of Canada disapproved of the use of probabilistic damages (at least to reduce an award). The issue in this case was whether two automobile accidents caused the plaintiff's back injury or whether it was

---

70   Above note 50.
71   *Ibid.* at 610.
72   *Ibid.* at 603 and 605.
73   [1996] 3 S.C.R. 458.

due to a pre-existing condition. The trial judge held that the accidents were a "minor contributing factor" and awarded 25 percent damages. The Supreme Court of Canada disapproved of this approach, stating:

> [The trial judge] awarded only 25 percent of the global damages because she held that the accidents were a "causation factor" of 25 percent. Taken out of context, this could be read as meaning that there was a 25 percent chance that the injury was caused by the accidents, and a 75 percent chance that it was caused by the pre-existing condition. In that case, causation would simply not be proven.[74]

The Court concluded that it was not appropriate to utilize probabilistic damages to resolve the problem of causal uncertainty in this case. If there was only a 25 percent chance that the accident caused the injury, the plaintiff would be entitled to no damages since causation would not be proved on the balance of probabilities. However, the Court interpreted the trial judge's comments as a finding that the accident played a smaller, but still *necessary*, role in producing the injury. This is a sufficiently substantial "material contribution" to take the case out of the *de minimus* range and lead to liability. In the result, the Court treated the case as one involving a thin-skulled plaintiff. While the plaintiff's pre-existing back condition was a major contributing factor, the ultimate condition would not have occurred but for the accident, and since the defendant must take the victim as found, the defendant was liable for the entire injury (for a discussion of the "thin-skull" rule, see Chapter 11). In reaching its decision, the Supreme Court summarized a variety of important points on causation:

1) The Court affirmed, following *Snell v. Farrell*,[75] that the plaintiff must establish on the balance of probabilities that the defendant's negligence caused or materially contributed to the injury in the sense that the injury would not have occurred "but for" the negligence. Where it is likely that the plaintiff's injuries would have occurred even in the absence of the defendant's negligence, there is no proof of causation.

2) Once it is shown that the defendant's negligence was a necessary, and non *de minimus* factor in causing the plaintiff's injury, the defendant is liable for 100 percent of the damages even if there were other concurrent (non-tortious causes operating).[76] Conversely, if

---

74   *Ibid.* at 476.
75   Above note 58.
76   In *Doern v. Phillips Estate* (1994), 2 B.C.L.R. (3d) 349 (S.C.), the plaintiff was injured by a driver fleeing a police pursuit. The police were held 25 percent

the injury would have occurred at the time in any event (because of the plaintiff's pre-existing condition), then the accident did not cause the injury. If the injury was caused by a combination of the pre-existing condition and the accident (and would not have occurred without the latter), then the accident is a necessary cause.

3) Once it is established that the defendant's negligence caused or materially contributed to the injury, the defendant is ordinarily liable for 100 percent of the damage associated with that injury, notwithstanding that the defendant's negligence was not the sole cause of the injury. The fact that other (non-tortious) factors were causative is not a grounds for a reduction in damages (as imposed by the trial judge).

4) Where an injury is divisible (i.e., the injuries are distinct and some are attributable to negligence and others are not) the defendant will only be liable for the injuries he caused.

5) Damages may only be increased or reduced on a probabilistic basis to adjust for contingencies with respect to future and hypothetical events and injuries, but not with respect to injuries that have already occurred. Future events (e.g., the chance that an injury may worsen, the chance that the plaintiff would have suffered the injury in any event, the chance that the plaintiff's condition may improve) are assessed according to probabilities and damage awards may be adjusted by percentage figures to reflect these probabilities. For example, if there were evidence of a substantial chance that the plaintiff in this case would have suffered the injury sometime in the future in any event, this might justify a reduction in damages. But past events and injuries must be proved on the balance of probabilities and once proved are treated as a certainty.[77]

It is difficult to state precisely where the line is drawn on the use of probabilistic damages. They are clearly available when the causal uncertainty is in relation to the extent of the plaintiff's future injuries (e.g., the chance of improvement or deterioration). They are also available in respect of opportunities of which the plaintiff has been deprived and which remain hypothetical (as in *Chaplin v. Hicks* or

---

liable based on their negligence during the pursuit. While the accident was caused most immediately by the fleeing driver, the police were also held liable on the basis of the "but for" test. Following *McGhee*, above note 54, Kirkpatrick J. held that the police had materially increased the risk of injury to the plaintiff, that the injury suffered was squarely within the ambit of that risk, and that the police therefore caused the harm.

77   *Mallett v. McMonagle*, [1970] A.C. 166 (H.L.).

the personal injury victim who lost the opportunity to pursue a particular career). In these cases the defendant's wrongful conduct has clearly caused the plaintiff a loss, but there is doubt about the extent or value of the loss. On the other hand, when the question is whether an injury or illness, which has in fact occurred, was caused by the defendant's wrong, the plaintiff must establish causation on the traditional balance of probabilities. The principle is usually explained in the following fashion: courts adopt a different approach depending upon whether they are assessing hypothetical events that might have occurred but for the accident, or that might yet occur in the future, and events that have in fact occurred. In the latter type of case, causation must be established on traditional grounds. Lord Diplock stated in *Mallett v. McMonagle*:

> The role of the court in making an assessment of damages which depends upon its view as to *what will be and what would have been* is to be contrasted with its ordinary function in civil actions of determining *what was*. In determining what did happen in the past a court decides on the balance of probabilities. Anything that is more probable than not it treats as certain. But in assessing damages which depend upon its view as to what will happen in the future or would have happened in the future if something had not happened in the past, the court must make an estimate as to what are the chances that a particular thing will or would have happened and reflect those chances, whether they are more or less than even, in the amount of damages which it awards.[78]

These distinctions are not entirely satisfactory, either in terms of logic or justice, and it is unfortunate that the development of the law has been halted at this point.[79] In cases like *Laferrière*, the defendant's negligence has indeed deprived the plaintiff of a valuable chance (to seek medical treatment). It is hard to discern why she should not receive

---

78 *Ibid.* at 176 [emphasis added].
79 McGregor attempts to rationalize this position by noting that the cases in which compensation may be awarded for loss of chance involve human activities and decisions that are inherently uncertain. On the other hand, in the personal injury cases where such losses are not compensable, there are no inherent uncertainties regarding the cause. Rather, it is a problem of lack of knowledge and this is an issue for the burden of proof, not the assessment of damages. However, he notes that, while this distinction appears logical, it leads to unjust outcomes. H. McGregor, *McGregor on Damages*, Second Supplement to 17th ed. (London: Sweet & Maxwell, 2005) at 8-032C [44].

compensation for this loss in the same way as the plaintiff in *Chaplin*. It is to be hoped that the Supreme Court will revisit this issue.

It is, of course, open to a legislature to utilize probabilistic damages as a means of recovery in problem situations. For example, British Columbia's *Tobacco Damages and Health Care Costs Recovery Act*[80] provides that the government may bring an "aggregate" action against tobacco manufacturers to recover the cost of health-care benefits caused by smoking. Quantification of damages would be based on an epidemiological assessment of the chances that smoking causes particular diseases in the population. The attribution of liability to specific manufacturers would be assessed in relation to that degree of probability and their market share of tobacco in the province. This statute was initially struck down on the basis that its attempt to attach liability to extra-territorial multinationals was overreaching, but its provision with respect to proof of damages was upheld.[81]

D. THE EFFECT ON DAMAGES OF SUBSEQUENT EVENTS

In assessing the extent of damages, especially when those damages extend far into the future, as in a personal injury case, courts must grapple with a variety of contingencies such as the possibility that the plaintiff's condition will improve or deteriorate or that circumstances will change somehow. As we have seen, these uncertainties are dealt with as contingencies and damages are assessed in a probabilistic fashion.

Sometimes, however, before trial, uncertainties become certainties. For example, the possibility that a personal injury victim's condition will deteriorate or improve may in fact be borne out by that person's death or recovery before trial. When this occurs, courts do, of course, take these events into account in assessing damages. Similarly, other events may intervene that change the course of things. In *Penner v. Mitchell*[82] it was held that any event that would otherwise be assessed as a future contingency will be taken into account if it in fact occurs before trial. If, after the plaintiff is injured, an event unrelated to the

---

80   S.B.C. 2000, c. 30.
81   *JTI-MacDonald v. British Columbia (A.G.)* (2000), 74 B.C.L.R. (3d) 149 (S.C.). The Act has subsequently been held to be constitutional, as it deals with torts occurring within the province: *British Columbia v. Imperial Tobacco Canada Ltd.*, [2005] 2 S.C.R. 473.
82   (1978), 10 A.R. 555 (C.A.) [*Penner*].

defendant's negligence intervenes so as to affect the nature of the plain-tiff's injury, that event will be taken into account in fixing damages. For example, in *Jobling v. Associated Dairies Ltd.*,[83] the damages awarded in a personal injury action were reduced when it was discovered that the plaintiff had a pre-existing natural condition that would have eventually totally disabled him. The award for lost income was reduced to the period between the injury and the time when the illness would have taken hold in any event. Another illustration of this principle is *Smith v. Shade*.[84] Following an injury to his ankle caused by the defendant's negligence, the plaintiff suffered a disabling knee injury. This injury was taken into account to reduce the plaintiff's damages for lost earning capacity since the knee injury essentially "obliterated" the effects of the ankle injury.

Conceptual problems arise when the subsequent event is also tortious. If the plaintiff is injured in the first accident so that she becomes unable to work, and is then injured equally seriously in a second accident, both defendants could theoretically plead that they did not cause the damage. The second defendant would argue that at the time of the second accident the plaintiff was already disabled and unable to work. The second accident did not, therefore, cause any lost income. The first defendant would argue, on the basis of *Penner* and *Jobling,* that the first accident caused only the loss of income in the period until the second injury, which would have ultimately disabled the plaintiff. Courts, however, have resisted this logic. In *Baker v. Willoughby*[85] the plaintiff's foot was injured by the first defendant and he subsequently lost his leg in an accident caused by the second defendant. The House of Lords held that the first defendant is liable to pay damages since they would be assessed on the day before the second injury, and that the second defendant is liable only for any increase in the loss suffered.

Cases dealing with damage to property raise similar issues but are in some respects treated differently. As in cases involving personal injury, where property is damaged by the defendant, but a subsequent non-tortious event intervenes, the defendant is responsible only for the harm caused to the point of the intervening event. In *Carslogie*[86] the defendant damaged the plaintiff's ship, but the ship was later damaged and delayed by heavy weather. The House of Lords held that the de-

---

83   [1981] 2 All E.R. 752 (H.L.) [*Jobling*].
84   (1996), 18 B.C.L.R. (3d) 141 (C.A.).
85   [1970] A.C. 467 (H.L.).
86   *Carslogie Steamship Co. Ltd. v. Royal Norwegian Government*, [1952] A.C. 292 (H.L.).

fendant was not liable for the lost use of the ship because the subsequent natural events would have caused the loss in any event.

Also as with personal injuries, where property is damaged in successive incidents, the second tortfeasor is liable only for the additional damage to the property. In *Performance Cars Ltd. v. Abraham*,[87] the plaintiff's automobile was damaged in a first accident and as a result required repainting. It was subsequently damaged in a second accident, which also would have required repainting. The plaintiff unsuccessfully sued the second defendant for the entire loss. The court held that the second defendant had damaged a car that already required a paint job. The second accident did not, therefore, cause the damage.

The decision of the Supreme Court of Canada in *Sunrise Co. Ltd. v. (The) "Lake Winnipeg"*[88] creates a disjunction between property cases and personal injury cases. The plaintiff's ship was forced aground by the defendant's ship as a result of the defendant's negligence. The damage would take twenty-seven days to repair and the plaintiff claimed its lost profit for that period. However, shortly after the first incident, the plaintiff's ship went aground again, resulting in damage that would also require that the ship be taken out of service. The defendant argued that the subsequent event should be taken into account in assessing damages since the loss would have inevitably been suffered. However, the Court held the defendant liable for the entire loss. L'Heureux-Dubé J. stated that "[t]he profit-making enterprise was brought to a halt by the meeting with the 'Lake Winnipeg' [first accident] … The second incident did not, therefore, have as a consequence a diminution in profit earning."[89] She also added that it makes no difference whether the second incident is tortious or non-tortious. In either event, the first defendant is liable for the entire damages. This holding is inconsistent with the personal injury cases (where the second non-tortious event is taken into account), and L'Heureux-Dubé J. makes it clear that she was not intending in this ruling to affect the law in respect of personal injuries.

---

87   [1962] 1 Q.B. 33 (C.A.).
88   [1991] 1 S.C.R. 3.
89   *Ibid.* at para. 30.

CHAPTER 11

REMOTENESS OF DAMAGES

A. INTRODUCTION

The common law places limits on the amount of damages recoverable for a tort or breach of contract, in order to avoid unduly burdening the defendant with an entirely unexpected or disproportionate degree of liability. As when a small pebble is thrown in a pond, the ripple effects from the commission of a tort or a breach of contract can spread far and wide. Even a minor breach of contract or tort may cause damage quite unforeseen by the parties and out of proportion to the culpability of wrong done. As a judge in one leading case explained, the relentless pursuit of the compensation principle, without limit, would result in liability for the most improbable and unpredictable consequences and would be unduly harsh on the defendant.[1] Thus, every system of law has a way of limiting the damages for which a defendant may be responsible. As Lord Wright explained,

> [t]he law cannot take account of everything that follows a wrongful act; it regards some subsequent matters as outside the scope of its selection, because "it were infinite for the law to judge the cause of causes," or consequences of consequences.... In the varied web of

---

1 *Victoria Laundry (Windsor) Ltd. v. Newman Industries Ltd.*, [1949] 2 K.B. 528 (C.A.) [*Victoria Laundry*].

affairs, the law must abstract some consequences as relevant, not perhaps on grounds of pure logic but simply for practical reasons.[2]

The principle of remoteness of damages is the law's primary means of guarding against unduly burdening the defendant with an inappropriate degree of liability. The question is whether, on the facts of the case, the damages claimed are too "remote" to be recoverable. The essential issue when addressing this question is whether it is fair to burden the defendant with the particular loss that has occurred. As Cromwell J.A. said in *D.W. Matheson & Sons Contracting Ltd. v. Canada (Attorney General)*, "remoteness imposes on damage awards reasonable limits which are required by fairness."[3]

B. REMOTENESS IN CONTRACT

1) The Rule in *Hadley v. Baxendale*

The test for whether a particular loss is too remote is one of "reasonable contemplation." The defendant will be responsible for a loss when that loss could be said to be within her reasonable contemplation at the time of entering into the contract. The leading case is *Hadley v. Baxendale*,[4] in which a carrier (Pickford's, a company owned by Baxendale) was late in delivering a broken mill shaft to a manufacturer. The item had been shipped as a prototype for the manufacture of a replacement. As a result of the late delivery, the plaintiff mill owner lost profits because the mill was idle for longer than necessary. The court held that the loss was too remote to be recoverable and provided the classic formulation of the rule:

> Now we think the proper rule in such a case as the present is this:—Where two parties have made a contract which one of them has broken, the damages which the other party ought to receive in respect of such breach of contract should be such as may fairly and reasonably be considered either arising naturally, i.e., according to the usual course of things, from such breach of contract itself, or such as may reasonably be supposed to have been in the contemplation of both parties, at the time they made the contract, as the

---

2   "*Liesbosch*," *Dredger v. "Edison," S.S. (Owners)*, [1933] A.C. 449 at 460 (H.L.) [*Liesbosch*].

3   *D.W. Matheson & Sons Contracting Ltd. v. Canada (Attorney General)* (2000), 187 N.S.R. (2d) 62 at para. 69 (C.A.) [*Matheson*].

4   (1854), 9 Exch. 341, 156 E.R. 145 [*Hadley*].

probable result of the breach of it. Now, if the special circumstances under which the contract was actually made were communicated by the plaintiffs to the defendants, and thus known to both parties, the damages resulting from the breach of such a contract, which they would reasonably contemplate, would be the amount of injury which would ordinarily follow from a breach of contract under these special circumstances so known and communicated. But, on the other hand, if these special circumstances were wholly unknown to the party breaking the contract, he, at the most, could only be supposed to have had in his contemplation the amount of injury which would arise generally, and in the great multitude of cases not affected by any special circumstances, from such a breach of contract. For, had the special circumstances been known, the parties might have specially provided for the breach of contract by special terms as to the damages in that case; and of this advantage it would be very unjust to deprive them.[5]

It is sometimes said that *Hadley* states two rules. The first is that damages are recovered only when they are the natural (usual) consequence of breach, or within the reasonable contemplation of the parties. The second is that "unusual" damages are recoverable when the special circumstances have been communicated to the defendant. In fact, it is simpler to formulate the principle as one rule: that the damages must be within the reasonable contemplation of the parties at the time of contract.[6] What is within their reasonable contemplation will simply depend upon what information and knowledge they have at the time of entering into the contract.[7] When a breach of contract caused losses for plaintiffs, due to their special vulnerability, of which the defendants were unaware, these were rightly considered remote.[8] However, the issue of remoteness does not necessarily hinge on the defendant's subjective belief or knowledge of risks, but, rather, what a reasonable person in the defendant's position would have known as a likely consequence of breach in the circumstances.[9]

---

5   *Ibid.* at 151 (cited to E.R.).
6   *Fidler v. Sun Life Assurance Co. of Canada*, [2006] 2 S.C.R. 3 at para. 54 [*Fidler*].
7   See *Somerville v. Ashcroft Development Inc.*, [2005] O.J. No. 3361 at paras. 68–69 (S.C.J.).
8   See *Turczinski v. Dupont Heating & Air Conditioning Ltd.* (2004), 246 D.L.R. (4th) 95 (Ont. C.A.), leave to appeal to S.C.C. refused (2005), 252 D.L.R. (4th) vi [*Turczinski*]; *Matheson*, above note 3 at paras. 72–74.
9   *Koufos v. C. Czarnikow Ltd.* ("*The Heron II*"), [1969] 1 A.C. 350 at 385 (H.L.) [*The Heron II*]; *Purolator Courier Ltd. v. Nav Air Charter Inc.*, 2002 BCSC 965 at paras. 28–35.

2) The Origin and Purpose of the Remoteness Rule

The general principle stated in *Hadley* is a useful starting point, but the rule of "reasonable contemplation" or "foreseeability" can provide only general guidance at best. The application of the rule to particular cases depends not so much on the verbal formula chosen as upon the court's sense of what is fair and appropriate in the circumstances. The rule, therefore, can be understood and applied only with some understanding of the motives and policies animating the desire to limit damages.

The rule in *Hadley* was consciously invented to serve the perceived needs of the time. Until 1854, there was no special rule about remoteness and the question of damages was ordinarily simply left to the jury. Why, then, did the courts decide to alter so fundamentally the way in which damages were awarded?

In a study of *Hadley*, Richard Danzig provides an illuminating analysis of the origin and underlying basis of the case.[10] The development of "rules" of law relating to damages, he suggests, was a response to both the economic and the legal times. Procedurally, fixed rules of damage calculation enabled a clearer delineation of jurisdiction over disputes between the superior and local courts, facilitated private settlement, and enabled the superior court system to assert greater control over the county courts and local juries.

Socially and economically, the rule in the case was appropriate to conditions in the middle of the industrial revolution. Commercial relations were becoming increasingly impersonal, complex, and interdependent. Errors could, therefore, lead to substantial unanticipated losses. The decision thus served to protect entrepreneurs from the potentially ruinous consequences of such errors. Even more specifically, the issue of a carrier's unlimited liability for losses had become a matter of significant public debate and the importance of developing a national transportation system (of which Pickford's was a part) would have been on the minds of the London-based superior court judges.

The desire to limit damages in this context may be further understood when we remember that the case took place at a time when instruments of entrepreneurial investment were less developed. It is significant, for example, that Baxendale was being sued personally (the case is not Hadley v. Pickford's). The principle of limited liability had not at the time been fully recognized and, at any rate, Pickford's was not incorporated.

---

10   R. Danzig, "*Hadley v. Baxendale*: A Study in the Industrialization of the Law" (1975) 4 J. Legal Stud. 249.

While social conditions have changed since 1854, the basic concerns underlying *Hadley* are still present and influence the way in which courts determine the recoverability of damages. It is not always fair, or good legal policy, to place every risk inherent in a transaction upon the breaching party. When parties enter into a contract they cannot be expected to be insuring each other against all possible risks associated with the transaction. The rule of remoteness likely reflects the reasonable understanding of the parties about the risks that they assume when entering into a contract. Indeed, if liability at common law were unlimited, the parties would likely want to include a clause in their contract limiting their liability very much like the rule in *Hadley*.

The rule is thought to strike a fair balance between the protection of the legitimate expectations of the plaintiff while avoiding unfair surprise to the defendant. Where a risk inherent in a transaction is obvious to one party and unknown and unexpected by the other, it is just to place the burden of that risk upon the one who knows of it. The remoteness rule also ensures that there remains some equivalence between the price charged for goods and services and the risks assumed by the provider. Economic considerations, too, provide support for the rule. Unlimited liability would be unduly chilling in ordinary commercial transactions, and without some limitation of liability, the price of many goods and services would be higher to reflect premium for risk. As well, the rule that a person is liable only for ordinary risks permits the parties to a contract to gauge the appropriate level of performance. Where there are special or unusual risks associated with a transaction, the rule gives the parties an incentive to inform one another so that they are able to take greater care (or at least to purchase the appropriate insurance). Finally, the rule is said to be efficient. It places risks upon the party who has the best information about them and who is best able to guard against their occurrence or to contract specifically with the other to assume the risk.[11]

3) Refining the Rule: The Semantics of Remoteness

The "reasonable contemplation" test may initially give the impression that the remoteness rule boils down to calculations about probabilities. And much judicial ink has been spilled in semantic exercises aimed at clarifying the required degree of foreseeability. In *Victoria Laundry*[12] (concerning recovery of lost profits by a commercial laundry owing

---

11 R.A. Posner, *Economic Analysis of Law*, 6th ed. (New York: Aspen, 2003) at 127.
12 Above note 1.

to late delivery of its boiler), the court stated that losses are recoverable when they are "reasonably foreseeable as liable to result from the breach."[13] This, in turn, suggested the court, means that the loss must be a "serious possibility," a "real danger," or "on the cards."[14] However, in the later case of *The Heron II*[15] (a claim for lost profits due to late delivery of a cargo of sugar), the House of Lords reconsidered this language. Lord Reid expressed dissatisfaction with the phrase "reasonable foreseeability" because it connotes a lower degree of probability than "reasonably contemplated" (since highly unlikely events are nevertheless foreseeable). In its place, Lord Reid preferred the use of the phrase "not unlikely,"[16] meaning "a degree of probability considerably less than an even chance but nevertheless not very unusual and easily foreseeable."[17] Adopting the reasoning in other leading cases on lost sales,[18] Lord Reid held that the loss need not be probable, in the sense of there being a better than even chance of its occurrence, but it must be "not unlikely." The law lords disagreed over whether the phrases "serious possibility" and "real danger" were acceptable.

The proliferation of semantic tests suggests that the issue of remoteness can be resolved simply by finding the right verbal formula that captures the exact degree of foreseeability required. This is misleading. While the degree of likelihood of a loss is clearly a relevant factor in determining whether the loss should be recoverable, it cannot be determinative. There is no single form of words that will be sufficiently precise to express the degree of probability or foreseeability required. The issue of remoteness cannot be left to mathematics, statistics, or semantics, and judicial discretion cannot be eliminated.

Indeed, the apparent probability of a loss occurring can easily be manipulated by the way in which the question is framed. For example, in *Parsons (H) (Livestock) Ltd. v. Uttley Ingham & Co. Ltd.*,[19] the issue was whether the defendant, who sold and improperly installed a food storage "hopper," should be liable for the loss of the plaintiff's pigs. Based on expert testimony, one level of court held that it was not foreseeable that pigs would contract *E. coli* from eating mouldy pignuts. Yet, on appeal, a different court held that it was easily foreseeable that pigs might get ill from eating improperly stored food.

---

13   *Ibid.* at 539.
14   *Ibid.* at 540.
15   *The Heron II*, above note 9.
16   *Ibid.* at 383.
17   *Ibid.*
18   *Re R. & H. Hall, Ltd. v. W.H. Pim (Junior) & Co's.*, [1928] All E.R. 763 (H.L.).
19   [1978] Q.B. 791 (C.A.) [*Parsons*].

Similarly, claims for lost profits have often been denied on the basis that the defendant had insufficient knowledge of the details of the plaintiff's business operations to foresee that a sale or business would be lost.[20] Yet framing the question more broadly, can it not always be said in a commercial contract that a breach is likely to result in lost profit? Cory J.A. stated in *Canlin Ltd. v. Thiokol Fibres Canada Ltd.*[21] (a claim for lost profits due to the supply of defective goods):

> The appellant's proposition [that such damages were too remote] appears to me to be one that flies in the face of reason and common sense. Most commercial contracts pertaining to the sale and delivery of material or goods must, of necessity, be entered into with a view to making a profit in the future. To say otherwise amounts to a denial of the profit motive in the free enterprise system.[22]

It is unlikely that any verbal formula regarding foreseeability can provide a mechanical test regarding the recoverability of damages. While the foreseeability of a risk is clearly an important factor, the real question will always be whether it is fair to allocate the loss to the defendant. Courts have recognized that there is much discretion in the application of the rule. As Zuber J.A. stated in *Kienzle v. Stringer*,[23]

> [t]he governing term is reasonable and what is reasonably foreseen or reasonably contemplated is a matter to be determined by a court. These terms necessarily include more policy than fact as courts attempt to find some fair measure of compensation to be paid to those who suffer damages by those who cause them.[24]

4) Application of the Remoteness Rule: Relevant Considerations

Whether a loss should be borne by the defendant is an issue of fairness and policy. To understand and apply the rule of remoteness, therefore, it is necessary to keep in the forefront of the analysis the reasons why we might desire to place limits on recoverability in the first place. At the most general level, the task of the court is to strike a balance be-

---

20   *B. Zar Enterprises Corp. v. Hitchen* (1982), 34 B.C.L.R. 87 (S.C.) [*B. Zar*]; *Matheson*, above note 3.

21   (1983), 40 O.R. (2d) 687 (C.A.) [*Canlin*].

22   *Ibid.* at 690. See also *C & B Corrugated Containers Inc. v. Quadrant Marketing Ltd.*, [2005] O.J. No. 1665 at para. 55 (S.C.J.).

23   (1981), 35 O.R. (2d) 85 (C.A.) [*Kienzle*].

24   *Ibid.* at 90.

tween the desire to compensate the plaintiff's loss and the equivalent desire to avoid burdening or unfairly surprising the defendant with unexpected liabilities. The primary function of the rule of remoteness, then, is to prevent unfair surprise to the defendant, to ensure a fair allocation of the risks of the transaction, and to avoid any overly chilling effects on useful activities by the threat of unlimited liability.

Two similar Canadian cases provide an illustration of the flexibility of the remoteness principle and also reveal several of the underlying considerations that will influence its application. In *Munroe Equipment Sales Ltd. v. Canadian Forest Products Ltd.*,[25] the Manitoba Court of Appeal held that the lessor of a faulty tractor was not liable to the lessee for lost profits on pulpwood sales when the tractor proved to be unreliable for the plaintiff's winter road-clearing operations (needed to bring the wood to market). The court held that the defendant had no way of knowing how much wood the plaintiff planned to remove, how quickly the work had to be done, or how much of the wood had been sold. The court found that the damages did not naturally flow from the breach and could not be said to be within the reasonable contemplation of the defendant at the time of the contract. By way of contrast, in *Scyrup v. Economy Tractor Parts Ltd.*,[26] the court held that the vendor of tractor parts was liable for lost profits (the loss of an excavation contract) when the tractor failed to operate properly. The court stated that "it is not unrealistic to ascribe to the defendant an awareness that his breach of contract in selling this defective equipment to the plaintiff would in the ordinary course of events result in damages in the form of loss of profits as here sustained."[27]

These cases were not decided by applying a mechanical rule regarding probabilities (even if it were possible to formulate such a rule). The reasons for the results of these cases must be sought elsewhere. While it may be true that some loss of revenue is both natural and foreseeable as the result of a defective tractor, it did not seem fair to the court in *Munroe* to burden the defendant with the entire risk that materialized. Miller C.J. was critical of the way in which the contract was made (the search for a tractor commenced only a few days before it was needed, and only when a representative of the plaintiff "bumped into" the defendant's salesperson). He was dissatisfied with the evidence that the failure to remove the wood from the bush was solely a result of the failure of the tractor (causation). And he was also doubtful that it was rea-

---

25   (1961), 29 D.L.R. (2d) 730 (Man. C.A.) [*Munroe*].
26   (1963), 40 D.L.R. (2d) 1026 (Man. C.A.) [*Scyrup*].
27   *Ibid.* at 1033.

sonable of the plaintiff to rely for its operation to such an extent upon a single piece of leased machinery. Miller C.J. concluded that the loss was unforeseeable because the extent of the work that the plaintiff planned to do with the tractor was out of proportion to the transaction:

> It appears to me that if it were a matter of such urgency to the defend-
> ant company that this tractor should bear the brunt of the roadwork,
> the defendant company would not have left the securing of the same
> until as late as December 1956 when hauling operations were ready
> to begin. It also seems logical to me that if the defendant company
> were going to hold the plaintiff company responsible in such large
> damages for any failure of a second-hand rebuilt unit, the defendant
> company should have made clear to the plaintiff the extent of the
> work to be done....[28]
>
> ...
>
> Had the plaintiff contemplated possible liability for such dam-
> age as claimed by the counterclaim, it is scarcely conceivable that it
> would have risked letting a second-hand tractor bear such respon-
> sibility.[29]

In the end, the way in which the remoteness principle is applied depends upon the court's assessment of a fair and reasonable allocation of risks between the parties. What is reasonable will depend upon the expectations of the parties about the ordinary risks inherent in that type of transaction and will be influenced by a number of factors that can be identified from the caselaw. First, the extent to which the defendant was actually aware of the risk will be an important consideration. Where the risk has been expressly brought to the defendant's attention, or is an obvious and usual one in this type of transaction, the defendant will bear that risk. On the other hand, where the risk goes beyond that ordinarily associated with this type of transaction, it will be less fair to burden the defendant with liability. One important factor that distinguishes *Munroe* from *Scyrup* is that, in the former case, the plaintiff's expectations regarding the use of the equipment seemed unusual and unreasonable to the court, whereas in the latter, the lost excavation work was precisely what would be expected.

Other important considerations in assessing a reasonable allocation of risk is the defendant's expertise and knowledge of the plaintiff's business. These are relevant as an indication of what the defendant can be taken to foresee as the probable result of breach, and of the risks that

---

28 *Munroe*, above note 25 at 739–40.
29 *Ibid.* at 741.

the defendant is willing to assume when entering into a transaction. In *Victoria Laundry* the fact that the defendants were engineers, with knowledge of the plaintiff's business, was of importance to the court, whereas the defendant in *Hadley* was a general carrier. Similarly, where the defendant is an expert in the industry, or a professional adviser, the ambit of liability may be wider because the defendant will be taken to know the circumstances and risks in greater detail. In contrast to situations where the defendant is, for example, a common carrier with no knowledge of the plaintiff's business,[30] it will be reasonable for the plaintiff to place a degree of reliance upon the defendant with respect to a wider range of risks when the defendant is an expert in the business in question. Additionally, a wider liability may be seen by the court as appropriate in order to impress upon professionals the importance of the obligations they undertake.[31]

Another set of considerations has to do with the proportionality among the magnitude of the risk, the nature of the defendant's promise, and the consideration paid for the promise. The nature of the goods and services offered, and the price charged, may often provide an indication of how the parties assumed that the risks would be allocated. In *Horne v. Midland Rly Co.*, Blackburn J. stated that "[t]he real meaning of the limitation as to damages is that the defendant shall not be bound to pay more than he received a reasonable consideration for undertaking the risk of at the time of making the contract."[32] In the *Munroe* case, discussed above, it seemed unfair to the court that such a large business risk should be borne by the defendant for the modest charge associated with the rental of a second-hand tractor. As Miller C.J. explained, "it is unreasonable to expect that such a burden of responsibility for damages as now claimed by the defendant should be assumed from the rental of a second-hand unit. Surely no reasonable person could contemplate, under the circumstances of the renting of this machine, that the lessor of one second-hand tractor was underwriting and virtually insuring the removal of all this pulpwood from the bush."[33]

In *B. Zar Enterprises Corp. v. Hitchen*,[34] the defendant agreed to sell land to the plaintiff for $156,000 but failed to close the transaction on time. The plaintiff subsequently sued for specific performance and also for the profit lost on a planned resale of the property to a third party

---

30   *Hofstrand Farms Ltd.* v. *British Columbia* (sub nom. *B.D.C. Ltd.* v. *Hofstrand Farms Ltd.*), [1986] 1 S.C.R. 228 [*Hofstrand*].

31   *Hodgkinson* v. *Simms*, [1994] 3 S.C.R. 377.

32   (1873), L.R. 8 C.P. 131 at 132–33 (Ex. Ch.) [*Horne*].

33   *Munroe*, above note 25.

34   Above note 20.

for $411,000. The court rejected the damages claim on the basis that the plaintiff's plan to resell the property was unknown to the defendant and the loss was therefore unforeseeable. This result can also be supported by pointing out the huge disproportion between the original sale price and the lost profits claimed by the plaintiff. It would be unfair to impose such a crushing burden of liability on the vendor.

Similarly, in *Kienzle* the court held that a solicitor should not be liable for the profit lost on a real estate transaction because of the failure of a prior transaction owing to a solicitor's negligence. Zuber J.A. stated:

> In the ordinary course, a client relies on his solicitor to guarantee the title that he certifies. The fee charged is calculated upon the sale price of the title certified and arguably the size of the risk assumed. It is not unreasonable to add to that risk consequential damages immediately concerned with the failure of marketability.
>
> This reliance, however, does not or should not extend to the loss of profits from secondary transactions which may be fuelled by funds expected from the marketing of the subject real property. This range of secondary transactions is unpredictable and limitless and so are the losses that may flow therefrom.[35]

Kienzle suggests a further factor that will be relevant — the custom of the trade. In specific areas the parties may have a well-developed sense of how the risks are allocated in a transaction. In such cases, the courts will be guided by the reasonable expectations of the parties. In addition, while seldom mentioned as a consideration, if one party customarily carries the insurance against a particular risk, that may be a factor that will influence the court. While it would be inappropriate to burden a party with liability for a risk simply because it has insurance, the fact that the parties usually arrange their insurance in a particular manner may be good evidence of their intentions regarding risk allocation.[36]

In summary, the courts strive to allocate the risks of a transaction in a way that is fair in light of the parties' reasonable expectations. In assessing what is fair, regard will be had to the actual or imputed knowledge of the parties, their expertise, the reasonableness of their expectations, the proportionality between the defendant's undertaking and the risks of the venture, the custom of the industry, and any other factors that reveal the intentions of the parties or that bear on the question of whether liability for that risk would be unduly surprising in the circumstances.

---

35 Above note 23.
36 *Photo Production Ltd. v. Securicor Transport Ltd.*, [1980] A.C. 827 (H.L.).

5)   Communication of Special Circumstances

The second branch of the rule in *Hadley* is that, where the special circumstances of a transaction are communicated to the defendant, the defendant may be liable for what would otherwise be considered an unforeseeable loss. Over the years, courts have placed different interpretations on this principle. Most simply, it suggests that, where a risk is specifically communicated to the defendant, the defendant will have actual knowledge of the risk and it will therefore fall within the ambit of what is "foreseeable." As opposed to this, other courts have held that the mere casual communication of special risks is not sufficient to shift liability to the defendant. Instead, there must be evidence of an undertaking by the defendant to assume that risk. Such an undertaking might be shown by a "special agreement" between the parties whereby the defendant expressly or by implication agrees to assume the additional risk of the transaction. Alternatively, such an undertaking might be inferred in circumstances where the defendant charges more for goods or services, indicating the inclusion of a premium for the risk.

The decision in *Hadley* itself provides some support for this latter interpretation. In explaining why a defendant will not be liable for unusual risks, Alderson B. states: "[H]ad the special circumstances been known, the parties might have specially provided for the breach of contract by special terms as to the damages in that case; and of this advantage it would be very unjust to deprive them."[37] In other words, the point of communication is to allow the parties specifically to address in their agreement how the risks are to be dealt with. Mere communication is not itself sufficient to shift the risk to the defendant. Indeed, there was evidence in *Hadley* that the fact that the mill had stopped had been casually communicated to the defendant, yet this was not sufficient in itself to shift the risk.[38]

One example of the "special agreement" interpretation is the case of *Horne*.[39] The defendant railway was late in delivering the plaintiff's goods to a customer and so the plaintiff lost the sale. The court awarded "ordinary damages" but not the loss of the especially lucrative profits that the plaintiff would have earned on the particular transaction. This was despite the fact that the plaintiff had specifically informed the defendant that a sale would be lost (though not that an exceptional profit was at stake). The court held not only that insufficient notice had been given of the unusual risk, but also that no notice would be sufficient

---

37   Above note 4 at 151 (cited to E.R.).
38   Danzig, above note 10.
39   Above note 32.

unless there was evidence of a special agreement by the defendant to bear the loss. Kelly C.B. stated:

> [E]ven if the notice given in the present case could be taken as having the effect contended for ... I do not think, in the absence of any express or implied contract by the company to be liable to these damages, that there could be any such liability imposed upon them.[40]

The court deemed this result fair in that it seemed wrong that merely informing a person of a risk should shift such a large liability to him. As Blackburn J. further observed, "if the carrier has notice of an extraordinary risk he may perhaps charge a higher rate of carriage to cover it."[41] The court was also influenced by the fact that as a common carrier the railway had no right to refuse to carry the goods. It would, therefore, be onerous to find that the railway's liability could be unilaterally increased by its customers merely informing it of the risks.

The modern tendency is no longer to require evidence of a "special agreement" before shifting the loss. This is because of changes in the economic and legal environment. First, business transactions are highly standardized and mass produced, and it is unrealistic in today's economy to imagine that customers are able to enter into "special contracts" with large firms regarding the risks associated with individual transactions. Second, firms are able to protect themselves against unusual risks through the use of exclusion clauses and limitation of liability clauses. Finally, the consequences of liability are not likely to be so ruinous. Large concerns are now insured and able to spread risks out over their entire business. Thus, in striking contrast to *Horne*, in *Cornwall Gravel Co. v. Purolator Courier Ltd.*,[42] a courier was held liable for a large lost profit on a construction contract, missed by the plaintiff when its tender documents were delivered fifteen minutes late. The Court took as sufficient communication of the "special circumstances" the fact that the plaintiff had informed the driver of the courier van that the document was a tender and that it was important that it arrive on time.[43]

---

40 *Ibid.* at 137.
41 *Ibid.* at 132.
42 (1978), 18 O.R. (2d) 551 (H.C.J.), aff'd (1979), 28 O.R. (2d) 704 (C.A.), aff'd [1980] 2 S.C.R. 118 [*Cornwall*].
43 See also *MJB Enterprises Ltd. v. Defence Construction* (1999), 170 D.L.R. (4th) 577 (S.C.C.). In this case, the plaintiff was awarded lost profits on a construction contract that the defendant had wrongly awarded to another company, in breach of the privilege clause in its tender document to offer the contract to the lowest compliant bidder, which would have been the plaintiff. Referring to *Cornwall*, Iacobucci J. stated: "If the lost profits were reasonably foreseeable to

Similarly, in *Newell v. Canadian Pacific Airlines Ltd.*,[44] the court awarded unusual damages for mental distress to the plaintiffs when the defendant airline failed to carry the plaintiffs' dogs safely (one died and one was injured when carried in the cargo compartment). In considering the plaintiffs' claim, the court held that, given that the plaintiffs had clearly indicated their concern for their pets, and offered to purchase the entire first-class cabin of the airplane for their dogs, the special circumstances had been communicated to the defendants sufficient to make them liable for the "vexation, frustration and distress" suffered by the plaintiffs in addition to their economic losses. A similar result was reached in *Kempling v. Hearthstone Manor Corp.*,[45] in which a disappointed purchaser of real estate was given damages for mental distress when the vendor's breach caused a "total disruption of lifestyle." In this case Picard J. held that the availability of damages for mental distress should depend upon the general rules of remoteness set out in *Hadley*. Generally, breach of an ordinary contract will not result in damages for mental distress unless the special circumstances of the case have been communicated to the defendant, but where those circumstances are known to the defendant, damages for distress are available despite the fact that the contract is an ordinary commercial arrangement. The subject of recovery for emotional and psychological harm is fully canvassed in Chapter 6.

In summary, the special notice rule no longer requires an express undertaking. Mere notice can be sufficient to shift a risk. However, it remains true that the more remote the risk, the more specific the notice will need to be. In these cases the special circumstances will have to be disclosed to the defendant in a meaningful way before a court can be confident that it is fair to shift the risk.

C. REMOTENESS IN TORT

1) General Principles

The basic principle of remoteness in tort is the same as that in contract. The leading case is *The Wagon Mound (No. 1)*,[46] which stated that the

---

the courier delivering the tender, then I believe that lost profits must be found to be reasonably foreseeable in the present instance. *Ibid.* at 599.

44   (1976), 14 O.R. (2d) 752 (Co. Ct.), discussed in Chapter 6, Sections C(2)(d) and C(3).

45   (1996), 41 Alta. L.R. (3d) 169 (C.A.).

46   *Overseas Tankship (U.K.) Ltd. v. Morts Dock and Engineering Co. Ltd.*, *The Wagon Mound (No. 1)*, [1961] A.C. 388 (P.C.) [*The Wagon Mound (No. 1)*]; followed in

test in tort is that the consequences must be "reasonably foreseeable" as the probable result. The case dealt with fire damage to the plaintiff's property when molten lead from a welding operation ignited oil on top of water in the harbour. The oil had been spilled by the defendant but it was highly unusual that it would burn. It was held that the defendant should not be liable in negligence because the damage was not foreseeable. Viscount Simonds explained that it would not be just for a slight act of negligence to result in unlimited liability even for unforeseeable consequences. Despite the language in this case suggesting that the damage must be "probable," later cases have held that the damage need only be "possible." Indeed, in another case arising out of the same incident (*The Wagon Mound (No. 2)*),[47] the Privy Council confirmed that the damage need only be a "real risk." In *McCann v. Hyndman*,[48] where the defendant doctor negligently failed to locate a loose balloon and tube previously implanted in the plaintiff's abdomen, the court conceded that no physician had heard of the particular injury that the plaintiff suffered in the circumstances—migration of the balloon through the diaphragm to infiltrate his lung —but nevertheless concluded that the injury was not remote. The court noted that a risk of harm to the plaintiff's internal organs was foreseeable in the circumstances, making his injury a foreseeable outcome of the defendant's negligence. Similarly, where there was a risk of harm to certain parts of the body, an injury to an eye, a part of the body not typically seen to be at risk from the activity in question, was nevertheless considered foreseeable.[49]

As with the concept of remoteness in contract, there is much debate about the precise semantic test to be used to describe the degree of foresight required. Likely, it is sufficient that a type of damage be reasonably foreseeable as a real possibility,[50] provided the possibilities are not so remote or fantastic to be rendered unforeseeable.[51] Such a general principle leaves a great deal of room for judicial discretion and the results in the cases will more often be the result of unarticulated

---

Canada in *R. v. Côté* (1974), [1976] 1 S.C.R. 595 [*Côté*]; *Price v. Milawski* (1977), 18 O.R. (2d) 113 (C.A.) [*Milawski*].

47 *Overseas Tankship (U.K.) Ltd. v. Miller S.S. Co. Pty., The Wagon Mound (No. 2)*, [1967] 1 A.C. 617 (P.C.) [*The Wagon Mound (No. 2)*].

48 (2003), 336 A.R. 360 (Q.B.), aff'd (2004), 354 A.R. 35 (C.A.).

49 *Michaluk (Litigation guardian of) v. Rolling River School Division No. 39* (2001), 153 Man. R. (2d) 300 (C.A.) [*Michaluk*]: the plaintiff, a twelve-year old, was injured in the eye by a coat hanger during an approved art class at school.

50 *Milawski*, above note 46; see also A.M. Linden & B. Feldthusen, *Canadian Tort Law*, 8th ed. (Markham, ON: LexisNexis Butterworths, 2006) at 371–74.

51 *Michaluk*, above note 49 at para. 22.

values than of the application of rules of probability. As in the case of contract, the basic question is whether, in respect of a type of damage that occurs, justice requires that the plaintiff or defendant bear those consequences. As one judge stated,

> the chain of cause and effect can be followed only to the point where the consequences of an act will be fairly accepted as attributable to that act in the context of the social and economic conditions then prevailing and the reasonable expectations of members of society in the conduct of each other.[52]

While it may seem initially attractive that a negligent defendant should bear all the consequences of her carelessness, there may come a point when it does not seem fair that a moment's inadvertence should result in liability for truly "freakish" consequences.[53] Fairness in loss distribution will depend upon a variety of factors. Undoubtedly, the social utility (or otherwise) of the defendant's behaviour will be a relevant consideration.[54] Where the defendant's activity is without redeeming social value, it is likely that the ambit of liability will be wide. Conversely, where the plaintiff's activity is one that society wants to encourage (e.g., rescuers), the plaintiff may be able to claim damages for extremely improbable events and injuries.[55] Similarly, the proportionality between the degree of the defendant's fault and the extent of the damages will influence a court. Other factors that likely play a role include the nature of the loss suffered by the plaintiff (a court may be more inclined to compensate for personal injury than for property damage or economic loss),[56] and the respective abilities of the plaintiff and defendant to spread a particular loss or to insure against it. In addition to the flexibility inherent in the general formulation of the remoteness rule, there are a number of modifications and exceptions that have developed over the years.

---

52   *Abbott v. Kasza* (1976), 71 D.L.R. (3d) 581 at 588 (Alta. C.A.), Clement J.A.
53   Linden & Feldthusen, above note 50 at 376.
54   *The Wagon Mound (No. 2)*, above note 47. However, *Michaluk*, above note 49, suggests that the possibilities test may be used even where the defendant was engaged in a socially useful activity, such as education.
55   *Videan v. British Transport Commission*, [1963] 2 Q.B. 650 (C.A.); *Chadwick v. British Transport Commission*, [1967] 2 All E.R. 945 (Q.B.D.).
56   *Parsons*, above note 19. See also *Michaluk*, above note 49.

2) The Rule in *Hughes v. Lord Advocate*: Type of Injury Foreseeable, Not Manner

In *Hughes v. Lord Advocate*[57] the House of Lords held that only the *type* of damage needs to be foreseeable, not the *manner* in which it occurs. In this case, it was deemed foreseeable that, when the defendant's employees left a lit paraffin lamp by a worksite, a curious young passer-by might play with the lamp and be burned. The fact that the burn occurred in a very unusual manner (when the lamp was dropped into a manhole, causing a large explosion, and the plaintiff fell in) did not make the plaintiff's injuries unforeseeable. So long as the type of injury suffered by a plaintiff is a foreseeable consequence of the defendant's negligence, the precise manner in which the injury occurs need not be foreseeable.[58] Similarly, in *Jolley v. Sutton London Borough*,[59] where a fourteen-year-old boy was rendered a paraplegic when an abandoned cabin cruiser on the defendant's property fell on him as he lay underneath it in an attempt to repair it, his injuries were not considered remote. The plaintiff and another boy had propped up the boat, thereby making it unstable. The Court noted that the boat was an attraction for children and, given their unpredictable nature, it was foreseeable that children would interfere with the boat even at the risk of some physical injury, and that what occurred was not different from what could be expected during normal children's play. Once such an outcome was foreseeable, neither the precise manner nor the extent of the injury need to be foreseeable. Only injury of a given description needs to be foreseen. In *Michaluk*, the court noted that "injury to the eye was not of a kind vastly different from the risk of other physical injury ... [it] was simply a variance of the more likely injury."[60]

By way of contrast, when the damage is not foreseeable, the defendant will not be liable. In *Trevison v. Springman*[61] the plaintiffs had left their house key with the defendant while they were away. They had asked the defendant not to tell her son about the key since they were concerned about his history of theft. The defendant's son stole the key, copied it, stole items from the house, and finally burned down the

---

57   [1963] A.C. 837 (H.L.). See also *Côté*, above note 46.
58   *Lauritzen v. Barstead* (1965), 53 D.L.R. (2d) 267 (Alta. S.C.T.D.); *Fox (Guardian ad litem of) v. Edwards*, [2001] B.C.J. No. 370 (S.C.); *Tooley v. Arthurs* (2002), 246 N.B.R. (2d) 160 (Q.B.).
59   [2000] 3 All E.R. 409 (H.L.). See also *Simmons v. British Steel plc*, [2004] UKHL 20 at para. 67, Lord Rodger.
60   *Michaluk*, above note 49 at para. 36.
61   (1995), 16 B.C.L.R. (3d) 138 (S.C.), aff'd [1997] B.C.J. No. 2557 (C.A.).

house in an attempt to avoid detection. The court held that the parent in this case might be liable to someone injured by her child, on the ground that she was aware of the child's propensity to theft and could reasonably have taken some additional measures to prevent it from occurring (by better safeguarding the key). However, while the parent might be liable for her son's theft, she is not liable for the arson damage. Arson was not within her son's repertoire of misdeeds and was not, therefore, a foreseeable consequence of the breach of her duty of care. Spencer J. distinguished *Hughes v. Lord Advocate* on the ground that the type of damage here was entirely different in kind from that which could have been foreseen by the defendant.

3) The Thin-Skull Rule: Type of Injury Foreseeable, Not Extent

The second important gloss on *The Wagon Mound (No. 1)* is the "thin-skull rule," which holds that the defendant takes the victim as found. Where the defendant's negligence causes some foreseeable injury to the plaintiff, the defendant will be liable for all the injury, even though its *extent* is beyond the norm owing to some pre-existing vulnerability. If a person is injured by negligence, it is no defence to a claim for damage that the person "would have suffered less injury, or no injury at all, if he had not had an unusually thin skull or an unusually weak heart."[62] This principle was confirmed even after *The Wagon Mound (No. 1)* in *Smith v. Leech Brain & Co. Ltd.*[63] Following a burn to his lip caused by molten metal, the plaintiff developed cancer. This was due to a pre-existing susceptibility and was not foreseeable. Yet some harm was foreseeable. Parker C.J. explained:

> The test is not whether these employers could reasonably have foreseen that a burn would cause cancer and that he would die. The question is whether these employers could reasonably foresee the type of injury he suffered, namely, the burn.[64]

The thin-skull rule has been applied in many cases of both physical and psychological harm. For example, a defendant was held liable for post-polio syndrome suffered by a polio survivor when he slipped and fell at the defendant's premises,[65] and also for the persistence of the

---

62 *Dulieu v. White & Sons*, [1901] 2 K.B. 669 at 679.
63 [1962] 2 Q.B. 405 [*Smith*].
64 *Ibid.* at 415.
65 *Chan v. Erin Mills Town Centre Corp.*, [2005] O.J. No. 5027 (S.C.J.).

plaintiff's injury from a motor vehicle accident due to her pre-existing degenerative condition.[66] As well, courts have held that a defendant will be responsible for the plaintiff's chronic-pain syndrome, even though the condition is the product of a pre-existing psychological susceptibility.[67] Similarly, where an emotional or psychological problem such as an excessive dependency upon caregivers,[68] or an eating disorder,[69] or a neurological disorder[70] is triggered by a minor physical injury, the defendant will be liable so long as the negligence triggered the condition. In *Gray v. Cotic*[71] the Supreme Court of Canada upheld a jury verdict holding the defendant liable for a suicide. The deceased blamed himself for an accident in fact caused by the defendant in which others were injured. He had a history of psychological problems and was especially vulnerable to a psychotic reaction to the accident. The defendant was held liable for all of the consequences, based on the thin-skull principle.

The thin-skull rule does not alter basic principles of causation or the assessment of damages. Its application is not intended to place the plaintiff in a better position than before the accident. The rule provides that the defendant is liable for the total extent of the injury caused by the negligence, even though that extent may not be foreseeable. But the rule does not mean that the defendant is liable for injuries that were already in existence or that were inevitable and therefore not caused by the negligence. For example, if in *Smith* it could have been shown that the plaintiff's cancer was inevitable even without the burn, the defendant would not be liable for the cancer or would be liable only to the extent that the burn accelerated the cancer's formation. This gloss on the rule is sometimes called the "crumbling skull" principle. The defendant is not liable for injuries that were inevitable. Major J. explained the distinction in *Athey v. Leonati*:

> The "crumbling skull" doctrine is an awkward label for a fairly simple idea. It is named after the well-known "thin skull" rule, which makes the tortfeasor liable for the plaintiff's injuries even if the injuries are unexpectedly severe owing to a pre-existing condition. The tortfeasor must take his or her victim as the tortfeasor finds the victim, and

---

66   *Zaruk v. Simpson* (2003), 22 B.C.L.R. (4th) 43 (S.C.) [*Zaruk*].

67   *Maslen v. Rubenstein* (1993), 83 B.C.L.R. (2d) 131 (C.A.); *Joel v. Paivarinta*, [2005] B.C.J. No. 84 (S.C.).

68   *Yoshikawa v. Yu* (1996), 21 B.C.L.R. (3d) 318 (C.A.).

69   *F.(K.E.) v. Daoust* (1996), 29 C.C.L.T. (2d) 17 (B.C.S.C.).

70   *Kollaras (Litigation guardian of) v. Olympic Airways S.A.*, [1999] O.J. No. 1447 (S.C.J.), aff'd [2000] O.J. No. 1104 (C.A.) [*Kollaras*]: trauma and stress from being struck on the head by a sliding door accelerated the onset of Alzheimer's.

71   (*Sub nom. Izquierdo Estate v. Cotic Estate*), [1983] 2 S.C.R. 2.

is therefore liable even though the plaintiff's losses are more dramatic than they would be for the average person.

The so-called "crumbling skull" rule simply recognizes that the pre-existing condition was inherent in the plaintiff's "original position." The defendant need not put the plaintiff in a position *better* than his or her original position. The defendant is liable for the injuries caused, even if they are extreme, but need not compensate the plaintiff for any debilitating effects of the pre-existing condition which the plaintiff would have experienced anyway. The defendant is liable for the additional damage but not the pre-existing damage.... Likewise, if there is a measurable risk that the pre-existing condition would have detrimentally affected the plaintiff in the future, regardless of the defendant's negligence, then this can be taken into account in reducing the overall award.... This is consistent with the general rule that the plaintiff must be returned to the position he would have been in, with all of its attendant risks and shortcomings, and not a better position. [72]

The fact that the plaintiff has a "crumbling skull" does not break the chain of causation or relieve the defendant entirely of liability. It goes to the assessment of damages.[73] The defendant will be liable for all of the consequences of an injury, but in assessing those consequences (and the amount of damages) the court will have regard to the plaintiff's actual condition at the time of the wrong or what her condition would have been but for the defendant's wrongdoing, that is, her "original position."[74] Damages will be reduced to reflect the likelihood of the plaintiff suffering the injury in question even without the defendant's wrongdoing. Where the defendant's wrongdoing aggravates a pre-existing condition that was manifest and disabling, damages for past and future losses will be limited to the extent of the aggravation. Otherwise, reduction is justified only where there is a measurable risk, or a

---

72   [1996] 3 S.C.R. 458 at 473–74 [*Athey*] [emphasis in original]. See also *K.L.B. v. British Columbia*, 2003 SCC 51 at para. 60 [*K.L.B.*].

73   See *Sparkes-Morgan v. Webb* (2002), 216 Nfld. & P.E.I.R. 112 at para. 18 (Nfld. C.A.). The British Columbia Court of Appeal has also emphasized that causation and the assessment of damages are separate issues and are governed by distinct principles: *A. (T.W.N.) v. Clarke* (2003), 22 B.C.L.R. (4th) 1 at para. 16 (C.A.), Smith J.A. [*Clarke*].

74   In *Smith*, above note 63 at 416, although the defendant was held liable for the unexpectedly severe consequences of the deceased's injuries, the employer was not liable for the plaintiff's entire losses. Damages were substantially reduced to reflect the fact that the deceased might have developed the fatal condition even absent the burn he suffered due to the defendant's negligence.

real and substantial possibility that the plaintiff would have suffered the injury even absent the defendant's intervention.[75] The principle is also applicable even where the plaintiff was unaware of and/or showed no symptoms of the pre-existing condition prior to suffering the injury from the defendant's wrongdoing.[76] However, no deduction on the basis of a crumbling skull is justified where there are treatment options that could potentially cure the plaintiff's condition if successful,[77] or where the plaintiff had coping strategies to deal with the pre-existing condition that she is no longer capable of using due to the injury from the defendant's wrongdoing.[78] In such cases, the injury from the plaintiff's pre-existing condition and the resulting losses cannot be considered inevitable and hence reduction of damages would be unjustifiable. On the other hand, recovery may be denied where the defendant's wrongdoing did not worsen the plaintiff's situation or where the plaintiff suffered no new injury due to the tort in question.[79]

The same principle applies to psychological injuries. Although the defendant may be liable for psychological conditions triggered by physical injuries (owing to a pre-existing susceptibility), where the psychological problems were likely to manifest themselves in any event, the defendant will not be liable for the entire harm. In *Malloch v. Moenke*[80] the plaintiff suffered soft-tissue injuries in an accident and went on to develop chronic pain due, she said, to a psychological reaction to the accident. There was evidence that the plaintiff had suffered from an anxiety condition before the accident. The issue for the jury was whether the accident "aggravated an active condition or triggered a latent and

---

75   *Athey*, above note 72 at para. 35; *McKelvie v. Ng* (2001), 90 B.C.L.R (3d) 62 at para. 13 (C.A.); *Hosak v. Hirst* (2003), 9 B.C.L.R. (4th) 203 at para. 10 (C.A.); *Zacharias v. Ley*, [2005] B.C.J. No. 2487 at para. 21 (C.A.); *Kielley v. General Hospital Corp.* (1999), 183 Nfld. & P.E.I.R. 1 at paras. 98–99 (Nfld. C.A.). In *Athey*, the deduction was not justified because, notwithstanding his vulnerability to back injury, there was no evidence that the plaintiff was likely to have suffered disc herniation without the accidents (in effect, it was a case of a thin, not a crumbling, skull). Also, in *Zaruk*, above note 66, although the court found that the plaintiff was predisposed to degenerative changes at a future date due to her pre-existing condition, this would not have materialized in the pre-trial period. Hence, there was no deduction from her award for past losses.

76   See *Niitamo v. Insurance Corporation of British Columbia* (2003), 16 B.C.L.R. (4th) 276 (S.C.); *Dufty v. Great Pacific Industries Inc.*, [2000] B.C.J. No. 1988 (S.C.); *Clarke*, above note 73 at paras. 28, 54, and 61–63, Smith J.A.

77   *Lyne v. McClarty* (2003), 170 Man. R. (2d) 161 at para. 36 (C.A.); *Kollaras*, above note 70.

78   *Johnstone v. Canada (Attorney General)*, [2006] B.C.J. No. 3247 at para. 49 (S.C.).

79   See *Sananin v. MacHale*, 2006 BCSC 672.

80   (1996), 20 B.C.L.R. (3d) 359 (C.A.).

quiescent condition, and if the latter, whether the problem would likely have erupted regardless of the accident."[81] The Court of Appeal upheld only a modest award to the plaintiff on the grounds that the plaintiff's condition prior to the accident was the major reason for her post-accident difficulties, and that the accident only temporarily worsened a condition that would have eventually existed anyway.

D. TORT VERSUS CONTRACT

There has long been debate about whether the rules of foreseeability are different in tort and contract. Some cases have stated quite unequivocally that the test for recovery in contract (reasonable contemplation) is more restrictive than the test in tort (reasonable foreseeability) and that tort law imposes a wider liability. The reasons for the difference, if any, are based on considerations of policy and fairness. The House of Lords stated in *The Heron II*:

> [In tort] The defendant will be liable for any type of damage which is reasonably foreseeable as liable to happen even in the most unusual case, unless the risk is so small that a reasonable man would in the whole circumstances feel justified in neglecting it. And there is good reason for the difference. In contract, if one party wishes to protect himself against a risk which to the other party would appear unusual, he can direct the other party's attention to it before the contract is made.... But in tort there is no opportunity for the injured party to protect himself in that way, and the tortfeasor cannot reasonably complain if he has to pay for some very unusual but nevertheless foreseeable damage which results from his wrongdoing.[82]

The position in Canada is different. It is now clear that there is no substantial difference in the rule in tort and contract. The Supreme Court of Canada has repeated on several occasions that the principles of remoteness are the same.[83] For example, in *Asamera Oil Corp. v. Sea Oil & General Corp.*, Estey J. stated:

> We therefore approach the matter of the proper appraisal of the damages assessable in the peculiar circumstances of this case on the following basis: that the same principles of remoteness will apply to the

81   *Ibid.* at 361–62.
82   Above note 9 at 385–86.
83   *Hofstrand*, above note 30; *BG Checo International Ltd. v. British Columbia Hydro & Power Authority*, [1993] 1 S.C.R. 12 [*BG Checo*].

claims made whether they sound in tort or contract subject only to special knowledge, understanding or relationship of the contracting parties or to any terms express or implied of the contractual arrangement relating to damages recoverable on breach.[84]

In *Canlin*, Cory J.A. stated:

> The test of determining what is a loss that directly and naturally results in the ordinary course of events from the breach of warranty may be phrased in the classical contract question, namely, are the consequences of the breach of contract such that a reasonable man at the time of the making of the contract would contemplate them as being liable to result or to be a serious possibility; or, in the classical tort question, namely, are the consequences of the act such that a reasonable man at the time the tort was committed would foresee that damages are likely to result. The questions are in reality the same. The affirmative answer to either question should lead to the same result. There is no difference between what a reasonable man might reasonably contemplate and what a reasonable man might reasonably foresee.[85]

The fact that there is no significant verbal difference in the tests was confirmed again by the Supreme Court of Canada in *BG Checo*.[86] However, there are some ways in which the tests might still be different. First of all, despite the broad language of the cases, it is likely that the time for assessing foreseeability is different in tort and contract. In tort, a defendant is liable for risks that are foreseeable at the time of the wrong. In contract, liability is based on the type and extent of risks that are foreseeable at the time of making the contract. In contract theory, the bargain is struck on the basis of risks as they are understood by the parties when they make the contract and they should not be liable for unassumed risks that become obvious later on.[87] In practice, it is unlikely that the timing rule makes a great deal of difference. When a risk is obvious at the time the defendant breaches, it is unlikely that the defendant will escape liability because that risk was not obvious at the time the contract was made. This is particularly true in the case of long-term contracts such as employment contracts, franchise agreements, and interdependent commercial relationships in which the parties are aware of the changing circumstances over time. For example,

---

84   (1978), [1979] 1 S.C.R. 633 at 673.
85   Above note 21 at 694–95.
86   Above note 83.
87   See *Turczinski*, above note 8 at para. 45.

in *Murano v. Bank of Montreal*,[88] where a bank was held liable for wrongfully calling the plaintiff's loan, Adams J. stated:

> [T]his case severely tests the reasonableness of this ancient rule.... Where a party can demand full payment of a loan at will, that party can assess daily whether to break off its contractual relationship. In the case of a demand loan, it can do so without breaching its contract provided it gives reasonable notice. In that particular context it seems strange to be thrown back to the original date of contract for the purposes of foreseeability. In fact, confining loss assessment to the formation of a long standing "at will" banking relationship seems artificial and may be inconsistent with the general trend of authority harmonizing rules in tort and contract. Indeed, in this case, judging the foreseeability of loss in light of the Bank's knowledge closer to the date of breach is not likely to upset contractual intentions given the expectations of the parties at the date of contract formation that the plaintiffs' changing conditions would be closely monitored.[89]

Despite the fact that there is no difference in the formulation of the remoteness test, the different circumstances in tort and contract cases mean that the test will often lead to different results. First, as the House of Lords explained in *The Heron II*, in most tort cases the parties are strangers. The plaintiff is typically an unknowing victim of harm and is not in a position to take steps to prevent that harm from occurring (and where the plaintiff can do so, principles of contributory negligence can be utilized to apportion liability). In contract cases the parties are acting intentionally and are typically aware of the risks and better able to take steps to guard against them. From this perspective, fairness and efficiency will often dictate that the rules of recoverability be somewhat broader in tort cases than in contract cases.

Second, unlike liability in tort, liability for breach of contract is absolute. In tort law, inevitable accidents and minor errors that cause harm may not lead to liability. Undue hardship to "innocent" defendants who cause harm can be avoided by the careful use of flexible liability rules regarding duty and standard of care. However, in contract law there are no excuses (or very few) for breach. Defendants are liable for breaches that are entirely unintentional and without fault. It seems probable that one way of "softening" the consequences of this strict regime is through a more "defendant-favourable" application of remoteness rules.

---

88   (1995), 20 B.L.R. (2d) 61 (Ont. Ct. Gen. Div. [Commercial List]), var'd on other grounds (1998), 41 O.R. (3d) 222 (C.A.).

89   *Ibid.* at 119–20 (Ont. Ct. Gen. Div. [Commercial List]).

Third, contract claims are typically for expectation losses. The plaintiff may have lost nothing but an anticipated benefit. Tort claims are more "real" in that they are concrete out-of-pocket losses. Such losses present a stronger case for compensation and are therefore less likely to be foreclosed by the application of remoteness rules.

Fourth, as indicated above, tort law has a ready tool for apportioning liability for risks between the plaintiff and defendant. When both are "at fault" the defendant's liability can be reduced through the application of contributory negligence principles. Until recently, these principles were not available in contract law. It may be suggested, then, that the rules of remoteness in contract served this double purpose. Even when the defendant has also clearly breached a contract, but the plaintiff is itself the author of its own misfortune, the court may limit the available damages through the application of remoteness principles.[90]

Finally, as Lord Denning pointed out in *Parsons*,[91] tort law is generally concerned with personal interests in physical and emotional well-being, whereas contract law is primarily concerned with economic interests. While his suggestion that the formal rules with respect to each be different has not borne fruit, it is likely that courts are, as a matter of practice, likely to apply the rules of remoteness more "generously" when faced with physical injuries than when faced with the loss of economic benefits.

E. REMOTENESS, MITIGATION, AND IMPECUNIOSITY

The issue of remoteness of damages is often intertwined with questions regarding mitigation of damages and causation. All three principles frequently come together when, following a tort or breach of contract, the plaintiff suffers additional losses because he lacked sufficient funds to take steps to mitigate the loss. For example, in a sale of goods case, the disappointed buyer may not have sufficient funds immediately to purchase a substitute and therefore suffers additional lost profits. Or frequently, where property is damaged, the owner may not have sufficient funds to do the repairs immediately and further damages are incurred as a result. In these cases the defendant will frequently make three arguments, all of which amount to the same thing: that the plain-

---

90 For example, *Freedhoff v. Pomalift Industries Ltd.*, [1971] 2 O.R. 773 (C.A.) [*Freedhoff*]; *Munroe*, above note 25.

91 Above note 19.

tiff has failed to mitigate and cannot claim the loss that could have been avoided; that the loss was not "caused" by the defendant but was caused by the plaintiff's failure to mitigate; and that the loss is too remote to be recoverable. However the issue is framed legally, at the bottom it is about risk allocation: Which of the two parties should bear the risk that the loss caused by the defendant might be aggravated because of the plaintiff's lack of funds?

While there is no absolute rule, the general presumption has been that the defendant is not liable for losses caused by the plaintiff's impecuniosity. Justice is generally served by compensating the plaintiff for foreseeable losses only. It would be unduly burdensome and surprising to make the defendant liable for every consequence of what may be a small or even "innocent" civil wrong. It may also be more "efficient" to allocate the risk of impecuniosity to the plaintiff. A particularly high-risk plaintiff may often be in a better position to anticipate and guard against special losses.

The leading illustration of the general principle is *"Liesbosch," Dredger v. "Edison," S.S. (Owners)*,[92] discussed earlier. Here, the steamship *Edison* had fouled the moorings of the dredger *Liesbosch*, dragging the latter into the open sea. The *Liesbosch* filled with water and sank. At the time of the incident, the dredger was engaged in fulfilling a contract between the plaintiff and a third party. Because of a lack of funds the plaintiffs were unable to replace the ship immediately and were forced to adopt the more expensive route of renting a ship to complete the contract. The House of Lords held that the plaintiffs were not entitled to the additional costs incurred because of their financial position. These losses, said the Court, resulted not from the defendant's tort but from their own impecuniosity. Lord Wright stated:

> But the appellants' actual loss in so far as it was due to their impecuniosity arose from that impecuniosity as a separate and concurrent cause, extraneous to and distinct in character from the tort; the impecuniosity was not traceable to the respondents' acts, and in my opinion was outside the legal purview of the consequences of these acts. The law cannot take account of everything that follows a wrongful act; it regards some subsequent matters as outside the scope of its selection, because "it were infinite for the law to judge the cause of causes," or consequences of consequences.[93]

---

92   *Liesbosch*, above note 2.
93   *Ibid.* at 460.

Liesbosch has been followed in other cases, though rarely is the result explained in terms of causation. Statements about which factor "caused" the loss are simply conclusions that do not provide a reason. Similar cases have been decided on the basis of remoteness.[94] For example, in *Freedhoff*[95] the plaintiff lost its skiing operation ultimately as a result of a ski-lift supplier's breach of contract to install a lift. The plaintiff was denied its claim for the loss of its property, which resulted from a combination of the defendant's breach of contract and the plaintiff's own impecuniosity, since the loss was held to be too remote.

As a universal or absolute rule, the exclusion of losses due to impecuniosity would be unfair. It goes against the spirit of the thin-skull rule that ordinarily the defendant is liable for all the harm caused, even if that harm is greater because of a pre-existing vulnerability (in this case financial) of the plaintiff. *Liesbosch* has been criticized on the basis that it is unfair to deprive a person of full compensation for her loss because of her lack of funds. Indeed, taken as a general principle, the principle can be said to discriminate against the poor.[96] Moreover, where the outcome of the case is uncertain, it is unfair to require the plaintiff to invest her own money in repairing or replacing property with the prospect that at the end of the day she may not recover. This was the view taken by the court in *Dodd Properties (Kent) Ltd. v. Canterbury City Council*.[97] Here, the plaintiff was awarded the cost of repairing his damaged building, which had increased substantially in the years leading to trial (during which time the plaintiff had done nothing). The court held that it was reasonable for the plaintiff to postpone the repairs given his "financial stringency" and the fact that the defendant was denying liability. Under the circumstances, it was a reasonable commercial decision to refrain from repairing the building until the outcome of litigation was known.

In *Lagden v. O'Connor*,[98] the House of Lords unanimously overruled *Liesbosch* on the issue of losses due to the plaintiff's impecuniosity. In this case, the plaintiff's car was damaged by the defendant's negligence. The plaintiff incurred higher consequential losses by using the services of a hire-car company while his car was being repaired, be-

94   *Compania Financiera Soleada S.A. v. Hamoor Tanker Corpn. Inc. ("The Borag")*, [1981] 1 All E.R. 856 (C.A.).
95   Above note 90.
96   S.M. Wexler, "The Impecunious Plaintiff: *Liesbosch* Reconsidered" (1987) 66 Can. Bar Rev. 129.
97   [1980] 1 All E.R. 928 (C.A.). See also *Alcoa Minerals of Jamaica plc v. Broderick*, [2002] A.C. 371 (P.C.).
98   (2003), [2003] UKHL 64, [2004] 1 A.C. 1067 (H.L.) [*Lagden*].

cause he could not afford to rent a car by himself. The majority held that the plaintiff was entitled to recover the higher cost in the particular circumstances due to his impecuniosity—that it was reasonably foreseeable that he would incur such higher costs. Their lordships said *Liesbosch* can no longer be considered authoritative and that the time has come to depart from that principle.[99] Lord Hope stated:

> It is not necessary for us to say that *The Liesbosch* was wrongly decided. But it is clear that the law has moved on, and that the correct test of remoteness today is whether the loss was reasonably foreseeable. The wrongdoer must take his victim as he finds him [or her].... This rule applies to the economic state of the victim in the same way as it applies to his physical and mental vulnerability. It requires the wrongdoer to bear the consequences if it was reasonably foreseeable that the injured party would have to borrow money or incur some other kind of expenditure to mitigate his [or her] damages.[100]

It is important not to overstate the effect of *Lagden*. The approach to impecuniosity will now be more specific to the facts of each case, and there will still be instances in which aggravated losses of the type under consideration here will properly be denied. In fact, the House of Lords did not purport to overrule its earlier decision in *Dimond v. Lovell*,[101] where the plaintiff was denied recovery of similar charges because they were considered remote. Recovery on the basis of impecuniosity is justified only where the plaintiff could not meet those expenses without personal sacrifices that she could not reasonably be expected to make.[102] Thus, the plaintiff's situation in *Dimond* was considered distinguishable, as there was no evidence that she could not have afforded to pay for rental charges without making personal sacrifices.

From a policy perspective, it is also important not to assume a new "rule" that losses caused by impecuniosity will now always be recoverable. One of the objectives of damages law is to give the parties incentives to minimize the costs from a tort or breach of contract. The approach taken in *Leisbosch* gives the plaintiff an incentive in advance to protect himself from aggravated damage. The easiest way for a

---

99   See Lord Nicholls, *ibid.* at para. 8.
100 *Ibid.* at para. 61.
101 [2002] 2 All E.R. 897 (H.L.) [*Dimond*].
102 *Lagden*, above note 98 at para. 9, Lord Nicholls. Some of their Lordships were sceptical of the use of the language of choice to determine plaintiffs who are impecunious and those who are not. Among other things, this is because how a person chooses to spend his resources would often be a matter of priorities for him. See Lord Hope at paras. 41–45, Lord Scott, and Lord Walker.

plaintiff to do this, of course, is to insure property. When the property is damaged, the plaintiff looks first to insurance for quick repair or replacement of the property. Especially in commercial cases and property damage cases, the defendant should not be saddled with the risk that the defendant is uninsured where there has been a deliberate decision not to insure and there is a need to safeguard the interests of impecunious victims.[103]

There may be other reasons to insulate the defendant from the consequences of the plaintiff's impecuniosity. In ordinary contract cases, if suppliers were made liable for the additional risks of dealing with "impecunious" customers, they might be reluctant to deal with them or would incur costly measures to avoid the special risks entailed. There is nothing wrong with running a commercial operation "on a shoestring," but it may be unfair to allocate the additional business risks of such an operation to its suppliers and others who deal with it. Thus, in situations where the parties are commercial enterprises dealing at arm's length, the defendant will rarely be liable for the additional losses caused by impecuniosity because such losses are unlikely to be reasonably foreseeable absent specific knowledge of the plaintiff's financial situation. In *R.G. McLean Ltd. v. Canadian Vickers Ltd.*,[104] the plaintiff suffered lost profits because the defendant supplied a defective printing press. Its claim for lost profits was cut off early by the court on the basis that it should have purchased a replacement machine. The argument that it could not afford to do so was met with the response that the defendant should not be responsible for the "frailties of the plaintiff's credit."

In the end, there is no absolute rule about impecuniosity. The question whether a defendant should be liable for additional losses attributable to the plaintiff's inability to mitigate will generally be treated as an issue of remoteness and will be decided according to considerations of policy and fairness. The crux of the matter is simply whether it is just in the circumstances to place the risk of loss on the defendant. Generally, in commercial contract cases, the plaintiff's impecuniosity is not an excuse for failure to mitigate in a timely fashion. The defendant should not be made an insurer of the plaintiff's business enterprise, especially when the plaintiff is operating at the margin. Similarly, in property damage cases, the usual expectation is that the plaintiff will have insurance and will be able to carry out repairs immediately after the damage.

---

103 *Rollinson v. Canada* (1994), 73 F.T.R. 16.
104 [1971] 1 O.R. 207 (C.A.).

Nevertheless, there are clear examples of situations where additional losses caused by impecuniosity will be recoverable. Most obviously, the contract itself, or the circumstances surrounding its formation, may alert the defendant to the problem of impecuniosity and may allocate the risk. Or, in cases where the contract provides that one party is responsible for financing a venture, and that party breaches the contract, the other party will not be expected to mitigate by immediately finding alternate financing and carrying on with the venture. In these cases the very subject matter of the contract is finance, and the defendant has assumed the risk of the venture by agreeing to provide funds. So, for example, in *General Securities Ltd. v. Don Ingram Ltd.*,[105] the defendant finance company was held liable for the loss of the plaintiff's car dealership when the defendant repudiated its contract to provide financing for the operation.[106] Other situations where courts are more forgiving of impecuniosity involve consumer contracts. For example, one of the factors that inclined the court in *Wroth v. Tyler*[107] to award damages assessed at the date of trial was that the plaintiffs were people of modest means and, in the circumstances of rising real estate prices, were not able to finance the acquisition of an alternative property. *Lagden* can also be justified along these lines. Similarly, where the defendant's wrong is a direct and obvious cause of the plaintiff's impecuniosity, the plaintiff may be excused from mitigating. In *Cash v. Georgia Pacific Securities Corp.*,[108] a stockbroker converted the plaintiff's shares by selling them without authorization. The shares represented a large part of the plaintiff's wealth. Since the broker had caused the plaintiff's impecuniosity, it was not open to him to argue that there was a failure to mitigate by not buying replacement shares quickly at a higher price. The measure of damages was held to be the value of the stocks at the time of their sale plus consequential damages, consisting of the commission paid for the sale, the loss of the opportunity to buy other shares, and the loss of the present value of the shares.

---

105 [1940] S.C.R. 670.
106 *Trans Trust S.P.R.L. v. Danubian Trading Co. Ltd.* (1951), [1952] 1 K.B. 285.
107 [1974] Ch. 30.
108 *Cash v. Georgia Pacific Securities Corp.*, [1990] B.C.J. No. 1315 (S.C.).

CHAPTER 12

MITIGATION, AVOIDED LOSS, AND TIME OF ASSESSMENT

A. MITIGATION OF DAMAGES

1) Introduction

Mitigation of damages is the principle that a plaintiff may not recover losses that could have been avoided by taking reasonable steps after the wrong. The principle applies in both tort and contract. The Supreme Court of Canada has quoted with approval the following statement from the House of Lords:

> The fundamental basis is thus compensation for pecuniary loss naturally flowing from the breach; but this first principle is qualified by a second, which imposes on a plaintiff the duty of taking all reasonable steps to mitigate the loss consequent on the breach, and debars him from claiming any part of the damage which is due to his neglect to take such steps.[1]

Another way of expressing the rule is that a plaintiff cannot recover "avoidable losses."[2]

---

1 *British Westinghouse Electric & Manufacturing Co. Ltd. v. Underground Electric Rlys Co. of London Ltd.*, [1912] A.C. 673 at 689 (H.L.) [*British Westinghouse*], quoted with approval in *Asamera Oil Corp. v. Sea Oil & General Corp.* (1978), [1979] 1 S.C.R. 633 at 661 [*Asamera*].
2 *Red Deer College v. Michaels*, [1976] 2 S.C.R. 324 [*Red Deer College*].

There are sound reasons underlying the obligation to mitigate. Most generally, mitigation is about fairness. Damages are not generally intended to be punitive. Following a tort or breach of contract, the plaintiff may not hold the defendant hostage to every loss that might occur. Where the plaintiff is reasonably able to avoid a loss, or to take steps to minimize it, it would be antisocial and punitive for the plaintiff to sit back and do nothing, thus incurring an "unconscionable accumulation"[3] of damages. The rule of mitigation has the effect of minimizing the total costs of the tort or breach of contract, thereby avoiding unduly burdening or surprising the defendant with an unexpected extent of liability. It should be borne in mind that not all breaches of contract are *mala fides* or even intentional. There is no general policy that contract breach should be punished. Similarly, most torts involve the unintended consequences of legitimate activities. The rule of mitigation reflects a recognition that "accidents happen" and that no useful purpose is served by allowing the damages to increase in their aftermath.

The basic insight that it is socially desirable to minimize the total costs of a civil wrong has been formalized by legal economists. The rule of mitigation is said to be efficient in that it provides an incentive to minimize the joint costs of an activity. More specifically, in breach of contract cases, mitigation permits "efficient breach." According to this notion, where the cost to the promisor of performing a contract is substantially more expensive than the loss to the other party from non-performance, the contract should not be performed. It is uneconomic, and oppressive, to force completion of such contracts when any losses to the innocent party can be compensated by damages. The theory also applies when the promisor is able, by breaching, to earn additional profits on an alternate transaction. Where the innocent party's loss can be fully compensated by an award of damages paid out of the additional profits, and there is still a net gain to be earned on the alternate transaction, it is efficient (joint value is maximized) to permit the breaching party to pursue the alternative transaction.[4] The rule of mitigation, requiring the innocent party to take steps to keep the costs of breach low, further promotes this result.

The rule of mitigation also ensures a fair allocation of risks between the parties. Often the plaintiff is in the best (or only) position to deal with the consequences of a breach of contract or tort. In such circum-

---

3   *Ibid.*
4   R.A. Posner, *Economic Analysis of Law*, 6th ed. (New York: Aspen, 2003) at 120. The Supreme Court of Canada has approved the idea of efficient breach: *Bank of America Canada v. Mutual Trust Co.*, [2002] 2 S.C.R. 601 at para. 31.

stances, it would be wrong to saddle defendants with post-breach risks over which they have no control. For example, where a buyer of goods breaches a contract of sale, the vendor has an obligation to resell the goods. If the vendor does not do so and the goods spoil, or the market price falls, that additional loss is caused as much by the vendor's inaction as by the buyer's breach. Additionally, while the vendor in such a case may choose to hold onto the goods rather than to resell them (in the hope that the market price will increase), the risk of such speculation should generally fall on the plaintiff's shoulders rather than the defendant's (if the price does in fact increase, the plaintiff will be permitted to retain the profit).

2) General Principles: Reasonableness

The objective of the rule of mitigation is to give the plaintiff an incentive to take steps to minimize the total costs of the tort or breach of contract, and to avoid unduly burdening the defendant with avoidable losses. The plaintiff is debarred from recovering losses that could *reasonably* be avoided. What is reasonable is a question of fact, not law, and the burden of proof is upon the defendant to demonstrate that the plaintiff could reasonably have avoided a loss or was unreasonable in her conduct.[5] In assessing reasonableness, the context is important. In the commercial context, plaintiffs must do what an ordinary business person would do in the circumstances. They must take actions that are consistent with their usual practices and may not let their feelings of hostility or anger get in the way. However, the plaintiff is not obliged to make extraordinary efforts or to take serious business risks or gambles to reduce a loss. The plaintiff need only do what is prudent under the circumstances. Given that the plaintiff is often facing difficult circumstances following an unexpected breach, the actions taken will not be judged against too high a standard. Nor will courts permit the actions taken by the plaintiff to be easily second-guessed by the defendant with the benefit of perfect hindsight. One court explained:

> Where the sufferer from a breach of contract finds himself in consequence of that breach placed in a position of embarrassment, the measures which he may be driven to adopt in order to extricate him-

---

5   *Red Deer College*, above note 2; *Coutts v. Brian Jessel Autosport Inc.* (2005), 40 C.C.E.L. (3d) 236 (B.C.C.A.); *Proctor Crushing Inc. v. Precision Surfacing Ltd.*, 2004 ABQB 713 at paras. 72–73 [*Proctor Crushing*]; *2438667 Manitoba Ltd. v. Husky Oil Ltd.*, [2007] M.J. No. 233 (C.A.); *Kern v. Steele* (2003), 220 N.S.R. (2d) 51 (C.A.).

self ought not to be weighed in nice scales at the instance of the party whose breach of contract has occasioned the difficulty.... The law is satisfied if the party placed in a difficult situation by reason of the breach of a duty owed to him has acted reasonably in the adoption of remedial measures, and he will not be held disentitled to recover the cost of such measures merely because the party in breach can suggest that other measures less burdensome to him might have been taken.[6]

The plaintiff is not obliged to take extraordinary risks in mitigating,[7] or to put his commercial reputation at stake, and courts will grant substantial deference to the plaintiff's choices following the breach so long as they are reasonable. One particularly dramatic example of deference to the plaintiff's choices is *Banco de Portugal*.[8] Through a breach in security the defendant printers enabled the forgery of the plaintiff's currency. The bank was able to tell good notes from bad within the series, and the defendant argued that the only real loss was the cost of printing the worthless notes (since the bank could simply have refused to honour the forged notes). However, instead, the bank redeemed all banknotes in circulation (both legitimate and forged). While the plaintiff could have reduced damages in the short run by simply refusing to honour the forged notes, the House of Lords permitted it to collect all its losses, accepting that the bank's action was reasonably necessary to preserve public faith in its currency:

> [F]or a country to find that what it believed to be a substantial portion of its legal wealth was nothing more than worthless pieces of paper instead of genuine notes of the Bank would have created an economic panic and confusion which would have caused the gravest damage to the credit of the Bank and might even have shaken the whole economic and commercial life of the country.[9]

Though the plaintiff is not obliged to take extraordinary risks, where she does do so, and successfully offsets the loss, that will be taken into account. For example, a dismissed employee is not obliged to become an entrepreneur, but if she does do so successfully, her earnings will be taken into account.[10] As Rand J. explained in *Karas*,

---

6   *Banco de Portugal v. Waterlow & Sons Ltd.*, [1932] A.C. 452 at 506 (H.L.) [*Banco de Portugal*].

7   *Karas v. Rowlett*, [1944] S.C.R. 1 [*Karas*].

8   Above note 6.

9   *Ibid.* at 471.

10   See *Cockburn v. Trusts & Guarantee Co.* (1917), 55 S.C.R. 264 [*Cockburn*], discussed in Section C, below in this chapter.

the steps which ought to be taken by an injured party must arise out of the consequences of the default and be within the scope of what would be considered reasonable and prudent action. There are obviously limitations to the class of venture, for instance, in respect of which the duty would arise, *but, where there has been an actual performance within those consequences, whether or not within the duty, the benefit* derived *may be taken into account.*[11]

Sometimes a plaintiff's failure to mitigate may be attributable to her pre-existing condition that prevents her from taking the steps necessary to mitigate her losses. Whether pre-existing conditions should excuse a plaintiff from the duty to mitigate depends on whether the defendant had actual or constructive knowledge of the plaintiff's condition. Knowledge of such condition could bring the plaintiff's inability to mitigate within the reasonable contemplation of the defendant as a possibility in the event of a breach.[12]

Occasionally the plaintiff is unable to mitigate because of a lack of funds, or the plaintiff's "impecuniosity" aggravates the loss suffered by reason of the breach. For example, in a sale of goods case, the disappointed buyer may not have sufficient funds immediately to purchase a substitute. Or frequently, where property is damaged, the owner may not have sufficient funds to do the repairs immediately. In both cases the delay may increase the loss (e.g., the price of acquiring a substitute or doing the repairs may increase) and the issue is whether those additional losses are recoverable.

Sometimes the issue of impecuniosity is dealt with as a problem of mitigation. The question is whether it was unreasonable for the plaintiff to delay. Other times it is dealt with as an issue of remoteness. The question is then whether the aggravated losses due to the plaintiff's impecuniosity were foreseeable. In this work, the problem is dealt with in that context and the relevant principles are fully discussed in Chapter 11.

---

11   Above note 7 at 8 [emphasis added].
12   See *Turczinski v. Dupont Heating & Air Conditioning Ltd.* (2004), 246 D.L.R. (4th) 95 (Ont. C.A.). In *Turczinski*, the plaintiff's failure to mitigate — find a replacement contractor to complete the work so she could rent out rooms — was due to emotional distress caused by her pre-existing mental condition. Since this condition was not known to the defendant, the plaintiff's increased losses from not being able to rent out the property for a longer time were not recoverable, because those losses were said to have resulted from her failure to mitigate.

3) Mitigation Applied

a) Sale of Goods

Several examples may illustrate what is ordinarily required by the rule of mitigation. In contracts for the sale of goods, the disappointed buyer of goods must ordinarily purchase substitute goods when the vendor has failed to deliver, and damages will be measured by the cost of procuring a substitute at the time of breach. Where the buyer does not purchase a substitute and suffers additional consequential losses as a result, those losses are not recoverable. Similarly, the disappointed seller of goods must resell the goods when the buyer refuses to accept delivery and damages will be measured by any loss on the sale.[13]

In both situations, the plaintiff is expected to take reasonable measures to salvage the transaction and minimize the resulting damage. Indeed, where a vendor of goods or services refuses to deliver goods in accordance with the terms of the contract, the buyer may nevertheless be obliged even to accept an offer of substitute performance from the same supplier (e.g., to deliver the same goods on different terms), so long as that offer is reasonable and is the next best offer the buyer can locate.[14] Along the same lines, the buyer of defective goods may have to accept an offer of a refund from the vendor rather than continue to engage in fruitless efforts to run the machinery or repair it. The buyer may not refuse reasonable offers and thus "'run up the damages' to the prejudice of the defendant."[15] In cases where the buyer is obliged to continue dealing with the vendor following breach, the buyer may be concerned that, in accepting the goods on different terms, or taking a refund, he is waiving his right of action and may be well advised to make it clear that he is preserving his right of action.

b) Property Damage

The obligation to mitigate arises in many other contexts. Where the plaintiff's property is delivered in unsatisfactory condition, the plaintiff is obliged to take steps expeditiously to have it repaired at a reasonable cost. Additional losses (e.g., lost profits and increased costs) flowing from unnecessary delays in repairs will not be compensated

---

13   *Hammond v. Daykin* (1914), 19 B.C.R. 550 (C.A.), var'd (1915), 8 W.W.R. 512 (S.C.C.).

14   *Payzu v. Saunders*, [1919] 2 K.B. 581 (C.A.) [*Payzu*]; *Westland Investment Corp. v. Carswell Collins Ltd.* (1996), 179 A.R. 272 (Q.B.); *Proctor Crushing*, above note 5 at paras. 111–19.

15   *R.G. McLean Ltd. v. Canadian Vickers Ltd.*, [1971] 1 O.R. 207 at 216 (C.A.).

without reasonable excuse.[16] In tort, the rule of mitigation applies as well. Where chattels have been damaged, the plaintiff has an obligation to act reasonably in repairing or replacing the article. For example, except in special circumstances, where an automobile is damaged, the owner must follow a reasonable route in repairing or replacing the vehicle and must do so in a timely fashion. Where the cost of repairing the damage exceeds the market price of a replacement, the owner is expected to follow the most "economic" path.[17] A court may deviate from this principle and permit the recovery of repair costs even though they exceed the replacement cost, when the plaintiff is able to demonstrate that the specific vehicle is of special value or use.[18] These principles are discussed more fully in Chapter 3 in the context of damages for harm to property.

c)   Wrongful Dismissal

In the context of employment contracts, an employee who is wrongfully dismissed has an obligation to take steps to secure alternative employment within a reasonable time. The onus to prove that the loss could be reduced through mitigation lies with the employer, who must demonstrate that the employee's efforts were unreasonable and that similar but not necessarily identical employment was available.[19] The standard of what is reasonable is judged largely from the employee's perspective, in light of her particular circumstances.[20] Taylor J. A. in *Forshaw v. Aluminex Extrusions Ltd.*[21] explained:

> That "duty" — to take reasonable steps to obtain equivalent employment elsewhere and to accept such employment if available — is not an obligation owed by the dismissed employee to the former employer to act in the employer's interests....
>
> The duty to "act reasonably", in seeking and accepting alternate employment, cannot be a duty to take such steps as will reduce the

16   *O'Grady v. Westminster Scaffolding Ltd.*, [1962] 2 Lloyd's Rep. 238 (Q.B.) [*O'Grady*]; *Dodd Properties (Kent) Ltd. v. Canterbury City Council*, [1980] 1 All E.R. 928 (C.A.) [*Dodd Properties*]. See the discussion of increased costs of repair in Section D(4), below in this chapter, and also in Chapter 2.

17   *Darbishire v. Warran*, [1963] 3 All E.R. 310 (C.A.).

18   *O'Grady*, above note 16.

19   *Red Deer College*, above note 2; *Zorn-Smith v. Bank of Montreal* (2003), 31 C.C.E.L. (3d) 267 (Ont. S.C.J.) [*Zorn-Smith*]; *Cimpan v. Kolumbia Inn Daycare Society* (2006), 54 C.C.E.L. (3d) 307 (B.C.S.C.).

20   See *Zorn-Smith*, *ibid.*; *Johnson v. Canwest Global Communications*, 2007 BCSC 981 [*Johnson*].

21   (1989), 39 B.C.L.R. (2d) 140 (C.A.).

claim against the defaulting former employer, but must be a duty to take such steps as a reasonable person in the dismissed employee's position would take *in his own interests*—to maintain his income and his position in his industry, trade or profession. The question whether or not the employee has acted reasonably must be judged in relation to his own position, and not in relation to that of the employer who has wrongfully dismissed him. The former employer cannot have any right to expect that the former employee will accept lower paying alternate employment with doubtful prospects, and then sue for the difference between what he makes in that work and what he would have made had he received the notice to which he was entitled.[22]

Whether the employee is obliged to accept an alternate (and less satisfactory) position with the same employer is somewhat more complex and there is no fixed rule. Some courts have found that it would often be unrealistic to expect a dismissed employee to take another position within the employer's organization while looking for work elsewhere, among other things, because it is unlikely that the parties can work in harmony after the termination.[23] Other courts have suggested the requirement to accept alternate employment will often arise in cases of constructive dismissal.[24] Where relations between the employer and employee have been damaged by the dismissal, the employee is not obliged to accept alternative and less satisfactory employment with the former employer.[25] However, some courts do require an employee who has been constructively dismissed, to look at the new position as a possible way of mitigating damages.[26] The terms and conditions of re-employment or re-assignment must be objectively reasonable. Factors of importance include whether there is a substantial change in the working conditions, reduction in responsibility, prestige, or pay, the nature of the employment relationship, and the extent to which harmonious relations are possible between the employer and employee and with fellow employees.[27] In *Farquhar*, Lambert J.A. explained:

---

22   *Ibid.* at 143–44 [emphasis in original]. See also *Stuart v. Navigata Communications Ltd.*, [2007] B.C.J. No. 662 (S.C.); *Plotogea v. Heartland Appliances Inc.*, [2007] O.J. No. 2717 (S.C.J.); *Smith v. Aker Kvaerner Canada Inc.*, 2005 BCSC 117 at para. 35 [*Smith*].

23   *Kuz v. CIBC Trust Corp.*, [1998] A.J. No. 1532 at para. 29 (Q.B.).

24   See *Farquhar v. Butler Brothers Supplies Ltd.* (1988), 23 B.C.L.R. (2d) 89 (C.A.) [*Farquhar*]; *Smith*, above note 22 at para. 41.

25   *Payzu*, above note 14.

26   *Mifsud v. MacMillan Bathurst Inc.* (1989), 70 O.R. (2d) 701 (C.A.).

27   *Mifsud*, *ibid.*: different position but everything else, including remuneration, remained substantially unchanged. He should have accepted the position in

The employee is only required to take the steps in mitigation that a reasonable person would take. Sometimes it is clear from the circumstances that any further relationship between the employer and the employee is over. One or the other or both of them may have behaved in such a way that it would be unreasonable to expect either of them to maintain any new relationship of employer and employee. The employee is not obliged to mitigate by working in an atmosphere of hostility, embarrassment or humiliation. But once the employer is clearly told, by words or equivalent action, that the termination is accepted by the employee, then, if the employer continues to offer a position to the employee, and the position is such that a reasonable employee would accept it, if he were not counting on damages, then the duty to mitigate may require the employee to accept the position, on a temporary basis while he looks for other work, even if it is roughly his old position before the constructive dismissal. Such circumstances may not arise frequently. Very often the relationship between the employer and the employee will have become so frayed that a reasonable person would not expect both sides to work together again in harmony. But sometimes it would be unreasonable for the employee to decline to continue in employment through the period equal to reasonable notice, while he looks for other work.[28]

As well, the re-employment or re-assignment should not prejudice the employee's interests; the position offered must be suitable to the employee's capabilities.[29] Opportunities for re-assignment may be undermined where the employer has engaged in bad-faith conduct in the course of

---

mitigation. See also *Evans v. Teamsters Local Union No. 31*, 2006 YKCA 14: failure to accept re-employment in one's former position on essentially the same terms, albeit temporary, amounts to failure to mitigate. *Cox v. Robertson* (1999), 69 B.C.L.R. (3d) 65 (C.A.): the close and personal nature of the employment relationship between a dentist and his dental assistant made it unreasonable for the plaintiff to have continued working for the employer. As well, a harmonious working relationship was not possible in the circumstances when the plaintiff was suing the defendant. See also *Turner v. Uniglobe Custom Travel Ltd.* (2005), 383 A.R. 70 (Q.B.); *Monti v. Hamilton-Wentworth (Regional Municipality)* (1999), 45 C.C.E.L. (2d) 230 at para. 51 (Ont. Ct. Gen. Div.); *Carscallen v. FRI Corp.*, [2005] O.T.C. 484 (S.C.J.) [*Carscallen*]; *Johnson*, above note 20.

28   Above note 24 at 94. See also *Lavinikas v. Jacques Whitford & Associates Ltd.*, [2005] O.J. No. 4580 at para. 112 (S.C.J.): the employee lost the respect of his superiors, and his authority over his subordinates was also diminished through the constructive dismissal. It would have been humiliating for him to continue working as general manager.

29   See *Tanton v. Crane Canada Inc.* (2000), 278 A.R. 137 (Q.B.).

dismissal, or no realistic position is open to the dismissed employee.[30] Where a plaintiff is determined to be entitled to an extended notice period for bad-faith conduct in the manner of dismissal, the award of *Wallace* damages is not subject to mitigation (discussed more fully in Chapter 6). The award is considered similar to severance pay. Hence, money earned or that could have reasonably been earned in mitigation is not deducted from *Wallace* damages. In support of this position, Weiler J.A. noted that the purpose of these damages is to compensate for intangible injuries, which cannot easily and totally be eliminated by finding other employment. To apply mitigation to these damages would undermine the purpose of *Wallace* damages.[31]

d) Personal Injuries

In the field of personal injuries, a plaintiff has an obligation to mitigate damages by taking reasonable steps towards medical treatment and re-habilitation. Again, the standard against which the plaintiff is judged is not one of perfection but what a reasonable person would do in the circumstances. The problem that frequently arises in these cases is that, given that medical care and rehabilitation are not guaranteed to succeed, where the plaintiff fails to mitigate, how is a court to determine the damages that might have been avoided had the plaintiff mitigated? The issue of mitigation in personal injury litigation is discussed more fully below.

4) Costs Incurred in Mitigating

A corollary of the rule of mitigation is that a plaintiff may recover additional costs reasonably incurred in taking steps to mitigate a loss. These costs are recoverable even if the attempt to mitigate is fruitless (so long as it was reasonable).[32] This principle provides additional encouragement to the plaintiff to mitigate, by providing a cushion against additional losses. For example, where the plaintiff spends money trying to repair faulty goods, but gives up when it is discovered that the

---

30 *Pauloski v. Nascor Inc.* (2002), 311 A.R. 67 at para. 97 (Q.B.); *Smith*, above note 22 at para. 41.

31 *Prinzo v. Baycrest Centre for Geriatric Care* (2002), 60 O.R. (3d) 474 at para. 72 (C.A.); *Carscallen*, above note 27; *McCulloch v. IPlatform Inc.*, [2004] O.J. No. 5237 (S.C.J.); *Jessen v. CHC Helicopters International Inc.* (2006), 245 N.S.R. (2d) 316 at para. 41 (C.A.).

32 *Farish v. National Trust Co.* (1974), 54 D.L.R. (3d) 426 (B.C.S.C.); *Ticketnet Corp. v. Air Canada* (1998), 154 D.L.R. (4th) 271 (Ont. C.A.), leave to appeal to S.C.C. refused (1998), 161 D.L.R. (4th) viii.

damage was more expensive than initially assumed, the money wasted on the attempted repairs is recoverable as damages.[33] The plaintiff is not, however, entitled to incur costs in mitigation that are not commercially prudent; the cost of mitigation must be reasonable in relation to the loss to be avoided.[34] For instance, where the plaintiff chartered an expensive ship to deliver goods on an urgent basis after the defendant's breach, its damages were reduced on the basis that there was no urgency and a less expensive means could have been found.[35]

5) Mitigation before Breach? The Problem of Anticipatory Repudiation

Difficult issues occur when a contract is repudiated by the defendant before the date of performance. The problem arises from trying to reconcile the doctrine of "election" with the rule of mitigation. The doctrine of election provides that, where a contract is repudiated in advance of performance, the plaintiff has the choice either to "accept" the repudiation, treat the contract as at an end, and sue for damages immediately, or to treat the contract as continuing, wait until the date set for performance, and demand or tender performance at that time.

In situations where the plaintiff "accepts" the repudiation, there is no real problem. In such a case, the breach "crystallizes" at the time the repudiation is accepted and the plaintiff has an obligation to mitigate. Damages are not necessarily assessed at the precise date the repudiation is accepted, but the plaintiff must act reasonably. *Roth (L) & Co. Ltd. v. Taysen, Townsend & Co. and Grant and Grahame*[36] provides an illustration. The purchaser of goods repudiated the contract on 29 May though the date of performance was not until August. The vendor sued in July but did not resell the goods until September. During this period the market had been falling steadily. The court assessed damages according to the price of the goods on the date the plaintiff sued. It held that, where the plaintiff elects to treat the repudiation as a breach, the damages are not *necessarily* assessed at the date the action is brought but that the plaintiff does have an obligation to mitigate. The court held

---

33   *Exchanger Industries Ltd. v. Dominion Bridge Co.* (1986), 69 A.R. 22 (Q.B.).

34   See *P.G. Restaurant Ltd. v. British Columbia (Northern Interior Regional Health Board)* (2004), 25 B.C.L.R. (4th) 242 (S.C.), rev'd on other grounds (2005), 38 B.C.L.R. (4th) 77 (C.A.); *UAP Inc. v. Oak Tree Auto Centre Inc.* (2002), 219 Nfld. & P.E.I.R. 292 (C.A.).

35   *Alcan Aluminium Ltd. v. Unican International S.A.* (1996), 113 F.T.R. 81 (T.D.), additional reasons (1996), 120 F.T.R. 44 (T.D.).

36   (1896), 1 Com. Cas. 306 (C.A.) [*Roth*].

that it was unreasonable, in the face of a steadily falling market, for the plaintiff to wait so long to resell the goods. As Waddams suggests, the unreasonableness of waiting is not really based on the fact that the price was falling (since it cannot usually be said to be "unreasonable" to fail to predict that the market price of a commodity will fall over a two-month period). Instead, the rule is about a fair way to allocate post-breach risks.[37]

The most serious mitigation problems arise when, on repudiation, the plaintiff does not "accept" the breach but instead elects to keep the contract alive and insists upon performance at the time specified in the contract. If the plaintiff truly has an unfettered election to keep the contract alive, then there can be no duty to mitigate. The case of *White and Carter (Councils) Ltd. v. McGregor*[38] illustrates the point. In this case the plaintiff sold advertising to the defendant (on plates attached to litter bins). The contract was to last for three years. On the same day that the contract was formed, the defendant cancelled it (repudiation). Nevertheless, the plaintiff went ahead, prepared the advertising, and charged the defendant the full price under the contract. Lord Reid affirmed the principle of election and concluded that the plaintiff had no duty to mitigate:

> The general rule cannot be in doubt.... If one party to a contract repudiates it in the sense of making it clear to the other party that he refuses or will refuse to carry out his part of the contract, the other party, the innocent party, has an option. He may accept that repudiation and sue for damages for breach of contract, whether or not the time for performance has come; or he may if he chooses disregard or refuse to accept it and then the contract remains in full effect.[39]

Despite the argument that the plaintiff should not be permitted to go ahead and incur useless expenses in performing the contract, the majority of the Court held that this is precisely what the plaintiff could do in this case. Essentially, the principle of election "trumps" the principle of mitigation.

> [I]t never has been, the law that a person is only entitled to enforce his contractual rights in a reasonable way, and that a court will not support an attempt to enforce them in an unreasonable way. One reason why that is not the law is, no doubt, because it was thought that

---

37   S.M. Waddams, *The Law of Damages*, 2d ed., looseleaf (Aurora, ON: Canada Law Book, 1991–) at para. 5.1420.

38   [1962] A.C. 413 (H.L.) [*White and Carter*].

39   *Ibid.* at 427.

it would create too much uncertainty to require the court to decide whether it is reasonable or equitable to allow a party to enforce his full rights under a contract.[40]

This case is controversial and much criticized. Several of the law lords vigorously dissented, pointing to the irrationality of the plaintiff's conduct and the waste caused by it. The case has been criticized by academic writers on the same ground. Stated as an absolute principle, the rule in *White and Carter* is unfair. If the plaintiff has no legitimate reason to carry on with the contract, it is wrong to run up damages needlessly at the expense of the defendant. Even the majority judgment, it seems, contains the seeds of a refinement of the rule. Lord Reid stated:

> It may well be that, if it can be shown that a person has no legitimate interest, financial or otherwise, in performing the contract rather than claiming damages, he ought not to be allowed to saddle the other party with an additional burden with no benefit to himself.[41]

As an illustration, Lord Reid gives the example of an expert, hired to travel abroad and prepare a report. If the employer cancels the contract before anything is done, it would be wrong, he conceded, to allow the expert to carry on with the work and, in its course, incur substantial expenditure and increase the damages. Yet Lord Reid apparently saw a distinction between this hypothetical and the case before him, saying only, "[T]hat is not this case. Here the respondent did not set out to prove that the appellants had no legitimate interest in completing the contract."[42] It is hard to see what legitimate interest the plaintiff had in continuing to fulfill this contract and how the actual case can be distinguished from the hypothetical. Perhaps the plaintiff did, in fact, have a legitimate reason to carry on with the contract because it needed to display customer advertising in order to advertise its own business and attract new customers. Or perhaps there was simply no evidence before the Court as to what expenditures were in fact needlessly incurred (perhaps all the work had already been done and there were no other customers for the plaintiff's garbage-can advertising). The onus of proof is, after all, on the defendant. However, in the absence of such an explanation, the result in *White and Carter* is hard to justify. The plaintiff's conduct must be reasonable in the circumstances. In *Reichman v. Beveridge*,[43] the English Court of Appeal stated that, where an

---

40   *Ibid.* at 430.
41   *Ibid.* at 431.
42   *Ibid.*
43   [2006] EWCA Civ 1659, [2007] Bus. L.R. 412.

innocent party has elected not to accept repudiation of a contract, he is entitled to enforce his contractual right by maintaining the contract in force and suing for the contract price, unless damages will be an adequate remedy and electing to keep the contract alive will be wholly unreasonable in the circumstances.

There is a strong indication in Canadian law that courts will not tolerate unreasonable and oppressive action by the plaintiff in these cases. In *Finelli v. Dee*[44] the Ontario Court of Appeal indicated that it would not follow *White and Carter*. In this case the defendant cancelled a contract to have his driveway paved but the plaintiff went ahead with the work and sued for the contract price. Laskin J.A. stated that he was "attracted by the reasons of the two dissenting members of the court"[45] in *White and Carter*, but that in any event the case was different because this was not a case where the plaintiff could carry out the contract without the cooperation and consent of the defendant. The plaintiff was not, therefore, entitled to the contract price.

Moreover, the "exception" conceded by Lord Reid in *White and Carter* (that a plaintiff might have a duty to mitigate where he has no legitimate interest in performing) has arguably become the rule in Canada. In *Asamera*[46] the Supreme Court of Canada, referring to *White and Carter*, held that a plaintiff may be able to justify a failure to mitigate only when the plaintiff is able to show a "substantial and legitimate interest in seeking performance as opposed to damages."[47] No cases after *Asamera* have permitted a plaintiff to use the doctrine of election to avoid its obligation to mitigate, except where the plaintiff has a legitimate claim to specific performance (these cases are discussed later in this chapter). This leads to a much more subtle statement of the rule in Canada. When a defendant repudiates a contract, the plaintiff has an election to sue immediately or to wait for performance. However, if the plaintiff elects to wait for performance, the plaintiff may not unnecessarily incur expenses performing its side of the bargain unless there is some real, fair, and substantial interest in doing so.

---

44   [1968] 1 O.R. 676 (C.A.).
45   *Ibid.* at 678.
46   Above note 1.
47   *Ibid.* at 668–69.

B. MITIGATION IN PERSONAL INJURY CASES

1) General Principles

Plaintiffs who are tortiously injured have an obligation to take reasonable steps to mitigate their injuries and cannot collect damages for losses that could be avoided. Mitigation in these circumstances ordinarily requires the plaintiff to seek appropriate medical treatment and to make an effort to get back to work when possible.[48] The plaintiff is not obliged to accept any employment, regardless of its compatibility with her training and work history,[49] but where there is a meaningful job opportunity with a viable employer, the plaintiff's wage loss claim will be reduced.[50]

Where the plaintiff fails to seek medical treatment, difficult issues arise. The courts must balance between respecting the autonomy of the plaintiff regarding decisions about medical treatment and their desire not to burden unduly the defendant with avoidable losses. *Janiak v. Ippolito*[51] is the leading Supreme Court of Canada decision on the issue and provides the test. There, it was held that an unreasonable refusal to undergo surgical treatment amounts to a failure to mitigate, and that damages will be reduced accordingly. The surgery in question entailed a 70 percent chance of success, and if successful would have provided almost complete recovery for the plaintiff's back injury.

The test of whether a refusal is unreasonable is based on a modified objective standard. The onus of proof is on the defendant to show that the plaintiff's refusal was unreasonable and the choices of the plaintiff will not be subjected to "an overly critical standard of review."[52] In determining what is reasonable, the ordinary person will have to consider medical opinion regarding the risks and benefits of the procedure. What are the chances of success? If successful, how completely will the procedure restore the plaintiff's health? What are the risks of the procedure? Where the medical opinions conflict, the plaintiff's refusal to go ahead will be more reasonable. Indeed, "as long as a plaintiff follows any one of several courses of treatment recommended by the medical

---

48   *Kero v. Love* (1994), 90 B.C.L.R. (2d) 299 (C.A.); *Freeswick v. Forbes* (1996), 1 O.T.C. 23 (Gen. Div.).
49   *Finlayson v. Roberts* (1996), 26 M.V.R. (3d) 66 (Ont. Ct. Gen. Div.).
50   *Leenstra v. Miller* (1994), 92 B.C.L.R. (2d) 366 (C.A.).
51   [1985] 1 S.C.R. 146 [*Janiak*].
52   *Ibid.* at 162.

advisers he consults he should not be said to have acted unreasonably."[53]

Janiak has been widely followed and applied. The rule may appear, on first inspection, to violate the principle of autonomy and free choice in the plaintiff's decisions regarding medical treatment. However, as the Supreme Court has subsequently explained,

> [a]lthough an injured party is free to decline medical testing, where such refusal is unreasonable and arbitrary, the defendant must not be made to bear the cost of the injured party's choice. Failure to take medical tests in order to determine the nature and extent of an injury raises the issue of the failure to mitigate damages.[54]

The issue of reasonableness is a question of fact and calls for subtle judgment based on multiple factors. There must be evidence of the value of the recommended treatment to alleviate the plaintiff's injuries. No reduction is justified in the absence of evidence that treatment would alleviate the plaintiff's condition.[55] In one case,[56] it was held that the plaintiff had not failed to mitigate his injuries by refusing surgery where there was only a 50 percent chance of improvement and significant additional risk from the treatment. The court did, however, hold that the plaintiff's failure to enter a retraining and counselling program was unreasonable and reduced his damages for lost earning capacity. Failure to closely follow a recommended exercise regimen and refusal to take painkiller injections that would enable the plaintiff to cope with rigorous exercises designed to maximize her chances of a cure, or at least minimizing the long-term adverse effects of her injuries, were found to be unreasonable.[57] Even where the refusal to undergo treatment results in death, the refusal may be reasonable. In *Law Estate v. Simice*[58] the British Columbia Court of Appeal affirmed that a reasonable decision by a patient to delay surgery did not break the chain of causation between the defendant doctor's negligence in diagnosing an aneurism and the patient's death (the aneurism burst after the originally scheduled surgery and the day before the rescheduled surgery). In *Bourgoin v. Leamington (Municipality)*,[59] the plaintiff's refusal to

53   *Ibid.*
54   *Engel v. Kam-Ppelle Holdings Ltd.*, [1993] 1 S.C.R. 306 at 315, rev'g (*sub nom. Engle v. Salyn*), [1990] 3 W.W.R. 277 (Sask. C.A.), rev'g (1988), 68 Sask. R. 312 (Q.B.).
55   *Renton v. Scott* (1999), 215 N.B.R. (2d) 263 (C.A.).
56   *Sandhu v. Kuntz* (1996), 18 B.C.L.R. (3d) 167 (C.A.).
57   *Cochrane v. O'Brien* (2002), 225 Nfld. & P.E.I.R. 285 (Nfld. C.A.) [*Cochrane*].
58   (1995), 17 B.C.L.R. (3d) 1 (C.A.).
59   (2006), 39 C.C.L.T. (3d) 41 (Ont. S.C.J.).

undergo amputation of her leg below the knee with a likelihood of pain relief and restoring function in the leg was not considered unreasonable. There was conflicting medical opinion as to whether the plaintiff should undergo amputation at that time but, more importantly, Nolan J. distinguised *Janiak*, noting: "Refusing a back operation as the plaintiff did in *Janiak v. Ippolito* is not the same thing as refusing to have a major limb removed. It is my view that our law is not such that a refusal of an amputation can be considered unreasonable with the result that a plaintiff could be found to not have mitigated his or her losses."[60]

2) The Psychological Thin Skull

Sometimes, a refusal to seek treatment will be based on a genuine (though objectively unreasonable) psychological, emotional, or moral reluctance to pursue a medical procedure. The issue in these cases is whether these subjective factors should be taken into account to excuse the plaintiff from the obligation to mitigate.

The issue was dealt with in *Janiak*. The plaintiff, who had an unusual fear of surgery, argued that his subjective characteristics should excuse him from the obligation to mitigate even if the surgery was "objectively" reasonable. The Court agreed that in some instances the thin-skull principle would apply.[61] The tortfeasor takes the victim as found. Damages for aggravated injuries due to some pre-existing infirmity of the plaintiff are recoverable. This principle applies even when the pre-existing infirmity is psychological in nature. The Court, however, drew two important distinctions. First, the Court made clear that the psychological infirmity must be *pre-existing*. Where the fear of surgery or inability to mitigate develops only after the tort (even as a consequence of the injury), the ordinary rules of recoverability apply and the plaintiff is held to an objective test of reasonableness. Second, the infirmity must be a genuine psychological disorder. Not every psychological or emotional state could be considered a psychological thin skull, or else the duty to mitigate would practically always be avoided. Thus, "a line must be drawn" between those plaintiffs who are capable of making a rational decision regarding their own care and those who are not.

> Accordingly, non-pathological but distinctive subjective attributes of the plaintiff's personality and mental composition are ignored in favour of an objective assessment of the reasonableness of his choice. So long as he is capable of choice the assumption of tort damages

---

60 *Ibid.* at para. 111.
61 Discussed in Chapter 11, Section C(3).

392 REMEDIES: THE LAW OF DAMAGES

theory must be that he himself assumes the cost of any unreasonable decision. On the other hand, if due to some pre-existing psychological condition he is incapable of making a choice at all, then he should be treated as falling within the thin skull category and should not be made to bear the cost once it is established that he has been wrongfully injured.[62]

Cases dealing with this problem are rare and it is unlikely that the test put forward in *Janiak* will provide much practical guidance. The distinction between pathological and non-pathological conditions is far from clear. The number of officially recognized mental disorders is expanding at a rapid pace so that many types of fear about medicine and surgery might be brought within a particular named illness.

3) Religious Scruples

The "objective" approach to mitigation cannot easily be adapted to deal with situations where the plaintiff's objection to medical treatment is based on religious or ethical grounds. According to the *Janiak* test, where a medical treatment is otherwise obviously required, religious or ethical objections would not provide an excuse from mitigating unless those objections rendered the plaintiff incapable of choice or could be assimilated to "pathological" conditions. There is little authority on this issue. In the U.S. case of *Lange v. Hoyt*,[63] heard in Connecticut, medical aid was refused for an infant based on the parent's beliefs as a Christian Scientist. This was said not to affect damages:

> While the test of conduct on the part of a plaintiff in promoting a recovery from injuries suffered is one of reasonable care and cannot be made to depend upon the idiosyncrasies of personal belief no matter how honestly held, courts cannot disregard theories as to proper curative methods held by a large number of reasonable and intelligent people.[64]

This case has been reconsidered and the test modified towards a more objective standard in Connecticut.

In *Williams v. Bright*,[65] the plaintiff, a Jehovah's Witness, was injured in a serious car accident. Surgery, potentially involving a blood transfusion, could restore the plaintiff to a near normal life. But she refused

---

62 *Janiak*, above note 51 at 159.
63 159 A. 575 (Conn. Sup. Ct. of Errors 1932).
64 *Ibid.* at 577–78.
65 658 N.Y.S.2d 910 (App. Div. 1997).

for religious reasons and remained confined to a wheelchair. At trial, the judge instructed the jury to determine if the plaintiff had acted reasonably in refusing the surgery, not by the standard of a reasonably prudent person, but by the standard of a "reasonable Jehovah's Witness." The Court of Appeal observed that the trial court had understood the issue as involving the plaintiff's right to the free exercise of her religion protected by the First Amendment to the United States Constitution; and that if the plaintiff's religious beliefs were not taken into account, this would wrongfully restrain the free exercise of her religion. "In effect, this plaintiff's religious beliefs were held, as a matter of law, to relieve her of any legal obligation to mitigate damages under the same standard required of all other persons similarly situated who do not share similar religious convictions."[66]

However, the Court of Appeal held that the state has an interest in the fairness of civil proceedings, and noted that no evidence had been led at trial as to the rationale for the plaintiff's refusal of a blood transfusion, or how widespread this particular conviction was among members of her faith. "The trial court, in accepting the sincerity of plaintiff Robbins' beliefs as a given and asking the jury to consider the reasonableness of her actions only in the context of her own religion, effectively provided government endorsement to those beliefs."[67] The court determined that evidence must be led by the plaintiff regarding the basis for her refusal of treatment, and that the charge to the jury should have been supplemented as follows:

> In considering whether the plaintiff acted as a reasonably prudent person, you may consider the plaintiff's testimony that she is a believer in the Jehovah's Witness faith, and that as an adherent of that faith, she cannot accept any medical treatment which requires a blood transfusion. I charge you that such belief is a factor for you to consider, together with all the other evidence you have heard, in determining whether the plaintiff acted reasonably in caring for her injuries, keeping in mind, however, that the overriding test is whether the plaintiff acted as a reasonably prudent person, under all the circumstances confronting her.[68]

4) Consequences of a Failure to Mitigate

Where the plaintiff has failed to mitigate, how should damages be calculated? There are two competing views. On the one hand, it has been

---

66   *Ibid.* at 912.
67   *Ibid.* at 914.
68   *Ibid.* at 916.

argued that the plaintiff's failure to mitigate breaks the chain of causation and cuts off the defendant's liability. This is based on the logic that, where the defendant demonstrates on a balance of probabilities that the treatment would have eliminated the plaintiff's injuries, no loss has been proved. The alternate view, which prevails in Canada, is that the failure to mitigate should be treated as a contingency and valued as a lost chance rather than a certainty. In other words, where the plaintiff refuses to undergo treatment, the damages should be discounted to reflect the chance that the surgery would have been successful. Another way of putting this is that the plaintiff should still be able to recover that portion of his loss that possibly would have occurred even had he pursued the treatment. In *Janiak*, the plaintiff's damages were reduced by 70 percent to reflect the probability that had he undergone the surgery he would have recovered. He was entitled to 30 percent of those damages to reflect the chance that, even with the surgery, his condition might not have improved. Such precise mathematical odds about the prognosis if the plainitff had undergone the recommended treatment makes the assessment of damages easier, but its absence is no reason not to reduce damage awards for failure to mitigate. Ultimately, what is being assessed here is the loss of chance to avoid or minimize detrimental consequences of the plaintiff's injuries.[69]

Thus, a court must estimate the value of the chance that the treatment would have eliminated or reduced the plaintiff's loss. It is wrong for a court to find that because, on the balance of probabilities, the treatment would have succeeded, the plaintiff is entitled to nothing for her loss.[70] This method of reducing damages for the chance that the plaintiff might have mitigated is used in ordinary commercial cases as well and is consistent with the measurement of future damages. For example, in *Apeco of Canada Ltd. v. Windmill Place*,[71] where the defendant breached a contract to lease warehouse space from the plaintiff, the plaintiff's damages for loss of rent were reduced to take into account the chance that the plaintiff would (or could) find another customer to lease the space sometime in the future.

---

69   *Cochrane*, above note 57. In this case, the plaintiff's damages were reduced for failure to mitigate, although there was no evidence of the odds of success had she undergone the treatment; but the reductions were modest — 7.5 percent reduction for loss of housekeeping capacity and 15 percent reduction for the other heads under general damages.

70   See also *Souto v. Anderson* (1996), 17 B.C.L.R. (3d) 238 (C.A.).

71   [1978] 2 S.C.R. 385 [*Windmill Place*].

C. AVOIDED LOSS

Determining whether a subsequent transaction does in fact cancel or mitigate a loss can be a complex question. In many cases, the second transaction, while initially appearing to mitigate the original loss, will not in fact do so because the second transaction is not a true substitute for the first. Instead, it is a transaction that the plaintiff could have entered into in any event. The basic test is whether the second transaction arises out of the circumstances of the breach, or whether it is independent of it. Only where the second transaction is directly related to the breach, and could not have been entered into "but for" the breach, will it be considered to mitigate the loss.

One aspect of the issue of avoided loss is the problem of "lost volume" discussed in Chapter 2. Where the defendant refuses to take delivery of goods, and the plaintiff is able to resell those goods to another customer, the second sale does not necessarily cancel the lost profit on the first. Depending on the state of supply and demand in the business, it may be that the plaintiff would have been able to make the second sale in any event and would, therefore, have earned two profits instead of one (where the plaintiff has sufficient supply of goods to satisfy all customers).[72]

A good example of the problem of avoided loss is provided by a case discussed above, *Windmill Place*,[73] where the defendant wrongfully cancelled a five-year lease of space in the plaintiff's warehouse. The plaintiff was able to re-let the space to a different customer six months later. The defendant argued that damages were limited to six months' lost rent, since the plaintiff had successfully mitigated its loss by finding a new tenant. The Supreme Court of Canada held that the subsequent transaction had not in fact mitigated the plaintiff's loss since portions of the warehouse were still vacant. The second lease could likely have been concluded even if the first one had not been broken since the plaintiff could have leased space in another part of the warehouse to the second customer. Thus, the vacancy created by the defendant's breach did not make the opportunity for the second lease. Where the second transaction is independent of the first, it will sometimes be referred to as "collateral" and will not be taken into account (deducted) in assessing the loss.

The problem of avoided loss arises in many other situations and it is far from easy to determine any bright-line rule. The main question to

---

72   *Thompson (W.L.) Ltd. v. Robinson (Gunmakers) Ltd.* (1954), [1955] Ch. 177.
73   Above note 71.

ask is whether the second transaction was a true substitute for the first, or whether it was a transaction that the plaintiff could have completed in any event. Phrased another way, the test is whether the profit on the second transaction was made possible only by reason of the loss of the first. Several cases illustrate this principle.

In *Cockburn*,[74] the defendant wrongfully dismissed the plaintiff (and went into liquidation). The plaintiff turned his ill fortune to good by purchasing the company's assets and selling them for a profit of $11,000. The steps taken by the plaintiff went far beyond what he was obliged to do in mitigation of his loss. Yet he was denied any compensation for his lost wages on the basis that the subsequent transaction mitigated (indeed eliminated) his loss. The Court commented:

> [W]hen in the course of his business he has taken action arising out of the transaction, which action has diminished his loss, the effect in actual diminution of the loss he has suffered may be taken into account even though there was no duty on him to act.[75]

While it may seem hard to give to the defendant credit for the plaintiff's skill and initiative, the Court appears to have been satisfied that the plaintiff's earnings were made possible only because of the breach of contract. The time and effort he employed to earn the profit had been owed to his employer prior to the breach and was freed up as a result of the breach, and therefore the profit could not have been earned but for the breach. Were the plaintiff to be awarded his lost salary plus the profit he earned on the subsequent transaction, he would be better off than had there been no breach in the first place.

In the result, gains realized by the plaintiff are taken into account only if they arise out of the breach and could not have been made but for the breach. A useful contrast to *Cockburn* is provided by the Supreme Court of Canada decision in *Karas*.[76] In this case the plaintiff was defrauded of a lease and lost his store. The profits he earned from running another store were not taken into account to reduce his damages because there was no evidence that running the second business was incompatible with the first, and the plaintiff's capacity to run that business was not "released" by the fraudulent loss of his first business. Rand J. explained the principles as follows:

---

74   Above note 10.
75   *Ibid.* at 269. The Court quoted this passage from the judgment by Lord Chancellor Haldane in *British Westinghouse*, above note 1 at 689.
76   *Karas*, above note 7.

It is settled, also, that the performance in mitigation and that provided or contemplated under the original contract must be mutually exclusive, and the mitigation, in that sense, a substitute for the other. Stated from another point of view, by the default or wrong there is released a capacity to work or to earn. That capacity becomes an asset in the hands of the injured party, and he is held to a reasonable employment of it in the course of events flowing from the breach.[77]

In *Erie County Natural Gas and Fuel Co. Ltd. v. Carroll*,[78] the defendant breached a contract to supply gas to the plaintiff for a seven-year period. But the plaintiff was able to purchase gas leases, meet its requirements, and in fact sell the leases at the end of seven years for substantial profit, thus apparently suffering no loss. Nevertheless, the plaintiff sought substantial damages on the theory that, had the defendant not breached its contract, the plaintiff would have had its gas needs provided and would have been able to sell rather than consume the gas from its own leases for a further profit. The trial judge did in fact award damages based on the value of the gas consumed, but the Court of Appeal overruled this "grotesque result." It held that the actions taken after the defendant's breach were taken as a substitute transaction, and that the damages should be limited, as usual, to the cost of obtaining the substitute (which in this case was in fact zero).

This result can be defended as fair. Again, while it may seem hard to give the defendant credit for the plaintiff's skill and good fortune, that benefit would not have been obtained but for the breach. The plaintiff was not in the business of gas production and the gas leases were intended to be a substitute only for the original gas required from the defendant. The plaintiff would not, but for the breach, have entered into the second transaction. Moreover, had the second transaction proved more expensive than it did, the plaintiff would have been "insured" against any loss. The defendant would have been liable for the costs incurred so long as the purchase of those leases was a reasonable step to take in mitigation of the breach of contract. Since the defendant would have borne that risk, it is fair to give the defendant "credit" for the full savings achieved on the second transaction.

Ascertaining whether a subsequent transaction avoids a loss is often difficult. Appearances can be deceiving. In *Jamal v. Moolla Dawood, Sons & Co.*,[79] the defendant refused to go through with a purchase of shares from the plaintiff. At the time of the breach, the market price of the

---

77   *Ibid.* at 8.
78   [1911] A.C. 105 (P.C.) [*Erie*].
79   [1916] 1 A.C. 175 (P.C.) [*Jamal*].

shares was lower than the contract price and damages (measured by the difference in value) would have been substantial. The plaintiff, however, delayed in selling the shares until the market price recovered and in fact was able to resell them at higher prices. The defendant claimed that the subsequent transactions avoided the loss caused by the breach. Despite the apparent elimination of the loss, the Court awarded damages to the plaintiff based on the difference between the contract price and the market price at the time of breach. At first glance, this case appears inconsistent with *Cockburn* and *Erie*. The subsequent favourable transaction was made possible by the defendant's breach and seems to have eliminated the plaintiff's loss. However, the result can be explained both logically and in terms of policy. The case can be considered as one of "lost volume." Shares are a fungible property and the plaintiff was in the business of buying and selling shares. Had the original sale gone through, it is at least possible that the plaintiff might have purchased other shares in order to undertake further transactions.

More important, the result in *Jamal* is consistent with the policy of mitigation and fair post-breach risk allocation. Had the plaintiff sold the shares at the time of the breach, the defendant would have been liable for the loss. Having chosen to retain the shares, the plaintiff took the risk that their price might fall even further and he would not then be able to claim any additional damages due to that decline. The result is therefore fair in that the plaintiff takes both the risk and reward of post-breach fluctuations in the value of the shares. Lord Wrenbury stated:

> If the seller retains the shares after the breach, the speculation as to the way the market will subsequently go is the speculation of the seller, not of the buyer; the seller cannot recover from the buyer the loss below the market price at the date of the breach if the market falls, nor is he liable to the purchaser for the profit if the market rises.[80]

Similar results have been reached in other cases involving contracts for the sale of commodities when the disappointed vendor delays in reselling. Subsequent profit earned from a favourable resale is not taken into account.[81] The same problem can arise in the case of a disappointed buyer. Where the cost of procuring substitute goods at the time of the breach is greater than the contract price, the buyer is ordinarily entitled to this difference. Where the buyer delays in procuring a substitute and

---

80   *Ibid.* at 179.
81   *Campbell Mostyn Ltd. v. Barnett Trading Co.*, [1954] 1 Lloyd's Rep. 65 (C.A.) [*Campbell*].

the price falls below the original contract price, this may seem to cancel the loss. However, based on the same logic and policy expressed in *Jamal*, the buyer in such circumstances is still entitled to damages based on the price of procuring a substitute at the time of the breach.

D. TIME OF ASSESSMENT

1) General Rule: Time of the Wrong

Another important issue related to the doctrine of mitigation is the question of the time at which damages should be measured and how courts should deal with losses (and benefits) that accrue subsequent to the breach. In many cases, the plaintiff will not be inclined, or able, to mitigate immediately, and during the period between the breach and the time when the plaintiff mitigates, the original loss is aggravated. The issue is whether the plaintiff is ever able to recover these additional losses. For example, where the plaintiff is unable to purchase substitute goods at the time of the breach, the price of those goods may increase. Where the plaintiff is unable to repair defective property immediately, the cost of repairs may increase, or lost profits may add up. If the plaintiff is obliged to mitigate immediately, these additional losses may not be charged to the defendant.

The starting point for measuring damages in tort and contract is the time of the wrong. Thus, in cases involving the sale of goods and property, damages are measured by the difference between the contract price and the value of the property at the time of breach. The "time of breach" rule (which is codified in the *Sale of Goods Acts*)[82] is a corollary of the rule of mitigation. At that point the disappointed party is expected to go into the market and purchase substitute goods. Any additional loss resulting from changes in price after that time is caused not by the breach but by the buyer's failure to mitigate. Similarly, the vendor of goods is expected to resell the goods at the time of the breach and, if the price subsequently falls, the vendor may not claim the additional loss. *Roth*[83] provides an illustration. The vendor of goods accepted the purchaser's repudiation and sued in July but did not resell the goods until September. During this period the price steadily fell. The court assessed damages according to the price of the goods in July, holding that it was unreasonable, in the face of a steadily falling market, for

---

82 See discussion in Chapters 2 & 3.
83 Above note 36.

the plaintiff to wait so long to resell the goods. As Waddams suggests, the unreasonableness of waiting is not really based on the fact that the price was falling (since it cannot usually be said to be "unreasonable" to fail to predict that the market price of a commodity will fall over a two-month period). Instead, the rule is about a fair way to allocate post-breach risks.[84]

The rule in tort is similar. Where the plaintiff suffers a tortious injury, she is expected to act expeditiously to mitigate damages, and increases in the loss suffered after that time may not be recoverable. For example, where the plaintiff's property has been damaged or destroyed by the defendant's tort, damages are assessed as the cost of repairs or replacement at the time of the wrong. If the plaintiff does not repair or replace the property until a later date, and the cost is then higher, the plaintiff will ordinarily be unable to claim the increased cost.[85]

The "time of the wrong" rule encourages the plaintiff to mitigate expeditiously and places the risk of subsequent losses on the plaintiff. Generally the defendant is at the mercy of the plaintiff and can do nothing to minimize damages at this point. It is best to place the risk of subsequent events upon the shoulders of the plaintiff. The rule also prevents the plaintiff from speculating at the defendant's risk. This point deserves illustration. Where the plaintiff is a disappointed buyer of goods and the price for those goods is fluctuating, if the plaintiff were permitted to postpone mitigation, there would be an incentive to delay on the chance that prices might drop and an even more advantageous transaction made. If the price increases, the plaintiff is no worse off because the defendant would bear the added cost of the substitute transaction. This is unfair to the defendant and provides the plaintiff with the wrong incentives. The rule is also administratively convenient. While somewhat arbitrary, any other rule would require courts in each case to inquire into the precise time, after the breach, that damages should be assessed.

There is an interesting corollary to the time of the wrong rule. Just as the plaintiff is not generally entitled to claim additional losses incurred after the breach, the plaintiff is entitled to retain additional gains realized after the date of the breach. In other words, the plaintiff takes the risk of additional losses after the breach and receives the benefit of a favourable turn of events. The case of *Jamal*,[86] discussed previously,

---

84   Waddams, above note 37 at 5.1420.
85   *Jens v. Mannix Co.* (1978), 89 D.L.R. (3d) 351 (B.C.S.C.), rev'd (1979), 30 D.L.R. (4th) 260 (B.C.C.A.).
86   Above note 79.

provides a good example. Following the buyer's breach of contract to purchase shares, had the vendor resold the shares immediately his loss would have been approximately 109,000 rupees. However, as a result of retaining them while the price increased, the vendor was able to resell them at a loss of only 80,000 rupees. Nevertheless, the purchaser was held liable for the larger sum, calculated by the difference in value between the contract price and the price at the date of the breach. In other words, the plaintiff is able to retain the benefit from post-breach events. As argued above, this is appropriate in light of the policies underlying mitigation. Had the plaintiff sold the shares at the time of the breach, the defendant would have been liable for the loss calculated at that time. Having chosen to retain the shares, the plaintiff took the risk that the price might fall even further and he would not be able to claim any additional damages because of that decline. The result is therefore fair in that the plaintiff takes both the risk and the reward of post-breach fluctuations in the value of the shares. Lord Wrenbury explained:

> In a contract for sale of negotiable securities, is the measure of damages for breach the difference between the contract price and the market price at the date of the breach—with an obligation on the part of the seller to mitigate the damages by getting the best price he can at the date of the breach—or is the seller bound to reduce the damages, if he can, by subsequent sales at better prices? If he is, and if the purchaser is entitled to the benefit of subsequent sales, it must also be true that he must bear the burden of subsequent losses. The latter proposition is in their Lordship's opinion impossible, and the former is equally unsound. If the seller retains the shares after the breach, the speculation as to the way the market will subsequently go is the speculation of the seller, not of the buyer; the seller cannot recover from the buyer the loss below the market price at the date of the breach if the market falls, nor is he liable to the purchaser for the profit if the market rises.[87]

Similar results have been reached in other cases involving contracts for the sale of commodities when the disappointed vendor delays in reselling. Subsequent profit earned from a favourable resale is not taken into account.[88]

Only in cases where the vendor does not have an obligation to mitigate immediately will a favourable later sale be taken into account. For example, as will be discussed below, the vendor of real estate is some-

---

87   *Ibid.* at 179.
88   *Campbell,* above note 81.

times not obliged to resell property immediately following breach. In such a case, if the value of the property increases after the breach, and the vendor later sells the property for more than the original contract price, that favourable resale will be credited to the damages payable by the defendant.[89] This is fair as a matter of risk allocation. In these limited circumstances, the law excuses the plaintiff from mitigating and places the risk of post-breach losses on the defendant (if the value of the property declines, the damages payable by the defendant will increase). By the same token, the defendant should also receive the benefit of a favourable turn of events.

2) Interest and Inflation

While damages are measured at the time of the wrong, the plaintiff will not ordinarily collect those damages for many months or years, until the dispute is settled or reaches a trial. As a result, the plaintiff may have to expend her own money to mitigate or repair a loss, or she may have to borrow money. These costs are taken into account through the award of pre-judgment interest. The rules regarding pre-judgment interest vary from province to province, but generally, the courts may give the plaintiff a commercial rate.[90] More generally, because the plaintiff does not usually receive the damages award until much later than the date of the wrong, she has been deprived of the use of that money in the interim. By the time the money is paid, its value may be eroded by inflation. In addition, the plaintiff will have incurred opportunity costs by not being in possession of that money to use or invest. Again, where damages are assessed at the date of the wrong, courts will award pre-judgment interest on the amount to compensate the plaintiff for the loss of use of this money. Conversely, in those exceptional cases (discussed below) where damages are measured at a date later than the wrong (or where the damages are incurred after the wrong), a court may adjust or refuse altogether to award pre-judgment interest.

3) Exceptions to the "Time of the Wrong" Rule

Despite its general attractions, the "time of the wrong" rule is not absolute. The courts are flexible and, taking into account the difficulties of mitigating immediately, will permit some flexibility with respect to

---

89 *Mavretic v. Bowman* (1993), 76 B.C.L.R. (2d) 61 (C.A.).
90 See M.A. Waldron, *The Law of Interest in Canada* (Scarborough, ON: Carswell Thomson Professional, 1992).

timing. Even in simple cases it may take time to organize financing, contact new suppliers, and arrange for delivery of goods or repair of property. A more accurate statement of the rule is therefore that the plaintiff is obliged to mitigate expeditiously, within a reasonable time following the wrong. What is reasonable will depend upon the nature of the transaction and the circumstances, but some general factors emerge from the cases. Where the subject matter of the transaction is unique or unusual, the plaintiff will be given additional time to locate a substitute. Indeed, where the subject matter is so unique that it is irreplaceable, the plaintiff may have reasonable expectation of specific performance and may therefore have no immediate duty to mitigate whatsoever (discussed below). Similarly, the innocent vendor will be permitted a reasonable amount of time to effect a resale when the property (e.g., real estate) is such that it cannot be resold instantly.[91] Where the defendant remains involved in the transaction even after the breach, and requests the plaintiff's indulgence or offers some type of substitute performance, the plaintiff may delay.[92] It may be commercially impracticable to mitigate immediately,[93] too risky,[94] or the plaintiff may have inadequate funds.[95] Each of these factors (which are discussed more fully below) will sometimes provide a justification for delay. The courts have considerable discretion in applying these factors. In each case, the court will be weighing the interests of each of the parties: attempting to do justice to the plaintiff by providing full compensation for her unavoidable losses, while avoiding oppression to the defendant.

The leading case is *Asamera*.[96] In this case the plaintiff had loaned shares to the defendant that the defendant failed to return on time. At the time of the breach (1960), the shares were worth $0.29. In the time leading to trial (1972), the price of the shares soared as high as $46.50 (and was $21 at the time of judgment). The plaintiff had not purchased replacement shares and sought damages based on the shares' highest intermediate price (reasoning that had he had the shares he could have sold them for a substantial profit).

---

91 *100 Main Street Ltd. v. W.B. Sullivan Construction Ltd.* (1978), 20 O.R. (2d) 401 (C.A.).

92 *Asamera*, above note 1.

93 *Canlin Ltd. v. Thiokol Fibres Canada Ltd.* (1983), 40 O.R. (2d) 687 (C.A.); *Dodd Properties*, above note 16; *Stronge v. Athol Forestry Cooperative Ltd.* (2006), 242 N.S.R. (2d) 185 (S.C.).

94 *Asamera*, above note 1.

95 *Wroth v. Tyler*, [1974] Ch. 30; *Dodd Properties*, above note 16.

96 Above note 1.

Despite older English authority to the contrary, the Supreme Court of Canada held that the plaintiff had a duty to mitigate by purchasing replacement shares after the breach. As a result, the plaintiff was not entitled to the lost profits suffered during the post-breach period. The Court held that the duty to mitigate was required by fairness and was in the interest of commercial enterprise, and that to ignore the duty to mitigate would result in "enormous hardships" and "massive distortions" in the damage claim. Estey J. stated:

> It is inappropriate in my view simply to extend the old principles applied in the detinue and conversion authorities to the non-return of shares with the result that a party whose property has not been returned to him, could sit by and await an opportune moment to institute legal proceedings, all the while imposing on a defendant the substantial risk of market fluctuations between breach and trial.[97]

However, the Court did not adopt an arbitrary "time of breach" rule but instead took a more flexible approach to the issue of timing. Damages were awarded based on a price of $6.50 per share, assessed seven years after the breach, based on an assessment of the plaintiff's circumstances and the practical considerations involved in replacing such a large number of shares. First, purchase of replacement shares at the time of the breach would have been unduly risky for the plaintiff, given the speculative and somewhat illiquid nature of the shares, the fact that the defendant had effective control of the company, and the adversarial nature of the relationship between the parties at the time of the breach. However, by 1967 the plaintiff was aware that the shares were not, in fact, going to be returned, and their value had recovered and stabilized so that it could no longer be said to be unreasonable to require the plaintiff to trade in the shares. Thus, in Canada, the presumptive position is that, while damages are assessed at the date of the wrong, courts have flexibility to take into account any special circumstances that make it unreasonable to require the plaintiff to mitigate immediately.

The time of assessment problem is also prevalent in cases involving damaged property. When property is damaged, the plaintiff is entitled to the cost of repairs, which must generally be undertaken in a timely fashion. Additional costs resulting from delays are generally treated as avoided losses. So, for example, in *O'Grady*,[98] the plaintiff's claim for loss of use of his motor car was reduced because he took too long to have it repaired. And in *Jens v. Mannix*[99] the plaintiff's claim for the cost of rebuilding his home, which had been ruined by an oil spill, was "rolled back" to the cost at the time of the tort, rather than the greatly increased costs at the time of trial. The court held that the plaintiff had no good excuse for failing to mitigate, despite the complexity of his situation.

However, the time of breach rule is not inflexible. Courts will permit the recovery of increased costs due to delay when the plaintiff has a reasonable excuse. A good illustration is the case of *Dodd Properties*.[100] The plaintiff's garage was damaged when the defendants constructed an adjoining building. The damage occurred in 1968, at which time the cost of repairs would have been £11,375. The plaintiff did not undertake the repairs at that time and at trial claimed the increased figure of £30,000 for repairs. The English Court of Appeal awarded the sum claimed. It held that it was reasonable for the plaintiff to wait under the circumstances. Of importance were several factors. The defendant was denying liability, so it was unclear that the plaintiff would actually recover the costs of repairing its building. The plaintiff was also facing a degree of "financial stringency" and testified that undertaking repairs at the earlier date would not have made commercial sense because the property would not produce sufficient income.

The result in this case is controversial. It seems unduly broad, and unfairly punitive, to relieve the plaintiff of its duty to mitigate merely because the defendant was denying liability. Taken to its extreme, this would undercut the obligation to mitigate in most cases. Moreover, as Waddams points out, from a commercial point of view, the defendant's liability is irrelevant to the decision whether and when to repair the building. If the repairs are worth doing (as a business investment), they are worth doing whether or not the defendant is liable.[101] If they are not worth doing with the plaintiff's own money (because repairing the building would be a bad investment), then it is unfair to charge the defendant with the full cost of those repairs. Finally, from the perspective of risk allocation, it is arguable that the plaintiff should look to its own insurance for speedy repairs to the building, sorting out the liability issues in due course. It would appear that the defendant in this case is bearing a risk that should ordinarily be borne (or eliminated) by property insurance. In the context of a commercial operation, where insurance is commonly expected, the plaintiff's "financial stringency" should not be an excuse from mitiga-

---

99 Above note 85.
100 Above note 16. See also *Radford v. De Froberville*, [1978] 1 All E.R. 33 (Q.B.).
101 Waddams, above note 37 at 1.2490.

tion.[102] Despite these criticisms of the specific result, the more general principle cannot be assailed. While the presumptive rule is that damages are assessed at the date of the wrong, courts have jurisdiction to take into account facts that make such an assessment unfair, and to assess damages at a later date when appropriate.

It is important to note that, where damages are assessed at a date after the wrong, as in *Dodd Properties*, the court may decline to award pre-judgment interest. By awarding the cost of repairs in trial-date dollars, the plaintiff in *Dodd Properties* was fully protected against inflation and other costs of being kept out of its money.

4) Specific Performance, Mitigation, and Time of Assessment

a) The Purchaser's Action

If the plaintiff is entitled to specific performance, there is no obligation to mitigate damages. The two concepts are incompatible since the plaintiff cannot have a legitimate claim to have the contract fulfilled while at the same time having an obligation to enter into a substitute transaction. So, for example, in a contract for the purchase of residential property, where specific performance is a common remedy because of the "uniqueness" of land, the purchaser may not have an obligation to mitigate damages by seeking a replacement since the purchaser may seek to have the actual contract performed. Even if, at the time of trial, the plaintiff is awarded damages instead of specific performance, any losses suffered between the breach and the trial will be compensable, since the plaintiff was reasonable in not mitigating. Where the value of the property has risen substantially in the period between breach and trial, the plaintiff will be entitled to the post-breach increase in value.

A good illustration of the relation between specific performance and mitigation is the case of *Wroth v. Tyler*.[103] The defendant agreed to sell his house to the plaintiffs for £6,000. The defendant's wife subsequently registered a matrimonial charge on the property that made it impossible to convey the home. The plaintiffs sued for specific performance. At the time of the breach, the value of the home was £7,500 and at the time of trial it was worth £11,500. At trial it was decided that specific performance was not available and the plaintiffs claimed damages instead. If damages were assessed according to the ordinary

---

102 See the detailed discussion of the effect of impecuniosity on damages in Chapter 11.

103 Above note 95.

rule (time of breach), they would be only £1,500. This would not, of course, enable the plaintiffs to purchase an equivalent house, which, at the time of trial, would now cost £5,500 more than the original price. Megarry J. held that the plaintiffs should be entitled to damages measured at the time of the trial. Two factors were particularly influential. First, at the time of the breach, the plaintiffs were unable to mitigate because they could not have raised the additional £1,500 necessary to purchase an equivalent house. The defendant was aware of this fact at the time. Second, the plaintiffs were reasonable in seeking specific performance of the contract and should not be penalized for the fact that the remedy was ultimately held to be unavailable.

Megarry J. found his authority to award damages "in substitution for specific performance" in the *Chancery Amendment Act* (*Lord Cairns Act*) of 1858, which states:

> In all cases in which the Court of Chancery has jurisdiction to entertain an application for an injunction … or for the specific performance of any covenant, contract, or agreement, it shall be lawful for the same court, if it shall think fit, to award damages to the party injured, either in addition to or in substitution for such injunction or specific performance, and such damages may be assessed in such manner as the court shall direct.[104]

Megarry J. reasoned that, if damages were to be a true substitute for specific performance (i.e., giving as nearly as possible what specific performance would have given), they must be measured at the date of the trial in order to give the plaintiffs sufficient funds to purchase a substitute: "[T]he court has jurisdiction to award such damages as will put the plaintiffs into as good a position as if the contract had been performed, even if to do so means awarding damages assessed by reference to a period subsequent to the date of the breach."[105]

After *Tyler*, a claim to specific performance will frequently excuse the plaintiff from the obligation to mitigate. While Megarry J. placed much emphasis on the *Lord Cairns Act* and the concept of "equitable damages," it has now been established that the same flexibility applies

---

104 *Ibid.* at 57. Most provinces and territories have the equivalent legislation. See the *Courts of Justice Act*, R.S.O. 1990, c. C.43, s. 99; *Court of Queen's Bench Act*, S.M. 1988–89, c. 4, s. 36; *Supreme Court Act*, R.S.P.E.I. 1988, c. S-10, s. 32; *Judicature Act*, R.S.A. 2000, c. J-2, s. 19; *The Queen's Bench Act*, S.S. 1998, c. Q-1.01, s. 66; *Judicature Act*, R.S.Y. 2002, c. 128, s. 27; *Judicature Act*, R.S.N.W.T. 1988, c. J-1, s. 42; *Law and Equity Act*, R.S.B.C. 1996, c. 253, s. 10.
105 *Wroth v. Tyler*, above note 95 at 60.

to the assessment of damages at common law.[106] Thus, when a purchaser of property has a legitimate claim to specific performance and reasonably pursues that claim, damages will not be tied to the date of breach but may be assessed at a later time. The time for assessment will be at trial, or the time when it becomes obvious to the innocent party that the contract is lost.

Thus, a claim to specific performance may displace the plaintiff's obligation to mitigate. However, the claim to specific performance must be "substantial and legitimate." Otherwise, the mere assertion of a claim would circumvent the law's strong policy in favour of mitigation. The claim to specific performance must be *bona fide* and must have a reasonable prospect of success before it will operate to suspend the obligation to mitigate; otherwise, a plaintiff could always defeat the obligation to mitigate simply by claiming specific performance.

This issue arose and was resolved in the *Asamera* case, discussed above. Among the reasons offered by the plaintiff for his failure to purchase replacement shares after the breach was that he expected actually to have the shares returned or intended to claim specific performance for their return. The Supreme Court of Canada rejected this on the basis that the claim was not sufficiently reasonable. Specific performance is available only when damages are inadequate, and shares are a fungible property that can easily be replaced.

> On principle it is clear that a plaintiff may not merely by instituting proceedings in which a request is made for specific performance and/or damages, thereby shield himself and block the court from taking into account the accumulation of losses which the plaintiff by acting with reasonable promptness in processing his claim could have avoided.... Before a plaintiff can rely on a claim to specific performance so as to insulate himself from the consequences of failing to procure alternate property in mitigation of his losses, *some fair, real, and substantial justification for his claim to performance must be found.* Otherwise its effect will be to cast upon the defendant all the risk of aggravated loss by reason of delay in bringing the issue to trial.[107]

b) The Vendor's Action
Whether a vendor of real property is entitled to damages assessed at a time later than breach is a complex question, and it is related to the issue of whether vendors of real estate should be entitled to specific

---

106 *Malhotra v. Choudhury*, [1980] Ch. 52 (C.A.); *Johnson v. Agnew*, [1980] A.C. 367 (H.L.).

107 Above note 1 at 667–68 [emphasis added].

performance. The issue arises when the vendor does not mitigate by re-selling the property at the time of the breach and its value subsequently declines. The question is whether she is entitled to the additional loss after the date of the breach. On the one hand, vendors have no real interest in completion of the contract other than financial. There is no reason why the disappointed vendor should not mitigate by relisting the property immediately, selling it as soon as possible, and claiming the difference between the actual sale price and the original contract price (if any). If the vendor fails to do so, and the price of the property drops between the time of breach and the time of trial, the vendor has no one to blame but herself.

However, for historical reasons (especially the dubious doctrine of mutuality), vendors of real estate have generally been entitled to specific performance. Thus, a vendor may reasonably expect that he has a legal right to specific performance. In such cases, where specific performance has been claimed, courts have sometimes compensated vendors for post-breach losses by assessing damages at a date later than the breach. In *Johnson v. Agnew*[108] the House of Lords confirmed that, where a vendor "reasonably continues to try to have the contract completed, it would to me appear more logical and just rather than tie him to the date of the original breach, to assess damages as at the date when (otherwise than by his default) the contract is lost."[109] This case has been followed by Canadian courts.[110]

It is submitted that this authority is now of dubious weight in Canada. There are a number of reasons why vendors of real estate will be less likely to receive damages assessed after the date of the breach. First, where it is clear to the vendor that the purchaser will not be able to complete the contract, it is more just (and common) to require the vendor to mitigate by relisting the property and limiting the plaintiff to damages assessed at a date when it would have been reasonable to sell the property. In *Ansdell v. Crowther*[111] the British Columbia Court of Appeal denied a vendor's claim to damages assessed at the date of the trial (the price had been falling), despite the fact that the vendor had claimed specific performance. The court held that the vendor was aware that the defendant would be unable to complete, and that the plaintiff should not have claimed specific performance but rather re-listed the property for sale. In these circumstances the damages will

---

108 Above note 106.
109 *Ibid.* at 499.
110 See, for example, *Kemp v. Lee* (1983), 44 B.C.L.R. 172 (S.C.).
111 (1984), 55 B.C.L.R. 216 (C.A.).

be measured by reference to the value of the property at a time when it likely could have been sold.[112] More generally, the right to specific performance is becoming increasingly restricted in real estate contracts (especially in claims by vendors). It is, therefore, much less likely that a decision by a vendor to retain the land after breach will be viewed as reasonable (though, in some cases, the conduct of the parties may still incline a court to award specific performance to a vendor[113]). These developments are discussed in the following section.

c)   Further Restrictions on Equitable Damages

Recent developments in the law regarding specific performance indicate that the vendor's right of specific performance (and hence the right to damages after the date of breach) will be further restricted. Indeed, these developments are affecting the claims to specific performance even by *purchasers* of real property, who may also be increasingly restricted in their claims to equitable damages. For centuries there has been a presumption that specific performance is available to purchasers of real estate as a matter of course.[114] This presumption is based on the sense that every parcel of land is unique, that no substitutes are available, and that damages are therefore inadequate and specific performance is the preferable remedy. However, over the past several decades, this presumption has come under question. Especially when the land is being purchased for an investment, or when it is one of a number of very similar parcels in an area, damages may be viewed as adequate.[115] It follows that, where a purchaser's right to specific performance is questionable, so will be the right to damages assessed at the date of trial. In these cases, courts will be reluctant to permit a purchaser to speculate at the vendor's risk. In *Buchanan v. Fisher*,[116] a disappointed purchaser of real estate was denied the increased value of the property after the date of the breach. The plaintiff should have mitigated by finding a substitute property, given that his interest in the property was as an investment only and it was inappropriate to sit

---

112 See also *MacLean v. Nietschmann Development Corp.* (1982), 39 B.C.L.R. 164 (S.C.); *Hargreaves v. Spence* (1983), 45 B.C.L.R. 367 (S.C.).

113 *Landmark of Thornhill Ltd. v. Jacobson* (1995), 25 O.R. (3d) 628 (C.A.).

114 *Roy v. Kloepfer Wholesale Hardware & Automotive Co.*, [1952] 2 S.C.R. 465 at 472; *Bashir v. Koper* (1983), 40 O.R. (2d) 758 (C.A.).

115 *Chaulk v. Fairview Construction Ltd.* (1977), 14 Nfld. & P.E.I.R. 13 (Nfld. C.A.); *McNabb v. Smith* (1982), 44 B.C.L.R. 295 (C.A.); *Domowicz v. Orsa Investments Ltd.* (1993), 15 O.R. (3d) 661 (Gen. Div.); *Electrohome Ltd. v. Gregg Properties Co.* (2002), 11 R.P.R. (4th) 270 (Alta. Q.B.), additional reasons 2003 ABQB 172.

116 (1993), 30 R.P.R. (2d) 317 (B.C.S.C.).

by and await the outcome of the trial before seeking out an alternate investment.

The Supreme Court of Canada has affirmed that specific performance may no longer be an automatic remedy for vendors or purchasers of real estate. In *Semelhago v. Paramadevan*[117] the Court held that the absolute rule was no longer valid, stating that

> [w]hile at one time the common law regarded every piece of real estate to be unique, with the progress of modern real estate development this is no longer the case. Residential, business and industrial properties are all mass produced much in the same way as other consumer products. If a deal falls through for one property, another is frequently, though not always, readily available.
>
> It is no longer appropriate, therefore, to maintain a distinction in the approach to specific performance as between realty and personalty. It cannot be assumed that damages for breach of contract for the purchase and sale of real estate will be an inadequate remedy in all cases.[118]

Sopinka J. went on to adopt the test from *Asamera* that, even in real estate cases, there must be some "fair, real and substantial justification" for the claim to specific performance. He concluded that "specific performance should, therefore, not be granted as a matter of course absent evidence that the property is unique to the extent that its substitute would not be readily available."[119]

The assessment of damages at a time later than breach must be approached with great caution. It is an exception to the general mitigation principle and exposes the defendant to potential hardship. Moreover, it may confer undesirable advantages on the plaintiff. Foremost among these is that the plaintiff is able to speculate at the risk of the defendant. The Supreme Court of Canada has clearly stated in *Asamera* that a mere claim to specific performance does not displace the obligation to mitigate, and *Semelhago* has stated that specific performance is no longer to be expected as an automatic remedy even in favour of buyers of real estate. In most situations, therefore, when the innocent party is the vendor, an attempt to resell the property should be made, except in extraordinary circumstances. Indeed, even when the innocent party is the buyer, unless the property truly is unique, and the plaintiff has a

---

117 [1996] 2 S.C.R. 415 [*Semelhago*].
118 *Ibid.* at 428.
119 *Ibid.* at 429.

legitimate reason to pursue specific performance, some attempt to find a substitute should be made.[120]

d) The Windfall Problem: Interest on the Purchase Price

When damages are assessed at the time of trial, the plaintiff may sometimes receive a windfall (in addition to the increased value of the property). This occurs in two ways. First, the plaintiff is awarded the full increased value of the subject matter of the contract while avoiding the costs that would have been incurred if the transaction had been completed. Second, the plaintiff may have entered into a collateral transaction at the time of the wrong and obtained profits and gains that are not taken into account. In both cases, the plaintiff is placed in a better position than if the contract had been performed.

These problems occur in real estate cases where the plaintiff is awarded the increased value of the property at the time of trial, without any deduction being made for the costs that the plaintiff might have incurred in order to "carry" the property during that time or, alternatively, without taking into account the additional earnings that the plaintiff has obtained from investing the purchase price elsewhere. To provide a simple illustration, assume a breach of contract by a vendor for the sale of property at a price of $100,000. At the time of trial three years later, the property is worth $120,000. If the plaintiff is awarded $20,000 in damages assessed at the time of the trial, he will be better off than if the contract had been performed. Assuming the plaintiff was going to pay cash for the property, the plaintiff will have retained the original capital sum, plus $20,000 damages, *plus earnings on the original capital* (e.g., investment income). Alternatively, if the plaintiff was intending to borrow the purchase price, the plaintiff will receive the full increased

---

120 Land is still considered unique even in the aftermath of *Semelhago*, especially in relation to residential real estate. As well, the concept of uniqueness has been liberally interpreted to mean a quality or combination of qualities that make the subject property particularly suitable for the plaintiff's purposes and that is difficult to duplicate elsewhere, to justify specific performance or equitable damages. Thus, courts have found some commercial properties sufficiently unique to warrant specific performance: *John E. Dodge Holdings Ltd. v. 805062 Ontario Ltd.* (2001), 56 O.R. (3d) 341 (S.C.J.), aff'd (2003), 63 O.R. (3d) 304 (C.A.), leave to appeal to S.C.C. refused, [2003] S.C.C.A. No. 145; *2475813 Nova Scotia Ltd. v. Lundrigan* (2003), 13 R.P.R. (4th) 197 (N.S.S.C.); *Cross Cree Timber Traders v. St. John Terminals Ltd.*, [2002] N.B.J. No. 77 (Q.B.); *Van Dyk v. Durno*, [2005] B.C.J. No. 1052 (S.C.); *DeFranco v. Khatri*, [2005] O.J. No. 1890 (S.C.J.); *Roma Construction Ltd. v. Excel Venture Management Inc.*, 2007 ABQB 396. The subject property must be unique to the purchaser and not to a third party: *Buckwheat Enterprises Inc. v. Shiu* (2001), 48 R.P.R. (3d) 72 (B.C.S.C.).

value of the land *without having to have incurred the costs* of earning that increased value (the mortgage interest). And in both cases, the plaintiff will receive the increased value of the property without having had to pay other carrying costs such as property taxation. It is submitted that, in accordance with the compensatory basis of contract damages, an adjustment should be made in the award to take into account the savings to the plaintiff resulting from non-performance. Of course, if possession of the land would have resulted in some additional pecuniary benefit to the plaintiff (e.g., rents or other income), the plaintiff should be compensated for those losses.

Despite the apparent overcompensation that occurs in these cases, courts have generally not made any deductions. The argument for a deduction was considered and rejected in *306793 Ontario Ltd. v. Rimes*[121] in which the purchaser of twenty-nine acres of land was suing for breach of contract. The purchase price of the land was $580,000 and at the time of trial the land was worth $145,000 more ($725,000). The vendor conceded that the plaintiff was entitled to specific performance or damages in substitution but argued that a deduction should be made to reflect the mortgage and carrying costs that the plaintiff would have incurred had the transaction closed. Those costs would have amounted to an estimated $120,000, thus reducing the damages to just $25,000. The logic of this approach is unassailable from one point of view. Had the contract been performed, the plaintiff would not simply be $145,000 better off, for the plaintiff would have incurred costs to earn that profit.[122] However, the Ontario Court of Appeal refused to make any deduction on the basis that an award of $25,000 would not be a "true alternative to specific performance." While the purchaser does receive a windfall, it is the same windfall that would have been received had specific performance been ordered (given that no adjustments are made in such a case).

The windfall problem was considered again, by the Supreme Court of Canada, in *Semelhago*,[123] which essentially confirmed the approach in *Rimes*. The plaintiff purchased a house under construction for $205,000. To complete the purchase he planned to use $75,000 cash on hand and to finance the remainder by mortgaging his existing house for six months (and selling it at the end of that period). The plaintiff claimed specific performance and damages, electing for damages at

---

121 (1979), 100 D.L.R. (3d) 350 (Ont. C.A.) [*Rimes*].
122 See J. Swan, "Damages, Specific Performance, Inflation and Interest" (1980), 10 R.P.R. 267.
123 Above note 117.

trial. The main issue was whether, in the assessment of damages, a deduction should be made for the carrying costs avoided by the plaintiff, and also to take into account that as a result of the breach he retained his old house and earned a substantial increase in value on it, which offset the loss on the new property.

The trial judge awarded $120,000 (the difference between the contract price and the value of the home at the time of trial) with no deductions. The trial judge recognized that this would result in a windfall to the plaintiff since the plaintiff had both avoided the costs of a mortgage and earned a substantial increase in value on his own home (of $110,000), which, as a result of the breach, he had not had to sell. However, the judge felt bound by *Rimes*. The Ontario Court of Appeal declined to follow *Rimes* and made a deduction from the award to reflect the costs that the plaintiff would have incurred (the carrying costs on the mortgage plus the notional interest earned on the $75,000 cash). The Court of Appeal did not deduct the profit made by the plaintiff by retaining his own home. The case was appealed on this last point to the Supreme Court of Canada.

Sopinka J., for the Supreme Court, declined to deduct the collateral profit earned by the plaintiff from retaining his original home. He stated that such a deduction would be inappropriate since the purpose of the award is to be a substitute for specific performance. "If the respondent had received a decree of specific performance, he would have had the property contracted for and retained the amount of the rise in value of his own property.... To make such deductions would depart from the principle that damages are to be a true equivalent of specific performance."[124] While not in issue before the Court, Sopinka J. also cast some doubt on the propriety of the deduction even of the interest charges that the plaintiff avoided on the planned mortgage.

In refusing the deductions, the Supreme Court did not deny that the plaintiff received a windfall. It is true that the plaintiff receives a windfall, but it is the same windfall that he receives had the Court ordered specific performance.[125] If the plaintiff had maintained his claim to specific performance, he would be entitled to possession of the property on payment of the purchase price, with no further deductions (which admittedly confers a windfall). Thus, in the end, the Supreme Court of Canada has not yet abandoned the notion that "equitable damages" (damages in substitution for specific performance) are not subject to

---

124 *Ibid.* at 427–28.
125 See P.M. Perell, "Damages and Fluctuating Land Values" (1996) 18 Advocates' Q. 401.

the general principles of common law. To make no deduction results in overcompensation and offends the common law principles, but specific performance would result in the same windfall and "equitable damages" are apparently intended to be a true economic equivalent of specific performance. Thus, the common law is "trumped" by the "imperative contained in s. 99 of the *Courts of Justice Act* [that the] damages that are awarded must be a true substitute for specific performance."[126]

Semelhago reveals a disparity between the rules of common law and the rules of equity. Equitable remedies historically are designed to remedy injustice caused by a strict application of the rules of common law. However, in this case, equity would seem to serve the opposite purpose. By awarding the entire increase in value, with no deduction of the expenses that the purchaser would have incurred (or the expenses that the vendor actually has incurred by retaining the property), the vendor is punished and the purchaser reaps a windfall. The Supreme Court only inferentially recognizes the injustice of this when, in *obiter*, it indicates that the right to specific performance in real estate cases will be increasingly restricted. If so, the plaintiff will have an obligation to mitigate, damages will not be assessed at a later date, and the problem of overcompensation will be avoided.

---

126 *Semelhago*, above note 117 at 426.

CHAPTER 13

DEDUCTIONS FROM DAMAGES: COLLATERAL BENEFITS

A. INTRODUCTION

1) The Issue Explained

Closely related to the issues of mitigation and "avoided loss" is the subject of collateral benefits. This subject arises whenever a plaintiff's loss (as a result of breach of contract or tort) is apparently ameliorated by a payment from a third party (or "collateral source"). The question is whether that payment should be taken into account in calculating the plaintiff's loss, thus reducing the damages payable by the defendant.

Collateral benefits problems arise in many contexts in civil litigation. For example, in wrongful dismissal and personal injury cases, the plaintiff may receive employment insurance, welfare, or other assistance that cushions the wage loss. In personal injury cases, the plaintiff's actual expenses for the cost of care and income losses may frequently be paid for by insurance or offset by income or benefits in kind from a variety of sources. Public health-care benefits will frequently cover many of the plaintiff's medical expenses. Family members and charitable institutions may provide care to the plaintiff free of charge. The plaintiff's wage loss may be defrayed, partly or in whole, by disability insurance, an employer's wage continuation plan, or a benevolent fund. In every case, the question is whether the benefits received by the plaintiff cancel the loss suffered.

2) Framework for Analysis

The tension over collateral benefits is acute. On the one hand, to permit the plaintiff to claim a loss or expense that is not actually incurred (or which is offset from another source) appears to overcompensate the plaintiff. For example, a person who is injured but continues to receive his salary from a disability fund will receive a "windfall" or "double compensation" if he is also permitted to claim lost income from the defendant. On the other hand, to exclude such losses from the plaintiff's claim gives to the defendant the benefit of the program, essentially "subsidizing" the defendant's negligence. For those who believe that tort law should play a deterrent role by charging wrong-doers with the full costs of their activities, such a subsidy undermines the social purpose of the law.

The law regarding collateral benefits is always evolving and the questions raised largely involve policy considerations. The "fundamental" policy of tort is compensation of the plaintiff, not punishment of the defendant, and from this perspective, a failure to deduct collateral benefits amounts to double compensation or a windfall to the plaintiff. In *Ratych v. Bloomer*,[1] McLachlin J. stated:

> The functional rational [*sic*] for the award of damages adopted in the trilogy of *Andrews*, *Thornton* and *Teno* underlines the necessity of using the plaintiff's actual loss as the basis of his or her damages. The award is justified, not because it is appropriate to punish the defendant or enrich the plaintiff, but because it will serve the purpose or *function* of restoring the plaintiff as nearly as possible to his pre-accident state or alternatively, where this cannot be done, providing substitutes for what he lost.
>
> The trilogy follows the modern trend in the law of damages away from a punitive approach which emphasizes the wrong the tortfeasor has committed. The link between the moral culpability of the tortfeasor and his obligation to pay damages to the person he injures is frequently tenuous in our technological and mechanical era. A moment's inattention is all that is required to trigger astronomical damages. The risks inherent in such activities as the use of our highways by motorists are increasingly recognized as a general social burden. In this context, the maxim that compensation must be fair to both the plaintiff and the defendant seems eminently reasonable ... That fairness is best achieved by avoiding both undercompensation and overcompensation.[2]

---

1   [1990] 1 S.C.R. 940 [*Ratych*].
2   *Ibid.* at 963 [emphasis in original].

Thus, an emphasis on "compensation" indicates a general rule of deductibility. As McLachlin J. concluded, it is implicit in the compensation principle that the "plaintiff should not recover unless he can demonstrate a loss, and then only to the extent of that loss."[3] Double recovery violates this principle. While this may seem to provide a benefit to the defendant, this concern is attenuated by the widespread use of liability insurance, since often it will be the third-party insurer who will be bearing the costs and not the defendant personally. Also persuasive is the point that McLachlin J. makes concerning the problem with assigning moral culpability to certain negligent actions commensurate with their often catastrophic results. With powerful machines (and complex science) comes the potential for great harm even when reasonable care is taken to prevent it.

However, tort law is often stated to have a deterrence function as well. Under the deterrence theory, tortfeasors should bear the full cost of their wrongdoing. This is said to provide incentives for those engaged in potentially harmful or dangerous activities to take into account the full societal costs of those activities. On this basis, collateral benefits should not be deducted from damages awards, since deduction would mean the benefit would inure to the defendant who would otherwise be required to pay the full cost of the wrongdoing. And in addition to deterrence, many find it disturbing that the wrongdoer should get "credit" for payments made to her victim. These notions were articulated by Cory J. in *Cunningham v. Wheeler*:[4] "Tort recovery is based on some wrongdoing. It makes little sense for a wrongdoer to benefit from the private act of forethought and sacrifice of the plaintiff."[5] Thus, a plaintiff may end up recovering more than her actual loss even if a court disapproves of this outcome.[6]

On this view, non-deductibility furthers the principles of deterrence and avoids the moral dilemma of giving the wrongdoer the benefit of payments intended for the plaintiff. It is said that the existence of liability insurance significantly undermines the deterrence rationale of tort law (since damage awards are paid by insurers, not by wrongdoers); however, as Calabresi has argued, even with insurance, tort law may serve a more general deterrence function.[7] Tort law causes the costs of

---

3   *Ibid.* at 981.
4   [1994] 1 S.C.R. 359 [*Cunningham*].
5   *Ibid.* at 401.
6   See *Zacharias v. Leys* (2005), 36 C.C.L.T. (3d) 93 at para. 40 (B.C.C.A.), Southin J.A.
7   G. Calabresi, *The Cost of Accidents: A Legal and Economic Analysis* (New Haven: Yale University Press, 1970).

certain activities (driving, manufacturing, and so on) to be "internalized" by the relevant actors. Even if the actors are insured, the costs of insurance in that field of activity should reflect the full cost of accidents so that all participants will take economically justified precautions to avoid accidents, or ultimately, if accidents in that field are too expensive (in terms of the cost of accidents), then the level of activity in that field will be reduced (or altered).

As will be seen in the following sections, the law of collateral benefits steers an uneasy course between the Scylla of overcompensation of the plaintiff and the Charybdis of subsidization of the defendant.

3) A Note on Subrogation and Trust

The concerns of both overcompensation and subsidy can be eliminated with advance planning. Subrogation is the legal means whereby one person (the subrogee) recovers money paid to another person (the subrogor). Where an insurer has paid benefits to its insured, to cover a loss for which a third party may be liable, subrogation gives to the insurer the right to recover those monies from the third party. Rights of subrogation may arise in equity, as the result of private contract, or may be contained in legislation (as in the case of workers' compensation legislation and some provincial health insurance legislation).[8] In most cases subrogation resolves the policy conflict explained above. The tortfeasor is liable to pay the full cost of the claim and thus is not subsidized. And overcompensation is also avoided by requiring the plaintiff to pay over the monies received in respect of the insured loss.

A result similar to subrogation can be achieved through the imposition by the court of a trust over a portion of the damages award received by the plaintiff, where the plaintiff's loss has actually been absorbed by a family member (e.g., where a family member provides nursing services).[9]

Another possible solution to the collateral benefits problem (similar to subrogation and the trust device) is to give to the provider of the plaintiff's benefits a direct right of action for reimbursement. For ex-

---

8   *Employment Insurance Act*, S.C. 1996, c. 23, s. 45. See also, for example, *Workers' Compensation Act*, R.S.A. 2000, c. W-15, s. 22; R.S.B.C. 1996, c. 492, s. 10; R.S.N.B. 1973, c. W-13, s. 10; S.N.S. 1994–95, c. 10, s. 30; R.S.P.E.I. 1988, c. W-7.1, s. 11; S.S. 1979, c. W-17.1, s. 40; R.S.N.W.T. 1988, c. W-6, s. 12; *Workplace Health, Safety and Compensation Act*, R.S.N.L. 1990, c. W-11, s. 45; *Workplace Safety and Insurance Act*, S.O. 1997, c. 16, s. 30.

9   See Chapter 4.

ample, under the Ontario *Family Law Act*,[10] specified family members can recover expenses incurred on behalf of a person who is injured or killed. Similarly, where a family member provides nursing, housekeeping, or other services to an injured person, the family member may recover the reasonable value of those services or the income forgone in providing them.

Despite the attractiveness of the devices of subrogation and trust as solutions, their use is limited and the collateral benefits problem continues to arise in a wide variety of contexts. The result in each case depends very much on the specific type of benefit and the circumstances under which it was acquired by the plaintiff. An insurer's right of subrogation or reimbursement may depend on the terms of the policy. As well, the right of subrogation may be lost where an insurer does not pursue or join in the action against the third party.[11] The *general* principle is a rule against double compensation. However, as will be seen below, there are so many exceptions to this rule that it can be said that the working rule is in fact the opposite. Indeed, the counter-rule even has a name: the "collateral source rule." This rule says that benefits received from a collateral source are not deductible; and the concept of "collateral source" has been given a broad interpretation. In the remaining sections, different types of collateral benefits are isolated and analyzed.

B. THE TREATMENT OF SPECIFIC BENEFITS

1) Gifts and Private Charity

The caselaw regarding private or charitable gifts is consistent in holding that these benefits should not be taken into account in determining the plaintiff's award. Courts are unanimous that the defendant should not receive the benefit of benevolent contributions from third parties to the plaintiff. The principal reason is the concern that, if the defendant were to take the benefit of gifts and charity, contributors would be shocked and private charity would dry up.[12] This was strongly articulated by the House of Lords in *Parry v. Cleaver*:

> It would be revolting to the ordinary man's sense of justice, and therefore contrary to public policy, that the sufferer should have his

---

10   R.S.O. 1990, c. F.3, s. 61(2).
11   *Wilson v. Great West Life Assurance Co.*, [2007] N.B.J. No. 92 at paras. 20–21.
12   *Redpath v. Belfast and County Down Rly*, [1947] N.I. 167; *M.B. v. British Columbia*, [2003] 2 S.C.R. 477 [*M.B.*].

damages reduced so that he would gain nothing from the benevolence of his friends or relations or of the public at large, and that the only gainer would be the wrongdoer.[13]

The rule against the deductibility of gifts has frequently been applied in Canada, and the Supreme Court of Canada has indicated that the rule is alive and well:

> The first exception to the rule against double recovery is the case of charitable gifts. If a plaintiff is injured and his neighbour brings him a basket of groceries or donates to him a sum of money, the law will not deduct the value of the basket from the damages which the negligent defendant must pay nor require that the monetary gift be called into account. This exception reflects the concern of the courts who initiated it that people should not be discouraged from aiding those in misfortune. Arguably, it also reflects the reality that in most cases it would be more trouble than it is worth to require the courts to hear evidence and rule on the value of charitable assistance.[14]

The application of the collateral source rule to gifts does mean that the plaintiff receives a "windfall." Occasionally the courts seek to avoid this result by ordering repayment to the donor under principles of trust or restitution, especially where there is evidence that this is what the parties intended, or, at the very least, acknowledging that the plaintiff has a moral obligation to repay the donor. In *Kask v. Tam*[15] the British Columbia Court of Appeal held that an oral agreement between the plaintiff and his employer that the plaintiff would be paid full salary while injured, subject to the plaintiff making restitution out of the litigation proceeds, amounted to gratuitous payments accompanied by a moral obligation to repay and the plaintiff was entitled to damages for lost wages. In *Rawson v. Kasman*,[16] the Ontario Court of Appeal awarded the plaintiff the costs of medical expenses paid for by her son, with the direction to pay the amount over to him.[17]

---

13   [1970] A.C. 1 at 14 (P.C.), Lord Reid [*Parry*].

14   *Cunningham*, above note 4 at 370. See also *M.B.*, above note 12.

15   (1996), 21 B.C.L.R. (3d) 11 (C.A.) [*Kask*]. See also *Frers v. De Moulin* (2002), 1 B.C.L.R. (4th) 131 at para. 164 (S.C.).

16   [1956] O.W.N. 359 (C.A.).

17   See also *Dawson v. Sawatzky*, [1946] 1 D.L.R. 476 (Sask. C.A.); *Bowers v. J. Hollinger & Co.*, [1946] O.R. 526 (S.C.).

2) Nursing and Other Gratuitous Benefits in Kind

In personal injury cases the plaintiff will frequently receive gratuitous "benefits in kind" from family members, such as nursing services and help with day-to-day tasks of living. The defendant will frequently argue that where family members are providing the plaintiff with help, there is no real "loss" to be compensated and that a monetary award will be a windfall. On the other hand, if the defendant receives "credit" for such benefits, there is little incentive for family members and others to continue with the services.

Generally, courts are reluctant to reduce awards to take into account benefits in kind, and they are usually brought within the "benevolence exception." In *Vana v. Tosta*,[18] the plaintiff and his children were injured in a motor-vehicle accident that also killed his wife. In an action brought under the *Fatal Accidents Act*,[19] the Ontario Court of Appeal reduced the award under the Act to take into account any services the plaintiff's family might render. In the Supreme Court of Canada, this aspect of the judgment was reversed. Spence J., speaking for the majority, stated:

> It is trite law that a wrongdoer cannot claim the benefit of services donated to the injured party. In the present case it amounts in my judgment to conscripting the mother and mother-in-law to the services of the appellant and his children for the benefit of the tortfeasor and any reduction of the award on this basis is and was an error in principle.[20]

It is in this context that the problem of "overcompensation" is most often solved through the use of the trust device. Especially where the plaintiff's claim is for the past cost of care, and there has been no actual expenditure because the care has been provided by a family member, the claim is awarded, but the court orders an amount to be held in trust and paid over to that family member. This was approved by the Supreme Court in both *Thornton v. Prince George School District No. 57*[21] and *Arnold v. Teno*.[22] This device required the defendant to pay the entire loss, while avoiding the problem of double compensation.

The issue of *valuing* the plaintiff's loss in these situations is interesting. Sometimes the court will award a modest conventional amount.

---

18   [1968] S.C.R. 71.
19   R.S.O. 1960, c. 138.
20   Above note 18 at 75.
21   [1978] 2 S.C.R. 267.
22   [1978] 2 S.C.R. 287.

More commonly, with proper evidence, the court may base the award on the notional costs of care that would have been incurred by the plaintiff but for the family assistance. Alternatively, where the caregiver has herself incurred costs to care for the plaintiff (for instance, given up employment or used up holiday time), the amount may be assessed by reference to those "opportunity costs" so long as they are not in excess of what it would have cost to purchase those services. This principle was expressly approved in *Crane v. Worwood*,[23] where the court held:

> [W]here a relative provides services needed as a result of the plaintiff's injuries, which could be provided by a third party, the plaintiff may be awarded damages for their reasonable cost. The maximum award under this head is the cost of obtaining the services outside the family. Where the opportunity cost to the care-giving family member is lower than the cost of obtaining the services independently, the court will award the lower amount.... But there is no authority for the proposition that the award should be the full amount of the [family care-giver's] opportunity cost if it exceeds the reasonable value of the services.[24]

3) Housekeeping Services

a) Personal Injury Cases

When we move away from "nursing services" provided by a family member to consider other "benefits in kind," the waters become murkier. As explained in Chapter 4, Canadian courts have recently recognized as a head of loss the diminished capacity to perform household work. This loss is treated as a pecuniary or economic loss, even though the plaintiff was not being paid a wage for performing this work. The question that has arisen is whether such an award can be made when the plaintiff's housework is taken over by a family member (usually a spouse).

The caselaw is divided. On one view, if a family member takes over the work, there is no real loss to compensate, and if the money is not going to be used to purchase outside help, the plaintiff will receive a windfall. This view, which also reflects stereotypes about the proper roles of men and women in families, finds expression in *Pickering v. Deakin*,[25] in which a male plaintiff was seriously injured. The trial court

---

23   (1992), 65 B.C.L.R. (2d) 16 (S.C.) [*Crane*]. See also *Bartosek (Litigation guardian of) v. Turret Realities Inc.*, [2001] O.J. No. 4735 (S.C.J.), aff'd (2004), 23 C.C.L.T. (3d) 161 (C.A.), leave to appeal to S.C.C. refused, [2004] S.C.C.A. No. 202.
24   *Crane, ibid.* at 38.
25   [1985] 1 W.W.R. 289 (B.C.C.A.) [*Pickering*].

made no award for the cost of housekeeping services as part of his cost of care because it assumed that the plaintiff's wife would continue to provide these services. The court reasoned that she had performed most of the housework before the accident and that there would be little marginal change in her workload due to the accident.

There are serious difficulties with this approach. It assumes that the wife will continue to provide these services without compensation and places her under social or moral pressure to do so. And if she fails to do so, it will leave the plaintiff seriously undercompensated. The Court of Appeal in this case partially recognized these problems and made an award of $116,000 to take into account the contingency that after twenty years (half the plaintiff's lifespan), he might no longer receive services from his wife owing to the possibility of divorce or death. This is clearly an improvement, but it also assumes that for the other twenty years the plaintiff will receive the services and that his spouse is not entitled to payment for them.

De Sousa v. *Kuntz*[26] confirmed the *Pickering* approach. The plaintiff was seriously injured as a result of medical negligence. His wife was forced to give up her employment in order to drive him to and from therapy, to bathe and dress him, and to take over the housework that they used to share. It was argued that an amount should be awarded in trust to compensate for this. The British Columbia Court of Appeal refused to make this award on the basis that

> household and nursing duties that you could expect a husband or wife to perform through the natural affection, friendliness and interdependence of the usual marital relationship is not compensable in a tort case as an actionable head of damages. It is only if a spouse has to take on a complete function like full-time nursing, a function that is outside the usual concept of what people undertake when they take their marriage vows, and outside the "worse" end of the "for better or worse" marriage scale, that additional compensation should be granted.[27]

The approach in *De Sousa* in fact penalizes a married couple who choose to care for one another and provides an incentive not to do so. It has led to lawyers advising their clients that "paid help should be substituted for family care givers at the earliest possible moment."[28]

---

26   (1989), 42 B.C.L.R. (2d) 186 (C.A.) [*De Sousa*].

27   *Ibid.* at 196–97.

28   *Personal Injury: Special Issues* (Vancouver: Continuing Legal Education Society of British Columbia, 1988) at 1.1.02.

The "for better or worse" approach law has been modified by *Kroek-er v. Jansen* in which the British Columbia Court of Appeal held that the loss of housekeeping capacity is a pecuniary loss and is compensable even when a spouse will be taking over some of those tasks.[29] The thirty-five-year-old female plaintiff was injured in an automobile accident, suffering, among other things, a diminished ability to perform heavy housework. After the accident she married, and her spouse assumed some of the household tasks that she otherwise would have done. In other words, their sharing was "dictated in part by the respondent's inability to do things she would normally do."[30]

It was argued for the defendant that no pecuniary loss had been suffered in respect of lost housekeeping capacity. The arrangement with her husband was such that no additional expenditure on housekeeping would be necessitated by the injury. The majority held that the earlier cases had been "overtaken by an evolution of judicial thinking" and that the loss of ability to perform housework is a pecuniary loss even when the services are replaced gratuitously from within the family. The Court of Appeal did, however, reduce the amount awarded by the trial judge from $23,000 to $7,000.[31]

In some jurisdictions, the problem has been addressed by legislation. In *Granger (Litigation guardian of) v. Ottawa General Hospital*, a child was brain-damaged and physically disabled as a result of medical negligence during her birth. She would require constant care throughout her life. The plaintiff parents received compensation for their past caregiving under Ontario's *Family Law Act* but were denied compensation for their claim for "extraordinary future care," including consulting with the full-time attendants, attending their daughter's medical appointments, and the time spent purchasing medication. Cunningham J. perceived these activities as "things any parent would do and [could] not characterize them as being extraordinary care."[32]

---

29   (1995), 4 B.C.L.R. (3d) 178 (C.A.).

30   *Ibid.* at 180.

31   In *West v. Cotton* (1995), 10 B.C.L.R. (3d) 73 at paras. 25–28 (C.A.), the court expressly held that *Pickering* and *De Sousa* have been overruled by *Kroeker*, and affirmed an "in trust" award for services rendered by the plaintiff's wife in the pre-trial period, but the amount was reduced to reflect the true value of those services. See also *McTavish v. MacGillivray* (2000), 74 B.C.L.R. (3d) 281 (C.A.); *Deglow v. Uffelman* (2001), 96 B.C.L.R. (3d) 130 (C.A.); *Tombe v. Stefulj*, 2002 BCSC 154.

32   (1996), 7 O.T.C. 81 at para. 244 (Gen. Div.).

b)   Fatal Accident Cases

The same issues arise even more starkly in fatal accident cases, where the issue of collateral benefits frequently merges with the issue of mitigation. In these cases, surviving family members may be suing for the loss of a parent or a spouse. They may be claiming for their financial losses and also for the loss of unpaid work around the house. As explained in Chapter 5, courts have recognized the substantial value of the household work provided by parents to children and spouses to one another. The issue that arises is how the claim should be treated when the surviving spouse forms a new relationship, or the children are adopted. Does this cancel or reduce the loss suffered?

Frequently, courts will hold that the remarriage does in fact cancel or reduce a spouse's loss. Where the survivor has remarried before the trial, a court will take the new spouse's income into account in assessing the loss. Even where there has been no remarriage, courts will frequently take the possibility of remarriage into account as a contingency that reduces the award.[33]

The issue of the effect of remarriage on claims by children is more complex. In *Tompkins (Guardian ad litem of) v. Byspalko*,[34] the award of damages to a child was not reduced by the provision of services by a stepmother. The court held:

> I find that the defendant's negligence here has deprived Nikki of a *source* of services and support she previously enjoyed free from her mother. She is at risk if for any reason her father and step-mother became unable or, particularly in the case of the step-mother who has no legal relationship to Nikki, unwilling to continue to serve or support her.[35]

However, a year later, in *Skelding (Guardian ad litem of) v. Skelding*,[36] the British Columbia Court of Appeal held that housekeeping services and financial support provided by a parent or step-parent were not classified as gratuitous and that they should be deducted from a damages award to avoid double compensation. In that case, the plaintiff children brought an action against their father under the *Family Compensation Act*[37] for the wrongful death of their mother in a motor-vehicle accident for which he was responsible. After the accident the father remarried

---

33   See discussion in Chapter 5.
34   (1993), 16 C.C.L.T. (2d) 179 (B.C.S.C.).
35   *Ibid.* at 192 [emphasis in original].
36   (1994), 95 B.C.L.R. (2d) 201 (C.A.) [*Skelding*].
37   R.S.B.C. 1979, c. 120.

and his second wife had a higher earning capacity. The issue on appeal was whether the remarriage should be taken into account in assessing the children's damages. Gibbs J.A. held that it should, explaining,

> [t]he sole question then is whether the housekeeping services and financial support provided by the parent and stepparent of the children fall into the category of gratuitous. They appear not to. There is, first and foremost, the societal concept of a positive duty upon persons standing in a parental relationship. Secondly, there are statutory duties imposed: specifically in the *Family Relations Act* and s. 215 of the *Criminal Code*, and implicitly in the *Family and Child Service Act*, R.S.B.C. 1979, c. 119; and the *Divorce Act*, R.S.C. 1985, c. 3 (2nd Supp.). It follows that the benefits received by the children from their parent and stepparent do not have the gratuitous aspect or coloration which would be present if they were received from non-parental persons out of a sense of concern or compassion or sympathy. Recovery by the children of damages for housekeeping services and financial support would, therefore, represent double recovery contrary to both *Ratych v. Bloomer* and *Cunningham v. Wheeler*.[38]

Perhaps not surprisingly, different considerations apply when a more remote relative adopts the children. The voluntary assumption of custodianship of a child does not extinguish that child's loss for the purpose of a fatal accident claim. In *Ratansi v. Abery*[39] it was held that the fact that their aunt had become legal guardian of the infant plaintiffs following the death of their parents did not eliminate the plaintiffs' claim to care, support, and housekeeping services. It would be against public policy to deduct gratuitous services received from a relative (as double recovery) because this would discourage the provision of such services. A similar situation arose in *Butterfield (Litigation guardian of) v. Butterfield Estate*,[40] where the children brought an action against their father's estate under the Ontario legislation after a motor-vehicle accident for which the father was solely liable killed both parents. Relying on the fact that the aunt and uncle of the children took them in, the court distinguished *Skelding* and granted the children's dependency claims.

---

38 *Skelding*, above note 36 at 214.
39 (1995), 5 B.C.L.R. (3d) 88 (S.C.).
40 (1996), 96 O.A.C. 262 (C.A.).

4) Private Insurance Benefits

Benefits received by the plaintiff through private insurance are not deductible from damage awards. This is the "insurance exception" to the general rule of deductibility, first recognized in *Bradburn v. Great Western Rly Co.*[41] The court reasoned that the plaintiff had paid for the insurance benefit and it should not be usurped by the defendant:

> [T]here would be no justice or principle in setting off an amount which the plaintiff has entitled himself to under a contract of insurance, such as any prudent man would make on the principle of, as the expression is, "laying by for a rainy day." He pays the premiums upon a contract which, if he meets with an accident, entitles him to receive a sum of money. It is not because he meets with the accident, but because he made a contract with, and paid premiums to, the insurance company, for that express purpose, that he gets the money from them. It is true that there must be the element of accident in order to entitle him to the money; but it is under and by reason of his contract with the insurance company, that he gets the amount; and I think that it ought not, upon any principle of justice, to be deducted from the amount of the damages proved to have been sustained by him through the negligence of the defendants.[42]

While the court in *Bradburn* was mixing concepts of causation and social policy in reaching this decision (that the accident did not cause the receipt of the insurance monies), later cases made it clear that the insurance exception rested on the injustice of permitting the defendant to usurp the benefit of insurance paid for by the plaintiff.[43] In addition, there is seldom any concern with "overcompensation" of the plaintiff in these cases because many insurance contracts will include a right of subrogation.

The private insurance exception is firmly established in Canadian jurisprudence,[44] and recently it has been reaffirmed by the Supreme Court of Canada. Speaking for the majority in *Cunningham*,[45] Cory J. stated:

---

41   (1874), L.R. 10 Ex. 1, [1874–80] All E.R. Rep. 195 [*Bradburn*].
42   *Ibid.* at 197 (cited to All E.R. Rep.).
43   *Parry*, above note 13.
44   *Canadian Pacific Ltd. v. Gill*, [1973] S.C.R. 654 [*Gill*]; *Trizec Equities Ltd. v. Guy*, [1979] 2 S.C.R. 756 [*Trizec*].
45   Above note 4. See Section B(5), below in this chapter, for a discussion of *Cunningham*.

I think the exemption for the private policy of insurance should be maintained. It has a long history. It is understood and accepted. There has never been any confusion as to when it should be applied. More importantly it is based on fairness. All who insure themselves for disability benefits are displaying wisdom and forethought in making provision for the continuation of some income in case of disabling injury or illness. The acquisition of the policy has social benefits for those insured, their dependants and indeed their community. It represents forbearance and self-denial on the part of the purchaser of the policy to provide for contingencies ...

... I can see no reason why a tortfeasor should benefit from the sacrifices made by a plaintiff in obtaining an insurance policy to provide for lost wages. Tort recovery is based on some wrongdoing. It makes little sense for a wrongdoer to benefit from the private act of forethought and sacrifice of the plaintiff.[46]

The private insurance exception is equally applicable in respect of mandatory insurance policies such as complusory automobile insurance because the plaintiff has paid for these benefits in the same way as private insurance policies.[47] Premiums need not have been paid by the plaintiff; it will suffice that they have been paid for by a third party on the plaintiff's behalf.[48]

5) Contractual Employment Benefits

a) Recent Legal Developments

Particularly difficult issues arise when an injured plaintiff receives disability payments or wage replacement through a term of an employment contract or collective agreement. In *Ratych*,[49] the issue before the Supreme Court of Canada was whether a police officer injured as a result of the tortious actions of the defendant was entitled to claim damages for lost wages when he had received full pay during that period pursuant to a collective agreement. In a split decision the Court held that wages paid by an employer pursuant to a contract of employment are not akin to insurance and therefore should be taken into account when

---

46   *Ibid.* at 400–1.
47   See *Dryden (Litigation guardian of) v. Campbell Estate*, [2001] O.J. No. 829 at paras. 229–37 (S.C.J.); *Cowles v. Balac* (2005), 19 C.C.L.I. (4th) 242 at paras. 191–98 (Ont. S.C.J.), aff'd (2006), 83 O.R. (3d) 660 (C.A.), leave to appeal to S.C.C. refused, [2006] S.C.C.A. No. 496 [*Cowles*].
48   *Cowles, ibid.* at paras. 199–204 (Ont. S.C.J.).
49   Above note 1.

awarding damages. McLachlin J. held that the general object of tort law is to compensate the plaintiff for the loss actually sustained — not to punish the wrongdoer.

> It is implicit in this that the plaintiff should not recover unless he can demonstrate a loss, and then only to the extent of that loss. Double recovery violates this principle. It follows that where a plaintiff sustains no wage loss as a result of a tort because his employer has continued to pay his salary while he was unable to work, he should not be entitled to recover damages on that account.[50]

The majority held the following as exceptions to the above rule: (a) where the plaintiff could establish that the third party was entitled to reimbursement on the principle of subrogation (thus avoiding double recovery by the plaintiff); (b) where the plaintiff could establish that he had some obligation to repay a third party, the trust device applied in *Thornton* could be used; or (c) where there was evidence that the plaintiff-employee had in fact suffered a loss or made a contribution to the fund equivalent to an insurance premium so that the benefit was akin to private insurance.

Ratych was applied in a number of subsequent cases in which wage benefits were deducted from damage awards in situations where the employee could not show a "loss or contribution" in exchange for the benefits so as to bring them within the insurance exception.[51] However, the case caused some confusion as courts struggled to define the breadth of the rule, and the decision in *Ratych* was subsequently modified by the Supreme Court in *Cunningham*.[52] There the Court entertained three joined actions to decide the issue of whether disability benefit payments received by injured plaintiffs under their collective agreements should be deducted from awards they received in tort actions. The different plaintiffs either made no contribution, or a very modest contribution, to the benefit plans in question. Assimilating the issue to the private insurance, the Court held that such employment benefits were not deductible if the employee paid for them. Moreover, even when there is no direct payment, such benefits will usually be bargained for and obtained as a result of a reduction in the hourly rate of pay. Thus, they are "paid for," albeit indirectly, "just as much as if [the employee] had bought and privately paid for a policy of disability insurance."[53] The Court also held

---

50   *Ibid.* at 981.
51   *Bloom v. Klein* (1992), 63 B.C.L.R (2d) 130 (S.C.).
52   Above note 4.
53   *Ibid.* at 403.

that proof of such a *quid pro quo* was not confined to collective agreements but might also be established in non-unionized situations so long as evidence could be brought to show that the employer had taken the cost of benefits into account in determining wages.

As Cory J. pointed out, this is a more just result. It is, he argues, unfair for the defendant wrongdoer to take the benefit of the plaintiff's forethought and sacrifice. Moreover, the *Ratych* rule is discriminatory, for to say that private insurance benefits are not deductible, while other contractual benefits are deductible, creates a double standard:

> To say that the exception applies only to private insurance, where actual premiums are paid to the insurance company, would create barriers that are unfair and artificial. It would mean that top management and professionals who could well afford to purchase their own insurance would have the benefit of the insurance exception, while those who made the same provision and made relatively greater financial sacrifices to provide for the disability payments through their collective bargaining agreement would be denied the benefits of the insurance exception. This would be manifestly unfair. There is no basis for such a socially regressive distinction.[54]

Cunningham does not technically overrule *Ratych*, since employment benefits will continue to be deducted if they have not been "paid" for. However, the more liberal understanding of how such benefits are paid for (e.g., through bargaining, forgone wages, or other *quid pro quo*) means that it will virtually always be possible to bring employment benefits within the insurance exception. Direct evidence that an employee gave up something for the benefit in the bargaining process is not required. In *Howes v. Rousta*,[55] the court said it could take judicial notice of the fact that all benefits have a cost to the employee in the bargaining process.[56] However, if they have not been paid for, then arguably they may be brought within the "charitable gifts" exception.

---

54 *Ibid.* at 403–4.

55 (2002), 27 Alta. L.R. (4th) 316 at para. 85 (Q.B.). See also *Gill v. Lindstrom*, [2002] B.C.J. No. 1616 (S.C.), var'd on other grounds (2004), 33 B.C.L.R. (4th) 325 (C.A.). In *Young v. Sutherland* (2000), 188 N.S.R. (2d) 112 (S.C.) [*Young*], the court was satisfied that the plaintiff paid for the disability benefits included in his severance package, and hence they were not deductible as this was the result of negotiation between the plaintiff and his employer. The employer would have unilaterally terminated the plaintiff's employment had he not agreed to the severance package.

56 Other courts have expressed the contrary view that they cannot presume that employees inevitably give up part of their compensation for employment bene-

The courts have continued to whittle away the deductibility rule in *Ratych v. Bloomer*. It is generally easy to demonstrate the required *quid pro quo* from the employee. Where it is not possible to demonstrate the *quid pro quo*, some courts have interpreted such benefits as "gratuitous" and therefore exempt under the rule in *Parry v. Cleaver*. In *Kask*[57] the plaintiff and his brother agreed that his wages from their business would continue while he waited for surgery following an accident caused by the defendant. The payment was not pursuant to any company policy, but there was an informal agreement that he would pay the company back from his damage award. After considering *Cunningham*, Donald J.A. noted how the courts are willing to presume in most cases that a salary continuance is "paid for" because such benefits are calculated as costs in the entire compensation package. Thus, he concluded:

> [w]hile Ratych survives to the extent of requiring some demonstration that the salary continuance was paid for in some way by the plaintiff *Cunningham* so lightened the burden of proof as to reverse the philosophical rationale in *Ratych* ...
>
> There will be few cases where the tortfeasor can escape paying compensation to an employee for lost time at work when the absence was covered by the employer or its insurer. Either the employer was obliged by contract to pay or to provide insurance coverage, in which case it can be easily shown that the benefit formed part of the overall compensation package, or the employer was under no obligation but continued the salary *ex gratia*, in which case the law says that the tortfeasor cannot take the benefit of another's generosity.[58]

In the result, the payment of salary was gratuitous, with a moral obligation to repay, and was held to be not deductible.

However, the principle in *Ratych* has not been universally abandoned. Not all employment benefits are "automatically" non-deductible from damage awards. Discretionary payments by an employer in the absence of any evidence that the employee paid for those benefits, and absent evidence of a right of subrogation in favour of the payor, are deductible. For example, in *Courtney v. Neville*,[59] the Nova Scotia Supreme Court held that *ex gratia* payments to the plaintiff made by

---

fits without evidence to that effect. *Cisecki v. Nipawin (Town)* (2000), 192 Sask. R. 161 (Q.B.); *Dionne v. Romanick*, [2007] B.C.J. No. 649 (S.C.).

57   Above note 15.

58   *Ibid.* at 18–19.

59   (1995), 141 N.S.R. (2d) 241 (S.C.).

the employer were to be deducted from the plaintiff's damages award for negligence against the defendant because the plaintiff was under no obligation to repay them. And in *Kozak v. Funk*,[60] the plaintiff, injured in a motor-vehicle accident, was unable to work. He received short-term disability benefits for which he contributed nothing, long-term disability for which he contributed half the premiums, and a severance package towards which he made no contribution. The court held:

> Where an employee makes any direct or indirect payment on account of wage indemnity or disability benefits received from the employer, no sum the employee receives is deductible from a damage award. Where the employee makes no contribution and the employer has no right of subrogation, all such sums the employee receives are deductible.[61]

Simply being a loyal employee is not sufficient to consitute evidence of consideration for disability benefits.[62]

b)   The Future: Alternate Views and Other Considerations

The treatment of employment benefits is not fully settled. It is important to appreciate that not all the arguments favour a rule of non-deductibility, and the concern about overcompensation is not to be entirely dismissed. The collateral source exception has been criticized as leading to overcompensation in the *Inquiry into Motor Vehicle Accident Compensation in Ontario*.[63] This report recommended that the collateral source rule be abolished in relation to *indemnity payments*. The distinction between indemnity and non-indemnity was explained as follows:

> An indemnity payment is one which is intended to compensate the insured in whole or in part for a pecuniary loss. Unemployment insurance benefits and employment disability benefits are examples of indemnity payments. A non-indemnity payment is a payment of a previously determined amount upon proof of a specified event, whether

---

60   [1996] 1 W.W.R. 79 (Sask. Q.B.).

61   *Ibid.* at 80.

62   *Young*, above note 55: a gratuitous payment of five-months' salary during an initial period of disability was deducted. There was no obligation on the part of the employer to continue paying the plaintiff's salary. The plaintiff was at the mercy of his employer, who felt that continuing to pay him was the right thing to do in the circumstances in light of his long service, but the court held this did not constitute payment for the benefit because it was not negotiated as part of his contract.

63   *Report of Inquiry into Motor Vehicle Accident Compensation in Ontario* (Toronto: Ministry of the Attorney General and the Ministry of Financial Institutions, 1988).

or not there has been pecuniary loss. Life insurance, employee retirement benefits and fixed-sum accident benefits are examples of non-indemnity payments. In principle, non-indemnity payments should not be considered in the discussion of the collateral source rule since they do not result in true overcompensation. Indemnity payments, on the other hand, can be clearly identified as duplicating an item of damage claimed from the tortfeasor and accordingly do constitute overcompensation.[64]

In Ontario, legislation has been enacted to require the deduction of wage continuation benefits to prevent double compensation.[65] Nor is the common law likely to remain static. In her dissent in *Cunningham*, McLachlin J. took the position that, ordinarily, the rule should be that collateral benefits are deductible in order to avoid double compensation. She would maintain exceptions for gifts and also for *non-indemnity* insurance and pensions.[66]

In reaching this conclusion, McLachlin J. carefully articulated several policy grounds for the deductibility principle. First, despite the fact that the plaintiff may have paid for the insurance, the practical reality is that the insurance benefits are intended to compensate for the loss suffered, and a failure to deduct them compensates the plaintiff twice for the same loss. Second, the deduction of such benefits is consistent with other legal principles such as mitigation and the principle of "avoided loss." As McLachlin J. states,

> The law has consistently refused to compensate a plaintiff because he or she took precautions which minimized the loss flowing from the negligent act. The defendant takes the plaintiff as the defendant finds the plaintiff. Sometimes this increases the damages a defendant must pay, as in the case of what the law calls the "thin-skulled" plaintiff. Sometimes it decreases the damages the defendant must pay. The point is this: the fact that the plaintiff is more or less vulner-

---

64   *Ibid.*, vol. 1 at 429.

65   Section 267(1)(c) of the *Insurance Act*, R.S.O. 1990, c. I.8 provides that damages awarded in automobile accidents shall be reduced by "all payments that the person has received or that were or are available for loss of income under the laws of any such jurisdiction or under an income continuation benefit plan and by the present value of any such payments to which the person is entitled."

66   An indemnity payment is one intended to compensate for a specific loss. Examples include unemployment insurance and disability benefits. A non-indemnity payment is one that is paid upon the happening of an event but does not require proof of a loss. Examples include retirement benefits, fixed-sum accident benefits, and life insurance that provides a fixed amount on the death of the policy holder without proof of loss.

able and hence suffers greater or lesser damages as a consequence of the defendant's negligence will not be reflected in the actual award of damages. The plaintiff will be compensated to the full extent of the loss, and no more, regardless of the measure of the plaintiff's personal vulnerability.[67]

McLachlin J. also dismissed the argument that deductibility undermines the deterrence objective of tort. There is, she says, little empirical data to support the view that tort law plays a significant role in deterring accidents. The fact that most liability cases involve large insurers means that individual defendants do not directly feel the consequences of a tort judgment (except perhaps through higher premiums). Nor does justice require non-deductibility. It is not generally the function of tort law to punish tortfeasors. Instead, the goal is to achieve corrective justice by having defendants restore losses suffered by plaintiffs. Where the plaintiff is fully compensated by insurance, there is no loss to be restored. The argument that justice requires the defendant to pay when there is no real loss, rests, in fact, upon unacknowledged punitive motives.

McLachlin J. also rejects the social inequality argument. While Cory J. stated that the problem with *Ratych* is that it favours "top management and professionals" who can afford to purchase private insurance, and discriminates against those who obtain benefits through collective bargaining, McLachlin J. denies that there is any evidence that the rule is, in fact, socially regressive in this way. First, it will be recalled, she is of the view that even privately obtained indemnity insurance should, in fact, be deducted. Moreover, she denies that there is any empirical basis for the assumption that the rule is socially regressive. Many self-employed persons who have to purchase private insurance may earn less, or pay more for that insurance, than employees who obtain their benefits as part of their overall wage packet. She asks, "Is the self-employed carpenter with private insurance in a better position than a deputy minister with employment sickness and disability plans? Clearly not. In the absence of further proof, the case that deduction of wage benefits is socially regressive is not made out."[68]

Finally, McLachlin J. argues that a general regime of deductibility would provide much greater certainty in the law than the majority's "open textured" and vague approach:

---

67 *Cunningham*, above note 4 at 382.
68 *Ibid.* at 386.

Lack of certainty as to when a deduction for a benefit should be made adds to the complexity of settlement negotiations and increases the number of cases which must be litigated. This in turn adds to the burden on the courts, delays resolution of the plaintiff's suit, and increases the cost to the general public. The desirability of a coherent, consistent rule which can be applied with certainty favours adhering as closely as possible to the fundamental principle of restorative, compensatory damages for actual loss suffered.[69]

c) Wrongful Dismissal Cases

The treatment of disability and wage continuation benefits in wrongful dismissal cases differs somewhat from tort cases because the plaintiff and defendant are not strangers. Thus, the court can look to their contractual intention to determine whether disability payments should be deducted.

The issue arises when employees are wrongfully dismissed during a period in which they are receiving disability payments (under workers' compensation or an employer's plan). Had they been working at the time, they would be entitled to their lost wages during the notice period. The question is whether that entitlement should remain unaffected by the fact that they are receiving wage replacement from another source during that period. Until recently, the caselaw has been conflicting. One line of cases likened disability payments to private insurance and exempted them from deductibility—reasoning that the employee in such a situation had entered into two separate contracts (one for insurance and one for reasonable notice of termination) and was entitled to both sets of benefits.[70] The other line of cases emphasized the problem of double recovery, as well as the anomaly that if, instead of receiving disability payments, the plaintiff found alternate employment, the wage from that new employment would be deducted from the wage-loss claim (as mitigation).[71]

The Supreme Court of Canada sought to provide a general rule for when such benefits are to be taken into account when assessing damages for wrongful dismissal. The issue before the Court in *Sylvester v. British Columbia*[72] was whether disability payments received by an employee during the notice period, from a plan established and funded solely by the employer, should be deducted from the damage award.

---

69   *Ibid.* at 388.
70   *McKay v. Camco Inc.* (1986), 53 O.R. (2d) 257 (C.A.).
71   *Salmi v. Greyfriar Developments Ltd.* (1985), 58 A.R. 364 (C.A.) [*Salmi*].
72   [1997] 2 S.C.R. 315.

The Court held that the deductibility of such benefits depended on the intention of the parties and that in this case it was not their intention that the plaintiff receive both disability and damages for wrongful dismissal. As to any presumption to be applied where such intention is not expressly stated, the Court held:

> The parties to an employment contract can obviously agree that the employee is to receive both disability benefits and damages for wrongful dismissal. There may also be cases in which this intention can be inferred. However, absent an intention by the parties to provide otherwise, an employee who is dismissed while not working but receiving disability benefits and an employee who is dismissed while working should be treated equally.[73]

An indication of the parties' intention not to have disability benefits deducted from damages for wrongful dismissal could be where the employee paid for the benefit, broadly defined. In *McNamara v. Alexander Centre Industries Ltd.*,[74] there was nothing in the employment contract to suggest whether the parties intended deductibility or non-deductibility of disability benefits from damages for wrongful dismissal. The court also assumed that the parties had not turned their minds to this issue when they negotiated the employment contract twenty-four years earlier. However, following *Sylvester*, the court proceeded to infer the intention of the parties from the circumstances, and found that a reasonable employer and employee considering the matter at the time of contract would have concluded in favour of non-deductibility of disability benefits from salary during the notice period. The court emphasized this position in *Sills v. Children's Aid Society of Belleville (City)*[75] (released the same day as *McNamara*), noting that, where an employee has somehow paid for the benefits, it is reasonable to infer that the parties intended the employee to be entitled to those benefits and salary for wrongful dismissal during the notice period. Simons J.A. noted:

> Absent an express provision precluding double recovery, in my view, the principles enunciated in *Cunningham* assist in determining whether an intention that there would be double recovery in the event of a wrongful dismissal can be inferred. I consider it reasonable to assume that an employee would not willingly negotiate and pay for a benefit that would allow her employer to avoid responsibility for a wrongful act. I consider it reasonable to infer that parties would

---

73   *Ibid.* at 324.
74   (2001), 53 O.R. (3d) 481 (C.A.) [*McNamara*].
75   (2001), 53 O.R. (3d) 577 (C.A.) [*Sills*].

agree that an employee should retain disability benefits in addition to damages for wrongful dismissal where the employee has effectively paid for the benefits in question.

The same reasoning applies to the suggestion in *Sylvester* that a disabled employee who receives adequate notice should not be treated differently [from] a disabled employee who is wrongfully dismissed—an employer should not be relieved of the obligation to pay damages for a wrongful act because of a benefit plan provided by the employee. Moreover, the concern expressed in *Sylvester*, that disabled employees who are wrongfully dismissed be treated the same as working employees who are wrongfully dismissed, simply does not arise where the employee has paid for the plan that provides a disability income.[76]

A contrary view was expressed in *Weber v. Capital Industrial Sales & Service Ltd.*,[77] where the court stated that parties would not reasonably contemplate that a dismissed employee should keep both disability benefits and salary for the notice period, where the benefits are an integral part of the employment arrangement.

Thus, disability benefits will generally be deducted from awards for lost wages in wrongful dismissal cases. There will, however, be exceptions. In *Sills*,[78] the plaintiff was wrongfully dismissed. At the time of the dismissal and subsequently, she was on disability leave and receiving her salary. The wages received were not deducted from the damages awarded, essentially on the basis of the private insurance exception. The court held that the amounts received by the plaintiff from the sick-leave bank should not be deducted because the plaintiff earned these as part of her compensation and as part of the trade-off in arriving at benefits and salaries. Similarly, the amount received by the plaintiff from the group disability insurance should not be deducted because it was provided by a private insurance plan to which the employee contributed. Further, the fact that the insurer had a right of subrogation under the policy was another indication that the benefits recovered by the plaintiff were not deductible from her claim for damages.

---

76 *Ibid.* at paras. 45–46. See also *Zorn-Smith v. Bank of Montreal* (2003), 31 C.C.E.L. (3d) 267 (Ont. S.C.J.) [*Zorn-Smith*]. In *Dowling v. TNT Logistics North America*, [2005] O.J. No. 2091 (S.C.J.) [*Dowling*], the court emphasized this point, and further noted that the usual provision in disability insurance contracts that benefits will be reduced if the employee earns money elsewhere cannot be interpreted to include long-term disability benefits.

77 (2001), 295 A.R. 365 (Prov. Ct.).

78 *Sills*, above note 75. See also *Kaiser v. Dural* (2002), 205 N.S.R. (2d) 194 (C.A.); *Dowling*, above note 76.

Some courts have held that no issue of double recovery arises where the employee "paid" for benefits and payments are made by a third-party insurer whereas salary is provided by the employer. The employee in such cases is entitled to payments from both sources and neither payor will be liable for payments in excess of its individual obligation. Like all employment benefits, direct contributions to the private insurance plan are not required so long as there is some evidence of consideration for the benefit as part of the employee's overall compensation package. On the other hand, double recovery remains a valid concern where both benefits and salary come from the same source, the employer.[79] As well, where the plan came into existence after the plaintiff was hired, one court has concluded that there was no evidence of contribution for the benefit as the disability plan was not a term of the plaintiff's contract. In such circumstances, the court said it had no choice but to apply the general rule of deductibility as stated in *Sylvester*.[80] The employee's contribution to the plan, even if 100 percent, may not necessarily be determinative of the issue of deductibility. Ultimately, it depends on the intention of the parties and the nature of the plan. Mandatory disability insurance plans that are integrated into the employment contract may not be perceived as akin to private insurance but rather as substitute salary/wages and, hence, benefits may be deductible from damages for wrongful dismissal.[81]

6) Pensions

Pensions, both private and public, are generally not deductible on the ground that they are paid for and should be treated in the same man-

---

79 *McNamara*, above note 74. See also *Dowling, ibid.*; *Zorn-Smith*, above note 76 at paras. 153 and 159 (in relation to short-term benefits). Courts may avoid the single-source concern and the resulting deductibility of benefits by reckoning the notice period after the end of the plaintiff's receipt of benefits (see *Rinaldo v. Royal Ontario Museum* (2004), 37 C.C.E.L. (3d) 1 (Ont. S.C.J.)) or by focusing on the intention of the parties as was done in *Zorn-Smith*.

80 *Kolaczynski v. Benz Sewing Machines Lts. (c.o.b. B&W Sewing Machine Co.)*, [2002] O.J. No. 1117 (S.C.J.). Presumably, the situation would be different where employees have subsequently bargained with the employer and the issue of disability benefits has been part of the negotiations.

81 Some courts have ruled in favour of the deductibility of disability benefits even where employees contributed to the plan, seemingly based on the presumed intention of the parties not to permit "double recovery." See *Reid v. Specialty Motor Cars (1970) Ltd.*, 2000 BCSC 247; *Martin v. Children's House Child Care Society*, 2006 ABQB 937; *Weber v. Capital Industrial Sales and Services Ltd.* (2001), 295 A.R. 365 (Prov. Ct.).

ner as insurance. The authorities for this proposition are the Supreme Court of Canada decisions in *Gill*[82] and *Trizec*.[83] In *Gill*, the Court held that "pensions payable under the Canada Pension Plan are so much of the same nature as contracts of insurance that they also should be excluded from consideration when assessing damages."[84] In *Trizec*, the Court found that a private company pension plan that the appellant contributed to derived from the appellant's contract of employment and that the payments made pursuant to it were akin to payments under a private insurance policy.

There is some dispute about whether the rule regarding pensions has been affected by *Ratych* and *Cunningham*. The British Columbia Supreme Court in *Burgess v. Lau*[85] held that the pension benefits of the plaintiff RCMP officer injured in a motor-vehicle accident should be deducted from an award of damages for lost wages. The court followed the principle against double recovery other than those arising from private insurance, from *Cunningham v. Wheeler*, stating:

> The purpose in contributing to a pension then is so the pension holder will be receiving income when he is no longer receiving wages from work. The expectation is not to be better off in the case of an accident but to have income when he retires or at a certain age and is no longer earning a wage from his employer. The plaintiff should be put in the same position he would have been if he were able to work and be retired at the same time. Accordingly, the plaintiff does not have the same type of wisdom which Cory J. refers to in his judgment [in *Cunningham*], that is, in paying into his pension he was not "making provision for the continuation of some income in the case of a disabling injury or illness," he was planning his retirement from employment.[86]

The Ontario Court of Appeal has taken a different view. In *Cugliari v. White*,[87] Canada Pension disability benefits were held to be akin to "paid for" private insurance and not deductible. The British Columbia Court of Appeal has also taken the same position with respect to superannuation pensions because these benefits "are of the same character

82   Above note 44.
83   Above note 44.
84   Above note 44 at 655.
85   [1996] B.C.J. No. 211 (S.C.).
86   *Ibid.* at para. 19.
87   (1996), 31 O.R. (3d) 42 (Div. Ct.), aff'd (1998), 38 O.R. (3d) 641 (C.A.). See also *Fraser v. Hunter Estate* (2000), 184 N.S.R. (2d) 217 (C.A.).

as CPP disability benefits and other pension payments, which have consistently been held to be non-deductible from tort damages."[88]

7) [Un]Employment Insurance Benefits

Employment insurance payments also raise the collateral benefit problem in both tort and contract cases (e.g., wrongful dismissal). Historically, they have not been deductible from damage awards. In *Jack Cewe Ltd. v. Jorgenson*,[89] the Supreme Court of Canada held that unemployment payments would not be taken into account in reducing a wage-loss claim for wrongful dismissal:

> The payment of unemployment insurance contributions by the employer was an obligation incurred by reason of respondent's employment, therefore, to the extent that the payment of those contributions resulted in the provision of unemployment benefits, these are a consequence of the contract of employment and, consequently, cannot be deducted from damages for wrongful dismissal. The situation is similar to contributory pension benefits which this Court recently decided [*in Trizec Equities Ltd. v. Guy*] should not be deducted in assessing compensation for loss of earnings.[90]

Even after *Ratych*, unemployment insurance payments have generally been held to be non-deductible by bringing them within the insurance exception. Since the unemployment insurance premium is paid in part by the employee, it may be assimilated to contributory insurance. Thus, in most provinces, benefits are not deductible from tort awards.[91]

However, it may be argued that a failure to deduct these benefits permits double compensation of the plaintiff and offends the compensation principle. This view has been expressed in *Boertien v. Carter*,[92] by Jenkins J.:

> Unemployment insurance benefits are realistically characterized as an employment supplement which has become a key component of

---

88   *Sulz v. British Columbia (Minister of Public Safety and Solicitor General)* (2006), 60 B.C.L.R. (4th) 43 (C.A.).
89   [1980] 1 S.C.R. 812.
90   *Ibid.* at 818.
91   *McDonald v. Nguyen* (1991), 138 A.R. 81 (Q.B.); *Regehr v. Nagle* (1993), 138 A.R. 229 (Q.B.); *Guthmiller v. Krahn* (2000), 268 A.R. 369 (Q.B.); *Khairati v. Prasad*, [2002] B.C.J. No. 513 (S.C.) [*Khairati*]; *Graham v. Lee*, [2004] B.C.J. No. 2052 (S.C.); *Briffett v. Gander and District Hospital Board* (1996), 137 Nfld. & P.E.I.R. 271 (Nfld. C.A.); *Webb v. Exide Electronics Ltd.* (1999), 177 N.S.R. (2d) 147 (C.A.).
92   (1995), 135 Nfld. & P.E.I.R. 91 (P.E.I.T.D.).

personal income safety net in a social welfare state.... Benefits have no meaningful relationship to premiums or to employment income, and utilization is seasonal and perennial. The program is statutory and compulsory, and not really a plan of any sort made between the employer and the employee.... On the remaining issue of whether on general grounds of legal principle deductibility is warranted, in my view, deductibility advances fundamental principles of compensation in tort law, as expressed by the Supreme Court of Canada. *Ratych v. Bloomer* sets out a general rule which requires wage benefits paid under an employment scheme to be brought into account, This does not specifically address unemployment insurance benefits. However, U.I. benefits fall within both the letter and the spirit of the rule.[93]

In Ontario, the *Insurance Act*[94] has replaced the common law as to the deductibility of some collateral benefits, and it has been interpreted to require the deduction of employment insurance benefits from damages awarded in an action pertaining to an automobile accident. In British Columbia, a person eligible for benefits under the *Employment Insurance Act* (Canada) is not entitled to benefits for injuries under the *Insurance (Vehicle) Act*, except where the amount under the latter exceeds the entitlement under the *Employment Insurance Act*.[95] Several other provinces have also moved to a rule of deductibility in personal injury cases.[96] In addition, the *Employment Insurance Act* has been amended to require the beneficiary to pay over to the fund the amounts received.[97] In some cases, courts have

---

93   *Ibid.* at 119. In *Khairati,* above note 91 at para. 313, Coultas J. said that *Boertien* should be restricted to its facts as the plaintiff in that case was a seasonal worker and EI benefits were an integral part of his income. Hence, the case should not be taken to favour a general principle of deductibility of EI benefits from damage awards.

94   Above note 65. See *Rutherford v. Niekrawietz* (1996), 38 C.C.L.I. (2d) 304 (Ont. Ct. Gen. Div.); *Estey v. Hinds* (1997), 25 O.T.C. 37 (Gen. Div.).

95   *Revised Regulation* (1984) under the *Insurance (Motor Vehicle) Act*, B.C. Reg. 447/83, s. 83. In *Kerpan v. Insurance Corp. of British Columbia*, [2006] B.C.J. No. 3079 (S.C.), the parties agreed that employment insurance benefits that the plaintiff had received were deductible pursuant to Regulation 447/83.

96   *Daley v. Alexander* (1998), 166 Sask. R. 84 (Q.B.), aff'd (1999), 180 Sask. R. 303 (C.A.) [*Daley*]; *Charters v. Hudson*, 2001 NBQB 148, aff'd (2002), 247 N.B.R. (2d) 280 (C.A.).

97   *Employment Insurance Act*, S.C. 1996, c. 23, s. 45, return of benefits by claimant:

If a claimant receives benefits for a period and, under a labour arbitration award or court judgment, or for any other reason, an employer, a trustee in bankruptcy or any other person subsequently becomes liable to pay earnings, including damages for wrongful dismissal or proceeds realized from the property of a bankrupt, to the claimant for the same period and pays the earnings,

ordered the defendants to pay over to the fund directly the amount of employment insurance benefits the plaintiff had received prior to trial.[98]

8) Workers' Compensation Benefits

The question of the deductibility of workers' compensation benefits arises most often in wrongful dismissal cases (when the employee who is receiving workers' compensation because of an injury is wrongly dismissed). It rarely arises in tort law because the legislation restricts most causes of action in tort for personal injury suffered on the job (and the legislation provides subrogation rights for any recovery where the employee is able to establish a cause of action in tort in respect of an injury for which benefits have been received).[99]

The prevailing view in most provinces is that workers' compensation benefits will be deducted from awards for both personal injury and wrongful dismissal. While the caselaw is conflicting,[100] most courts have rejected the private insurance analogy[101] and have held that workers' compensation provides an indemnity for lost wages, thus cancelling any loss.[102] Given the history of workers' compensation, courts tend to view deductibility as more consistent with its policy. Workers gave up their common law rights of action against employers in a trade-off for no-fault accident compensation benefits paid for by levies on employers. In light of this, several courts have concluded that

> [t]he very purpose of workers' compensation benefits attests to the incompatibility of their non-deductibility from damages for wrongful dismissal. Not to do so would be tantamount to circumventing the entire raison d'être of the system and impose liability for damages which has been foregone in the trade-off in which the worker's right of action was surrendered. It would serve to circumvent the no fault insurance characteristic inherent in the concept of workers' compensation.[103]

---

the claimant shall pay to the Receiver General as repayment of an overpayment of benefits an amount equal to the benefits that would not have been paid if the earnings had been paid or payable at the time the benefits were paid.

98 *Rice v. Tillsonburg & District Multi-Service Centre* (1996), 26 C.C.E.L. (2d) 289 (Ont. Small Cl. Ct.).

99 *Workers Compensation Act*, R.S.B.C. 1996, c. 492. s. 10(6).

100 No deduction was made in *Fleming v. Safety Kleen Canada Inc.* (1996), 20 C.C.E.L. (2d) 140 (Ont. Ct. Gen. Div.).

101 *Pastachak v. Bienfait (Town)* (1996), 143 Sask. R. 139 (Q.B.).

102 *Salmi*, above note 71.

103 *White v. F.W. Woolworth Co.* (1996), 139 Nfld. & P.E.I.R. 324 at 347 (Nfld. C.A), leave to appeal to S.C.C. refused (1997), 161 Nfld. & P.E.I.R. 90 (note); followed

9) Welfare Benefits

On occasion, the plaintiff will receive welfare benefits while awaiting trial in the context of personal injury or wrongful dismissal. In *Boarelli v. Flannigan*,[104] the Ontario Court of Appeal held that these benefits were akin to charity or gifts and thus should not be deducted. Dubin J.A. stated that welfare payments are "benefits provided to persons in need, independent of any cause of action such person may have or assert, and as a benefit provided to him not in diminution of any claim the injured person may have for damages."[105] Moreover, as the court pointed out, if the legislature is concerned about overcompensation, it is able to include a right of subrogation in the statute.

> There is no difference in principle between benefits received under social welfare legislation and those received by way of private or public benevolence. The injured party has received a reward as a result of the injury and it is no concern of the defendant. In many statutes a right of subrogation is established, the loss is borne by the tortfeasor and the question of overlapping compensation is thereby avoided. It is for the appropriate legislative authority to determine whether the right of subrogation should be included in those statutes which are now silent in this respect.[106]

The law on welfare benefits became uncertain, particularly after the decisions in *Ratych* and *Cunningham*. Some courts continued to follow *Boarelli*, holding that welfare benefits have replaced private benevolence and charity in the modern state and should be exempted from deductibility on the basis of the private-charity exception.[107] However, other courts expressed concern that the plaintiff is doubly compensated and have suggested that it was open to courts to reconsider the issue. In *M.(M.) v. F.(R.)* the British Columbia Court of Appeal held that welfare benefits should be deducted from an award.[108] It held that *Ratych*[109] had

---

in *Dowsley Estate v. Viceroy Fluid Power International Inc.* (1997), 34 O.R. (3d) 57 (C.A.). See also *Enwin Utilities v. I.B.E.W., Local 636* (2004), 130 L.A.C. (4th) 179 (Ont. Arbitration Board); *Antonacci v. Great Atlantic & Pacific Co. of Canada* (2000), 48 C.C.E.L. (2d) 294 (Ont. C.A.); *Merk v. I.A.B.S.O.I., Local 771* (2006), 284 Sask. R. 124 (Q.B.), aff'd 2007 SKCA 6.

104 [1973] 3 O.R. 69 (C.A.) [*Boarelli*].
105 *Ibid.* at 73.
106 *Ibid.* at 69.
107 *Daley*, above note 96.
108 (1997), 101 B.C.A.C. 97 (C.A.).
109 Above note 1.

implicitly overruled *Boarelli*.[110] Essentially, the court took the view that, in principle, wage replacement benefits, including welfare, should be deductible unless they can be brought within the "insurance exception" (paid-for benefits) or the "charitable gift exception." Welfare benefits, the court held, are neither, and "were they not to be deducted, that would result in double recovery to the extent of those payments."[111] Where the amount of social assistance was not deducted from a damages award, the court sometimes included an order for the plaintiff to reimburse the collateral source.[112]

In *M.B. v. British Columbia*,[113] the British Columbia Court of Appeal refused to follow *M.(M.)* and *Jones*. The court held that welfare benefits should not be deductible from damages for past income loss because this is a collateral matter between the plaintiff and the government, and should not influence the assessment of damages. However, the Supreme Court of Canada favoured deductibility of welfare benefits to avoid double recovery.[114] The Court rejected the plaintiff's argument that, because social assistance benefits are based on need, they are akin to charity, and therefore must fall within the charitable gift exemption. The Court reasoned that although charitable gifts and social assistance benefits share a common purpose—to relieve need—the rationales for charitable gifts are conceptually different; namely (1) the possible ramifications of deductibility (that it will discourage charity); and (2) the difficulties of assessing the monetary value of benefits in kind. Neither of these issues arises in relation to social assistance benefits; benefits are provided by the government from general tax revenues as an entitlement, and there is no difficulty in ascertaining the monetary value of benefits. Social assistance benefits are, in fact, income replacement intended to meet recipients' basic needs. Entitlement to benefits depends on meeting certain criteria so there is no concern about deductibility discouraging future availability of assistance.

As well, the Court rejected a policy-based exception of non-deductibility for social assistance as being contrary to public policy. Among other things, the Court noted that, since benefits are publicly funded, a rule of non-deductibility would mean that taxpayers will pay for the same loss twice; first through the social safety net and then through

---

110 Above note 104.

111 Above note 108.

112 *Jones v. Trudel*, [1998] B.C.J. No. 1748 (S.C.), aff'd (2000), 74 B.C.L.R. (3d) 263 (C.A.).

113 (2002), 99 B.C.L.R. (3d) 256 (C.A.).

114 *M.B.*, above note 12; followed in *H.L. v. Canada (Attorney General)*, [2005] 1 S.C.R. 401.

a tort award (since taxpayers also bear general increases in insurance costs).[115] In addition to fairness, the rule of non-deductibility was also rejected on the ground of efficiency, as such a rule might force legislatures to institute recoupment schemes to recover past benefits from tort damages. Such schemes are inefficient loss-distribution mechanisms compared to a simple rule of deductibility. Further, there is both academic and judicial support for deductibility in Canada and elsewhere.

Deductibility of welfare benefits is intended to prevent the plaintiff from obtaining a windfall for being a tort victim, but ignores the potential benefit to the defendant who is subsidized by taxpayers. This was not an issue in *M.B.* and *H.L.*, as the government was both the source of the benefits and the defendant. However, where the defendant is a private entity, deductibility will not necessarily benefit the public. The potential benefit to private entities can be avoided through the establishment of repayment schemes by governments, but this raises the same efficiency concerns as the Supreme Court identified in *M.B.* Alternatively, plaintiffs can be made to undertake to repay the government, as was done in *Jones*.[116]

10) Health Insurance Benefits

Provincial health insurance programs provide basic medical services free of charge. In addition, there are various programs that provide benefits in kind in the form of extended-care facilities, home assistance, and the like. Each province has a different regime regarding the treatment of health benefits because the rules regarding subrogation vary across the country.

In some provinces (such as Ontario and Alberta) the health-care fund has subrogation rights. In these provinces, therefore, health-care benefits are not deducted from awards. They are included in the claim and paid over to the fund. In provinces where the health insurer has no right of subrogation, health benefits are generally deducted from the plaintiff's claim—since the claim would be for costs or losses that

---

115 This is based on the fact that tort damages are usually satisfied with insurance funds, which are considered quasi–public because members of the public contribute to these funds through insurance premiums and the purchase of goods and services.

116 For a discussion of some of the potential problems with the deductibility of welfare benefits, see E. Adjin-Tettey, "Deducting Past Welfare Benefits May Unfairly Impact Aboriginal Claimants" *The Lawyers Weekly* (24 June 2005).

were never incurred by the plaintiff.[117] One example is the decision of the British Columbia Court of Appeal in *Wipfli v. Britten*.[118] The infant plaintiff was injured by the negligence of the defendant doctor. The cost of institutional care necessitated by the injury was provided under the British Columbia *Hospital Insurance Act*. The plaintiff's claim for damages did not include a claim for the cost of care in the six years prior to trial (which had been fully paid under the Act), but it did include a claim for future care. The Court of Appeal denied this claim:

> [T]he damages award for the cost of that [future] care should not have included amounts that would not be incurred by the plaintiff due to the British Columbia *Hospital Insurance Act*. That Act provides universal subsidies with no premiums or costs payable by the beneficiaries and given its legislative history and government policy concerning provision of free hospital care, it was inconceivable that the scheme would ever be substantially modified. The only possible cost to the plaintiff for institutional care was $7.50 per day pursuant to s. 5(4) of the Act.[119]

A similar approach was taken by the Manitoba Court of Appeal in *Tronrud v. French*,[120] where the cost of medical equipment needed by the plaintiff as a result of injuries attributable to the defendant's negligence was deducted from the damages award because the items "[were] supplied and maintained by the Government without charge to the plaintiff."[121] Defendants have also been relieved of care costs where there are social programs that injured plaintiffs can rely on for assistance.[122]

These cases appear to be in conflict with the line of authorities holding that other public benefits are non-deductible. The Manitoba Court of Appeal held in *McLeod v. Palardy*[123] that damages should, in fact, be awarded to the plaintiff for the cost of future home-care as-

---

117 *Schaeffer v. Mish*, [1950] 4 D.L.R. 648 (Sask. C.A.); followed in *Flaherty v. Hughes*, [1952] 4 D.L.R. 43 at 51 (B.C.C.A.). See also *Curtis v. Mayne* (1960), 24 D.L.R. (2d) 506 (Nfld. S.C.); *Fortus v. Allegretti* (1994), 156 A.R. 337 (Q.B.); *Stein v. Sandwich West (Township)* (1995), 77 O.A.C. 40 (C.A.) [*Stein*].

118 (1984), 56 B.C.L.R. 273 (C.A.) [*Wipfli*]; followed in *Semenoff v. Kokan* (1991), 59 B.C.L.R. (2d) 195 (C.A.).

119 *Wipfli*, *ibid.* at 274.

120 (1991), 75 Man. R. (2d) 1 (C.A.).

121 *Ibid.* at 6.

122 See *Krangle (Guardian ad litem of) v. Brisco*, [2002] 1 S.C.R. 205 [*Krangle*]; *Boren v. Vancouver Resource Society for The Physically Disabled*, 2003 BCCA 388 [*Boren*].

123 (1981), 124 D.L.R. (3d) 506 (Man. C.A.).

sistance even though such care was available from the Department of Health without charge. Huband J.A. stated:

> In my view the learned trial Judge was right to follow the decision in the *Boarelli* case. Indeed, the plaintiff's claim, in the instant case, is a stronger one than the plaintiff's in *Boarelli v. Flannigan*. In that case the welfare payments had been received by the plaintiff and there could be no speculation as to amount. In the present case, whether and for how long the plaintiff would qualify under a Government home care programme is speculative. Moreover, the criteria for determining who qualifies for assistance is subject to both legislative and administrative change.[124]

While these cases appear to be consistent with the rule against double recovery, they may not necessarily be in the best interest of plaintiffs or society—especially regarding the deductibility of *future* anticipated benefits. The point regarding the uncertain nature of the availability and continuation of public benefits merits consideration. Notwithstanding the judicial optimism about the permanence of such programs voiced in *Wipfli* and *Krangle*, it seems reasonable for the courts to take into account the likelihood of existing public health service plans being maintained at their current levels over the time period when a plaintiff may need to rely on them, particularly where programs are not statutorily guaranteed but rather discretionary. If there is a real chance that services provided today will not be available tomorrow, the award for future-care costs should reflect this possibility, at least by way of contingency allowance.[125] As well, even where the benefit is expected to continue into the future, some award for future-care costs will still be necessary where the plaintiff might require more care than is available under the publicly funded program.[126]

Jacobsen v. Nike Canada Ltd.[127] considered the question of the effect of less certain government subsidies on a personal injury award; in this

---

124 *Ibid.* at 526–27.

125 *Krangle,* above note 122. The cost of future care was awarded for the period until the plaintiff turned nineteen, after which time he was expected to move into a publicly funded group home. His parents were concerned about their legal obligation to support him if that program were no longer available or proved insufficient for his needs. The Supreme Court was confident that, as a universal benefit, the program would continue to be available to the plaintiff but, in any event, allowed a contingency award of 5 percent of his future-care cost for the possibility that the benefit would not be fully available in the future.

126 *Boren*, above note 122.

127 (1996), 19 B.C.L.R. (3d) 63 (S.C.).

case, the precise issue was whether subsidized home care should be taken into account in reducing a damage award to a catastrophically injured plaintiff. The case differed from *Wipfli* because the benefits at issue were not universal, but income-based, and there was no evidence that they would always be forthcoming to the plaintiff. Indeed, given that the plaintiff would have income from the award, it appeared likely that he might lose the subsidy and would have to pay for this care. For these reasons, the court refused to take the benefits into account. In reaching this conclusion, Levine J. noted that the decision in *Wipfli* to deduct health-care benefits was based on judicially expressed confidence that hospital care and services in British Columbia would always be available and would never change. Given the significant pressure under which the health-care system finds itself currently, the same confidence could not be expressed about the benefits in the present case.

> It is common knowledge in the community, and I take judicial notice of the fact that in 1996, 12 years after *Wipfli* was decided, the health care system in Canada is under significant financial pressure. Governments at all levels are seeking ways to increase their revenues and reduce their costs. It is certainly conceivable that subsidized health care services such as those now available to the plaintiff will not be available in the future as they have been in the past.
>
> I do not consider that the principles on which *Wipfli* and *Semenoff* were decided are generally applicable to all government subsidies for health care costs. In the absence of evidence that the subsidy provided for long term care is subject to the same legislative safeguards and universality as was the case with the medical and hospital costs at issue in those cases, I am of the view the plaintiff would not be adequately compensated for the cost of his future care if the award were reduced because a subsidy may be available.[128]

As well, no reduction in future-care costs is warranted where the benefit in question is not universally available, has limited funding, and is intended to be a last resort. In *Fullerton (Guardian ad litem of) v. Delair*,[129] the court distinguished *Krangle*, noting that the program that is expected to benefit the plaintiff in this case is discretionary and subject to competing budgetary constraints. As well, the program is needs-based and intended as a relief for those not entitled to tort damages, or awaiting the outcome of litigation. There is usually a long

---

128 *Ibid.* at 103–4. The uncertainty of continued program funding was also mentioned as a factor against deductibility in *Stein*, above note 117.
129 (2006), 55 B.C.L.R. (4th) 252 (C.A.).

waiting list for the program, so making the tortfeasors responsible for the plaintiff's loss rather than expecting him to rely on the publicly funded program ensures that families on the waiting list who have no tort claim or cannot afford the necessary care can access the program.

C. CONCLUSION

The categorical approach to collateral benefits outlined above will provide guidance in most cases. However, in the case of new forms of employment benefits, private and public insurance, and benefits in kind, the courts will continue to decide the issue on a case-by-case basis and according to the weight of the underlying policy considerations. The issue of collateral benefits raises a conflict between two basic concerns. On the one hand, the courts do not generally seek to punish civil defendants and are reluctant to confer windfalls upon plaintiffs. These considerations weigh in favour of deducting benefits received by the plaintiff. On the other hand, courts are reluctant to subsidize wrongdoing and undermine the deterrence function of the law. In balancing these two competing principles, the following considerations will be brought to bear:

- First, in the case of future benefits that the plaintiff has not yet received, the courts will be reluctant to make any deduction if there is any risk that the benefit will not be forthcoming. Where there is uncertainty about the future, the courts should lean against making a deduction on the ground that a risk of undercompensating the plaintiff is graver than a risk of overcompensation.
- The second consideration is whether there will be adverse social effects if the benefit is deducted. For example, in situations where there is a strong deterrence role to be played by the law of tort, this may weigh against a deduction. On the other hand, in situations where losses are largely spread through insurance, a deduction may be more appropriate. Another example of adverse social effects is the approach taken to benevolent contributions (charity, gifts, services in kind from family members). To deduct the value of such contributions from the damages award will demoralize third parties and sap any incentive to behave altruistically (since the real beneficiary is the tortfeasor). Courts consistently mention such adverse effects as a reason for making no deduction.
- A third consideration is whether there is any right of subrogation by statute, by contract, or in equity. If there is a right of subrogation

in the donor of the benefit, this will eliminate any concern about double compensation of the plaintiff, and the collateral benefit will not be deducted from the award. Along these same lines, courts will be influenced by the existence of a legal or moral obligation upon the plaintiff to repay the donor, especially where this moral obligation can be enforced by way of restitution or a constructive trust. If the plaintiff has an obligation to repay the benefit from an award, or if it can be impressed with a trust, there will be no double compensation.

- Fourth, where the benefit is part of a public benefits scheme (welfare, workers' compensation, medicare) to which the plaintiff has not paid a premium, the court may be more inclined to deduct the award from damages. Courts often reason that it is not generally the intent of such schemes that beneficiaries be doubly compensated.
- Where the benefit can be analogized to private insurance, for which there has been a payment by the plaintiff, or some other *quid pro quo*, or a loss of those benefits in respect of future needs (e.g., sick days), the benefit will not be taken into account. The tortfeasor should not be given credit for the plaintiff's prudence and sacrifice.
- A final consideration is the question whether the benefit is a true indemnity for the plaintiff's loss, or more in the nature of a contractual obligation triggered by the occurrence of a contingency, or a coincidental payment. If the payment is a true indemnity (intended to compensate a loss and calculated by the amount of the loss), it is more likely to be taken into account since it does in fact cancel the plaintiff's loss. If the payment is a non-indemnity payment, then it is not directly related to the loss suffered by the plaintiff and does not lead to overcompensation.

CHAPTER 14

JUDICIAL OVERSIGHT OF REMEDY STIPULATION

A. INTRODUCTION

1) Remedy Stipulation and Liquidated Damages

It is not uncommon, in both tort and contract cases, to find that the parties have sought in advance to specify an amount of damages for breach of duty. Exclusion clauses and limitation clauses contained in written agreements and in posted notices frequently seek to limit both liability and the amount of damages that may be claimed for tort or breach of contract. These clauses are inserted for the benefit of the breaching party. Conversely, contracts sometimes contain "liquidated damages" provisions that specify a fixed amount of damages for breach and are generally included for the benefit of the plaintiff. Other clauses, such as "acceleration clauses" and clauses providing for forfeitures of deposits, also serve to stipulate the remedy. The essential question in any case is whether or not the courts will enforce the stipulated remedy at the suit of the plaintiff upon breach. Exclusion clauses are controlled by the substantive law of contract regarding notice of terms and unconscionability. As such, they will not be dealt with here. Instead, this chapter is concerned with stipulated damages provisions, generally called "liquidated damages."

2) The Advantages and Disadvantages of Stipulated Damages

There are many advantages to permitting parties to stipulate the damages upon breach of contract. In situations where damages will be difficult to prove, they provide a form of insurance to the parties that in the event of breach their losses will be fully recompensed. They reduce "judicial risk," reduce the difficulty and cost of proving damages, and achieve savings for both the parties and the judicial system. The principle of freedom of contract weighs in favour of permitting a wide scope for liquidated damages clauses. The parties know best what is at stake in the transaction and how to arrange their affairs. Each enters into the agreement with her eyes open, knowing what the consequence of breach will be.

Despite these arguments in favour of stipulated damages, there are competing principles at play, including the law's desire to protect weaker parties and its dislike of penalties and punitive damages. These considerations suggest that courts should police stipulated damages clauses carefully. Stipulated damages provisions will often appear to be punitive or coercive. The law of contract rarely permits punitive damages or specific performance, and the question is whether the parties should be permitted to agree between themselves to a result that a court would not consider appropriate. Moreover, such clauses may be an indication of overbearing by one party and thus raise the issue of unconscionability.

B. LIQUIDATED DAMAGES AND PENALTIES

1) Basic Concepts

The most common way of stipulating a remedy is to include in a contract a clause requiring that a fixed sum be payable for breach. Historically, such provisions, aimed at securing performance of a contract, took the form of penal bonds and penal clauses.[1] Penal bonds were instruments under which one party promised to pay the other a sum of money. The bond would be void only if the promisee performed a certain act. Penal clauses were included in the contractual instrument itself. Courts of equity, however, provided relief against bonds and forfeitures, and legis-

---

1   S.M. Waddams, *The Law of Damages*, 2d ed., looseleaf (Aurora, ON: Canada Law Book, 1991–) at para. 8.40.

lation in the seventeenth and eighteenth centuries ultimately rendered such penal provisions unenforceable. So long as the harm suffered by one party would be fully compensated by an award of damages, the bond or penalty would not be enforced. However, these developments did not put an end to all stipulated damages clauses. Instead, the courts distinguished between penalty clauses (which were unenforceable) and liquidated damages clauses (which were enforceable).

2) The Tests

Since the courts have held that liquidated damages clauses are enforceable and that penalty clauses are not, it is not surprising that most contracts providing for the payment of a certain sum upon breach expressly describe the payment as "liquidated damages and not as a penalty." The courts have held that the form of the words used by the parties, however, is not conclusive as to the effect of the clause.[2] The basic test to distinguish a penalty from a liquidated damages clause is described in *Dunlop Pneumatic Tyre Co., Ltd. v. New Garage & Motor Co. Limited.*[3] Lord Dunedin stated: "The essence of a penalty is a payment of money stipulated as in terrorem of the offending party; the essence of liquidated damages is a genuine covenanted pre-estimate of damage."[4] In the examination of any particular clause to determine on what side of the line it falls, the following guidelines from *Dunlop* are often cited:

(a)   It will be held to be [a] penalty if the sum stipulated for is extravagant and unconscionable in amount in comparison with the greatest loss that could conceivably be proved to have followed from the breach ...

(b)   It will be held to be a penalty if the breach consists only in not paying a sum of money, and the sum stipulated is a sum greater than the sum which ought to have been paid ...

(c)   There is a presumption (but no more) that it is a penalty when "a single lump sum is made payable by way of compensation, on the occurrence of one or more or all of several events, some of which may occasion serious and others but trifling damage" ...

---

2   For example, see *Craig v. Dillon* (1881), 6 O.A.R. 116 (C.A.); *Shatilla v. Feinstein,* (1923), 16 Sask. L.R. 454 (C.A.) [*Shatilla*]; *Moose Jaw Industrialization Fund Committee Ltd. v. Chadwick,* [1943] 2 W.W.R. 219 (Sask. K.B.); *Huffman v. Spalding,* (1989), 57 D.L.R. (4th) 589 (Man. C.A.): agreed system of fines struck down without regard to reasonableness.

3   *Dunlop Pneumatic Tyre Co., Ltd. v. New Garage & Motor Co., Limited* (1914), [1915] A.C. 79 (H.L.) [*Dunlop*].

4   *Ibid.* at 86.

On the other hand:

(d) It is no obstacle to the sum stipulated being a genuine pre-estimate of damage, that the consequences of the breach are such as to make precise pre-estimation almost an impossibility. On the contrary, that is just the situation when it is probable that pre-estimated damage was the true bargain between the parties.[5]

a) Proportionality

Thus, the basic test is whether the clause is a fair and reasonable attempt to estimate damages in advance. The most important factor is the proportionality of the amount stated in the clause in light of what is at stake in the agreement. In other words, is the amount a *bona fide* attempt to quantify those stakes in advance, or is it extravagant or unconscionable in light of those stakes?

In *Hughes v. Lukuvka,*[6] the British Columbia Court of Appeal upheld as liquidated damages the forfeiture of a $5,000 deposit paid on a $60,000 home. Similarly, the court in *Craig v. Mohawk Metal Ltd.*[7] upheld a deposit of 2 percent of the purchase price as liquidated damages. In both cases, the courts held that the measure of damages was fair and reasonable in the circumstances, considering the value of the contract and the potential loss contemplated by the parties at the time the agreement was made. In *Federal Business Development Bank v. Fredericton Motor Inn Ltd.,*[8] the plaintiffs granted the defendants a loan commitment on the grounds that they would pay roughly 1 percent of the committed sum should they decline to take the loan. The court held:

> While the description of damages prescribed in a contract as "liquidated damages" is not conclusive that they in fact are such … Having regard to the size of the credit agreed upon, viz. $550,000; and the proportion at which the agreed damages were stipulated in relation to that amount, viz. something under 1%, in my view the liquidated damages agreed represent in the circumstances a genuine pre-estimate of the loss likely to flow from the breach and must therefore be considered in fact as liquidated damages.[9]

---

5   *Ibid.* at 87.
6   (1970), 14 D.L.R. (3d) 110 (B.C.C.A.) [*Hughes*].
7   (1975), 9 O.R. (2d) 716 (H.C.J.) [*Craig*].
8   (1980), 32 N.B.R. (2d) 108 (Q.B.T.D.) [*Fredericton Motor*]. See also *Bowlen v. Digger Excavating (1983) Ltd.* (2001), 286 A.R. 291 (C.A.): deposit of 1.75 percent of total purchase price not unconscionable.
9   *Fredericton Motor, ibid.* at 112–13.

Even where the stipulated amount appears to be a substantial proportion of the value of the transaction, it would nevertheless not be considered a penalty so long as it is a genuine pre-estimate of damages. In *Lam v. Ernest & Twins Ventures (PP) Ltd.*,[10] the stipulated liquidated damages of 30 percent of the contract price were found not to be a penalty but, instead, a genuine pre-estimate of the vendor's damages, among other things, because the amount of the actual loss in fact exceeded the 30 percent deposit.

By way of contrast, where the amount stipulated as damages is necessarily and substantially beyond the actual loss that could be suffered by the plaintiff, that amount will be regarded as a penalty. In *H.F. Clarke Ltd. v. Thermidaire Corp.*,[11] the defendant entered into an exclusive distribution agreement with the plaintiff and agreed not to sell competitors' products. The defendant agreed that if it violated the non-competition clause, it would pay an amount equal to its gross profit from the sale of competing products as liquidated damages. The defendant broke the agreement and made gross profits of $200,000. The trial court and the Ontario Court of Appeal upheld an award for this amount as a genuine pre-estimate of damages. Though the sum was in excess of the amount that would have been awarded in an action for damages, these courts held that it was a "businesslike and reasonable" arrangement. The Supreme Court of Canada reversed this decision, holding that the sum was a penalty, given that it was in excess of any amount that could reasonably be claimed as damages. The Court was much influenced by the fact that, even on its own calculations, the plaintiff had lost net profits of less than half the sum claimed.

---

10   (2001), 42 R.P.R. (3d) 173 (B.C.S.C.) [*Lam*]. *Colliers Macaulay Nicolls Inc. v. Park Georgia Properties Ltd.* (2003), 15 R.P.R. (4th) 132 (B.C.S.C.): a remedy clause of 3 percent commission payable to a real estate agency was a genuine pre-estimate of damages, though there was no correlation between the amount and the plaintiff's efforts under the agreement. *Tkachuk Farms Ltd. v. Le Blanc Auction Service Ltd.* (2006), 290 Sask. R. 203 (Q.B.): 14 percent commission on gross sale proceeds not a penalty.

11   [1976] 1 S.C.R. 319 [*Thermidaire*]. See also *National Bank of Canada v. Merit Energy Ltd.* (2001), 294 A.R. 36 (Q.B.), aff'd as to other issues (2001), 93 Alta. L.R. (3d) 43 (C.A.); *Private Lender Inc. v. Little* (2003), 13 Alta. L.R. (4th) 321 (Q.B.): amount demanded from mortgagor was at least ten times the mortgagee's actual loss. See also *MTK Auto West Ltd. v. Allen*, 2003 BCSC 1613 [*MTK*], where the amount claimed as liquidated damages was more than three times the greatest loss that could be sustained under the agreement. In striking down the clause as a penalty, Kirkpatrick J. noted, among other things, that the amount was set without any consideration of the plaintiff's potential loss in the event of default. To enforce the remedy clause would simply give the plaintiff a windfall.

The Supreme Court's decision has been criticized. There was no evidence of inequality of bargaining power or unconscionability in the case. Both parties were sophisticated traders who agreed to the "gross profit" formula with their eyes open. Moreover, the use of the net-profit figure as a standard of comparison may not be fair to the plaintiff. To give the plaintiff only its loss of net profits would not compensate the plaintiff for intangible losses caused by the sale of competing products. The gist of the wrong in this case is not simply that the defendant made unauthorized sales, but that it directly competed with the plaintiff for market share. The loss suffered by the plaintiff is not simply the lost profits on the specific sales, but loss of goodwill, name identification, and market share. These are losses that are difficult to calculate and extend far into the future. Moreover, as the Ontario Court of Appeal pointed out, to take "net profit" as the standard of comparison is to charge the plaintiff for all the advertising, promotion, and administrative costs incurred by the defendant to commit the unauthorized acts and "put down" the plaintiff in a competitive venture.

The questionable result in this case reinforces the argument that courts should not apply mathematical rules to test the fairness of stipulated damages clauses. Instead, even if the sum is an overestimate, courts should simply apply well-developed principles of unconscionability to determine whether the clause is unfair or oppressive as between the parties.[12] In *Liu v. Coal Harbour Properties Partnership*,[13] the British Columbia Court of Appeal adopted such an approach to hold that the vendors are entitled to keep deposits that appear high, even when the vendor sold the property for a substantially higher amount than the defaulting party was willing to pay, so long as the amount was a genuine pre-estimate of damages in the circumstances. In this case, the subject property was a condominium development that was yet to be constructed. Given the longer time horizon and the uncertainty of costs involved in such projects, forfeiture of the 20 percent deposit was found to be a genuine pre-estimate of the damages at the time of the contract and therefore not unconscionable.[14]

---

12   C.J. Goetz & R.E. Scott, "Liquidated Damages, Penalties and the Just Compensation Principle: Some Notes on an Enforcement Model and a Theory of Efficient Breach" (1977) 77 Colum. L. Rev. 554; Waddams, above note 1 at para. 8.200.

13   (2006), 56 B.C.L.R. (4th) 230 (C.A.).

14   See also *Blackcomb Skiing Enterprises Limited Partnership v. Schneider*, 2000 BCSC 720.

b) Trivial Breach

Under *Dunlop*, a stipulated damages clause can be struck down where it provides for the payment of a lump sum on the occurrence of a number of events where some or one of those events may be a trivial breach resulting in nominal damages. In *Unilease Inc. v. York Steel Construction Ltd.*,[15] the defendant leased copiers from the plaintiff. The lease provided for repossession and accelerated payment of any remaining lease payments on default. The Court of Appeal held that the "event of default" contemplated serious events, such as the bankruptcy of the defendant, and trivial events, such as late payment of a lease instalment. On this basis, the provision was struck down for being a penalty. The "trivial breach" principle is not so much a rule as a factor to be taken into account in assessing whether the clause is a genuine pre-estimate of damages, or an attempt to impose an unreasonable penalty.[16]

c) Unconscionability

Waddams and others argue that the underlying basis for upholding or striking down liquidated damages clauses is the principle of unconscionability.[17] He points to the speeches of the lords in *Dunlop*, where they held that such clauses are enforceable so long as they are not "extravagant and unconscionable." Since unconscionability principles are now recognized as a defence in contract law, he argues that they should be recognized as applying to liquidated damages clauses, for the "open recognition of unconscionability as the basis of relief will greatly facilitate the rational development of this branch of the law."[18] Dickson J. stated in *Elsley Estate v. J.G. Collins Insurance Agencies Ltd.*:[19] "It is now evident that the power to strike down a penalty clause is a blatant interference with freedom of contract and is designed for the sole purpose of

---

15   (1978), 18 O.R. (2d) 559 (C.A.) [*Unilease*].
16   See also *Brenaul-Pattam Leasing Inc. v. Capriotti*, [1994] O.J. No. 787 (Gen. Div.), rev'd [1997] O.J. No. 1039 (C.A.). But see *Indianhead Financial Services Ltd. v. Nucro-Technics Ltd.* (1981), 14 B.L.R. 319 (Ont. Co. Ct.): amount represented a genuine pre-estimate of lessor's damages and lessor had no opportunity to mitigate; *Langille v. Keneric Tractor Sales Ltd.* (1985), 67 N.S.R. (2d) 404 (C.A.), aff'd [1987] 2 S.C.R. 440: liquidated damages not enforceable but lessor entitled to a reasonable amount for damage suffered; *Canadian Western Bank v. Watson Lake Bus Lines Co.* (2006), 17 B.L.R. (4th) 197: clause enforceable as the genuine intention of the parties.
17   Waddams, above note 1 at para. 8.2000.
18   *Ibid.* at 8.130. In *Hunting Wood Homes Ltd. v. Mohan*, [1988] O.J. No. 861 (Dist. Ct.), the court held that the test of oppression in *Elsley*, below note 19, had superseded the *Dunlop* tests for determining the enforceability of liquidated damages clauses.
19   [1978] 2 S.C.R. 916 [*Elsley*].

providing relief against oppression for the party having to pay the stipulated sum. It has no place where there is no oppression."[20] On this view, *Thermidaire* would be an anomaly, since the agreement was entered into by two equal parties, with eyes open and no evidence of oppression.

Relief from oppression was also explicitly mentioned in the case of *Hurdal v. Club Monaco Inc.*[21] The case involved the recovery of a deposit paid by the plaintiffs to secure a clothing-store franchise. The $75,000 deposit represented the whole of the franchise fee. After incurring unanticipated costs, the plaintiffs decided not to continue with the franchise plans and requested the return of their deposit. The defendants informed them that the deposit was considered liquidated damages for failure of the franchise agreement. The court held that the agreement was invalid on other grounds, but it also considered the validity of the forfeiture clause:

> The sum is described as a penalty. Being extravagant and unconscionable it is clearly a penalty. Though parties are free to contract, courts have the power to strike down penalty clauses to provide equitable relief from oppression. There has been no genuine pre-estimate of damages. The sum reflects the total franchise fee. It is not a fair pre-estimate of damages. The amount is unfair and objectively unreasonable. It falls to the court to determine what is reasonable in the circumstances.[22]

Similarly, in *Place Concorde East Limited Partnership v. Shelter Corp. of Canada*,[23] the Ontario Court of Appeal affirmed the trial judge's decision that a post-default rate of interest on promissory notes that was 4.25 percent higher than the pre-breach rate was in the nature of a penalty clause. This was found to be extravagant, unconscionable, and commercially unreasonable, and therefore unenforceable.

In *Prudential Insurance Co. of America v. Cedar Hills Properties Ltd.*,[24] the plaintiff lender entered into a loan agreement with the defendants for $6.4 million. The agreement included an "interest rate standby fee" of $100,000 in consideration of the plaintiff reserving funds and fixing the mortgage rate. It provided that the defendants would forfeit this fee if they failed to complete the loan transaction. The defendants

---

20   *Ibid.* at 937.
21   [1996] B.C.J. No. 958 (S.C.).
22   *Ibid.* at para. 26.
23   (2006), 270 D.L.R. (4th) 181 (Ont. C.A.). See also *Jeancharm Ltd. (t/a Beaver International) v. Barnet Football Club Ltd.*, [2003] EWCA Civ 58: an annual interest rate of 260 percent constituted a penalty and hence was unenforceable.
24   (1994), 100 B.C.L.R. (2d) 312 (C.A.).

found alternate funds and the plaintiff sued for the $100,000. At trial the provision was struck down as a penalty; however, the Court of Appeal permitted the plaintiff to recover the deposit on the basis that the stipulated sum was not unconscionable. Goldie J.A. stated that the effect of *Elsley* is that a clause stipulating a sum payable upon breach will be struck down only if it is oppressive. Thus, "[e]ven a stated penalty clause will not be struck down unless oppression is demonstrated."[25] This view has also been affirmed in *869163 Ontario Ltd. v. Torrey Springs II Associates Ltd. Partnership*,[26] which found that a remedy clause in a commercial contract that stipulated that certain promissory notes were to be deemed paid in the event of a default, could be regarded as a penalty clause. However, this did not necessarily make it void. The court noted that there should be no blanket prohibition on penalty clauses, either at common law or equity. Sharpe J.A. noted that courts have been enforcing penalty clauses in the interest of upholding freedom of contract, provided they are not unconscionable. Thus, penalty clauses will be enforceable unless they are shown to be extravagant, unreasonable, or otherwise unconscionable.[27]

Determining unconscionability turns on an assessment of the bargaining power of the parties, their level of sophistication in commercial dealings, the gravity of the breach, and the difference between the amount to be forfeited and the actual losses. These matters will be critical in determining whether or not a penalty clause is enforceable.[28] For instance, in *Iyer v. Pleasant Development Inc.*,[29] the plaintiffs were first-time home-buyers, whereas the defendants were a developer building houses in a subdivision, a licensed real estate agent, and an on-site sales representative for the developer. The Ontario Superior Court of Justice noted that, given the inadequate explanation in the contract that the purchaser would lose the deposit in the event of a breach, a forfeiture of the deposit was not justifiable in the absence of proof of damages. As well, allowing the vendor to keep the deposit of $10,000 was found to be grossly disproportionate to the vendor's losses, if any. This would have simply resulted in a windfall for the vendor

---

25   *Ibid.* at 321.
26   (2005), 76 O.R. (3d) 362 (C.A.), leave to appeal to S.C.C. refused, [2005] S.C.C.A. 420.
27   See also *MTK*, above note 11; *Nortel Networks Corp. v. Jervis* (2002), 18 C.C.E.L. (3d) 100 (Ont. S.C.J.). In *Bobbiduncan Holdings Ltd. v. Pawelek*, [2007] BCCA 312 [*Bobbiduncan Holdings Ltd.*], a remedy clause that was three times the actual damages suffered by the respondents was found to be a penalty clause, but was nevertheless held to be enforceable.
28   *32262 B.C. Ltd. v. See-Rite Optical Ltd.* (1998), 216 A.R. 33 (C.A.); *MTK, ibid.*; *Global Entertainment v. Yeo* (2005), 7 B.L.R. (4th) 213 (Alta. Prov. Ct.).
29   [2005] O.J. No. 3407 (S.C.J.). See also *Tsui v. Zhao*, [2006] O.J. No. 3032 (S.C.J.).

and was therefore unconscionable. On the other hand, in *Busby*,[30] the British Columbia Supreme Court upheld a termination fee as enforceable, among other things, because it had been negotiated between sophisticated parties of equal bargaining power as the amount to defray the defendant's cost.

d) Time of Application of the Tests

Generally, the characterization of a clause as liquidated damages or penalty is to be made at the time the parties entered the contract.[31] For example, in *Maxwell v. Gibsons Drugs Ltd.*,[32] the employment contract between the parties provided for $2,000 in liquidated damages in the event of wrongful dismissal. At the time the contract was entered into, the defendant employer contemplated that the longest the plaintiff might be out of work in the event of a wrongful dismissal was three months, resulting in a loss of $3,000. The court upheld the amount as fair and reasonable in the circumstances.[33]

However, there are recent cases that indicate that the courts may be willing to consider whether the provision is reasonable by examining the actual loss sustained as a result of the breach. Generally, this approach has been used to strike down a liquidated damages clause where the actual loss suffered by the plaintiff has been minimal. The fact that the plaintiffs in *Thermidaire* had sustained losses equal to less than half the amount stipulated in the non-competition agreement was one of the reasons Laskin C.J.C. gave for holding the provision unreasonable.[34] In several other cases it is apparent that, in reaching the conclusion that a liquidated damages clause was unreasonable, courts have compared it to the actual loss suffered as a result of the breach.[35] Thus, whether or not the remedy clause is oppressive may be determined by reference to circumstances that exist when the clause is invoked.[36]

---

30 *Busby + Associates Architects Ltd. v. Good Fortune Investments Ltd.* (2001), 15 B.L.R. (3d) 93 (B.C.S.C.). See also *Lam*, above note 10.

31 *Dunlop*, above note 3; *Clydebank Engineering & Shipbuilding Co. v. Don Jose Ramos Yzquierdo y Castaneda*, [1905] A.C. 6 (H.L.); *Commissioner of Public Works v. Hills*, [1906] A.C. 368 (P.C.) [*Hills*]; *Jobson v. Johnson*, [1989] 1 All E.R. 621 (C.A.).

32 (1979), 103 D.L.R. (3d) 433 (B.C.S.C.).

33 See also *Fredericton Motor*, above note 8; *Hughes*, above note 6; *Craig*, above note 7.

34 Above note 11.

35 *R.C.A. Victor Co. v. Pelletier* (1968), 68 D.L.R. (2d) 13 (N.B.C.A.) [*R.C.A.*]; *Canadian Acceptance Corp. v. Regent Park Butcher Shop* (1969), 3 D.L.R. (3d) 304 (Man. C.A.) [*Canadian Acceptance Corp.*]; *Infinite Maintenance Systems Ltd. v. ORC Management Ltd.* (2001), 5 C.P.C. (5th) 241 (Ont. C.A.), leave to appeal to S.C.C. refused, [2001] S.C.C.A. No. 105.

36 *Axton Industries Ltd. v. Bobbiduncan Holdings Ltd.*, 2006 BCSC 1204 at para. 21 [*Axton Industries*], var'd on other grounds, *Bobbiduncan Holdings Ltd.*, above note 27.

3) Consequences of Finding of Liquidated Damages or Penalty

Where the stipulated sum is struck down as a penalty, the plaintiff is still permitted to recover provable damages. In *Thermidaire*, although the Supreme Court struck down the $200,000 liquidated damages as a penalty, the plaintiff was able to recover $92,000 in actual damages.[37]

Where the court holds that the stipulated sum is a genuine pre-estimate of damages, the clause will generally be taken to operate for the benefit of *both* parties. In other words, even if provable damages are greater than the stipulated sum, the stipulated sum will act as a ceiling on what the plaintiff can recover. For example, in *Love v. Robinson*,[38] the agreement of sale and purchase stipulated that the purchaser's $1,000 deposit would be forfeited as liquidated damages for breach of contract where the purchaser failed to close. The court held that the vendor's recovery was restricted to the deposit despite greater proven losses.[39] The Supreme Court of Canada has also determined that stipulated damages will ordinarily be a ceiling on damages. In *Elsley*[40] the plaintiffs purchased an insurance business from the defendant, hiring him back as an employee. The contract contained a clause whereby the defendant would not compete with the plaintiffs for a period of five years after termination of employment and provided liquidated damages in the amount of $1,000. After seventeen years the defendant resigned and started his own insurance agency, taking away many of the plaintiffs' clients. The trial court and Ontario Court of Appeal awarded an injunction and damages for the commissions lost to the plaintiffs as a result of the defendant's breach. However, the Supreme Court of Canada held that the penalty clause operated as a ceiling on damages and reduced the award to $1,000. Dickson J., speaking for the Court, stated:

> If the actual loss turns out to exceed the penalty, the normal rules of enforcement of contract should apply to allow recovery of only the agreed sum. The party imposing the penalty should not be able to obtain the benefit of whatever intimidating force the penalty clause may have in inducing performance, and then ignore the clause when it turns out to be to his advantage to do so. A penalty clause should function

---

37 See also *Hills*, above note 31; *Shatilla*, above note 2; *R.C.A.*, above note 35; *Unilease*, above note 15: the Court of Appeal overturned the liquidated damages award and directed a new trial to assess actual damages sustained by the plaintiff.
38 [1981] 4 W.W.R. 517 (Sask. Dist. Ct.).
39 See also *Gisvold v. Hill* (1963), 37 D.L.R. (2d) 606 (B.C.S.C.); *Dorge v. Dumesnil* (1973), 39 D.L.R. (3d) 750 (Man. Q.B.).
40 Above note 19.

as a limitation on the damages recoverable, while still being ineffective to increase damages above the actual loss sustained when such loss is less than the stipulated amount. As expressed by Lord Ellenborough in *Wilbeam v. Ashton* [(1807), Camp. 78]: "Beyond the penalty you shall not go; within it, you are to give the party any compensation which he can prove himself entitled to." Of course, if an agreed sum is a valid liquidated damages clause, the plaintiff is entitled at law to recover this sum regardless of the actual loss sustained.

In the context of the present discussion of the measure of damages, the result is that an agreed sum payable on breach represents the maximum amount recoverable whether the sum is a penalty or a valid liquidated damages clause.[41]

It is a matter of debate, as discussed below, whether it is an absolute rule that the stipulated sum is a ceiling on recoverable damages. Waddams argues that the true principle is that the stipulated sum will be a ceiling on recovery only where this is the intention of the parties. In other words, the issue should be determined on the true construction of the contract. Where the plaintiff's losses far exceed the liquidated damages, and the parties did not intend the stipulated sum to be a maximum, the courts may allow the plaintiff to recover the full amount of proven damages.[42] Pitch and Snyder add the further argument that in some cases the fact that actual damages substantially exceed the stipulated sum may indicate that it would be unconscionable in the circumstances to hold the plaintiff to his bargain.[43] In these cases it is open to the courts to hold that the parties never intended the liquidated damages clause to act as a limitation of liability.

Subsequent cases have not interpreted *Elsley* uniformly. Most cases at least start from the presumption that the stipulated sum is a ceiling on damages.[44] However, where the circumstances show that it would be

---

41   *Ibid.* at 937.
42   Waddams, above note 1 at para. 8.220.
43   Pitch & Snyder appear to accept this proposition. H.D. Pitch & R.H. Snyder, *Damages for Breach of Contract*, 2d ed., looseleaf (Toronto: Carswell, 1989–) at 6§5(a): "The courts are unwilling to restrict a plaintiff to the quantum of damages specified in a liquidated damage clause where the plaintiff's damages far exceed that sum and to do so would be totally unreasonable."
44   In *Erskine Building Corp. v. First College Grenville Holdings Inc.* (1993), 13 C.L.R. (2d) 51 (Ont. Div. Ct.), a construction contract between the parties provided that the owner's damages resulting from the builder's failure to complete the project on time were limited to $3,000 per day. The court held that an agreed sum payable on breach represents the maximum amount recoverable whether the sum is a penalty or a valid liquidated damages claim.

unconscionable to treat it as such, the courts will not follow the rule absolutely. The Court in *Elsley* surely did not mean to state that the presumptive rule trumps the more general principles of unconscionability.

In *Lozcal Holdings Ltd. v. Brassos Development Ltd.*,[45] a land sale agreement specified that the deposit would be held as liquidated damages upon the purchaser's default, yet the vendor was allowed to recover their full loss. The Alberta Court of Appeal's decision was based on principles of construction:

> Certainly ... the parties may, by their contract, govern the arrangements between them, and if they provide that the vendor's damages in the event of breach by the purchaser were to be limited to the deposit paid, it would have been competent for them to do so. The question here is whether they have done this by providing that the deposit shall be "forfeited as liquidated damages."
>
> In my view, if the intention were to limit the purchaser's liability, that could have been easily said, and the court should not import into the words "as liquidated damages" (particularly when they appear in a printed form) any such intention. It seems to me that very much more express language is required.[46]

In *Harchies Developments Ltd. v. Ewanchuk*,[47] the amount of the stipulated liquidated damages ($5,000) relative to the value of the transaction ($91,500), and the absence of unequivocal language limiting the plaintiff's remedy to that amount, were taken as indications that the parties did not intend the plaintiff's damages to be limited to the deposit. The plaintiff's damages were therefore to be assessed in accordance with the normal rules of contract damages.

Similarly, in *Quantum Management Services Ltd. v. Hann*,[48] the plaintiff brought an action against a former senior employee for breach of a non-competition provision of his employment contract. The defendant employee argued that damages were limited to a liquidated damages provision in the contract. The court held that the defendant was in breach of his fiduciary duty not to exploit the employer's confidential information and corporate opportunities and that the liquidated dam-

---

45   (1980), 22 A.R. 131 (C.A.) [*Lozcal*]. See also *Mitchell v. Paddington Homes Ltd.* (1977), 3 B.C.L.R. 330 (S.C.); *Raymer v. Stratton Woods Holdings Ltd.* (1988), 65 O.R. (2d) 16 (C.A.); *Fern Investments Ltd. v. Golden Nugget Restaurant* (1987) *Ltd.* (1994), 149 A.R. 303 (C.A.); *504148 Alberta Ltd. v. Seventies Homes Canada Inc.*, 2005 ABQB 382.

46   *Lozcal, ibid.*

47   (2006), 64 Alta. L.R. (4th) 314 (Q.B.).

48   (1989), 69 O.R. (2d) 26 (H.C.J.), aff'd (1992), 11 O.R. (3d) 639 (C.A.).

ages clause did not extend to limit damages for breach of that duty. Therefore, the plaintiff was allowed to recover damages over and above the stipulated sum.

However, to reiterate, these cases are exceptions to the more general principle. In the absence of contrary evidence, courts assume that stipulated damages operate in favour of both parties and are a ceiling on damages, and express language is not necessary to limit recovery to the amount of liquidated damages.[49] As Baynton J. stated in *Lac La Ronge Indian Band v. Dallas Contracting Ltd.*,

> [T]he courts are obviously reluctant to permit a party to have it both ways so to speak. It would be unfair to permit a party to enforce a liquidated damages clause in a contract in instances where the liquidated damages exceeded the actual damages if that party was permitted to abandon the agreed upon liquidated damages and claim actual damages in instances where they exceeded the liquidated damages. The purpose of a liquidated damages clause is to avoid litigation by genuinely "pre-estimating" and "pre-determining" potential damages.[50]

4) Relation between Liquidated Damages and Specific Relief

There is considerable caselaw concerning the effect of a liquidated damages clause on a plaintiff's right to an injunction. As a general rule, the existence of a liquidated damages provision does not deprive the plaintiff of her right to specific performance or an injunction (where such relief is otherwise available as a matter of law).[51] For example, in the context of contracts for the sale of real estate, the principle has been applied on the basis that "a purchaser has no right to say that he will put an end to the agreement, forfeiting his deposit."[52]

However, where both remedies are available, there is a potential for overcompensation of the plaintiff. If an injunction or specific performance will achieve for the plaintiff the full benefit of the contract, the enforcement of a liquidated damages clause would confer a windfall upon the plaintiff. For example, in *Snider v. McKelvey*,[53] the Ontario Court of

---

49 *Cikes Developments Ltd. v. Jung*, [1985] B.C.W.L.D. 4283 (C.A.); applied in *Fraser v. Van Nus* (1987), 14 B.C.L.R. (2d) 111 (C.A.).

50 (2001), 206 Sask. R. 13 at para. 114 (Q.B.), var'd (2004), 254 Sask. R. 6 (C.A.).

51 *Jones v. Heavens* (1877), 4 Ch. D. 636.

52 *Crutchley v. Jerningham* (1817), 2 Mer. 502 at 506 (Ch.), Lord Eldon. See *Fleisher v. Rosenbloom* (1988), 53 Man. R. (2d) 247 (Q.B.).

53 (1900), 27 O.A.R. 339 (C.A.).

Appeal refused to award both an injunction and damages specified in a sales agreement between the parties, on the basis that to do so would be to allow the plaintiff double recovery. To award both would allow the plaintiff to obtain the "performance of the agreement *in specie* and also what he was only entitled to recover in the case of its non-performance."[54] This principle has also been applied to non-competition clauses contained in employment contracts that stipulated the damages payable upon breach by the employee. For example, in *General Accident Assurance Corp. v. Noel*,[55] the court held that the plaintiff must elect between an injunction or liquidated damages.

However, awarding both liquidated damages and an injunction will not inevitably amount to double compensation if the court can be satisfied that the liquidated damages provide compensation for the harm that has occurred until the time of trial and that an injunction is still necessary to prevent further breaches. The Supreme Court affirmed this in *Elsley*, in which the plaintiff sought an injunction to enforce a non-competition clause as well as damages for breach. The Court held:

> In the case of a gross underestimate of damages as, presumably, in the present case, the plaintiff may receive an amount equivalent to the liquidated damages sum, plus an injunction, and therefore appear to have double relief. But such is not the case. The injunction relates to the latter part of the period in respect of which the restrictive covenant imposes restraint, the damages (not exceeding the stipulated liquidated damages) relate to the period prior to the granting of the injunction and are in substitution for injunctive relief during that period.[56]

Dickson J. then went on to provide a summary of the rules regarding the relationship between liquidated damages and injunctions:

1. Where a fixed sum is stipulated as and for liquidated damages upon a breach, the covenantee must elect with respect to that breach between these liquidated damages and an injunction.
2. If he elects to take the liquidated damages stipulated he may recover that sum irrespective of his actual loss.
3. Where the stipulated sum is a penalty he may only recover such damages as he can prove, but the amount recoverable may not exceed the sum stipulated.

---

54   Cited in *Elsley*, above note 19 at 931.
55   [1902] 1 K.B. 377.
56   *Elsley*, above note 19 at 935.

4. If he elects to take an injunction and not the liquidated sum stipulated, he may recover damages in equity for the actual loss sustained up to the date of the injunction or, if tardy, up to the date upon which he should have sought the injunction, but in either case, not exceeding the amount stipulated as payable upon a breach.

5. Where a liquidated damages sum is stipulated as payable for each and every breach, the covenantee may recover this sum in respect of distinct breaches which have occurred and he may also be granted an injunction to restrain future breaches.[57]

C. DISGUISED PENALTY CLAUSES

As explained previously, the wording used by the parties is not conclusive as to whether a clause will be upheld as a legitimate pre-estimate of damages or struck down as a penalty. Penalty clauses in disguise do not escape the scrutiny of the courts. Clauses providing for the forfeiture of a deposit or of payment owing under a contract may be penalties.[58] "Discounts" for prompt payment or performance may be a form of penalty clause, since in substance such provisions really specify a higher "price" for breach.

Acceleration clauses are a common contractual provision stating that a stipulated sum will be payable upon breach of a land or chattel lease. Either the whole or part of the rent due under the lease becomes due and payable upon breach. Acceleration clauses are subject to judicial supervision. For example, where in a long-term lease of equipment the entire future rent can become due on default, this may be a penalty and a windfall to the plaintiff (who recovers the entire rent and is able to re-let or sell the equipment).[59] However, in other situations, acceleration clauses will be upheld. Payment of the entire price as damages may in fact be a genuine estimate of damages when the plaintiff has fully performed and there is no opportunity to mitigate. Cases dealing with the construction of signs and the lease of advertising space may illustrate this principle. The plaintiffs in *Neonette Sign Co. v. Stankovic*[60] custom-built a sign for the defendants. The lease contained an acceleration clause stipulating that the remaining unpaid rental payments would be

---

57 *Ibid.* at 938.
58 *Frank H. Davis of Georgia Inc. v. Rayonier Canada (B.C.) Ltd.* (1968), 65 W.W.R. 251 (B.C.S.C.).
59 *Unilease,* above note 15; *Canadian Acceptance Corp.,* above note 35; *International Harvester Credit Corp. of Canada v. Dolphin* (1978), 12 A.R. 541 (T.D.).
60 (1961), 66 B.C.L.R. 269 (C.A.).

payable as damages upon breach. The court held that the provision was a genuine pre-estimate of damages, based on the fact that the sign was unsaleable and lacked any salvage value.[61]

In the recent case of *Claude Neon Ltd. v. KDJ Enterprises Ltd.*,[62] the court held that such clauses should be enforceable unless highly unreasonable. The clause in this case read:

> The parties agree that these payments are liquidated damages for the Owner's design, manufacturing, sales, finance, depreciation and administrative costs and the Owner's anticipated profit allocated to the uninterrupted completion of this Agreement, and not as a penalty.[63]

Geatros J. upheld the clause as a genuine pre-estimate of damage. The court quoted the following passage from *Sign-O-Lite*:

> The law must not lose sight of the principle of freedom of contract, particularly in the commercial context. There are strong arguments to allow parties to commercial contracts to stipulate the results arising from the nonperformance of their obligations. It allows for flexibility in the contracting process and allows the promisor to offer an assurance of performance while quantifying liability for damages and making the costs of breach predictable. It thereby is of some assistance to the parties in avoiding recourse to the courts and thus it is truly in the interests of contracting parties that the costs of nonperformance be ascertainable within their contract. In my view, a high standard of unreasonableness should be applied to such cases before an accelerated damages provision is struck down as a penalty.[64]

---

61   See also *Direct Leasing Ltd. v. Chu* (1976), 71 D.L.R. (3d) 303 (B.C.S.C.); *Alwest Neon Signs Ltd. v. Henze* (1989), 105 A.R. 343 (C.A.).

62   (1995), 136 Sask. R. 66 (Q.B.) [*KDJ*]. See also *652013 B.C. Ltd. v. Kim*, [2006] O.J. No. 423 (S.C.J.).

63   *KDJ*, *ibid.* at 70.

64   *Ibid.* at 73, quoting from *Sign-O-Lite v. Henry and Bowlerade*, [1993] O.J. No. 1138 (Gen. Div.).

TABLE OF CASES

INDEX

ABOUT THE AUTHORS

Jamie Cassels, B.A., LL.B., LL.M., Q.C., is Vice President Academic and Provost of the University of Victoria. He is also Professor of Law, and former Dean, at the Faculty of Law, University of Victoria. Prof. Cassels' areas of expertise are Contracts, Torts, Remedies, and Legal Theory, and he has written several books and numerous articles on these subjects, including *The Uncertain Promise of Law: Lessons from Bhopal* (Toronto: University of Toronto Press, 1993), and, with Craig Jones, *The Law of Large Scale Claims* (Toronto: Irwin Law, 2005). Professor Cassels is the recipient of several awards for teaching and scholarship, including the 1999 Canadian Association of Law Teachers Award for Academic Excellence and the national 3M award for Teaching Excellence.

Elizabeth Adjin-Tettey, B.A. (Hons.), LL.M., LL.M., D.Jur., is an Associate Professor at the Faculty of Law, University of Victoria, where she has been teaching since 1998. Professor Adjin-Tettey's teaching and research interests are in the areas of torts, remedies, insurance, and critical race and feminist theories, and she has written several articles and book chapters in these areas. Her recent work has focused on the marginalizing effects of traditional torts and remedial principles, examining issues such as the implications of parental responsibility legislation for under-privileged parents, inequities in the assessment of damages for impaired working capacity, and judicial responses to historical abuse claims by Aboriginal plaintiffs.